DESERTS

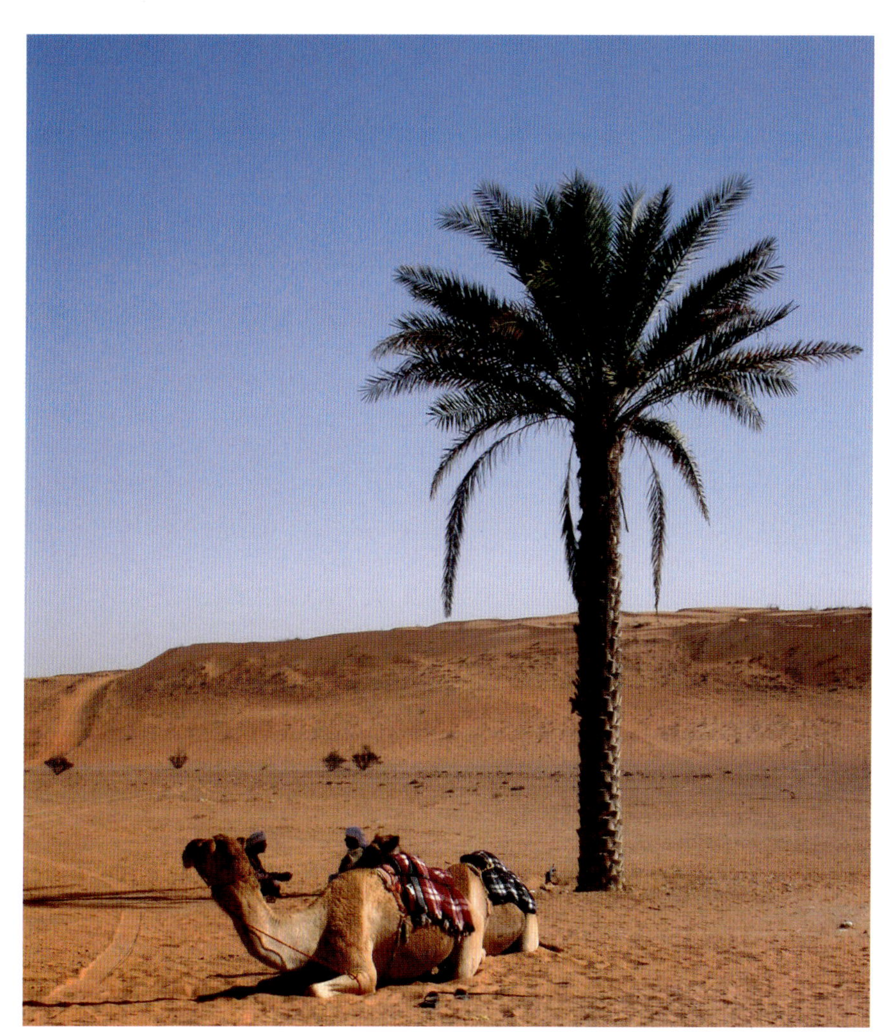

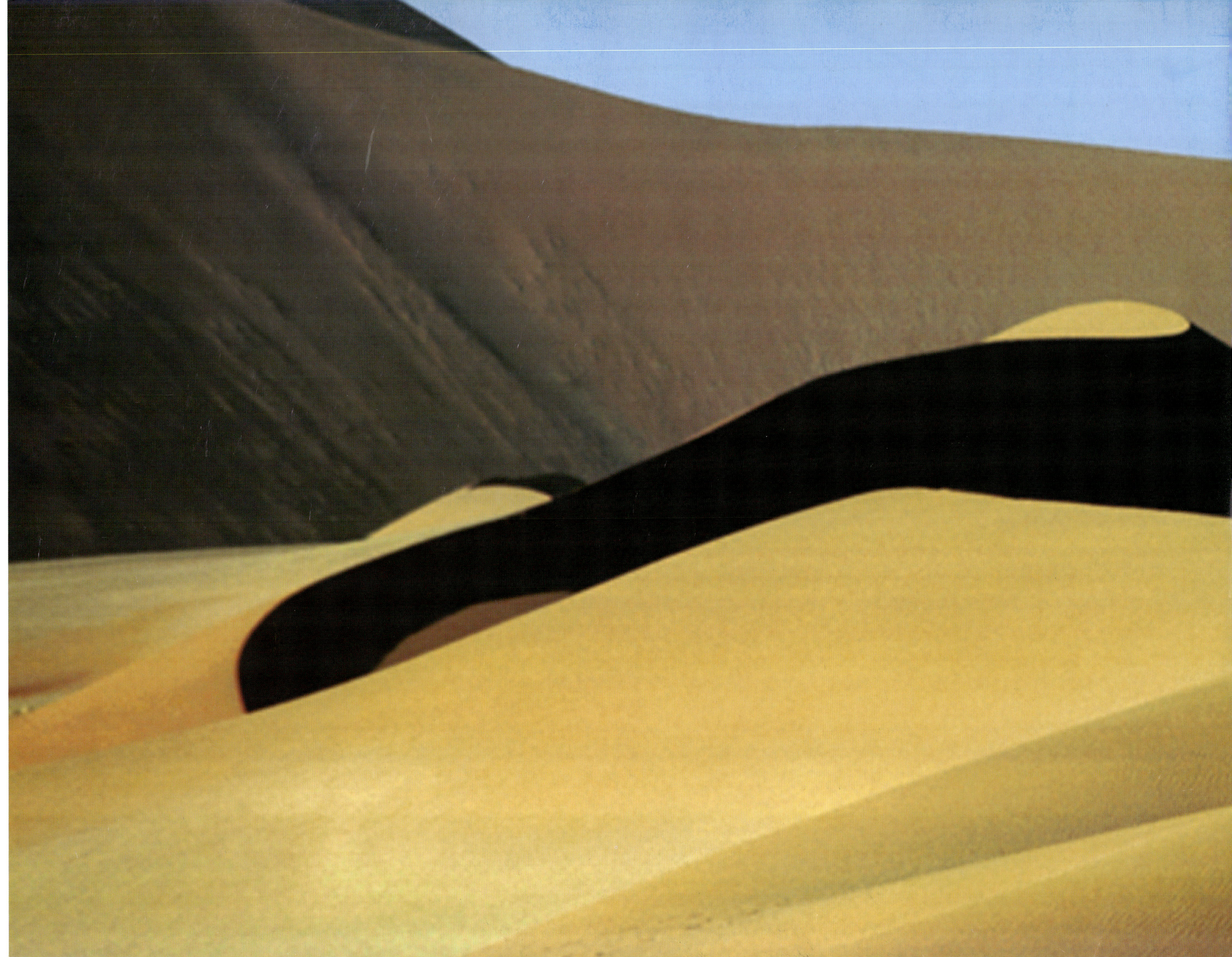

DESERTS

David Miller

CHARTWELL
BOOKS, INC.

This edition published by

CHARTWELL BOOKS, INC.
A Division of
BOOK SALES, INC.
114 Northfield Avenue
Edison, New Jersey 08837

ISBN 0-7858-2076-0

Cataloging-in-Publication data is available from the Library of Congress

The Author
David Miller is an author with over sixty published works to his credit. He has a Bachelor of Arts degree from the Open University in the United Kingdom and is currently studying for a PhD. Apart from many books on naval and other military matters, his recently published works include *The Wreck of the Isabella* (Pen & Sword, 1995), *Lady de Lancey at Waterloo* (Spellmount, 2000) and *Richard the Lionheart* (Weidenfeld & Nicolson, 2003).

Project Manager: Ray Bonds

Designer: Danny Gillespie

Map: Mark Franklin

Color reproduction: anorax

Printed in: China

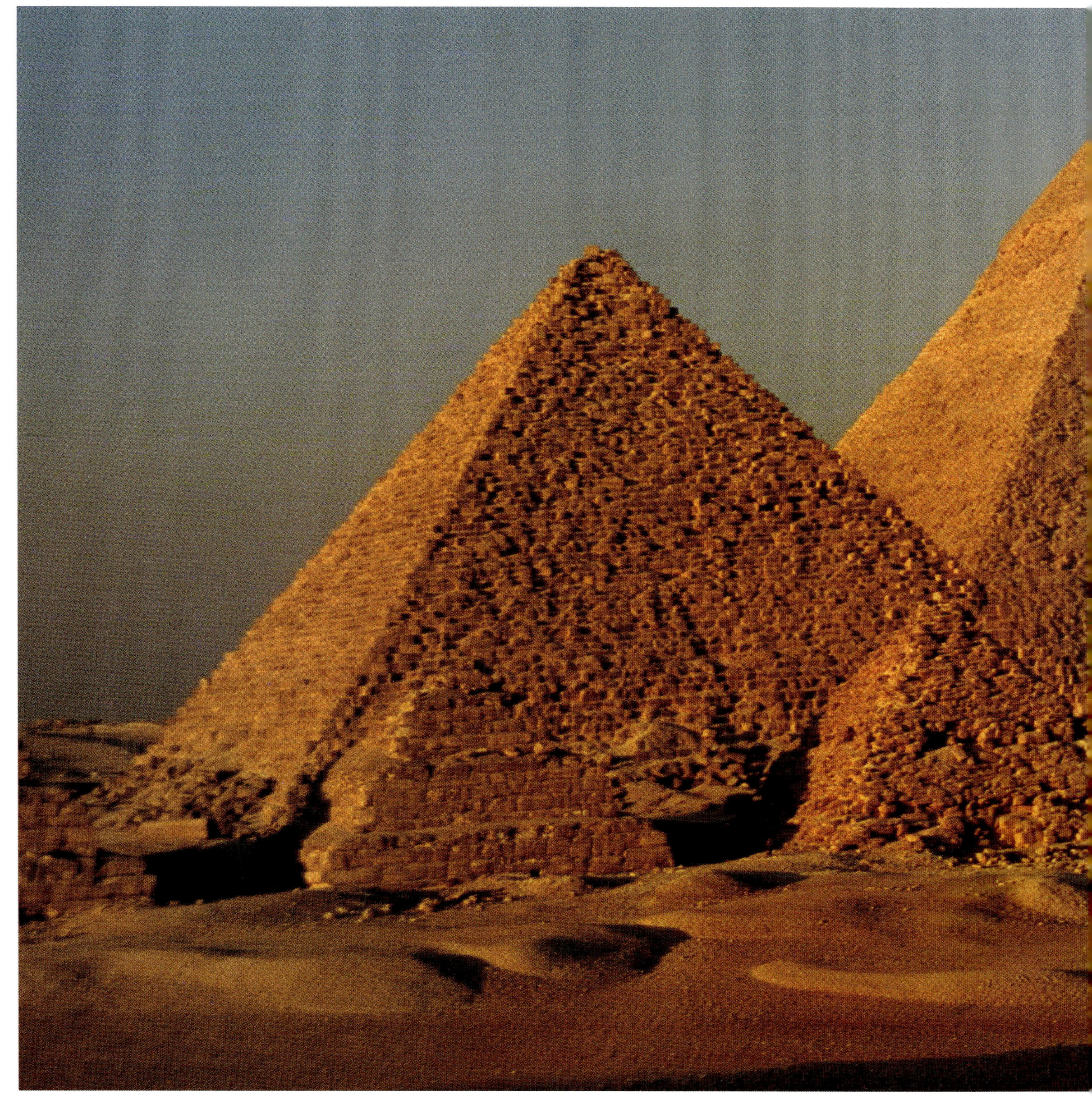

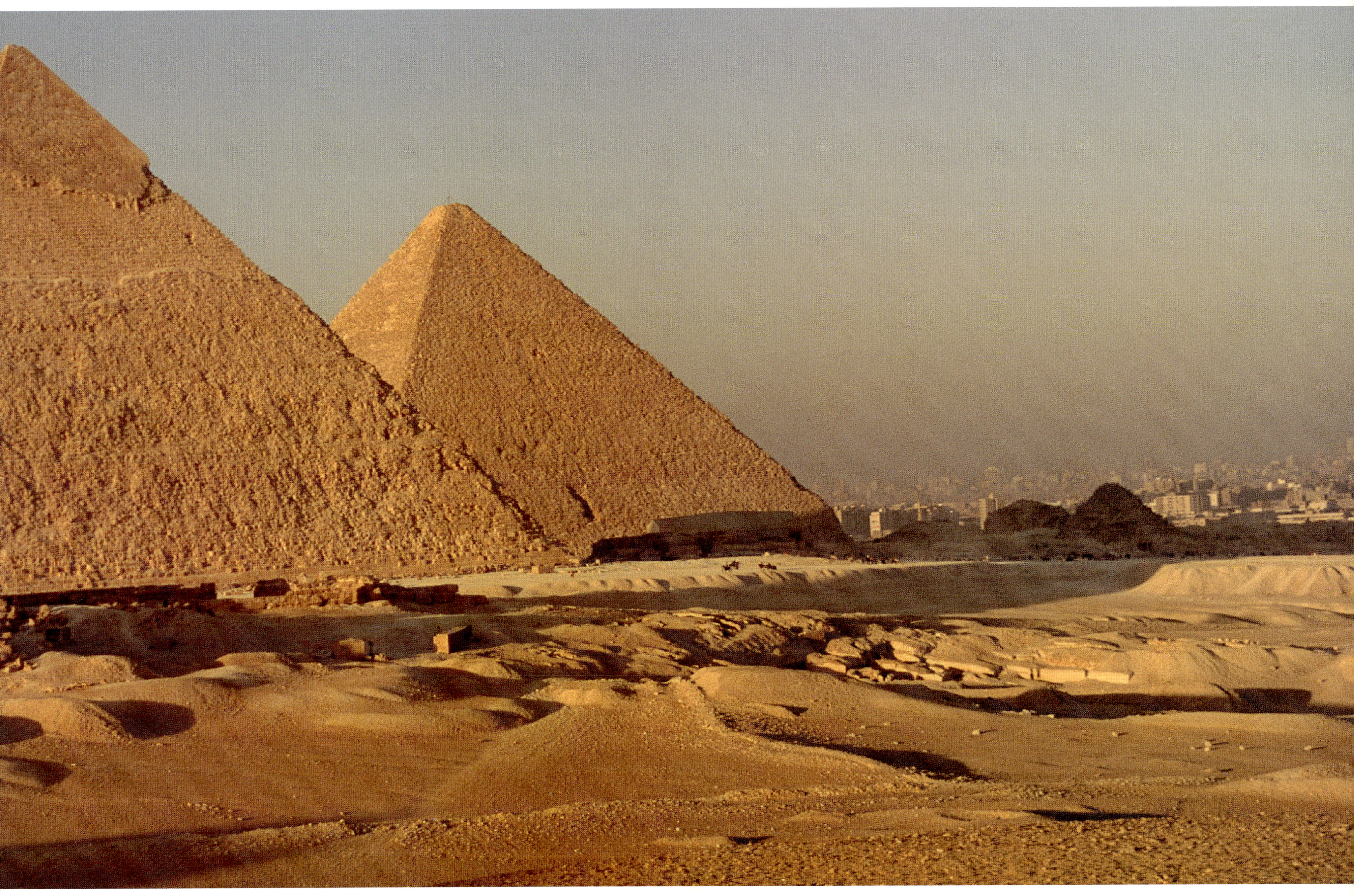

Page 1: Camels and a palm tree typify people's perception of deserts.
Simon Butler/fotoLibra

Pages 2–3: Sand dunes in the Sossusvlei, Namibia, in southern Africa.
Carole Rawlinson/fotoLibra

Pages 4–5: The Great Pyramids of Giza, Egypt.
Kenneth Garrett/Getty Images

Right: A long and dusty road in the Namib Desert, southern Africa.
Lutz Wahlers/fotoLibra

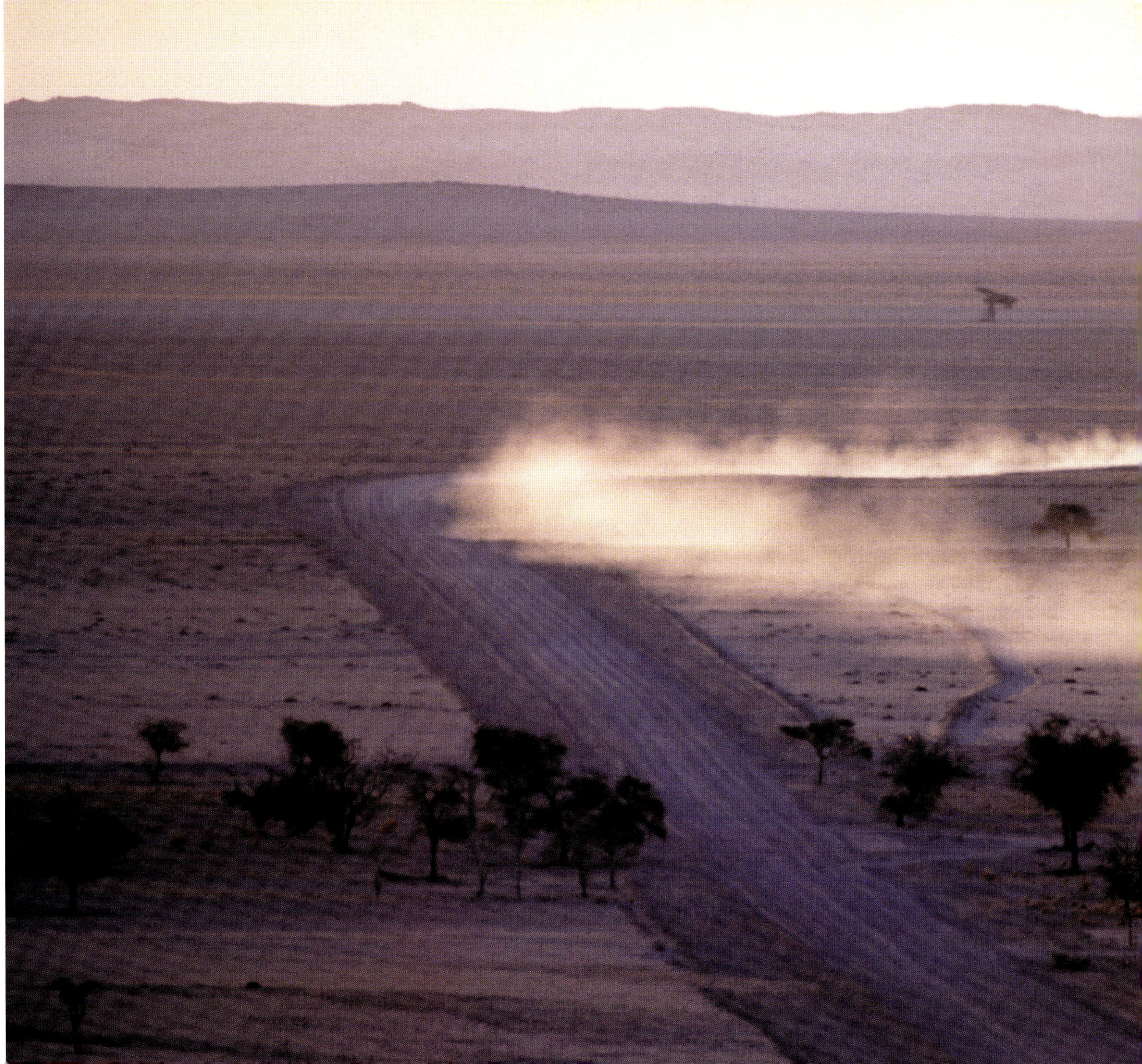

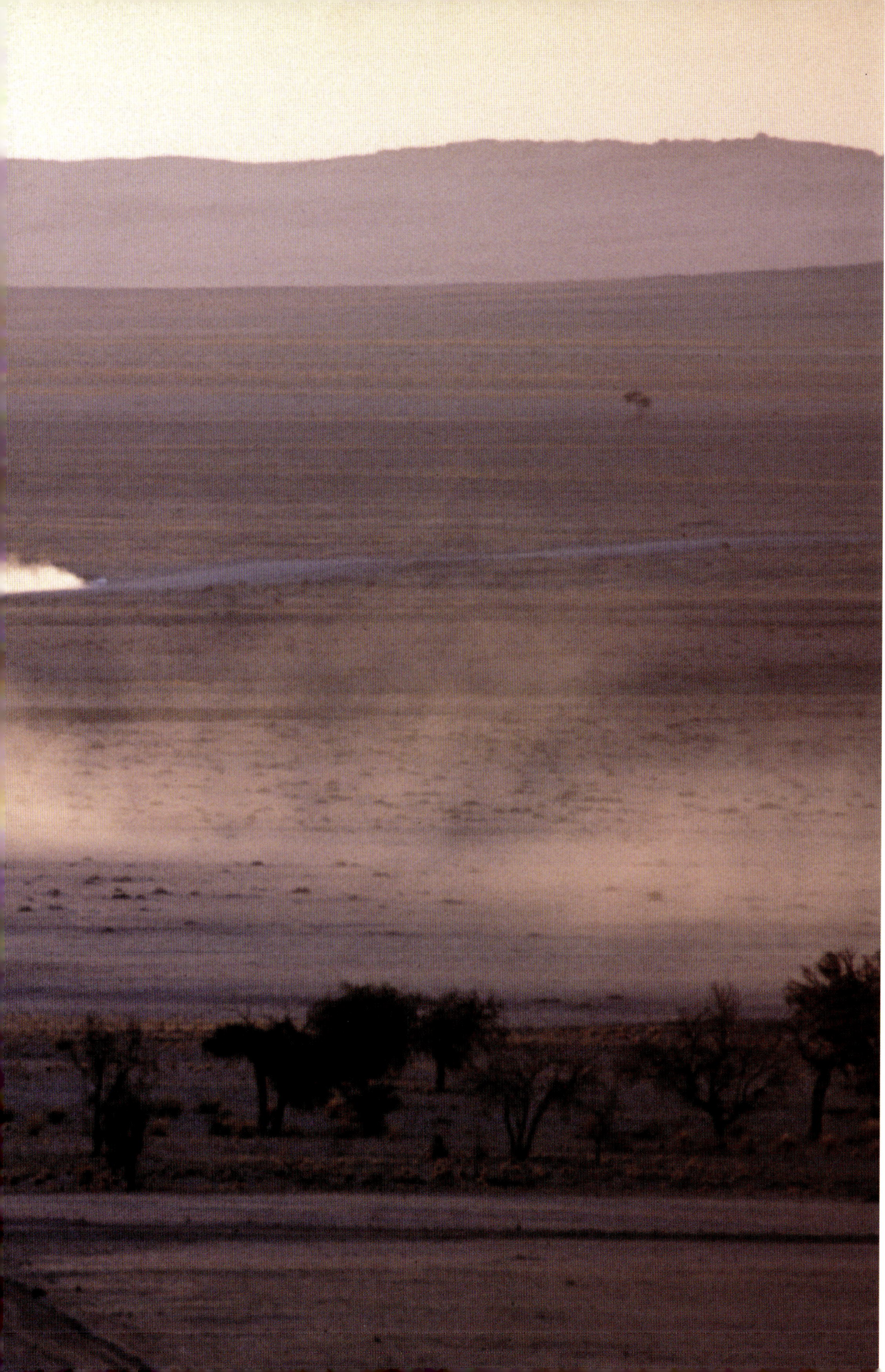

CONTENTS

INTRODUCTION

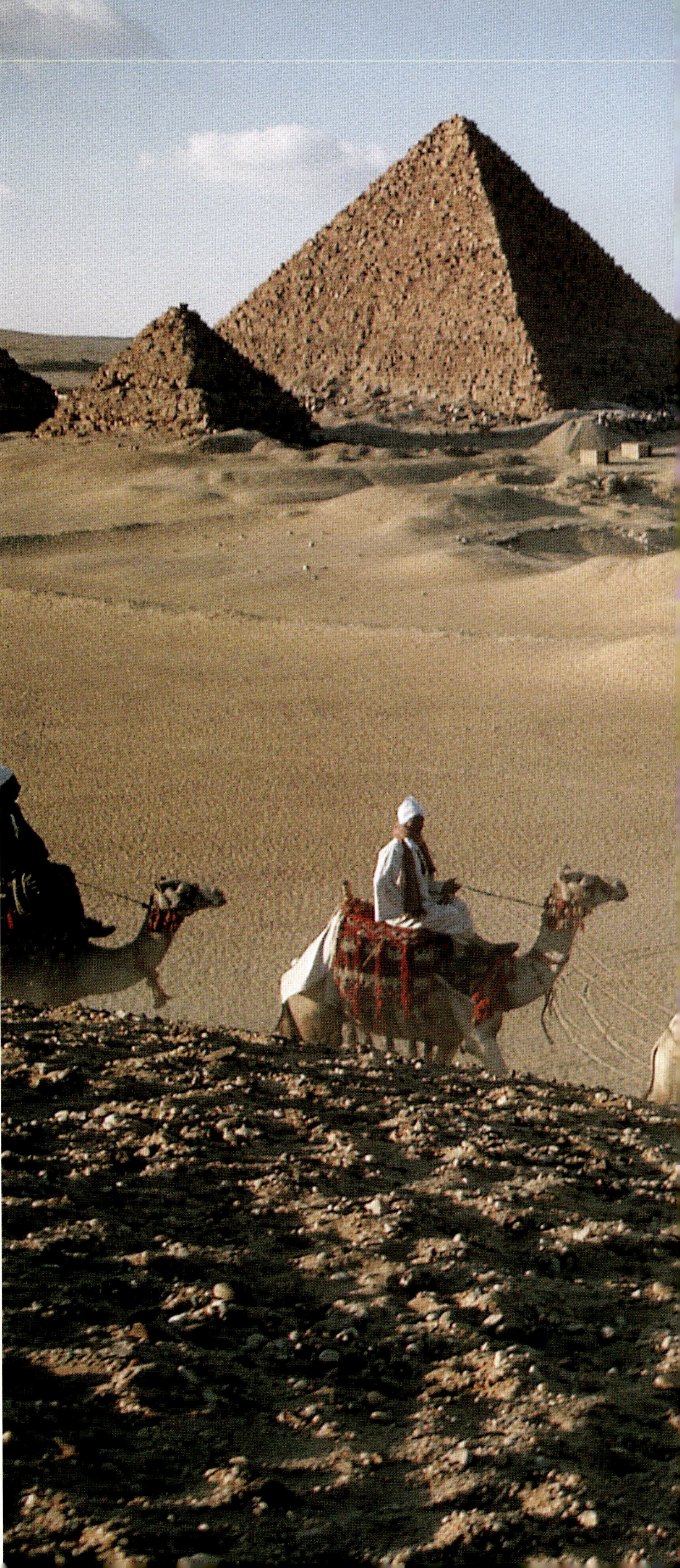

Right: This caravan of camels wending its way slowly past the Great Pyramids at Giza in Egypt represents the traditional Western view of a desert and its people. According to such preconceptions, desert terrain features only shifting sands and a scorching sun, while the people and their nomadic way of life have remained unchanged for many centuries. As this book shows, such traditional views have, in many ways, always been simply wrong, while in other instances, where they may once have contained a grain of truth, that is no longer the case. *Jonathan Blair/Corbis*

The world has a surface area of 196,940,000 square miles, of which 57,506,000 are land, and of that some 19 million square miles are made up of deserts. Thus, no less than one-third of the land available for human life is, to a large extent, uninhabitable, at least in significant numbers of people. Some deserts are too hot for human life and others too cold, some are covered in sand and others in gravel, but they all have one thing in common—they are very, very dry, having either little water or, in some cases, none at all.

Because deserts are such mysterious and apparently forbidding places, epic movies such as *Lawrence of Arabia* and more routine productions about the French Foreign Legion in the Sahara or Westerns about frontier life and exploration in the United States have enabled viewers to explore them by proxy in the security and comfort of their own movie theaters or homes. Thus, the sand dunes of Africa's Sahara and the rugged grandeur of Death Valley and Monument Valley in the United States have become part of the public consciousness. Unfortunately, however, such movies have also given the impression that deserts are unremittingly dangerous, whereas the human body is actually quite well adapted to such conditions, and what has often been forgotten are the techniques developed to come to terms with them.

Definitions

Deserts are not confined to any particular latitude or longitude, nor are they at any specific height above sea level, being found at both Poles and at the Equator and located in heights from over 8,000 feet above sea level to 500 feet below—both, as it happens, in China. Deserts can be categorized in various different ways, but the most widely accepted system is based on the amount of precipitation (i.e., rainfall) over a calendar year, something that is quite straightforward to measure. Thus, areas are divided into three groups: *semi-arid*—between one and two inches of rainfall per year; *arid*—less than one inch; and *extremely arid*—more than twelve months without any rainfall whatsoever. Using these criteria, *extremely arid* and *arid* lands are classified as deserts, while *semi-arid lands* are known as grasslands or steppes. In a further subdivision, they are divided into four main types: hot and dry; semi-arid; coastal; and cold deserts.

Hot and Dry Deserts

The most important hot and dry deserts in North America are the Chihuahuan, Great Basin, Mojave, and Sonoran, with others across the world in Ethiopia. Australia, Asia, and Central and South America. In such deserts the daylight hours are usually warm to hot during most of the year, but extremely hot in summer, while the nights are cold, sometimes below freezing, throughout the year. These conditions are the result of a lack of humidity as the rainfall is so very low; less than about a half-inch per year in some cases. In these deserts the surface is usually either coarse soil, rock or gravel, with effective drainage, which means that there is no sub-surface water. If there is any wind, fine dust or small sand particles are quickly blown elsewhere. The naturally occurring animals (as opposed to those imported by Man) are generally small, live in burrows, and move about in the cool of the night.

Semi-arid Deserts

Semi-arid deserts have moderately long and dry summers, and warm but slightly wetter winters, and, like the hot and dry deserts, cool nights. The surface ranges from fine-textured sand to loose gravel or small rocks and sand. Again, animals tend to be small and to live in burrows, coming out to forage and hunt only at night. Vegetation is usually more plentiful and, in the United States, usually has spines to reduce evaporation or leaves with a glossy surface to reflect heat. Again, there are numerous insects and small animals, all of which have one or more techniques in either body or behavior to minimize the effects of the heat.

Coastal Deserts

The world's coastal deserts are situated on the western edges of continents, near the Tropics of Cancer and Capricorn. They are more complex than other deserts because they are located at the junction of atmospheric, oceanic and terrestrial systems, which interact with each other in unique ways. These deserts, such as the Atacama in Chile and the Skeleton Coast Desert in Namibia, continue right down to the shore. They tend to have cool winters with temperatures of about 41 degrees Fahrenheit to just below freezing, interspersed with fairly long warm-to-hot summers, with temperatures ranging from 55 to 75 degrees Fahrenheit. Average rainfall is between three and five inches, but often

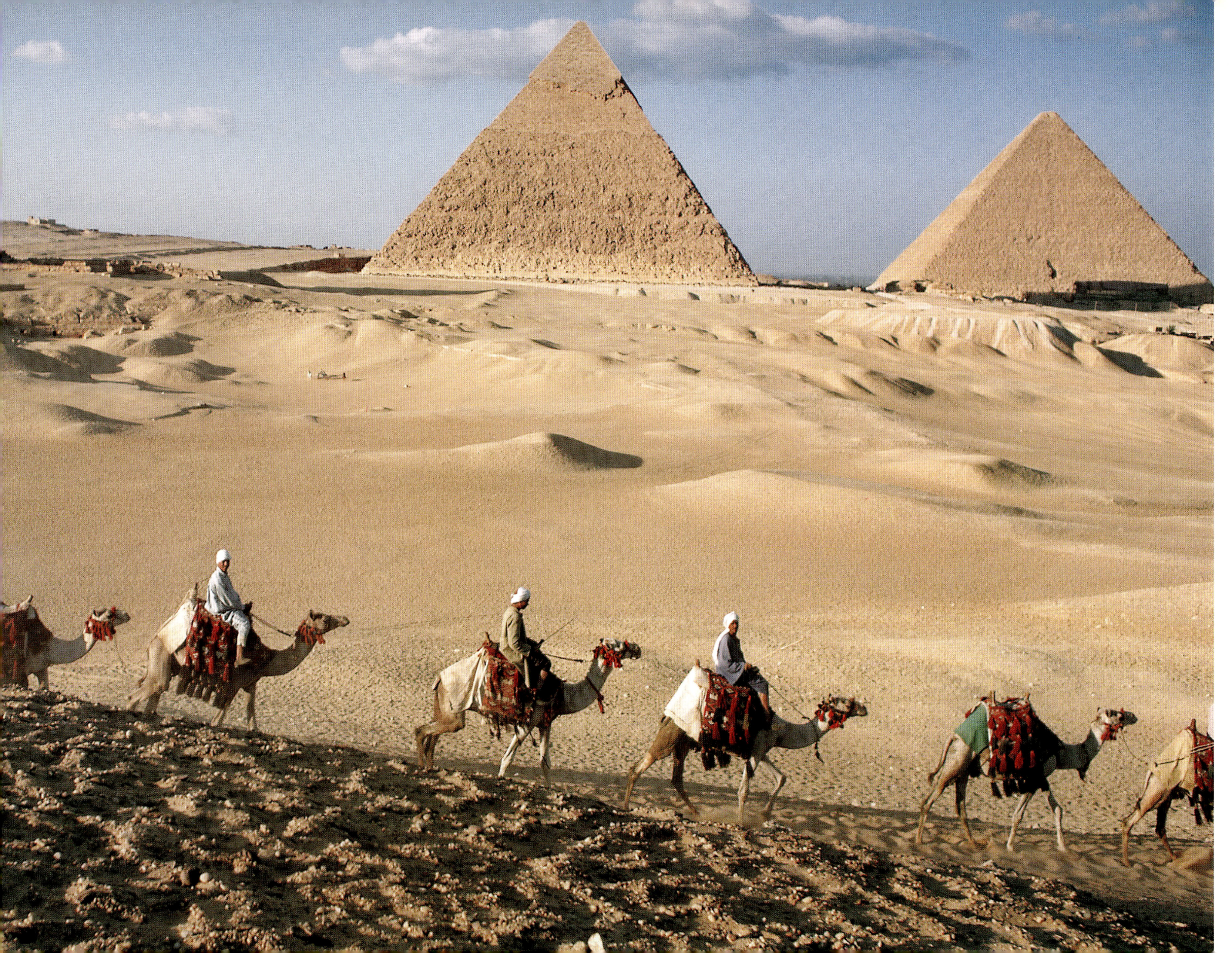

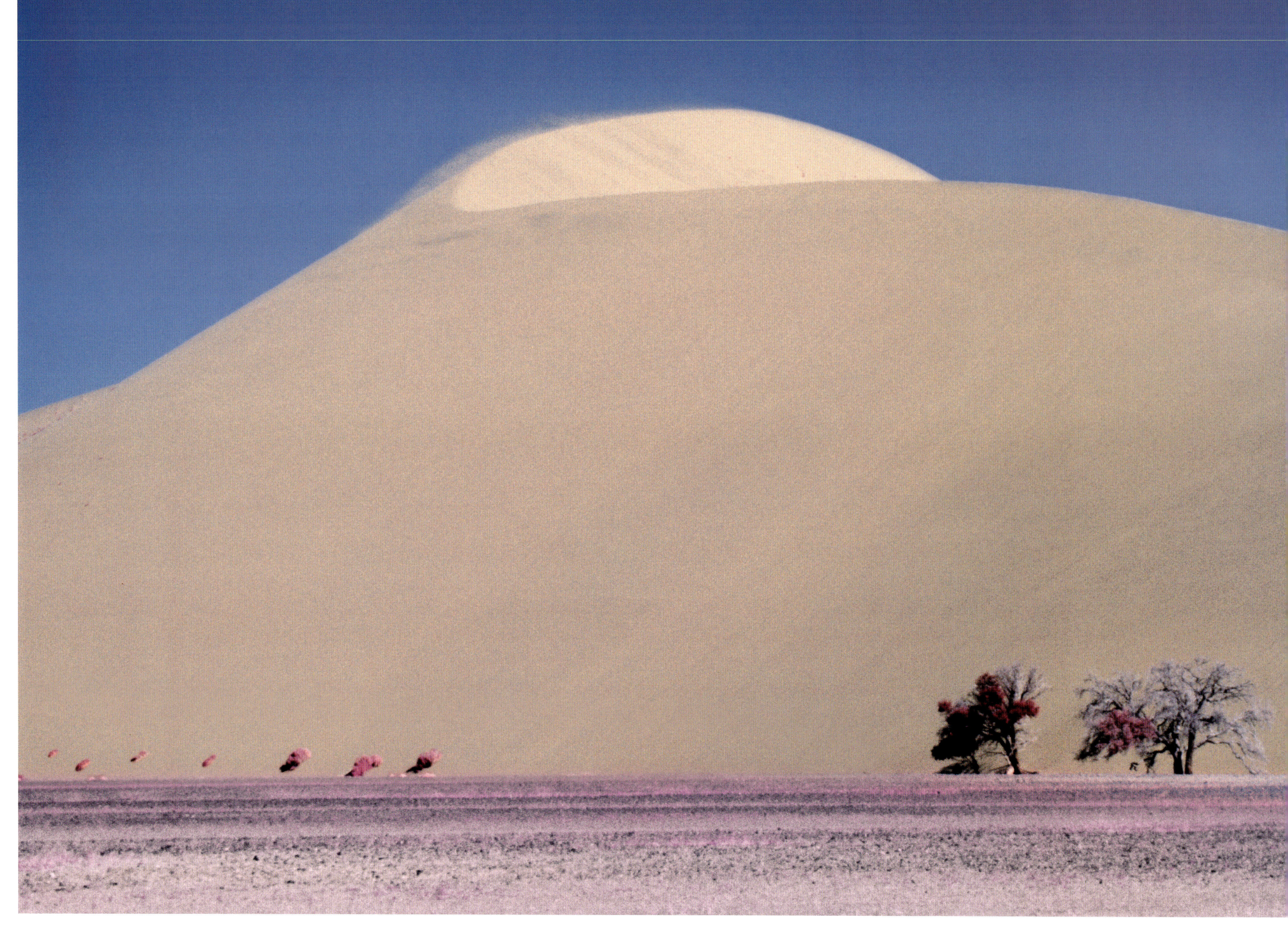

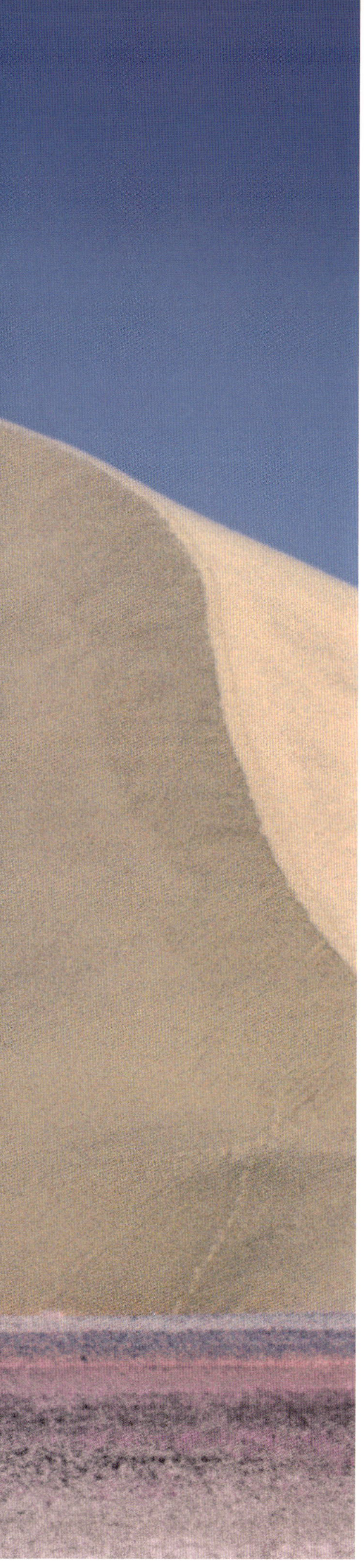

LEFT: The splendor of the sand dunes of the Sossusvlei in the Namib-Naukluft National Park, which soar up to 1,000 feet or more above the surrounding plains, making them the highest dunes in any of the world's deserts. The dunes are bereft of any vegetation, but on the rocky plain below some Camel's Thorn shrubs eke out their lonely and struggling existence. *Michele Westmorland/Corbis*

less, as in the Atacama Desert, where measurable rainfall occurs at an average frequency of between five and twenty years. The surface is generally sandy and fairly porous. Coastal deserts are particularly susceptible to fogs, the result of upwelling cold currents immediately off the shore. Animal and plant life has long since adjusted to the local conditions and, in particular, to the lack of water.

Cold Deserts

Deserts are not all hot, and the Antarctic is just as bereft of life as the Sahara or the Gobi. These cold deserts have very cold winters, with typical temperatures of between 28 to 25 degrees Fahrenheit (although the "wind-chill factor" can make it much colder) and short, moderately warm summers, with temperatures rising to about 78 degrees Fahrenheit. Animal life is minimal, with only a few sea lions, seals and penguins as examples.

Sand Dunes

Among the visually most striking sights in any desert are the sand dunes, which offer superb images for artists, photographers and moviemakers. The sweeping curves, geometrical wind ripples, and pure colors result in striking pictures, one of whose unintended outcomes has been to give many city dwellers the impression that deserts are made up of nothing but such sand dunes. In reality, nothing could be further from the truth and, although it appears that they have never been accurately measured, dunes probably account for no more two percent or so of the surface of the world's desert surfaces.

Dunes require three elements: sand, and plenty of it; wind of sufficient strength to raise the grains and move them to a new position; and a surface that will cause the grains to settle. The grains may simply be blown to a new, but essentially similar, place on the desert floor, but, if the wind direction and speed are reasonably constant, they will cause the grains to move up the windward slope and then tumble over the "slip-face," thus causing the dune to move in a down-wind direction. Indeed, a speed of thirty feet per year is by no means uncommon. Although sand storms occur, lifting grains to considerable heights, normally when the wind picks up grains they rarely rise more than a few feet above the surface. Most desert sand dunes consist of hard crystalline grains of quartz or feldspar, which are made up of aluminum silicates of calcium, potassium or sodium. There are, however, also brilliant white sands, which are formed from grains of gypsum.

Shapes

The most common dune form is crescent-shaped where the mounds are generally wider than they are long, with the slip-face on the concave side of the dune. Such crescentic dunes form as the result of winds blowing in one steady direction, and some of these can move with relative rapidity, sometimes as much as 300 feet per year.

Parabolic dunes are U-shaped and usually result from the arms being held still by vegetation while the apex points towards the wind. Linear dunes, whose length is much greater than their width, may occur in total isolation or, more usually, in parallel with each other, although the lines may be several miles apart. Star dunes have a high central column with three or more arms radiating outwards, and grow upwards rather than laterally. Some have been found that are 1,500 feet high.

Wind Ripples

In many cases the wind simply picks up grains and moves them over a relatively short distance and drops them again. This tends to create a series of low ripples whose line is at right angles to the direction of the prevailing wind and which make seemingly elaborate geometrical patterns, whose visual impact is heightened when the sun is at a low angle in the early morning or late afternoon.

Singing Dunes

One of the unusual properties of some, although by no means all, dunes is that they make a noise, whose nature seems to depend largely on the listener. This noise is variously described as singing, squeaking or booming, while one of the most famous songs to come out of the American West is the ballad of the "shifting, whispering sand." Such noises occur only when the sands are very dry—never in rain or high humidity—and where the grains are more smoothly spherical than usual. In some cases at least, it appears to be the result of a surface layer moving over a static lower layer, with the latter serving as a sounding board. The sound is usually generated naturally but can be created artificially by a human sliding down the slip face of a dune. There are several areas in the USA where such dunes are found, including Nevada, at Sand Mountain, near Fallon; California, at Kelso Dunes, near Kelso; and Eureka Dunes in the Northeast.

Flora and Fauna

Despite the arid nature of sand dunes, many animals and insects have adapted to the conditions to be found there, most by taking advantage of the fact that temperature drops very rapidly with depth, so they live in burrows and are also capable of burying themselves very quickly if threatened. Snakes have adapted to moving on the surface of dunes, but some of these also appear to be capable of moving short distances laterally while maintaining a constant depth of a few inches beneath the surface. Lizards also burrow, but move across the surface on long legs with toes that are specially adapted to ensure minimal contact with the hot surface.

Plants, too, have adapted themselves to survive. One of the most extraordinary sights in the world occurs when rain falls on an apparently empty and lifeless sand dune and within days, if not hours, the sand is covered by a solid carpet of verbena or sunflowers in a riot of color, usually accompanied by delicate scents. Then, after a few days—and as suddenly as they appeared—the plants are overcome by the searing sun and die, but always leaving their seeds to bide their time and await the next opportunity to bloom.

There are also shrubs, such as desert buckwheat and mesquite, which survive by deploying long and dense roots to take advantage of every bit of moisture that can be found. The United States is also home to the sand food plant, which is a parasite and latches on to a host plant, such as desert buckweed, in order to survive.

Many insects also make their home in the sand dunes. Among these is the ant-lion, which digs a circular pit in the sand and then waits for passing prey to fall into the trap from which the steep walls prevent any escape, whereupon the waiting ant-lion pounces and sucks them dry. Another insect, the sand wasp, digs complicated burrows and then spends most of its life catching small insects and bringing them home for its young to feed on.

Thus, dunes are not the lifeless heaps of sand of popular imagination, but are very specialized habitats, that are home to some of the hardiest and most determined survivors on Earth.

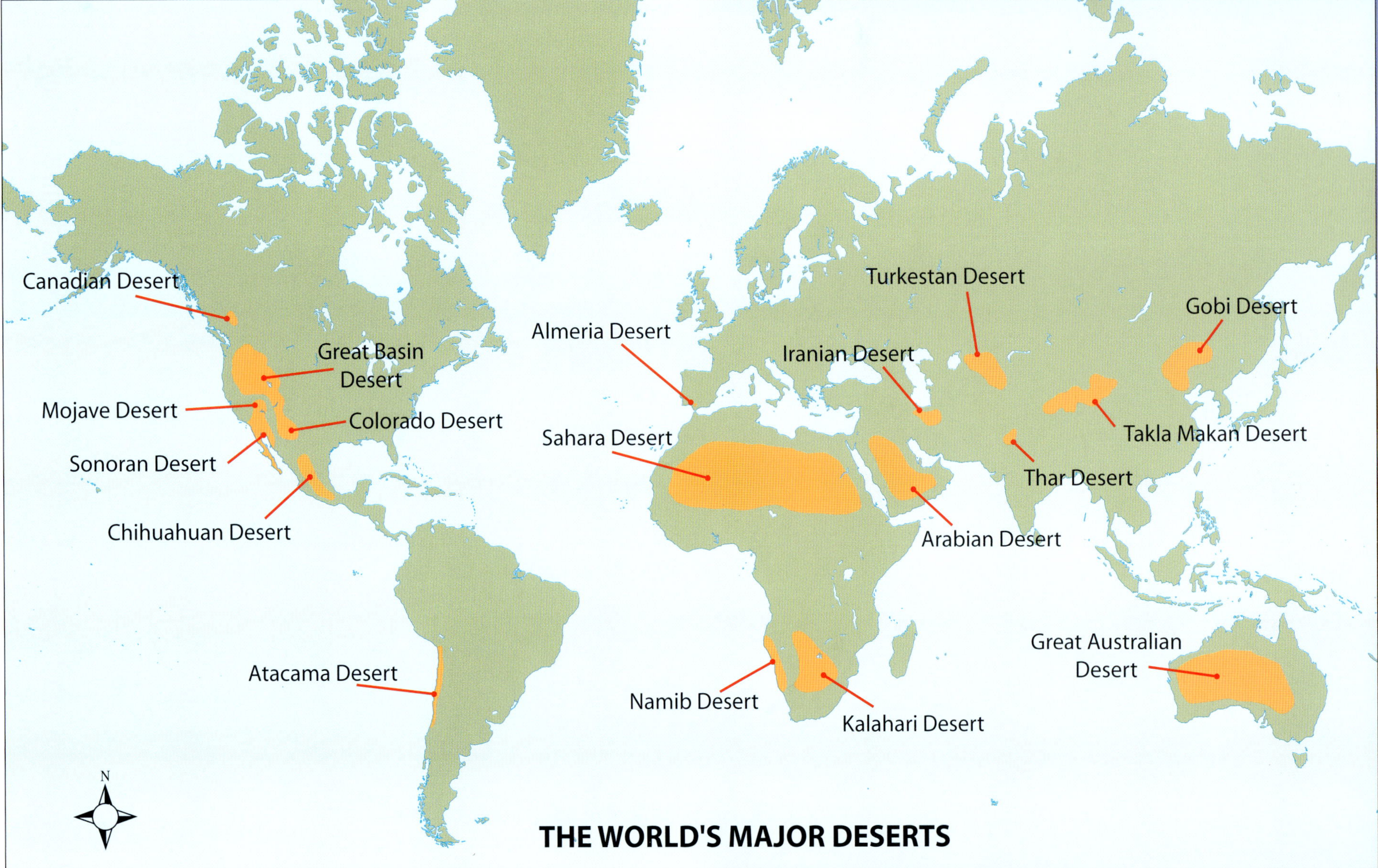

THE DESERTS OF NORTH AMERICA

It is generally considered that there are four distinct desert areas in North America, with the Great Basin Desert described as a "cold desert" and the remaining three—Chihuahuan, Mojave, and Sonoran—as "hot deserts."

Great Basin Desert

With an area of some 190,000 square miles, the Great Basin Desert is the largest desert located entirely within the United States. It stretches north-to-south from the Columbian Plateau to the Mojave and Sonoran deserts, and east-to-west from the Sierra Nevada to the Rockies, with portions in the states of Idaho, Nevada, and Utah and a small corner of Oregon. Classified as a "cold desert," it lies to the north of the other deserts and the greater part is at heights between 4,000 and 6,500 feet. Rainfall is between seven and twelve inches per year and is reasonably evenly distributed across the whole area. The vegetation is generally low in height and plants tend to be grouped by species, with a single species dominating particular areas.

Some authorities include the Colorado Plateau as part of the Great Basin Desert; others regard it as a separate entity, named the Navajoan Desert. Some areas within the Great Basin are given their own names, including the Black Rock, Escalante, Great Sandy, Red, Sevier, and Smoke Creek Deserts.

Chihuahuan Desert

The Chihuahuan Desert has a total area of some 200,000 square miles, making it the largest in North America. Most of it lies in Mexico. That part lying in the United States occupies the extreme west of Texas and small areas of southeastern New Mexico and Arizona. Most of the desert is high—between 3,500 and 5,000 feet—with cool winters and extremely hot summers, with only small areas receiving more than ten inches of rain per year. A small part of the Chihuahuan Desert to the

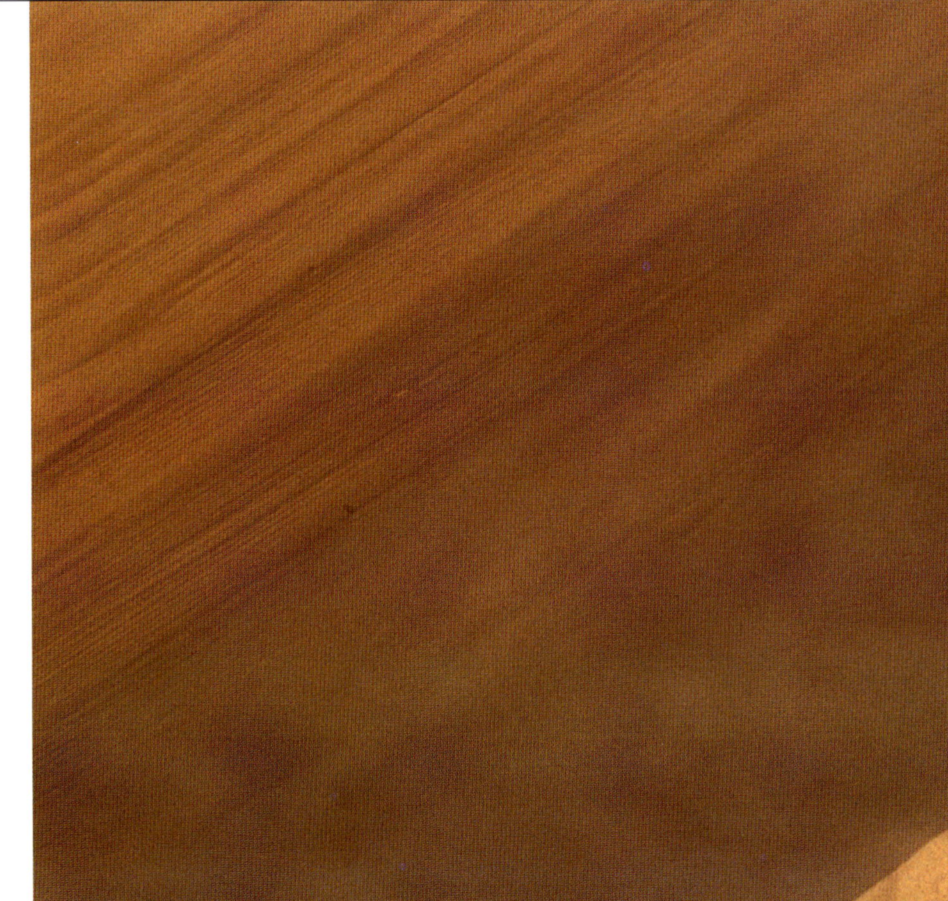

RIGHT: "Erg" is the Arab term for a sprawling sea of sand dunes, and this is Libya's Erg Murzuq, deep in the south of the country and in the heart of the Sahara. The area has been desperately dry for centuries but recent exploration has shown that deep below the surface are huge fossil aquifers holding great reserves of pure, fresh water. A project known as "The Great Man-Made River" is in progress to bring the water across terrain such as this to irrigate the coastal belt and, it is hoped, drive the desert sands a little further inland.
Sergio Pitamitz/Corbis

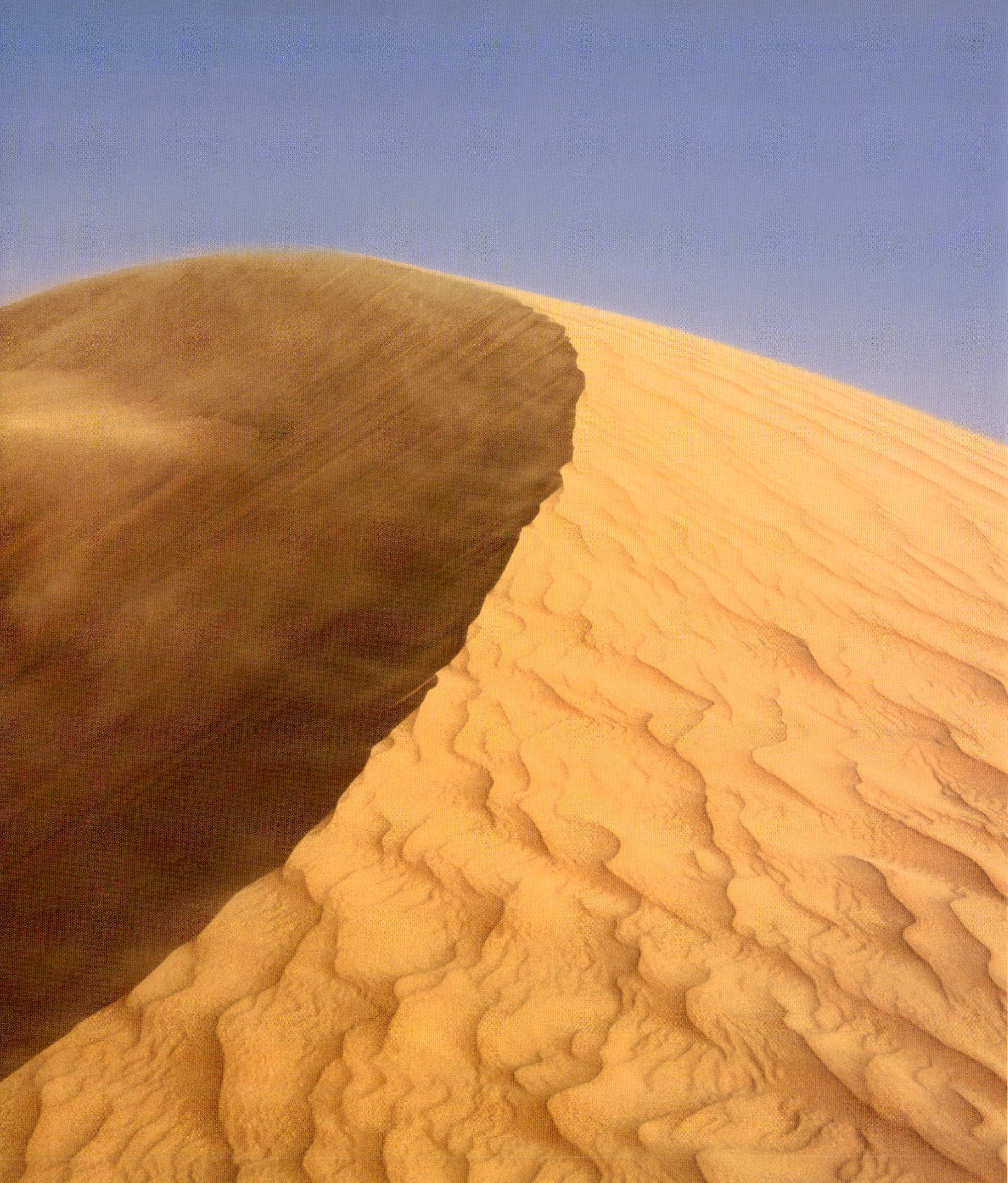

west of the Pecos River is known as the Trans-Pecos Desert; it covers 32,000 square miles, most of which is under private ownership in the form of very large ranches.

Mojave Desert

The Mojave Desert covers an area of some 25,000 square miles between the Sonoran and Great Basin deserts, including southeastern California and portions of Arizona, Nevada, and Utah. One of its most famous features is Death Valley. It is characterized by an average rainfall of less than five inches per year, almost all of which arrives during winter. The summer is very hot, extremely dry, and windy, while winter temperatures are below freezing. Vegetation is sparse, although the Mojave is home to over 200 separate species of plants. Some mining takes place, mainly for gold, iron, silver, and tungsten. Some authorities divide the Mojave into two quasi-separate entities, the North and South Mojave Deserts, with the dividing line running east-to-west through Las Vegas, Nevada.

Sonoran Desert

With an area of 120,000 square miles, the Sonoran is the third largest—as well as by far the hottest—of the North American Deserts. It covers the southern parts of Arizona and California, much of Baja California, and about half of the Mexican state of Sonora, from which it takes its name. Vegetation is comparatively plentiful by desert standards, while irrigation schemes have transformed some areas into fertile agricultural land. As with the other major deserts, parts of the Sonoran Desert are sometimes considered to be deserts in their own right. These include the Arizona Upland, Borrego, Colorado, Magdalena, Vizcaino, Yuha, and Yuma Deserts.

Canadian Desert

The Canadian Desert is situated in the South Okanagan-Similkameen Valley of British Columbia, and lies at the northern end of the Great Basin Desert. This very small area receives greater annual rainfall and has lower average temperatures than the much larger deserts south of the border, but it is nevertheless a desert habitat and meets the criteria of a desert.

AFRICAN DESERTS

Sahara Desert

The Sahara Desert stretches across most of northern Africa, with a total area of 1,791,500 square miles, making it about three times the size of the state of Alaska. The popular picture of the Sahara is of a vast sea of rolling sand dunes, but while there are certainly some such areas of dunes, the major part of the desert is gravel or stony plains, with the occasional salt flat. Rainfall is both very low and irregular, and life centers on the oases and their associated springs or wells, although vast underground aquifers have recently been discovered. There are also several

Desert	Location	Area (sq miles)	Surface	Vegetation	Animals	Comments
Arabian	Arabian Peninsula	900,000	Gravel, sand, extensive dunes	Acacia, oleander, saltbush	Camel, gazelle, lizard, jackal	Nomadic Bedouin
Australian (includes Gibson, Great Sandy, Simpson, Sturt, Victoria)	Australia	890,00	Sandy: Great Sandy, Victoria, Simpson. Stony: Gibson, Sturt	Acacia, casuarina, eucalyptus, saltbush, grass	Dingo, fat-tailed mouse, kangaroo, marsupial, mole, bandicoot	Aborigines
Chihuahuan	North Central Mexico, Arizona, New Mexico, Texas	175,000	High plateau: stony areas, sandy soil	Cacti, flax, creosote bush, lechuguilla, mesquite, poppy	Coyote, kangaroo rat.	Largest US desert
Kalahari	Southwestern Africa	200,000	Sand dunes, gravel	Acacia, aloe	Gazelle, gerbil, squirrel, hyena, jackal, springbok	Bushmen
Mojave	Southwestern United States (Arizona, California, Nevada)	25,000	Sandy soil, gravel, salt flats	Creosote bush, verbena, joshua tree, mesquite	Bighorn sheep, chuckwalla, coyote, jackrabbit	Death Valley located in this desert
Monte	Argentina	125,000	Sand and soil	Cactus, creosote bush, paloverde	Armadillo, cavy, jaguarundi, puma	Similar to the Sonoran Desert
Sahara	Northern Africa	3,500,000	Mountains, rocky areas, gravel plains, salt flats, huge areas of dunes.	Acacia, grasses, tamarisks	Antelope, dorcas, gazelle, fennec fox	Largest desert in the world. Over 2 million inhabitants (mostly nomads)
Sonoran	Southwestern United States (Arizona, California) and parts of Mexico (Baja Peninsula, Sonora)	120,000	Sand, soil, gravel	Agave, globemallow, creosote bush, lily, mesquite	Gila monster, rats	
Thar	India, Pakistan	77,000	Sand dunes, gravel plains	Acacia, euphorbias, grasses, shrubs	Black buck, camel, jackal	

HOT DESERTS OF THE WORLD

mountain ranges, which enjoy slightly greater rainfall and more moderate temperatures.

Some experts claim that the Sahara was the result of the first known case of desertification, which started about 3000BC and was the result of over-grazing by domesticated animals, particularly pigs. For many centuries the Sahara has been very sparsely populated, with the majority of its inhabitants located on the outer fringes, although hardened and desert-wise people such as the Tuareg have long conducted camel-trains across the arid waste, maintaining overland trade and making considerable profits in the process.

Namib Desert

The Namib Desert is a large coastal desert in Namibia, in southwestern Africa. It stretches for some 1,000 miles along the coast of the Atlantic Ocean and is between 30 and 100 miles deep, giving it a total area of approximately 19,000 square miles. It is generally thought to be about 80 million years old, making it the world's oldest continuous desert region, being almost totally barren and with an average rainfall of less than one inch a year. It includes an area of sand dunes with a maximum height of about 1,100 feet, the highest in the world. The coast is notorious for its dense fogs, which in times past led many ships to be wrecked and cost many sailors their lives, leading to the northern part being named the Skeleton Coast. Signs of creeping desertification are clear from the fact that some wrecks are now up to forty yards inland, indicating that the desert is gradually creeping out to sea. The main financial value of the Namib lies in its tungsten, salt, and diamond mining, although there is also a growing tourist industry.

Kalahari Desert

The generally accepted extent of the Kalahari Desert includes most of Botswana, as well as parts of South Africa, Namibia, and Zimbabwe, an area of some 193,000 square miles. It is characterized by extensive areas of red-brown sand with no permanent surface water, although it is not a true desert within the usual definition of the word, since parts receive up to about ten inches of rainfall, and the true arid area is in the southwest. The Kalahari is noted for its game reserves, which protect many species of animals birds and reptiles. The main inhabitants are the Bushmen who have lived there for at least 20,000 years, but those living within the borders of Botswana have been compulsorily relocated into villages, allegedly for their own benefit. The name "Kalahari" comes from a local word meaning "the great thirst."

ASIAN AND SOUTH ASIAN DESERTS

Arabian Desert

The Arabian Desert covers a huge area (714,786 square miles) of predominantly arid and sparsely populated desert. In the north it borders on Jordan and Iraq, on the west the Red Sea, on the east the Gulf, and the south the Indian Ocean. Although termed the Arabian Desert, it is actually made up of a number of identifiable desert regions, which abut on each other. In the north is the An-Nafud Desert (25,000 square miles) which is connected by a corridor of sandy terrain known as the ad-Dahna Desert to the Rub' al Khali (= empty quarter) in the south. The Rub' al Khali has an area of 250,000 square miles—approximately the same as Texas—composed mainly of sand lying on a bed of gravel or gypsum, with the dunes reaching heights of 1,000 feet or so. The sands are mainly silicates, approximately 80 percent quartz, the remainder feldspar. The majority of the population is grouped around water sources, such as wells and springs, and along the coast, but as elsewhere there is a drift towards the towns.

Gobi Desert

The Gobi Desert, one of the largest in the world, lies within the People's Republic of China and the Mongolian Republic. It is some 1,000 miles from southwest to northeast and 500 miles from north to south, covering an area of approximately 450,000 square miles. The surface is predominantly bare rock although there are sandy areas. Some authorities state that the western end of the Gobi, plus the desert basin of Lop Nor, form a separate desert, designated the Taklamakan. The nomadic herders of the Gobi have always been small in number, but they are decreasing rapidly in the face of the attractions of urban life.

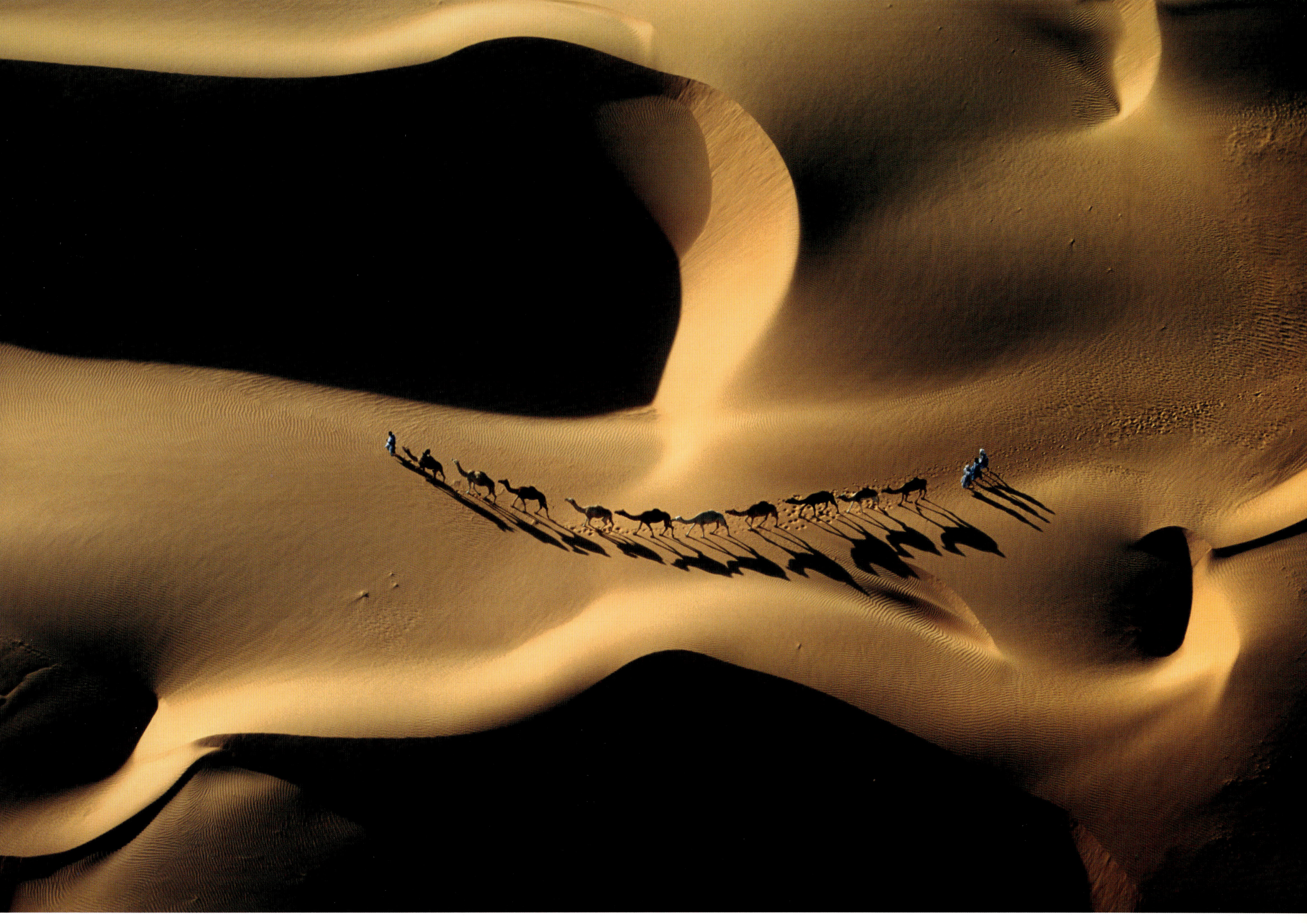

PAGE 15: A camel train in the western Sahara Desert, near Nouakchott, capital of Mauritania, a small republic on the Atlantic coast of Africa. The country's natural supplies of fresh water are very limited and some 80 percent of the terrain is desert, a figure that is increasing slowly, and the country is constantly hot, dry and dusty. Mauritania achieved independence from France in 1962, at which time some 66 percent of its population were nomads, but this figure has reduced dramatically to no more than about six percent today and scenes such as that seen here are becoming progressively rarer.
Yann Arthus-Bertrand/Corbis

RIGHT: The popular picture in the West of deserts is that they are covered in sand dunes, but as this picture of the Gobi Desert shows, this is by no means always correct. Here a gravel-covered plain has a scattering of low-lying bushes, with not a single dune in sight. In the middle distance on the left is a collection of *gers*, the Mongolian circular tent. In the far distance are the snow-capped Altai Mountains.
Steve Bein/Corbi

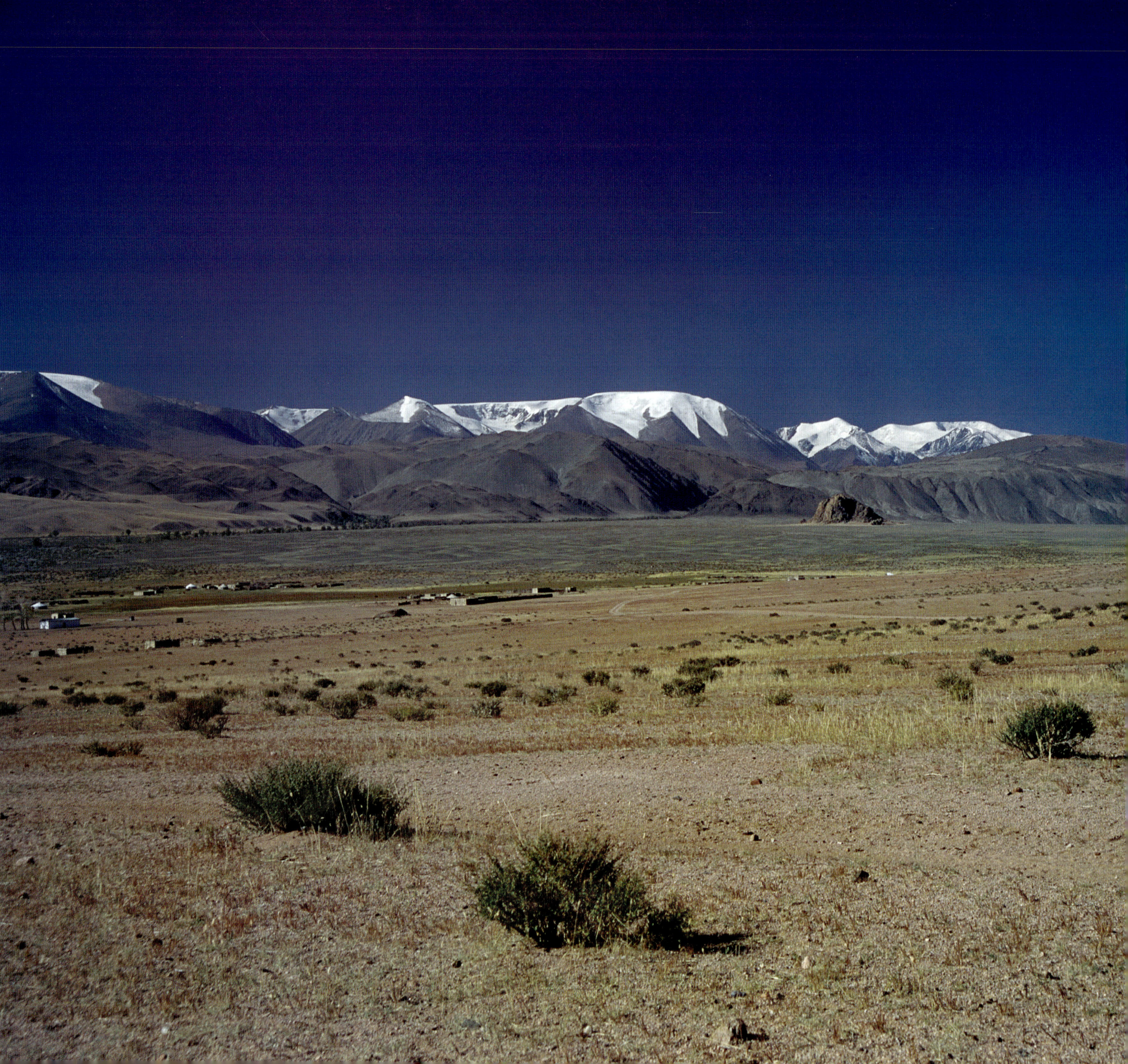

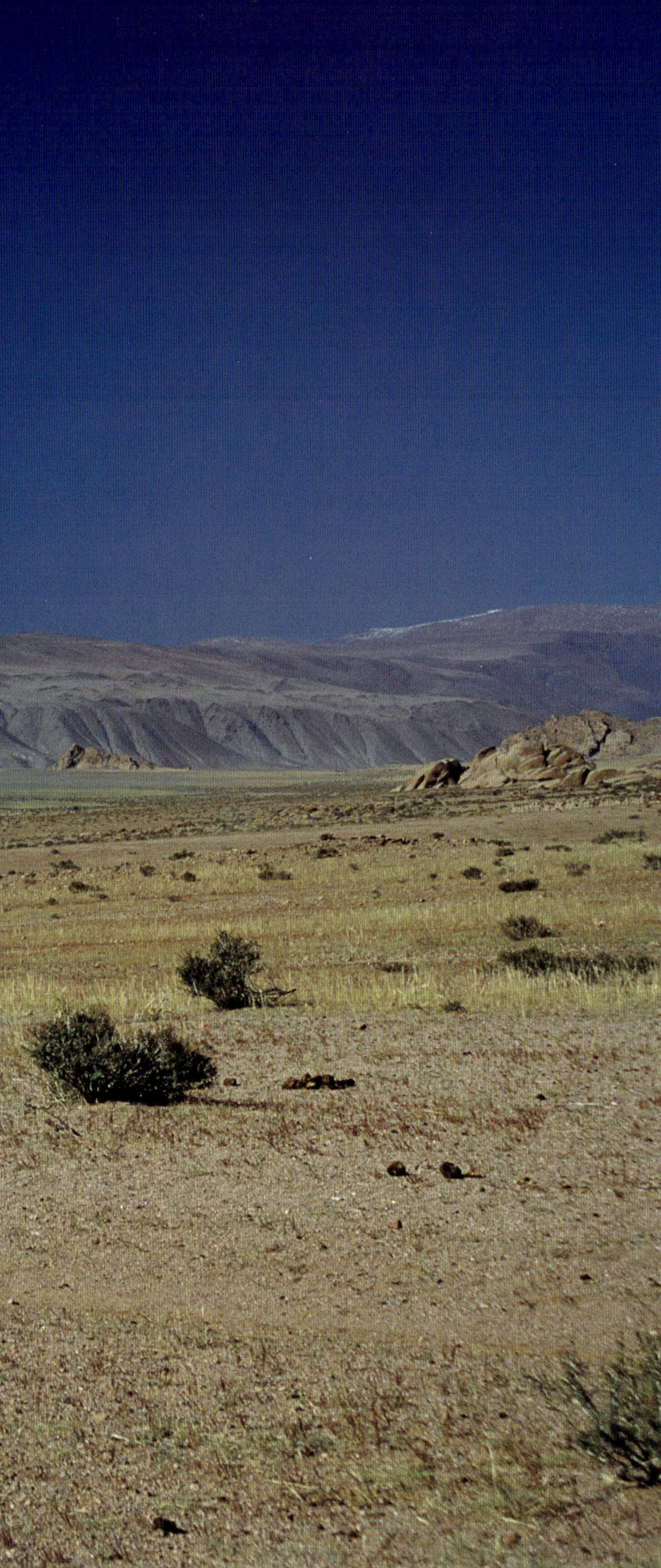

Great Indian Desert

The Great Indian Desert is about 500 miles long and 250 miles wide, covering an area of some 77,000 square miles, and is split politically between India, which calls it the Thar Desert, and Pakistan, where it is known as the Cholistan Desert. Its approximate boundaries are the Indus River in the west, the Sutlej River in the northwest, the Arvalli Hills in the east, and the Rann of Kutch, a large salt marsh in the south. The surface is mainly static dunes, rock outcrops, and salt pans, but about ten percent of the area is moving sand dunes. Annual rainfall is less than ten inches per year and vegetation is non-existent in many areas, but there is some sparse shrub- and grassland.

Iranian Desert

The Iranian Desert (whose full name is the Southern Iranian Nub-Sindian Desert) covers an area of some 135,700 square miles in the south of the country and extending into southern Iraq and western Pakistan. It is generally similar to the southwestern states of the United States, with scrub-filled, generally rocky plateau, and high daytime temperatures of up to 110 degrees Fahrenheit that fall to about 50 degrees at night. The area was generally unknown outside the Middle East until 1980 when U.S. Special Forces suffered grievous losses at a rendezvous named as "Desert One," during their failed rescue attempt of the U.S. Embassy hostages.

Sinai Desert

The Sinai is a triangular-shaped peninsula, lying between the Red Sea and the Gulf of Ababa, with mountains in the south, rising to over 7,000 feet, but the remainder is desert that extends northwards to the Mediterranean coast. The desert has an area of approximately 23,000 square miles and is virtually uninhabited apart from a small number of nomadic Bedouin and military patrols. The Sinai has considerable religious significance to no fewer than three world religions, Christianity, Islam, and Judaism, and Mount Sinai itself was the place, according to the Hebrew Bible, that Moses was handed the Ten Commandments. This religious significance has led to repeated fighting over this barren desert for many years. At first glance the Sinai appears lifeless, but there is, in reality, plenty of animal, reptile, bird, and plant life. Most of the animals and birds are nocturnal, emerging from their lair, burrow or nest only in the cool of the night.

Turkmen and Aral Kara Kum Desert

The Turkmen Kara Kum Desert lies to the east of the Caspian Sea stretching 500 miles from east to west and 300 miles from north to south—a total area of 135,000 square miles, which includes almost the whole of the state of Turkmenistan. It is usually considered to consist of three elements: the Trans-Unguz, the highest part, in the north, whose surface has been scoured by high winds; Central Kara Kum, a low-lying area, mainly sand dunes; and the southeastern Kara Kum, which is mainly sand marshes. The inhabitants are Turkmen, who in past times were nomadic, but over the past century have formed farming settlements and small market towns, while oil and gas have brought new economic and employment opportunities. The Turkmen Kara Kum has hot, dry summers (up to 93 degrees Fahrenheit) and cold winters (25 degrees Fahrenheit), although there is little snow, while the annual rainfall varies from almost three inches in the north to as much as six inches in the south. Animals are relatively few in total numbers, but of diverse species, including cats, foxes, gazelle, hares, and hedgehogs. The much smaller Aral Kara Kum, with an area of approximately 15,440 square miles, lies to the northeast of the Aral Sea.

THE PEOPLES OF THE DESERTS

All humans originated in arid areas, but over the millennia the vast majority have moved to more hospitable environments. Some, however, remained in the deserts, either to live there or by developing the ability to move over them, although, as will be seen from this general survey, their numbers are reducing rapidly.

The Middle Eastern Bedouin

The Bedouin (*Bedu* = desert dweller) is a generic Arabic term applied to the nomadic peoples who originated in the Arabian Desert, but subsequently spread to the Negev and Sinai Deserts as well. Assembled into groups known as "tribes," some Bedouin settled in oases, while others led a nomadic existence based on moving from one oasis to another to find water and grazing for their camels. But, while some still pursue such a traditional way of life, many have become urbanized.

There have been two dramatic developments that have impacted on the way of life of the Bedouin. The first is the achievement of modern statehood, which has not only imposed political boundaries across what used to be simply open desert where anyone was free to wander as they wished, but has also involved increasing numbers in the running of a modern state. The second has been the discovery of oil, which, for those in the areas concerned, has resulted in almost untold riches, resulting in a rejection by the younger generations of the physically and mentally demanding nomadic life and harsh conditions of the desert. Some struggle to maintain the traditional culture, values, and way of life, but there are fewer of them every year.

The Tuareg of the Sahara

It is estimated that some two million people live in the geographical region known as the Sahara Desert, of whom approximately two-thirds live in small towns and oases, where they irrigate the land to produce fruit, vegetables, and cereals, and grazing for their animals, particularly goats. They also harvest the dates from the palm trees. The remainder, possibly some 600,000 to 700,000 (nobody is certain of the actual number) still follow the traditional nomadic way of life and, like the Bedouin in the Middle East, they are dependent on the camel for transportation as they move from one oasis to another in search of sustenance for themselves and their herds of sheep and goats.

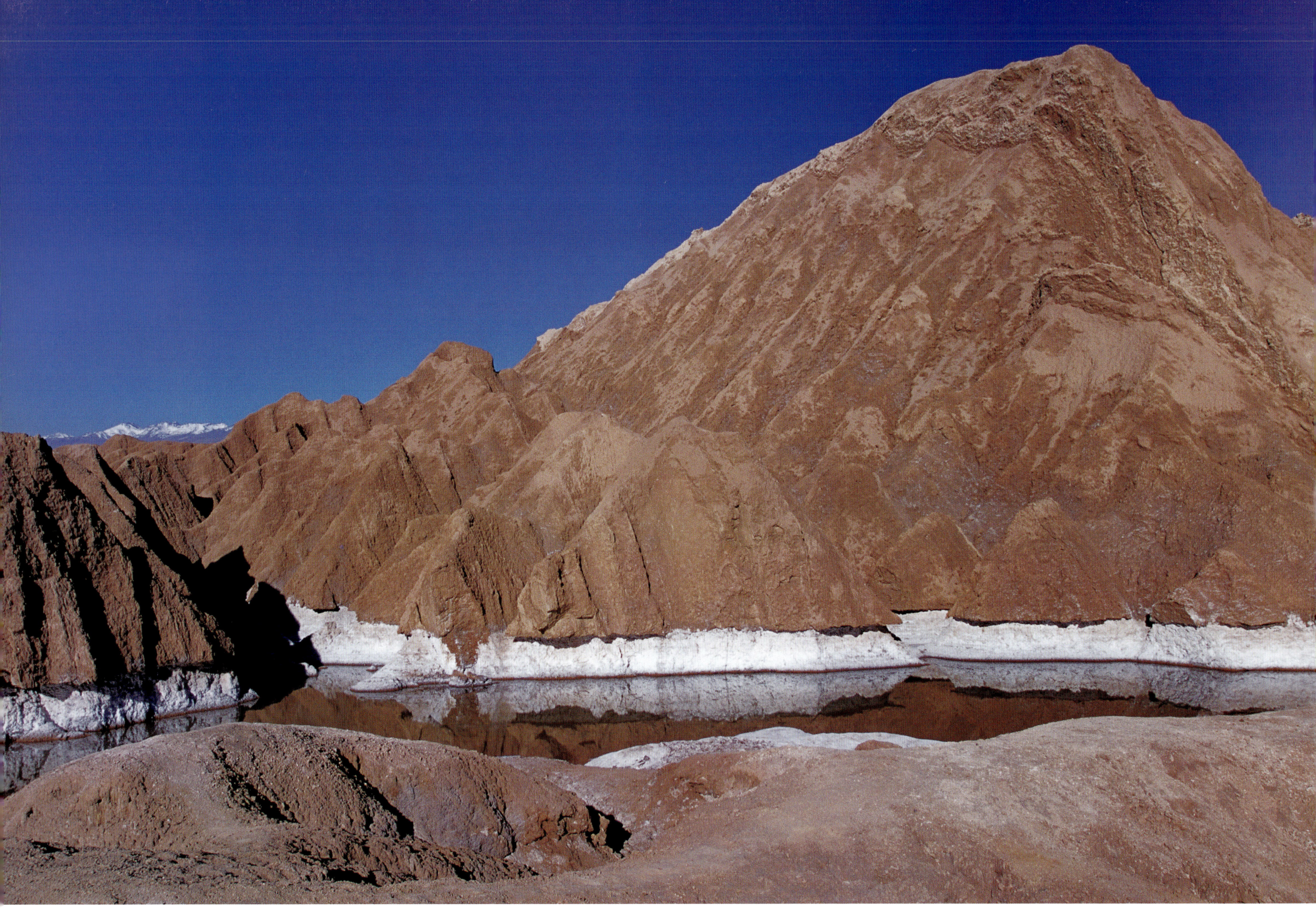

The Tuareg belong to the Berber ethnic group and for at least two millennia they operated the caravans that moved people and goods across the inhospitable central Saharan region between the northern Mediterranean coast and the great cities on the southern fringe of the Sahara. Today, the Tuareg homeland stretches across a wide swathe of the central Sahara, encompassing parts of the modern states of Algeria, Burkina-Farso, Libya, Mali, and Niger, and there is a political movement seeking the establishment of a Tuareg state. Another ethnic group, the Toubou (Tébu) live in the Tibesti Mountains in Chad, from where they traded with Algeria and Libya for many centuries.

The Himba of Southern Africa

The Himba people inhabit the Kunenen region (formerly known as Kaokoland) of Namibia, where they pursue a nomadic, pastoral way of life, concentrating on raising cattle and goats. Like other inhabitants of southwestern Africa, the Himba have had to cope not only with harsh living conditions, but also with a series of man-made disasters. They managed to avoid the European colonial expansion of the 17th and 18th centuries, only to be forcibly incorporated into the embryonic German empire in the 1880s. The various local tribes rebelled against the Germans' harsh rule, whereupon, under direct orders from Berlin, the colonial administration set out, quite deliberately, to exterminate them, in particular the Himbas and a related tribal group, the Herreros. The Himbas moved northwards to their present territory but were later the victims of the South African policy of apartheid and then became innocently involved in the civil wars that led to the establishment of independence in Angola and Namibia. Having successfully survived all of those, albeit with depleted numbers, the Himbas' way of life is now threatened by a huge hydro-electric scheme, which, if implemented, would result in a large part of their tribal lands being submerged for ever.

In northern Africa, the Bedouin and Tuareg respond to the desert heat by dressing in long flowing robes and turbans, which are designed to keep them cool and protect their skins. The Himba, on the other hand, wear as little as possible, although the women, who are renowned for their beauty, cover themselves with a mixture of herbs, ochre (a pigment based on iron oxide) and butter fat, giving their skins a glowing, reddish color. They also have intricate hairstyles and wear elaborate jewelry.

The Aboriginal People of Australia

The continent of Australia is marginally greater in area than the contiguous states of the United States of America (2,966,368 compared to 2,965,487 square miles), and of that some 80 percent is arid or semi-arid and around 18 percent is true desert. The Aboriginal people of Australia arrived some 40,000 years ago, at a time when present-day Australia and Tasmania were joined to each other and were, in turn, joined to what is now New Guinea. When the land masses separated, the Aborigines were cut off from the remainder of the human race and developed a lifestyle that stayed effectively unchanged for tens of

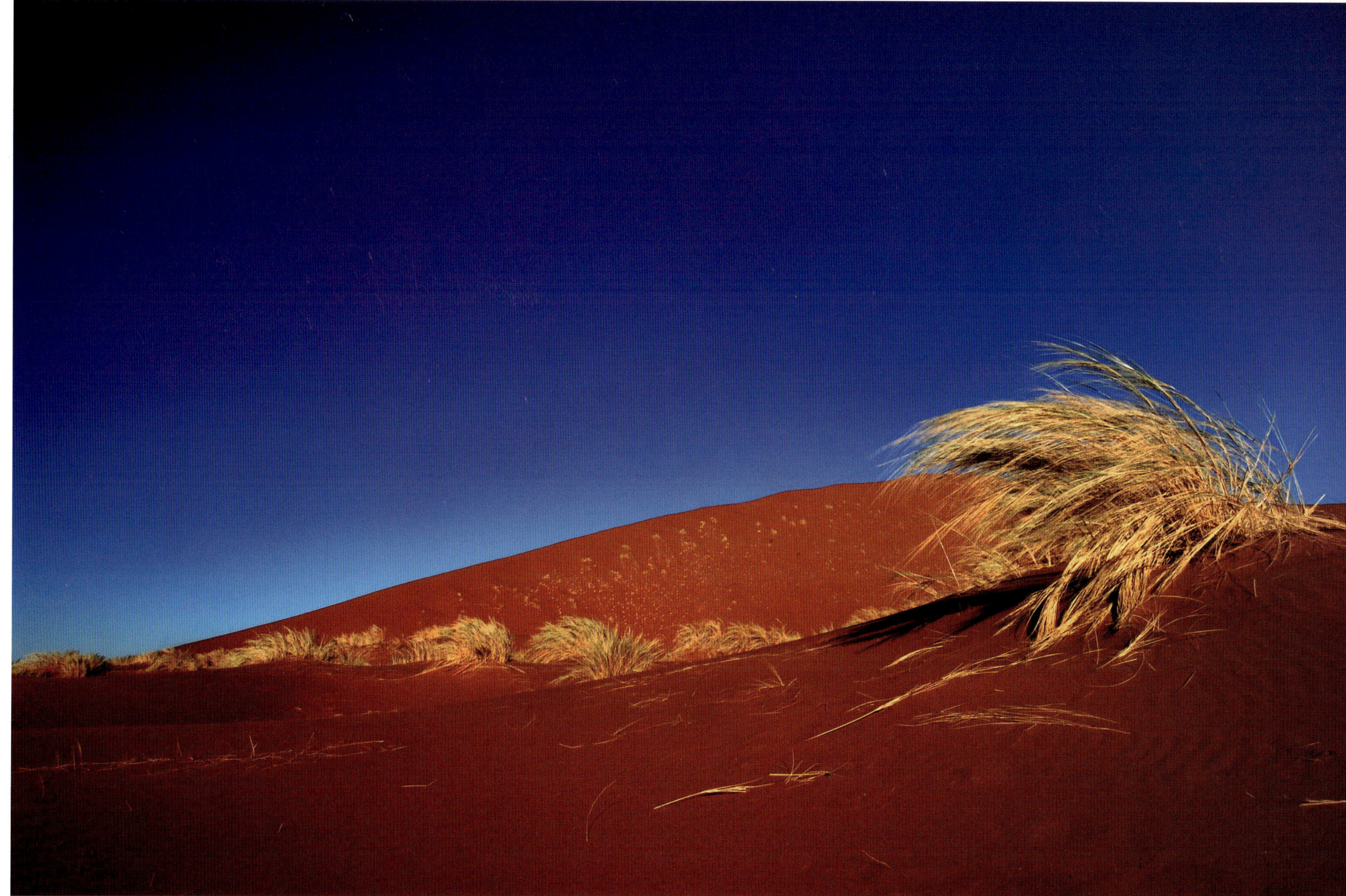

Left: One of the better known areas in the Atacama Desert is the chillingly named *Valle de la Muerte* (= Valley of the Death). There is, however, a belief among some authorities that this is a mispronunciation of the original name, *Valle de Marte* (= Valley of Mars), which stemmed from its perceived likeness to the surface of that planet, a belief that is supported by its proximity to *Valle de la Luna* (= Valley of the Moon).
Ludovic Maisant/Corbis

Above: Various plants will grow in desert conditions, such as this Namib Dune Grass (*Stipagrostis sabulicola*), which is found only among the dunes. It is reed-like, with individual stems reaching heights of up to about six feet. As with these examples, it roots itself in sand hummocks, where little other vegetation will ever be found. In order to gain full benefit from any precipitation, the Dune Grass spreads its roots in all directions; some are up to 60 to 70 feet in length and all are close to the surface.
Tjaart van Staden/fotoLibra

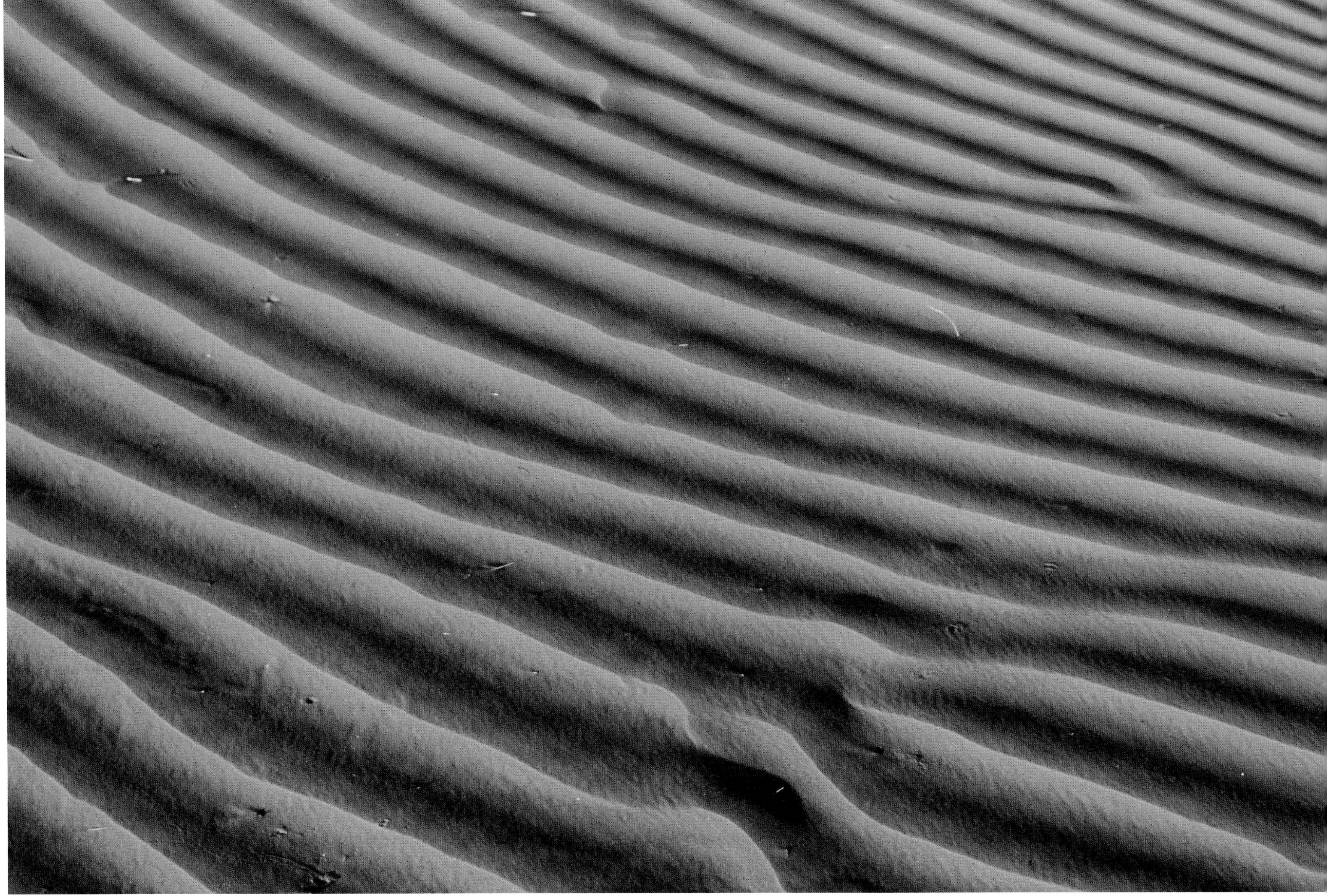

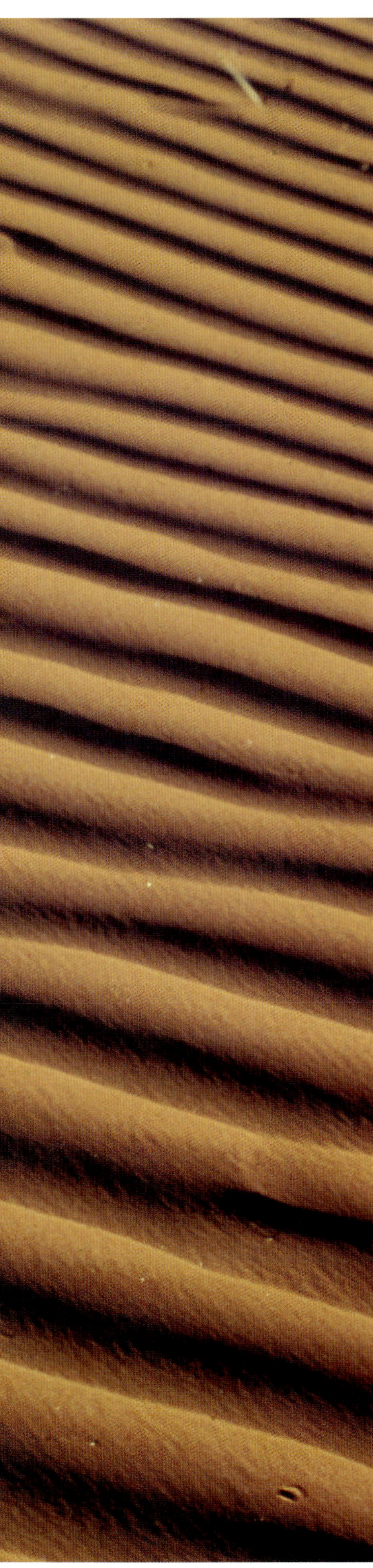

LEFT: The rippling effect on desert sands is due to the action of the wind, which tends to prise individual grains from their current location and then blow them a distance, which depends upon the velocity of the wind and the mass of the grain. The grain then encounters another ripple—in effect, a low ridge—and always on the windward side, thus building it up and creating beautiful patterns, which are always roughly parallel with each other, at right angles to the prevailing wind, and nearly, but never quite completely, symmetrical.
Lutz Wahlers/fotoLibra

thousands of years. They were spread over almost the entire continent and, while some were in the coastal area, a proportion made their homes in or on the edge of the deserts; there was no form of unity and each group went its own way.

There was some contact in historical times with Melanesians and people from what is now Indonesia, but no significant and continuing contact with outsiders took place until the first British settlers arrived in 1788. It is impossible to say how many Aborigines there were at that time, quoted figures ranging from as few as 250,000 to as many as 750,000, so about half-a-million seems a reasonable estimate. But, while well adapted to conditions in Australia, the Aborigines found themselves ill-equipped, both physically and mentally, to resist the expansion of the colonists, the vast majority of whom looked upon them as little more than an inconvenient nuisance. As a result, the Aboriginal population was decimated, either through contracting imported European diseases such as influenza, or as a result of deliberate action by the colonists.

The ill treatment of the Aboriginals continued well into the 20th century, as the white settlers tried to work out what to do with them. There were attempts at separate development and at totally doing away with Aboriginal culture, language, and customs. Beginning in the 1980s efforts were made to redress past wrongs, and much tribal property has been returned to the original owners, such as the huge rock, known to the settlers as Ayer's Rock but to the Aborigines as Uluru. Today there are about 485,000 people of Aboriginal origin, of which only a small, but nevertheless significant, proportion still live in the desert.

Native American Desert Peoples

The four major deserts in the southwest of the United States—Chihuahuan, Great Basin, Mojave, Sonoran—have been the homes of groups of Native Americans for many centuries, and each group responded in its individual way to the inhospitable conditions. All depended upon hunting, but they varied in the degree to which they also cultivated the land; some, where conditions were favorable, even used irrigation to improve yields. What they had in common, both with each other and with other desert peoples around the world, was their need to locate their settlements near water and to conserve that precious commodity in every way possible.

After several centuries of persecution from European settlers moving ever westward, many Native American groups still survive in the United States, but there is space here to mention only a few. The largest single group of Native Americans is the Navajo Nation, with 250,000 members living in an area of some 17.5 million acres of the Great Basin Desert, which includes parts of Arizona, New Mexico, and Utah. This is one third of all Indian lands and is larger in area than that of the states of Connecticut, Delaware, Maryland, Massachusetts, and Rhode Island combined. The major Apache groups comprise the Western Apache, based in Arizona, and the Jicarilla and the Mescalero, both of which are based in New Mexico.

The Piman peoples are centered in the Sonoran Desert, with the Akimel O'odam residing in the Gila River and Salt River areas, while the Tohono O'odham live in the San Xavier and Gila River areas. Some 10,000 Paiute people live in reservations scattered across the Great Basin Desert regions of Arizona, California, Idaho, Nevada, Oregon, and Utah. The Paiute adapted to high desert conditions by gathering pine nuts, roots, and seeds, and by hunting birds and fish, while during fall they hunted jackrabbits and antelope, but the rapid reduction in both species is causing concern.

Mongolia

The population of Mongolia was estimated to be approximately 2,800,000 in mid-2005, of which ethnic Mongols formed about 85 percent. In the past, virtually all the inhabitants were nomads, criss-crossing the Gobi Desert in search of grazing and water, but the past few decades have seen a definite drift towards the towns, while even those in rural areas are tending to settle rather than keep on moving. Nevertheless, there are still some who follow the old way of life.

Mongolian town dwellers refer to the nomads as "the five animal people" on account of the animals they keep: camels, cattle, goat, horses, and sheep, although, confusingly, they also keep Tibetan yaks, making six! Of these, by far the most important in terms of status and value is the horse; apart from being a means of transport, the mares are also the source of milk, which is fermented to produce a very potent drink. The Bactrian camels have two humps and are capable of surviving in both extreme heat and cold, and, with the yak, are used for transportation, especially for the *ger*, the collapsible wood-framed, skin-covered tent, which is used throughout the year, but with the addition of an iron stove in winter.

Atacama Desert

Approximately one million people live in or on the fringes of South America's Atacama Desert, mostly in towns and fishing villages on the coast, or in the numerous mines, but there are still some who remain in the oasis villages and in the farms along the northern edge. On the desert itself there are many descendants of the pre-Columbian indigenous peoples, including Aymara Indians in the Lake Titicaca area, and the Atacama Indians, who herd alpacas and llamas, and grow a limited variety of crops.

The great majority of these people were overrun by the Incas and then by the Spanish, and were treated harshly by both. Following independence from Spain they were then treated as a second-class group by their urbanized compatriots and have either been left to fend for themselves or have been exploited by mining companies. Only now is their traditional way of life seen as of value and worth preserving.

Common Experiences

The peoples of the world's deserts have more in common than any of them probably realize. Their ancestors chose to live in a harsh and demanding environment, where simply to survive was a major triumph.

RIGHT: The Atacama Desert, in Chile, is probably the most arid place on Earth, with some parts known to have received no rain whatsoever in forty years. A group of American scientists recently ran the same tests as used to detect life on Mars and found no trace whatsoever of any living organism. The Spanish soldier/poet Alonso de Ercilla y Zúñiga (1533-94) served in Chile between 1557 and 1562, and in his famous poem, La Araucana, he wrote of the Atacama that it was "…a land without men, where there is not a bird, not a beast, nor a tree, nor any vegetation." Nothing has changed.
Joel Sartore/Contributor National Geographic/Getty Images

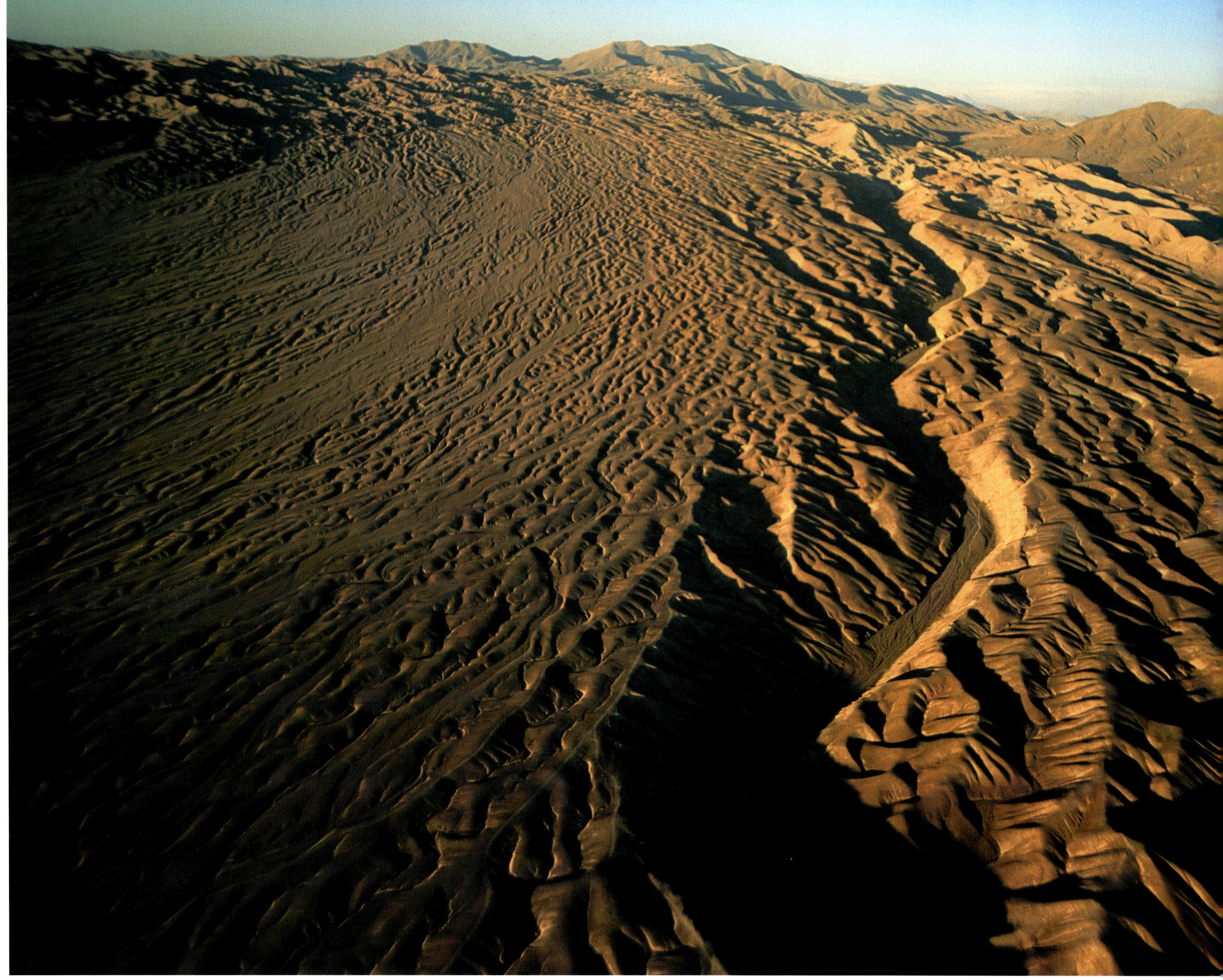

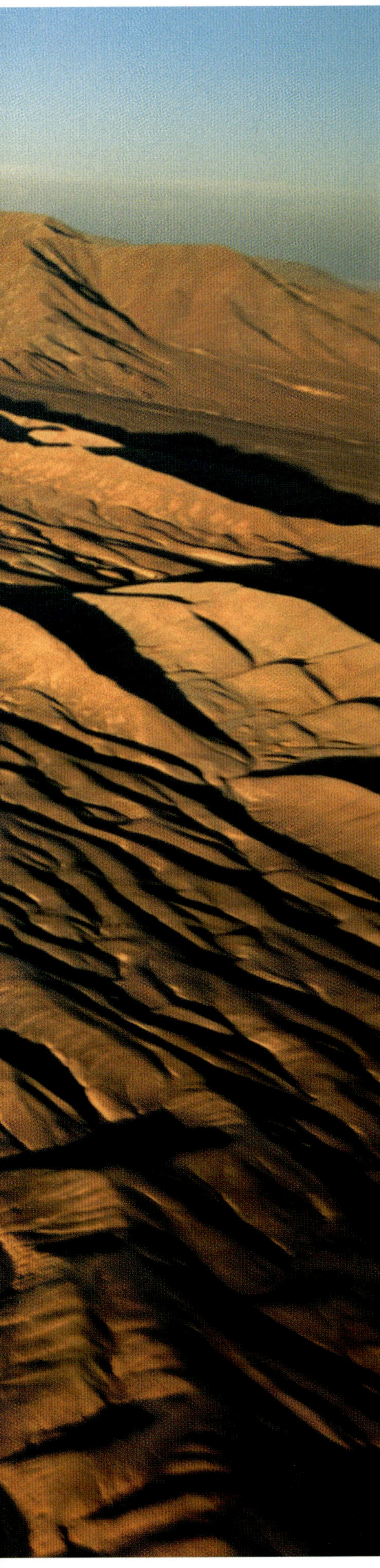

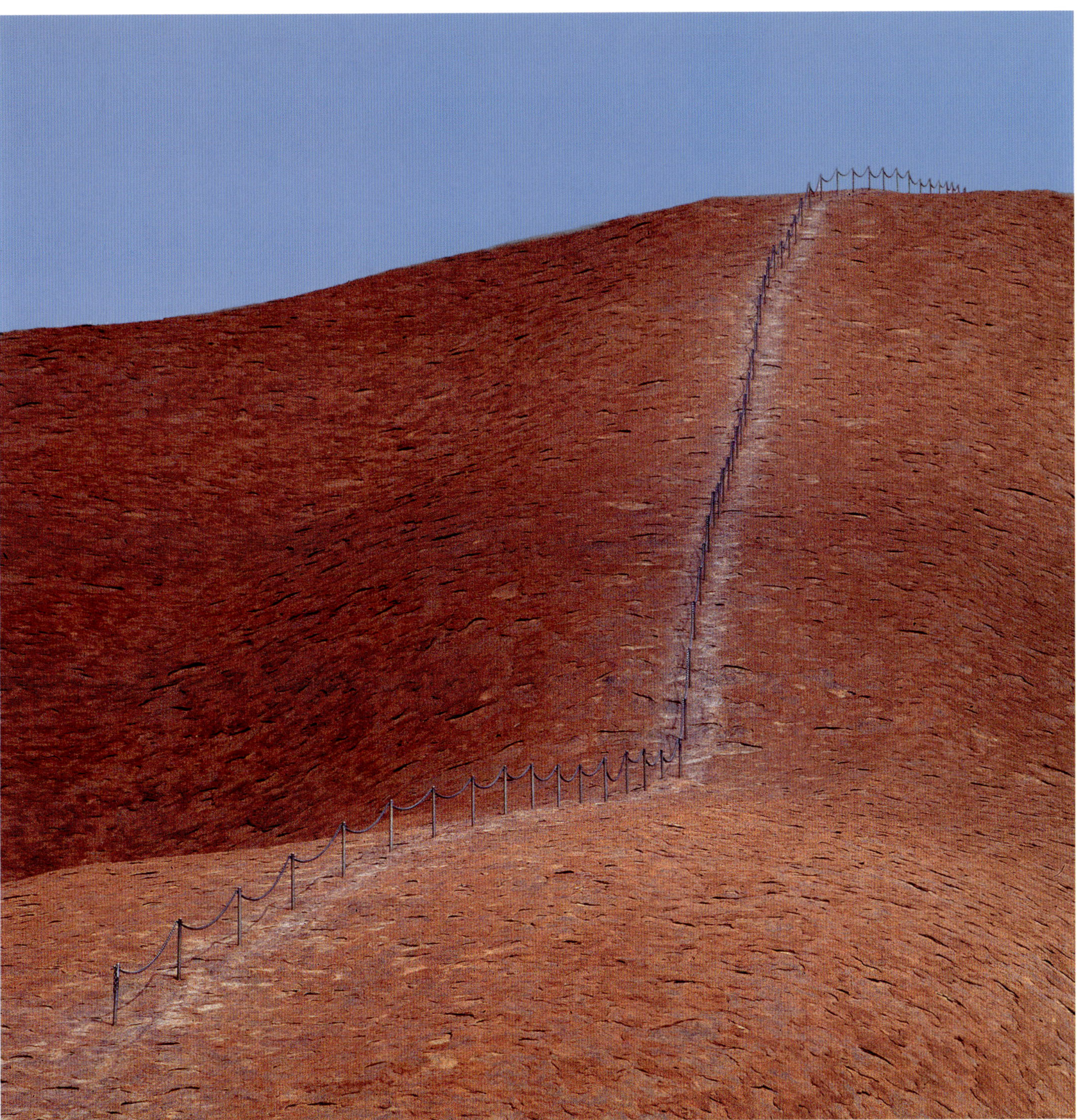

ABOVE: The unique Uluru (Ayer's Rock) in Australia is a great draw for tourists, many of whom inevitably want to climb it, following the path that has been carefully marked out, as seen here. Before starting their climb, the tourists must pass notices politely ask them not to walk on what the local Aboriginal peoples regard as sacred ground, but many disregard the request and press on.
Lorenzo Menghini/FotoLibra

In addition, their nomadic way of life meant that they could live only in small and self-contained communities, with little cohesion or cooperation between groups. As a result, while some groups, such as the Tuareg, Bedouin, and Aymara Indians, could defend themselves when subjected to isolated attacks, they stood little chance against powerful invaders. Thus, they were easily overpowered by the Incas or Ottomans, and later by the Europeans as they expanded from the 17th century onwards. Nevertheless, many of these imperial powers tended to leave these desert dwellers to their own devices, provided that they did not resist the imposition of taxes and an alien political and legal system.

From the mid-19th century onwards two further influences were brought to bear. The first of these was commercial exploitation of the deserts by companies, usually from another part of the world, which found vast deposits of minerals and oil that had lain undisturbed for many centuries. Finally came the simple attractions of urban life, which offered a more secure income, greater comfort and much less hardship. It is this last that caused the most serious depletion in desert dwellers, particularly in the second half of the 20th century and continuing into the 21st, but a swing in the opposite direction is becoming just discernible, as the attractions of a quieter, more traditional and better-ordered way of life come to be appreciated.

WEATHER

Apart from the fact that deserts are usually very hot and very dry, many of them also suffer from notorious phenomena known as the sandstorm, which, in a slightly less damaging context, is also known as a dust storm. These events also have local names such as *simoon* in northeast Africa and *haboob* in the Sudan. These sandstorms are usually caused by the intense heat of the ground warming the air above it which then rises, causing cooler air to rush in, become heated and, in its turn, also to rise, lifting sand and dust as it goes. The circular nature of this system creates a vertical column, which moves laterally across the desert, usually led by a vertical face of sand, which can be several thousand feet high. This column has a scouring effect on anything, including humans, in its path, and can rearrange the desert floor by obliterating roads, removing topsoil, moving sand dunes, and covering anything in its path with a layer of sand, which sometimes can be quite thick.

Indeed, sandstorms starting in the Gobi Desert have become a serious problem in north-east China, depositing thick layers of sand on areas that were, until very recently, distant from the desert as well fertile and crop-bearing. As a result, Beijing is now considered to be under threat and sandstorm warnings are now a routine element of all daily radio and TV weather forecasts in northern China. There can be no doubt that poor agricultural methods contribute to the prevalence of sand storms, and that Man can, to a certain extent, take corrective measures. Sandstorms are also, however, a purely natural phenomenon and were regularly reported, for example, by British Commonwealth and German troops fighting in the North African desert during World War Two, when the arrival of such storms meant that both sides simply stopped fighting and hunkered down under cover until it was over, each soldier's aim being personal survival.

DESERTIFICATION

Desertification is not, as many seem to think, the process of deserts regaining land that was once desert, but of deserts taking over land that was previously fertile. In the past, deserts have grown primarily due to natural processes, but in modern times they are spreading as a result of misuse or neglect by Man. Thus, the events that took place in the early 1930s, when large areas of the United States' Mid-West changed from highly productive arable land to a dust-bowl, were the result of over-stressing the environment through intensive farming, as is the continuing disaster in the Sahara, which has caused several hundred thousand deaths and led to the collapse of the agricultural economies in at least half-a-dozen countries.

In Asia, the Gobi Desert is expanding at a rate of 950 square miles per year, which is causing very serious concern not only in China and Korea, but also in Japan and North America. This is because such events do not only affect the area immediately adjacent to the desert, but can also have effects far way. For example, as described above, in China the edge of the Gobi Desert is no more than 150 miles from Beijing and each spring fine particles of dust from the Gobi settle over people, automobiles, and buildings, clogging machinery, closing airports, destroying crops, and driving farmers off their land.

Sometimes the cause is not readily apparent, desertification often being the result of the interactions between more than one cause. For example, large numbers of animals in the same area or following the same route, such as the approach to a water-hole, will, over time, increase the amount of fine, powdery material, which then blows away in the wind, increasing erosion in the original place and probably causing desertification elsewhere. The situation is compounded by the animals grazing on local plant life and their herders collecting firewood, both of which are totally comprehensible activities, but which combine to eliminate the plants that bind the soil together, increasing erosion further.

In some cases the demarcation between desert and non-desert is very clear, for example, by mountains or forests, but often there is an almost literal "line in the sand," on one side of which is desert and the other cultivation. In other cases the transition is much more gradual and it is these "transition zones" that prove the most vulnerable, both to natural influences and, in particular, to the influence of people.

Unfortunately, in the past, desertification has not always been easy to identify, and has not occurred according to recognizable patterns. As a consequence, the fact that desertification is taking place usually becomes generally known only after it has happened and when starving mothers and children appear on Western TV screens, or vast dust clouds deposit layers all over people's houses and factories.

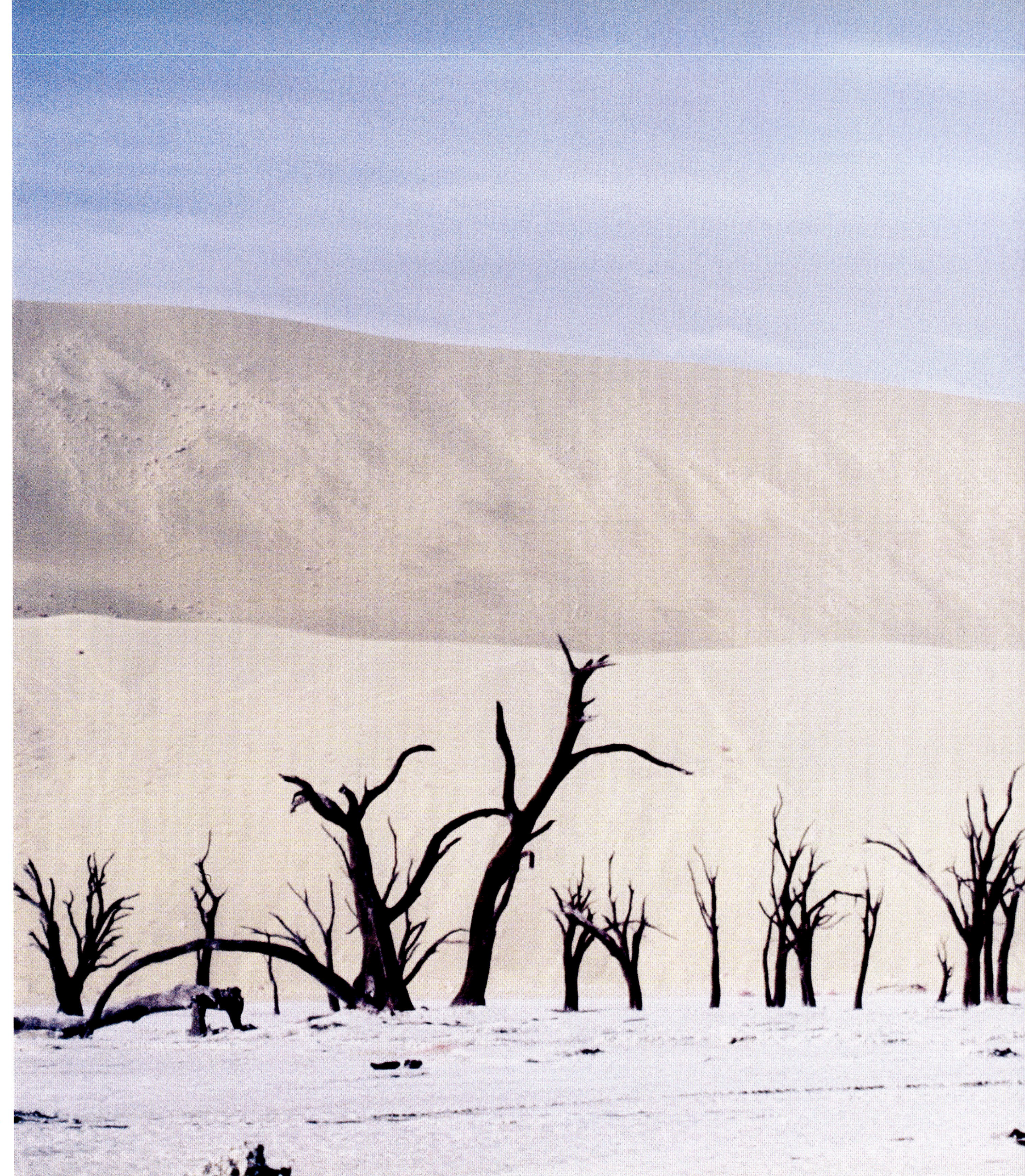

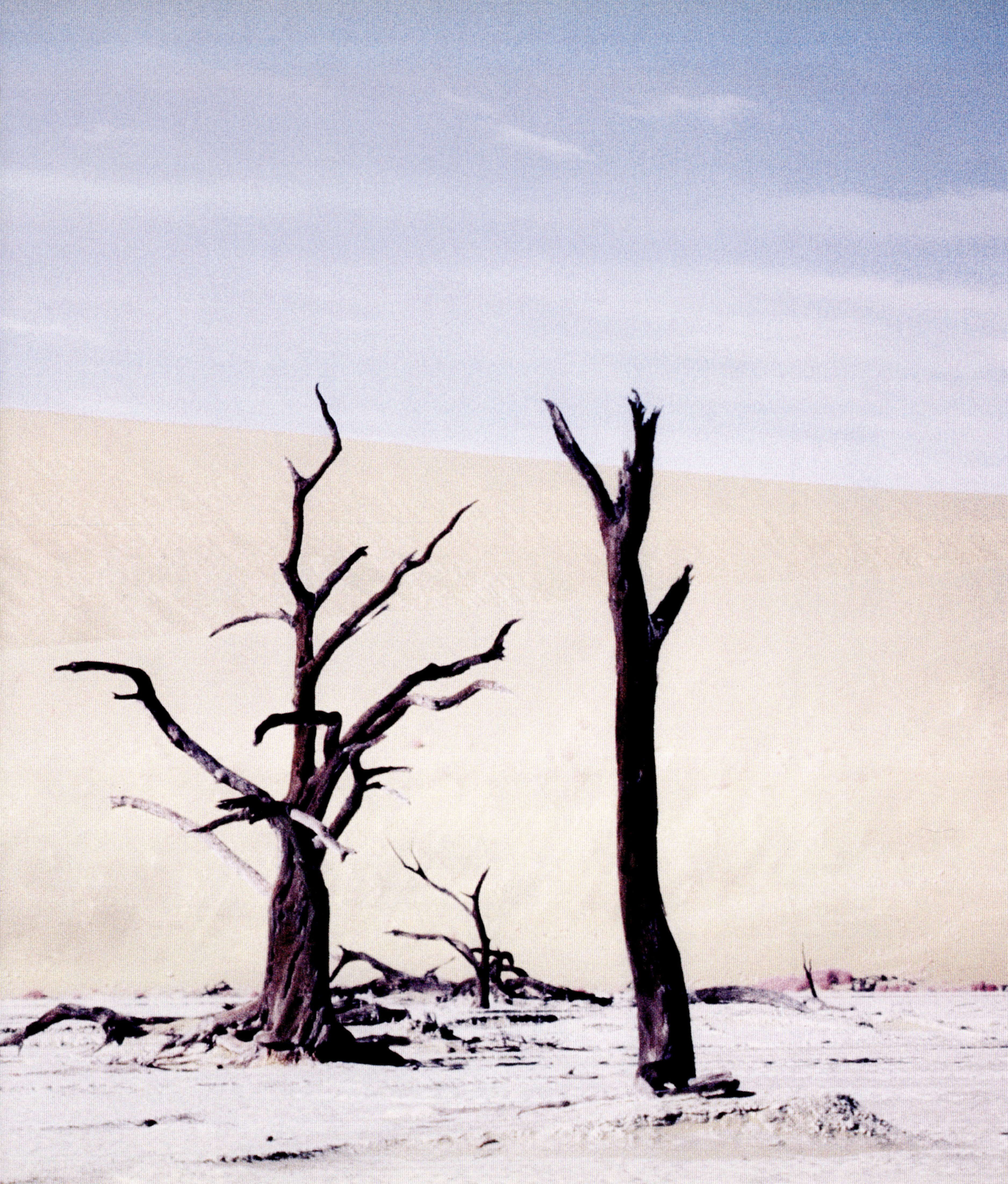

LEFT: The Sossusvlei sand dunes in the Namib-Naukluft National Park. The 20,000 square mile national park is the largest conservation area in the country of Namibia, on southwest Africa's Atlantic coast, and is carefully managed to ensure that its unique flora and fauna will survive for future generations. In the foreground are well preserved but long-dead trunks of Camel's Thorn, a shrub of the acacia family found in many desert environments, and whose leaves exude a sweetish, gelatinous gum.
Stuart Westmorland/Corbis

GLOBAL MONITORING

Desertification is often very difficult to recognize on the ground, but one of the many benefits of satellites has been the ability to take photographs of the same place and at the same time of the year over a period of several years, thus enabling experts to detect where changes are occurring and at what rate. This, allied to more and better organized ground observations, will eventually mean that the process of desertification and the problems it causes will be better understood.

These systems will enable a global picture to be built up, but the problem of desertification can also be tackled at the local level, by individuals, municipalities, and by government, all of which have a role to play. Sand movement can be reduced or eliminated by the judicious placing of mats, boulders or fences and the planting of grass, shrubs or trees to stabilize the situation.

This last problem is of special significance in China, where it is planned to create a "Green Wall of China" which will be some 2,800 miles long and, it is hoped, will not only stop the advance of the desert but also enable it to be, at least partially, rolled back, To achieve this, nine million acres of trees will be planted, consisting of a sand fence, an outer belt and an inner belt separated by a six-foot wide gravel platform. An extensive control system is also being put in place both to monitor the entire defense system (because that is what it is) and to supervise remedial action, where necessary. Nor is the problem simply one of the expansion of the Gobi into inhabited areas of China, as the dust-clouds are being carried right across the Pacific, and it is not impossible that they could pick up toxins, say from a factory chimney, and carry them to Japan or the United States, which could cause an immense diplomatic row.

The events in the USA in the 1930s and in China and the Sahara today are serious warnings. Man cannot go on taking from the Earth; some controls must be imposed on agricultural, industrial and leisure activities; and the deserts must be looked after properly or they will wreak a terrible vengeance.

LEISURE ACTIVITIES

A problem of growing significance is the ever-increasing use of deserts for leisure activities. It is perfectly understandable that people with time and money available for leisure pursuits should want to see the more remote places in the world, and it is equally understandable that the people in those areas, many of whom are extremely poor, should want to make money out of such tourism. There is a danger, however, that the construction of the necessary facilities, ranging from airports through access roads to luxury hotels, allied to the pressure exerted by ever-increasing numbers (on the water supply, for example) will cause a breakdown in the already delicate eco-system.

A far more obtrusive activity is the use of deserts by automobiles, including four-wheel drive vehicles and motorcycles. The drivers of such vehicles revel in the freedom that the open spaces give them, without speed limits and with the challenge of surmounting considerable obstacles. There is also an apparently insatiable desire for golf courses, which, in order to provide the necessary amount of grass, require about the same amount of water as a town with 12,000 inhabitants. The irony is that people who go to such beautiful areas for their leisure activities are actually making a serious contribution to their ruin, thus destroying what it is that they are going to see.

CONCLUSION

Deserts have an attraction all their own. First, there is the innate fear of a relatively unknown and apparently very hazardous environment, which has been played upon by countless movies and stories. Second, there is their sheer size, which tends to exaggerate the dangers. Third, there is their strangeness, with bleak, barren vistas and strange creatures, some of them quite unlike anything found in fertile areas. Finally, and much more recent, is a rarely articulated fear that somehow this hostile environment is spreading and threatening to engulf ever-increasing areas of developed land.

It is certain that Man has, over the past fifty to sixty years, done a great deal to upset the age-old balance. The mineral resources of the deserts are being exploited on a scale never seen before as modern prospecting and surveying finds yet more deposits of oil, minerals, and precious stones, which are then extracted so long as there is the slightest chance of a profit. Sometimes it is the expansion of traditional activities that causes the problem, as, for example, in northern China, where the ever-increasing numbers of cattle are grazing at an intensity the land cannot maintain, so the plants disappear and the land becomes desert.

There are also instances of the "law of unintended consequences," where action to solve a problem in one place has caused a problem of equal or greater size elsewhere. Thus, water from two rivers feeding the Aral Sea, the Amu-Dar'ja and Syr-Dar'ja, are being extracted and used for irrigation that has increased agricultural production upstream but has also resulted in a major ecological disaster at the Aral Sea itself. This is contracting so fast that, where it was once the world's fourth largest lake, it is now the eighth and is slipping further down the table, and the land exposed by the Aral is becoming almost instant desert.

The problem of over-using deserts for leisure is comparatively small at the moment and, in most instances, is very strictly localized. People have a right to enjoy Nature's facilities, but that right is not boundless and, if the result of enjoyment today is to deprive future generations of that right absolutely, then surely things have gone too far.

Above all, deserts are part of our natural heritage, and for all their hardness they are also places of great beauty. The symmetry of the sand dunes, the patterns of the wind ripples, the purity of the colors, the might and complexity of some of the natural features must not be lost. The unique flora and fauna of the deserts are also worthy of preservation. Some of the animals may be ugly by conventional standards and the snakes dangerous, and their lives may be a perpetual struggle, but they have evolved over thousands of years and deserve to still be here in another thousand years.

With the peoples of the deserts it is a different matter. Life in the desert has always been a hard and constant struggle, and in any weakening on the part of the human Nature will always triumph. While the desert people knew of no other existence, they could see no alternative but to continue the life they were born into. But, once they came under the influence of outsiders and realized that there was a possibility of a more comfortable and less challenging life they started to drift into collective farms or into the towns and cities. Who can blame them, as there is little enjoyment in serving solely as a curiosity to be stared at by tourists? But, there can be no doubt that the loss of these people and of their culture and way of life is also a loss for the world at large.

COLD DESERTS OF THE WORLD

Desert	Location	Area (square miles)	Surface	Vegetation	Animals	Comment
Antarctic	Antarctica continent	5,500,000	98% thick ice 2% barren rock	Lichen, moss (small amounts only)	Sea lions, seal	Coldest, driest area on Earth. No indigenous population
Aral Kara Kum	Kazakhstan, northeast of Aral Sea	15,440	Sand ridges, dunes	Grasses, shrubs, bushes, trees	Fox, gazelle	Extension of Kara Kum (see below)
Atacama	Coastal areas of Peru and Chile	54,000	Sand dunes, pebbles	Grasses, cactus	Llama, Peruvian fox	Few thousand people (mostly farmers, miners) live in desert. Large deposits of sodium nitrate (used to make gunpowder)
Gobi	Northern China and Southern Mongolia	450,000	Sandy soil, gravel	Camel's thorn, grasses	Camel, gazelle, gerbil, jerboa, lizards, onager, wolf	Government encouraging nomads to settle on government-run farms. Gobi = desert
Great Basin	Western United States (Idaho, Nevada, Oregon, Utah)	158,000	Sand, gravel, clay, extensive salt flats	Greasewood, sagebrush, shadscale	Bighorn sheep, jackrabbit, mice, antelope	Includes Great Salt Lake
Iranian	Afghanistan, Iran, Pakistan	150,000	Coarse soil, stones, salt flats	Grasses, low trees, shrubs	Monitor lizard, onager, oryx	Includes world's largest salt flat
Kara Kum	Turkmenistan	135,000	Sand ridges, dunes, clay deposits	Grasses, shrubs, bushes, trees	Hare, hedgehog, cat, fox, gazelle	Very sparse population. Kara Kum = black sands
Namib	Atlantic coast of southwestern Africa	52,000	Sand dunes on coast, gravel inland.	Aloe, grass, lichens	Mole, jackal	Namib Desert coast is world's primary source of gemstones.
Takla Makan	Western China	600,000	Sand dunes, rocky soil	Grasses, shrubs	Bactrian camel, jerboa, gazelle	"Takla Makan" = "place of no return"
Turkestan	Parts of Middle East, southwestern Russia	215,000	Extensive stretches of sand dunes.	Alhagi shrub, saxaul tree, sedges	Tortoise, gazelle, gerbil, antelope	

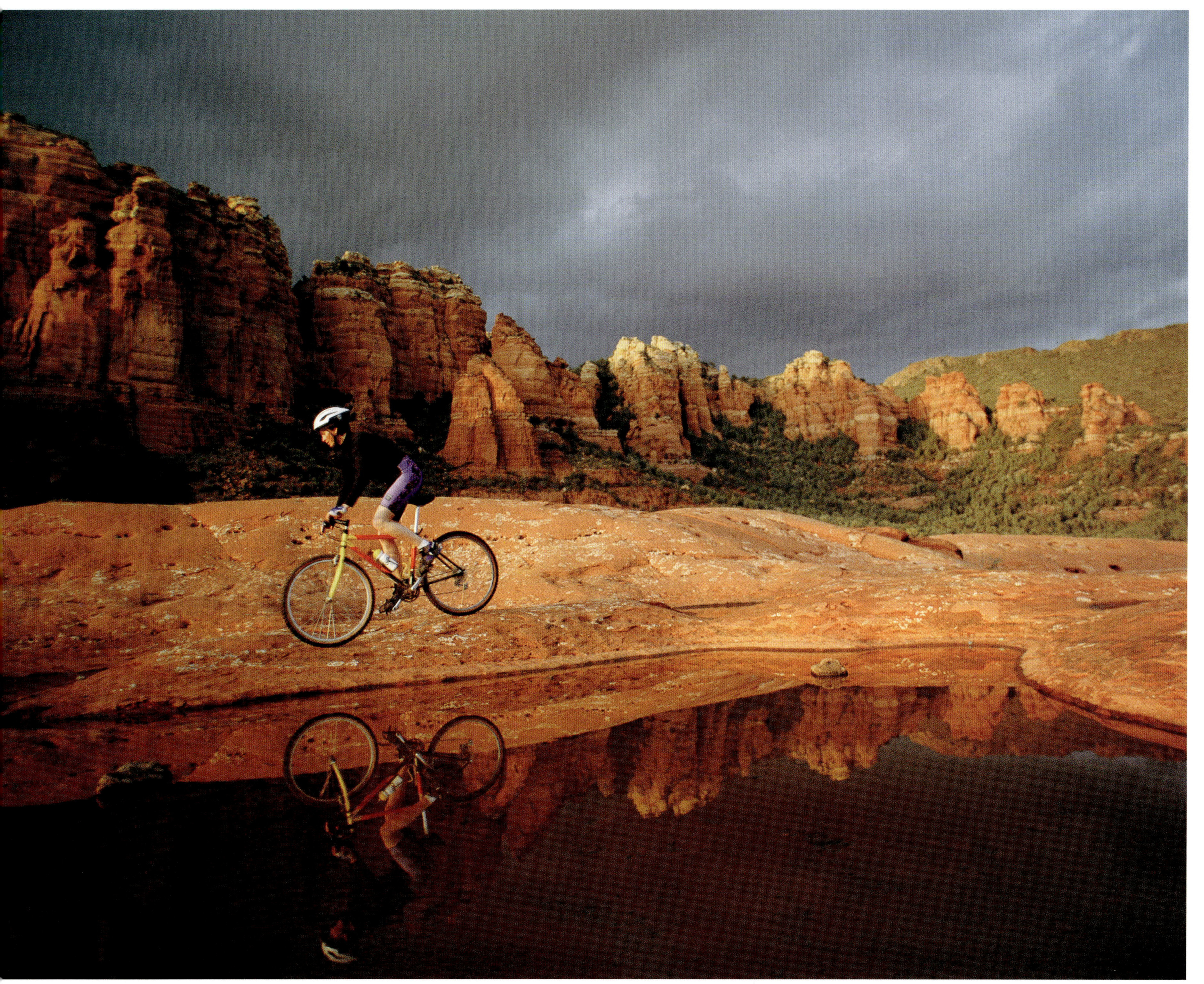

LEFT: Where once intrepid settlers battled the heat and drought in their wagon trains, today's adventurers go by bicycle. This biker is in the Sonora Desert, a vast and generally inhospitable area, which covers approximately 120,000 square miles of two US states, south-west Arizona and south-east California, as well as parts of two Mexican states, Baja California and Sonora. It is the hottest desert in North America, but parts can record sub-zero temperatures at night.
Dugald Bremner/National Geographic/ Getty Images

THE WORLD'S GREAT DESERTS

The world's deserts are spread over all the major continents; even Europe has its very own—the small but very arid Almeria Desert in Spain. In combination, these deserts cover approximately 10 percent of the world's land surface, rendering this area almost uninhabitable and virtually unusable for agriculture or raising animals. To most town-dwelling Westerners, it is the hot-dry desert with a scorching sun beating down on rolling sand dunes that is considered the most typical, but, in reality, such scenery forms only a small proportion of desert terrain. Gravel-covered plains or bare rock are far more widespread—even if they are considerably less photogenic. Four of the greatest and most fascinating deserts are located in North America, some of them with stunning scenery—like that in Monument Valley—that is without equal anywhere else in the world.

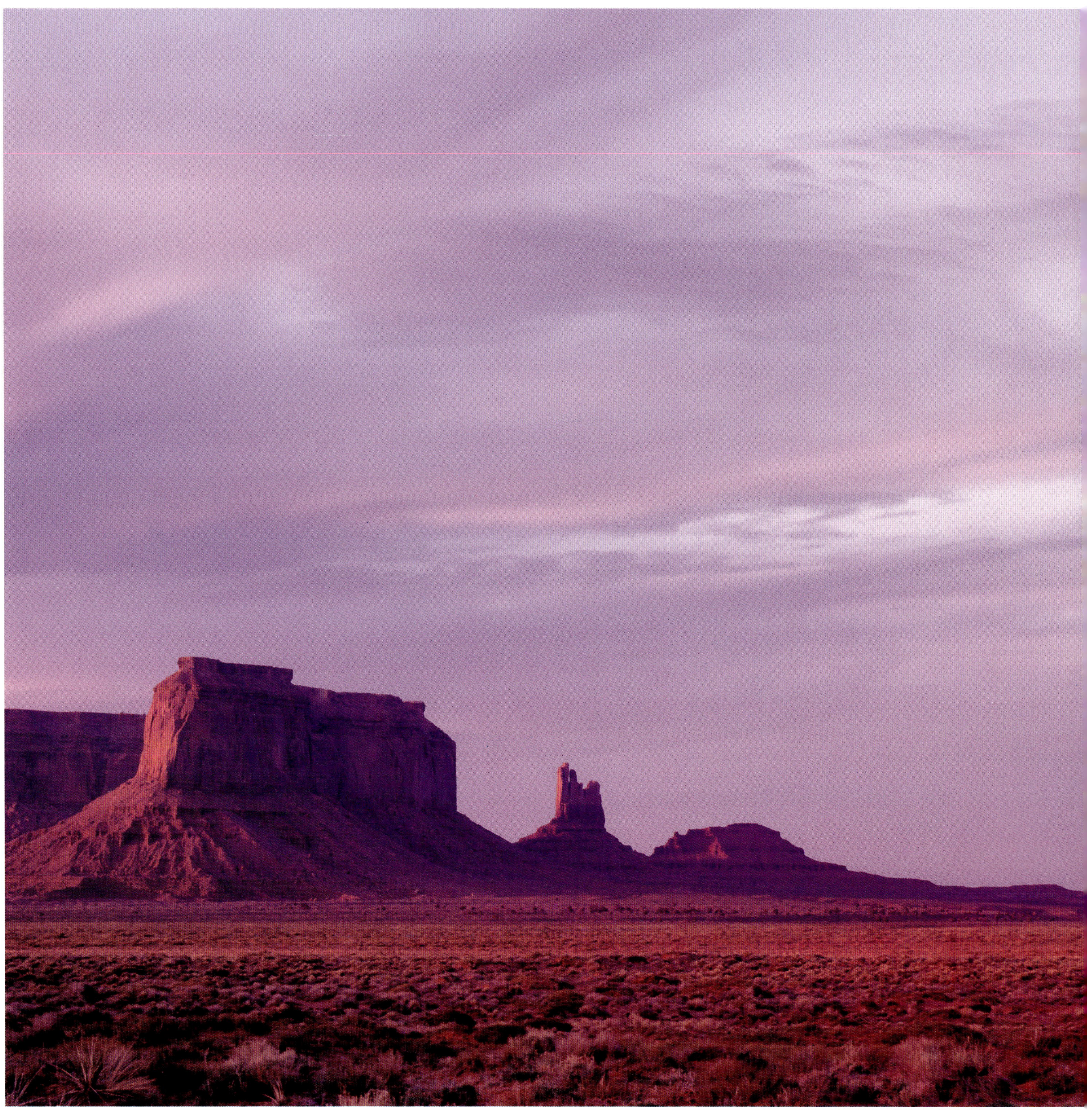

Right: Monument Valley has attained iconic status, its tall, deep red sandstone buttes and mesas, which rise to heights up to 1,000 feet above the desert plain, having been seen around the world in many hundreds of Western movies. The valley covers an area of some 2,000 square miles in northeastern Arizona and south-eastern Utah and is part of the Navajo Tribal Park.
Pete Saloutos/Corbis

Pages 30–31: Looking west across Monument Valley, Utah, towards an oncoming fall storm. As this aerial picture makes clear, to call this place a "valley" is something of a misnomer, since it is actually a wide and very flat plain.
Wark/AirPhotoNA

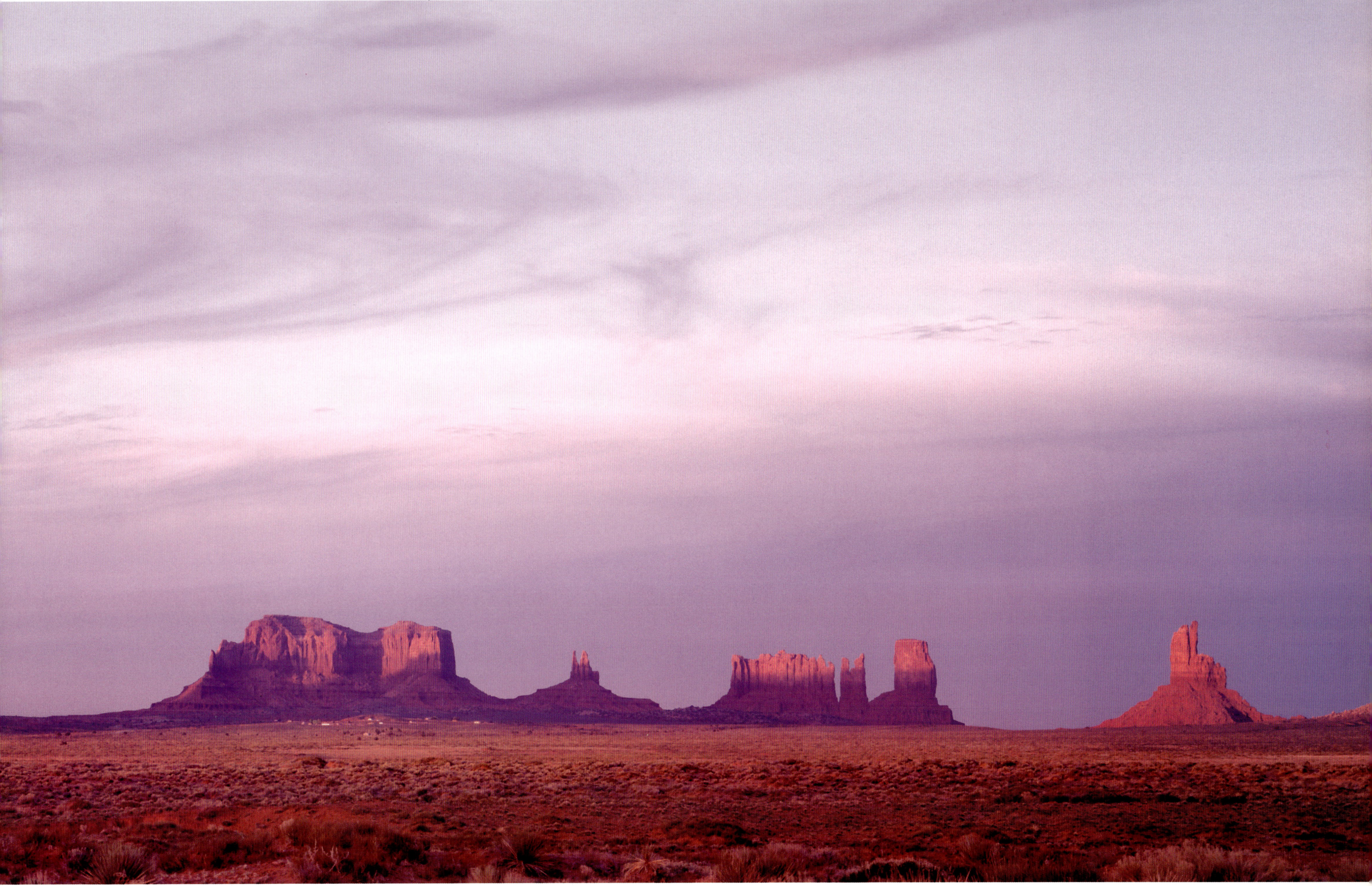

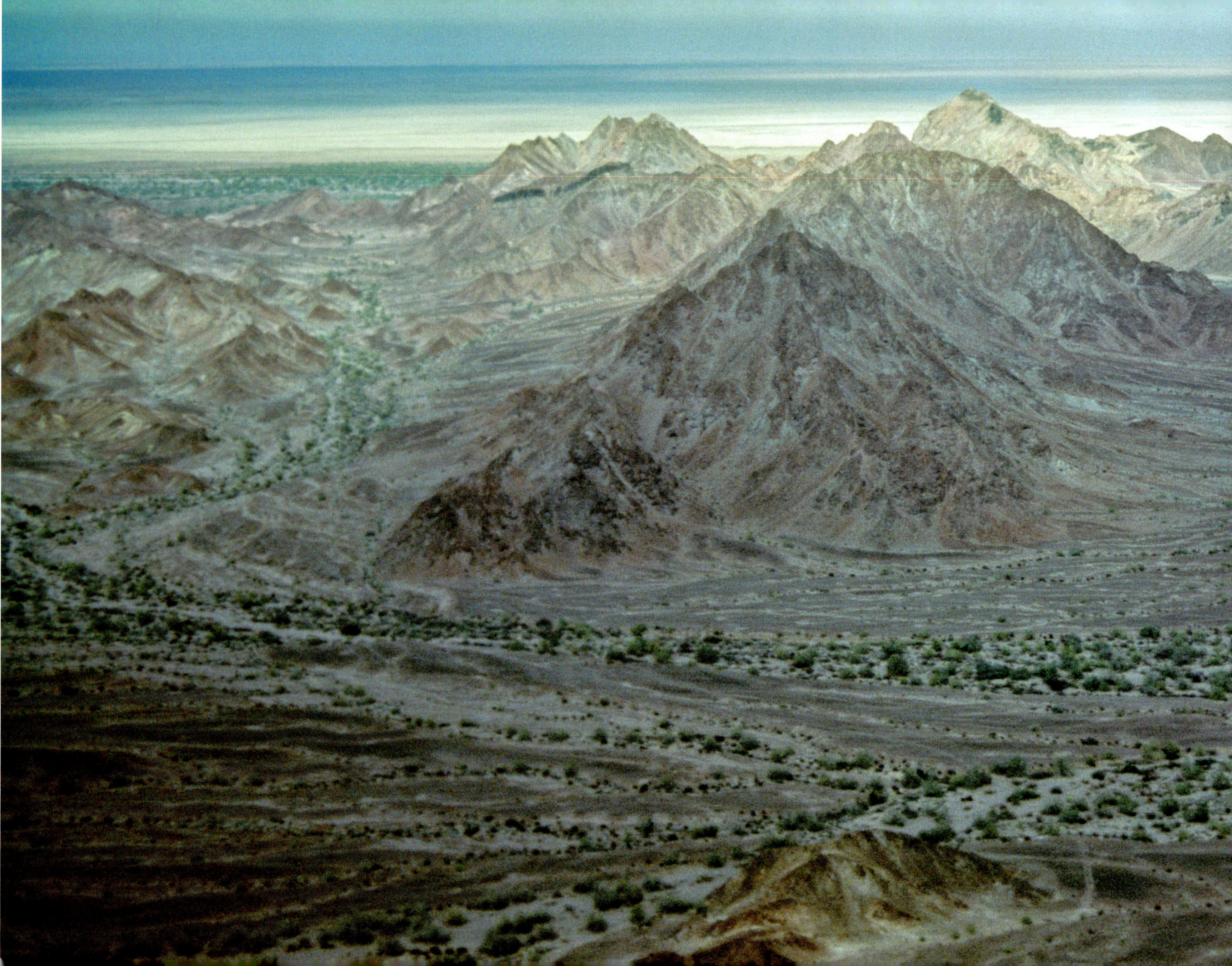

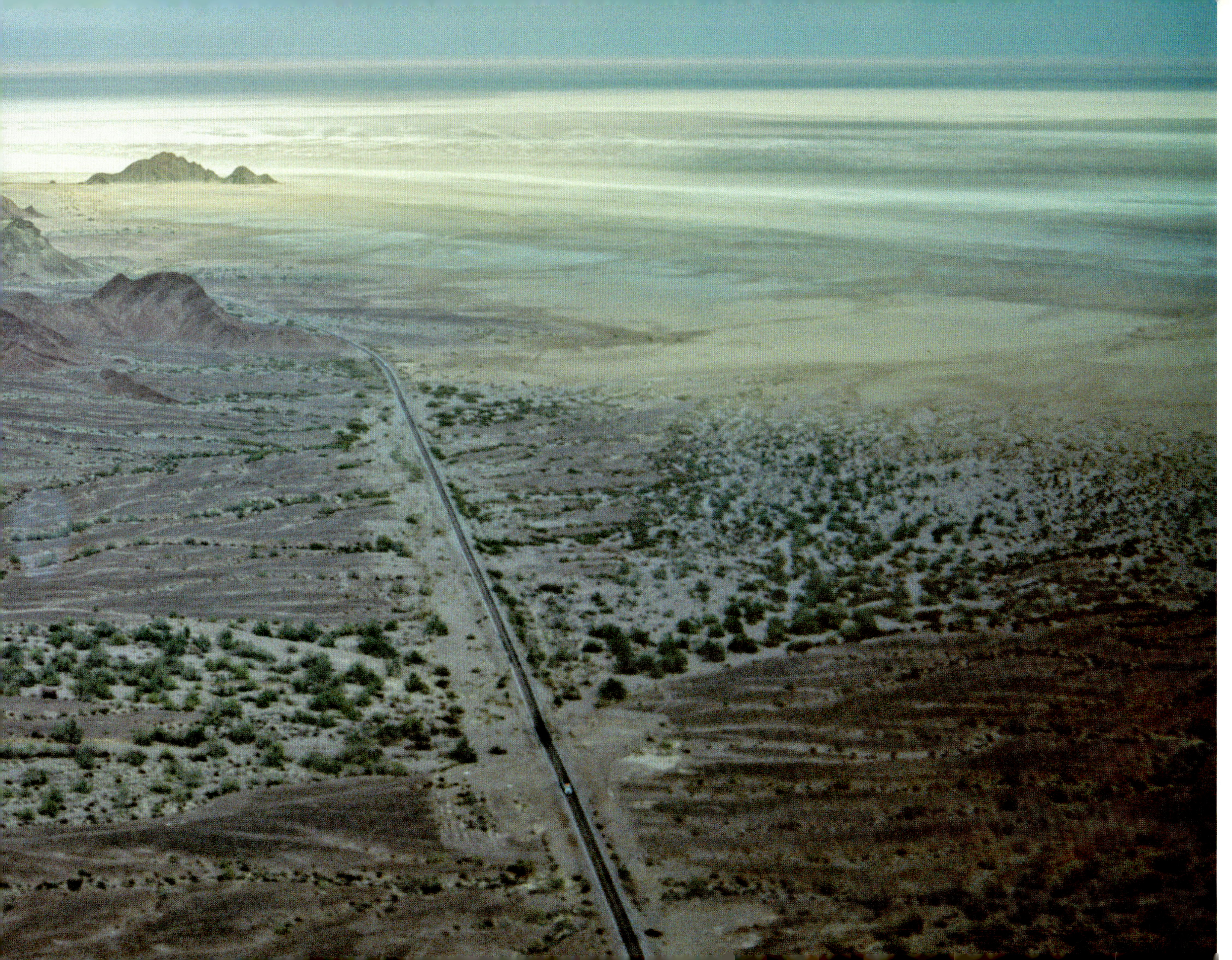

RIGHT: Canyonlands National Park in Utah is the result, first, of rock-building processes many millions of years ago that saw sediment, which had been washed down from nearby mountains by mighty rivers, compacted into solid rock. Then, some ten million years ago, the Earth's tectonic plates moved, pushing what is now the Colorado Plateau upwards, thus exposing them to erosion by rivers and weather. Most pictures of Canyonlands show the bare rock in summer, but here it is covered in a mantle of snow.
ML Sinibaldi/Corbis

FAR RIGHT: The Mitten Buttes in Monument Valley glow red because of the iron oxide in their siltstone. They also show very clearly the layers that have gone into their formation, each of which can be identified and dated by geologists. The Mittens were used as a backdrop in John Ford's 1939 movie *Stagecoach*, which not only made John Wayne a star but also gave these two buttes a similar status. Since then they have been used in countless Westerns, as well as for advertising products such as cigarettes and automobiles.
ML Sinibaldi/Corbis

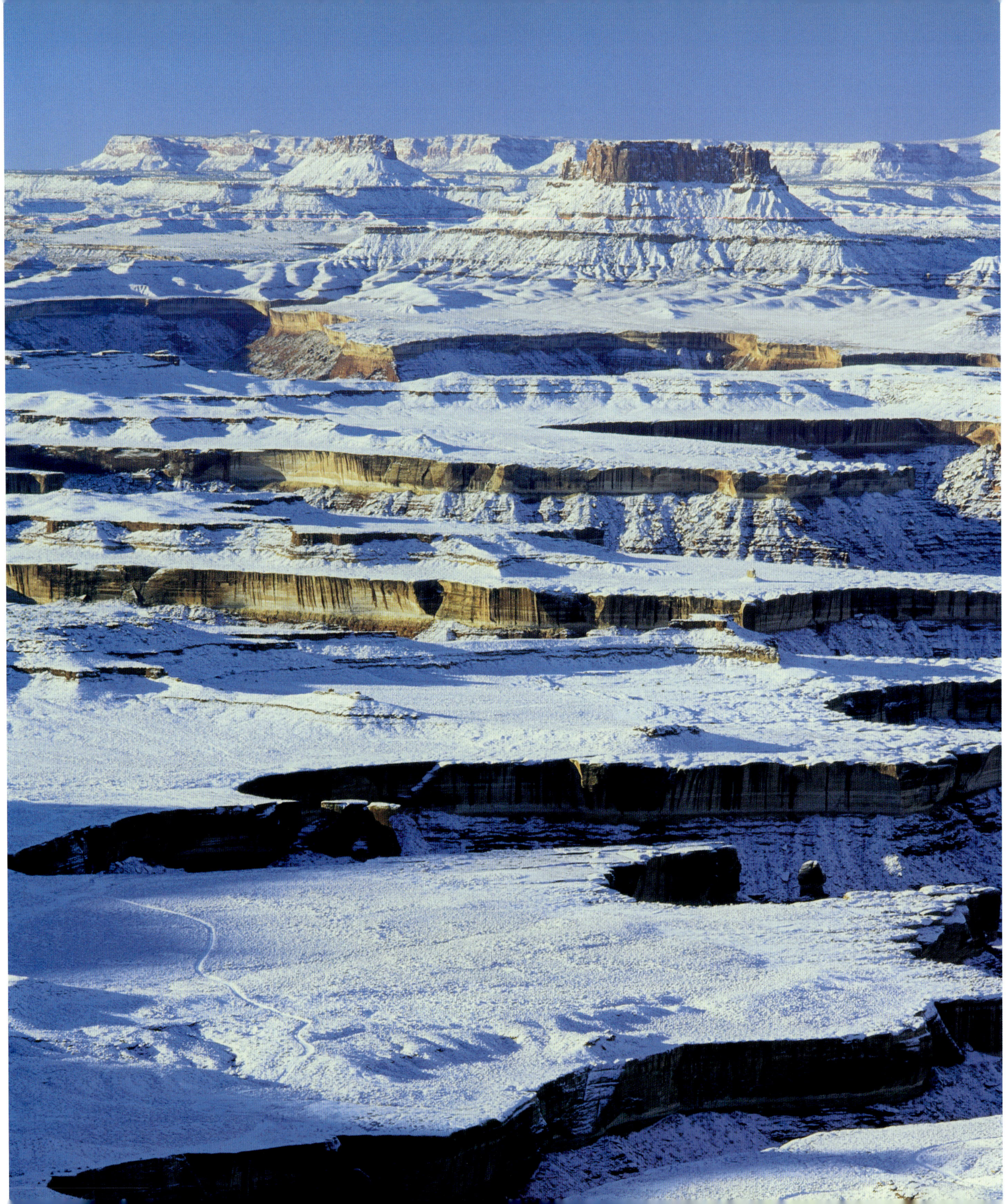

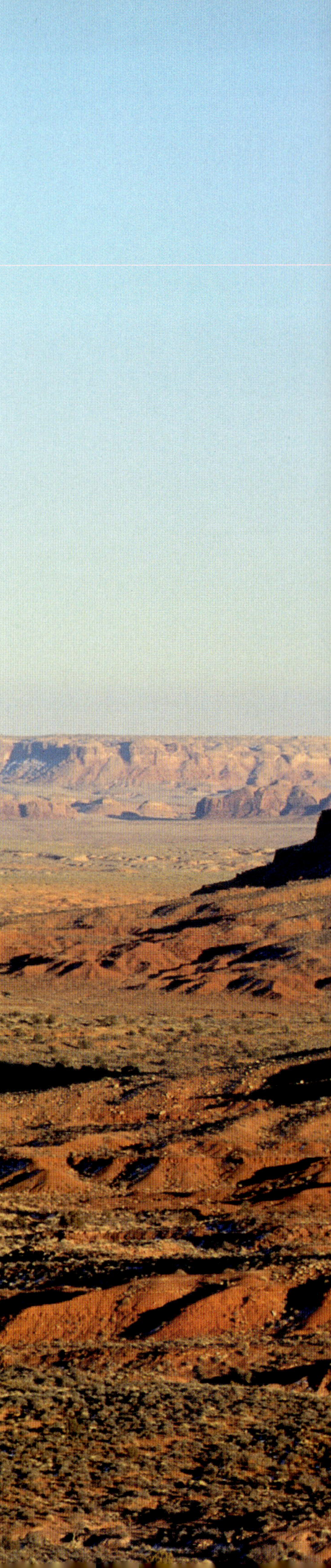

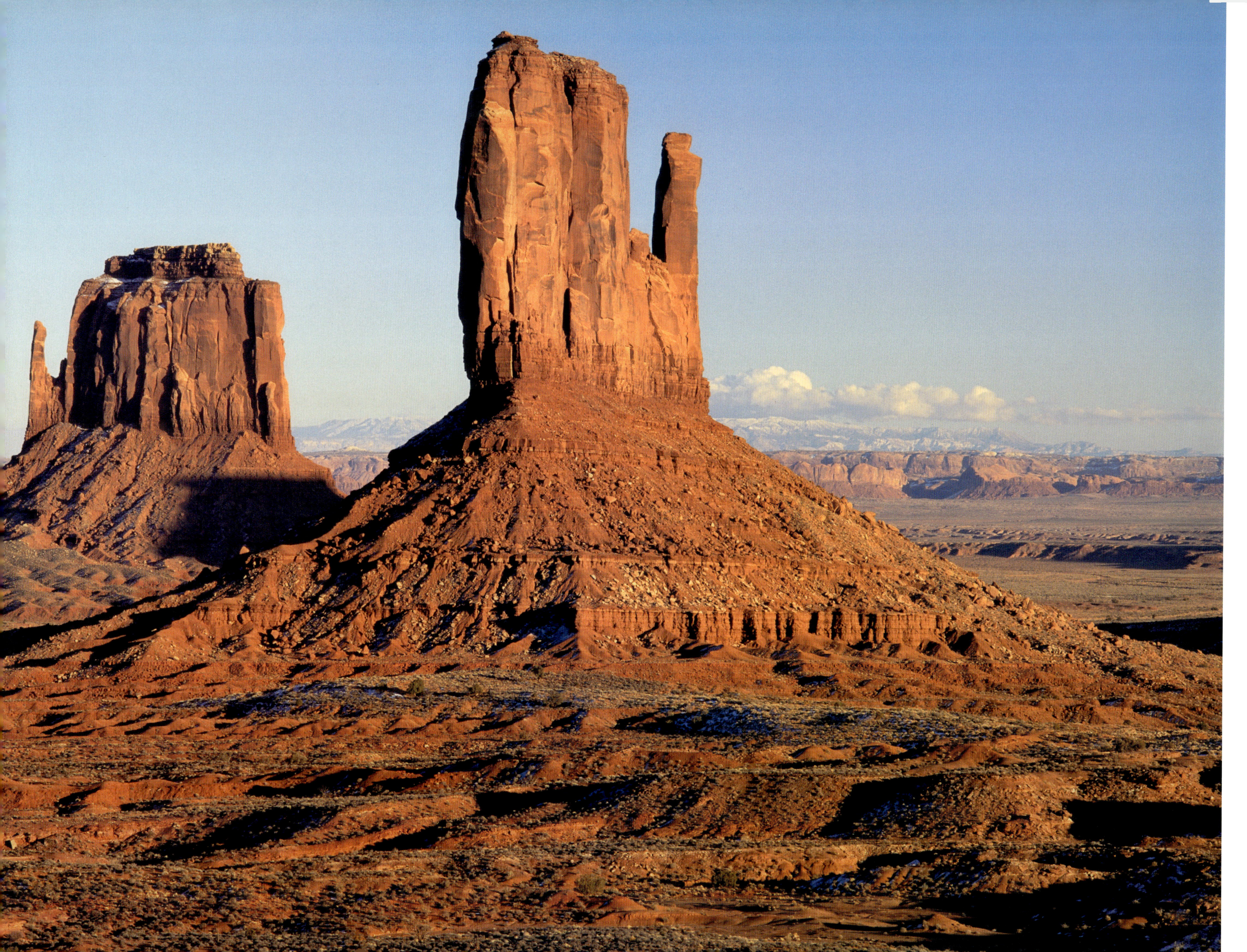

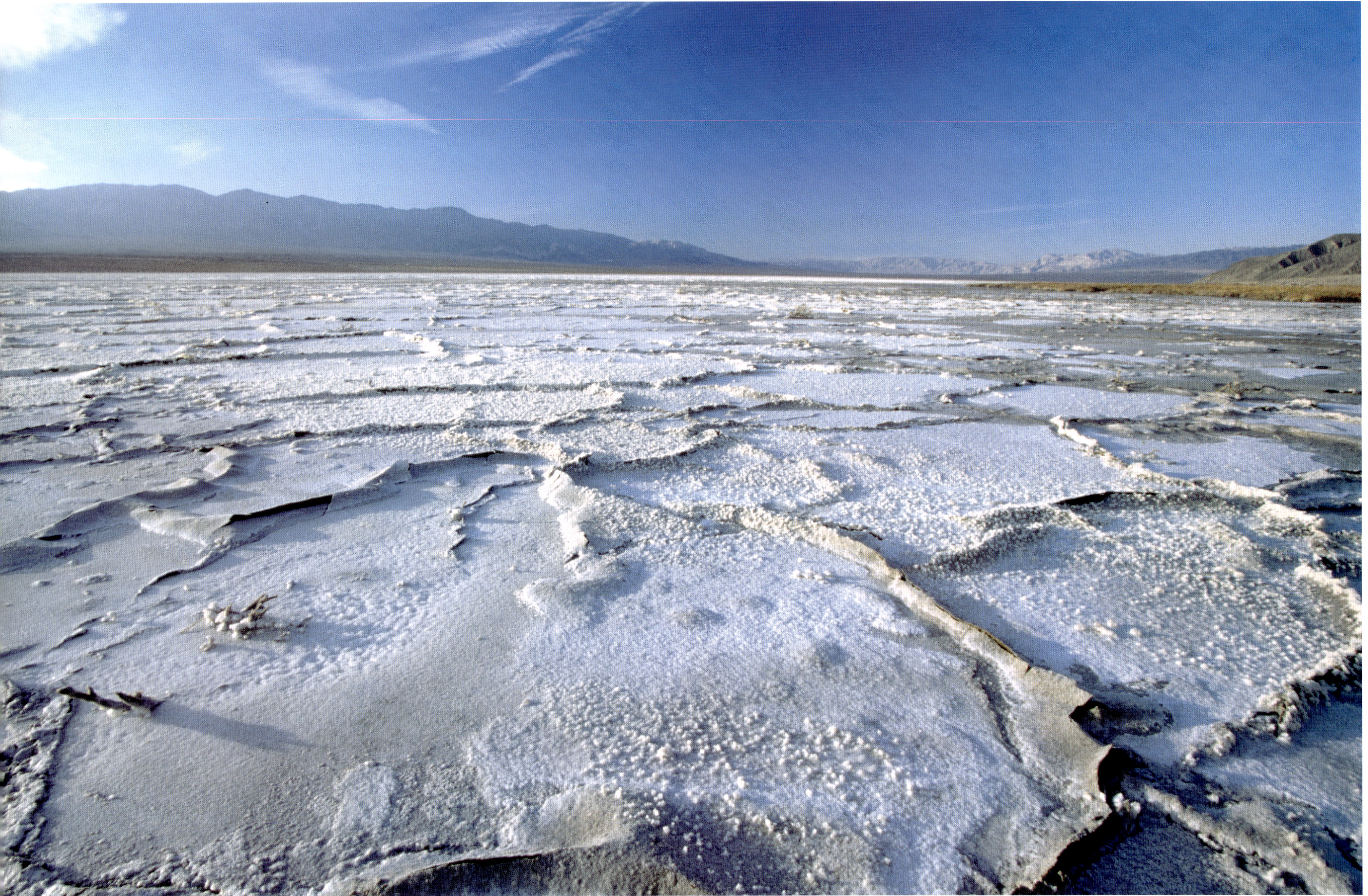

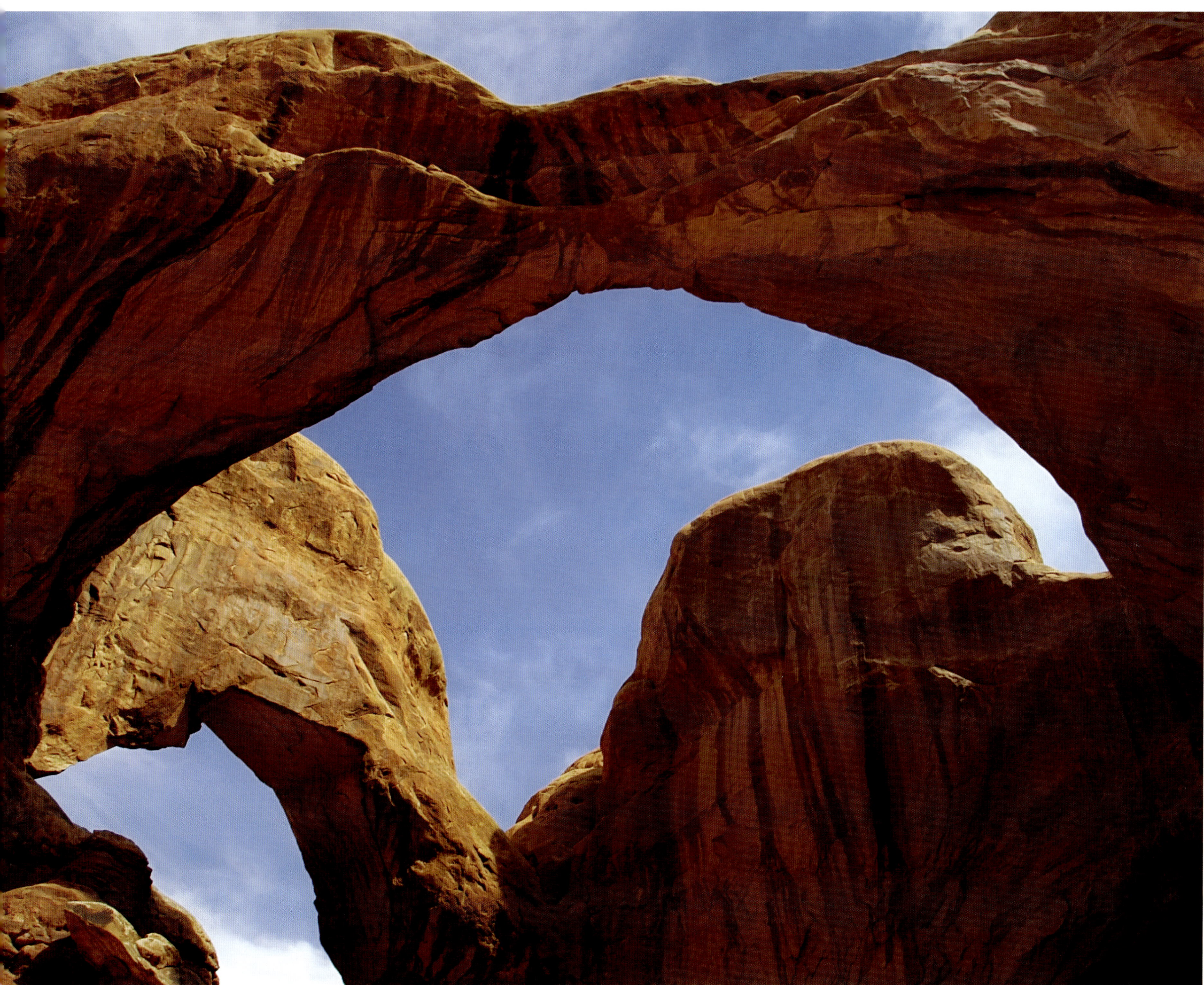

Left: Arches National Park in Utah contains more natural arches than anywhere else on Earth. Seen here is one of the major attractions—the Double Arch—but there are many more, all of which have been formed by the forces of Nature over millions of years and whose many layers can be "read" by experts to produce a detailed history of each one.
Marek Skrzypek/fotoLibra

Far Left: Death Valley in California was named by one survivor among thirty prospectors trying to find an overland shortcut to California during the 1849 Gold Rush, and which had lost twelve of their number while crossing the badlands. The valley lies some 280 feet below sea level and is the driest known place in the Continental United States, with an average rainfall of under two inches per year. The valley is also one of the hottest places on Earth, with average summer temperatures of well over 100 degrees Fahrenheit, the record being 120 degrees, recorded in 1917.
Gabe Palmer/Corbis

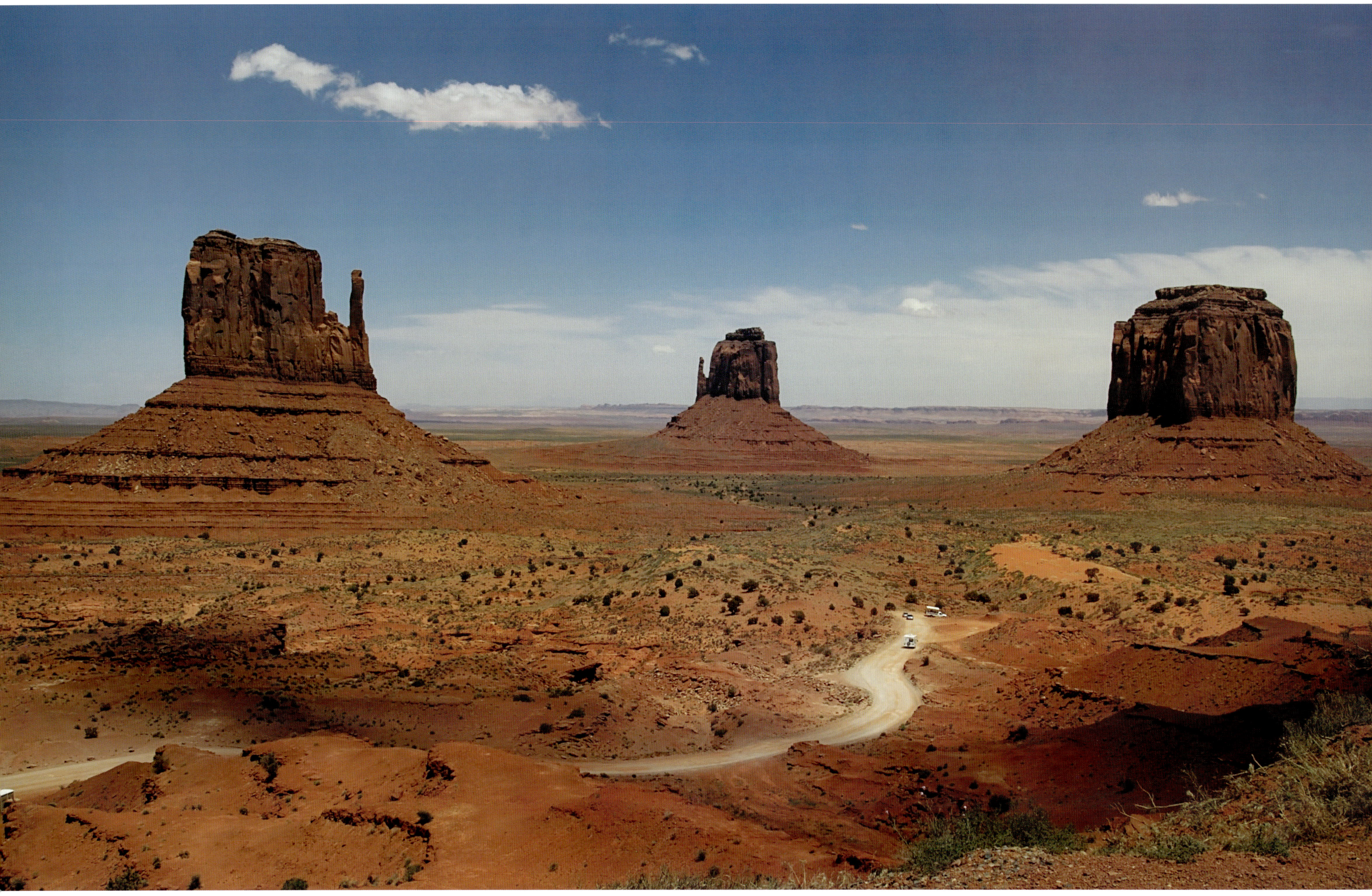

Left: In Monument Valley, the two Mitten Buttes (left and center) are named for their obvious resemblance to such gloves, but Merrick Butte (right) is named for a former soldier of that name who, with another ex-soldier named Mitchell, tried silver prospecting in the area on ground that the Navajo Indians considered sacred. Merrick and his comrade were duly killed for affronting the gods, but his name lives on in this magnificent butte.
Marek Skrzypek/fotoLibra

Right: The scene is Death Valley, California, and most people looking at it will feel instinctively that a stagecoach is just about to race into view hotly pursued by outlaws on horseback. Many of the thousands of Westerns produced by Hollywood throughout the 20th century were set among such scenery, which was not only nearby but also cost little or nothing to use, making this desert country a familiar sight around the world.
Neil Nathan/fotoLibra

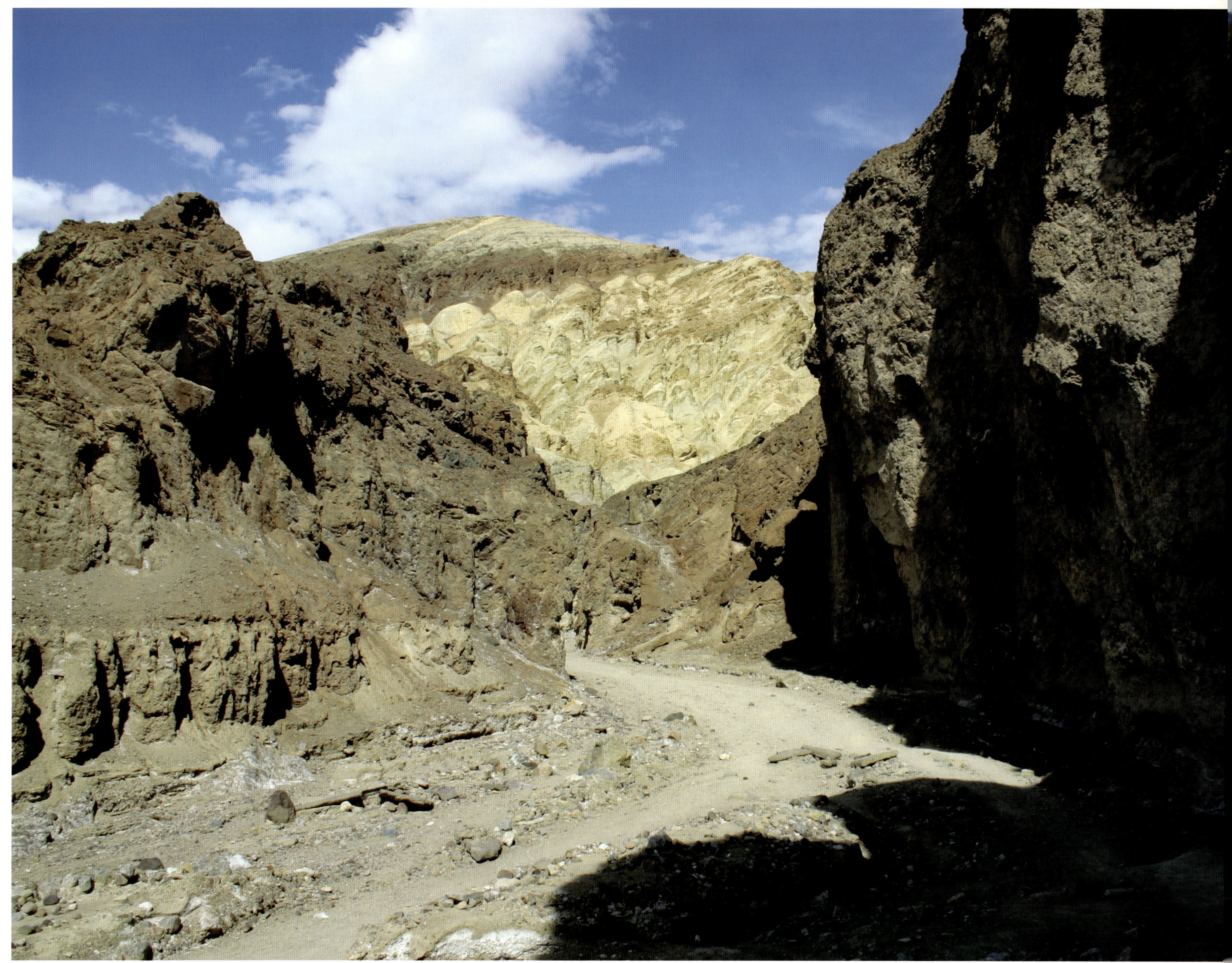

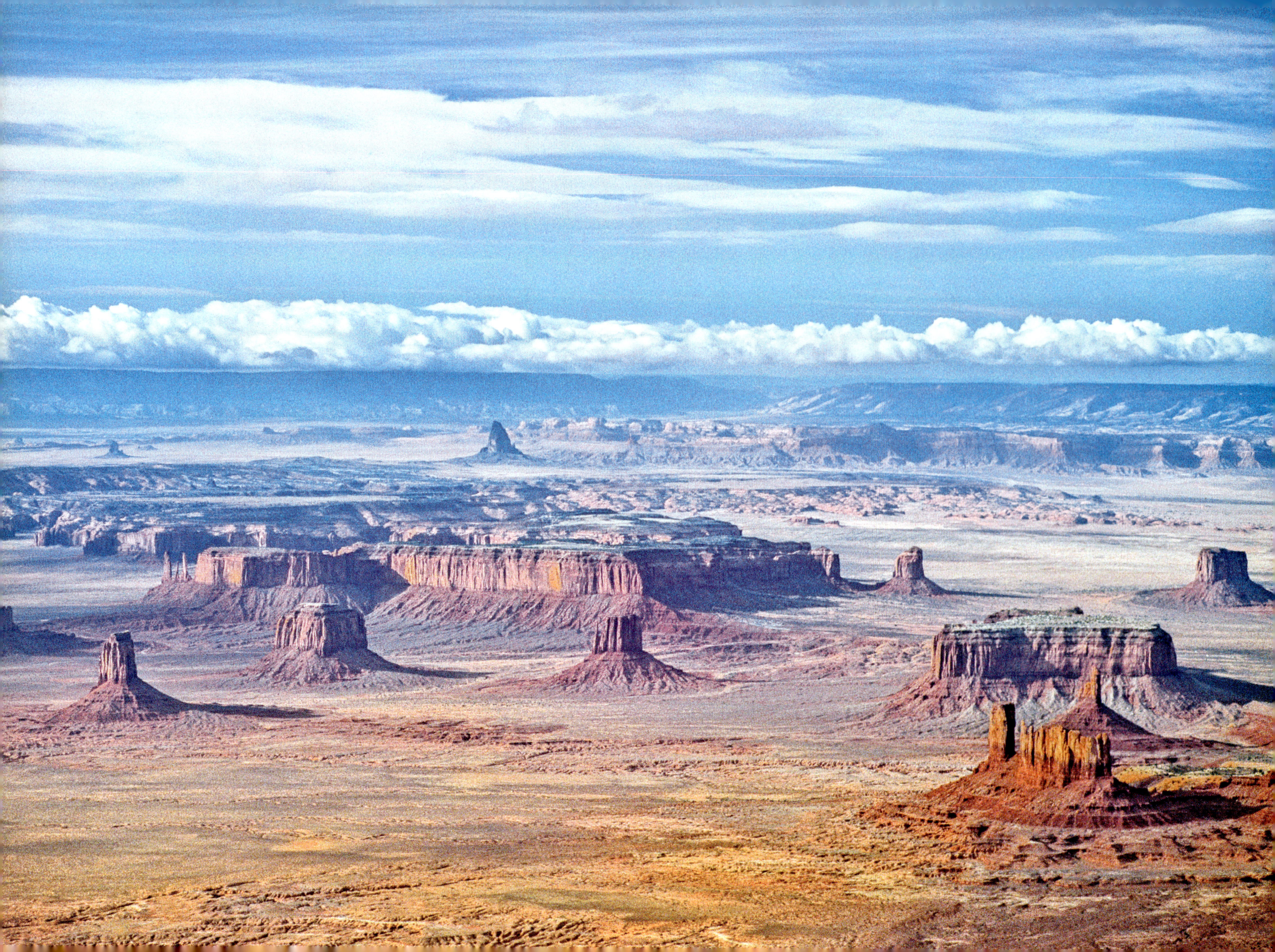

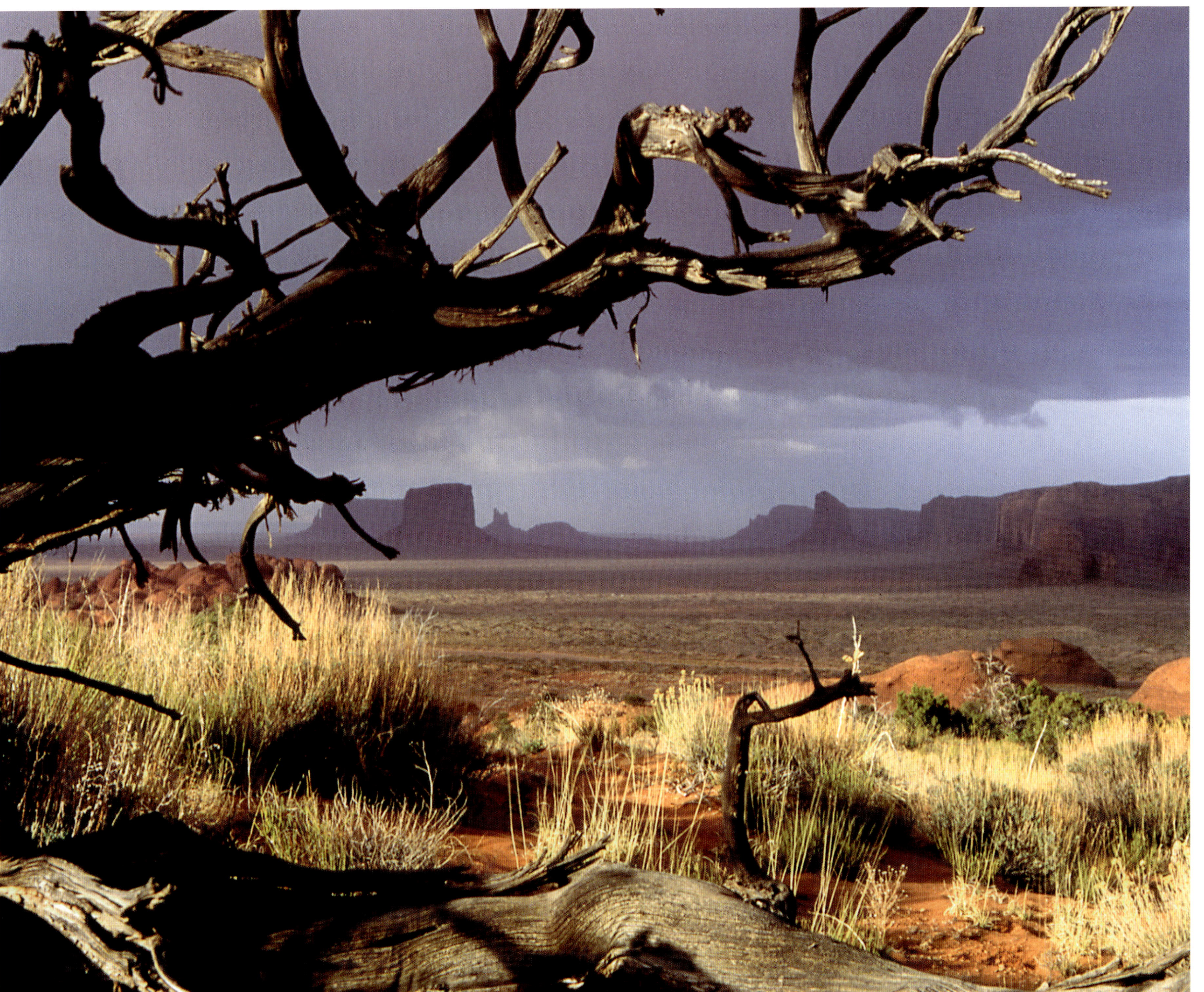

LEFT: Most pictures of Monument Valley in Utah concentrate on the might and very impressive buttes, but this picture shows the greater reality of wide, seemingly endless, flat plains and occasional clumps of grass, with the dried-out and well preserved remains of long-dead trees.
Geoffrey Lipscombe/fotoLibra

FAR LEFT: Monument Valley Navajo Tribal Park, showing The Castle (foreground), Brigham's Tomb (background), and Eagle Rock Mesa (right).
Wark/AirPhotoNA

PAGE 40: Bryce Canyon is a small National Park in southwestern Utah, named for Ebenezer Bryce (1830-1913), a Scottish carpenter who was converted to the Mormon religion and emigrated to the United States to join Brigham Young in his move eastwards. The canyon contains some unique geological formations and beautiful scenery, but the down-to-earth Scotsman's only known comment on the canyon was that it was "a helluva place to lose a cow."
Geoffrey Lipscombe/fotoLibra

PAGE 41: Zion National Park is located east of St. George, Utah, and includes a variety of life zones within its 230 square miles. This towering structure shows with great clarity the traces of each geological period that has gone into its construction.
Geoffrey Lipscombe/fotoLibra

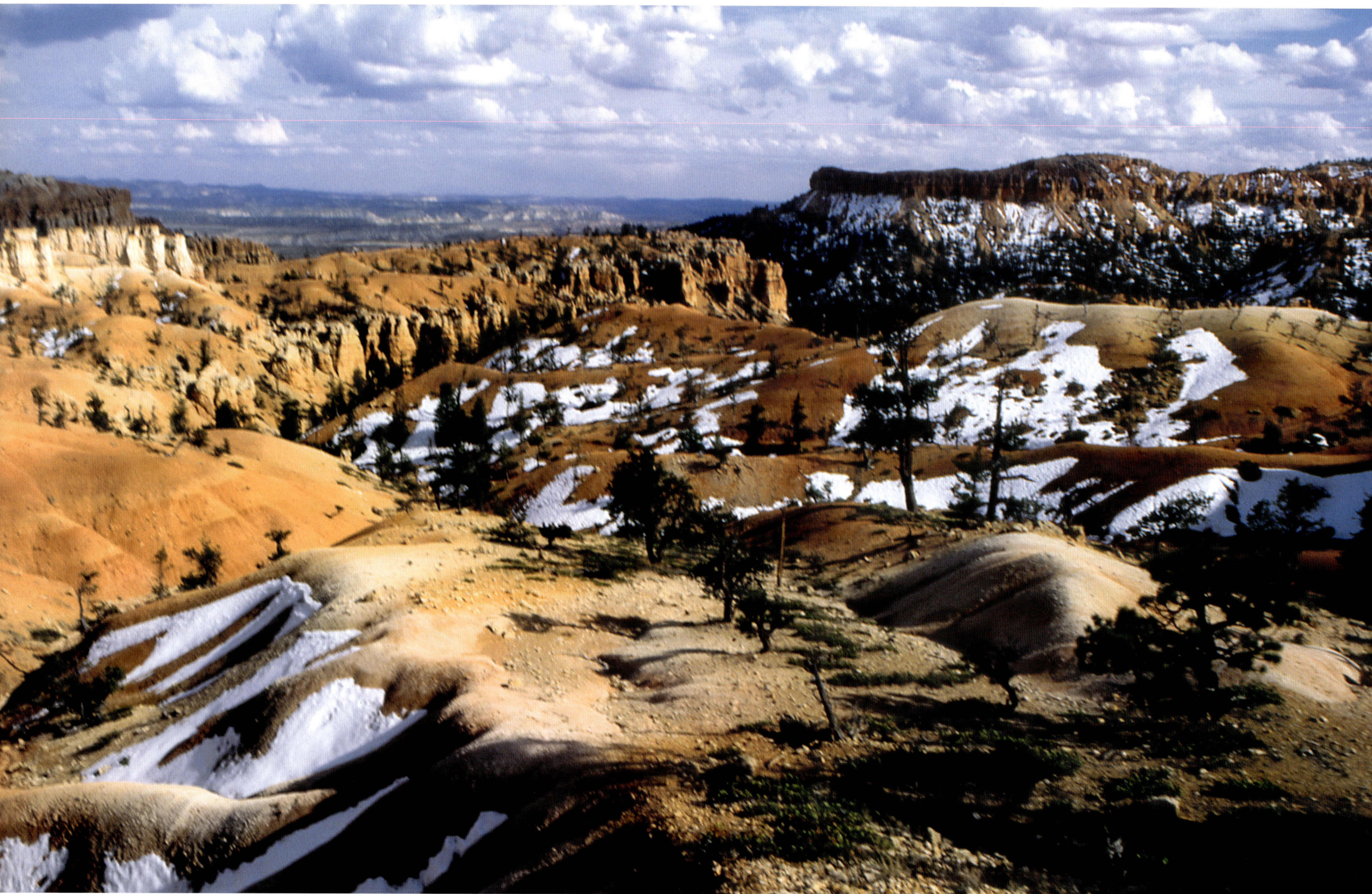

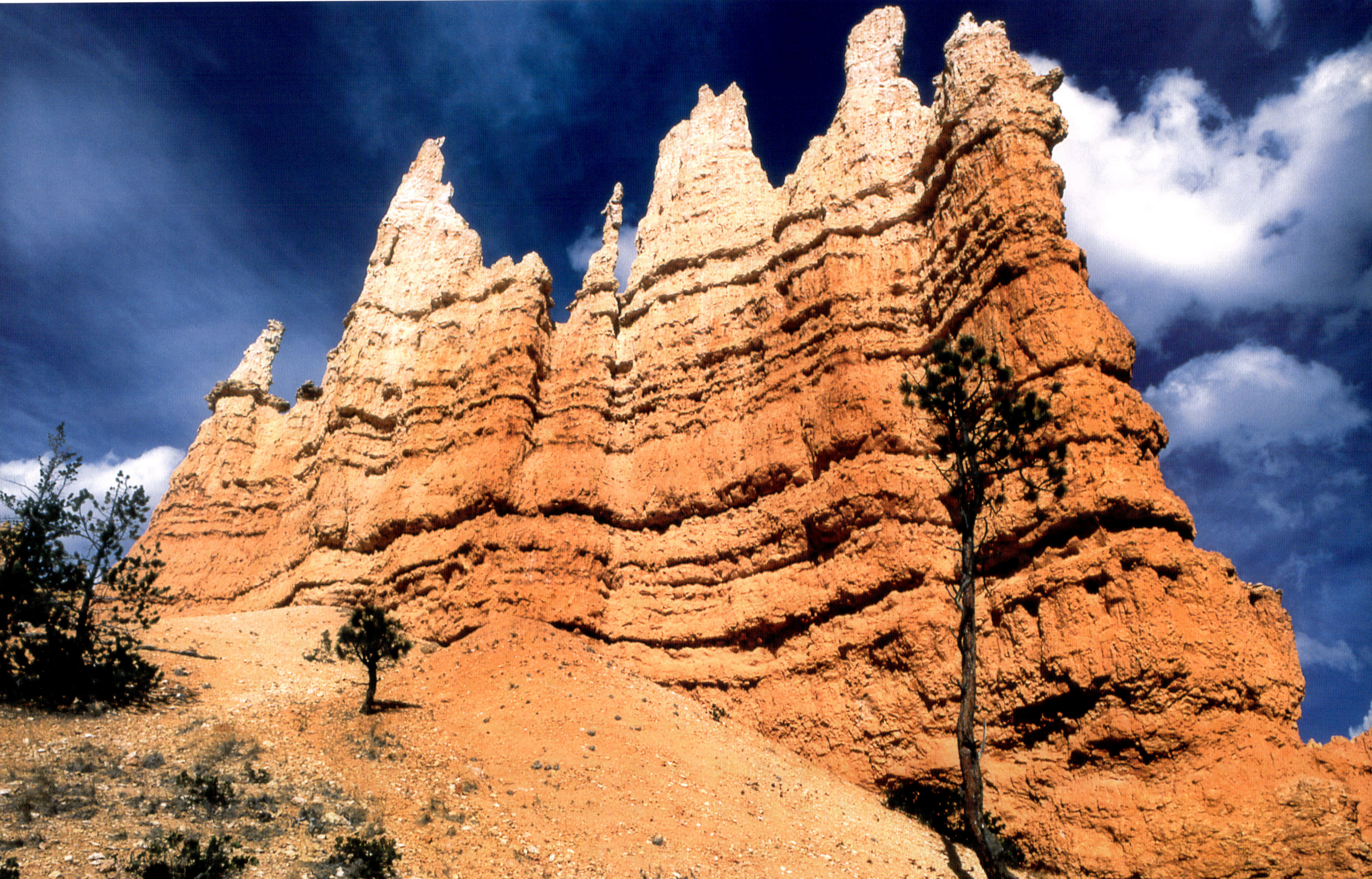

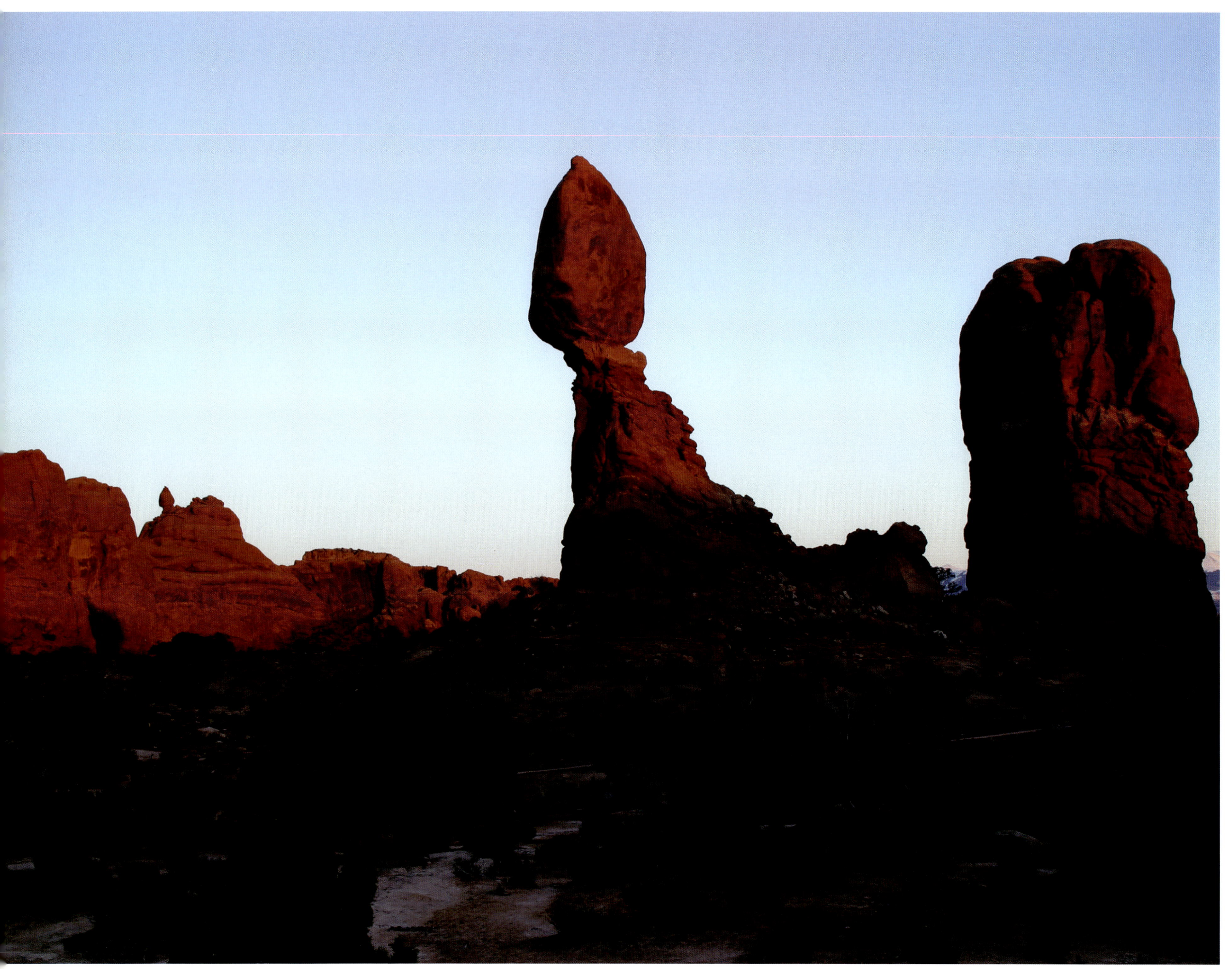

LEFT: The famous Balanced Rock in Arches National Park, Utah, is an example of a geological feature named a "hoodoo." This is not a black magic term, but is the name for the curiously shaped rock pillars that develop as a result of erosion by wind or water, particularly in areas where soft and hard sedimentary layers alternate with each other. In this case a 55-foot high, 3,500-ton slickrock sandstone caprock stands atop a softer layer, which rests, in its turn, on a Navajo Sandstone base, and they have been eroded at different rates.
George Frandsen/fotoLibra

RIGHT: These fantastic shapes and patterns in a Utah desert are sandstone buttes, which are the result of the erosion of petrified sand dunes.
Eastcott Momatiuk/Getty Images

PAGE 44: Geologists and scientists can often offer convincing explanations for the some of the more bizarre sights in the natural world, such as the Australian Pinnacles and the Balanced Rock in Arches National Park. There are occasions, however, such as with this ball-shaped rock atop a delicately-necked pedestal in a Wyoming desert, where any explanation would be wasted and all Man can do is to look and wonder.
Richard Olsenius/Getty Images

PAGE 45: Dune riders power their way across Sand Mountain, Nevada, which lies two miles off U.S. Highway 50 and about 1½ hours from Carson City. This great feature is about 2½ miles long and 600 feet high and is regularly used by all-terrain vehicles and three- or four-wheeled dune buggies, as well as by sand boarders. The facility is managed by the U.S. Bureau of Land Management, which has to strike a balance between the beliefs and rights of the Native Americans, the pursuit of leisure by visitors for whom the Sand Mountain is an off-roader's dream, and ecologists seeking to protect rare species.
Philip Schermeister/Getty Images

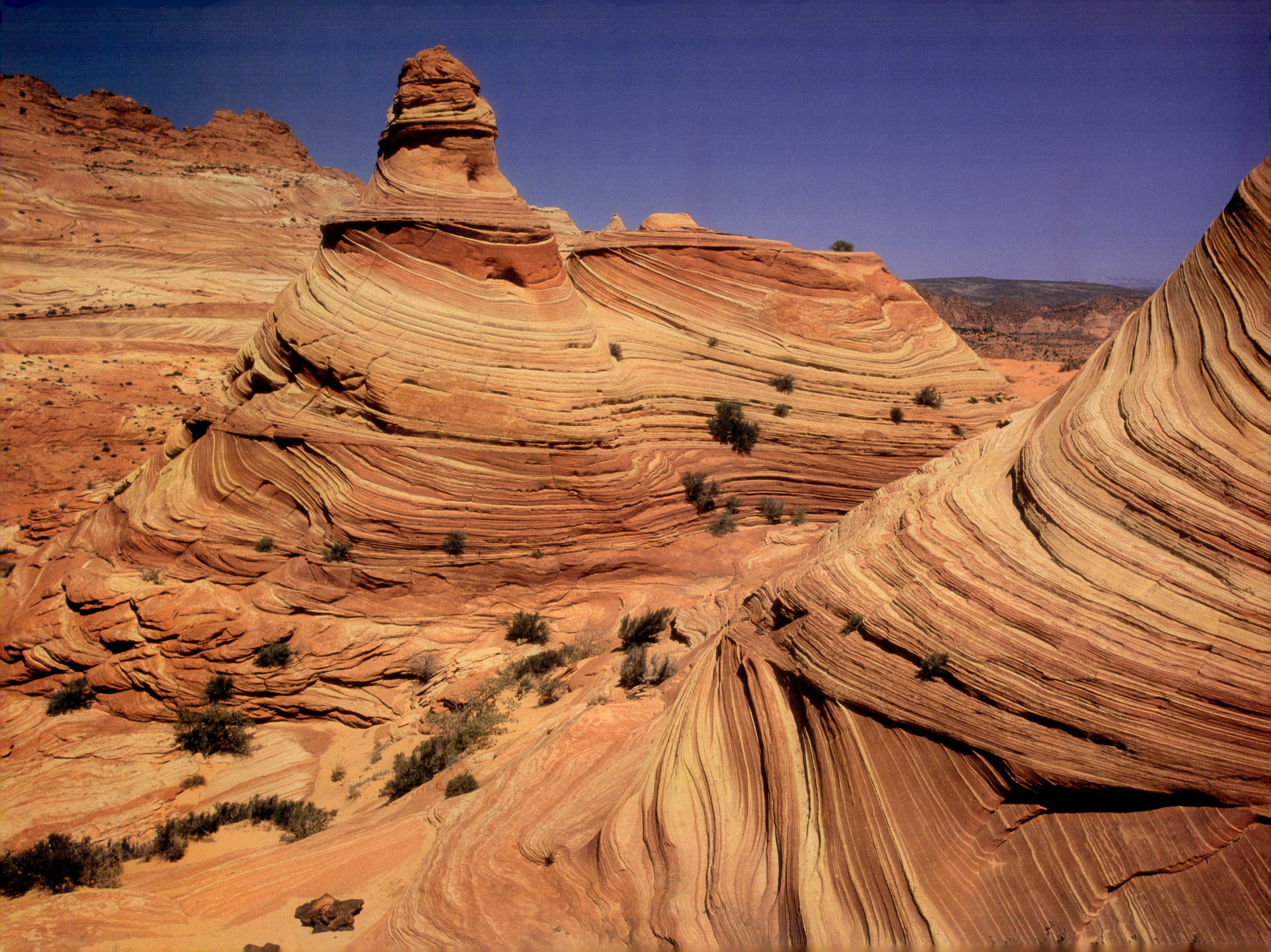

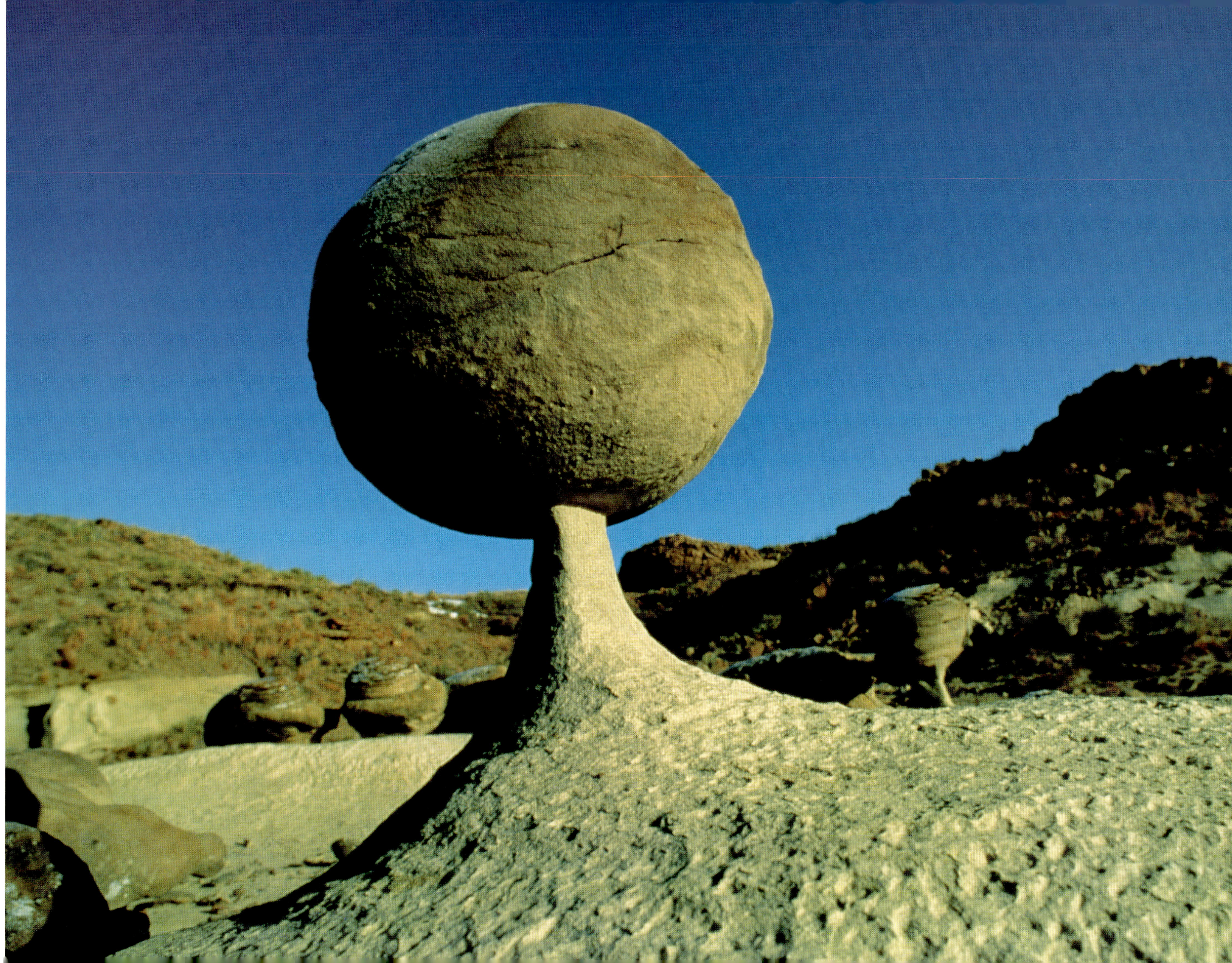

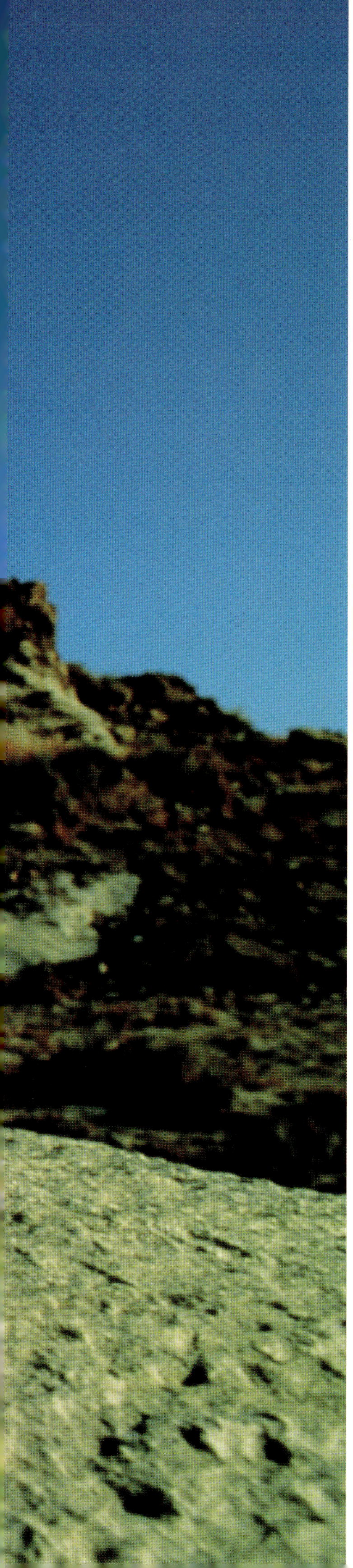

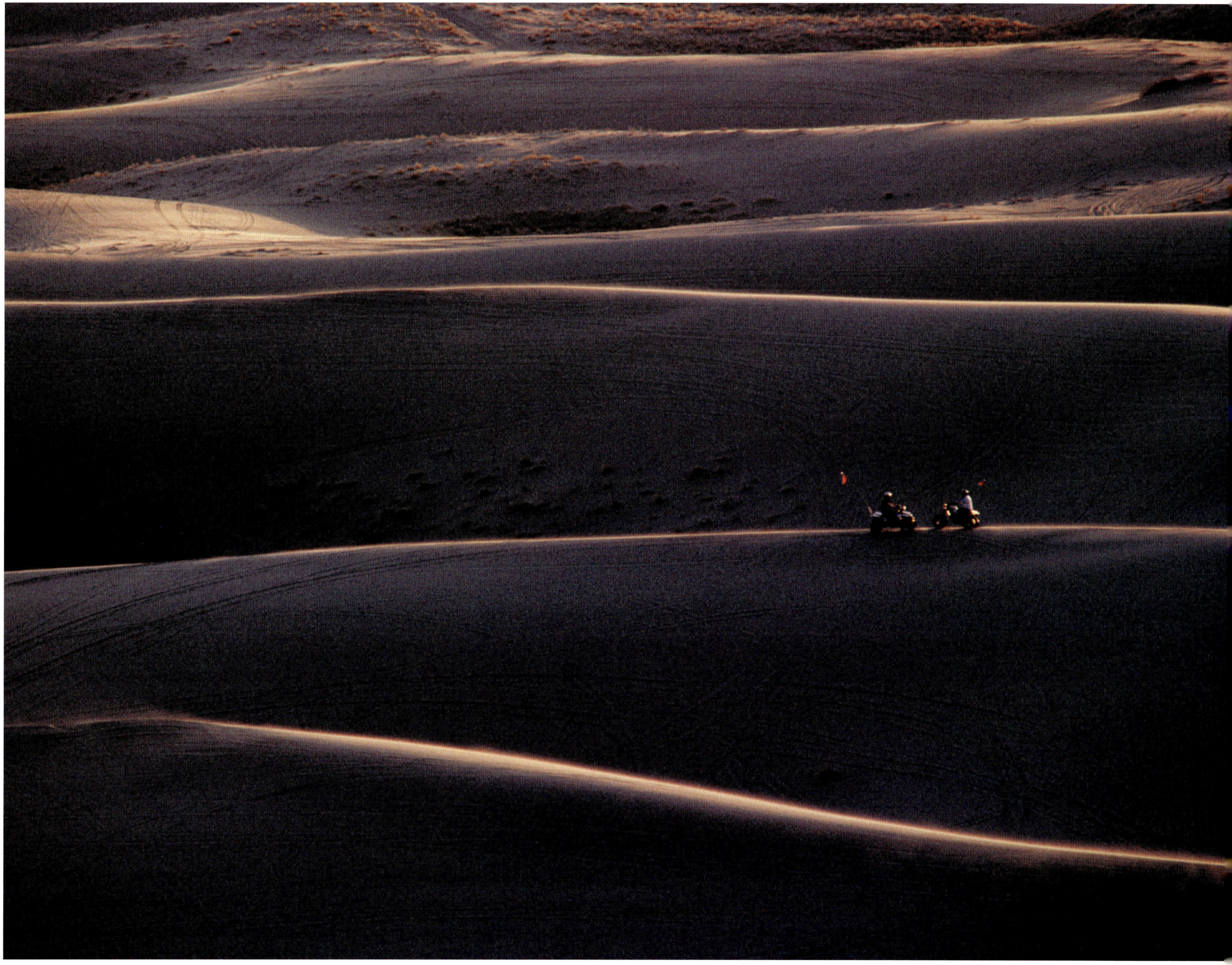

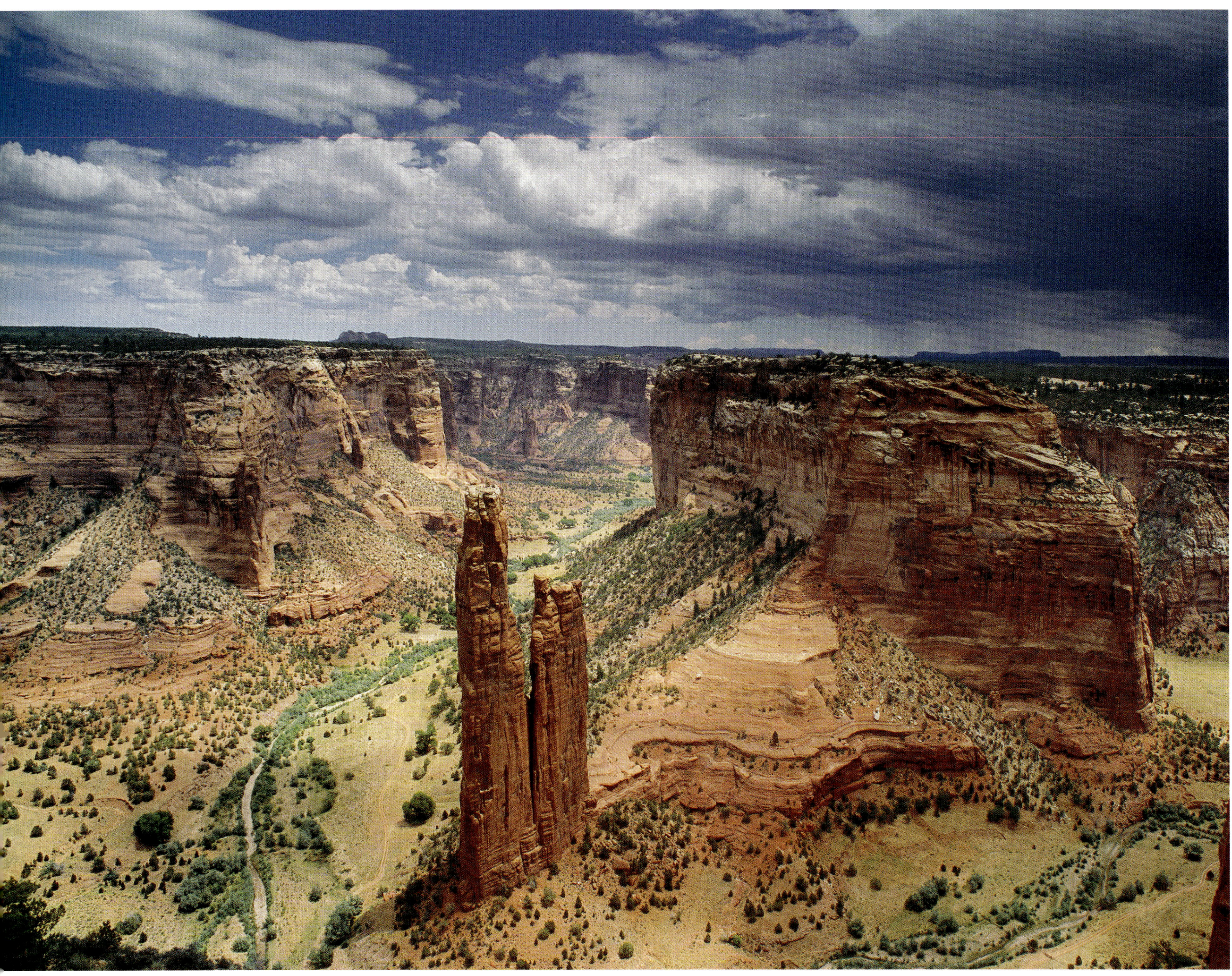

Left: The Canyon de Chelly National Park is composed entirely of land belonging to the Navajo people and among its many attractions are Spider Rock, towering some 800 feet above the canyon floor. It was the home of the deity Spider Woman who lived on the platform at the top and protected the Navajo Nation, as well as teaching them how to weave on a loom.
Bill Hatcher/Getty Images

Right: Away from the great buttes in Arizona's Monument Valley, the scenery is different but no less impressive. Here a semicircle of ancient sandstone spires, known to the Navajos as the *Ye Bi Chai*, with the Totem Pole on the right, creates one of nature's cathedrals.
Paul Chesley/Getty Images

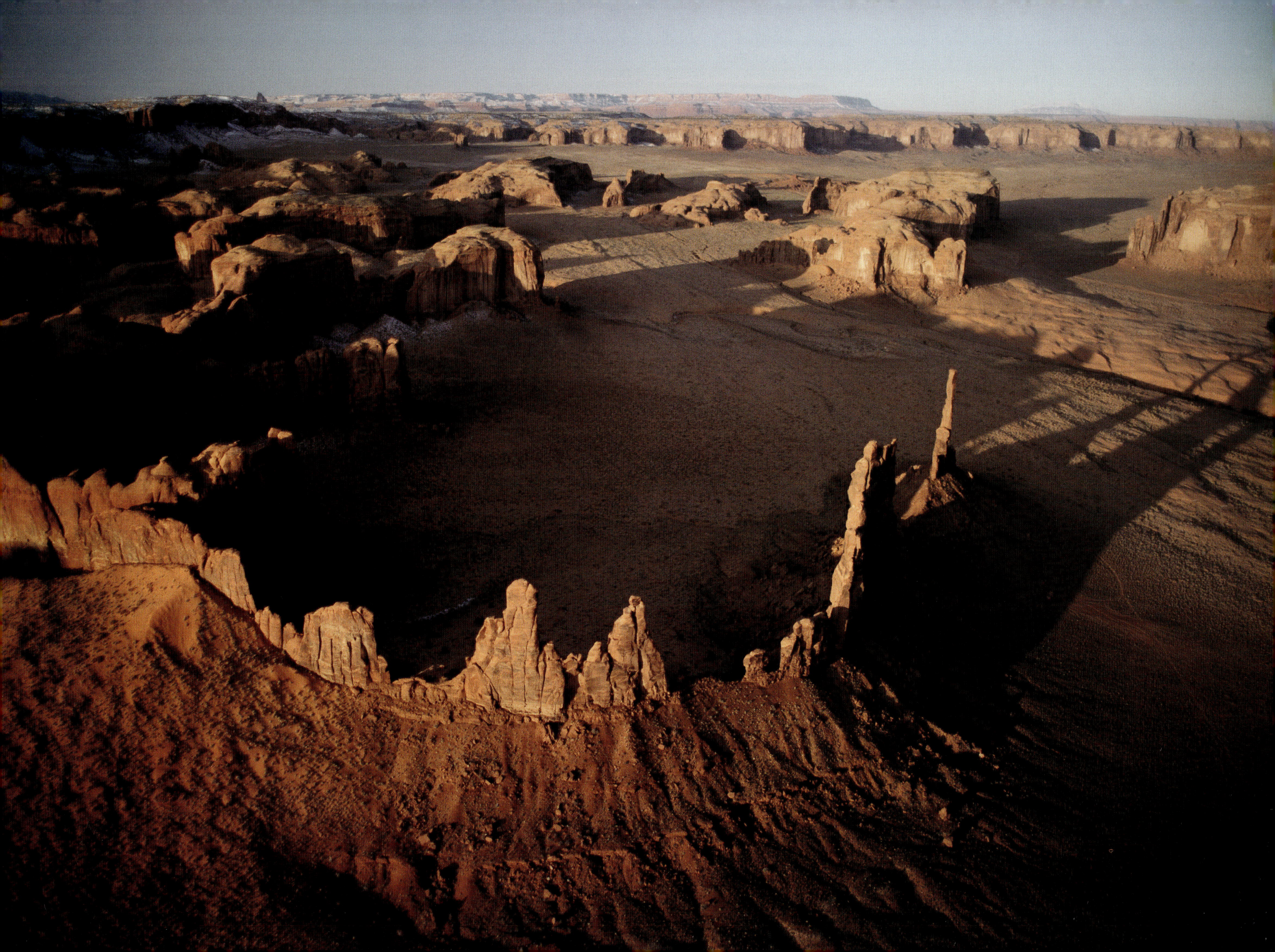

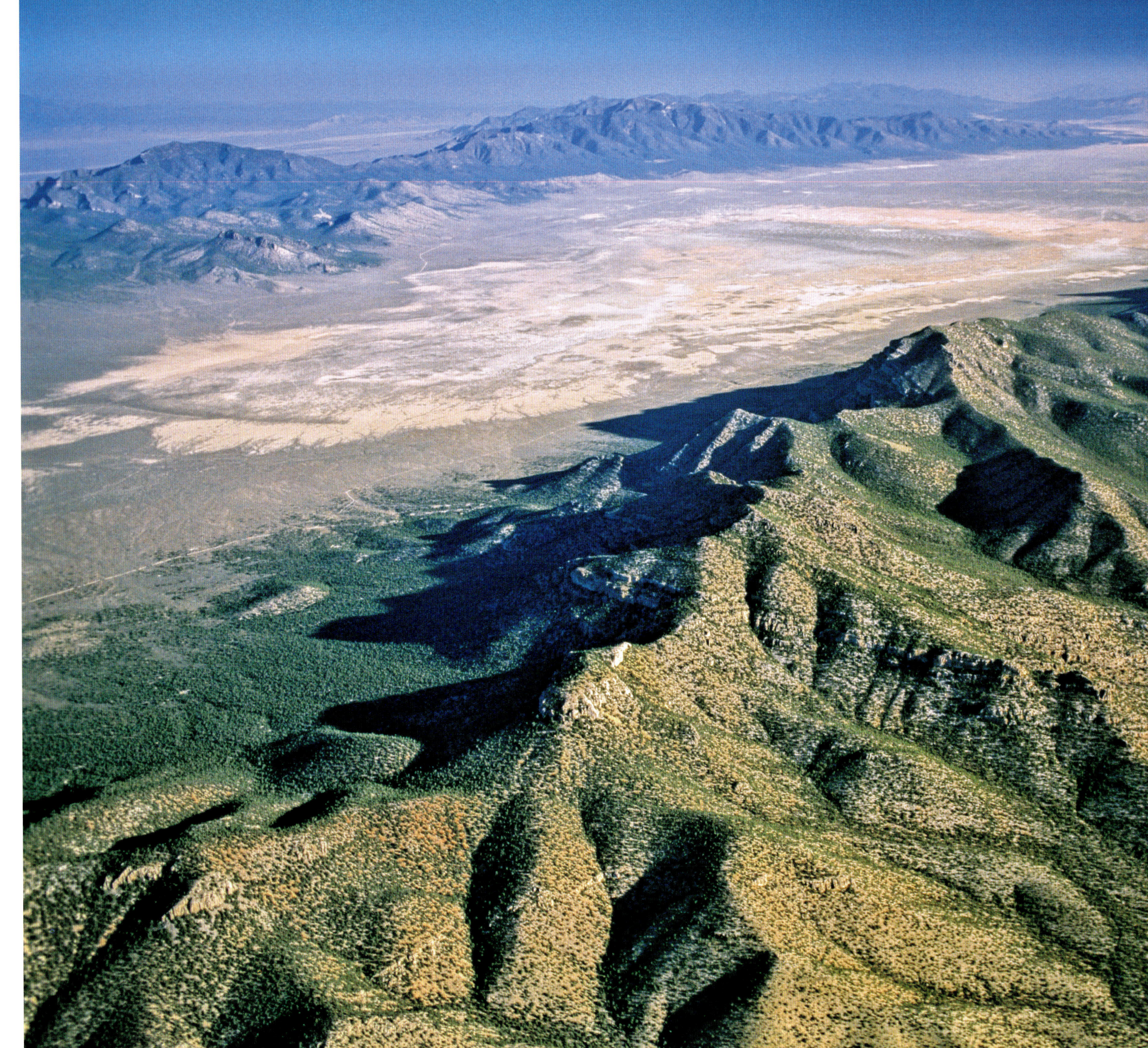

RIGHT: Schell Peak Mountain Range in Nevada's White Pine County has heavily wooded lower slopes, making it appear from the air to be a verdant mountainous island, set in a desert sea. Beyond the range is Cave Valley, part of the Great Basin Desert.
Wark/AirPhotoNA

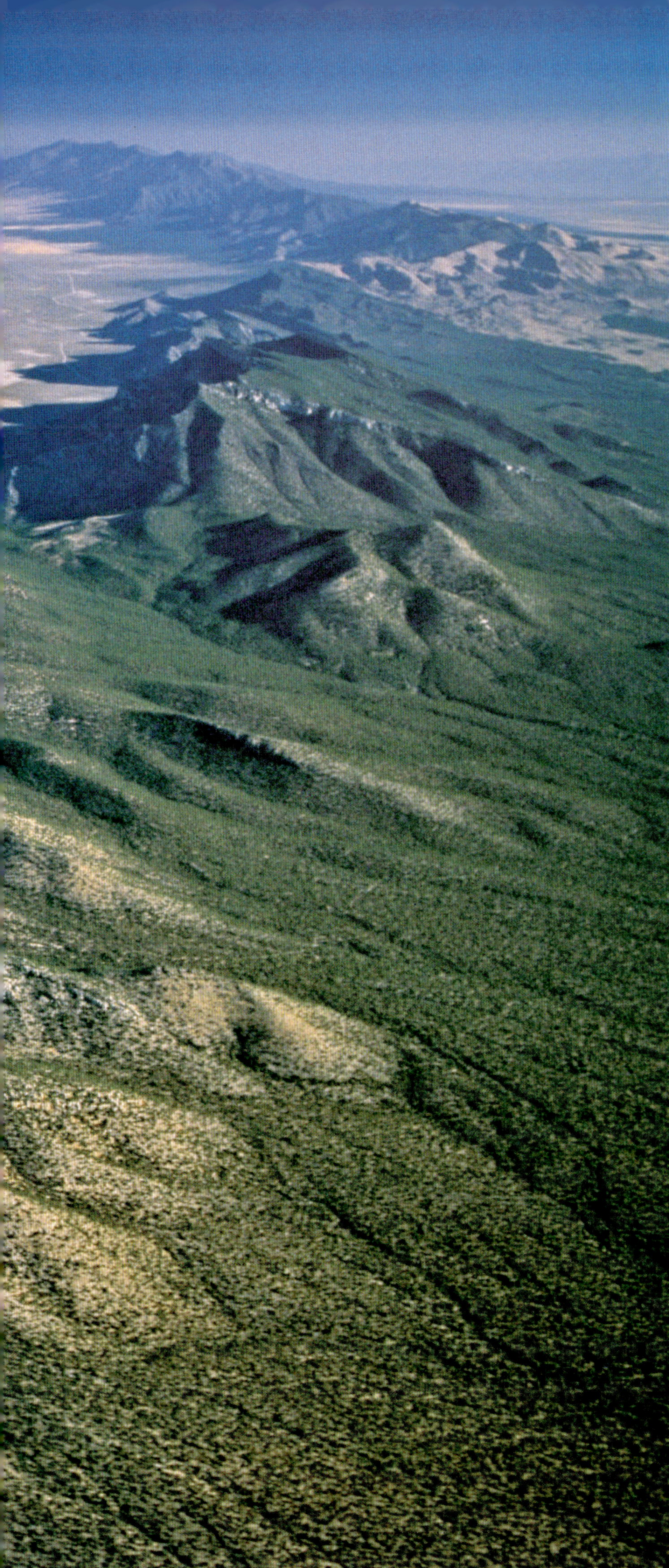

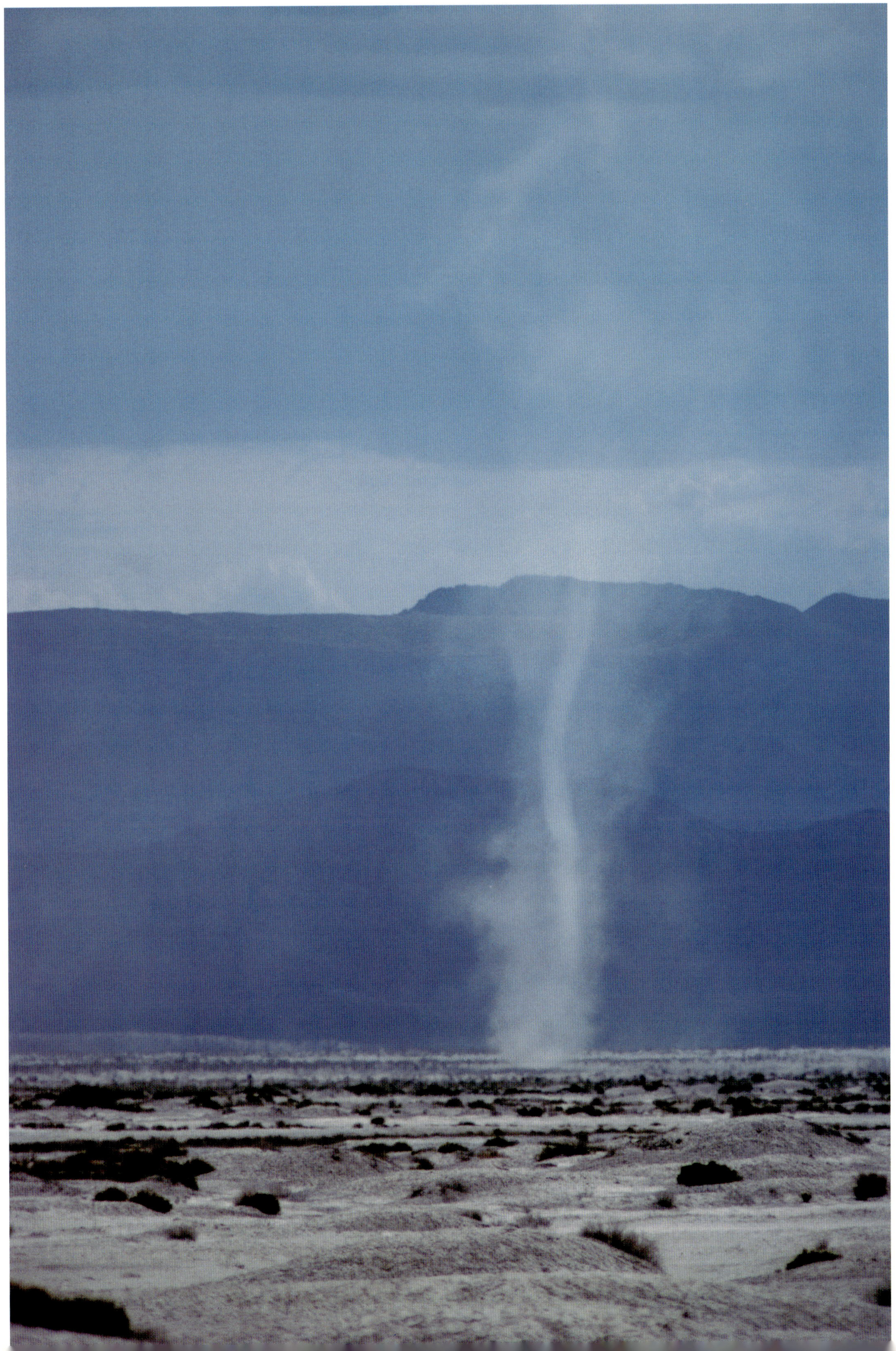

LEFT: A dust devil forms in Black Rock Desert, north of Reno, Nevada, a dried out lakebed, known as a playa, which locals claim to be the largest flat spot on the Earth's surface. Dust devils occur in desert areas on sandy surfaces, where the sun heats the surface and thus the thin layer of air immediately above. This hotter air seeks to rise but is prevented by the cooler air above until some external cause enables it to break through. It then rises rapidly, sucking more air in at its foot, and carrying dust and debris with it. The result is a funnel-like chimney, which can last from a few minutes to several hours. *James P. Blair/National Geographic/Getty Images*

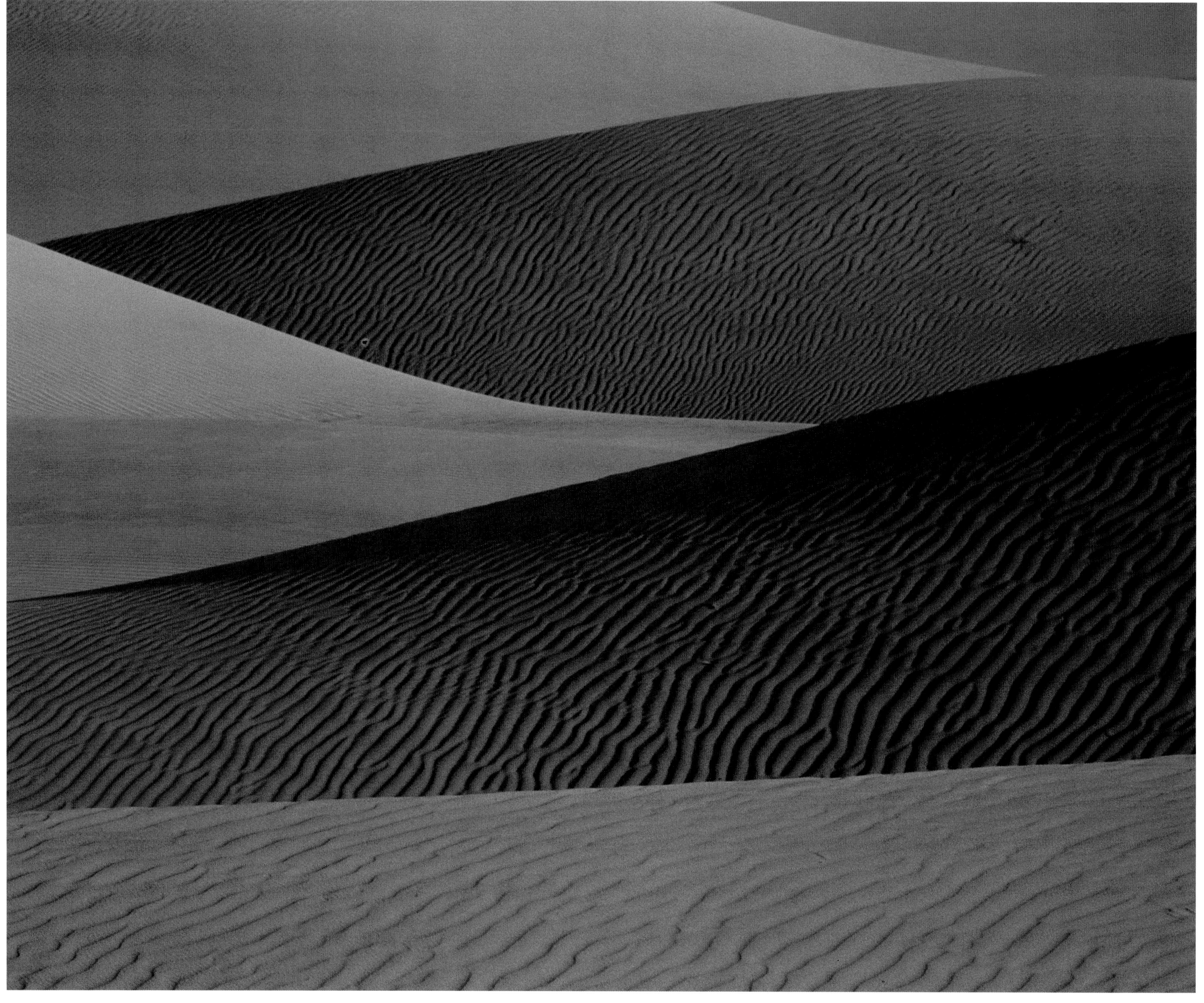

Left: Sand dunes in the Death Valley National Monument in California, with the ripples that indicate that the wind is gradually moving the dune in a direction at right angles to the line of the ripples.
Michael K. Nichols/Getty Images

Right: New Mexico's White Sands are in an area of constant southwesterly winds, which results in a permanent state of movement as individual grains are moved from one "ripple" to another and, at the outer edges, constant encroachment onto adjacent land.
Andrew Brown/Corbis

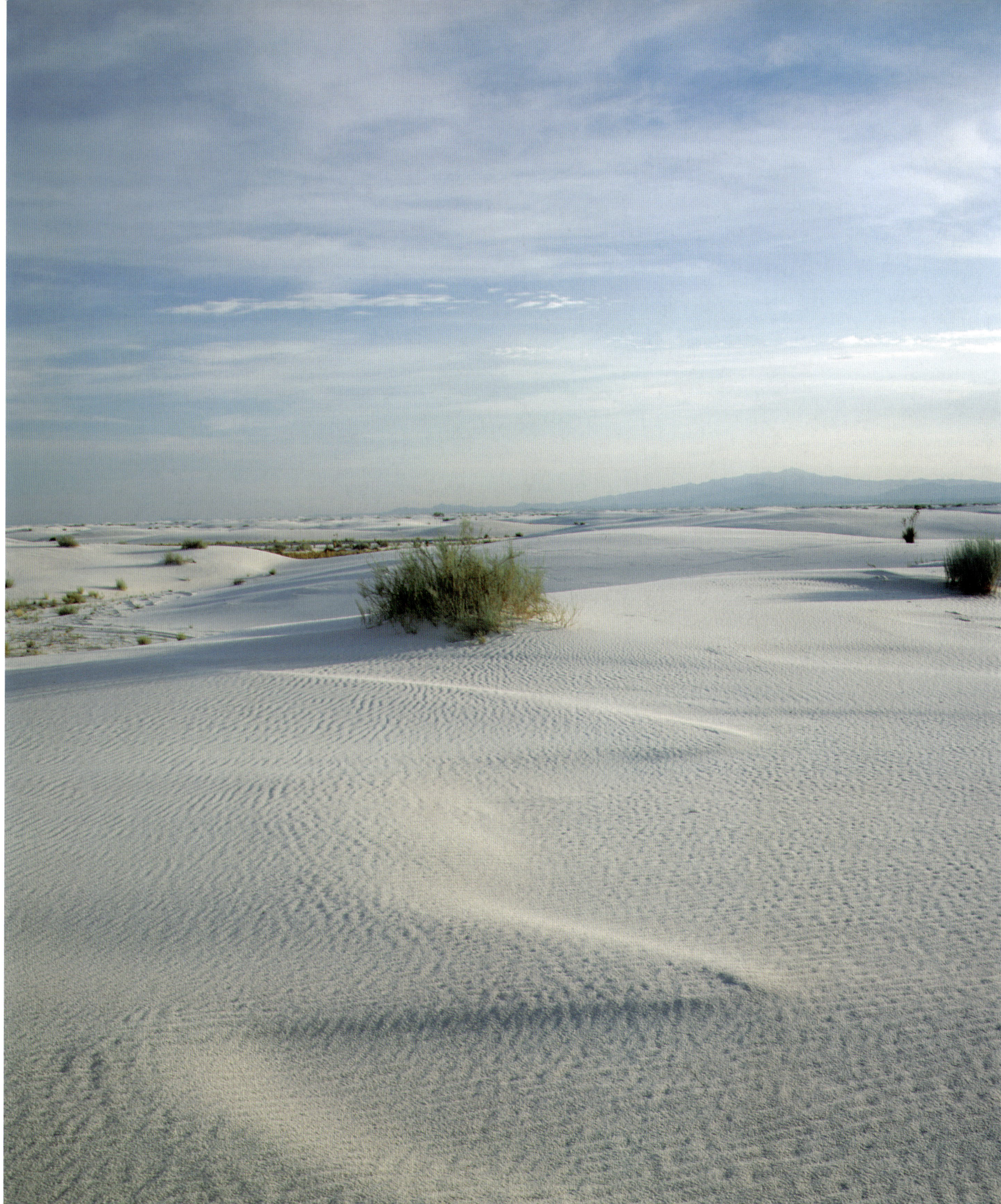

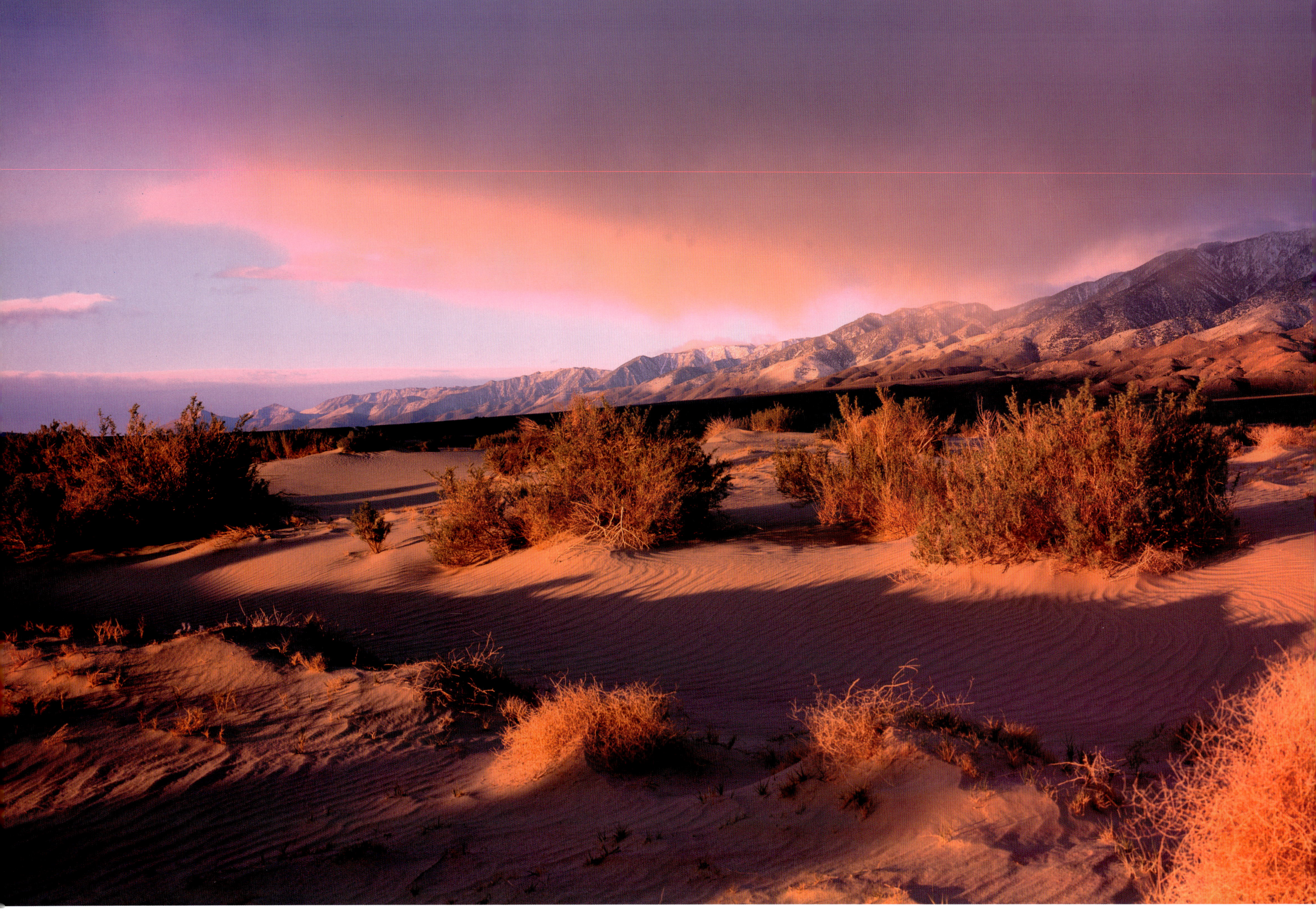

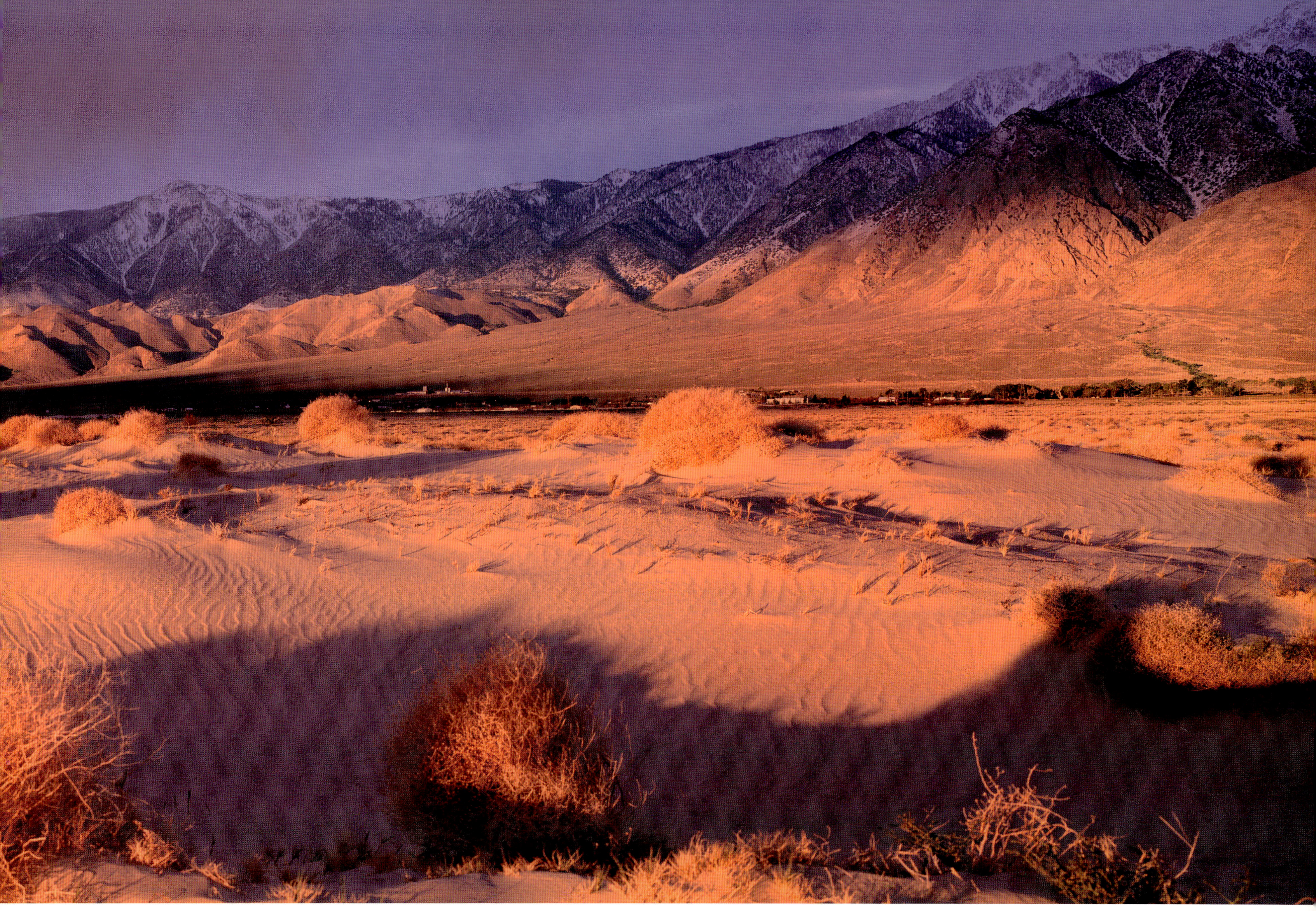

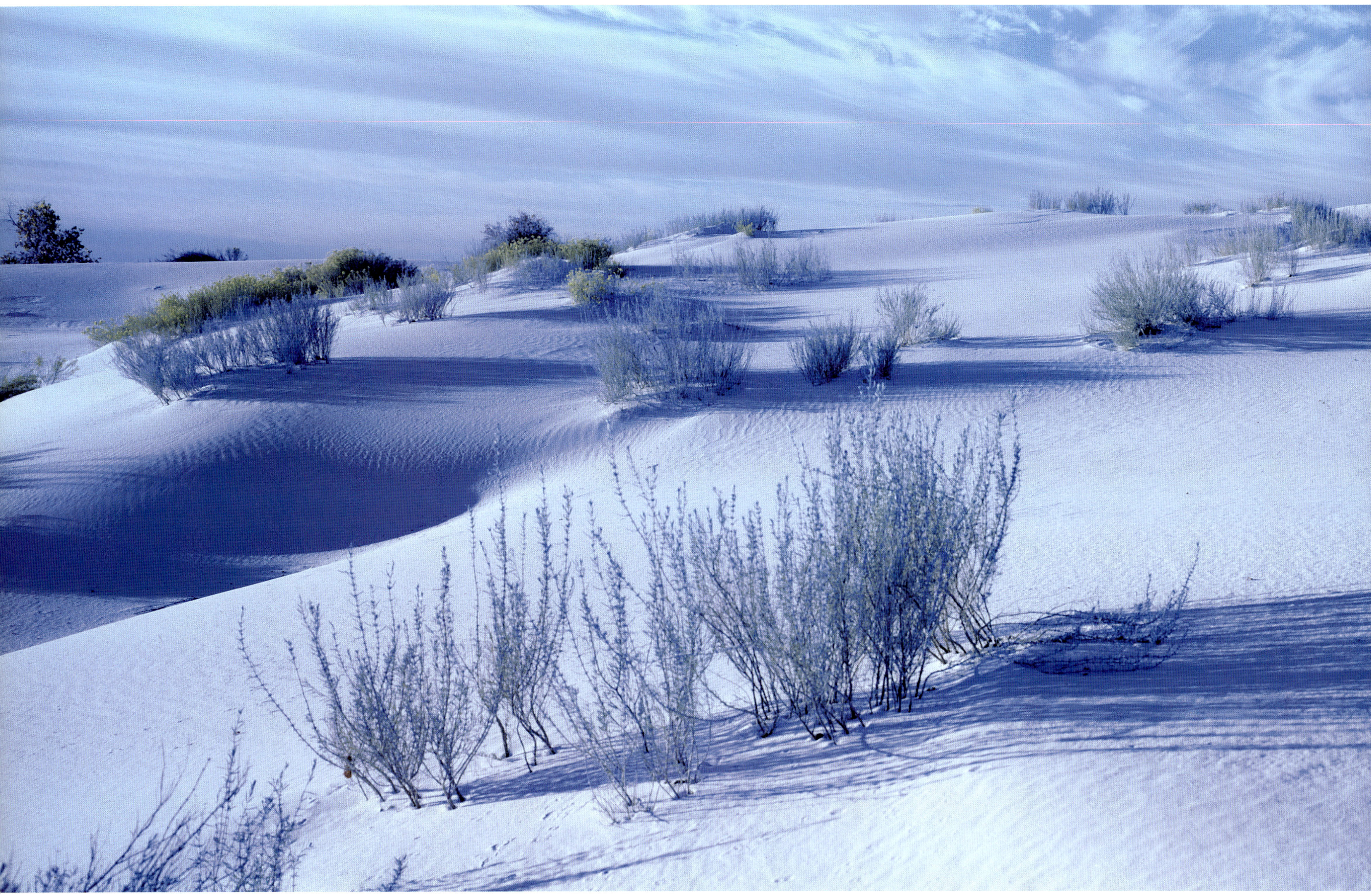

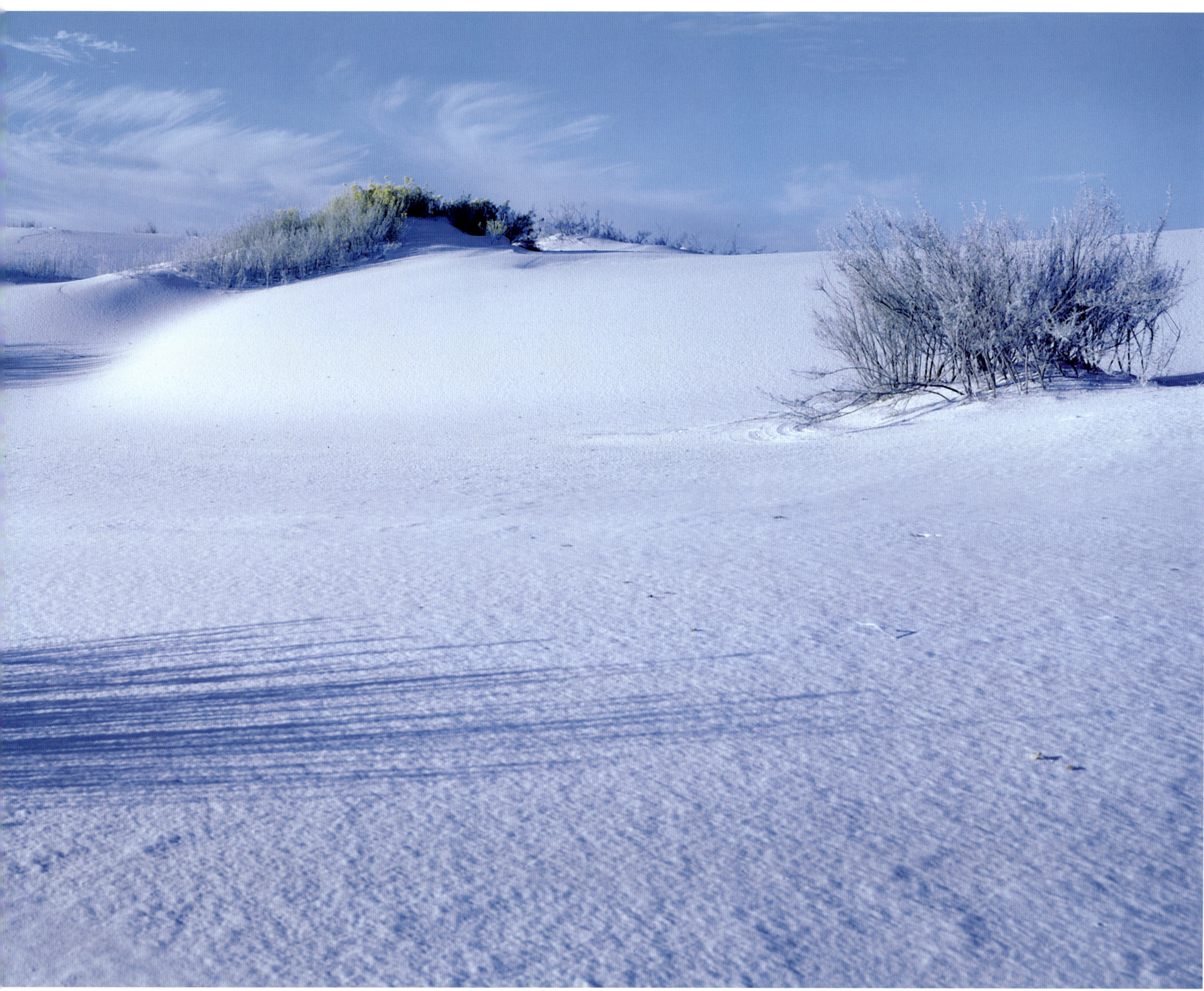

Pages 52–53: A view of the Mojave Desert, taken from the town of Olancha, California, population 134, looking across typical desert scenery towards the South-East Sierras In the distance, a sandstorm is building up and heading towards the photographer.
Pete Saloutos/Corbis

Left: The Chihuahuan Desert in New Mexico is home to a great natural wonder, the White Sands. These sands, which are actually grains of gypsum (hydrated calcium sulphate), cover an area of some 275 square miles at the northern end of the desert and have created a unique environment in which only a few plants and animals have learnt to survive, partly because of the nature of the gypsum, but also because the sands are permanently on the move.
Pete Saloutos/Corbis

Page 56: Around the world vast efforts are being put into irrigation schemes that seek to turn arid desert into productive, crop-bearing, farming country. Some, like this one in Buckeye, in Maricopa County, Arizona, have been successful, but others have failed.
Wark/AirPhotoNA

Page 57: The Barrenger Meteorite Crater in the Arizona Desert has been the subject of endless scientific theorizing. It is approximately one mile in diameter and 570 feet deep, and it is now generally accepted that it was caused by a meteorite some 50,000 years ago. That meteorite was probably about 150 feet in diameter, made predominantly of nickel-iron, and weighed some 300,000 tons. Its speed at impact was about 40,000 miles per hour, resulting in a force equivalent to 20 million tons of TNT, or five times the power of the largest thermonuclear weapon ever tested.
Charles O'Rear/Corbis

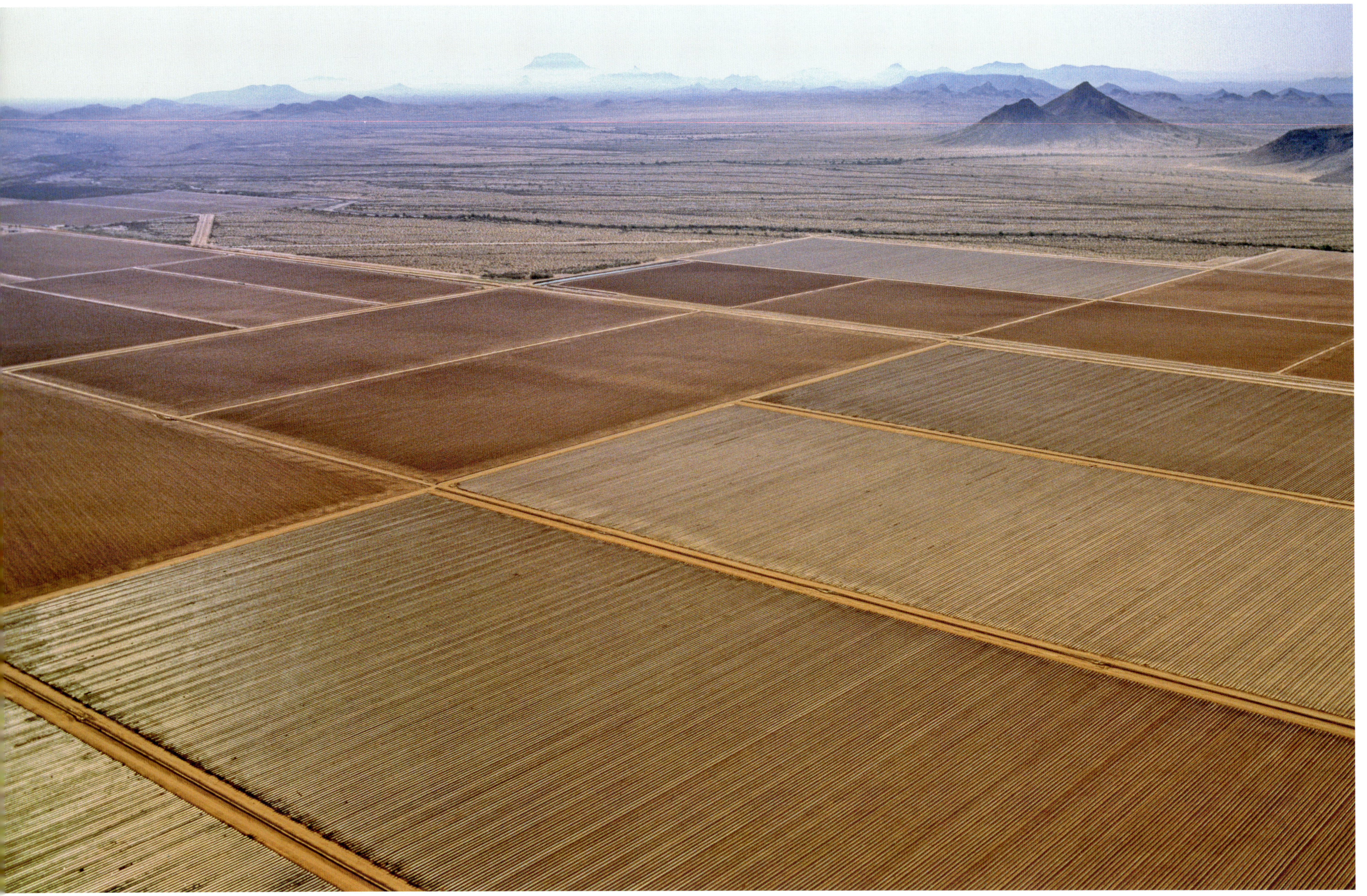

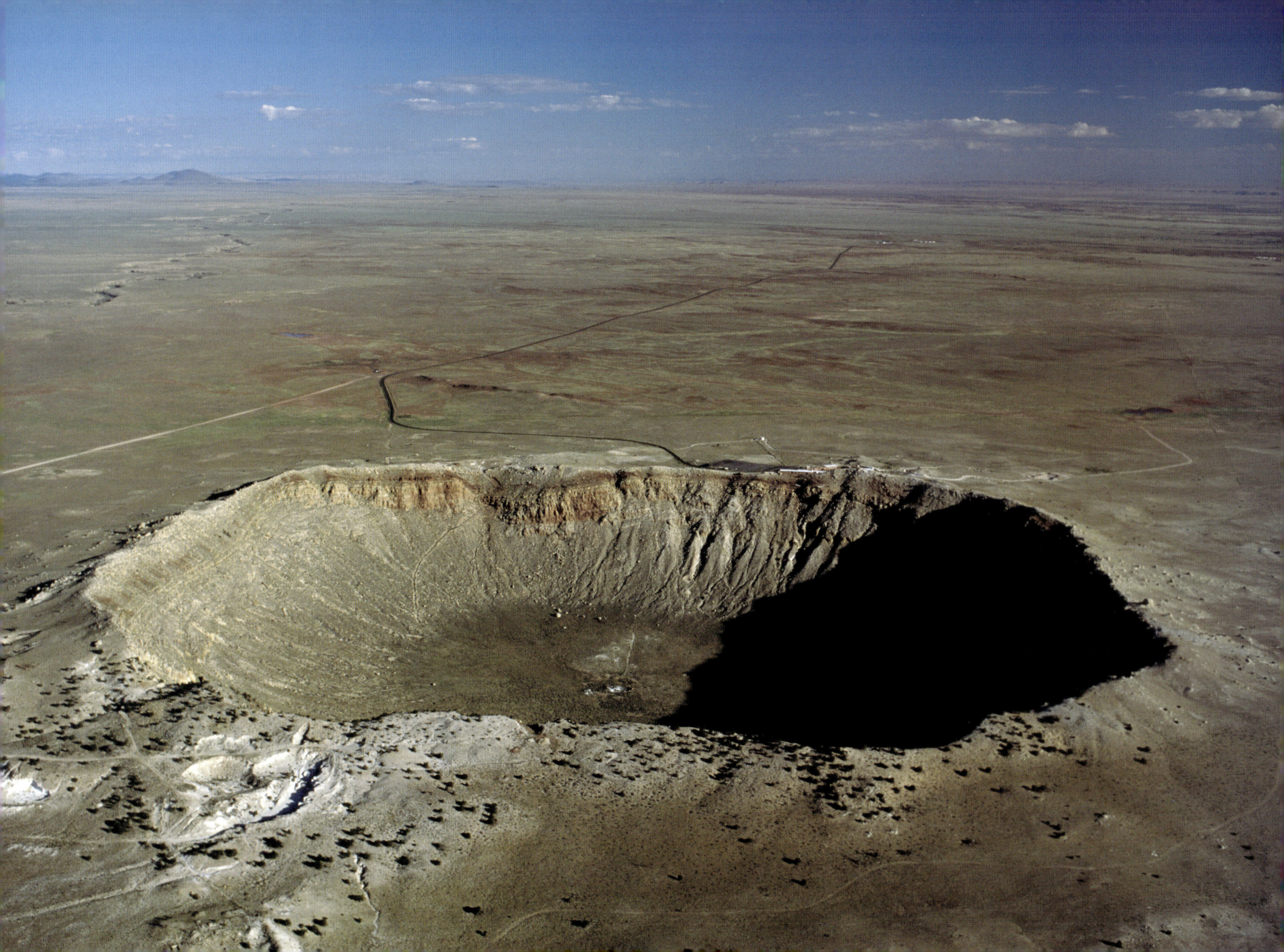

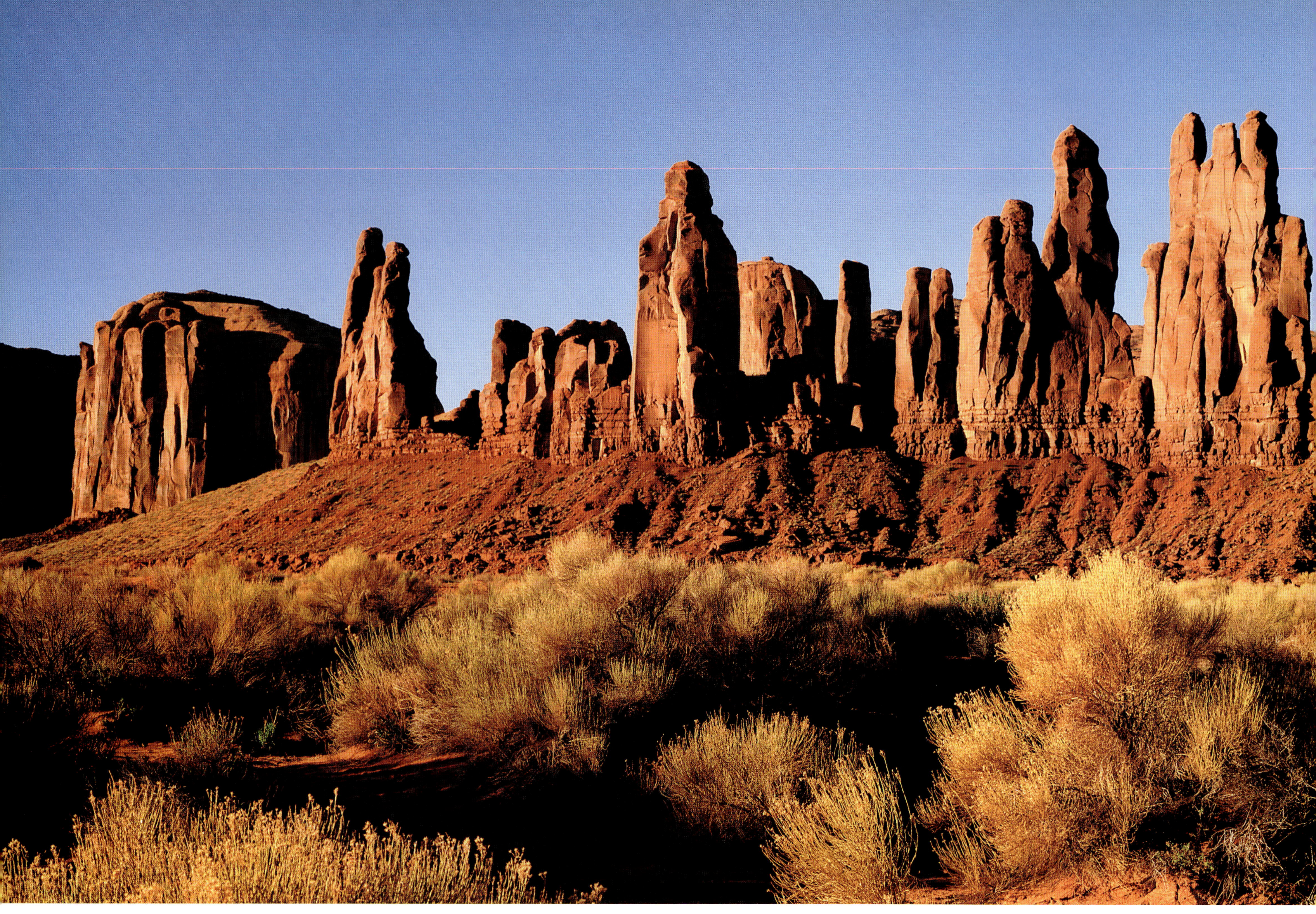

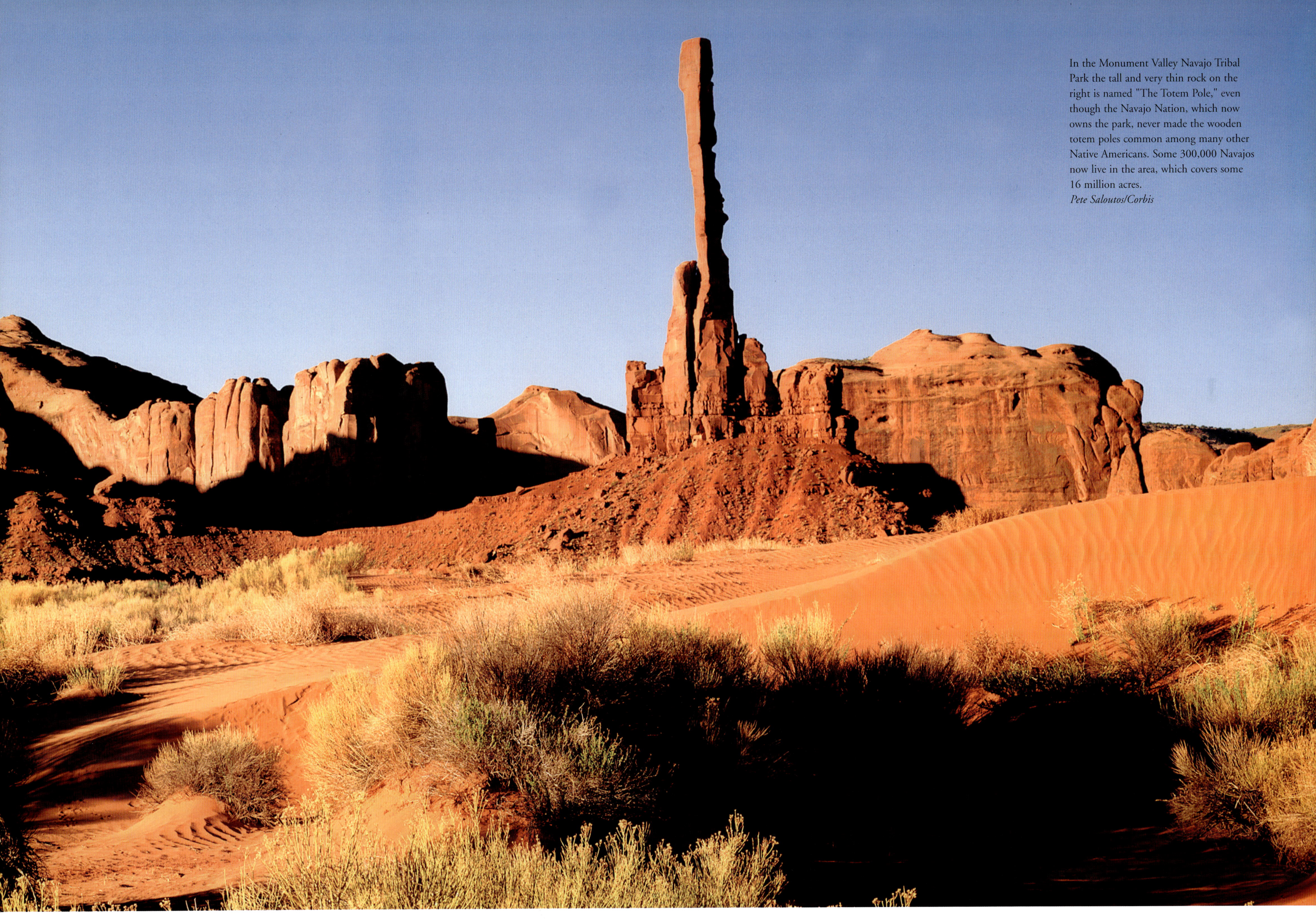

In the Monument Valley Navajo Tribal Park the tall and very thin rock on the right is named "The Totem Pole," even though the Navajo Nation, which now owns the park, never made the wooden totem poles common among many other Native Americans. Some 300,000 Navajos now live in the area, which covers some 16 million acres.
Pete Saloutos/Corbis

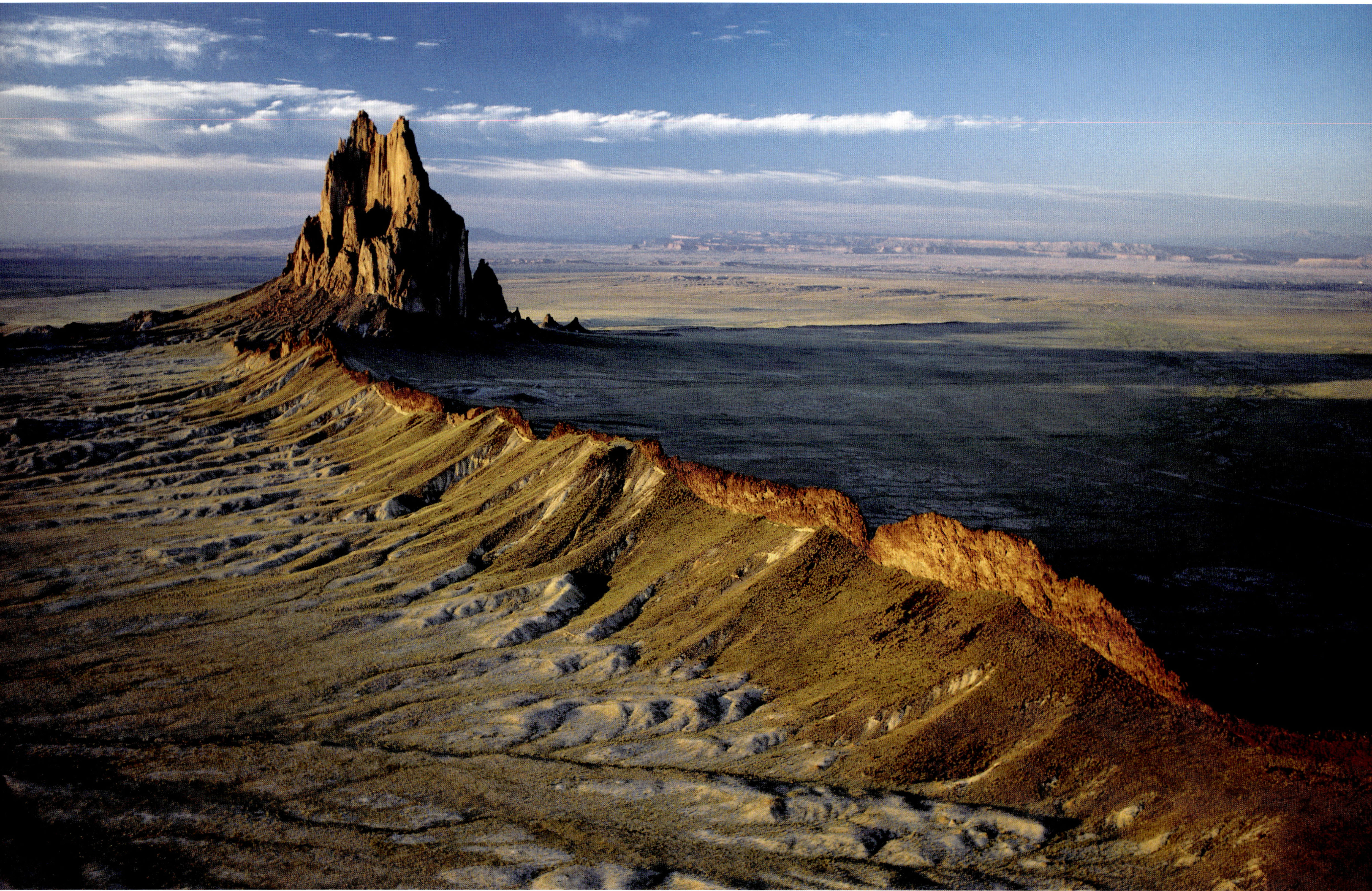

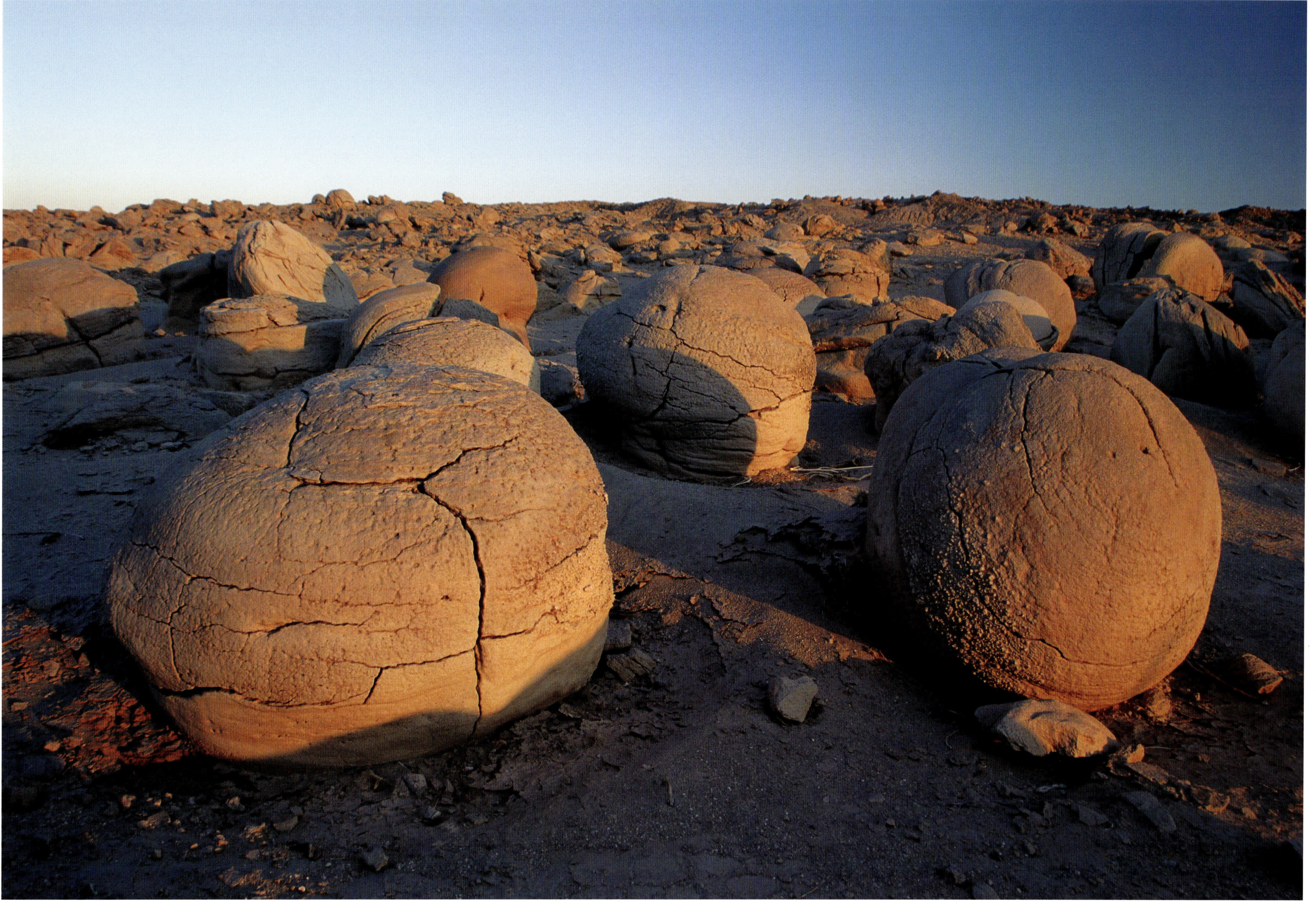

Page 60: Shiprock Peak towers some 1,800 feet above the surrounding plain of the Navajo National Park. It gained this name among 19th century explorers from the East Coast, due to its supposed resemblance to a clipper ship of the time, but it is known as *Tsé Bit' A'í* to the Navajo, who own it and who have placed a ban on climbers scaling it, since it is considered a sacred place.
Danny Lehman/Corbis

Page 61: The Anza-Borrego Desert State Park covers an area of some 600,000 acres in California and Arizona, making it the largest desert state park in the Continental United States. The park is a two hour drive from San Diego and attracts some 600,000 visitors a year, who come to see desert flora and fauna at first hand, as well as boulder fields like this, which look little different from the pictures beamed back from the Moon during the American astronauts' lunar explorations.
Richard Cummins/Corbis

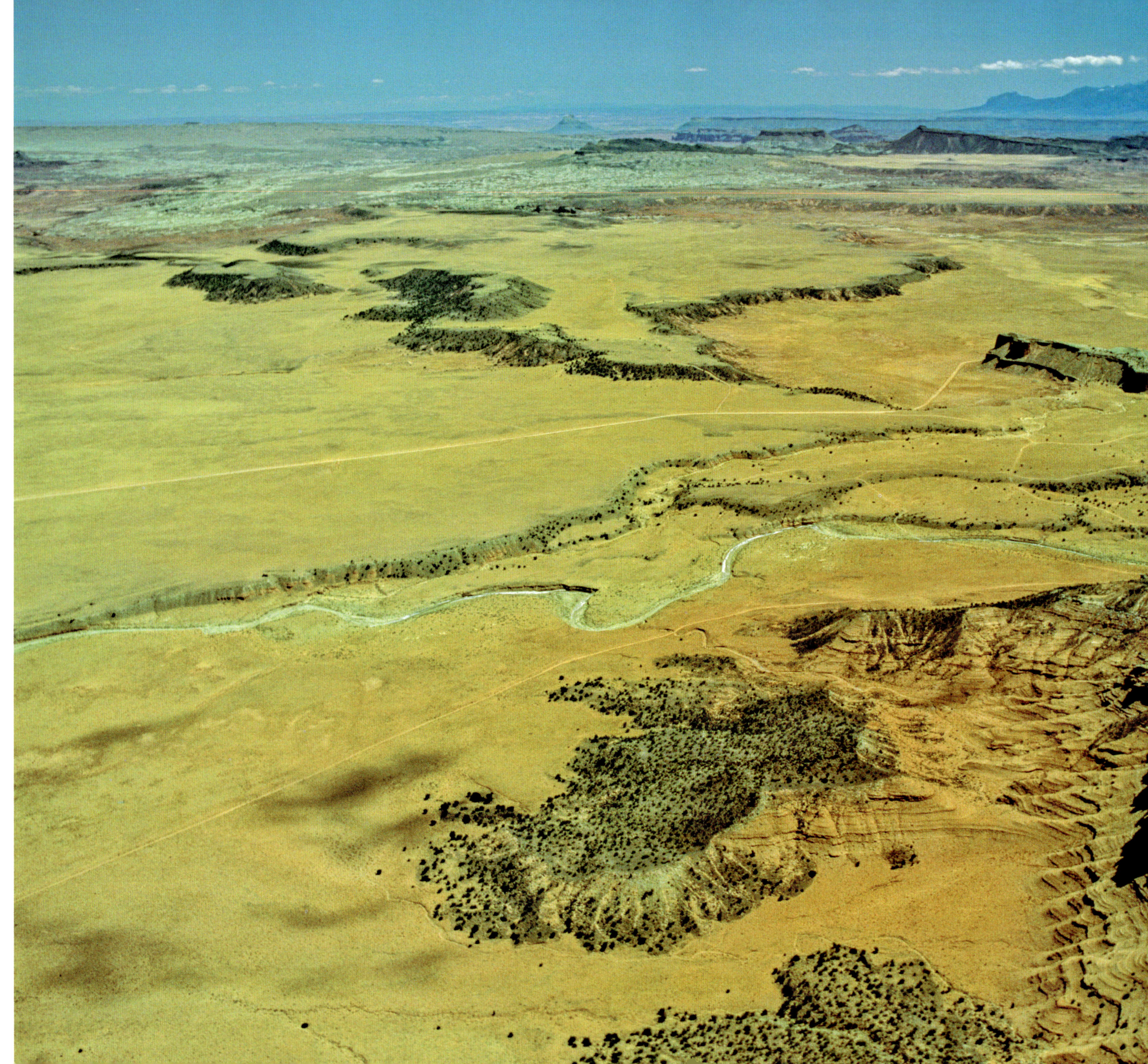

Right: Marble Canyon consists of vertical cliffs each side of the Colorado River, lying below Glen Canyon Dam and the man-made Lake Powell, and the Grand Canyon, proper. It gets its name from the many very colorful rocks, but only rafters on the river can properly appreciate them.
Wark/AirPhotoNA

Far Right: There are men and women for whom deserts exert an irresistible fascination. There is something almost magical about the vast open spaces, the loneliness, the silence, the challenge of moving and surviving, and, as with this walker in the Mojave, seeing only your own footsteps on an apparently virgin surface.
Gordon Wiltsie/Getty Images

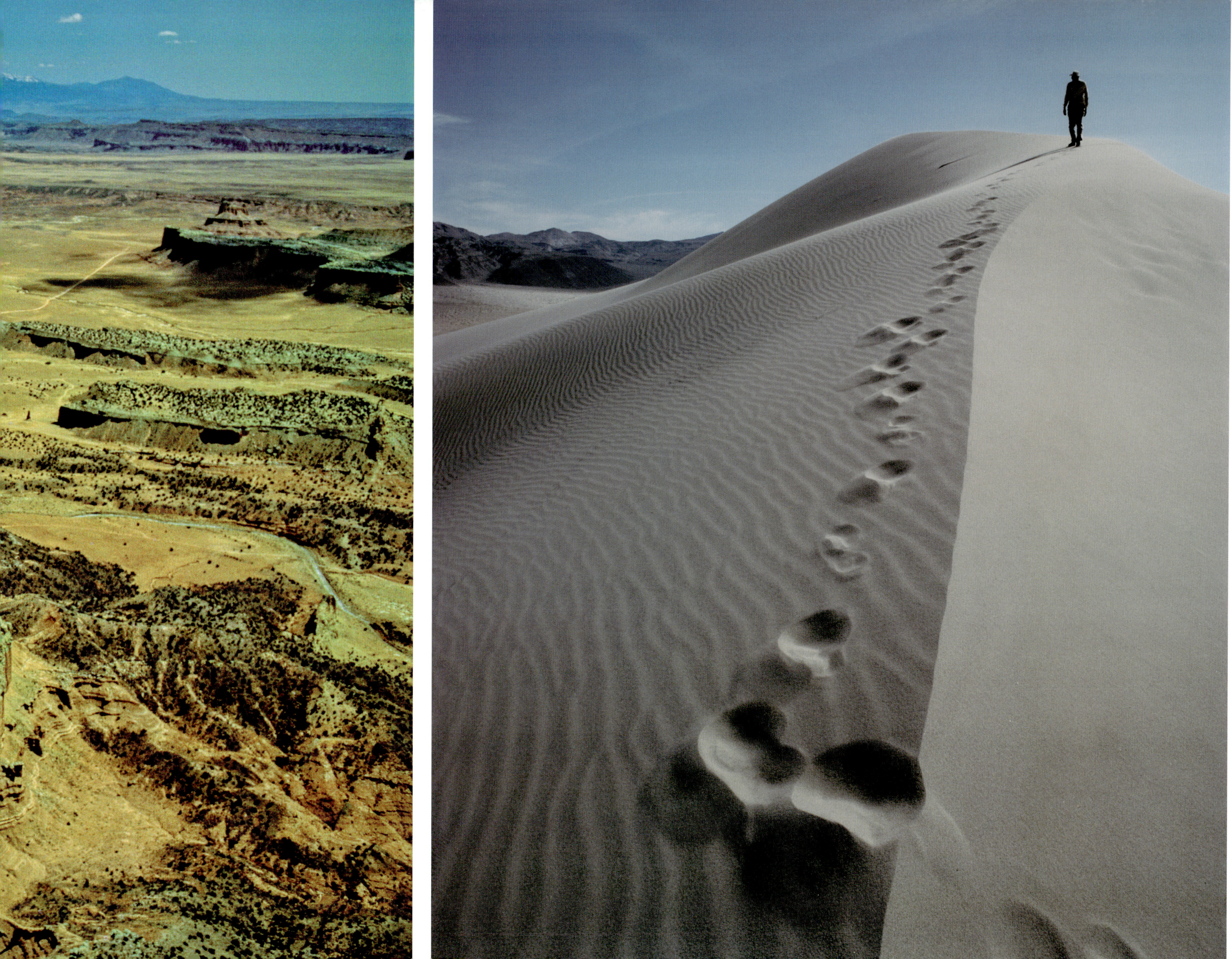

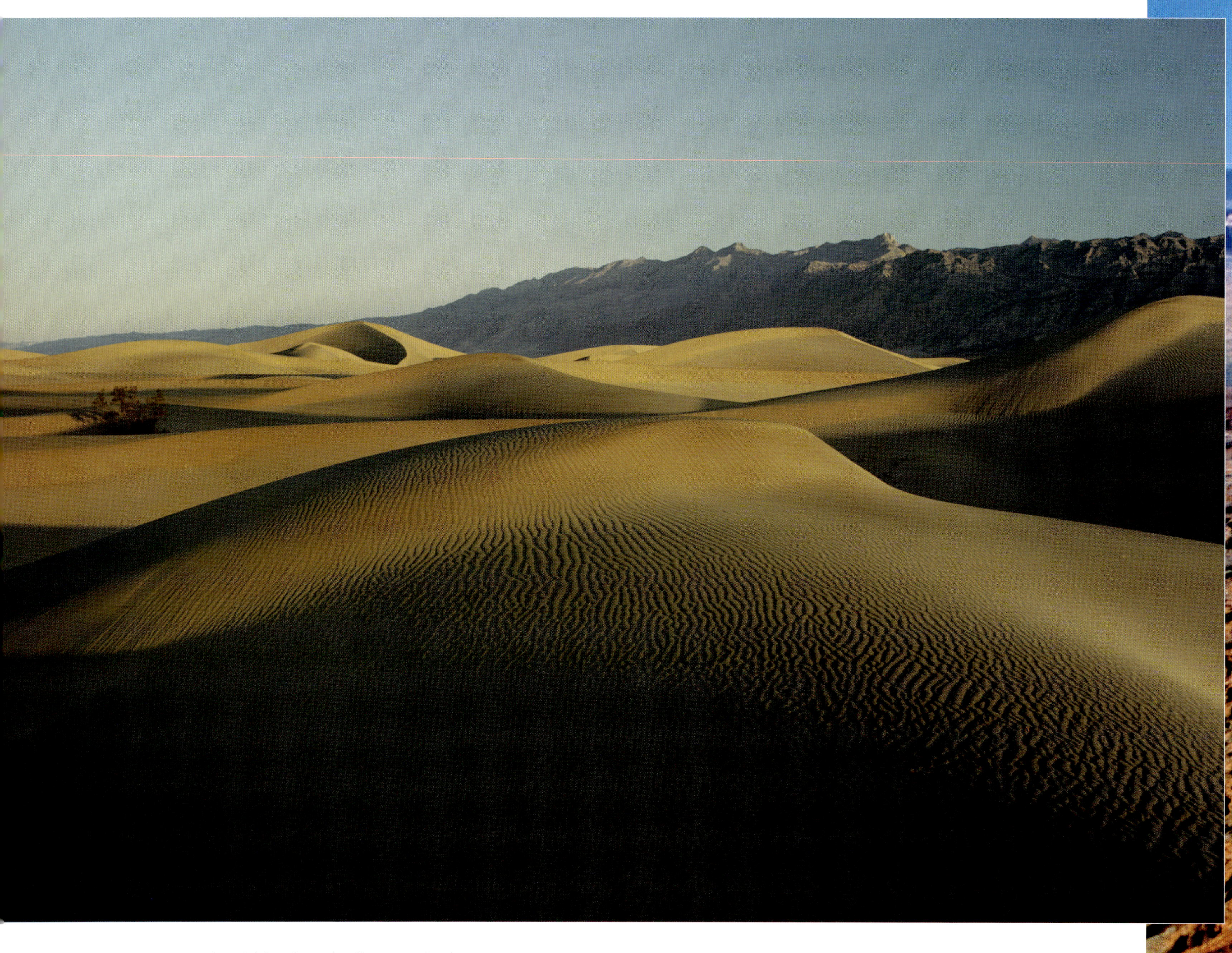

ABOVE: Mesquite Sands in California's Death Valley National Park. Mesquite is a common plant in America's southwestern deserts, being found in three varieties: Honey, Screwbean, and Velvet. All are deep-rooted and bear characteristic pods, which provide a food source for humans, wildlife, and livestock. Native Americans used mesquite as food, and also the bark for basketry, fabrics, and medicine, and the roots for firewood, while bees feeding on mesquite flowers produce delicious honey.
Gordon Wiltsie/Getty Images

RIGHT: Last Chance Creek in Emery County, Utah. America's trekkers, explorers, settlers, and gold prospectors gave many descriptive names to the places they lived in or passed through, and there are many "last chances" in the West, denoting a degree of desperation and despair among some of those, now nameless, individuals who pushed America's frontier ever westwards.
Jim Wark/AirPhotoNA

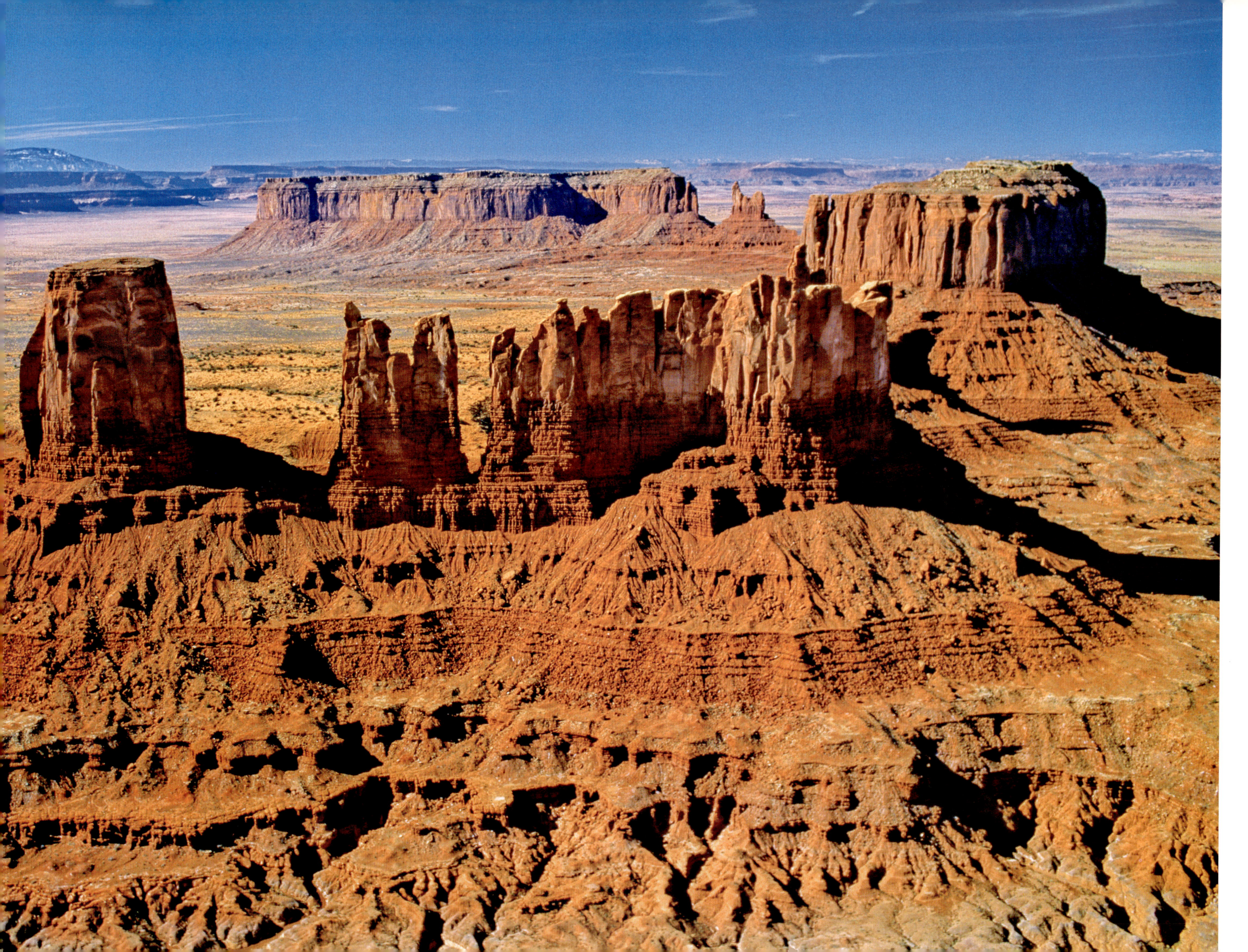

RIGHT: This part of California's Death Valley National Park is typical desert scenery with rolling sand dunes and mountains in the distance. It looks totally inhospitable and waterless but, even so, a few incredibly hardy plants have managed to survive, meaning that they must somehow have found just enough water to bloom.
Otto Rogge/Corbis

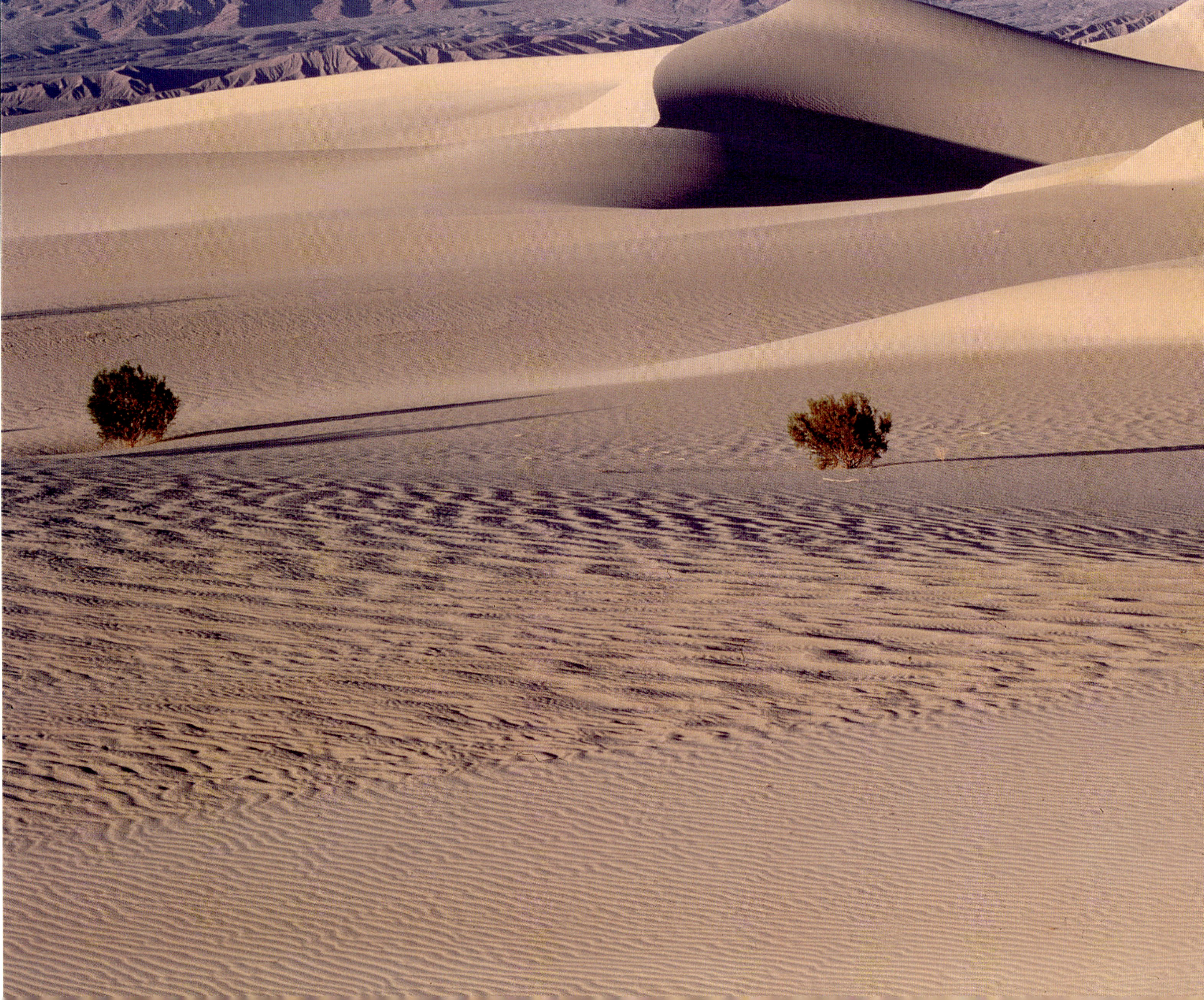

PAGES 68–69: When President Theodore Roosevelt visited the Grand Canyon in 1903 he was so impressed that in 1908 he raised its status from national game reserve to national monument, and in 1919 Congress upgraded it yet again to a national park. More recently, in 1979, it was designated a World Heritage Site. The Grand Canyon is 277 miles long and, while width and depth vary from place to place, it is typically about 5,000 feet deep and 10 miles wide.
James Randklev/Corbis

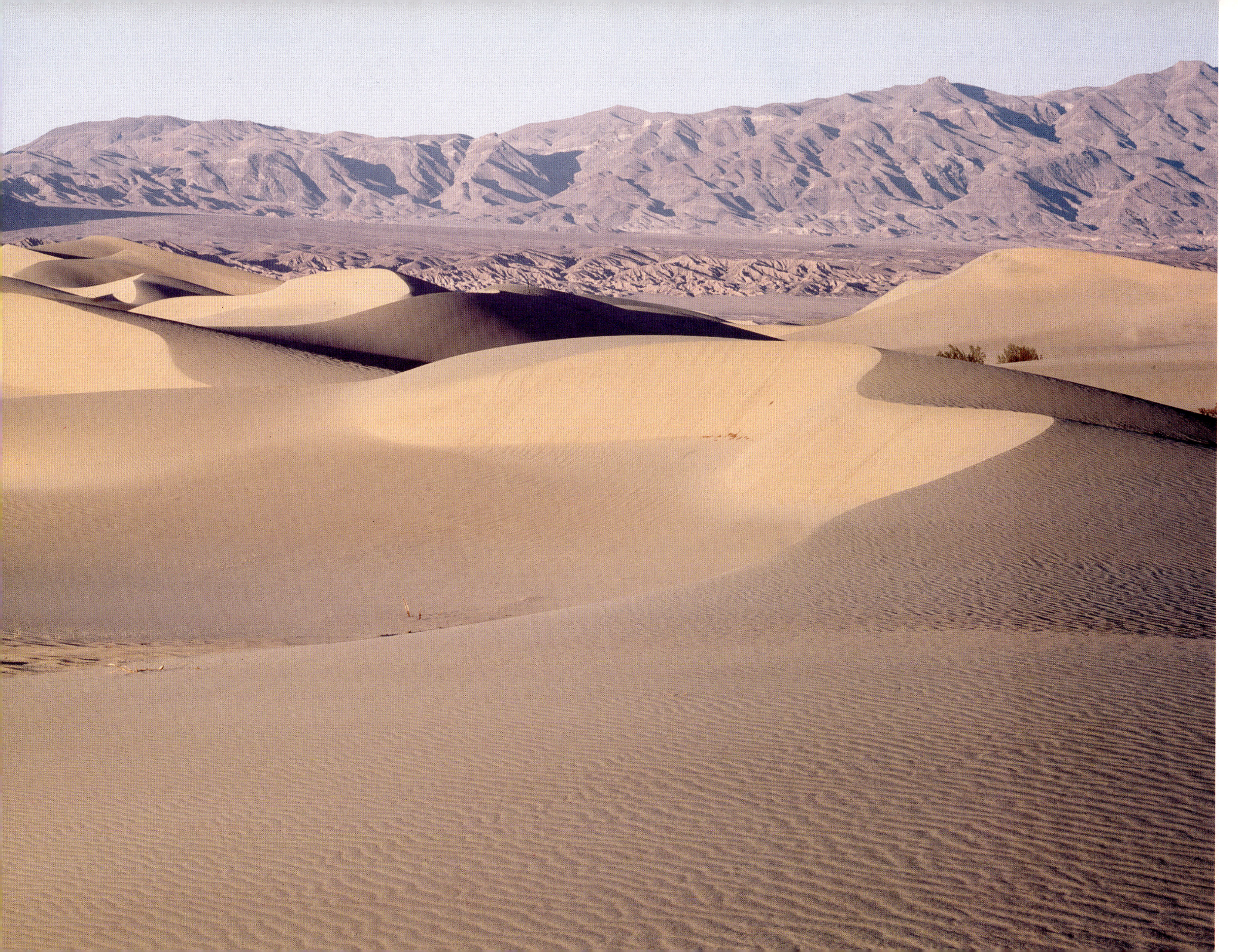

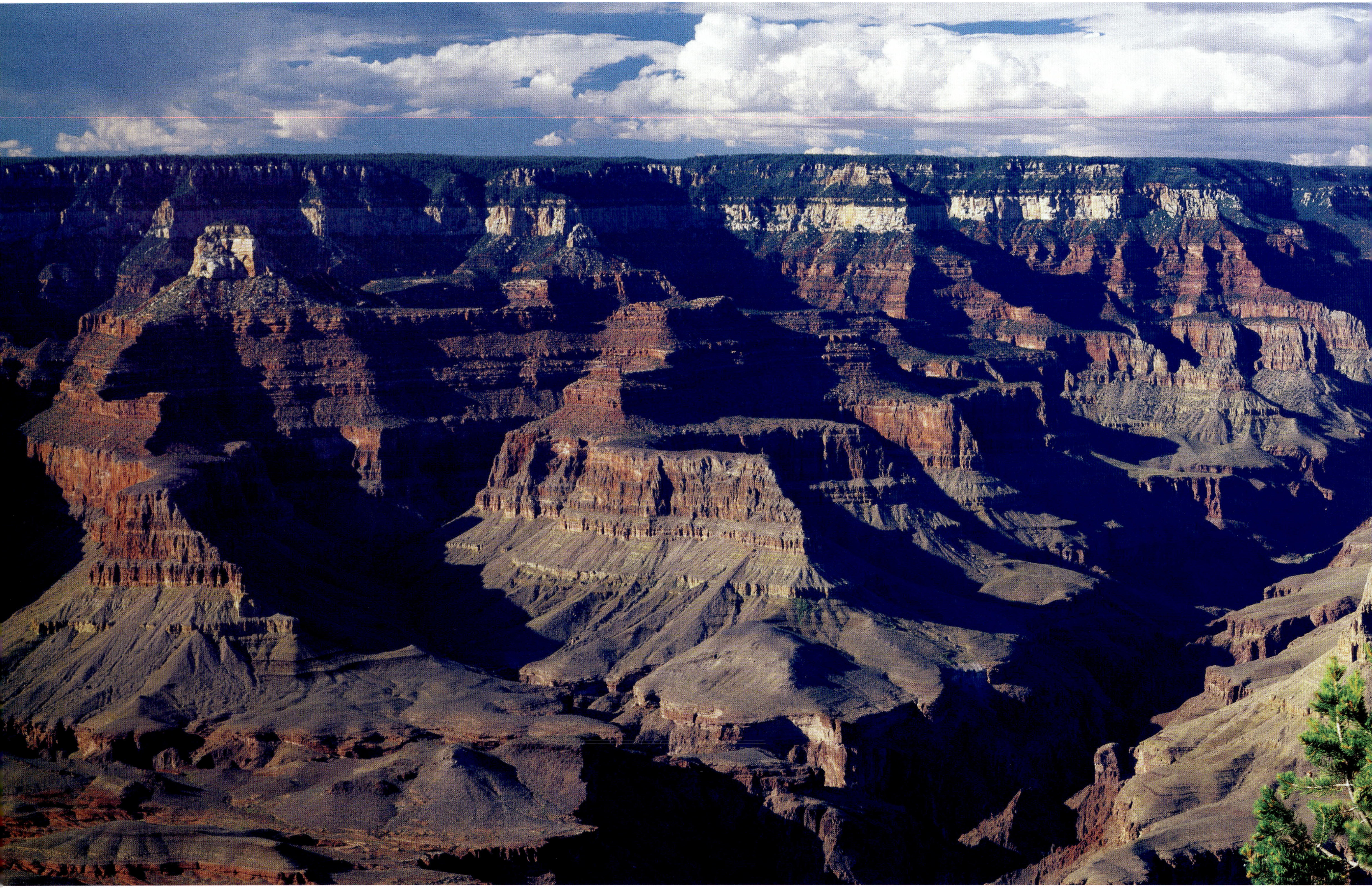

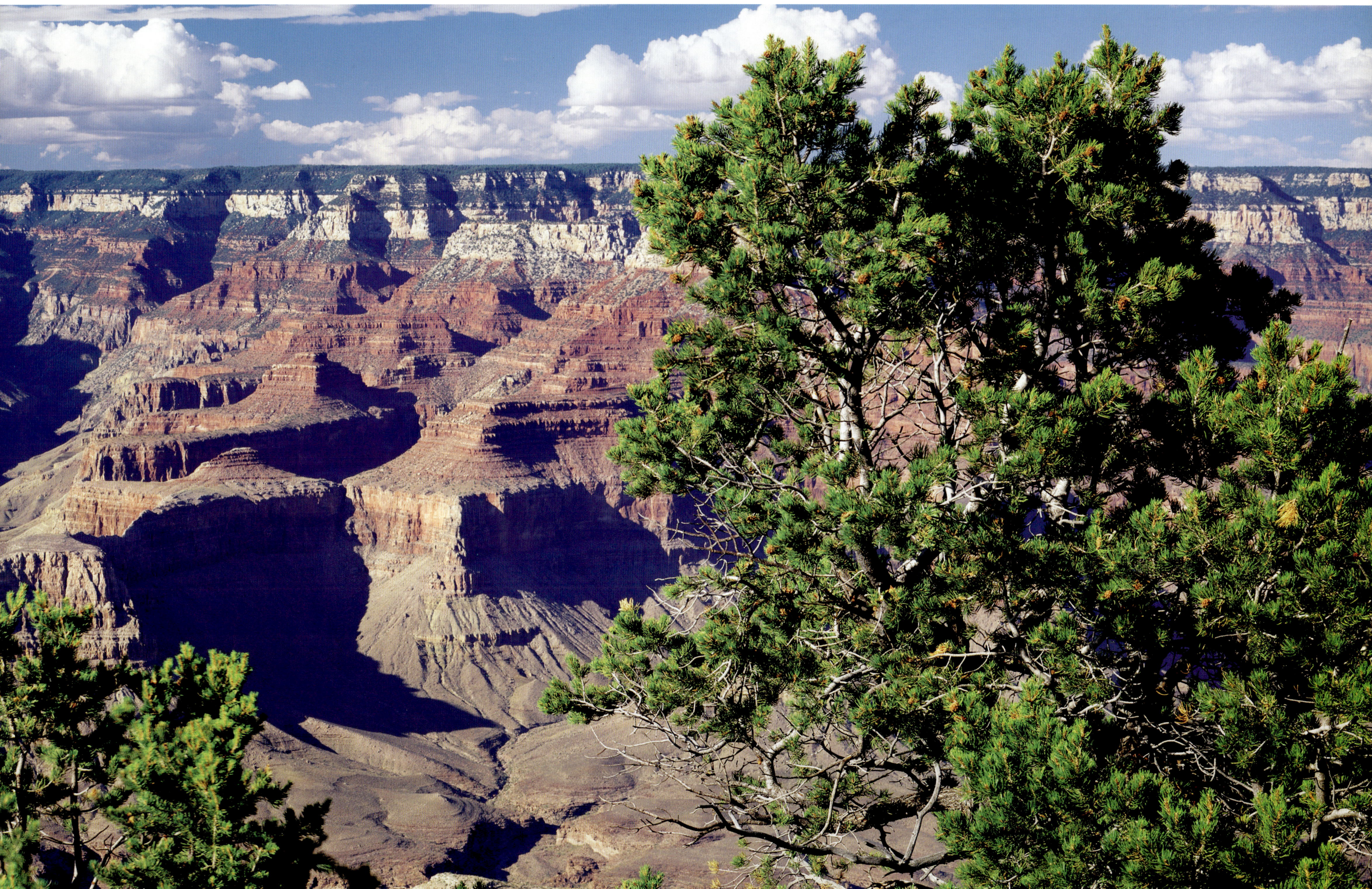

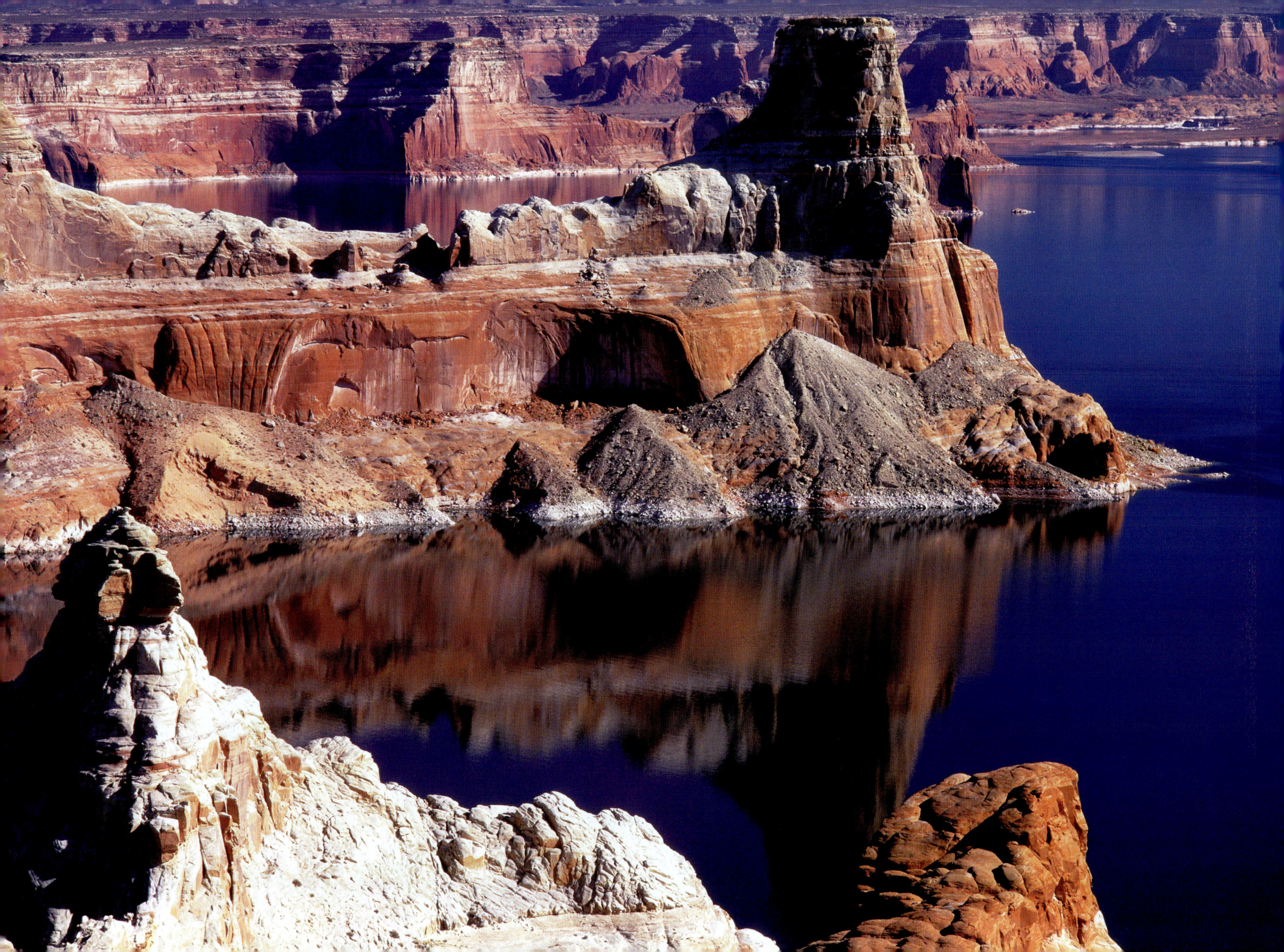

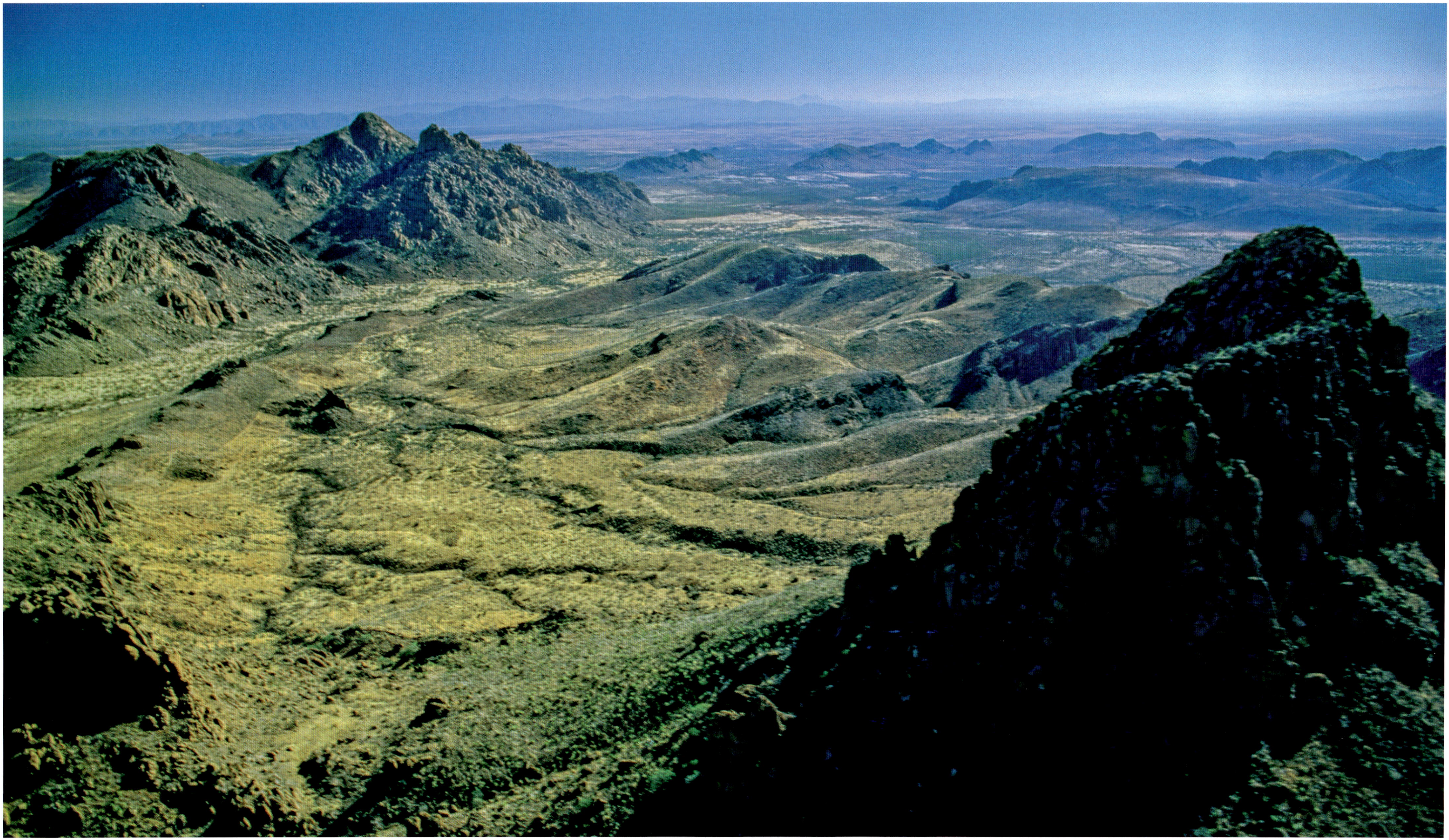

LEFT: Lake Powell in Colorado was created by the construction of the Glen Canyon Dam, which was completed in 1963. It then took fourteen years for the lake to fill to its planned level, and it is now some 186 miles long. The water inflow comes from melting snow feeding rivers, which then flow into Lake Powell, while the outtake is carefully controlled at the dam. Although it still holds huge amounts of water, the lake is currently considerably below maximum capacity due to several years of drought.
ML Sinibaldi/Corbis

ABOVE: The bleak scene in the Sonoran Desert, near the town of Ajo, Arizona, which lies midway between Tucson and San Diego. The picture is taken from an aircraft looking southwards across the border into Mexico.
Wark/AirPhotoNA

PAGES 72–73: The Organ-Pipe Cactus National Memorial is located in Arizona and extends over some 300,000 acres of the Sonoran Desert. It contains many plants that have adapted to the harsh desert conditions, but is named for the Organ-Pipe Cactus, which can grow up to 23 feet in height, making it the second tallest (after the Saguaro) in the United States. This cactus bears fruit, which has been eaten by Native Americans for centuries, it being edible in its natural state, or it can be made into a jelly or fermented into a beverage.
James Randklev/Corbis

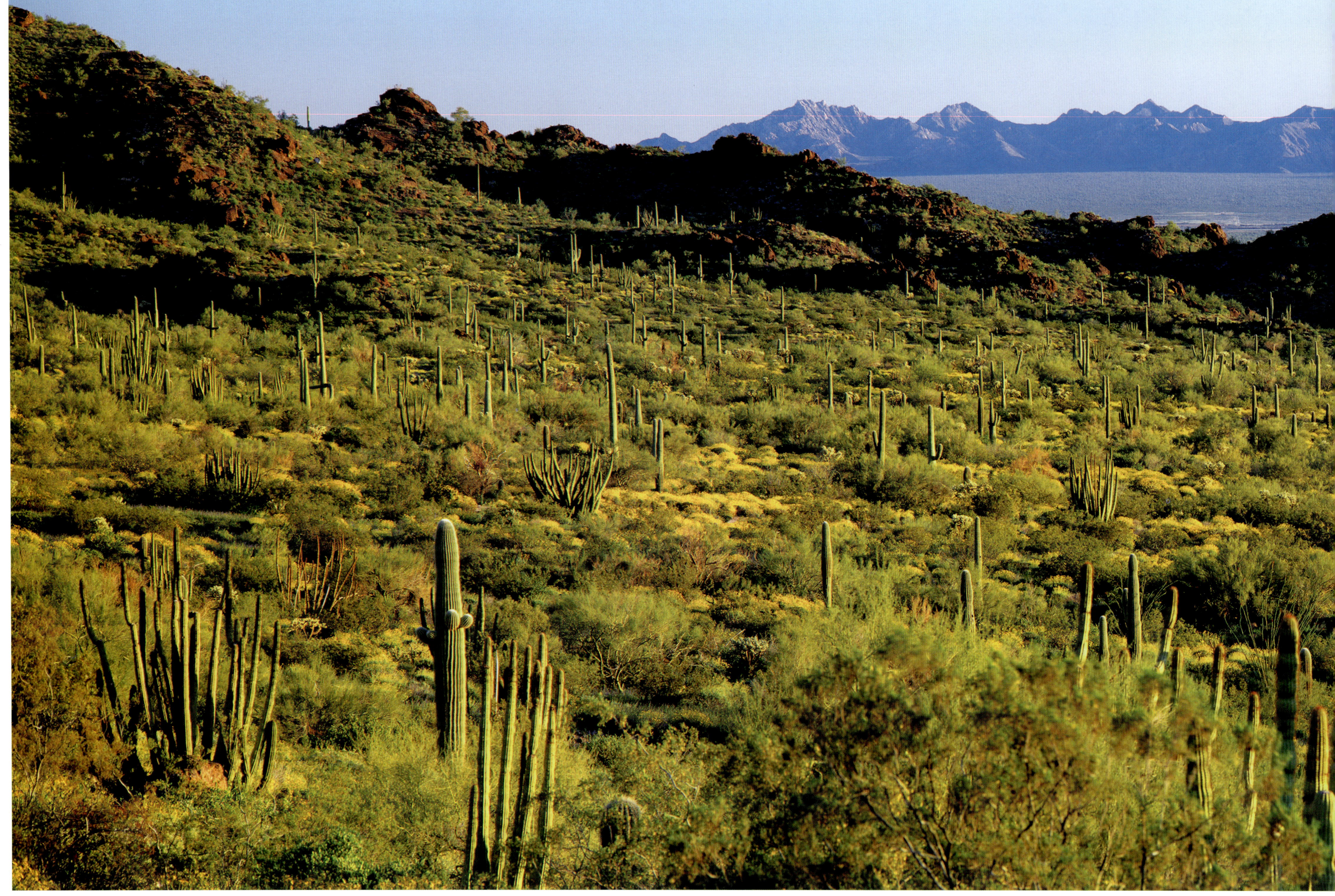

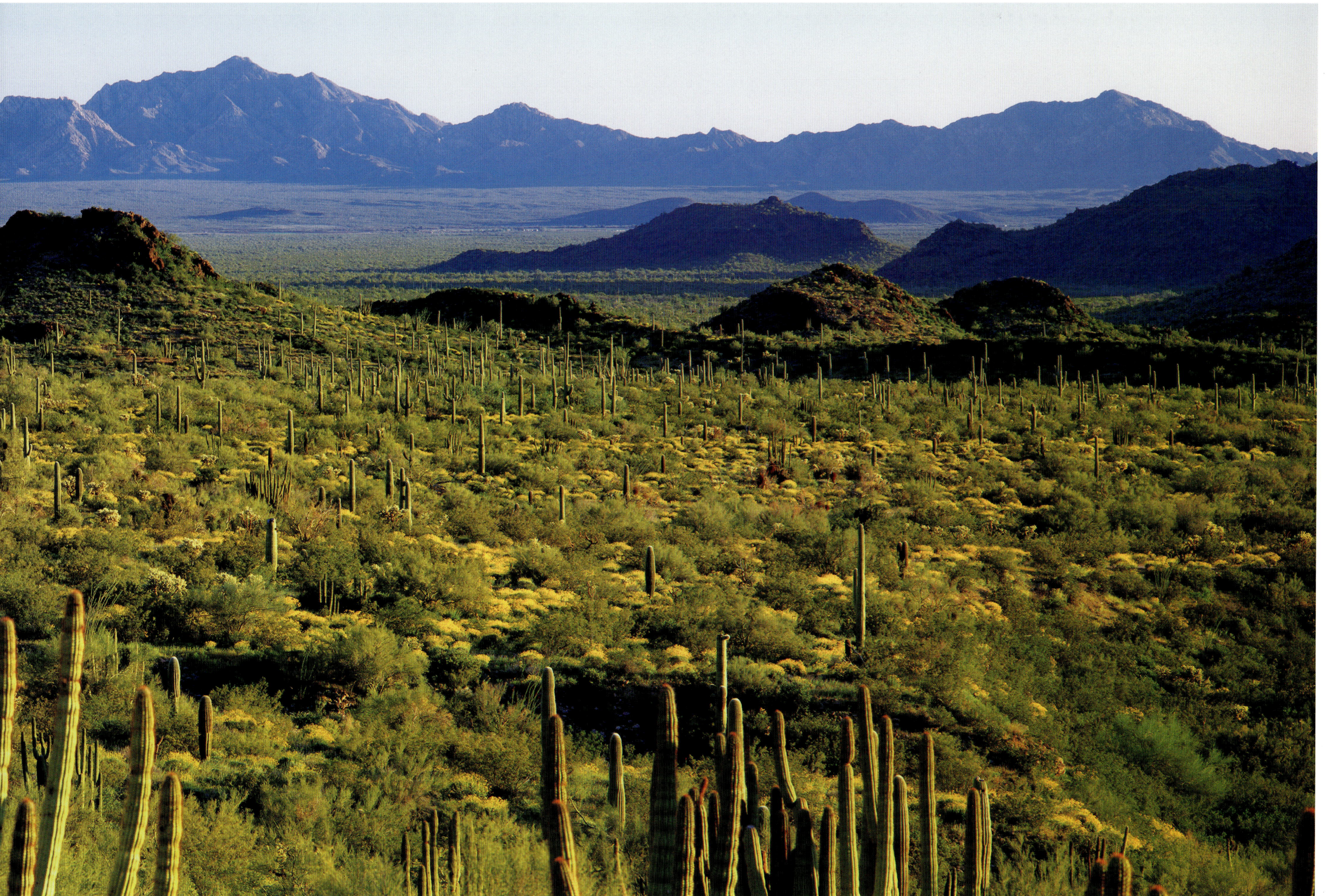

Right: Mexico's Baja California Peninsula extends southwards from the border with the USA's State of California some 800 miles to the Tropic of Capricorn. This long and narrow peninsula includes two deserts, the Vizcaino along the Pacific coast and the San Felipe to the east on the shores of the Gulf of California.. These deserts are further south than those in the United States and have a milder, more sub-tropical climate, without the same extremes of temperature.
Wark/AirPhotoNA

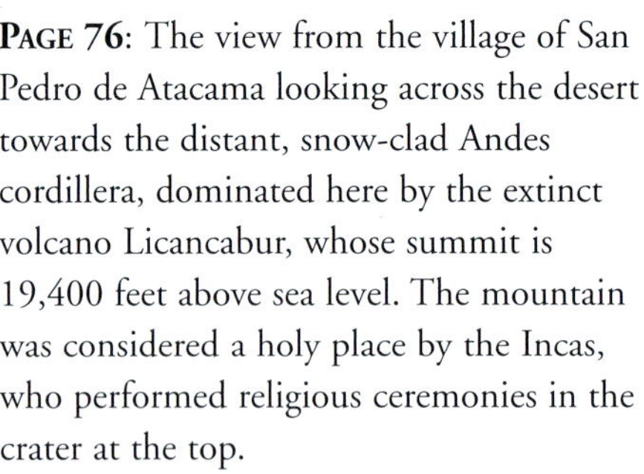

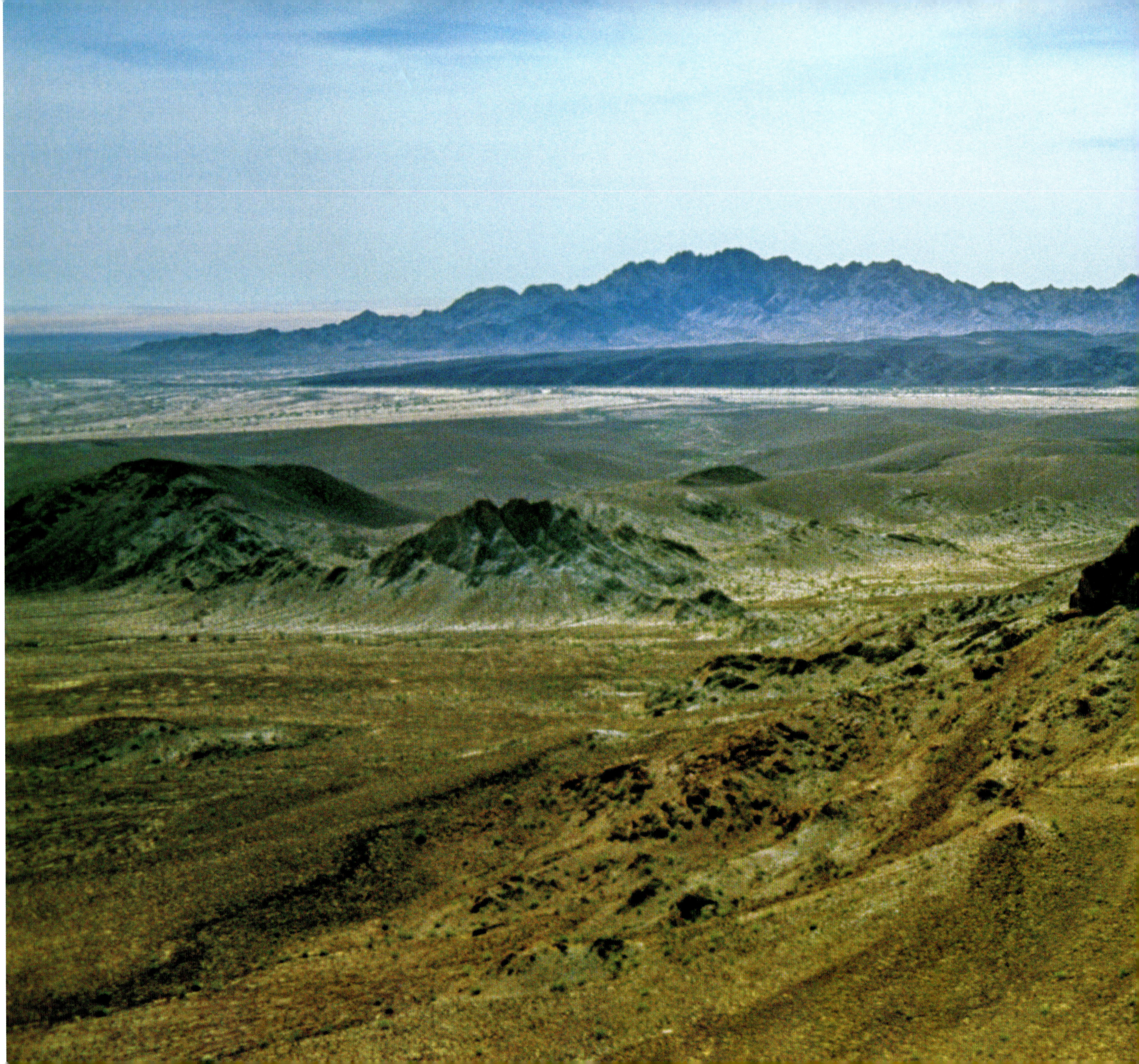

Page 76: The view from the village of San Pedro de Atacama looking across the desert towards the distant, snow-clad Andes cordillera, dominated here by the extinct volcano Licancabur, whose summit is 19,400 feet above sea level. The mountain was considered a holy place by the Incas, who performed religious ceremonies in the crater at the top.
Pablo Corral Vega/Corbis

Page 77: The Cerro Dragón (dragon hill) towers over the Chilean port of Iquique, whose houses can be seen through the gloom, and marks the forward edge of the Tarapaca Desert, which is, itself, the northern extension of the Atacama Desert. Iquique and the surrounding desert area were part of Peru until being captured by Chile in the War of the Pacific in 1879-84.
Joel Sartore/Getty Images images

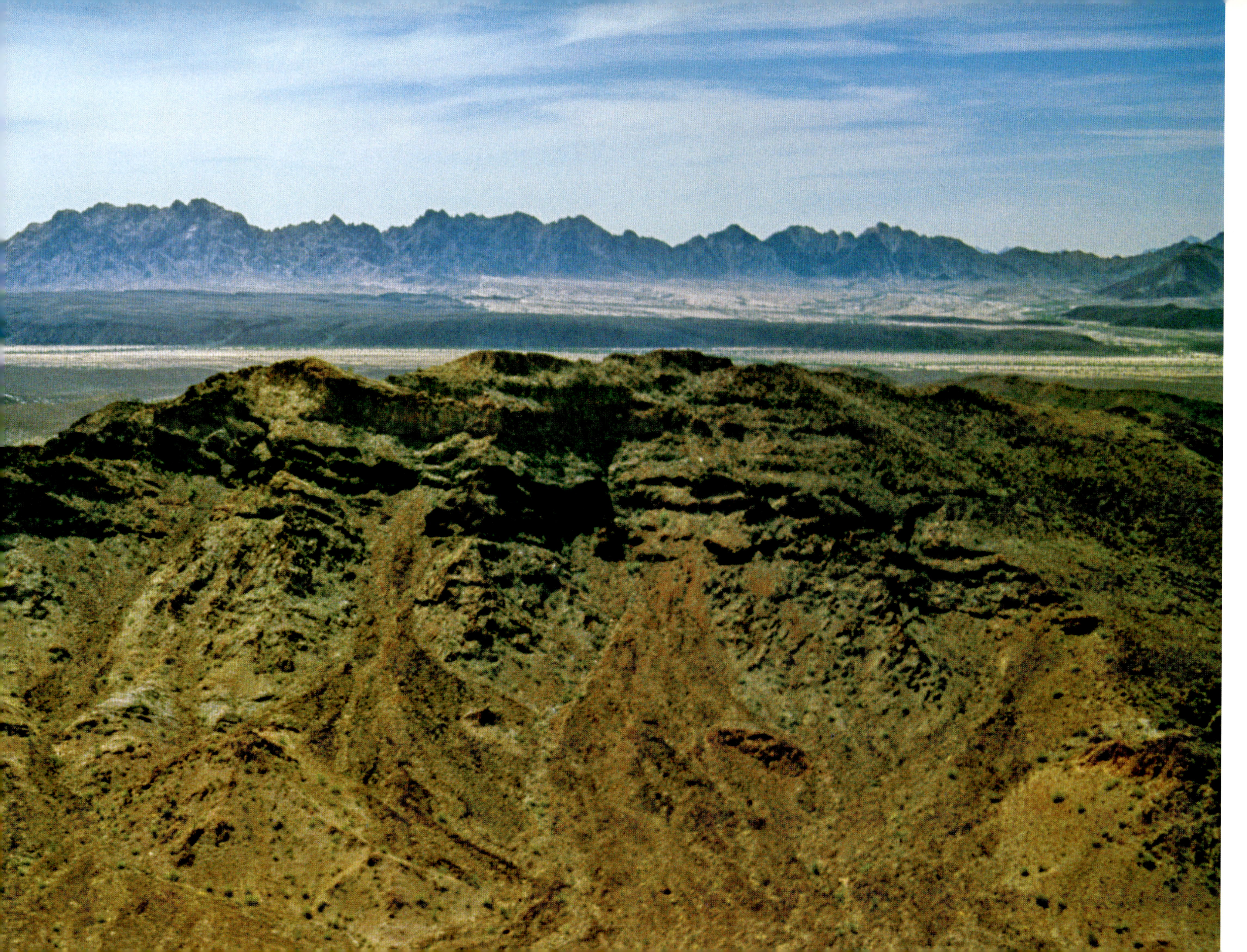

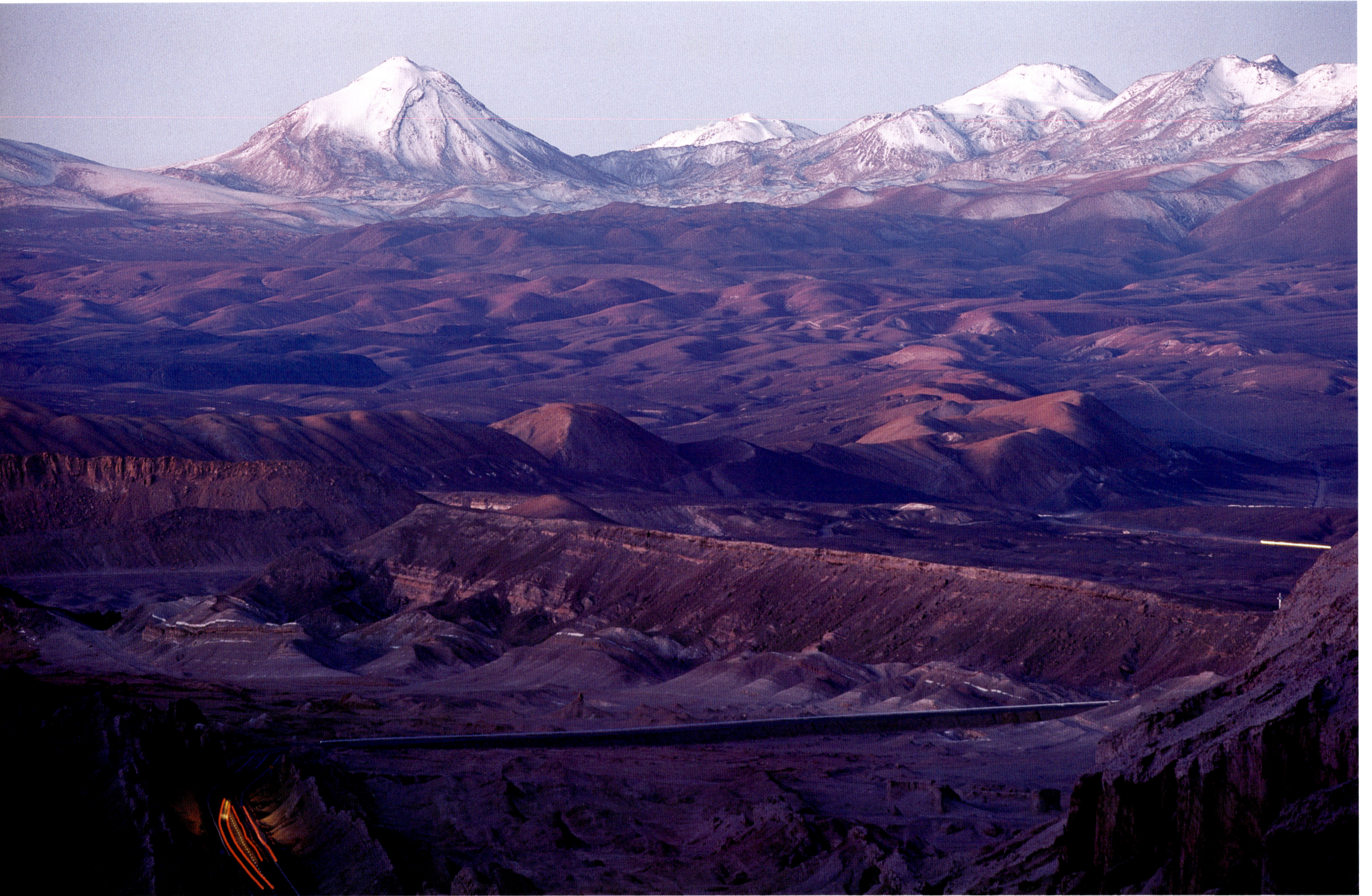

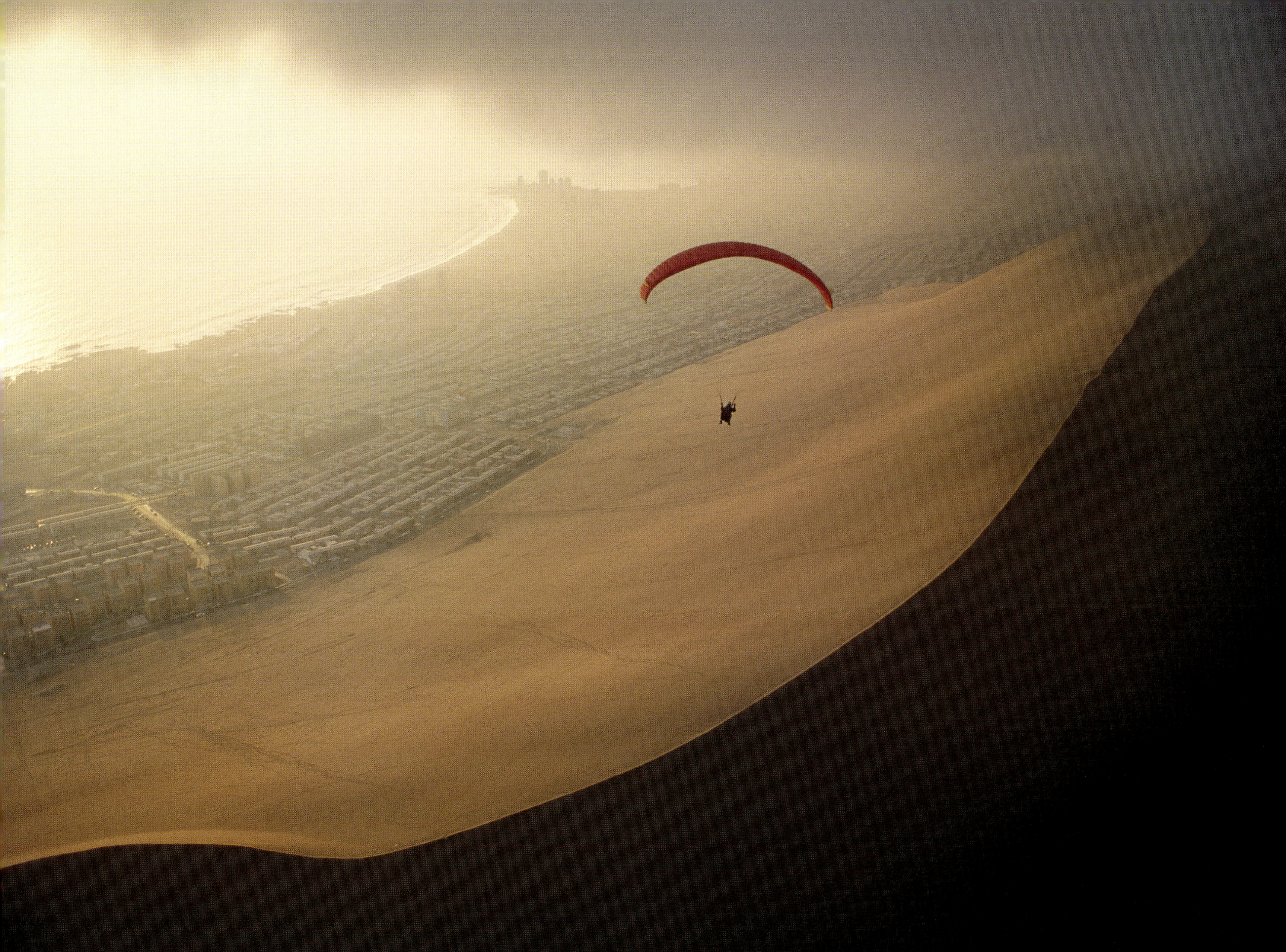

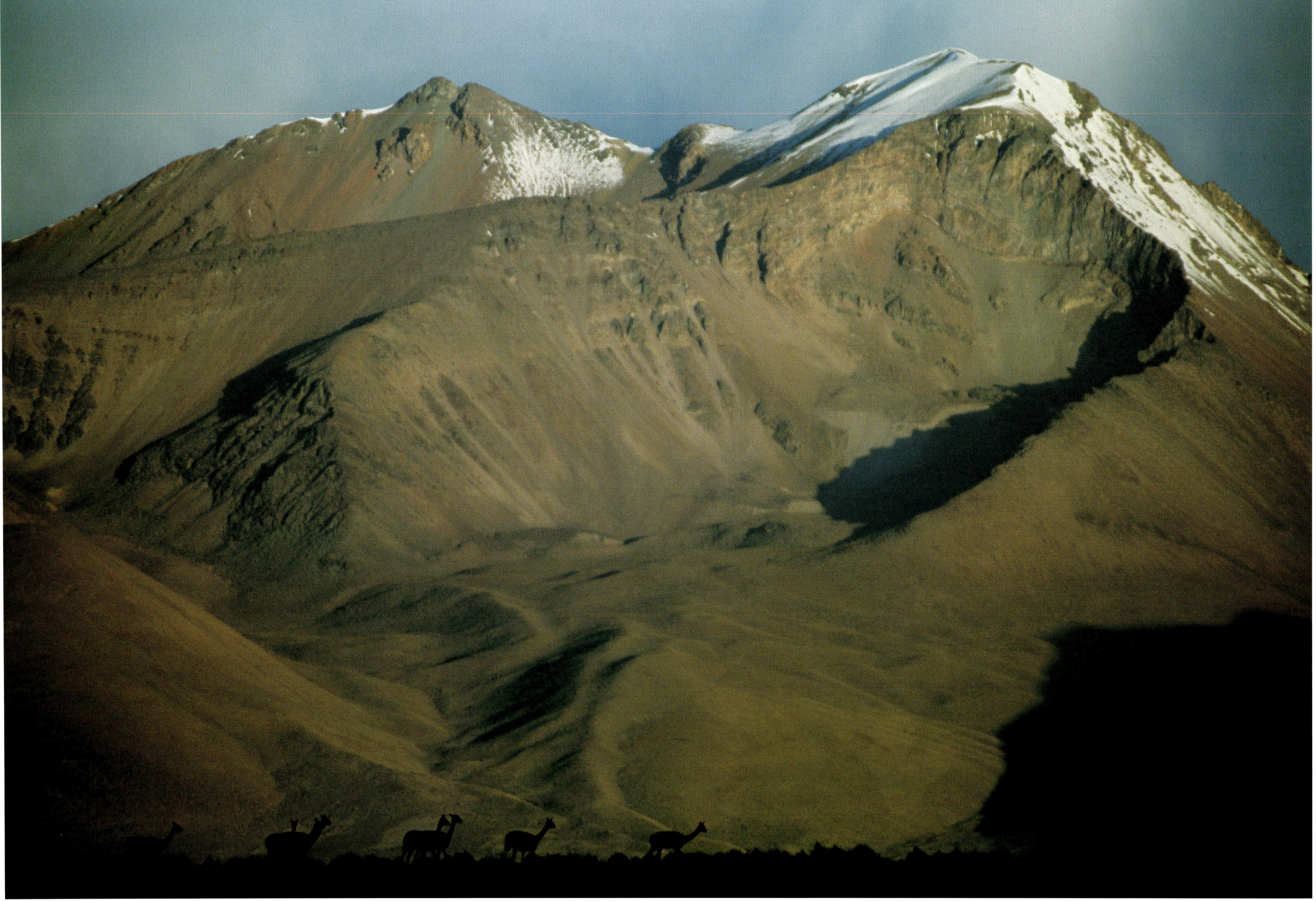

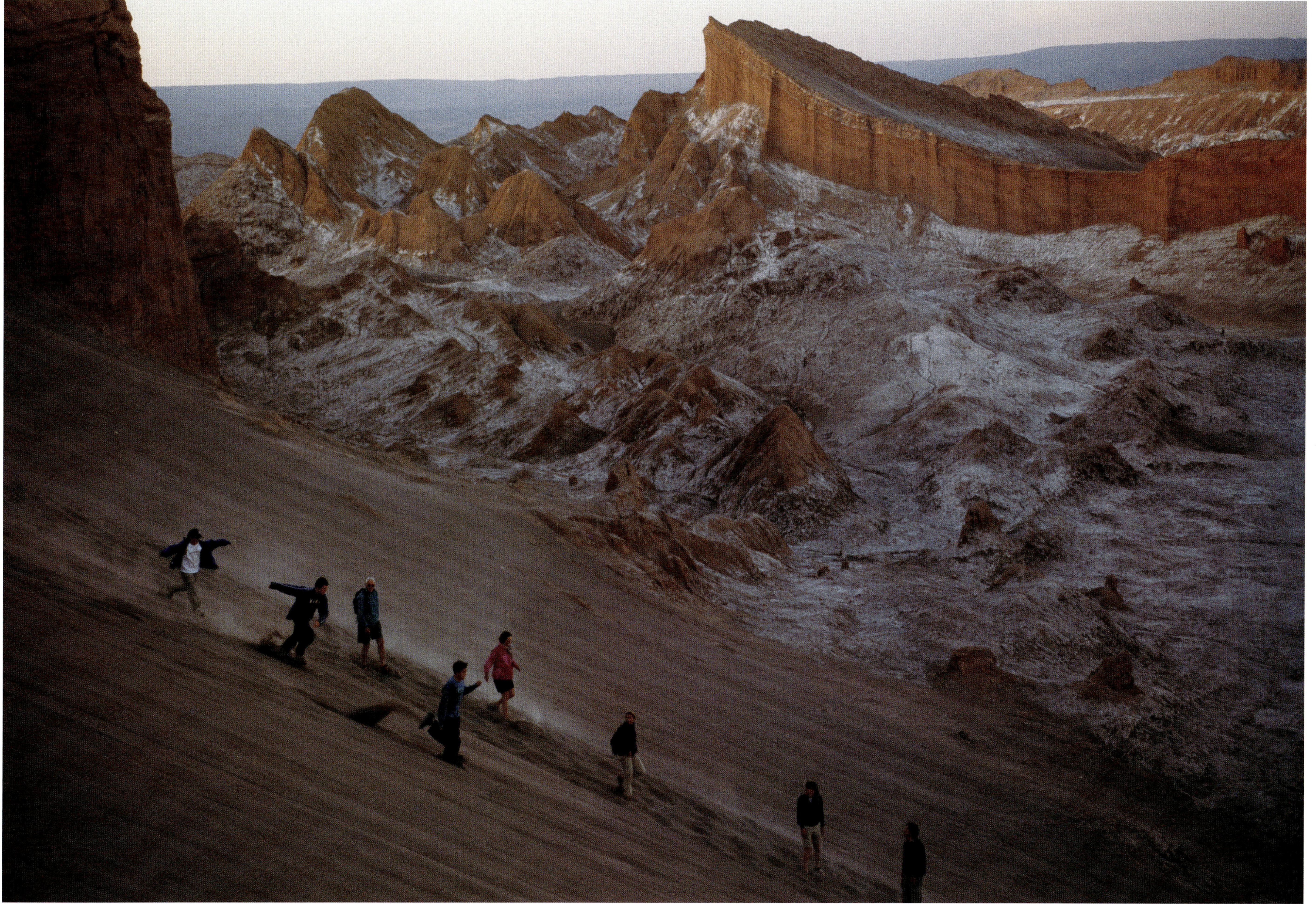

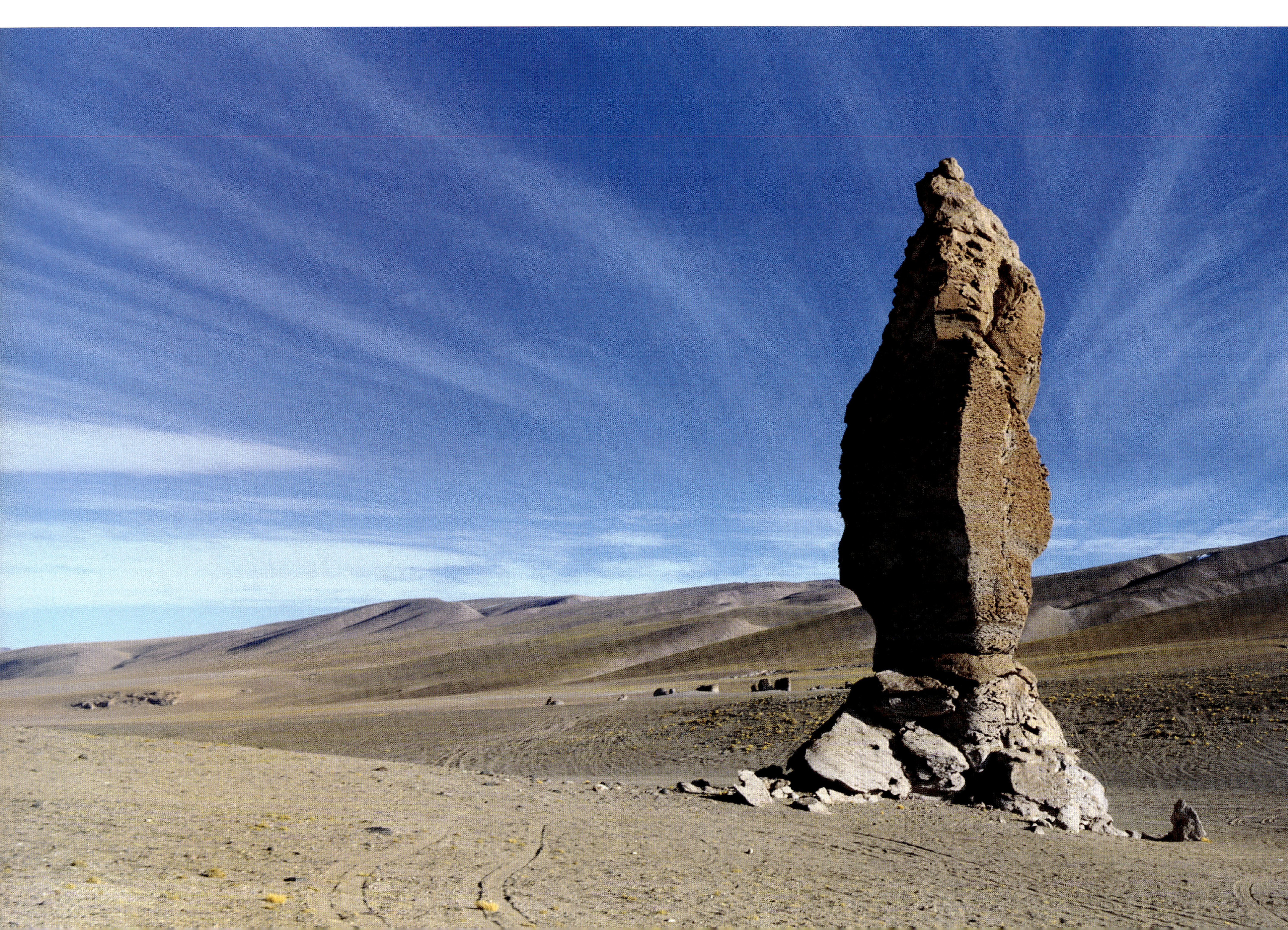

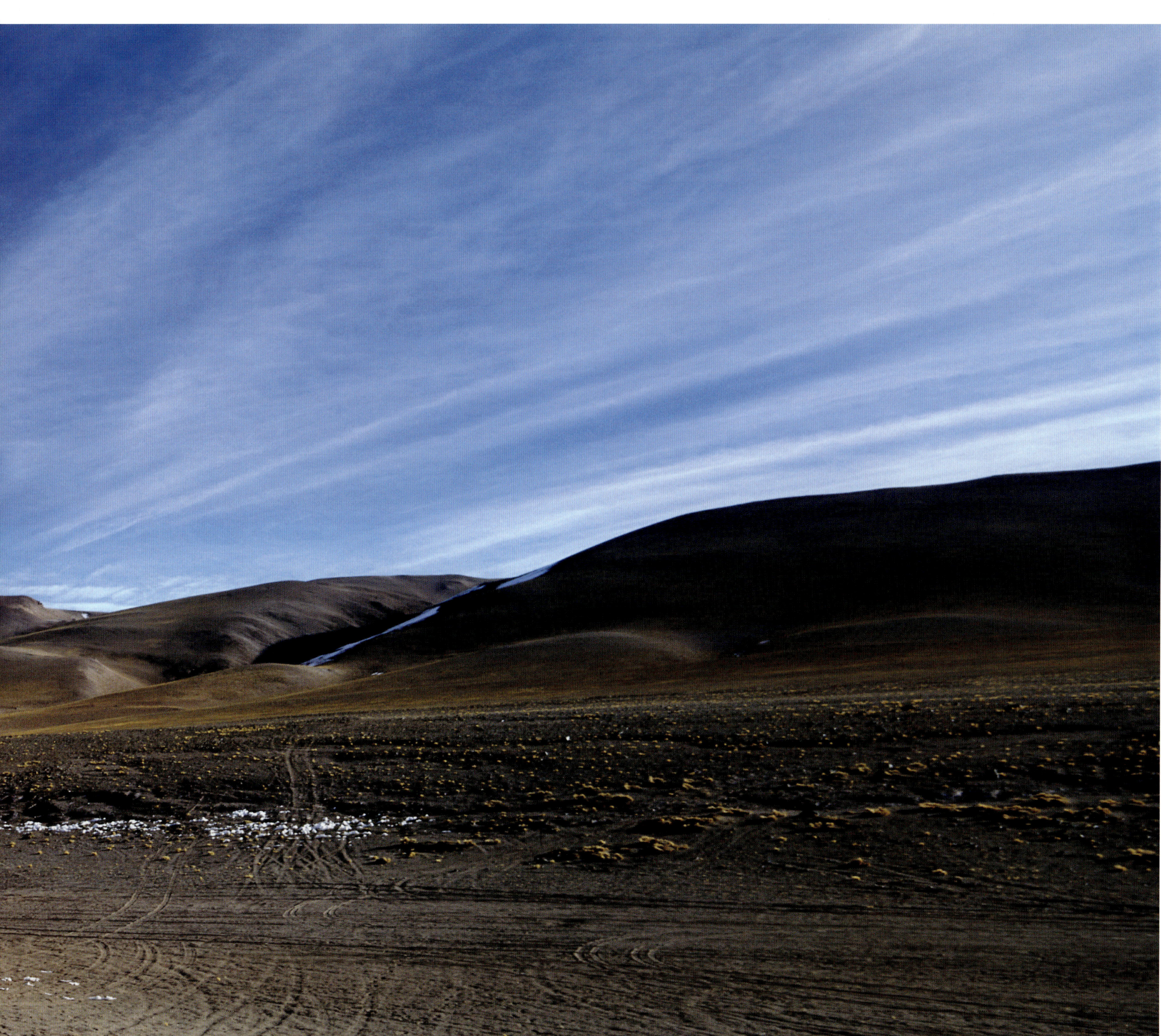

Page 78: A herd of llamas move silently across Chile's Atacama Desert, silhouetted against the snow-capped peaks of the Andes. The Andes mountain system runs north-south along the western side of the South American continent, parallel to the Pacific coast. Its highest peak is Acanagua, at 22,385 feet the highest mountain in the western hemisphere. It is on the Argentine side of the border with Chile.
Joel Sartore/Getty Images

Page 79: Tourists at play in Chile's Valley of the Moon. Striking a balance between preserving such geological treasures and the requirements of an ever-increasing number of tourists is becoming a problem for many national and park authorities around the world. Sometimes tourists are invasive, driving four-wheel-drive vehicles or, as here, playing games, but even well behaved and considerate tourists can exert pressure simply through their numbers and requirements for transportation, accommodation, and feeding.
Joel Sartore/Getty Images

Left: A solitary rock pedestal in the Atacama Desert in the Paso de Jama on the road from El Aguilar in Argentina to San Pedro de Atacama in Chile. The pass is 13,800 feet above sea level.
Hubert Stadler/Corbis

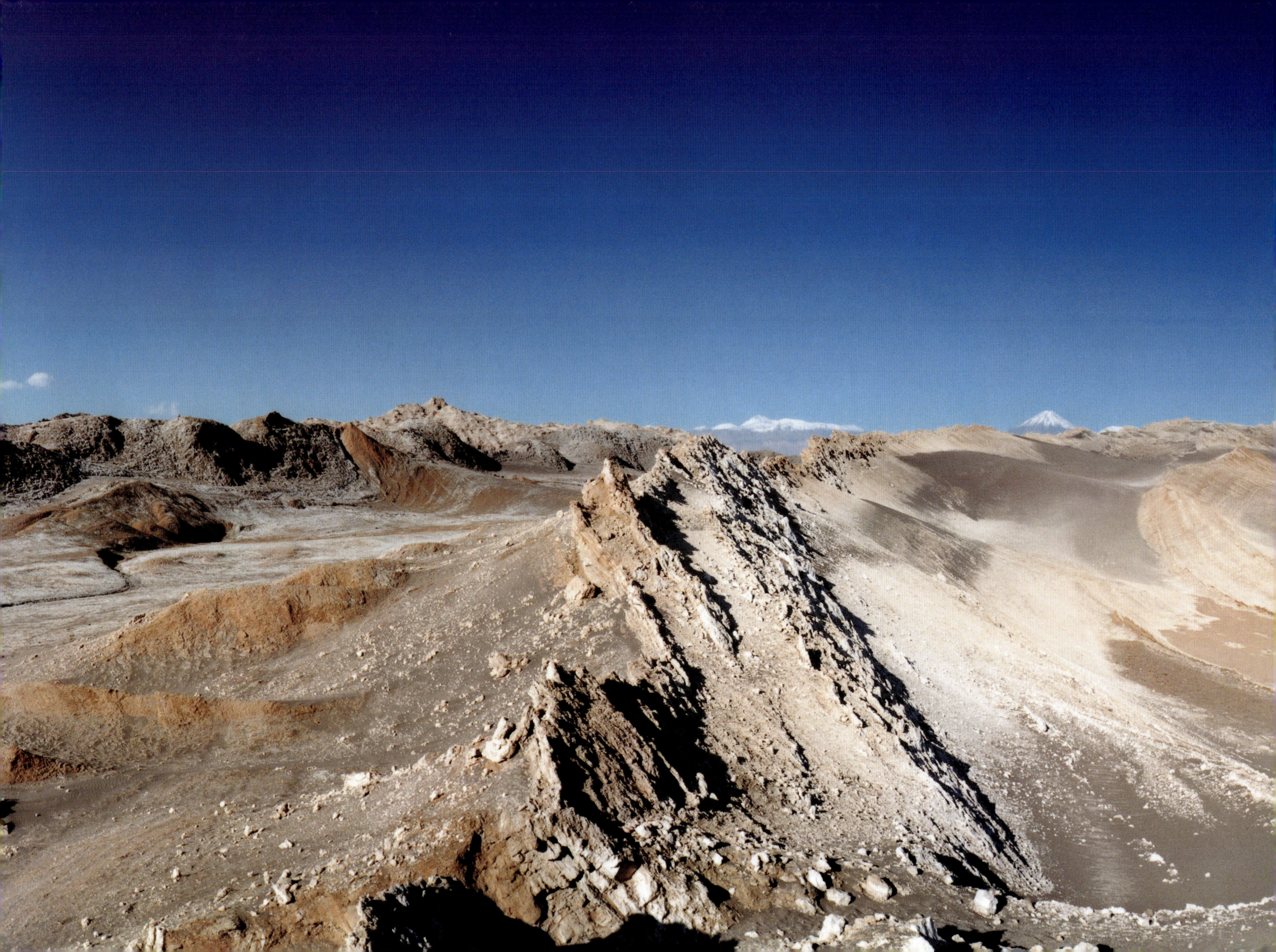

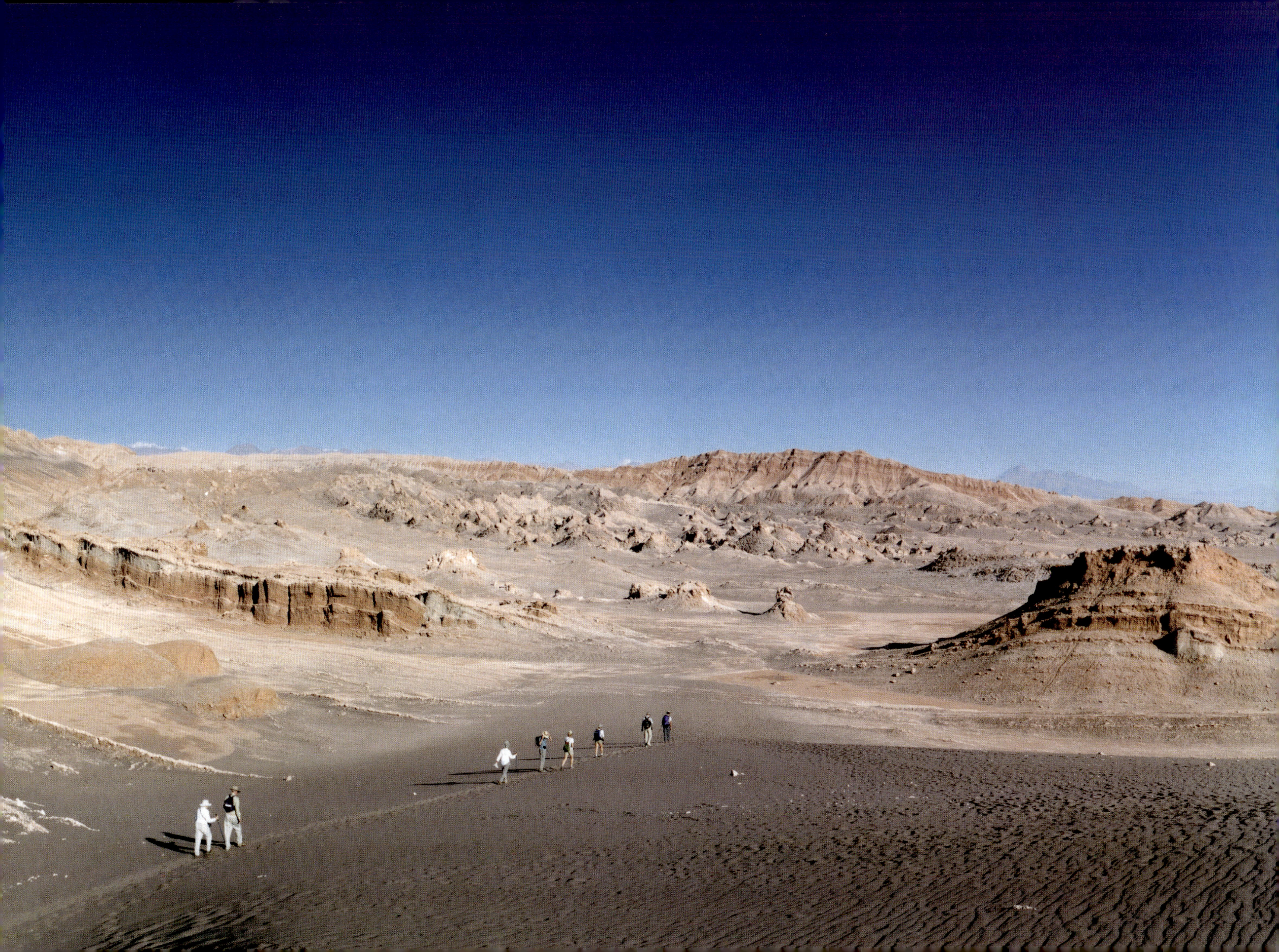

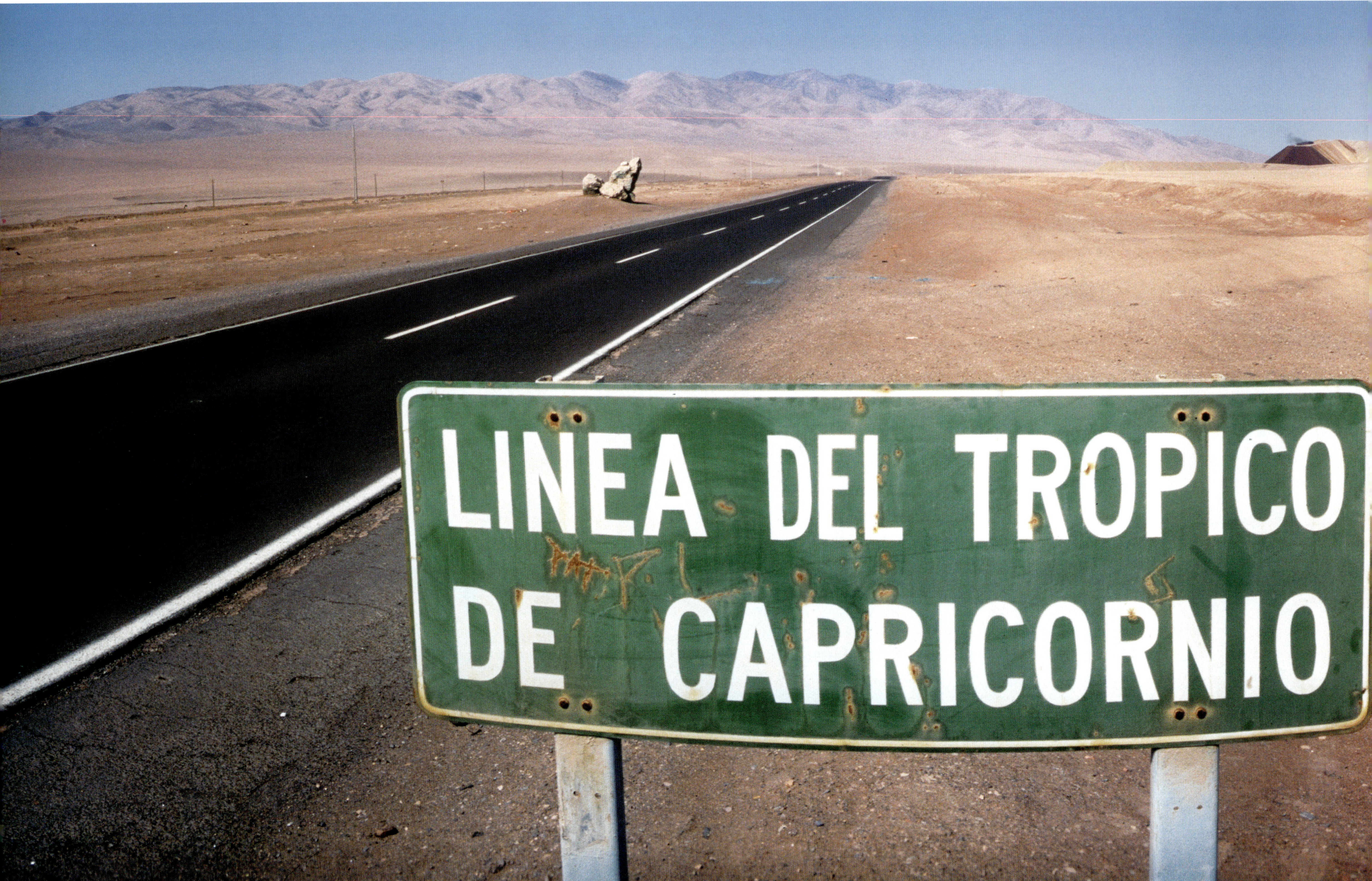
LINEA DEL TROPICO
DE CAPRICORNIO

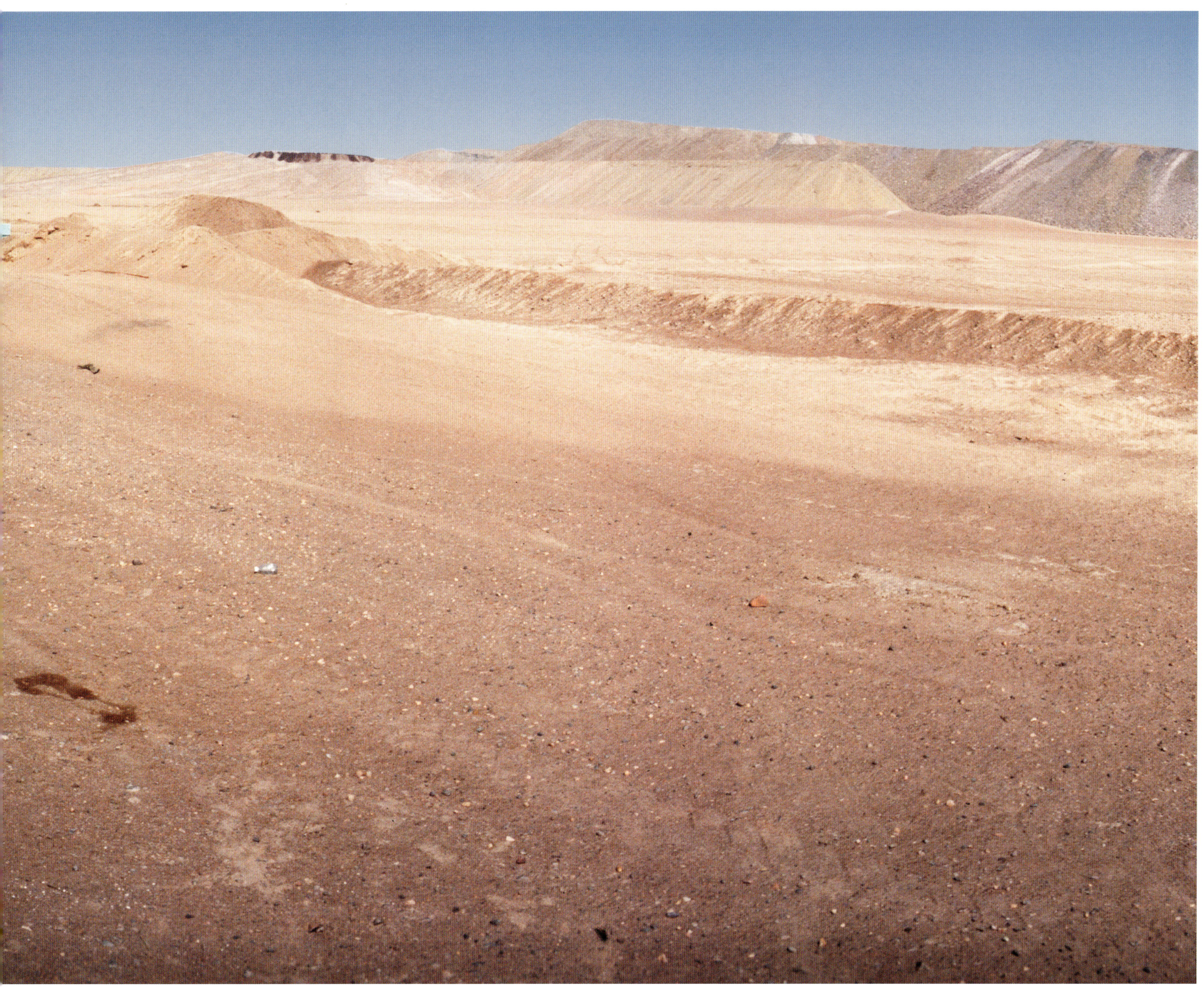

PAGES 82–83: Hikers crossing the Valley of the Moon (Valle de la Luna) in Chile, a place otherwise totally without life of any sort and which, not surprisingly, is renowned for its utter silence. The valley is part of the Cordillera de la Sal (Salt Mountain Range) and has an atmosphere all its own, which results in people wanting to see it and to walk through it, but not to linger.
Macduff Everton/Corbis

LEFT: The Tropic of Capricorn—23 degrees 30 minutes south—marked here by a roadside sign in Chile's Northern Desert, placing it on approximately the same latitude as Alice Springs in Australia and Windhoek, the capital of Namibia, in Africa, both of which are also surrounded by desert terrain. The line of the Tropic of Capricorn links the southernmost points on the Earth's surface where the sun is directly overhead at midday, which occurs about December 22 annually.
Charles O'Rear/Corbis

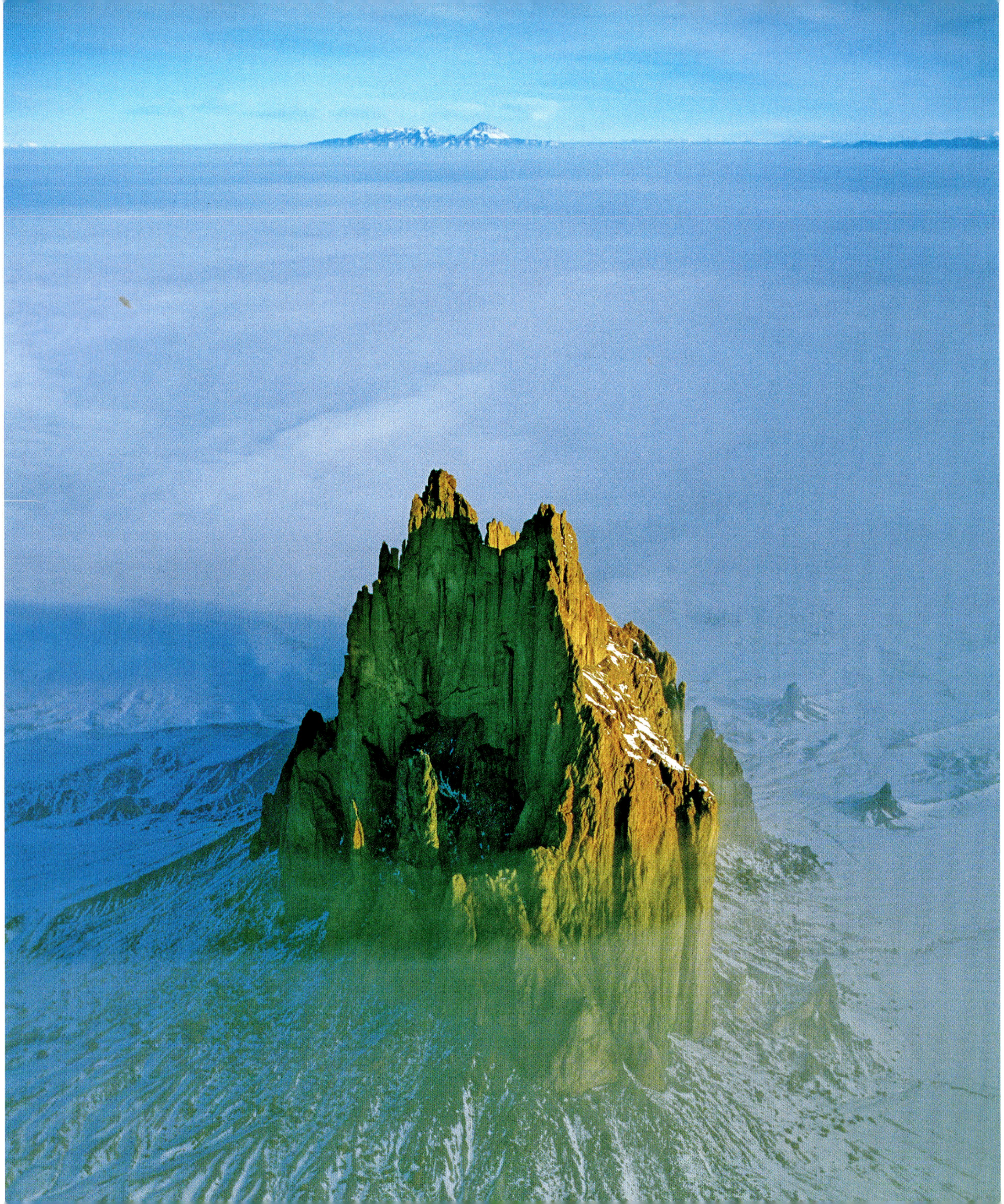

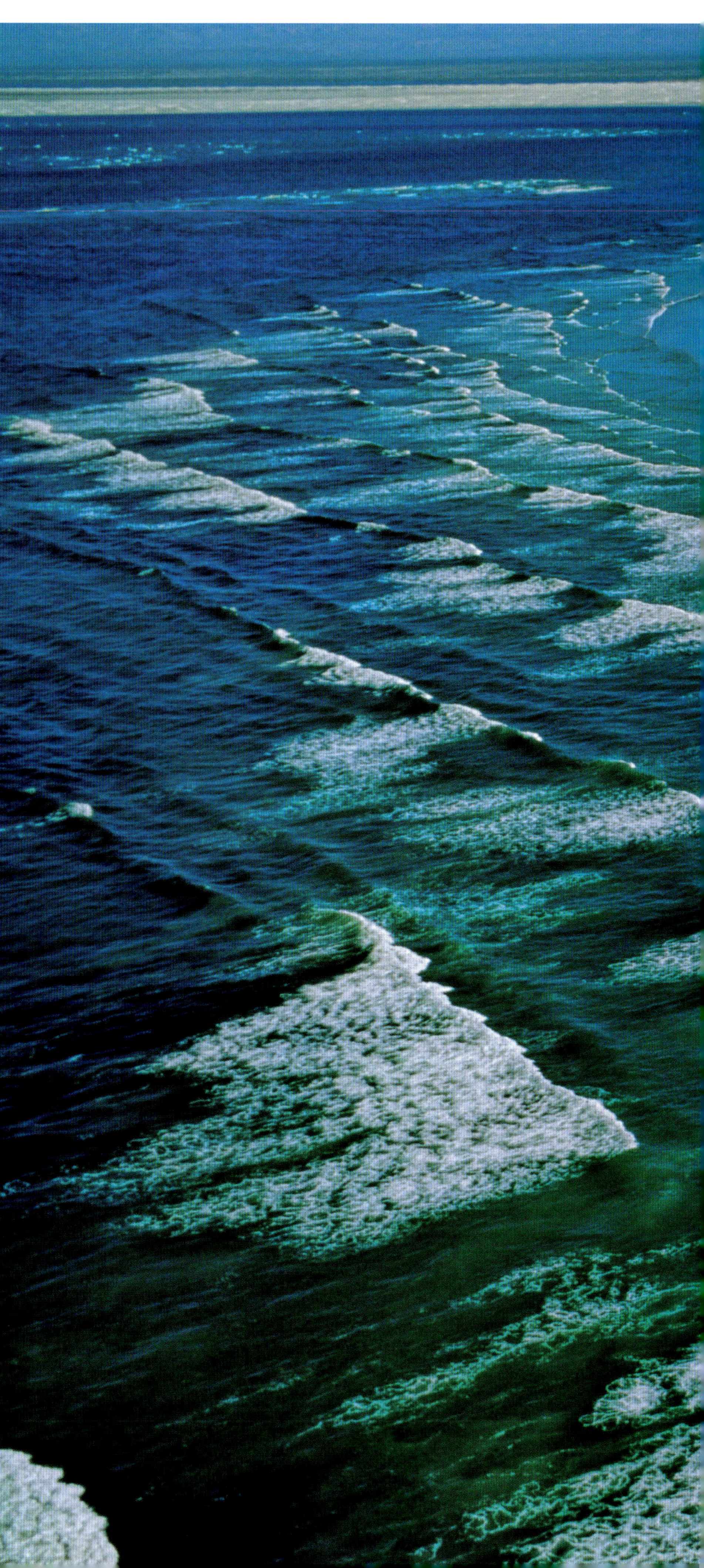

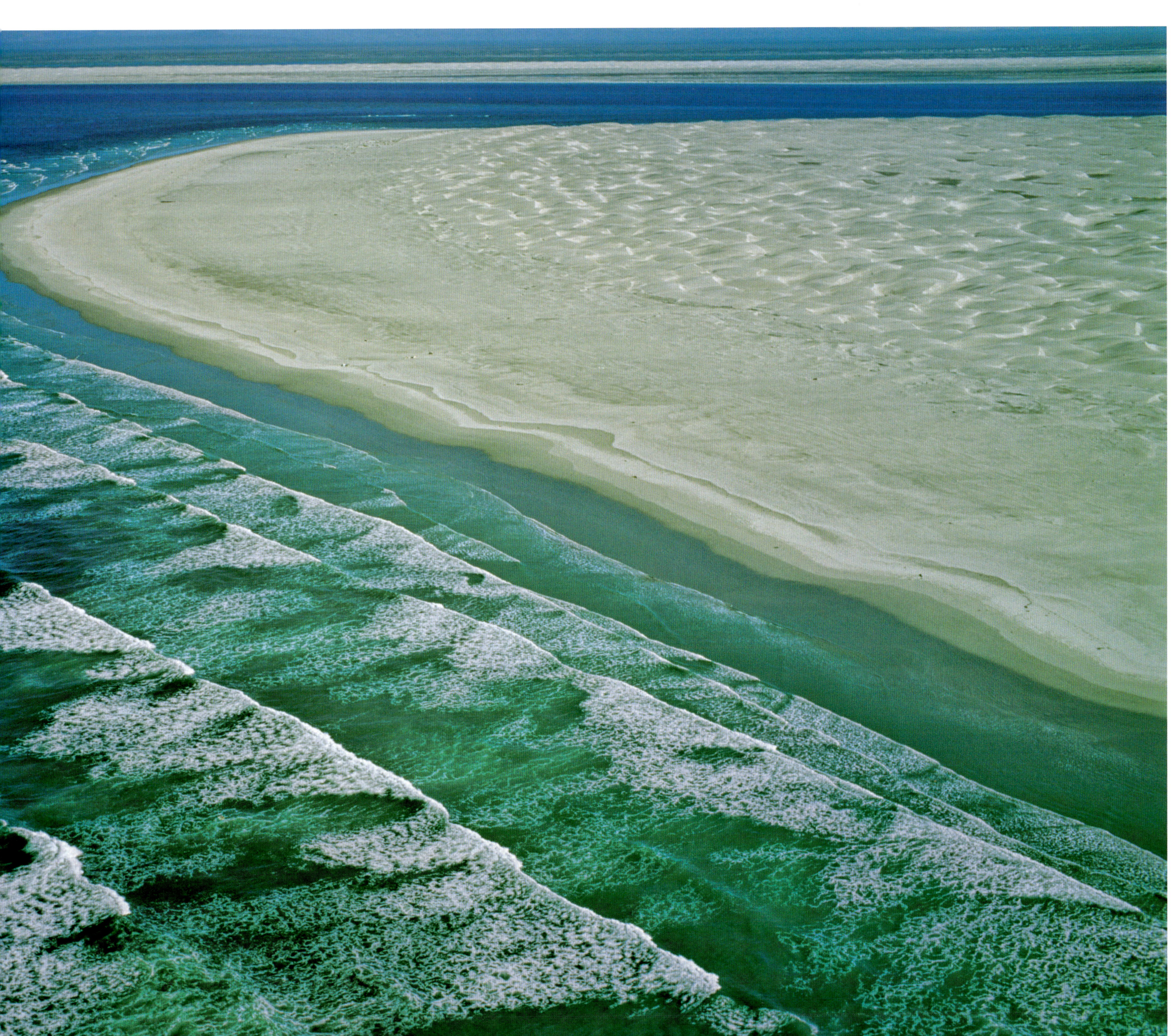

Far Left: The scene in Chihuahua State, Mexico, north of Chihuahua City, looking northwards towards the border with the United States.
Wark/AirPhotoNA

Left: The desert meets the Pacific Ocean on Mexico's Baja California Sur at the Baja de las Ballenas (Bay of the Whales). The bay is so named because it is to these waters that the California Gray Whales travel every year in late fall-early winter to have their young in one of Nature's great spectacles when these mammals are clearly visible from the shore.
Wark/AirPhotoNA

Pages 88–89: Benedict Allen is a modern explorer who has undertaken many daring expeditions, which are based on him making contact with local tribesmen and learning from them how to overcome the conditions, which would defeat an untrained outsider. One of his treks was to cover 1,000 miles along Namibia's Skeleton Coast for which he learnt about survival from the Himba tribesmen, as well as training three camels to carry his equipment. Here he crosses the beach at Sandwich Bay accompanied by a friend and local conservationist, Tommy Hall.
Adrian Arbib/Corbis

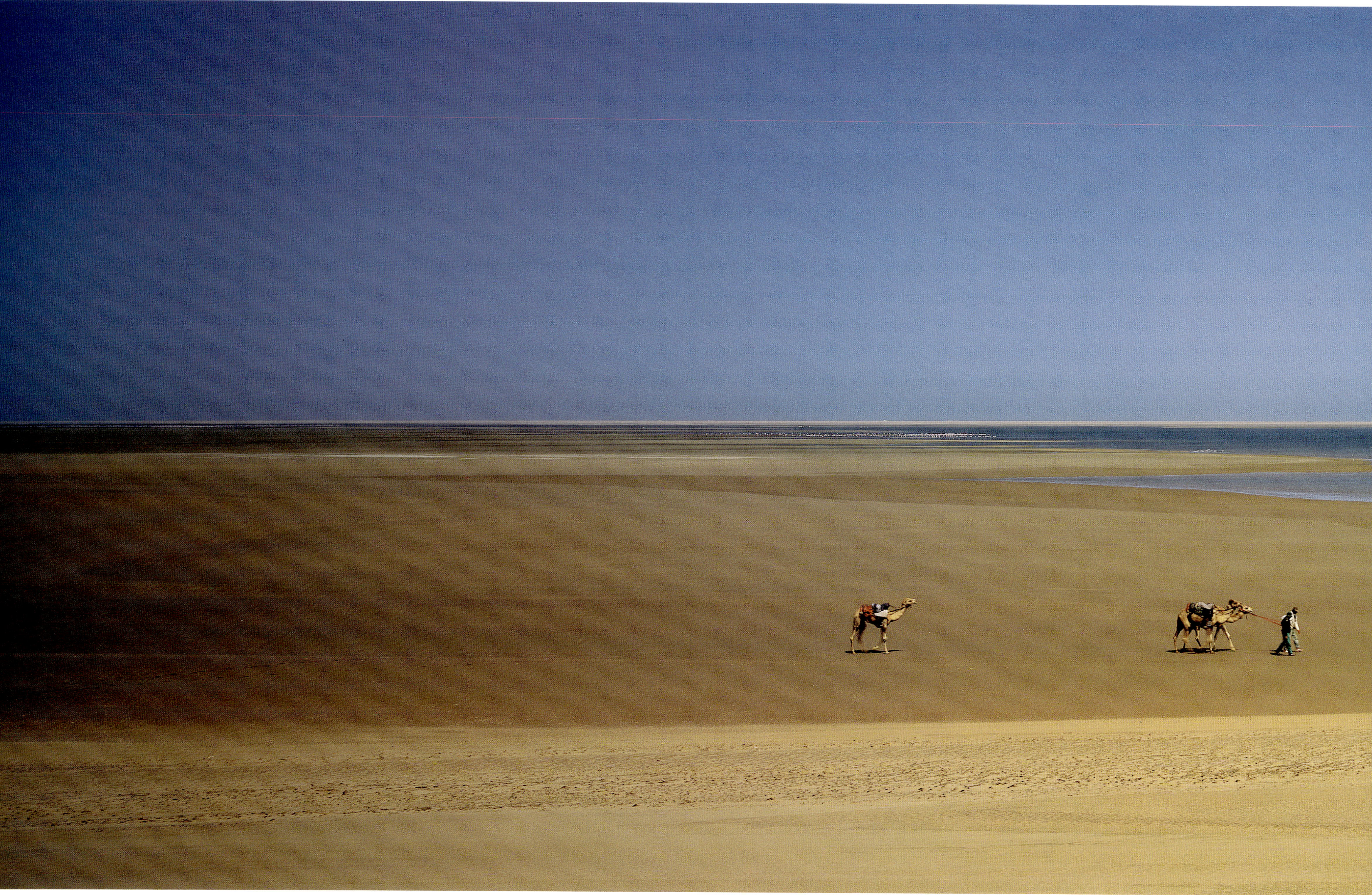

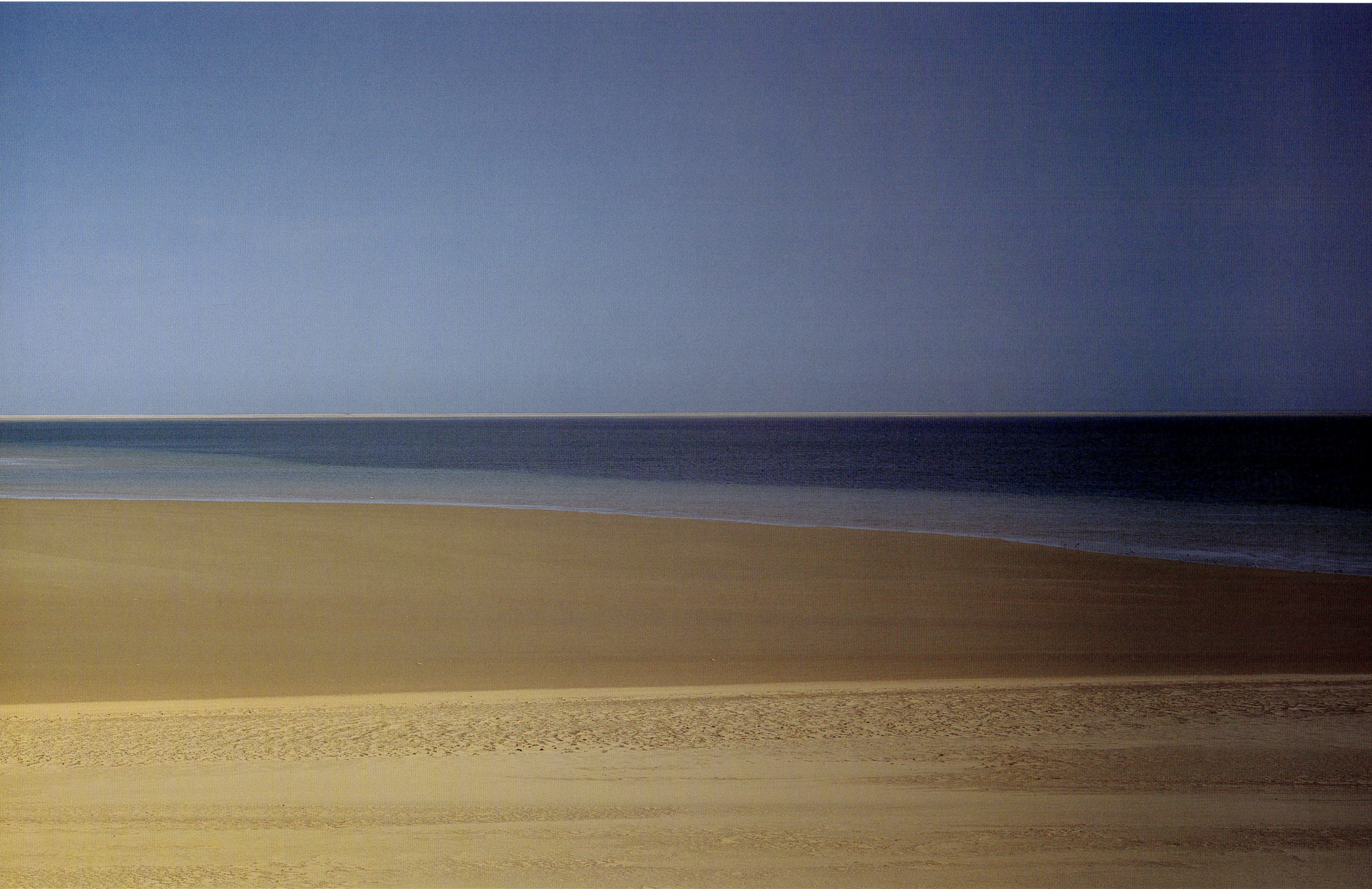

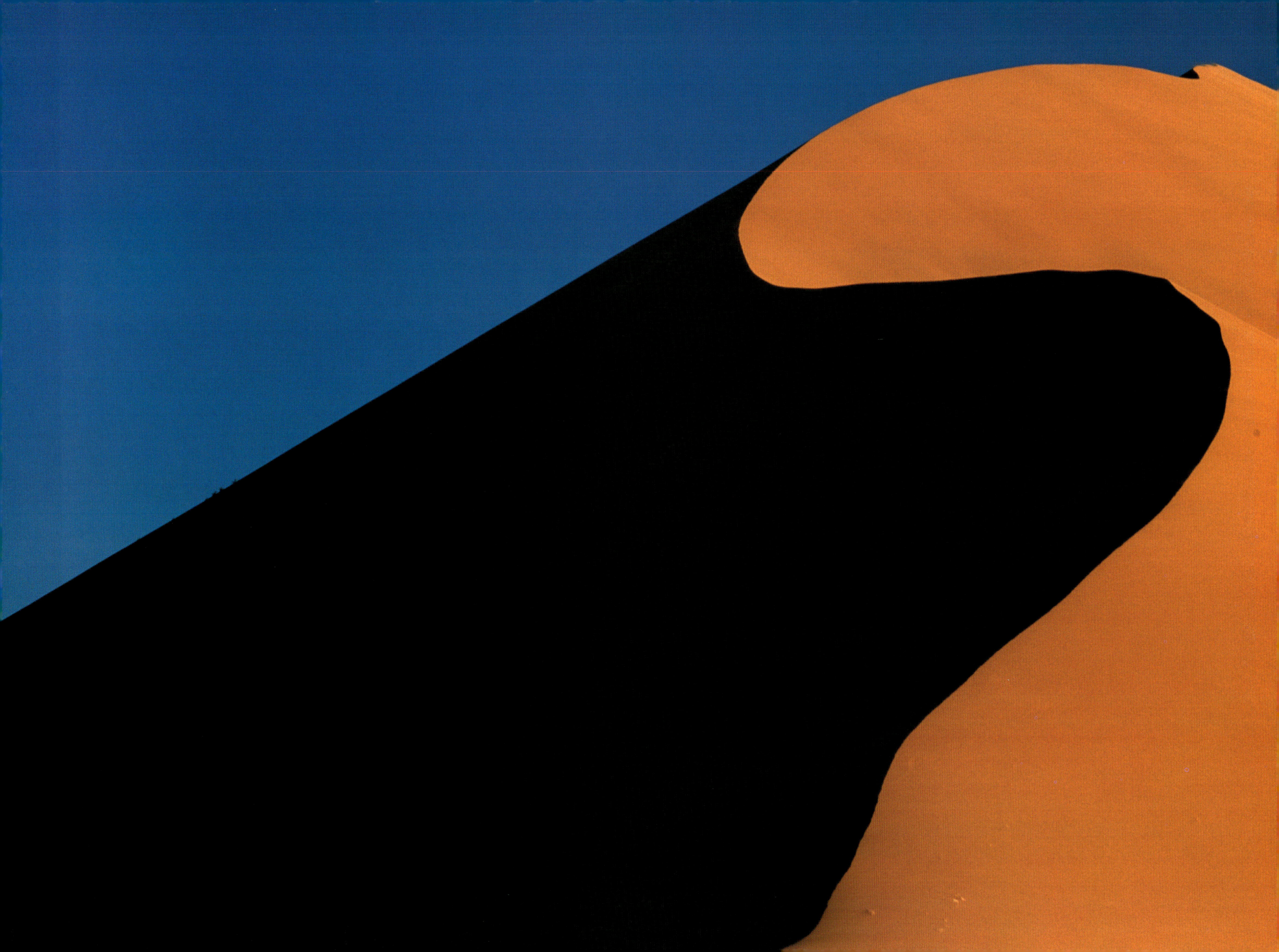

LEFT: Anyone who doubts that deserts can be beautiful need look no further than this picture of a sand dune in Namibia's Skeleton Coast Park. The sweep of the curve along the ridge, the almost mathematical straightness of the hillside on the left, and the purity of the only three colors—tan in the sunlight, black in the shadow, and azure-blue sky—make a picture even the most gifted artist would find difficult to produce.
Gavriel Jecan/Corbis

BELOW: Dead Vlei in Namibia is a parched salt flat, which very occasionally receives a little rain, turning the dry surface into a glutinous mud in a matter of minutes. There are a few dead trees, some of which are over 500 years old, dating back to the time when a river flowed through the valley. Dead Vlei has proved popular with film crews and has even been used as the setting for a commercial ad for bottled water.
Tjaart van Staden/fotoLibra

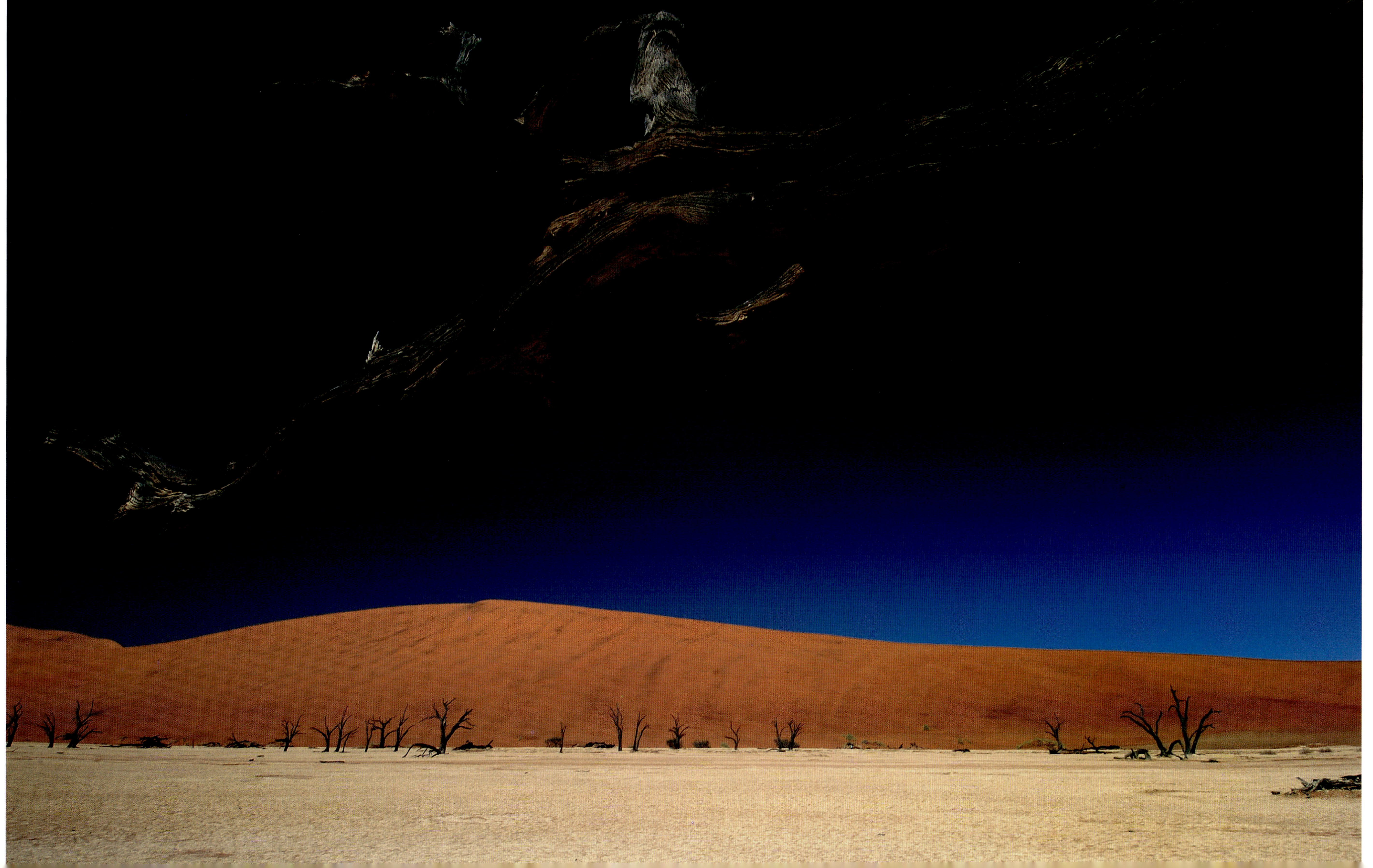

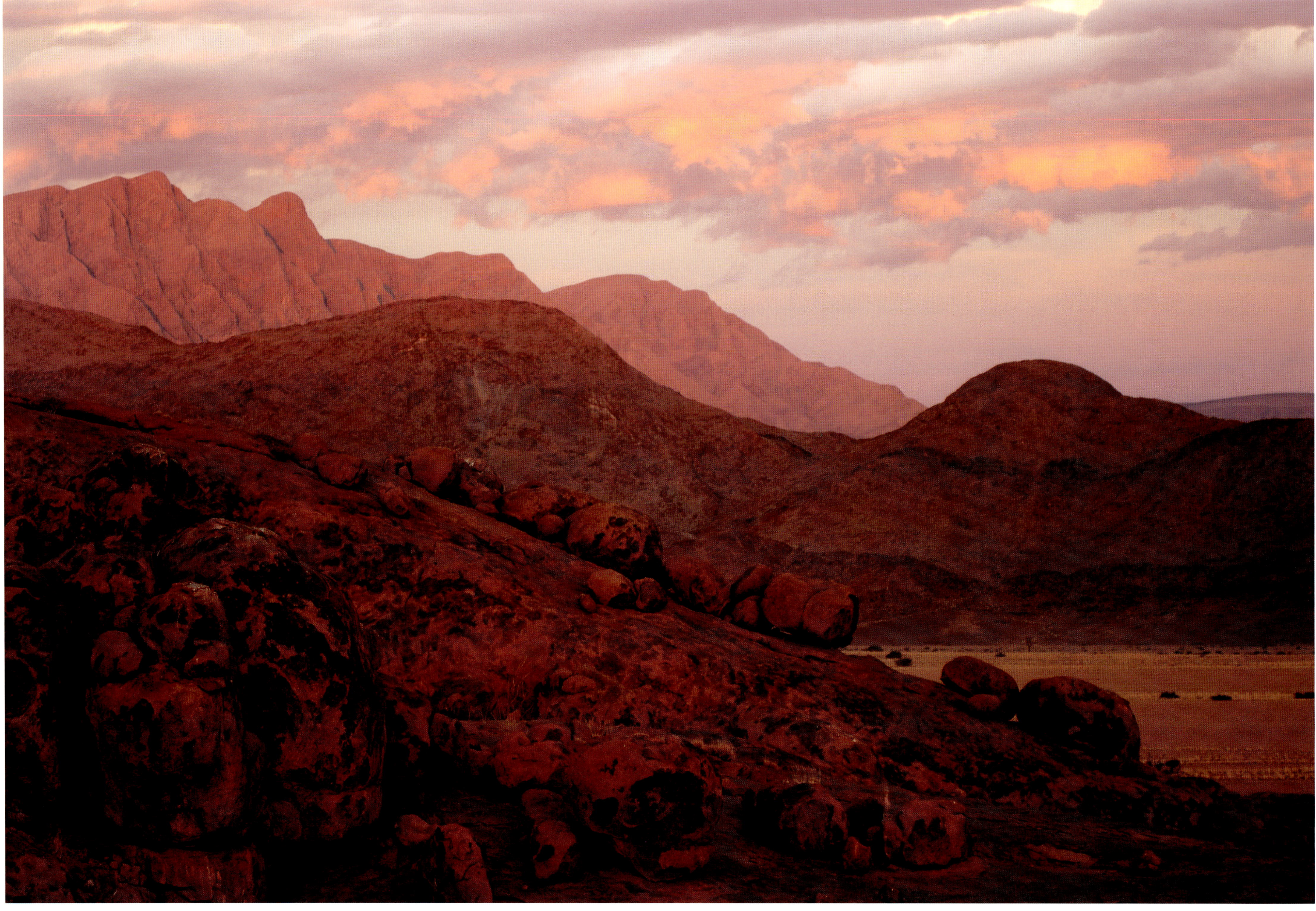

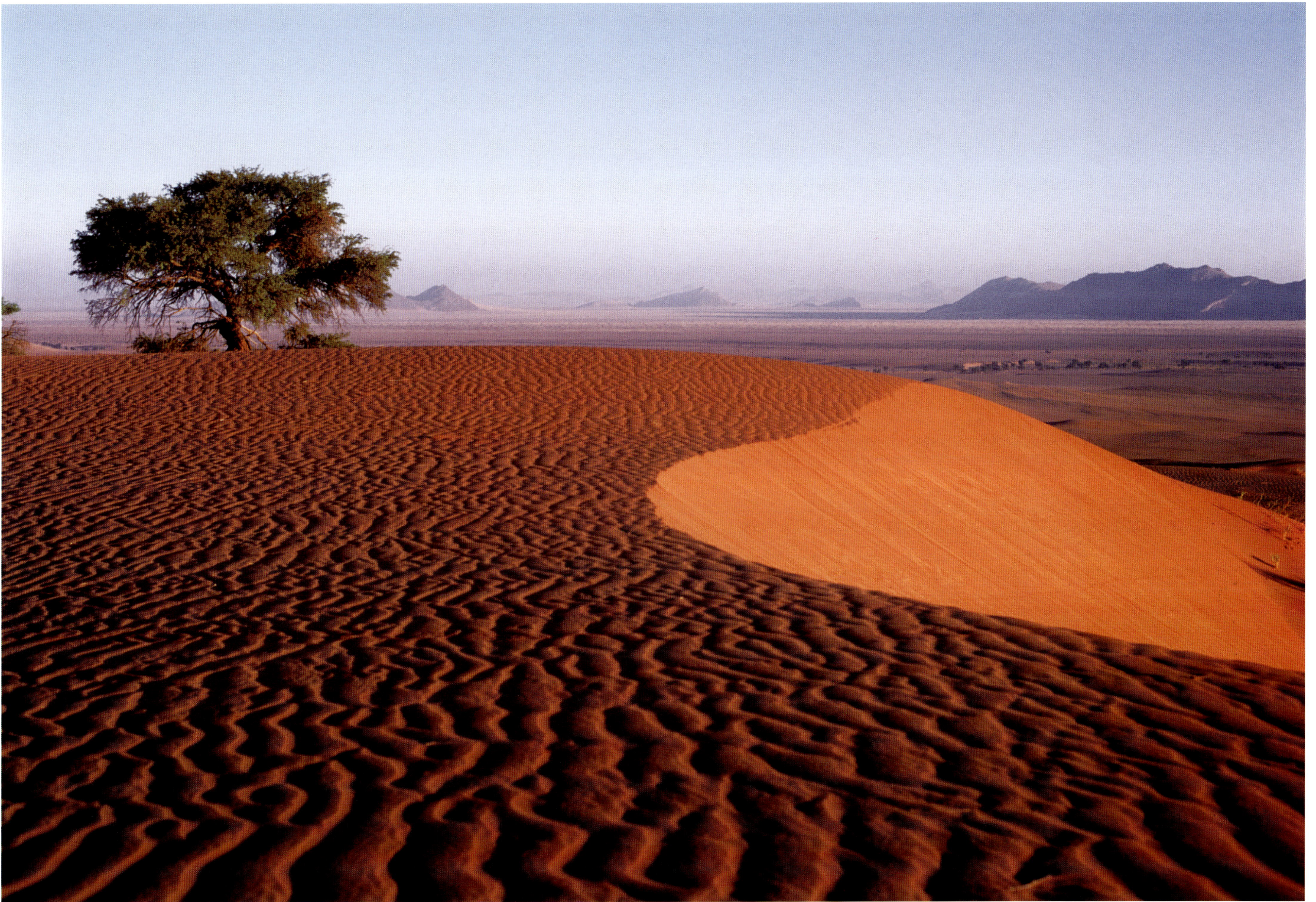

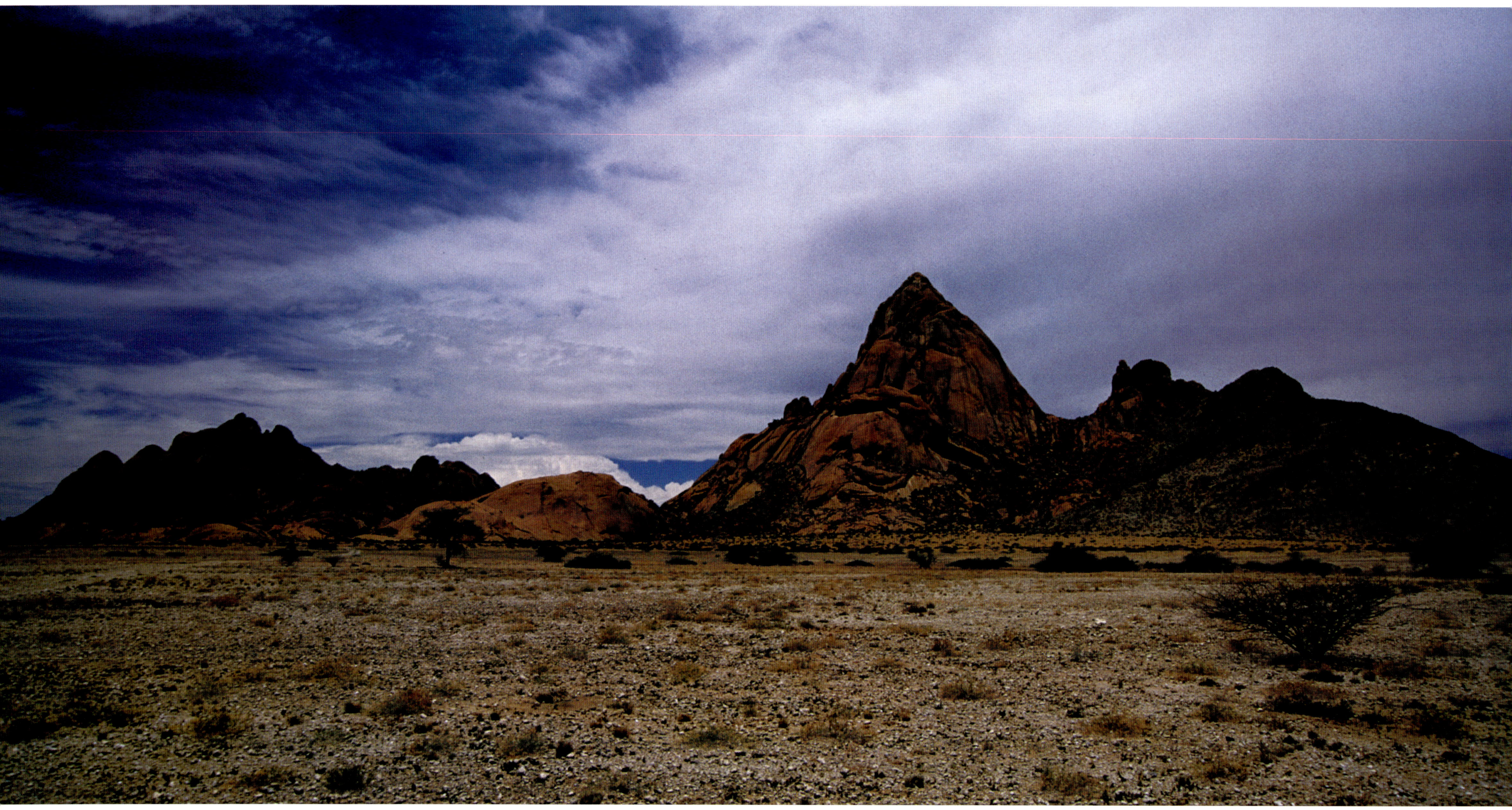

PAGE 92: Black Mountain in Namibia's Sossusvlei at sunset. There is a marked contrast between the very flat sandy valley and the rugged hills, with, in the foreground, an extensive field of boulders, many of which look as though they should have rolled down the hillside long ago.
Tjaart van Staden/fotoLibra

PAGE 93: Early morning among the sand dunes of Namibia. The rills on the plateau etch deep patterns in the sand, but the break at the edge is sudden and complete with a steep and even slope to the plain far below. Despite the dryness, a lone tree has managed not only to establish itself but also to thrive and grow to a considerable height.
Lutz Wahlers/fotoLibra

ABOVE: The Spitzkoppe is not the highest mountain in Namibia, but it is certainly the most striking, and the similarity of its silhouette to that of the Matterhorn have made it the best known. The summit is 5,905 feet above sea level, and 2,300 feet above the surrounding Kakoveld plain, and the climb is highly rated by mountaineers, although it is not attempted in summer since the rock is too hot to touch. It is decorated with much San (Bushmen) artwork, whose present-day descendants still consider it a sacred place.
Lutz Wahlers/fotoLibra

RIGHT: These dunes in the Sossuvlei in Namibia are classified as crescentic. They form under pressure from winds that constantly blow in the same direction. The slip face on such dunes is on the concave side, thus the dunes seen here are slowly moving towards the camera.
Lutz Wahlers/fotoLibra

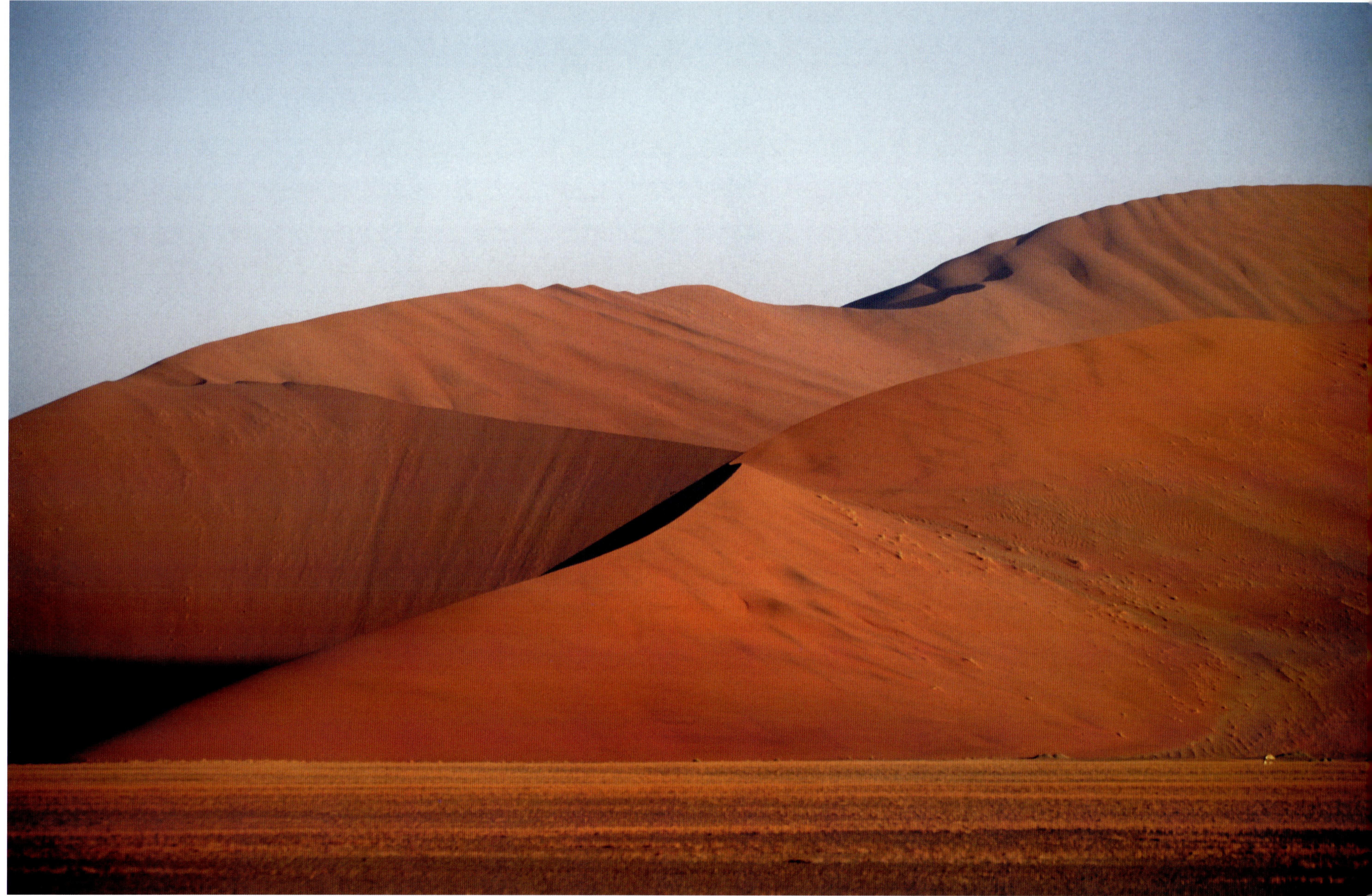

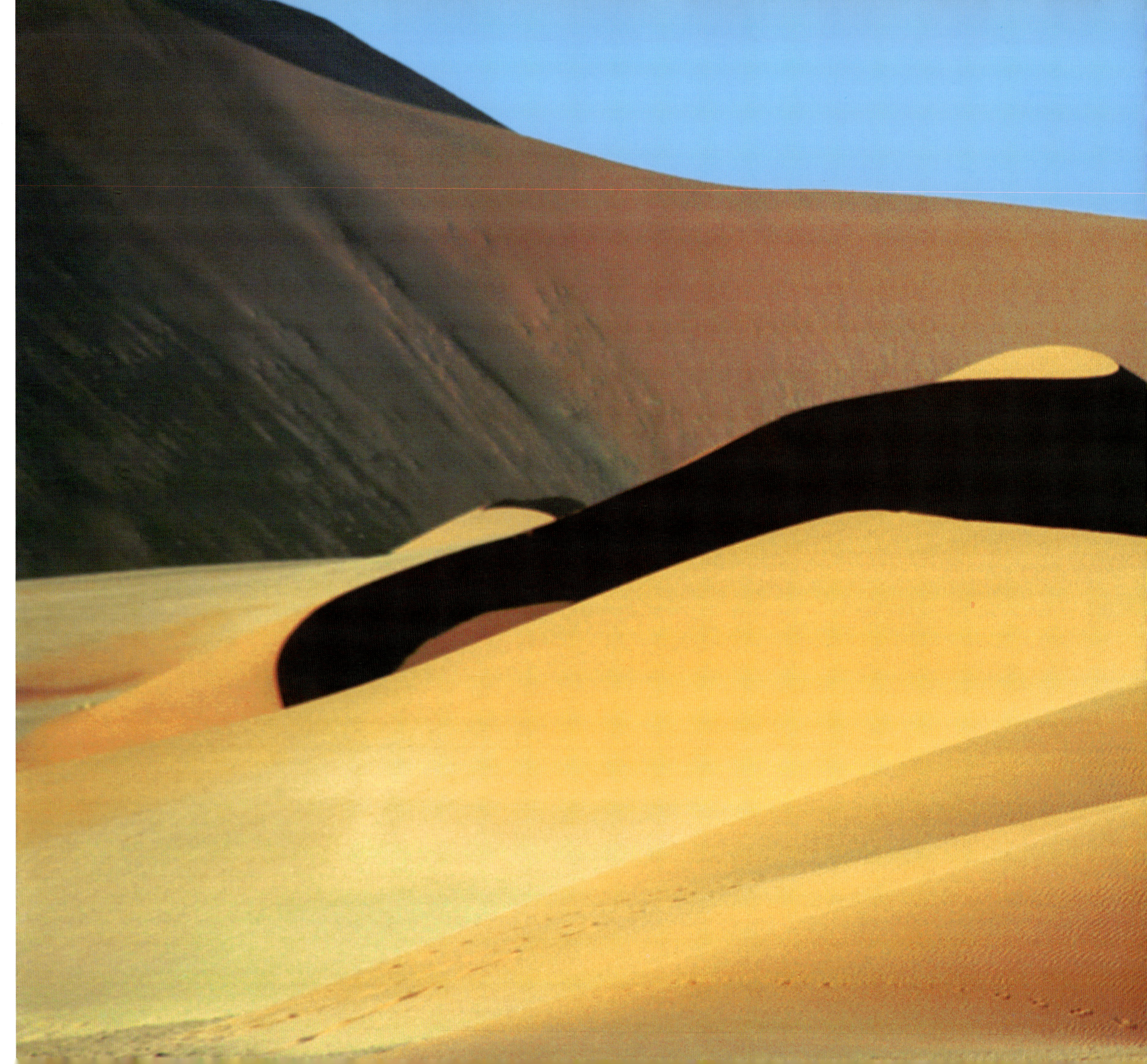

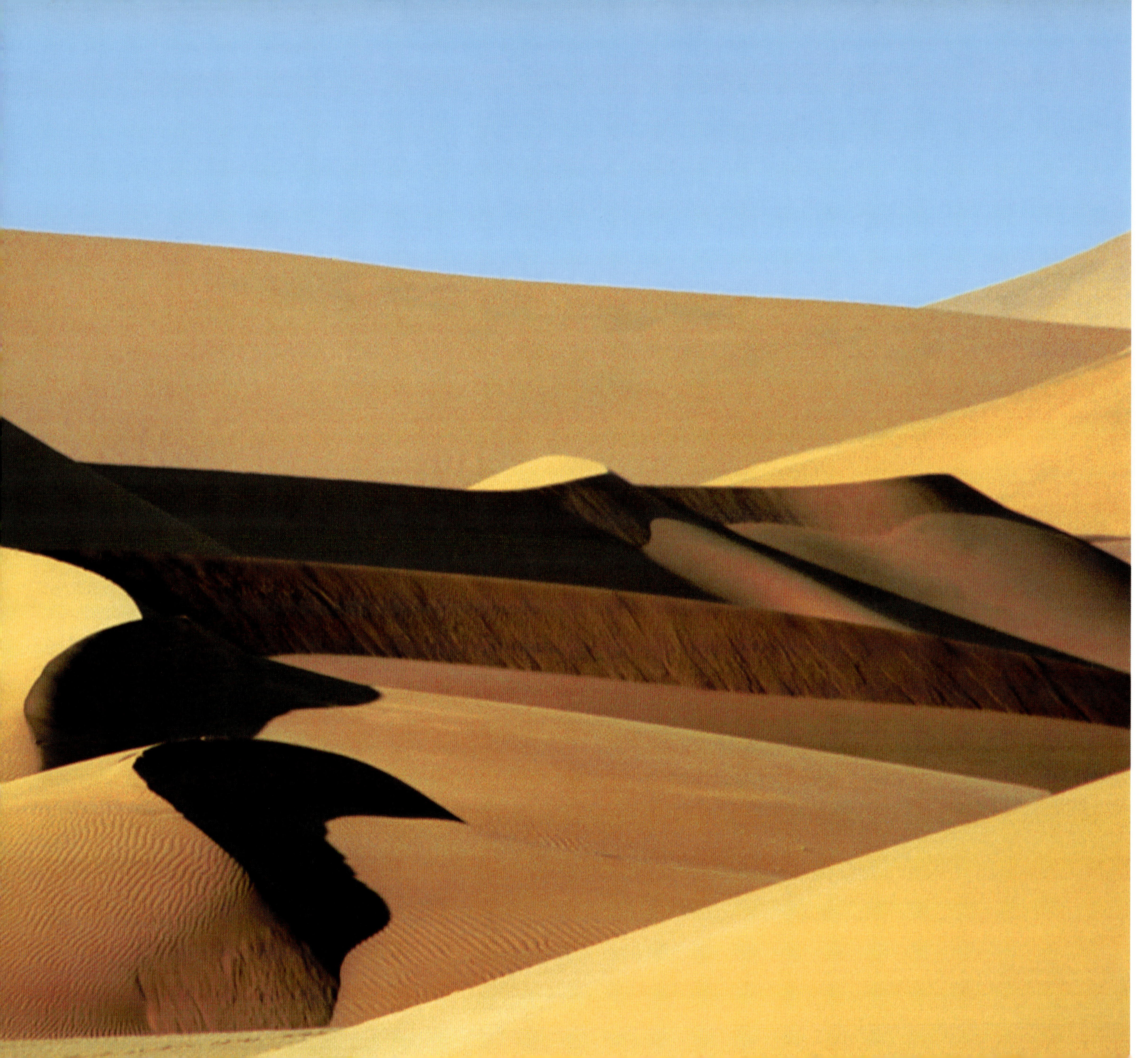

Left: The timeless beauty of the sand dunes of Sossusvlei in Namibia. The dunes look static but, in reality, are moving very gradually from left to right in this picture.
Carole Rawlinson/fotoLibra

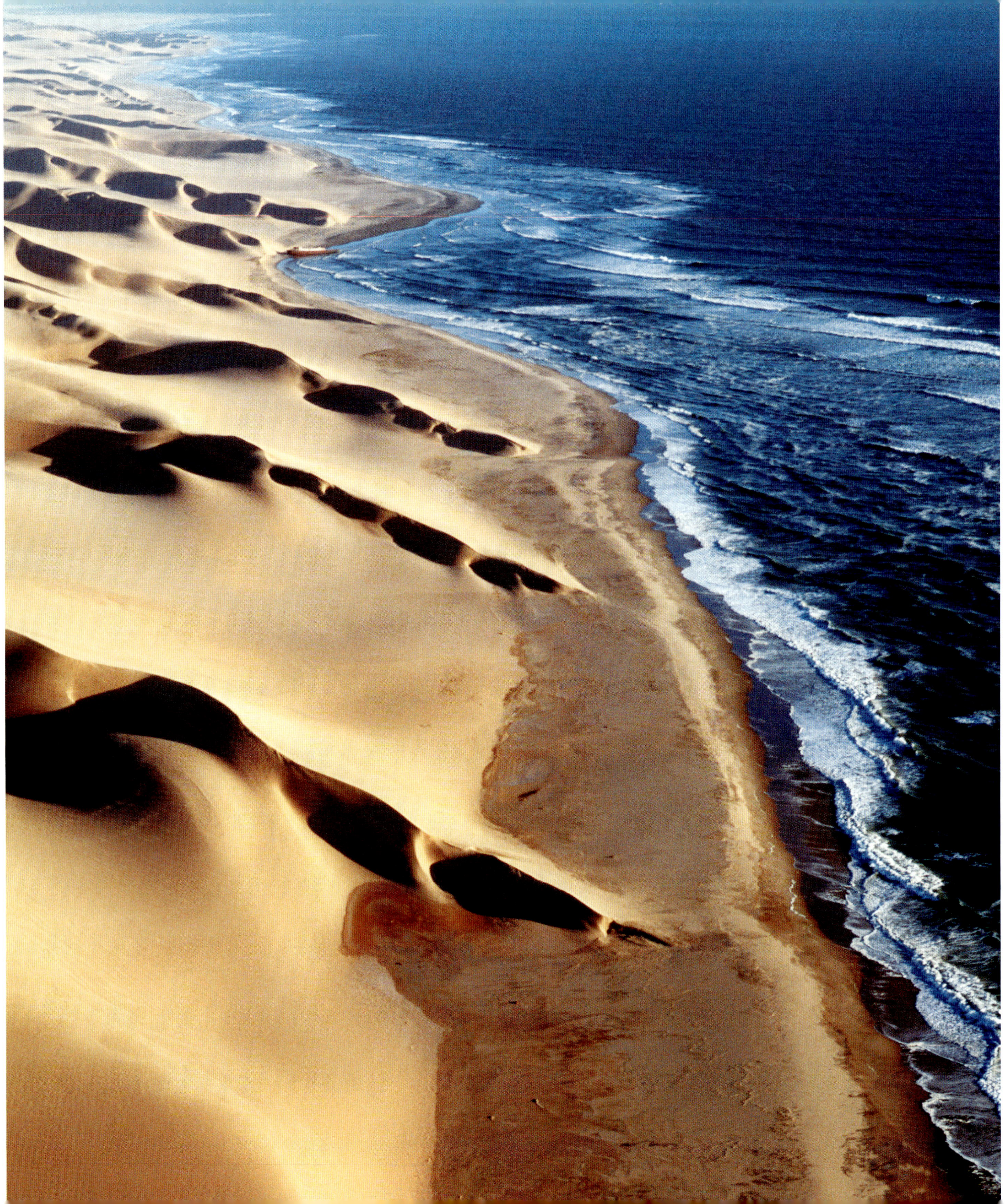

Left: The Namib Desert extends right to the Atlantic Ocean, as this picture makes clear. Annual rainfall is at most three inches a year—sometimes very much less—but frequent thick fogs come in from the Atlantic to create sufficient moisture for more species to survive than would otherwise be possible, and both flora and fauna have adapted to take advantage of this.
Martin Harvey/Corbis

Right: It was very difficult to make an objective analysis of dunes when the only way of crossing them was on foot—an inevitably physically demanding, if not exhausting, process. Aerial photography, as here in Morocco, was a considerable improvement, but it is satellite imaging that has enabled geologists and geographers to examine deserts, classify dunes according to five types, and to measure their movement; some dunes, for example, have been seen to move at a rate of about 110 yards per year.
Cory Langley/Corbis

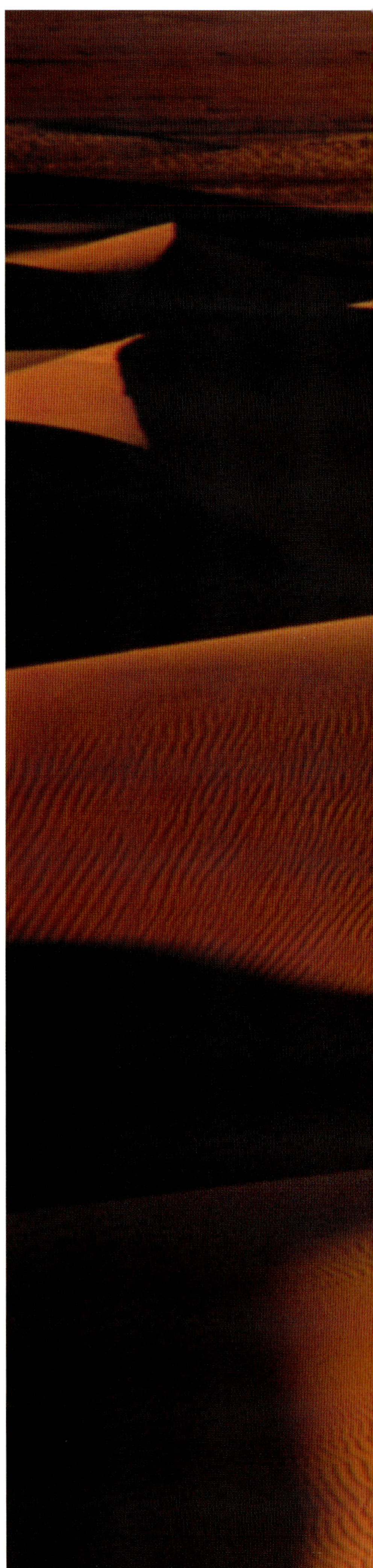

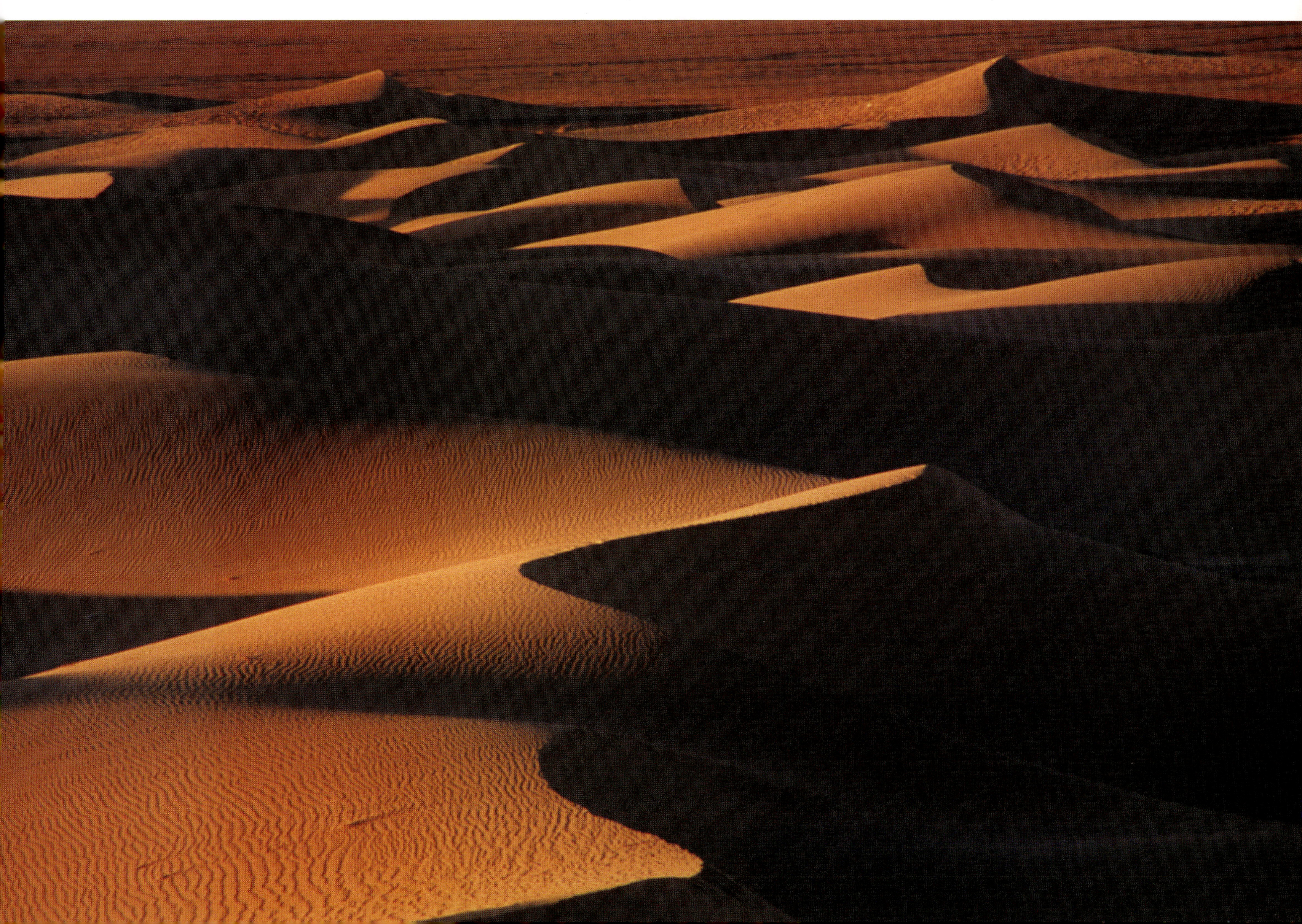

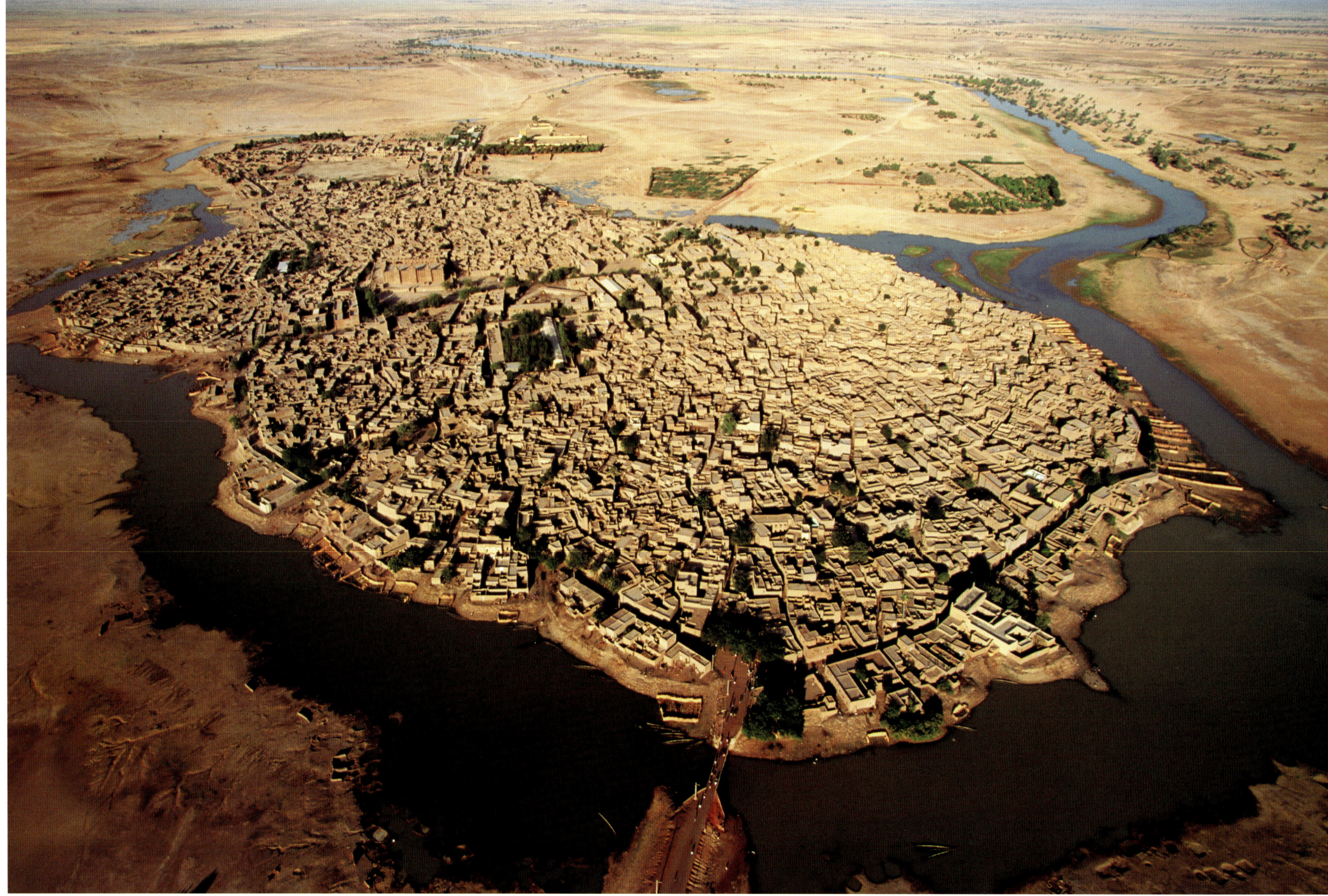

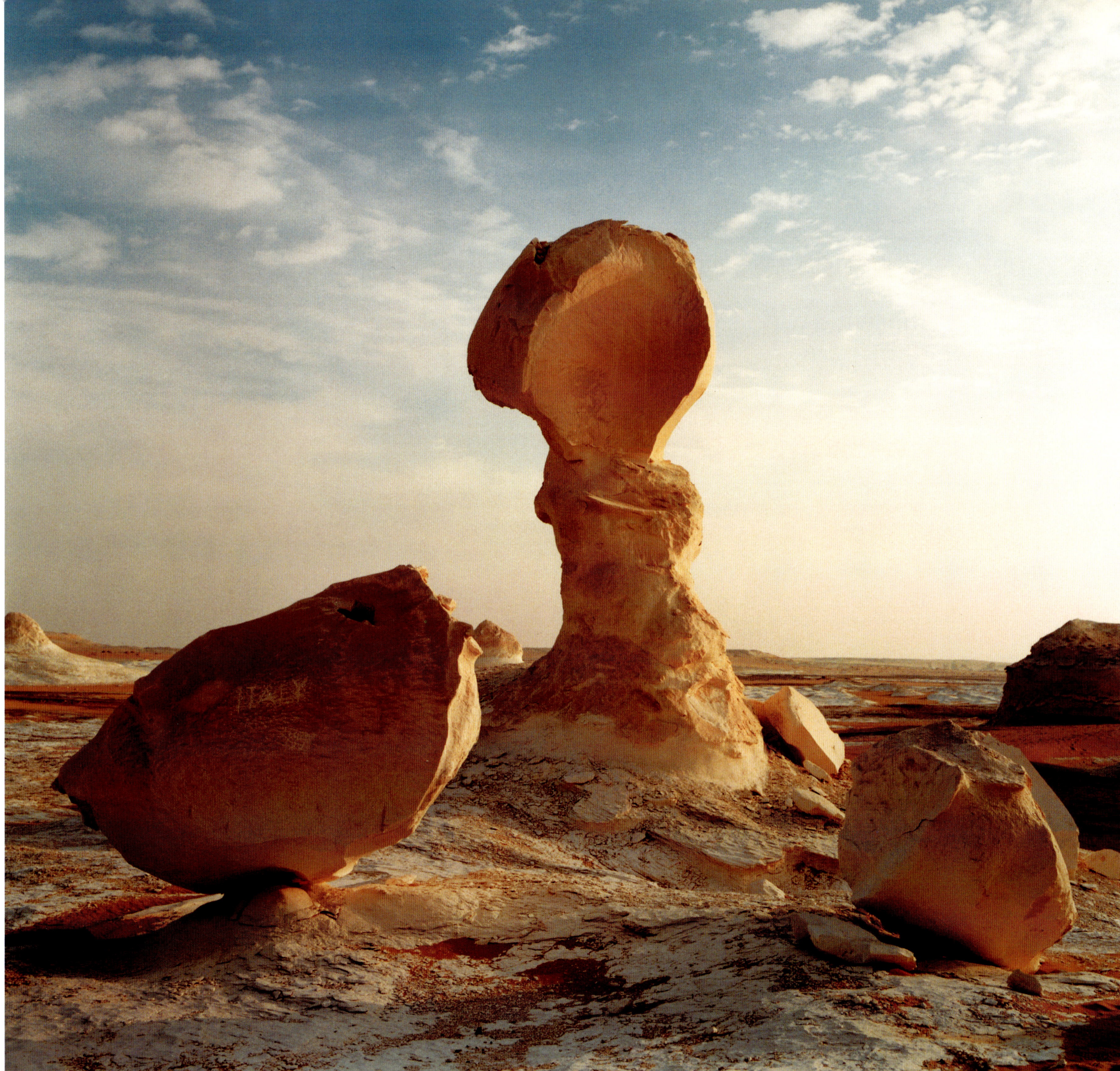

FAR LEFT: Djenné in Mali, Africa, is the oldest known city in sub-Saharan Africa, having been continuously occupied since about 250BC. Completely surrounded by the Sahara Desert, it lies across various traditional trade routes and also has direct riverine connection with the city of Timbuktu. Djenné's heyday was in the 18th and 19th centuries, after which it lost trade to Mopti, a town some fifty miles to the northeast, situated at the junction of the Niger and Bani Rivers.
Yann Arthus-Bertrand/Corbis

LEFT: Farafra Oasis in Egypt is located immediately to the east of the Great Sand Sea. Although mentioned in many ancient records, the oasis contains few sites of historical significance, but is famed for the White Desert, located some miles to the northeast. This area is chalk white and littered with rocks eroded by wind and time into strange shapes, as seen here. A charming local legend has it that some centuries ago the villagers so lost track of time that they had to send a delegation to a nearby town to discover what day of the week it was.
Rob Howard/Corbis

Right: Sandstone formations at Egypt's Wadi el-Rayan, declared a protected area in 1989. It is one of the most important fossil sites in North Africa, including that of the carcass of a whale estimated to be forty million years old. The Protected Area covers 680 square miles of which some 44 square miles are taken up by two artificial lakes, which were created in the 1970s to receive excess agricultural drainage water, but have since become an important habitat for birds and other wildlife.
Rob Howard/Corbis

Far Right: These crescentic dunes at the Egyptian end of the Sahara are moving inexorably from left to right in this picture. The slopes and purity of line of the dunes contrast with the flat, gravelly plain in the distance.
George F. Mobley/Getty Images

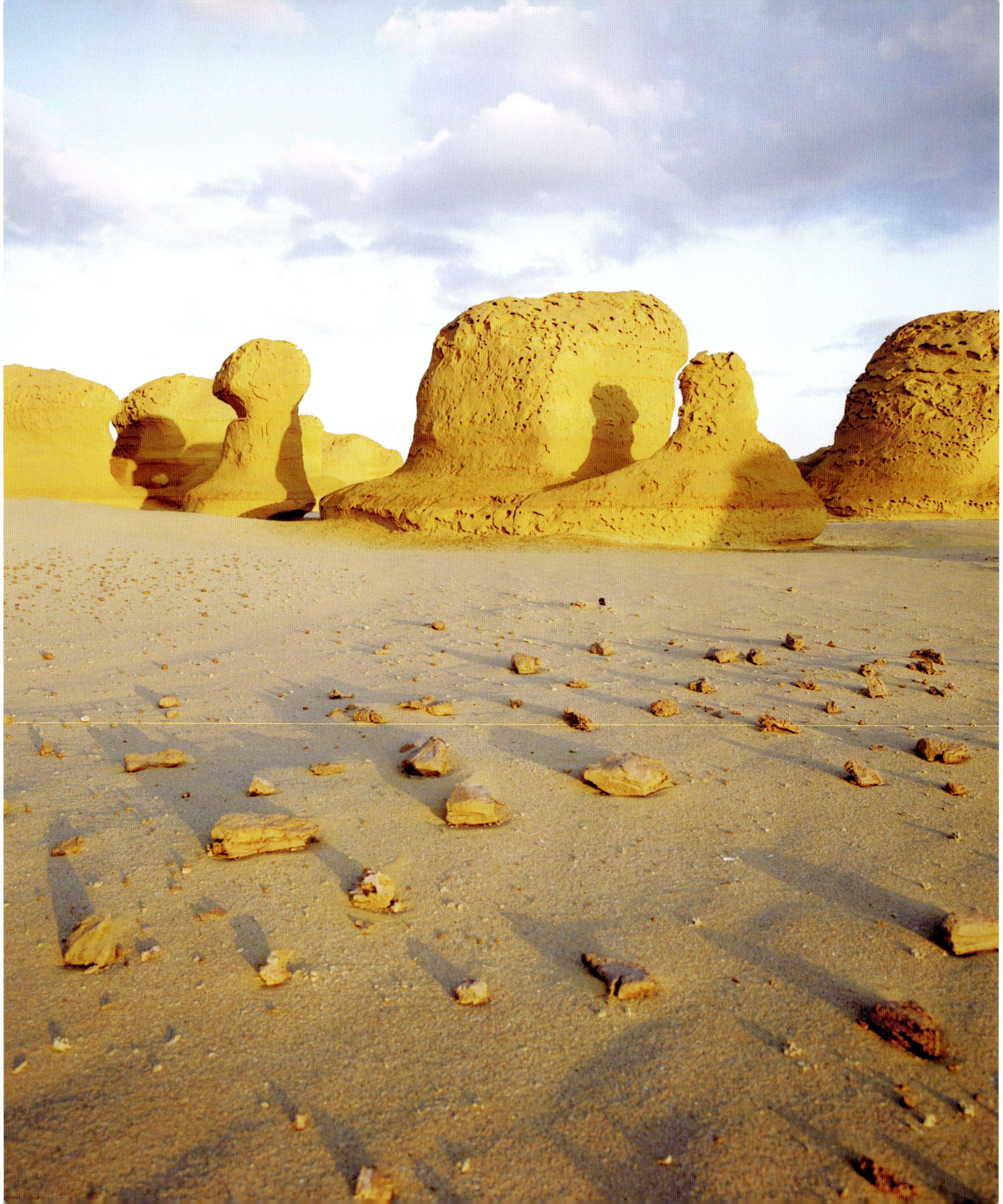

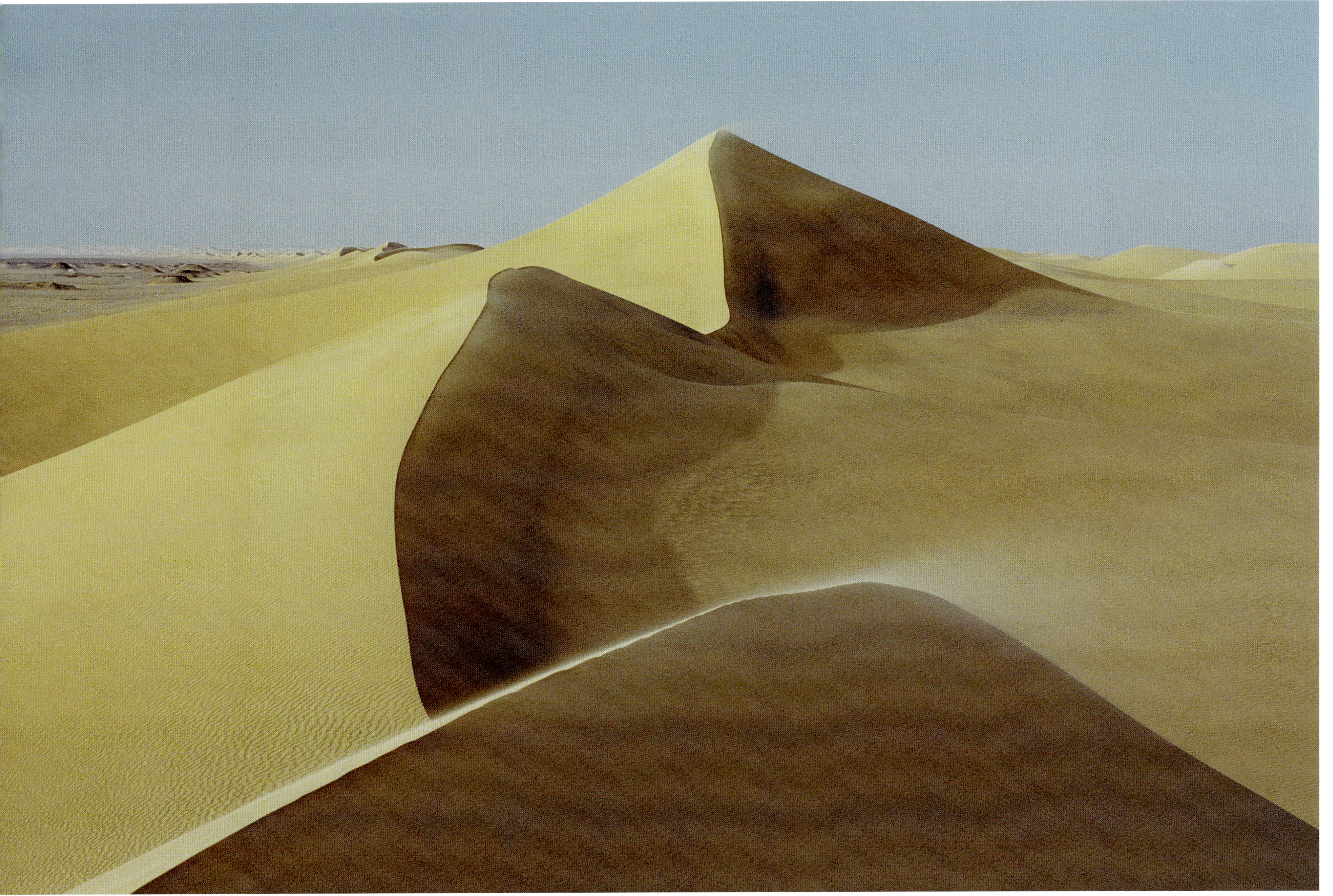

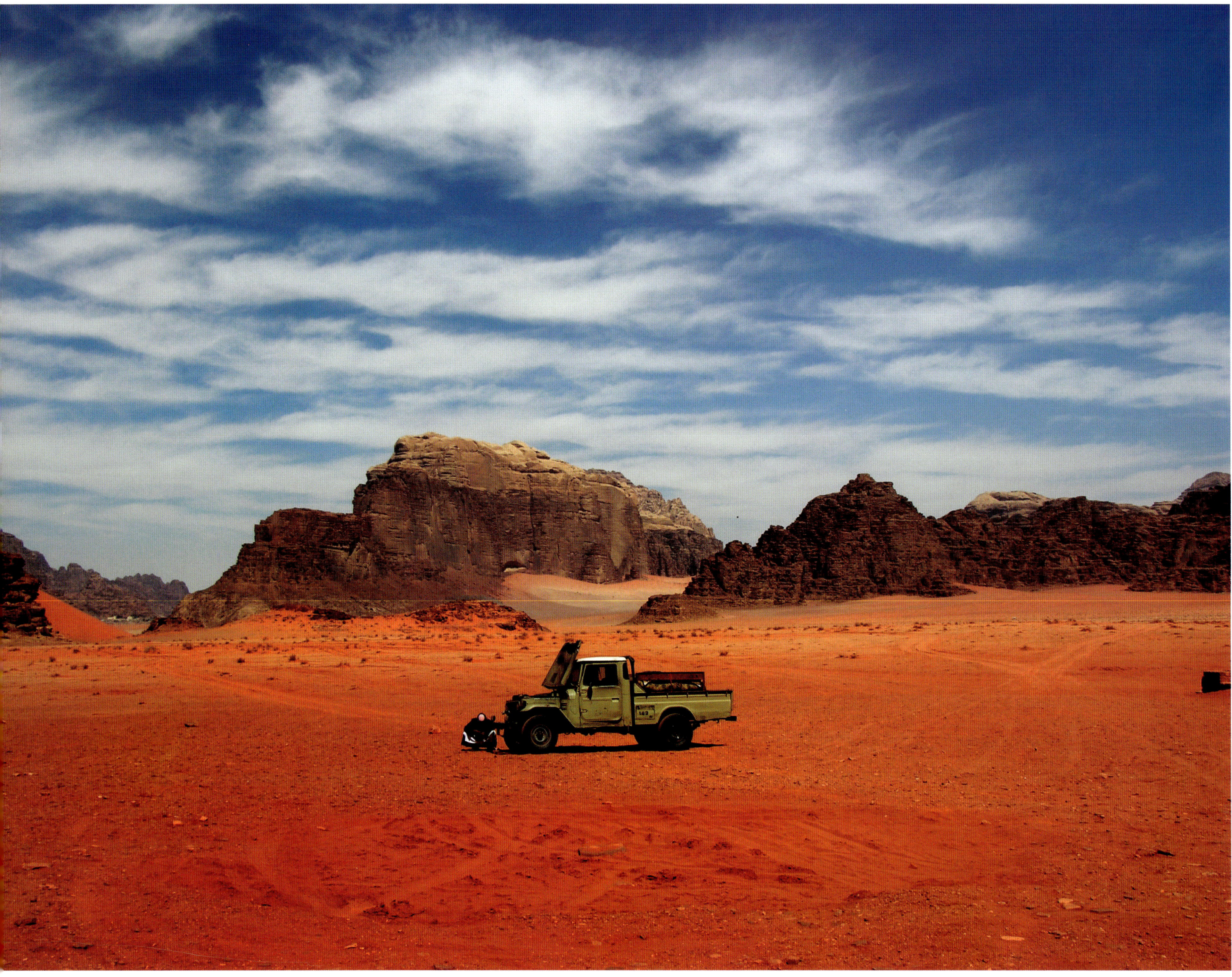

LEFT: A broken-down four-wheel-drive vehicle receives first aid from its anxious driver. Deserts are extremely inhospitable places and whether it's an experienced driver like this Jordanian in the Wadi Rum, or an unprepared Californian family setting out into the Sonoran Desert in their automobile, the costs of a mechanical breakdown or becoming immobilized in sand can be very high, even fatal.
Terry Bugden/fotoLibra

RIGHT: Jordan's Wadi Rum. This small but important country is composed mainly of desert and hills of the type seen here, which are attractive to tourists who, by definition, are passing through, but will not adequately support a large indigenous population. Jordan's challenge is to strike a balance by protecting a unique part of the world's heritage while providing an adequate lifestyle for its people.
Yann Arthus-Bertrand/Corbis

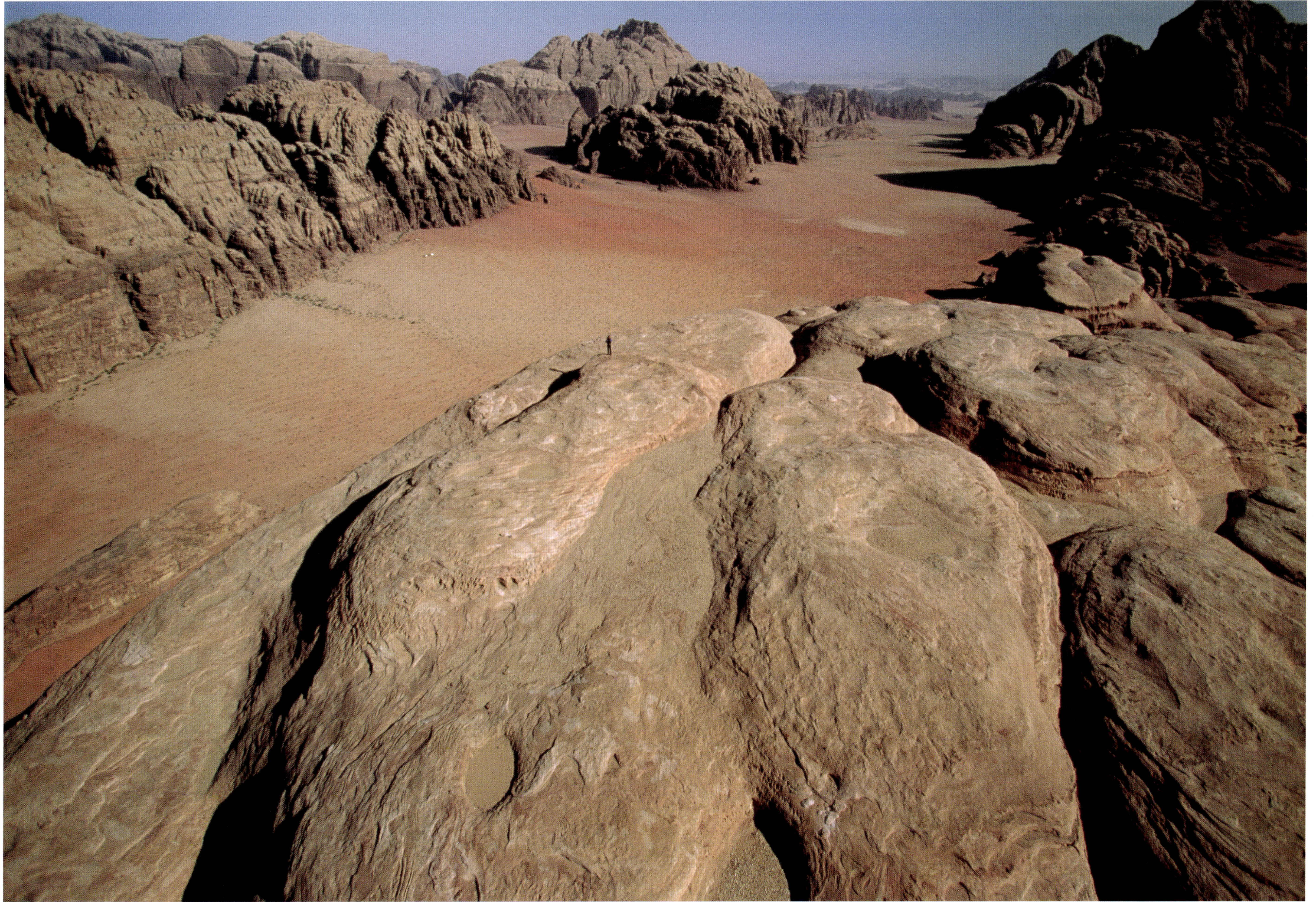

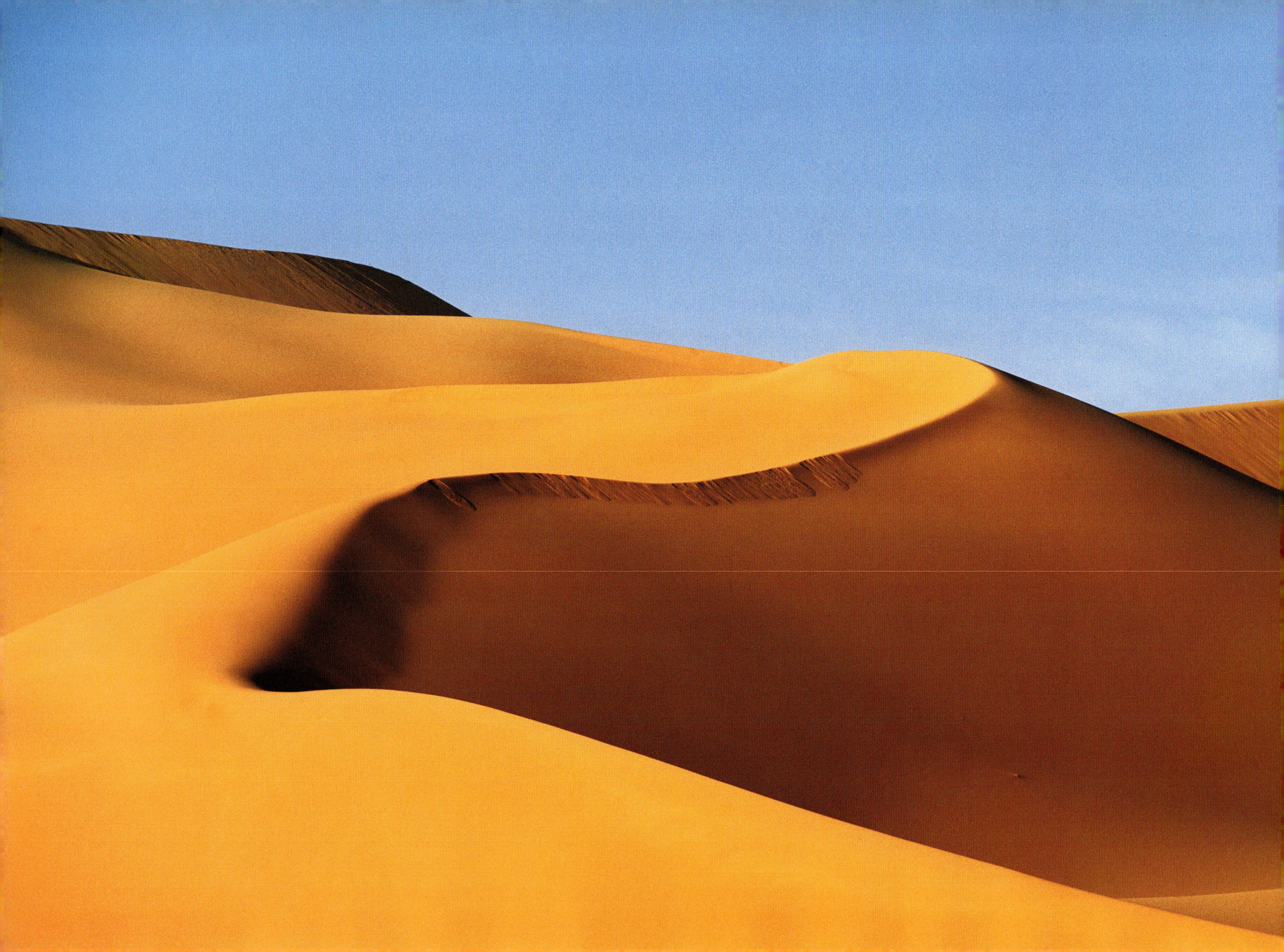

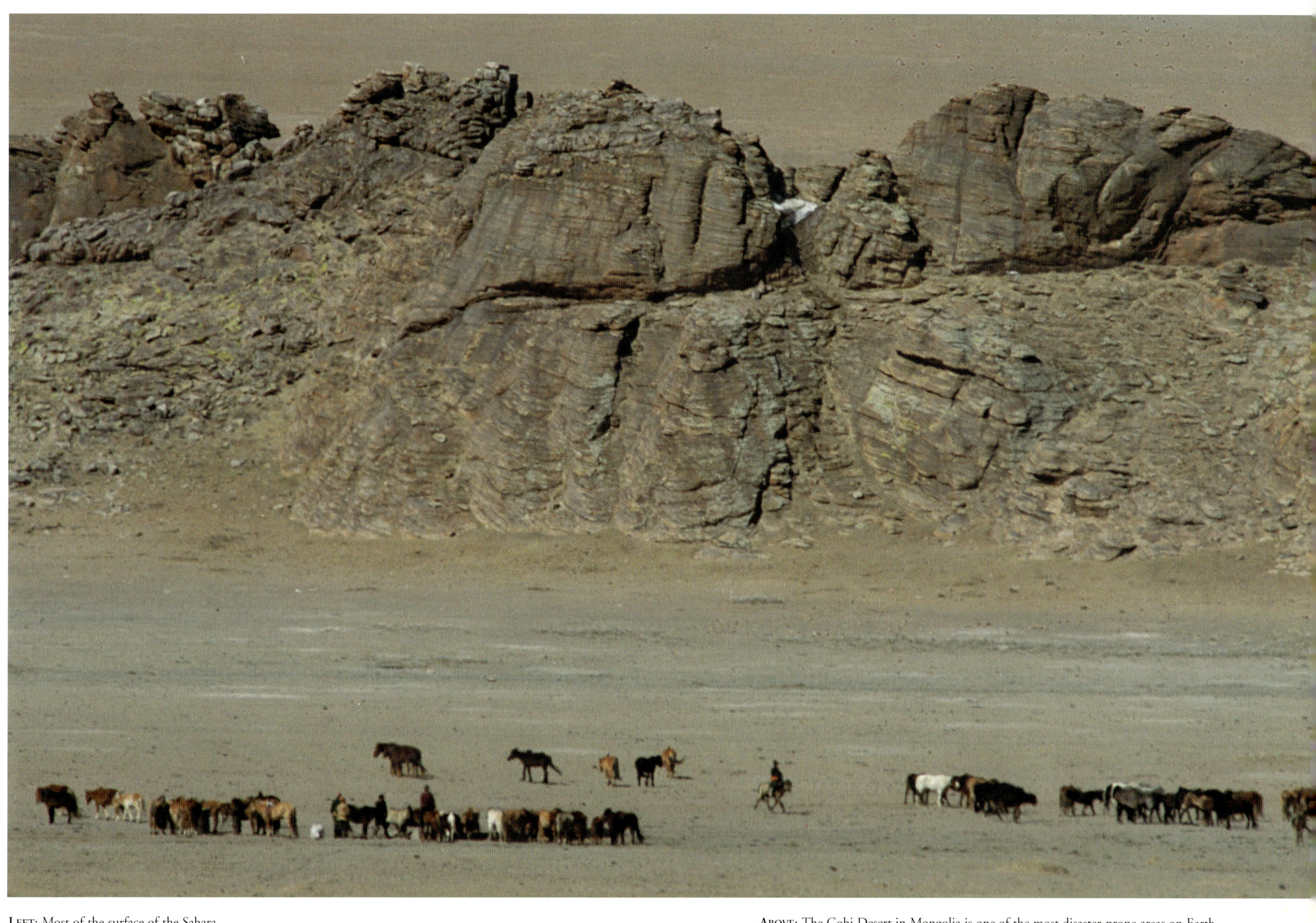

Left: Most of the surface of the Sahara Desert is bare stone and pebbles, but there are also large areas of sand dunes, as here in the Erg Murzuq in southern Libya. As in Namibia, these dunes have a linear grandeur and consistency of coloring all their own.
Sergio Pitamitz/Corbis

Above: The Gobi Desert in Mongolia is one of the most disaster-prone areas on Earth. The hardy nomadic herdsmen such as these face a litany of natural threats, including blizzards, heavy snow, dust storms and zuds, which are a local phenomenon, combining heavy snow, very low air temperatures and strong winds. In addition, there can be floods, earthquakes, and wildfires (where there is something to burn), drought, and the increasing encroachment of the desert on cultivated land (desertification).
Jacques Langevin/Corbis

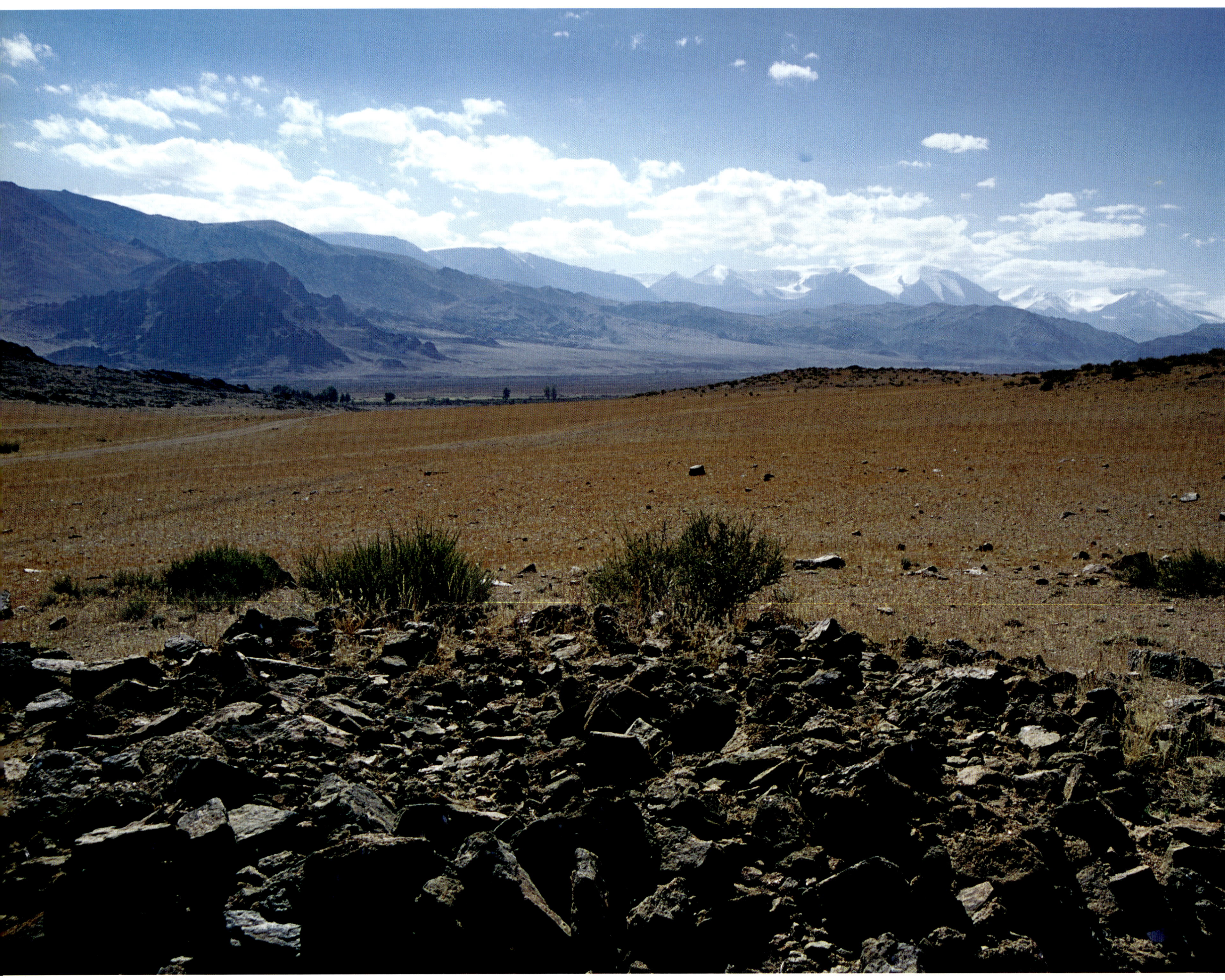

Left: The Gobi Desert covers an arc of land some 1,000 miles long and 500,000 square miles in area, making it one of the largest deserts in the world. In political terms it is split between northern China and southern Mongolia and, contrary to popular images of a desert, is not all sand-covered, with many areas being covered with rock, as shown here.
Steve Bein/Corbis

Right: The Hongorin Els sand dunes in the Gobi Desert are among a small number of desert fields around the world that emit acoustical energy. The sounds appear to be variable, being described as booming, roaring or squeaking, or like a musical instrument such as a bass violin or a trumpet, but, for want of a more accurate term, the word normally used is "singing." Common factors are that the sand grains must be dry and well rounded, and the dunes high and steep.
Dean Conger/Getty Images

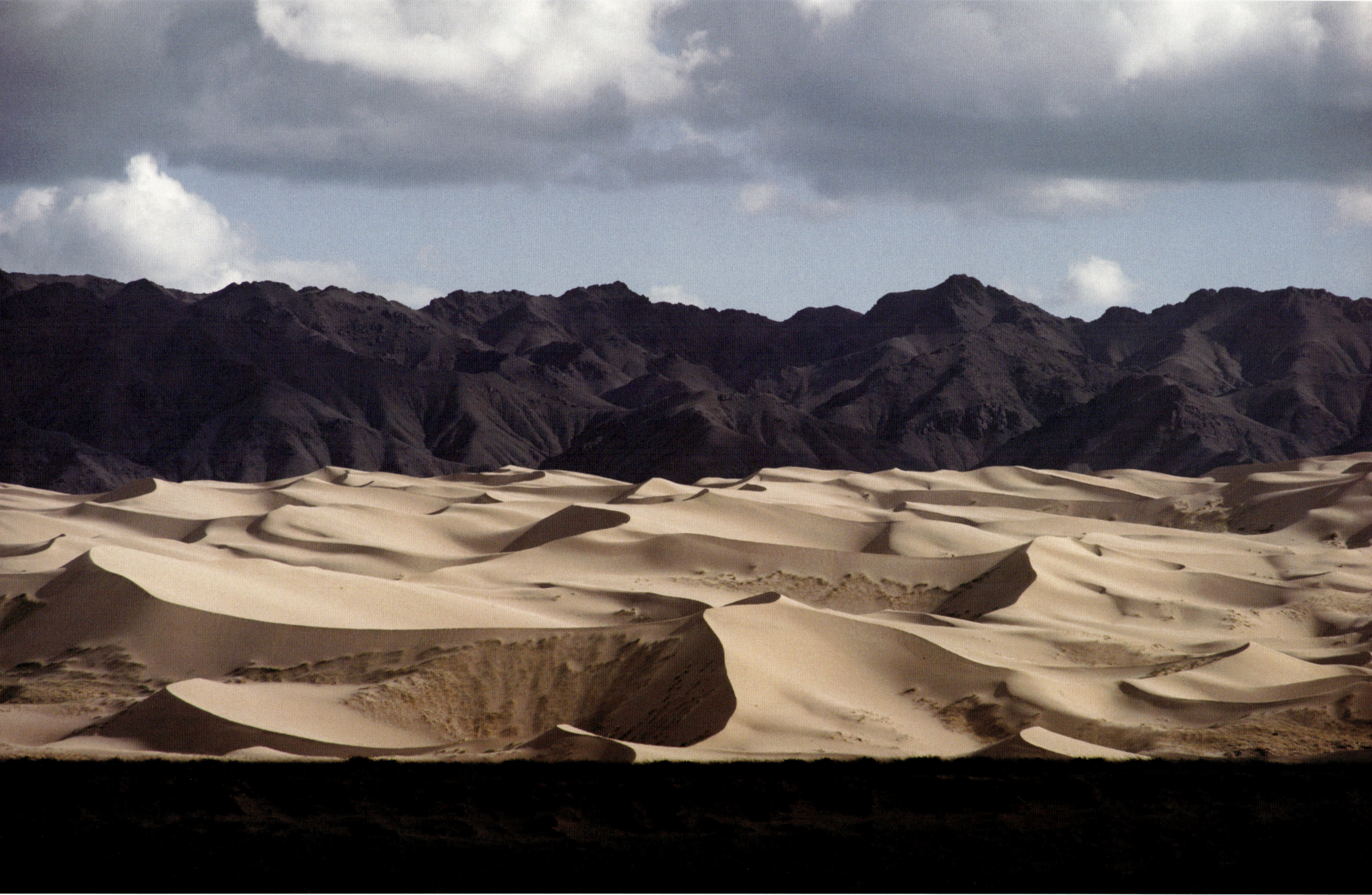

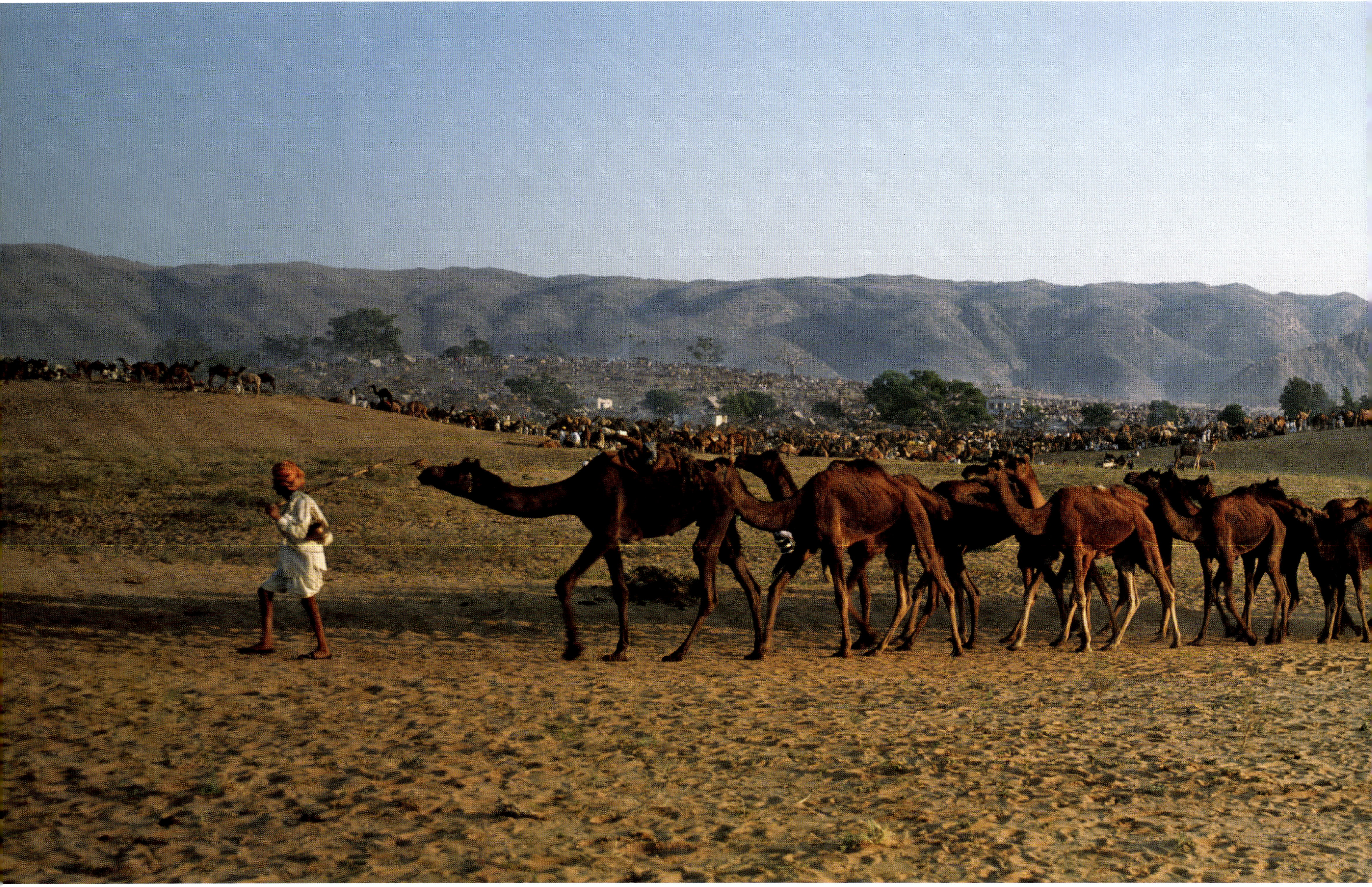

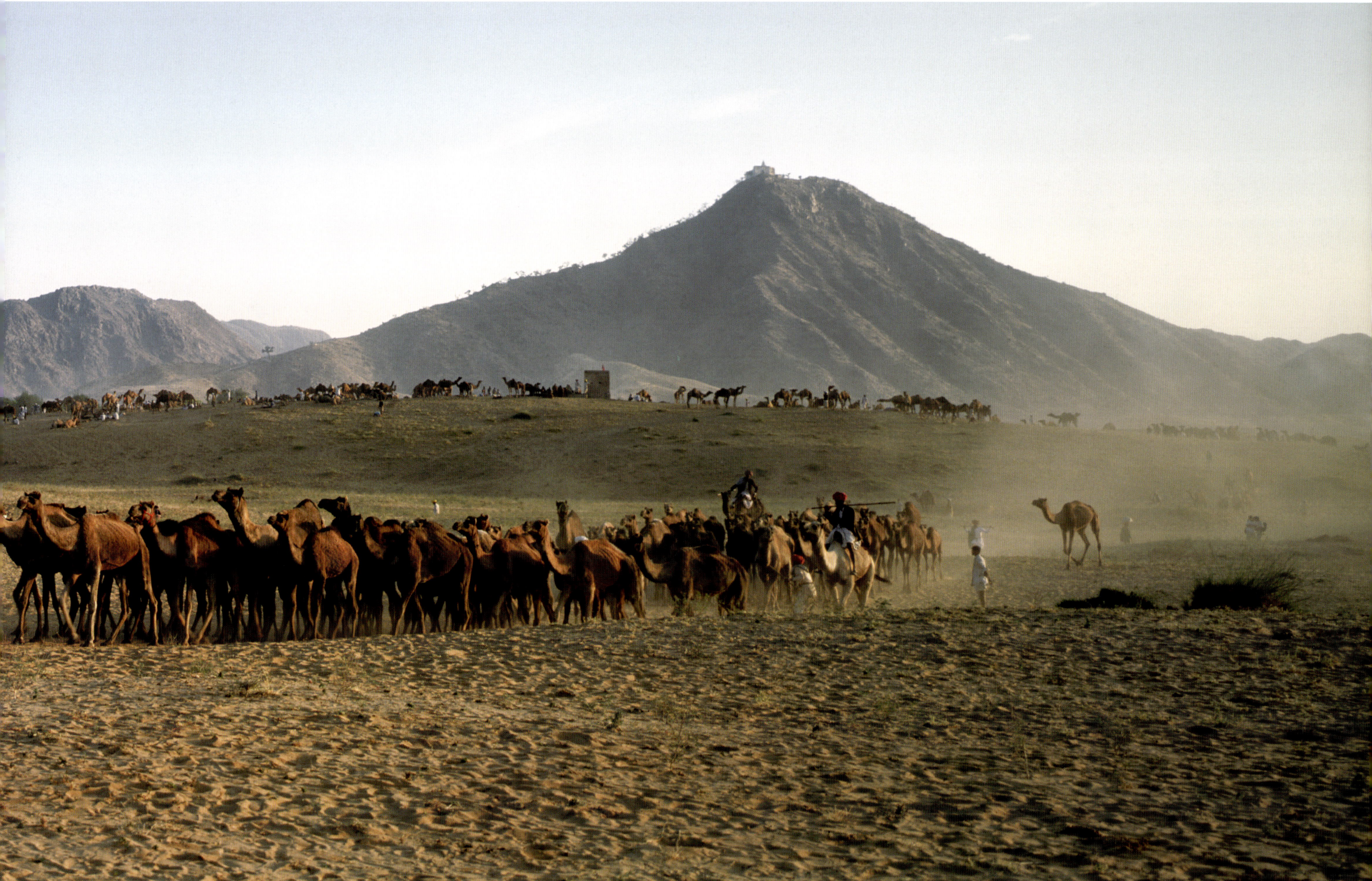

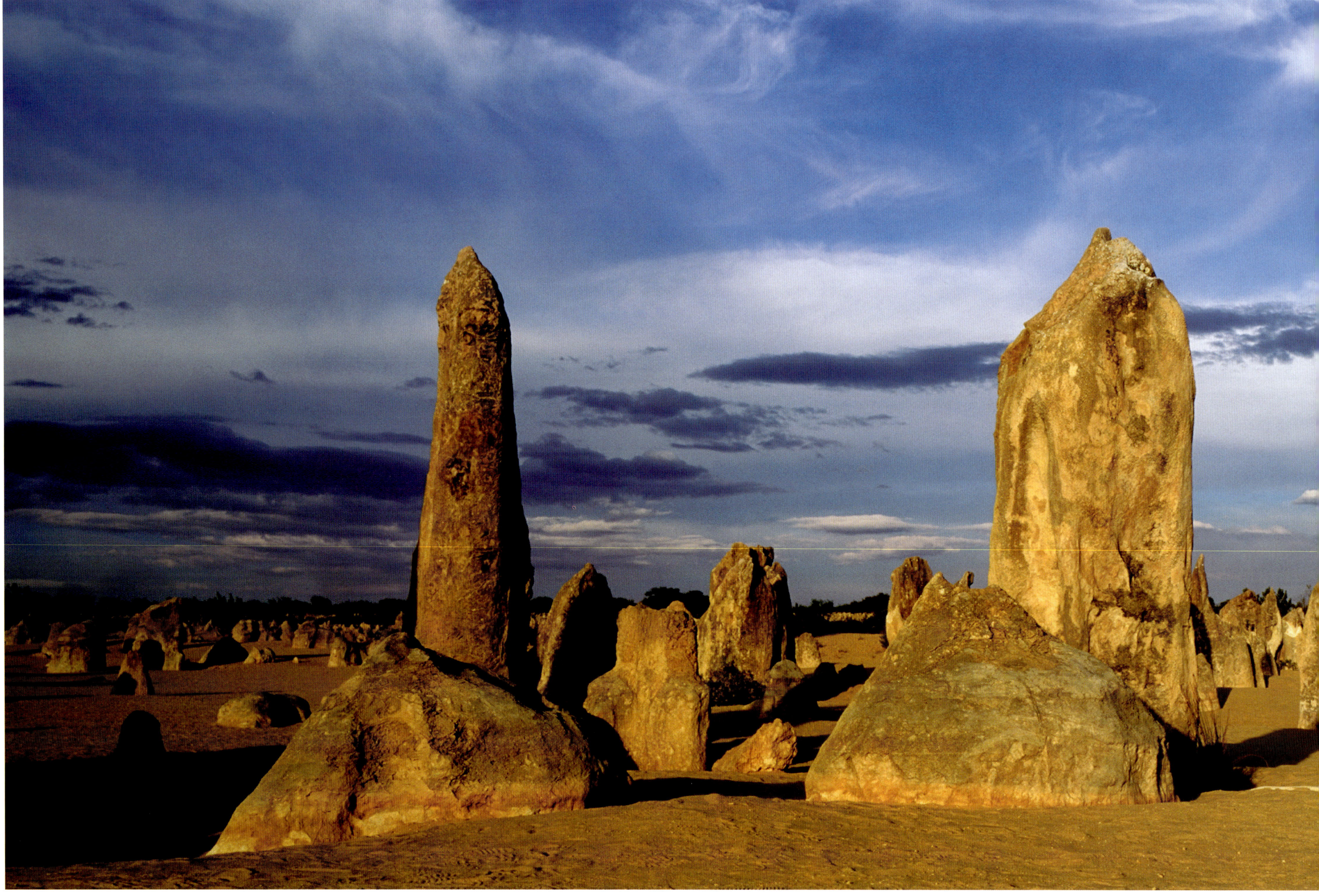

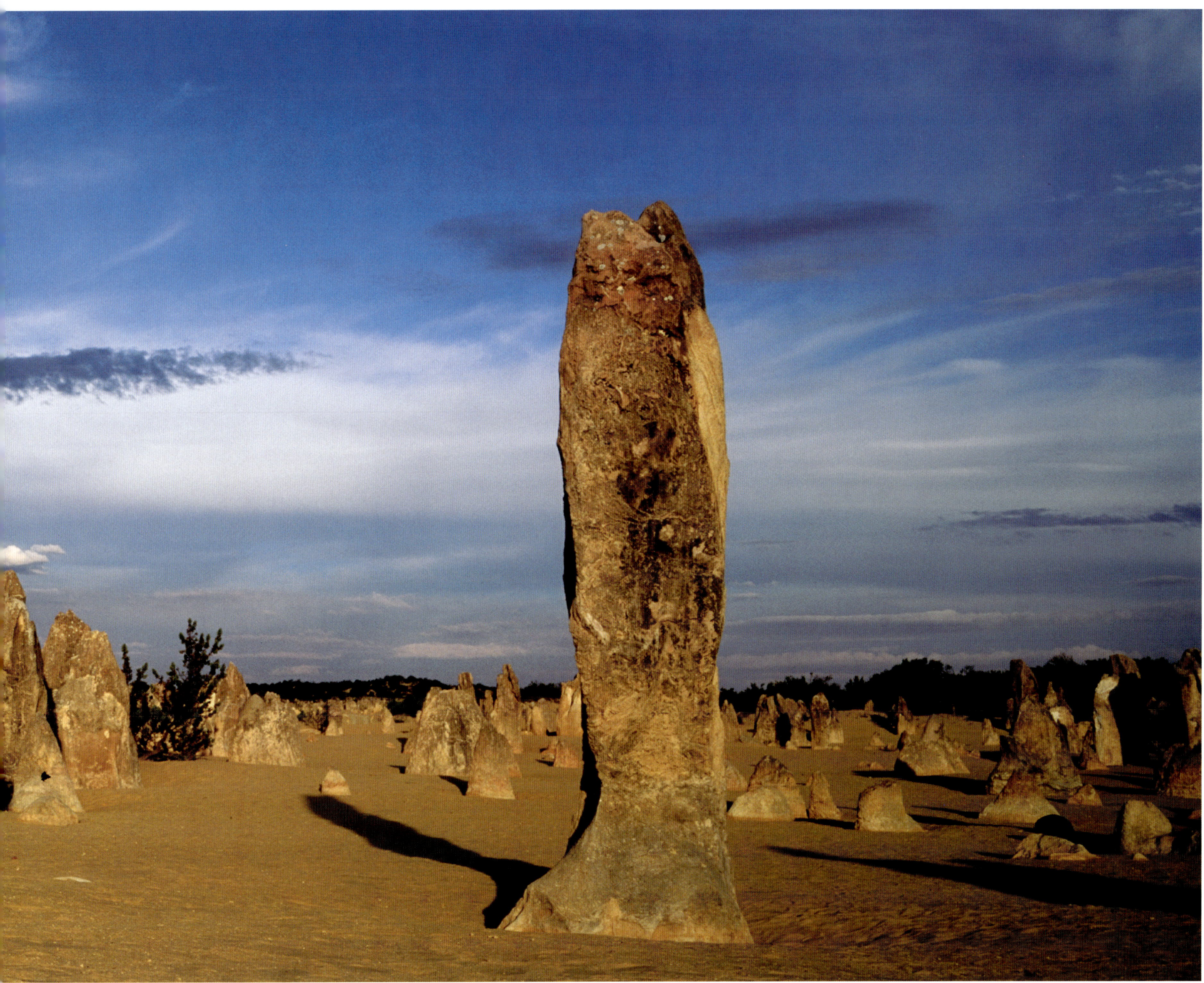

PAGES 110–111: Rajasthan is known in India as the "desert state" so it is unsurprising that there should be large herds of camels. These are paraded, traded and raced at the annual Pushkar Mela (mela = fair), which lasts for nine nights and ten days in November. The city of Pushkar is sacred to Hindus, who believe that the lake, which lies on the edge of the desert, was created by Lord Brahma himself. Here a herder brings a train of camels to the market for trading.
Lindsay Hebberd/Corbis

LEFT: The Pinnacles Desert lies within Australia's Nambung National Park, near the coastal town of Cervantes, and features thousands of these limestone monoliths, varying in height from several inches to over twenty feet. They are the roots of long-dead trees and shrubs, which have been covered and fossilized in a limestone jacket. In the course of time the loose sand has moved on, leaving the pinnacles exposed, but it appears that this cycle of exposure and burial may have been repeated at least twice, with the latest exposure taking place within the last three or four centuries.
Grenville Brown/fotoLibra

Right: The Lake Mungo National Park is situated in the southwestern corner of Australia's New South Wales, where conditions are harsh and drought almost endemic. One of its striking features is a lunette (ie, crescent-shaped) of orange and white dunes and rocky outcrops around part of what used to be Lake Mungo (long since dried up), which is designated with typical Australian humor as the "Walls of China."
Dave G. Houser/Corbis

Far Right: These monoliths in the Pinnacles Desert in Australia were first seen by exploring Dutch sailors in the 17th century. They thought they were the remains of some long-abandoned city.
Lorenzo Menghini/fotoLibra

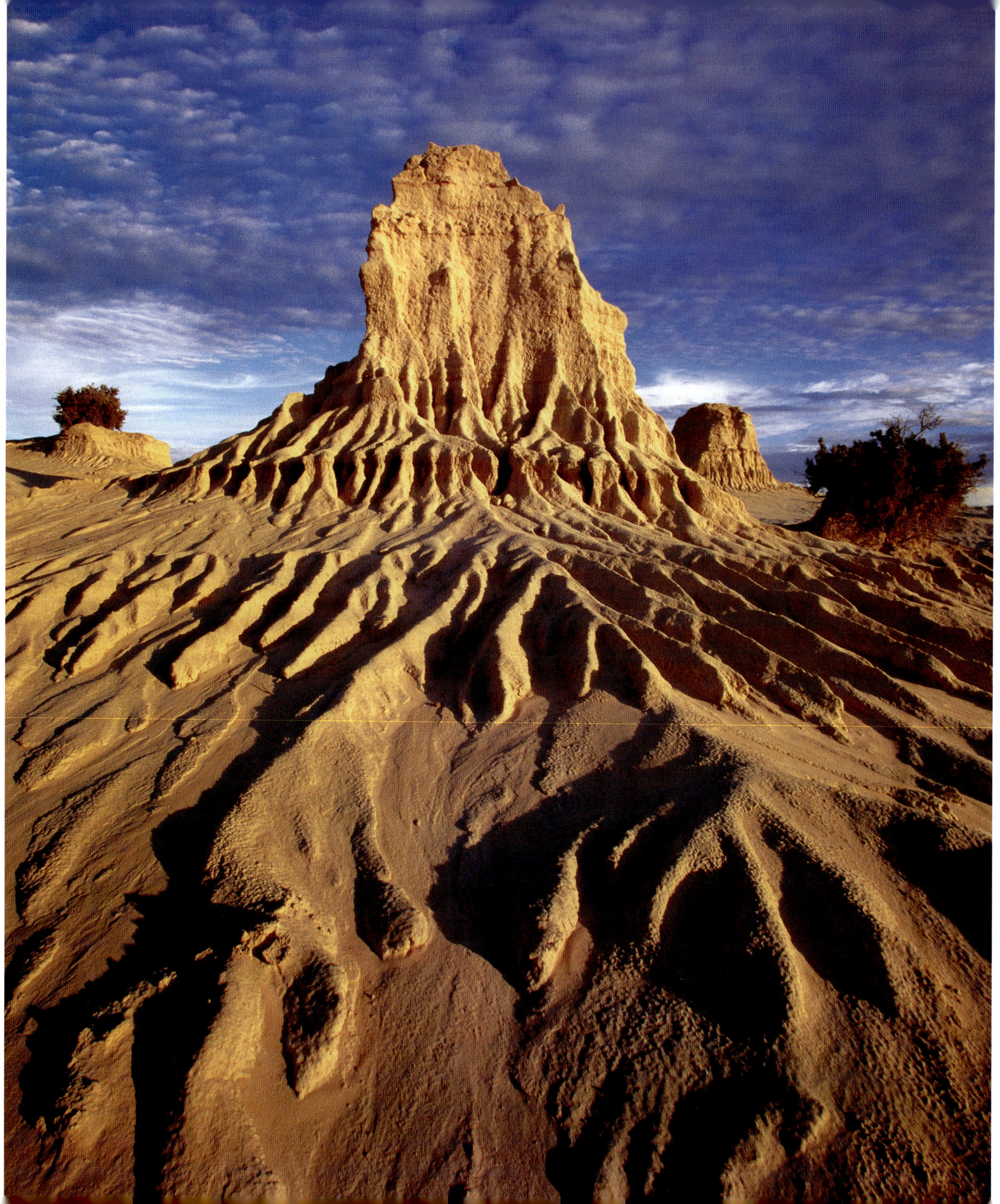

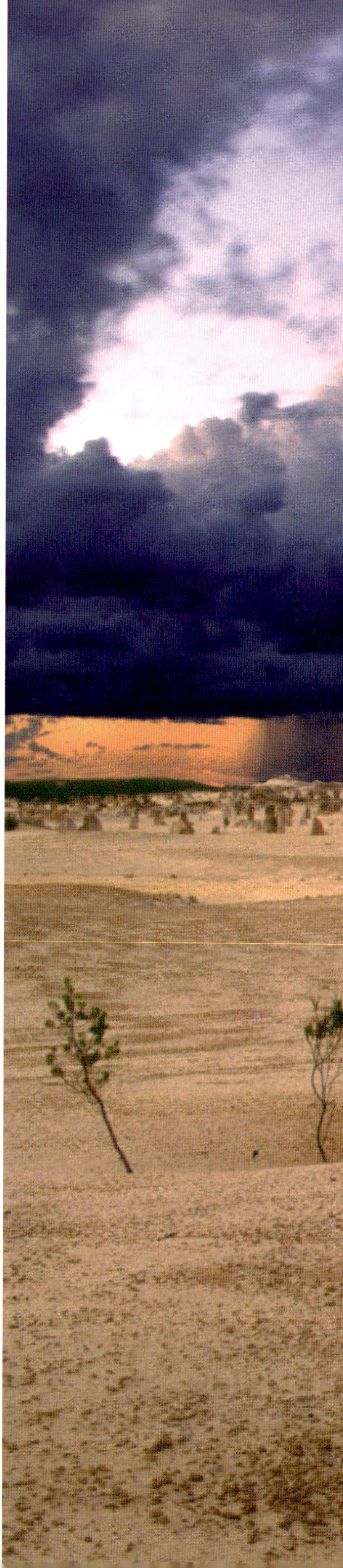

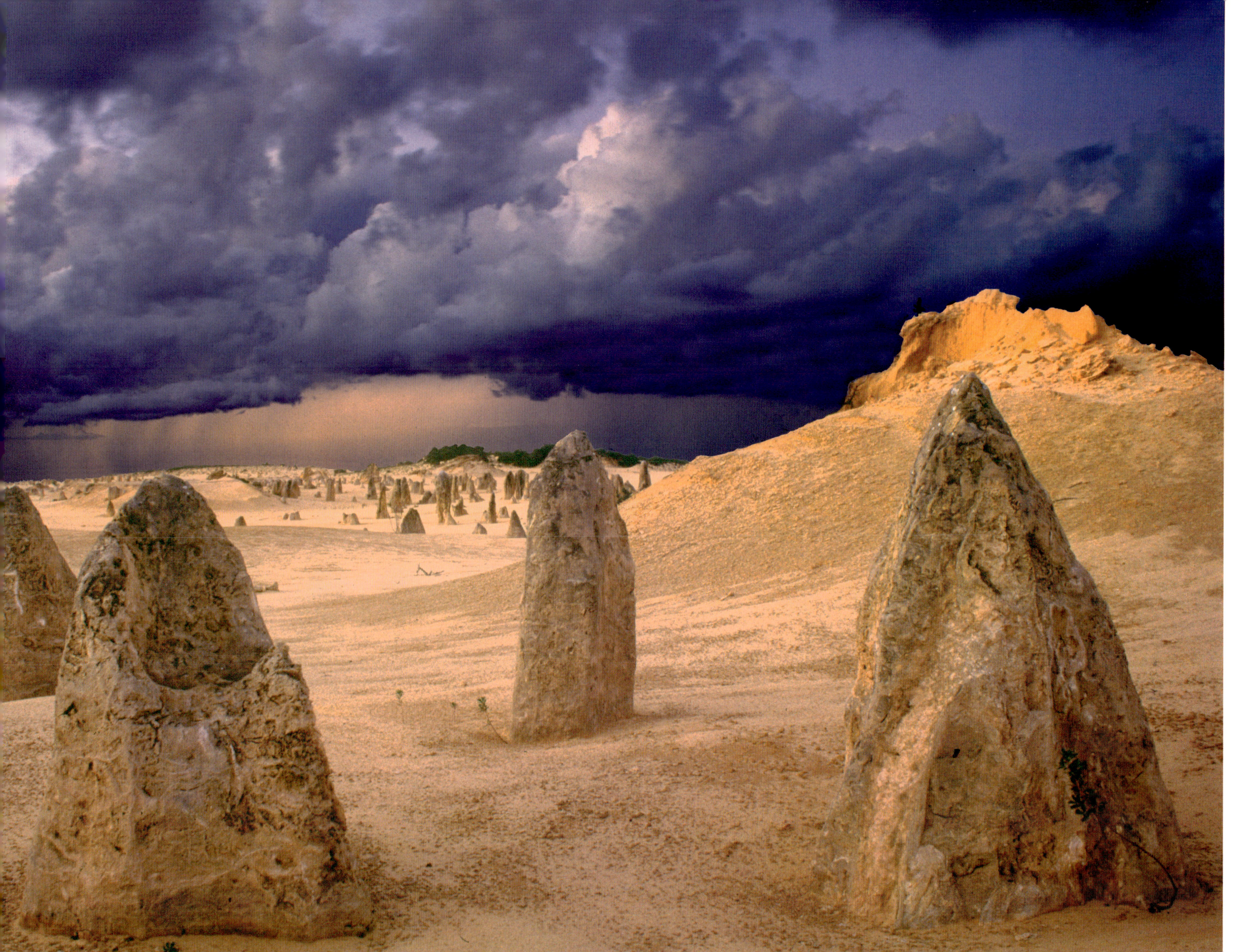

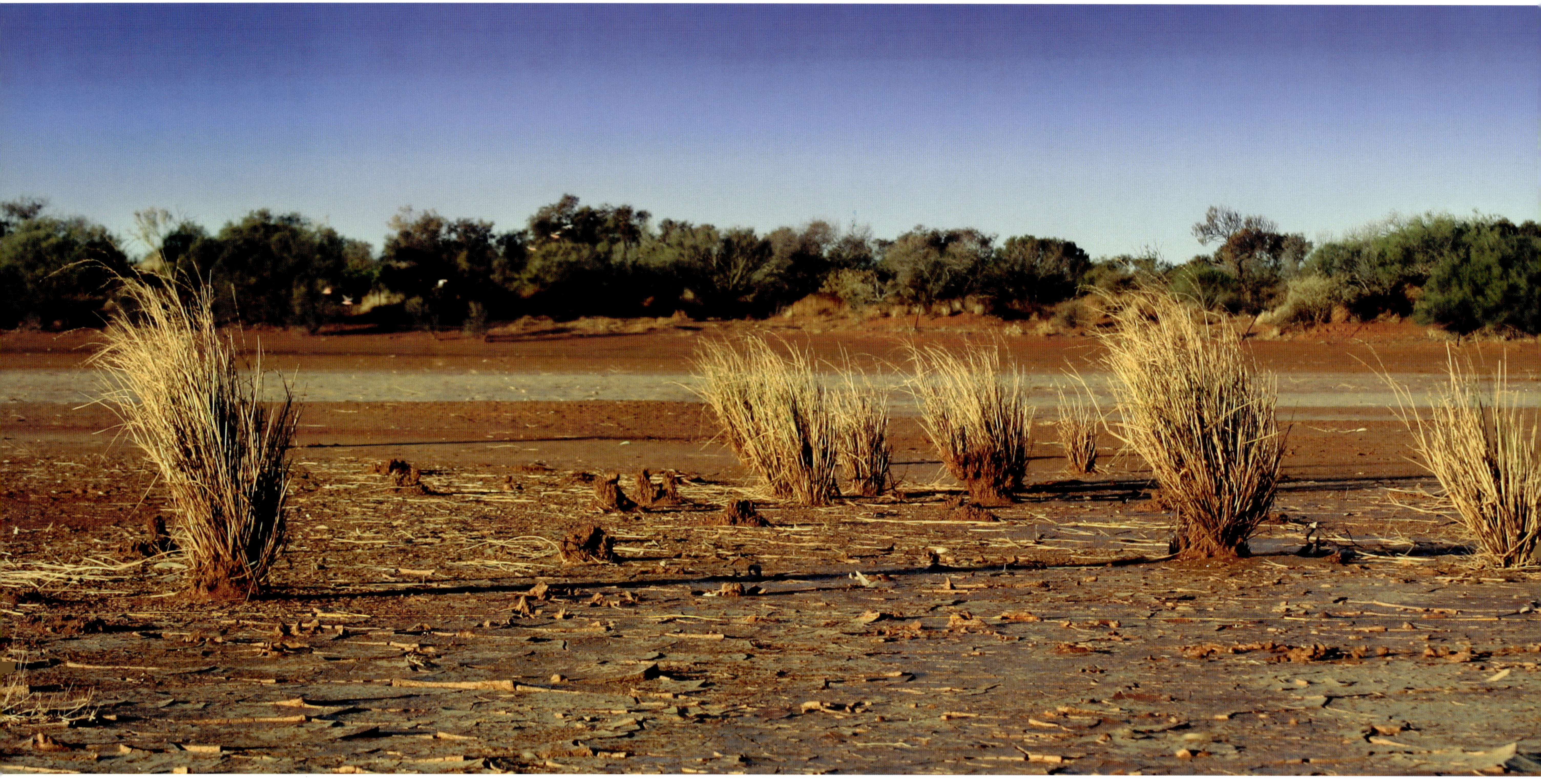

Above: The roadside on the Sir Charles Kingsford Smith Mail Run, where the clay has solidified and then cracked under the unrelenting heat of the desert sun. This road runs between Carnarvon (some 560 miles north of Perth in Western Australia) and Meekatharra and is named after a heroic Australian pioneer aviator, whose first job in the 1920s was to carry the mail along this route, although he mostly used an airplane rather than ride a horse through such a hostile environment. The official start of the route (or perhaps its end?) is at the municipal public toilet in Carnarvon.
Karl Monaghan/fotoLibra

Right: As seen here, Shelburne Bay on Cape York, Australia's most northerly peninsula, is blessed with an area of silica sand of the purest white. This is exceptionally beautiful, but it is also very attractive to the glass industry, and there is one mine that exports its product almost entirely to Japan. More mining companies want to move in and the situation has developed into a three-way contest between conservationists, government, and commercial interests. Local conservationists and the traditional Aboriginal owners have banded together, but they face an uphill fight.
Thad Samuels Abell II/Getty Images

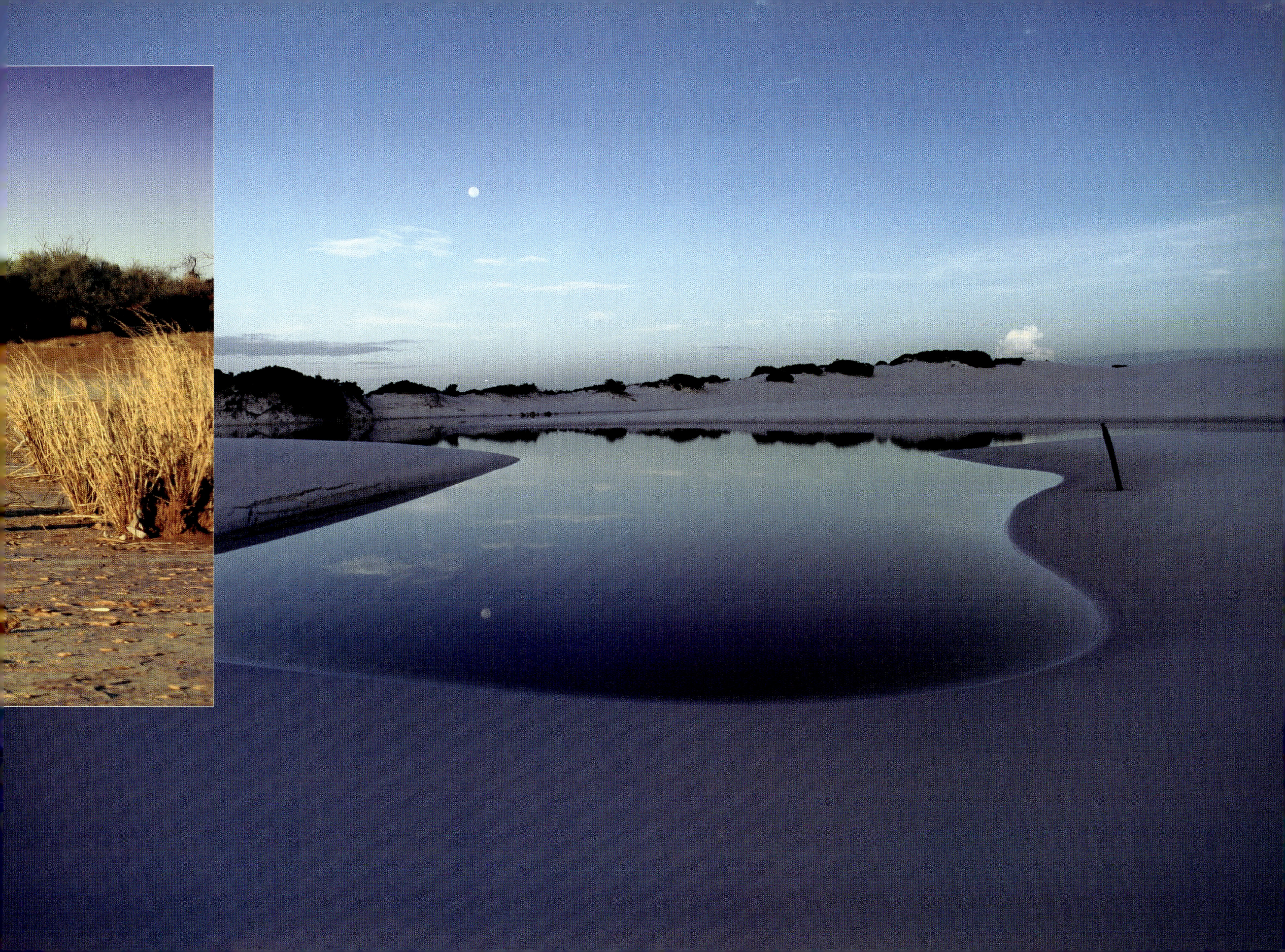

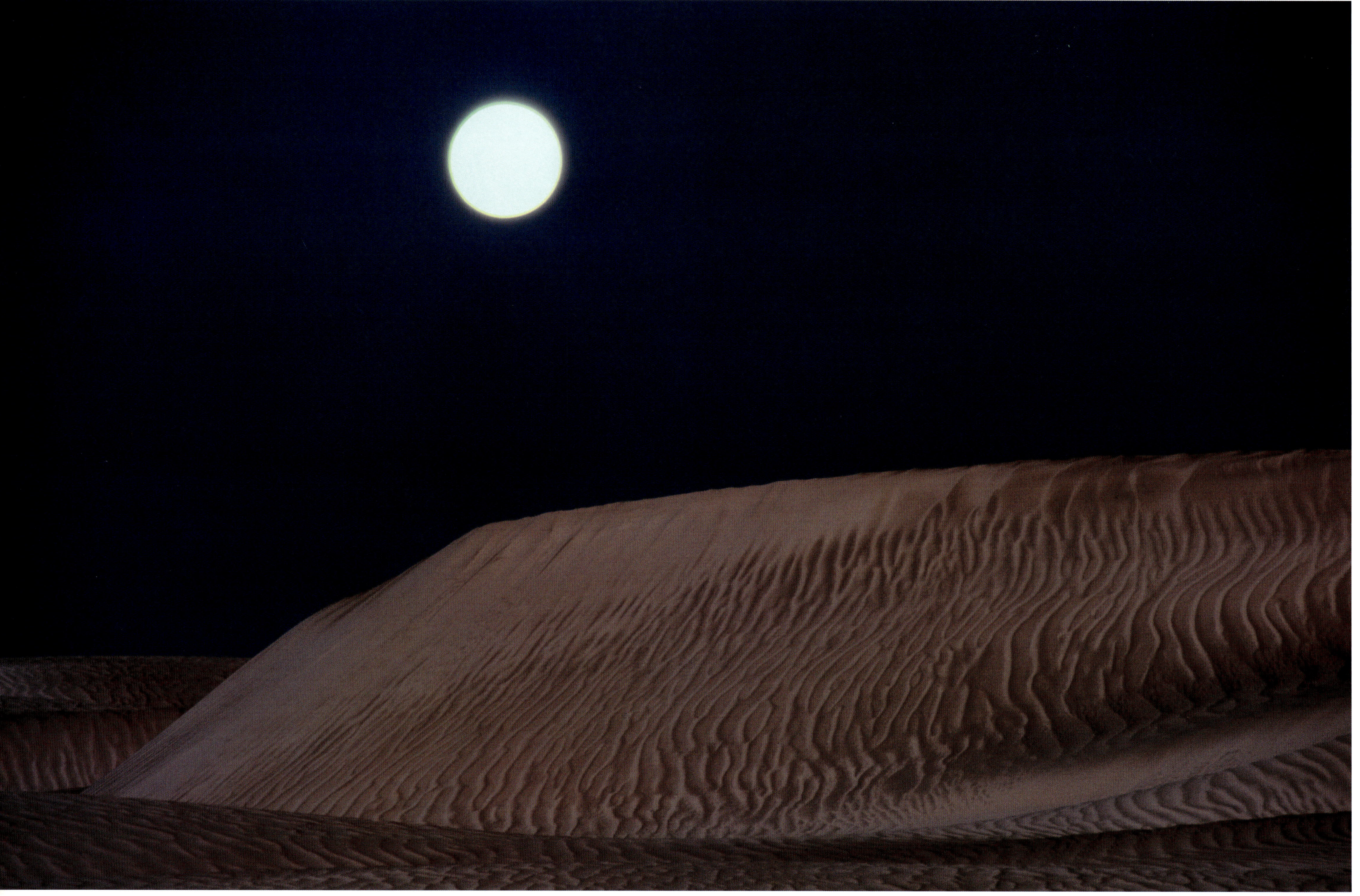

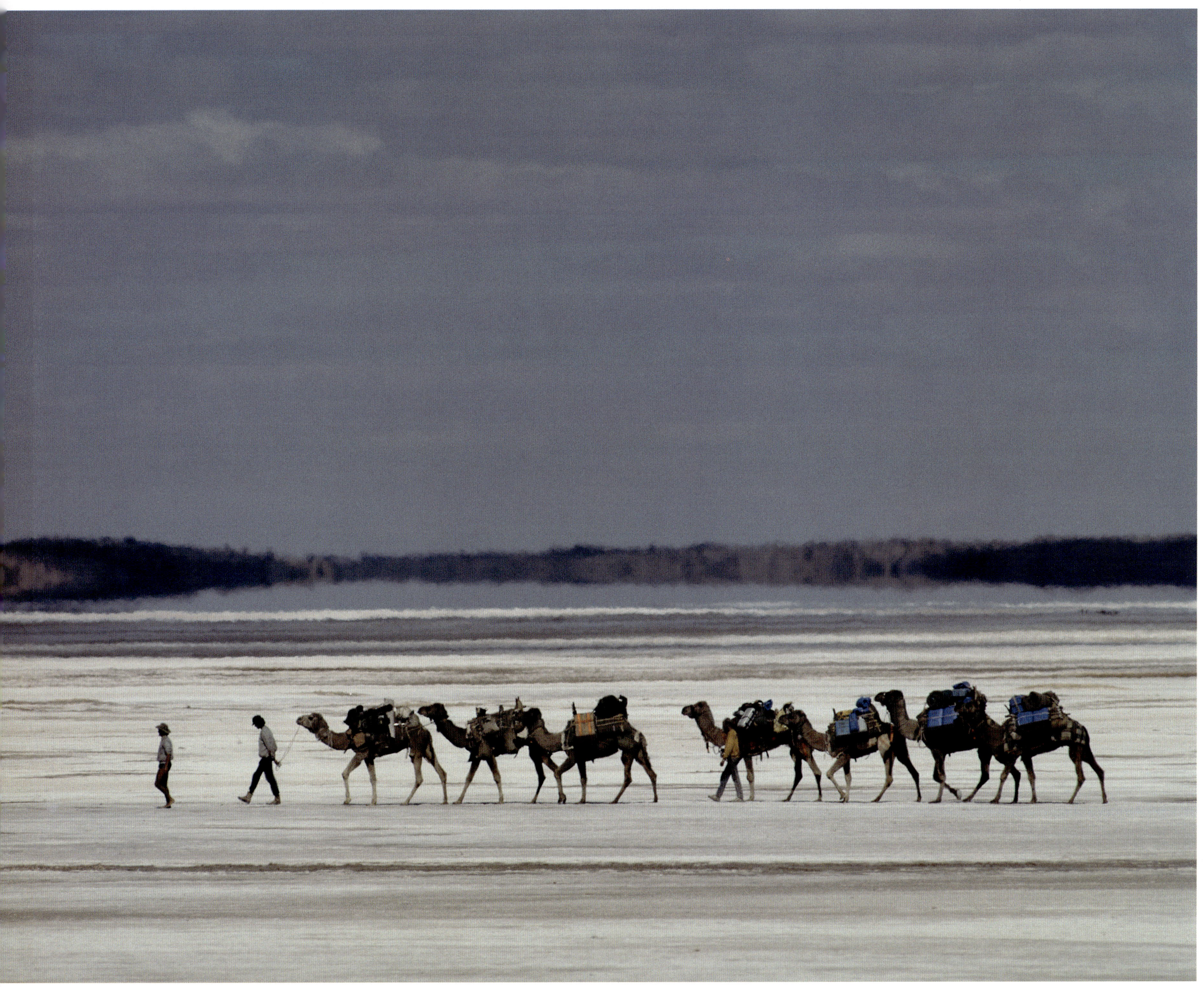

Far Left: Moonlight over St. Clair Bay on the South Australian coast brings out the quantity and patterns of the rills on the sand dunes in a way never quite achieved in the daytime.
Medford Taylor/Getty Images

Left: It was realized early in Australian history that camels would be valuable in exploration and in supplying outlying farms, mines, and settlements, and the first animal arrived in October 1840. Some 10,000 were imported and others were bred in local studs, while most cameleers came from Afghanistan. The introduction of the automobile and the expansion of the railways put an end to the need for camels and from the 1920s onwards their numbers have decreased rapidly, although some remain, and these shown here were seen crossing a dried salt lake in the Simpson Desert in 2003.
Medford Taylor/Getty Images

Page 120: This is only one of hundreds of such objects in an area of Australia's Northern Territory known as "The Devils Marbles." These are huge, red-colored granite boulders up to 23 feet in diameter, many of which, like this one, seem to be precariously balanced at the edge of a larger rock. The site is considered sacred by Australia's Aboriginal people, who believe them to be the eggs of the Rainbow Serpent.
L. Clarke/Corbis

Page 121: Ownership of Uluru (formerly Ayer's Rock) was returned to the Aboriginal people by the Australian government in 1985. Unfortunately, the handover document included the stipulation that tourists be allowed to climb to the summit, something that upsets the Aboriginal owners to whom it is a sacred site, especially as the climbing route crosses one of their "dreaming tracks." Despite signs asking them not to do so, many tourists attempt the climb, although most give up part way and several die each year, usually from heart failure or exhaustion.
Yann Arthus-Bertrand/Corbis

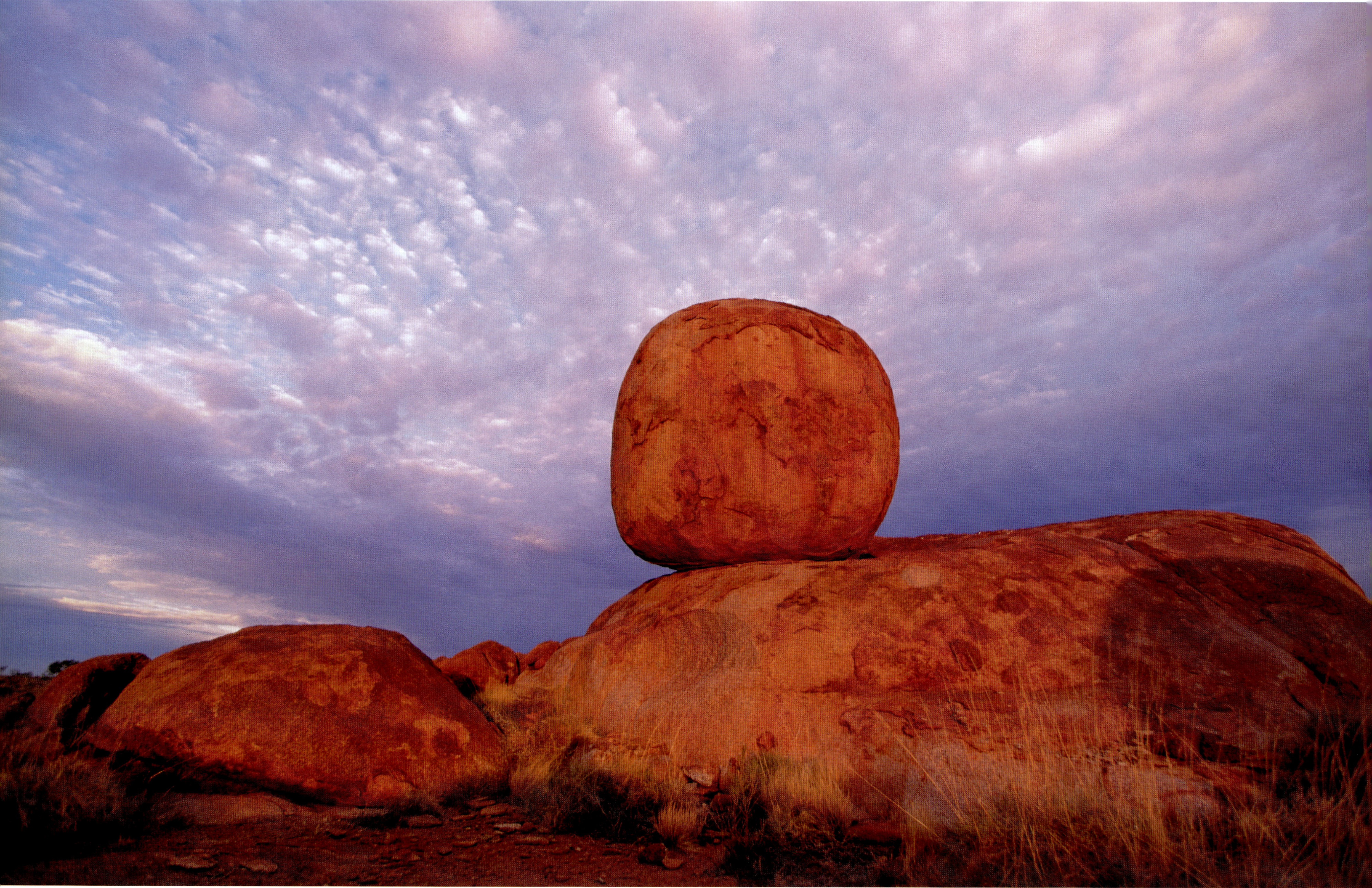

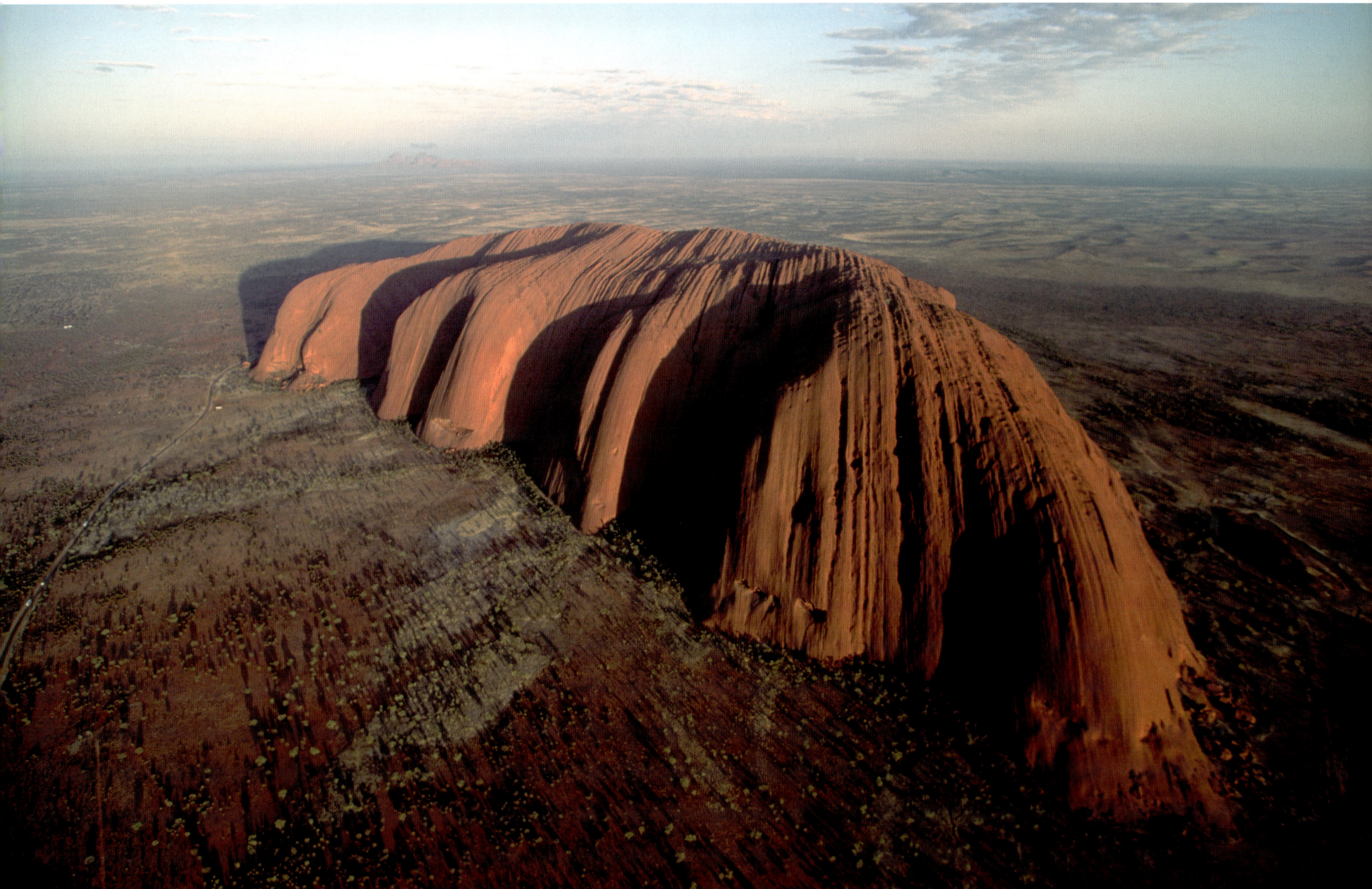

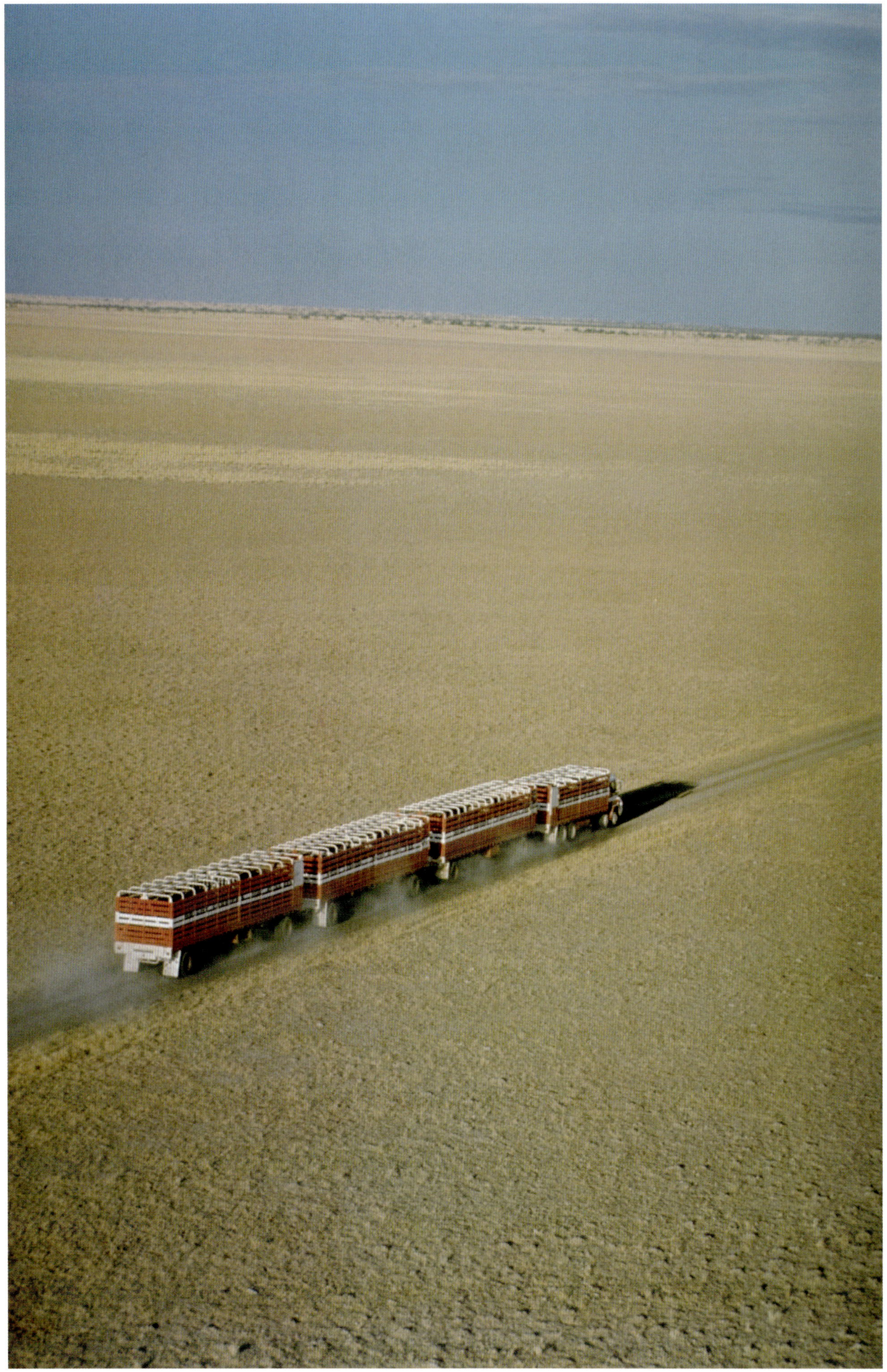

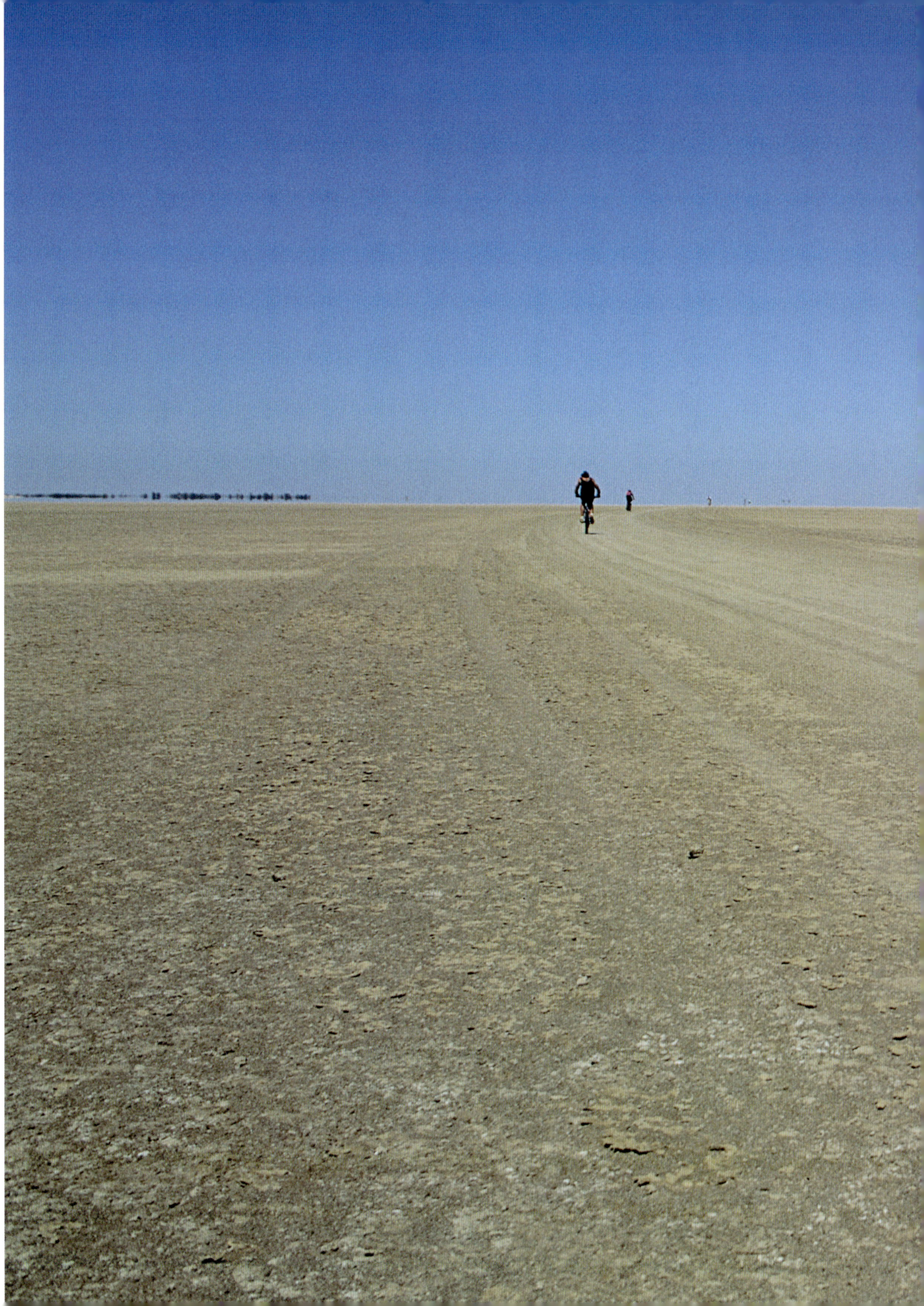

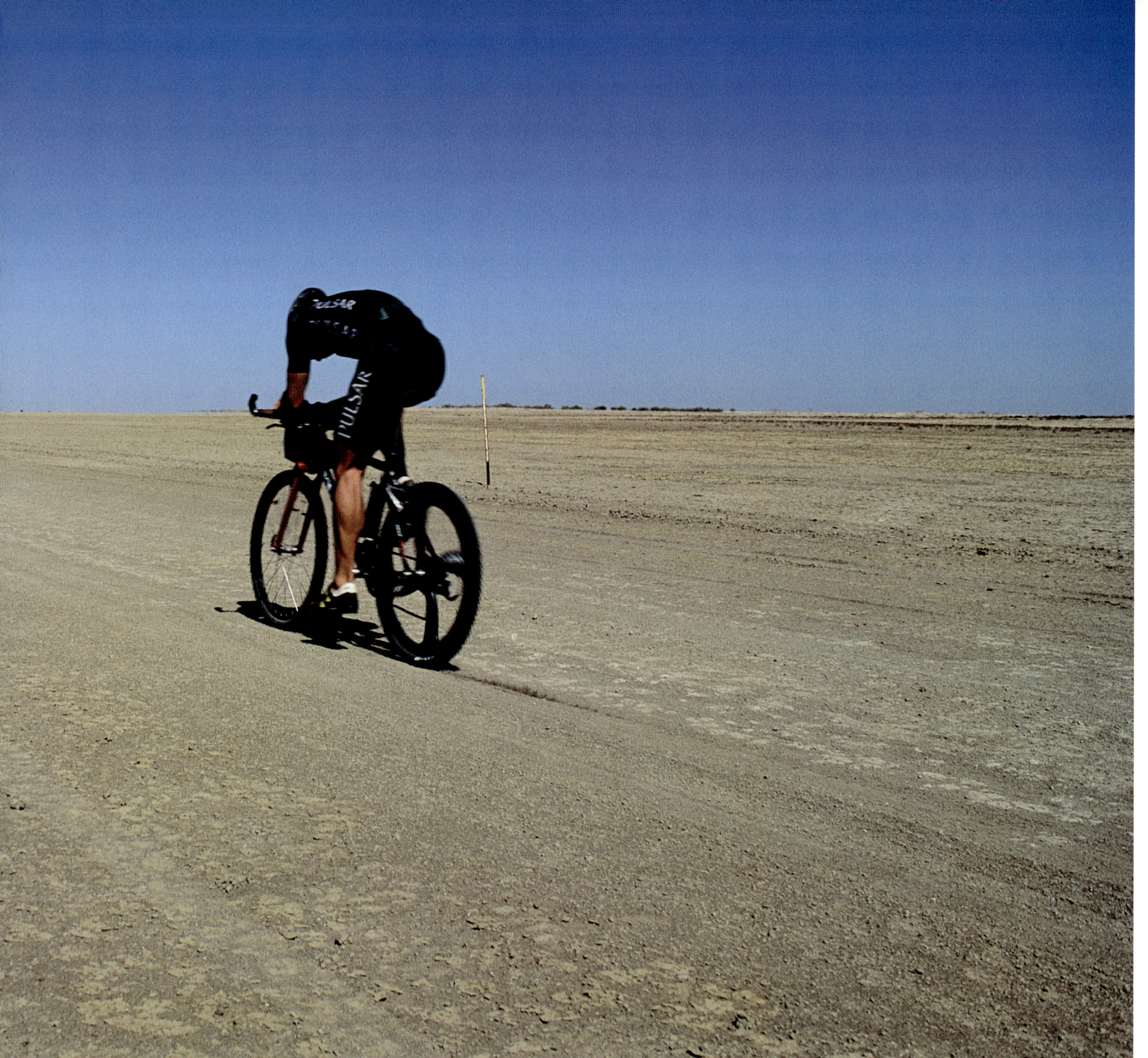

Far Left: Cattle road trains such as this are a common feature of modern life in the Australian "outback." These rigs consist of a large and very powerful diesel prime-mover drawing up to four trailing vans, which in many cases have twin decks, enabling one unit to move hundreds of cattle over great distances across the wild and inhospitable desert.
Douglass Baglin/Corbis

Left: Australia's Crocodile Trophy race takes place annually in Northern Queensland and takes the riders over some 1,243 miles of the "outback" from Townsville to Port Douglas. It is reputed, with considerable justification, to be the hardest, longest and most grueling bicycle race in the world.
David Adamas/ The Cover Story/Corbis

DESERT FLORA & FAUNA

Just as humans living in deserts have had to adjust to the conditions around them, so, too, have animals, reptiles, insects, trees, vegetables, and flowers. Sometimes animals adjust quite quickly, as, for example, the horses that were abandoned in the Namib and North American Deserts, but usually it takes millennia to develop the techniques necessary for desert survival. Thus, for example, the sidewinder snake has a unique method of moving that minimizes contact with the hot sand, while the camel can store sufficient water to enable it to survive many days without replenishment.

Desert plants are lean and mean, optimizing their leaf and root structures for survival with very little water. One of the most extraordinary sights occurs when an apparently barren stretch of sand receives only a very small amount of rain, whereupon seeds, like those of the Australian Billybutton, whose existence was neither noticed nor suspected, turn into flowers that bloom, covering vast stretches in the most beautiful colors. Within days the flowers fade, the petals fall, the stems wither, and all is as before, except that a new batch of seeds is lurking in the sand, awaiting the next brief shower of rain.

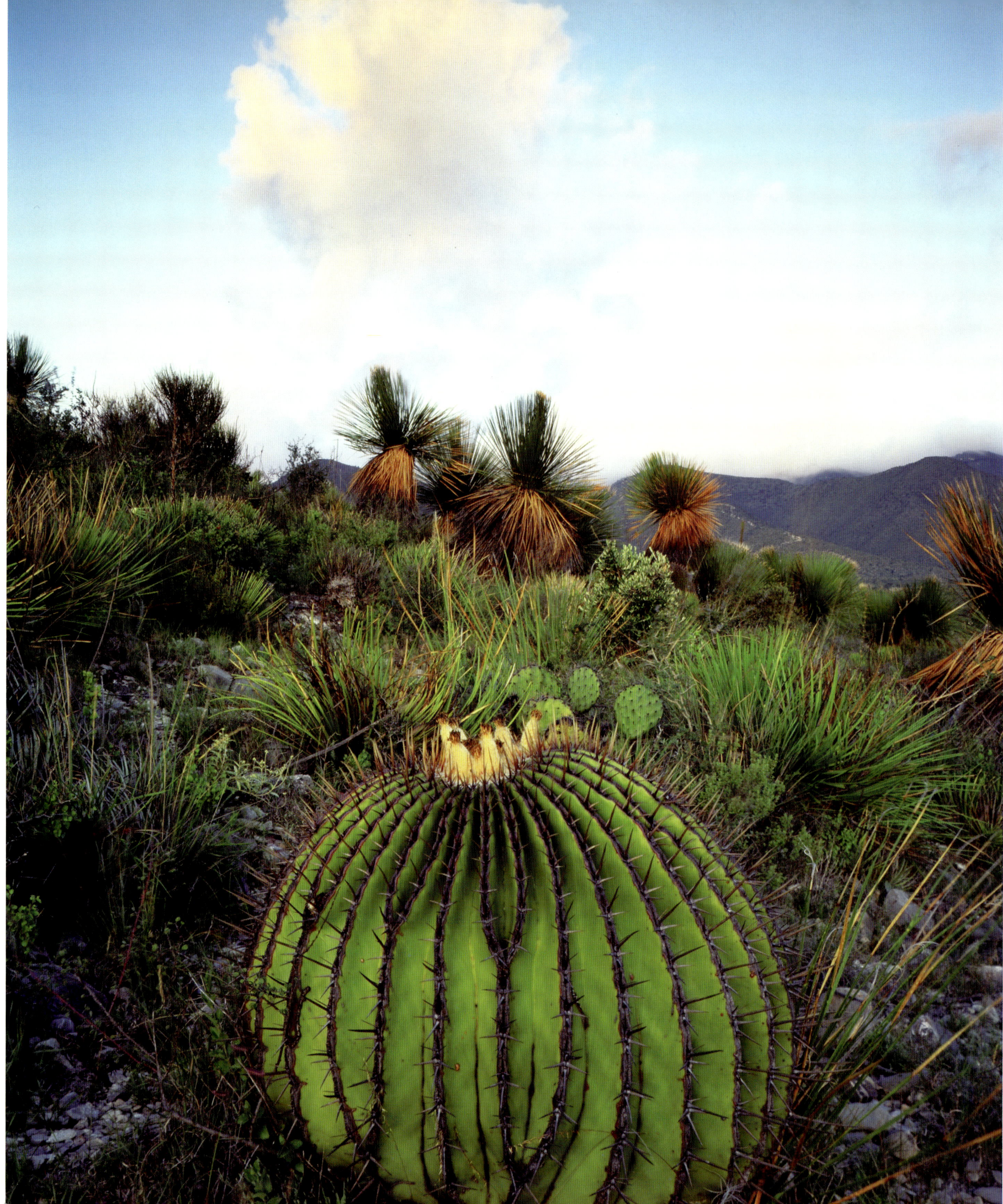

Right: A fishhook barrel cactus in the Chihuahan Desert in Mexico's Estado de Nuevo León. This is the largest type of cactus in the American Southwest and has up to twenty-five vertical ribs in order to present the maximum possible surface area. Its survival techniques include very slow growth, a massive but very shallow root system, and the ability to store large quantities of water.
George H. H. Huey/Corbis

Pages 126–127: Chile's Pan de Azúcar National Park covers some 106,000 acres of the Atacama Desert region and extends from its famous beaches on the Pacific coast inland to this 2,600 feet high plateau. The area is rich in plant life, such as these cacti, and is home to the world's smallest cactus—so tiny that guides have to point it out to doubting tourists.
Hubert Stadler/Corbis

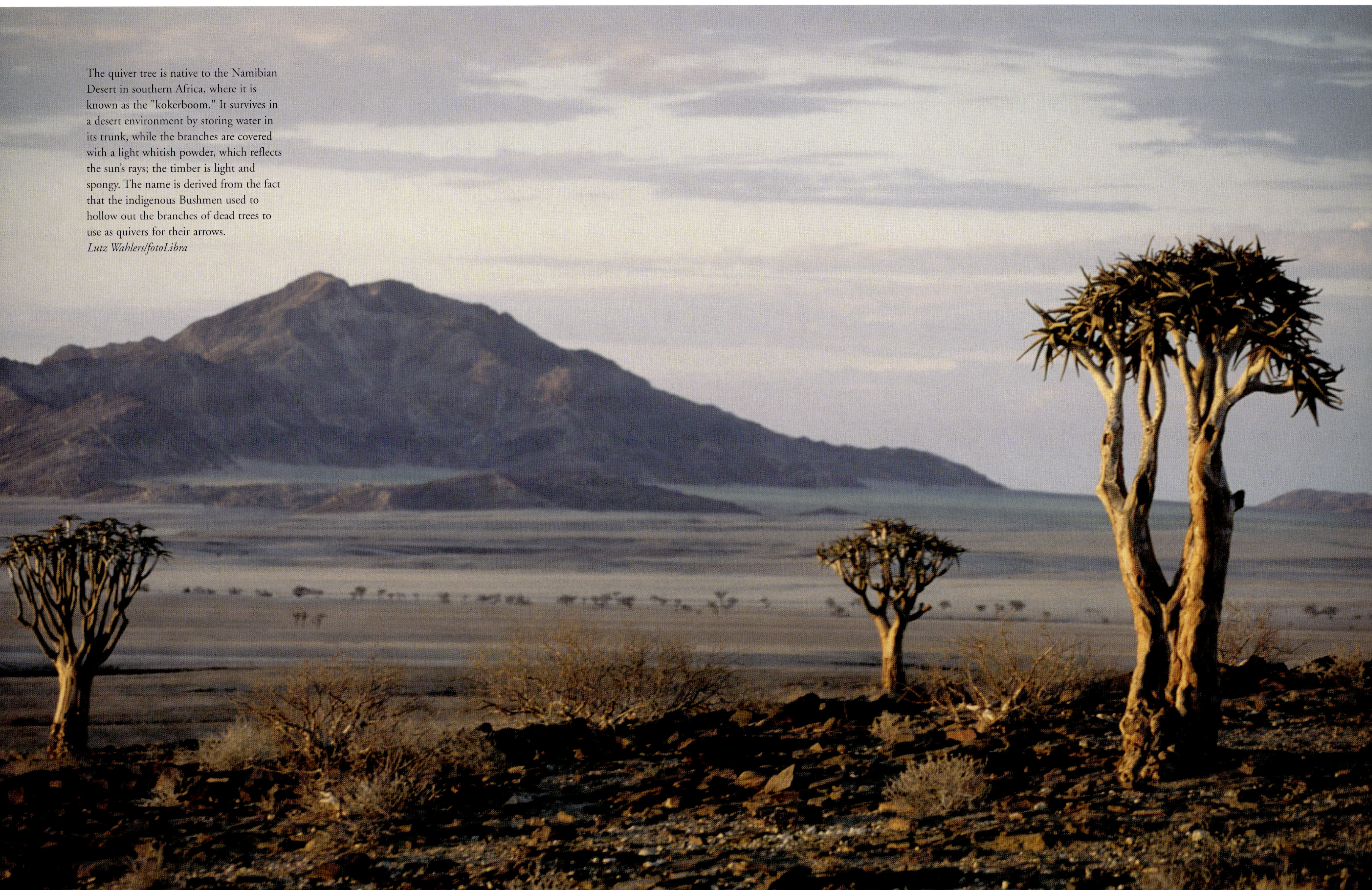

The quiver tree is native to the Namibian Desert in southern Africa, where it is known as the "kokerboom." It survives in a desert environment by storing water in its trunk, while the branches are covered with a light whitish powder, which reflects the sun's rays; the timber is light and spongy. The name is derived from the fact that the indigenous Bushmen used to hollow out the branches of dead trees to use as quivers for their arrows.
Lutz Wahlers/fotoLibra

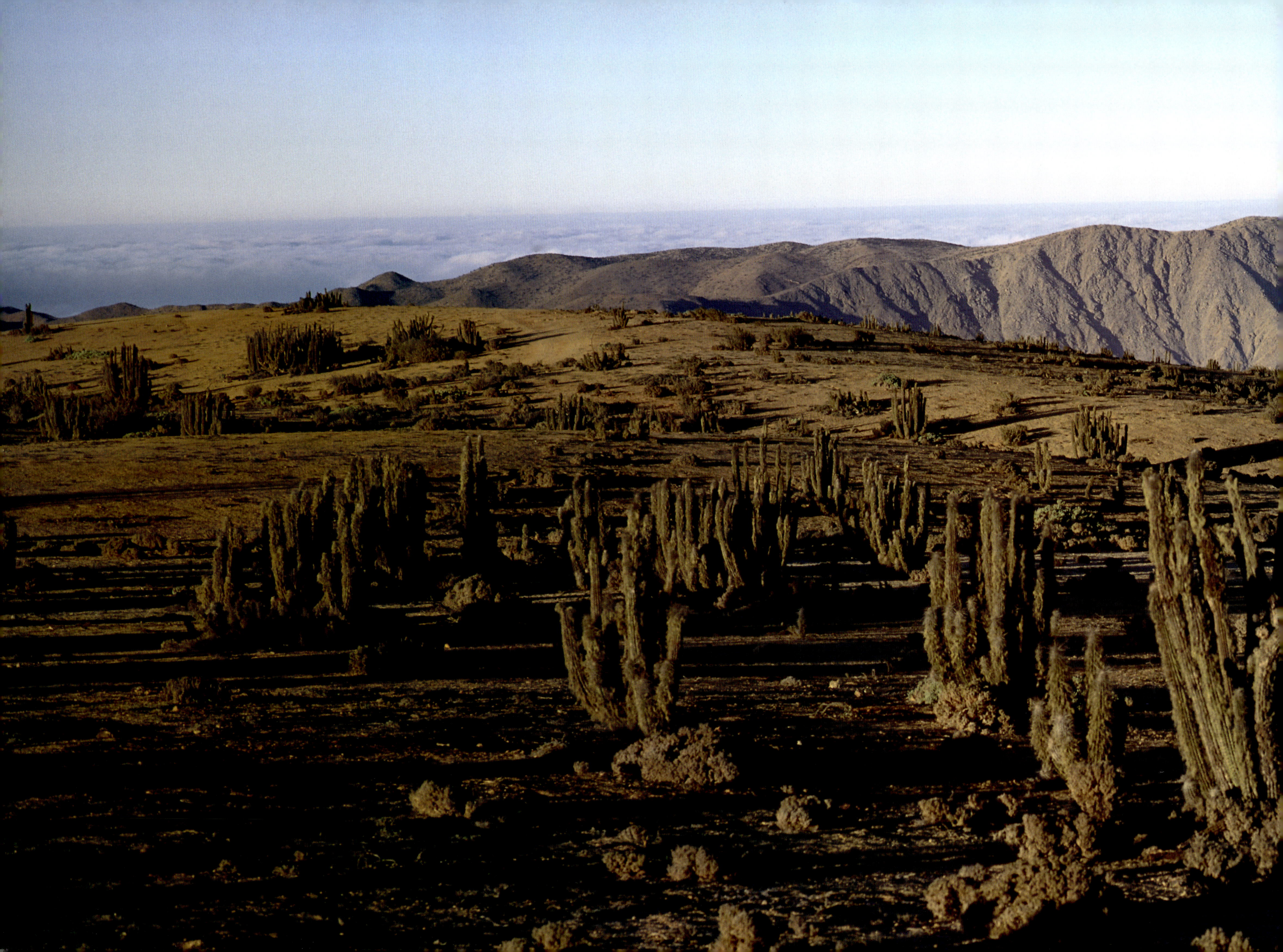

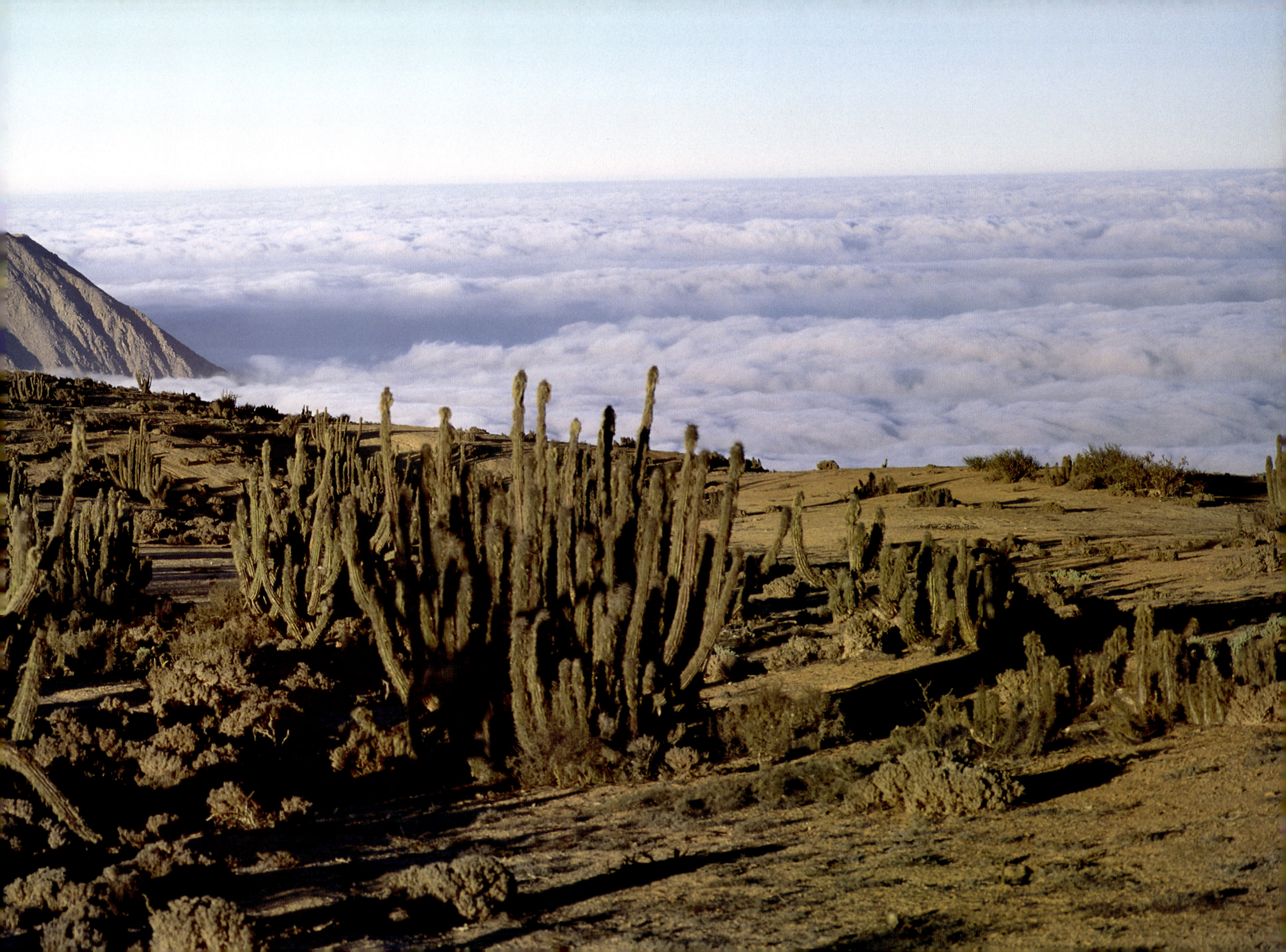

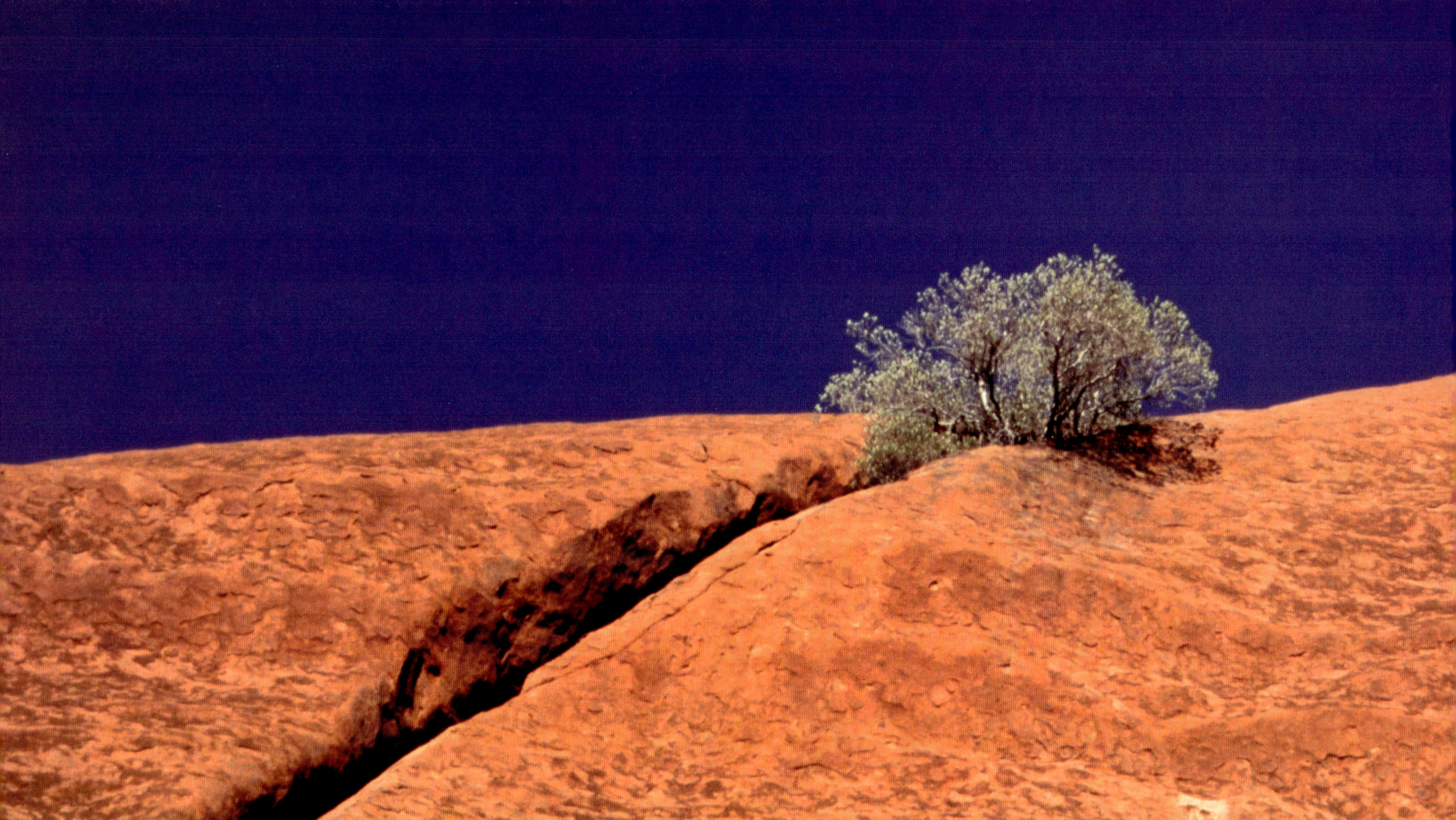

Above: The ability of plants to survive in the desert environment is awe-inspiring. They can put down roots in places such as this crack on Mount Uluru (Ayer's Rock) in Australia, where logical reasoning would indicate that they do not have the remotest chance of survival.
Amanda Raby/fotoLibra

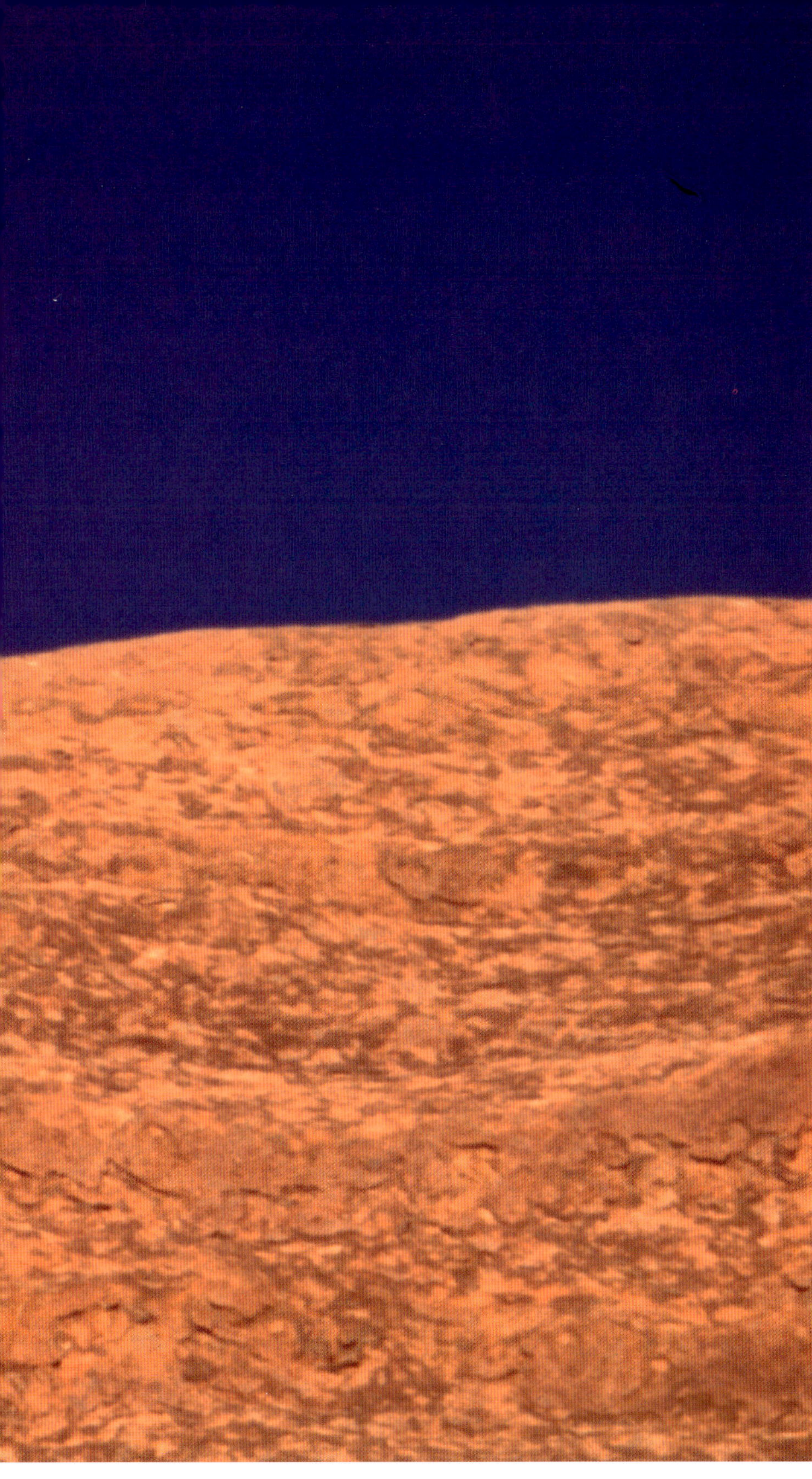

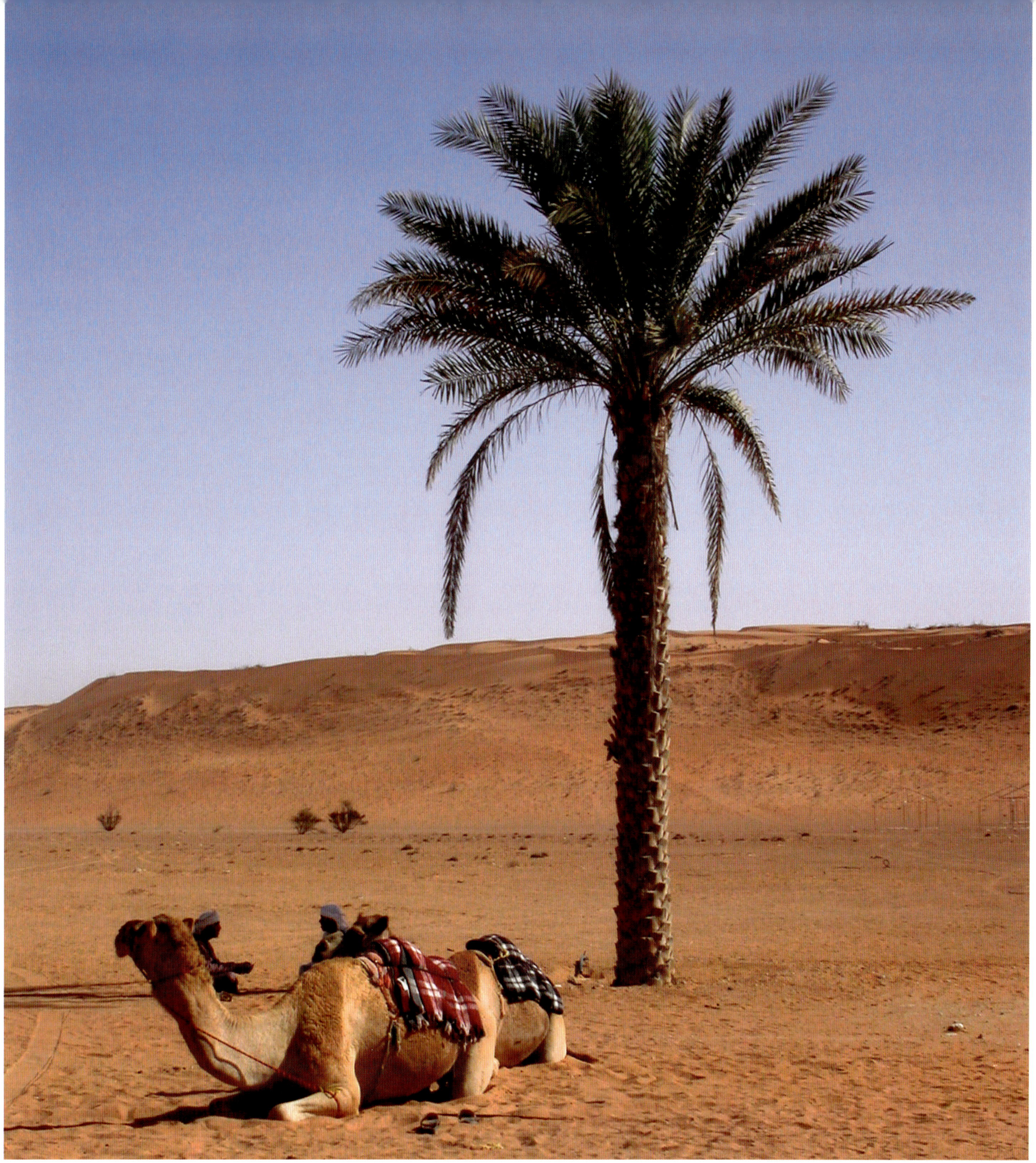

Right: The westerner's traditional picture of the desert, with a pair of camels, a lone palm, some low bushes in the distance, sand stretching to the horizon, and the sun beating down from a cloudless sky. All that is missing is a company of soldiers of the French Foreign Legion advancing down the side of the dune. *Simon Butler/fotoLibra*

RIGHT: The cholla cactus is found in most of North America's desert regions, these being in the Joshua Tree National Park, a 794,000-acre facility created in 1994, which embraces the Mojave and Colorado Deserts. Also in this picture is a solitary Joshua Tree, so named by the Mormon pioneers, who believed it to be a sign of Joshua from the Old Testament, beckoning them on towards the Promised Land.
Nigel Henbrey/fotoLibra

FAR RIGHT: The saguaro cactus has a very tall stem, some 18 to 24 inches in diameter, usually with upward curving branches, resulting in the archetypical image of a cactus, seen in so many Western movies. It is found in the Sonoran Desert of extreme southeastern California, southern Arizona, and adjoining northwestern Mexico.
Joanna B. Pinneo/Getty Images

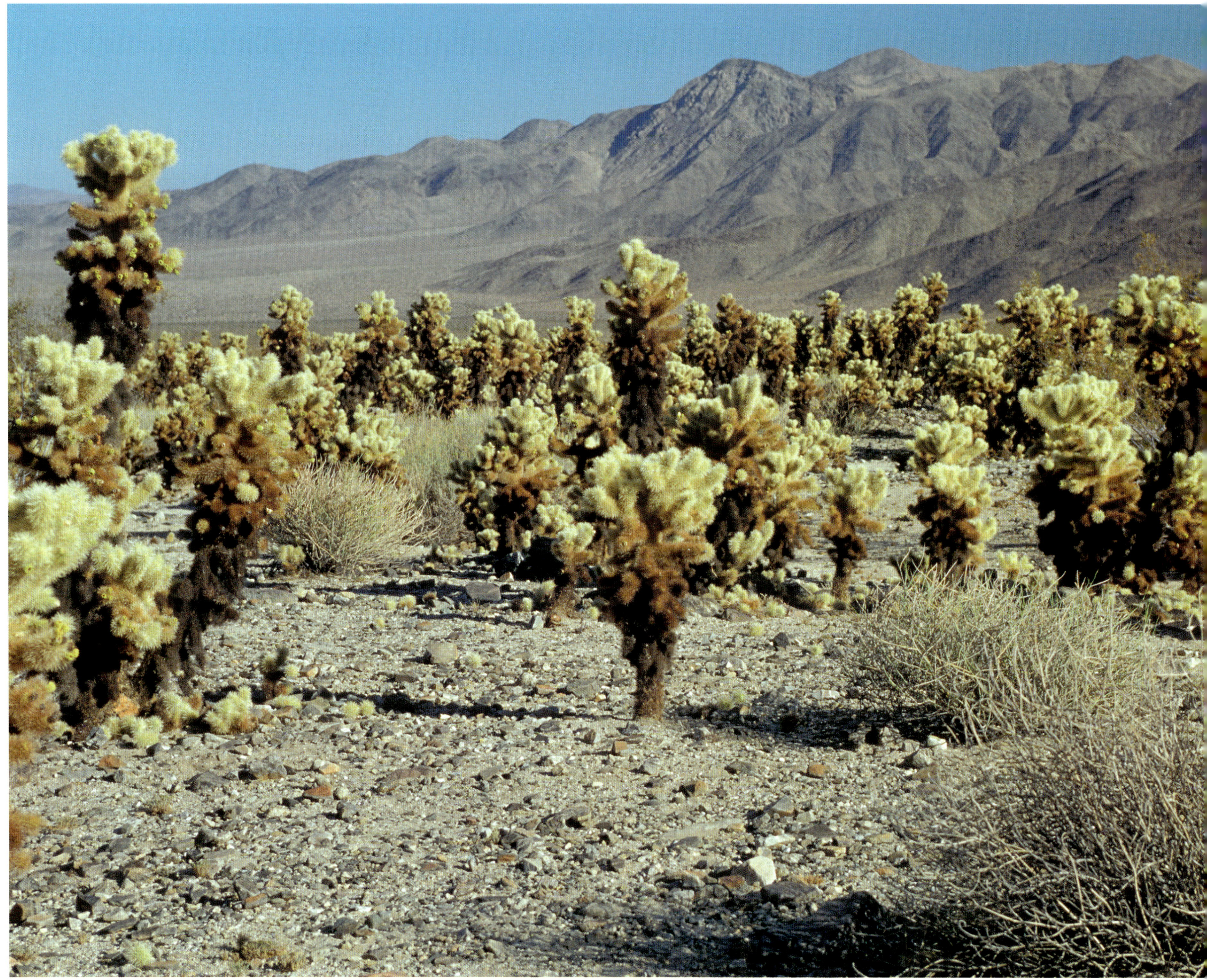

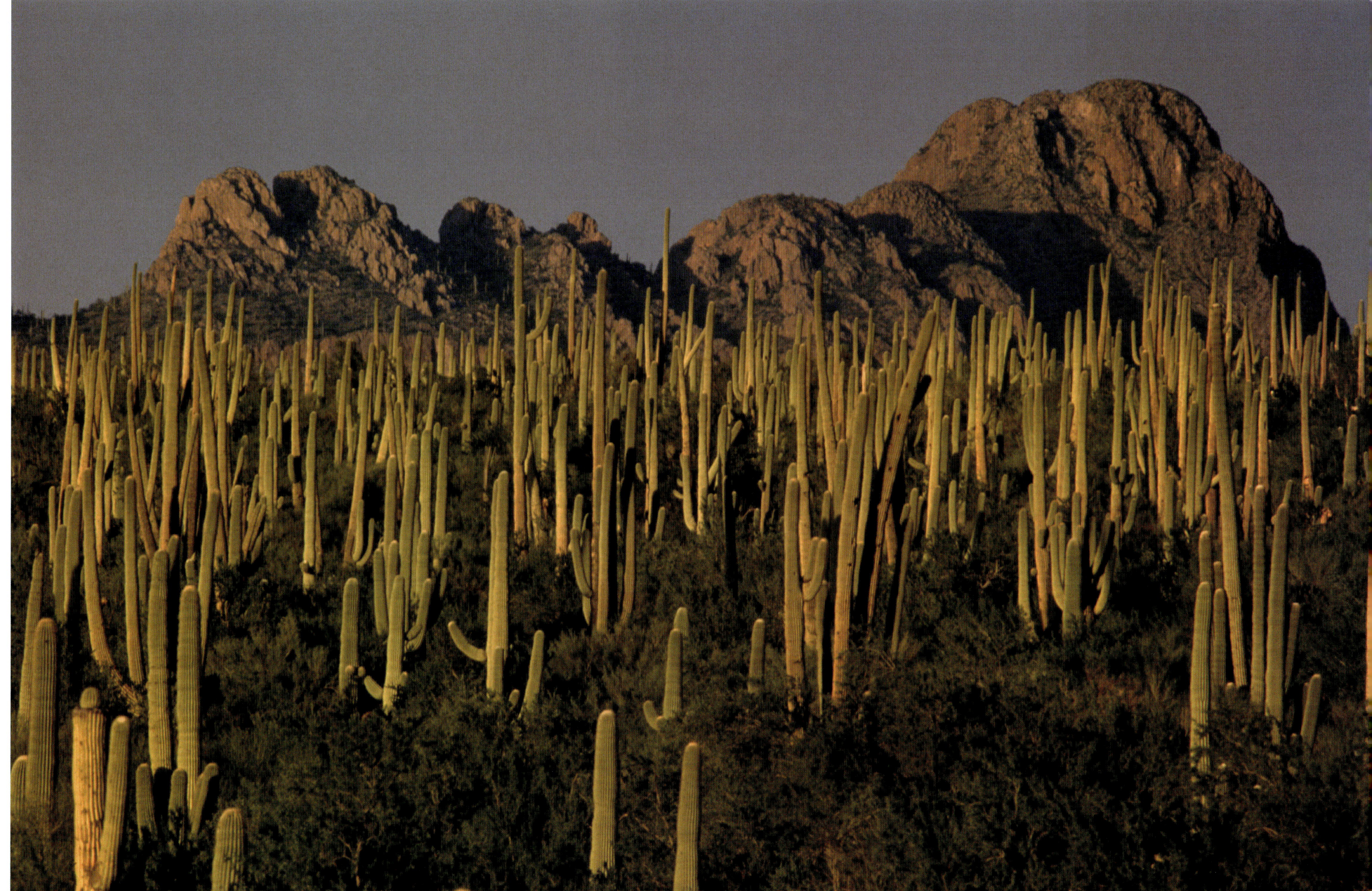

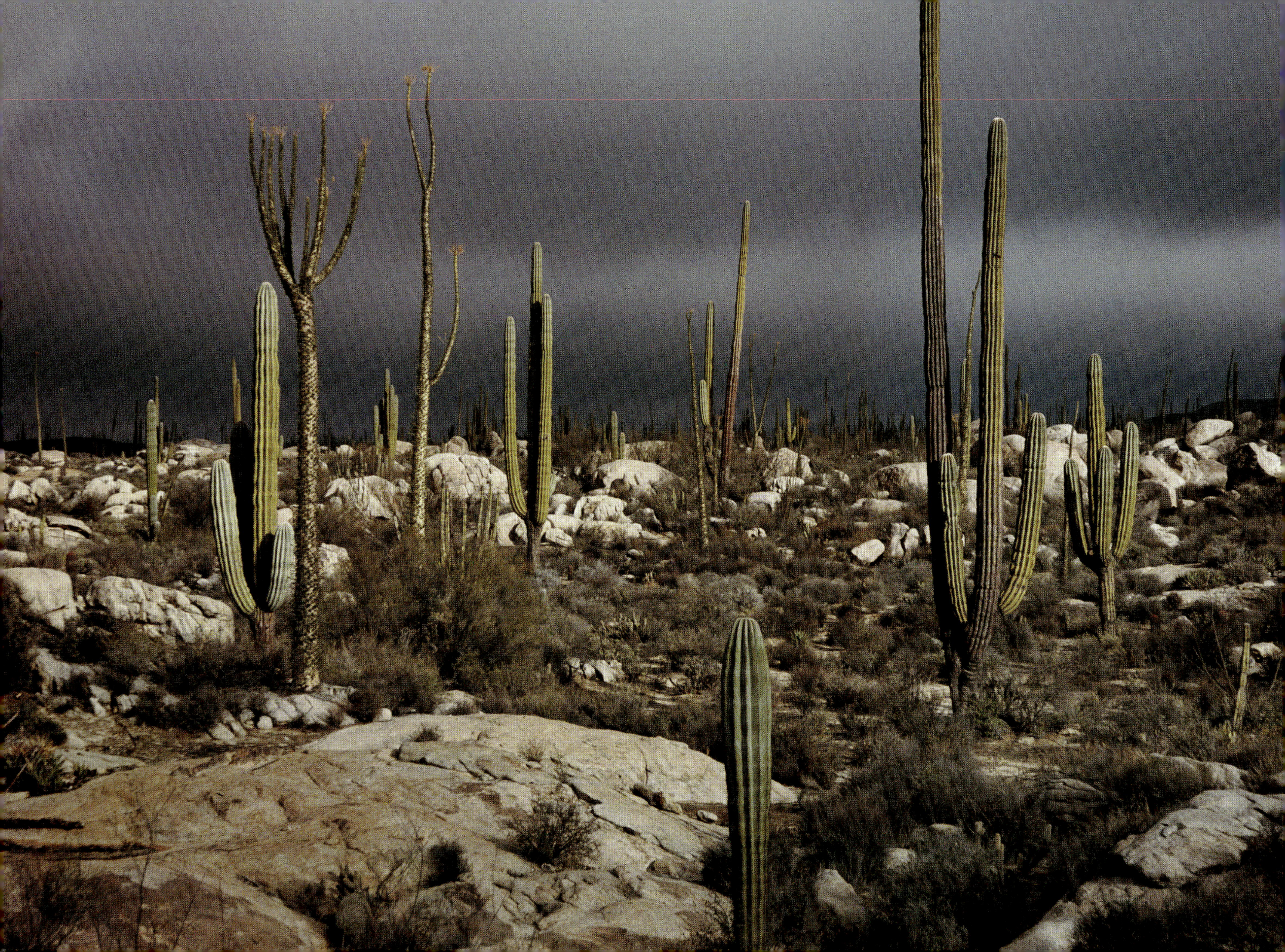

Left: The cardón cactus, the world's largest cactus, is very tall with vertical ribs, which perform photosynthesis through the skin, thus having no need for leaves. The boojum tree has no leaves, either, and appears lifeless. When first seen in 1922 its discoverer found it so very unusual that he exclaimed, "It must be a boojum," referring to a mythical creature in Lewis Carroll's book *The Hunting of the Snark.* The two are often found together on Mexico's Baja Peninsula.
Stephen Sharnoff & Sylvia Dunn/Getty Images

Right: As with so many desert flowers, the seeds of the Australian Billybutton daisy remain dormant in the sand, waiting for a tiny drop of rain to start the process by which they will grow and bloom at a very rapid rate. Then their moment—and the rain—having passed, they die in the heat and wither, as here, but their seeds will lie in the sand, waiting for their moment to come again.
Medford Taylor/Getty Images

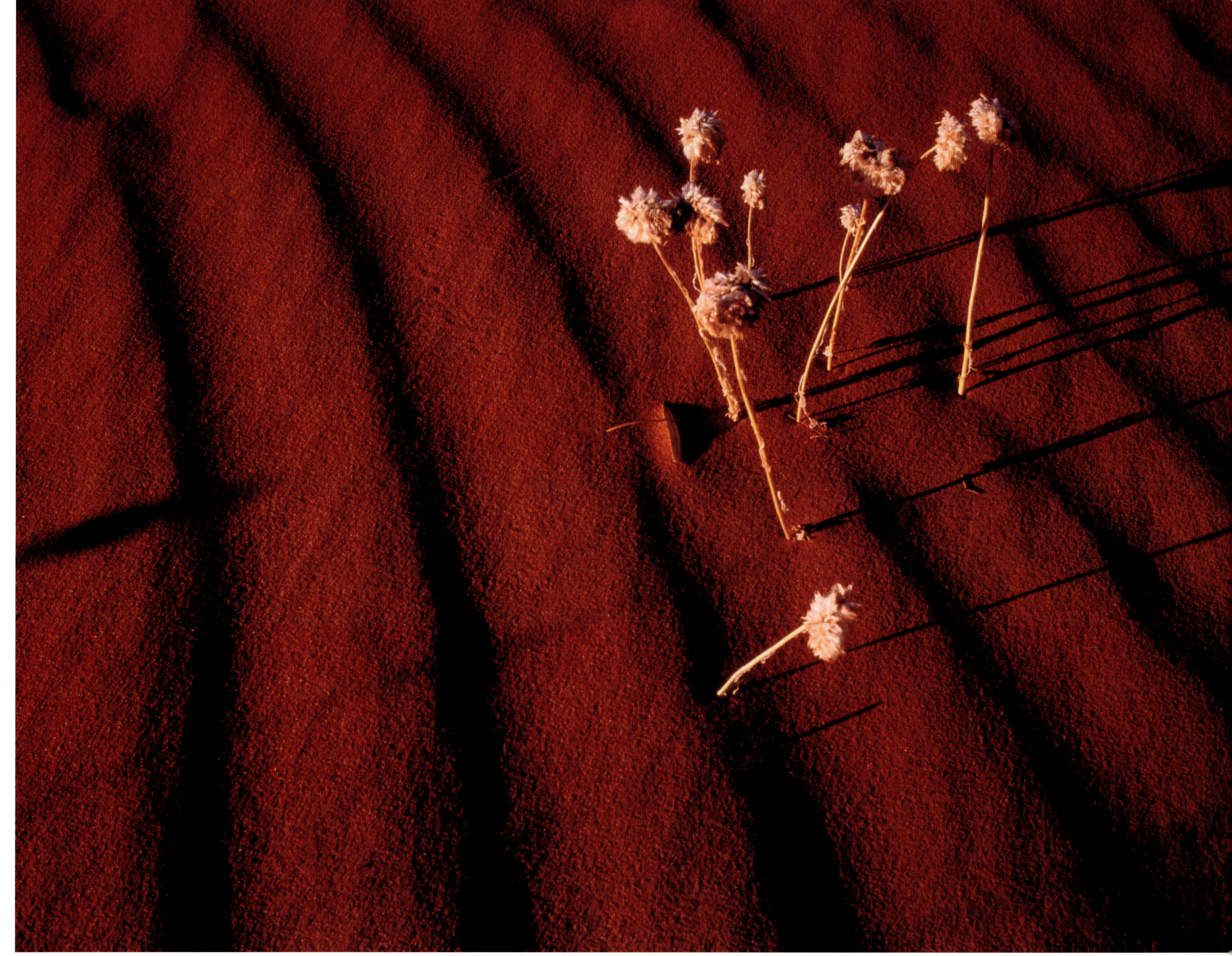

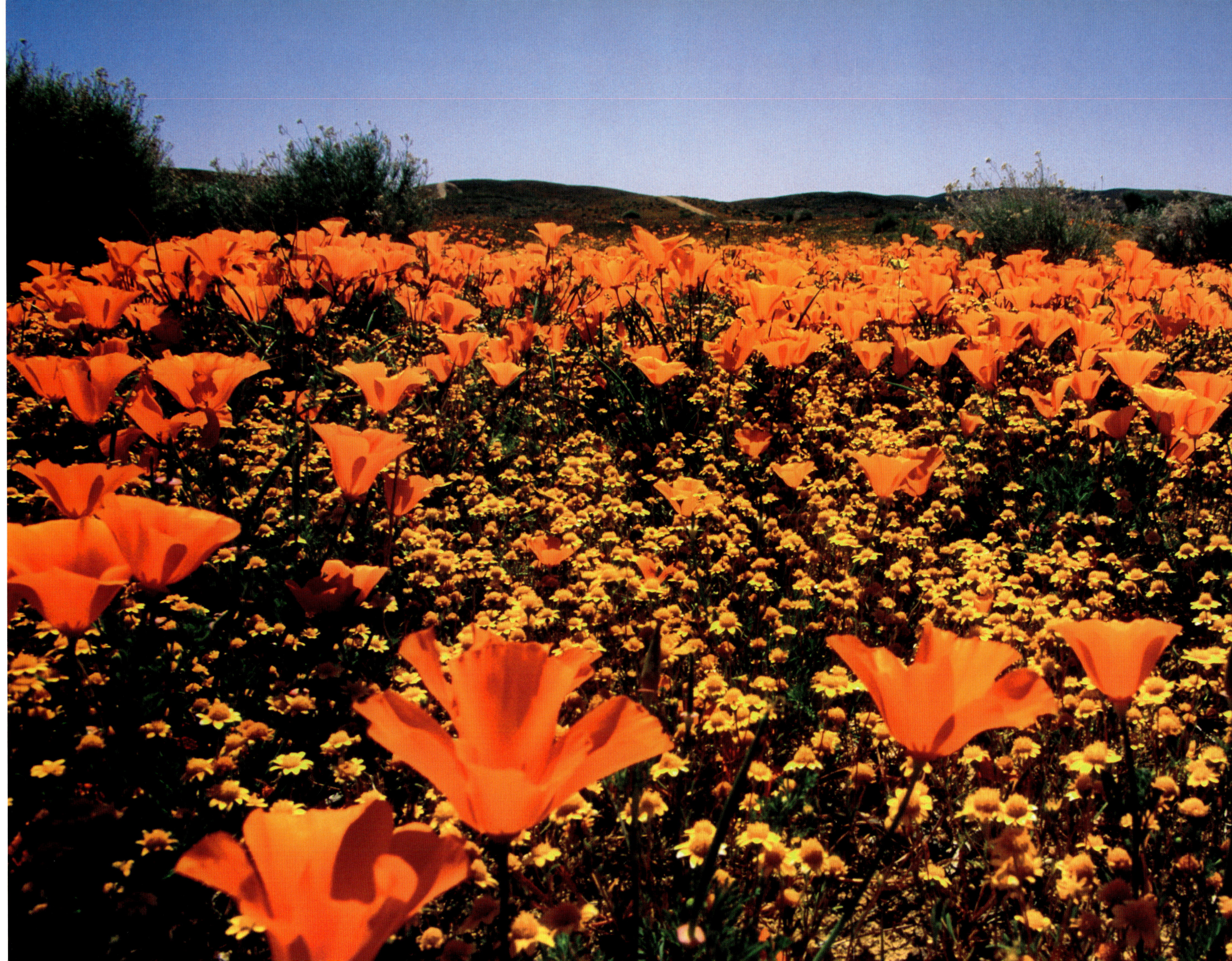

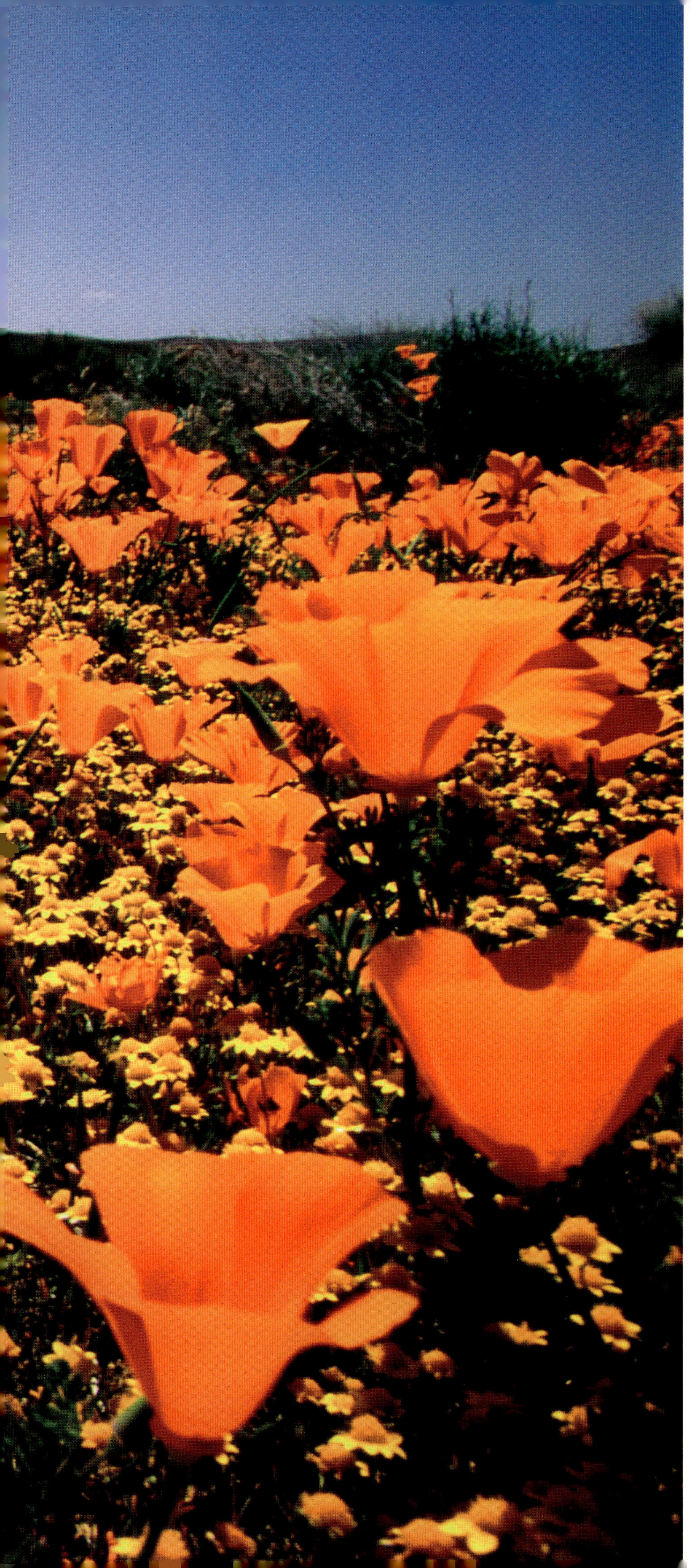

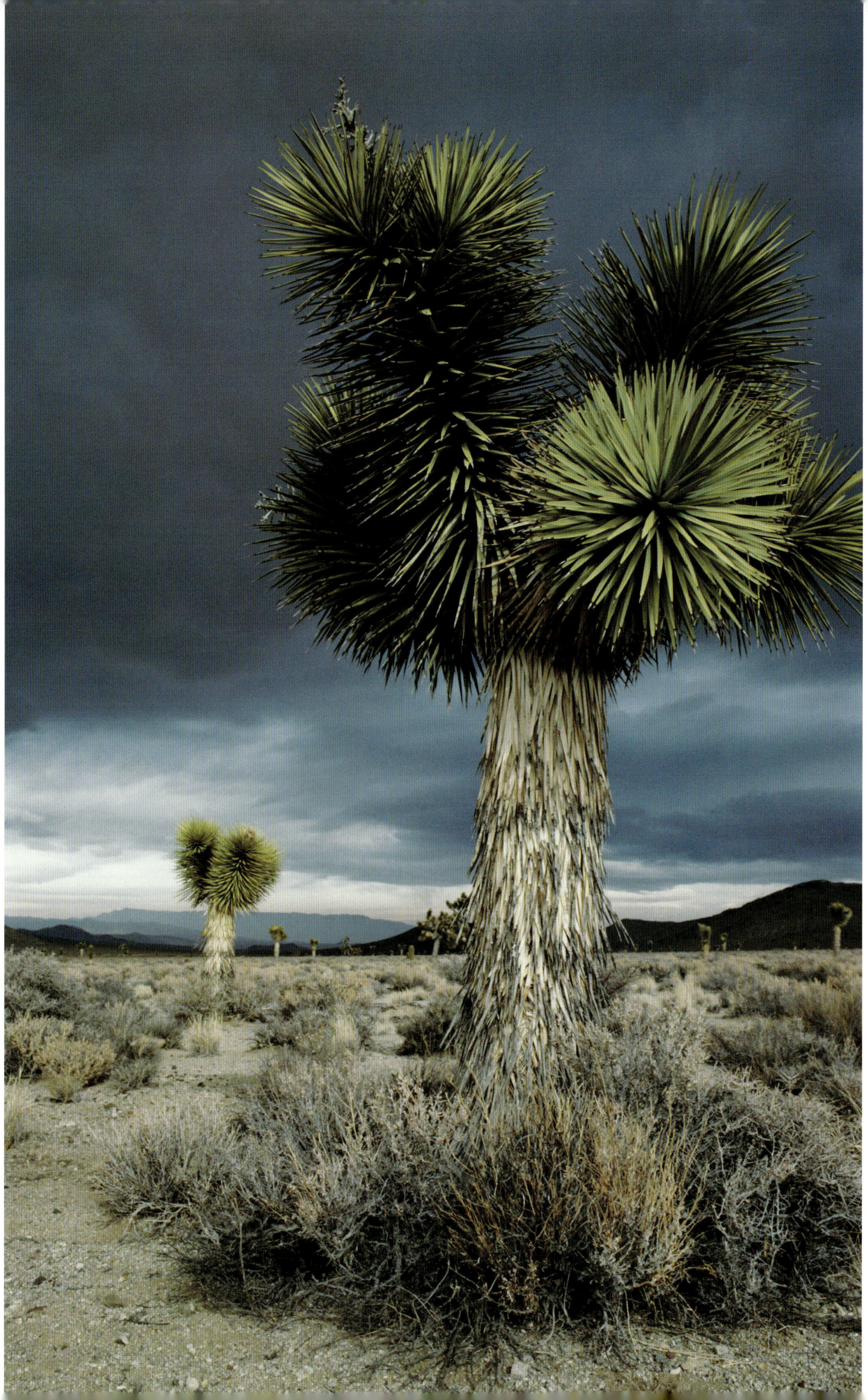

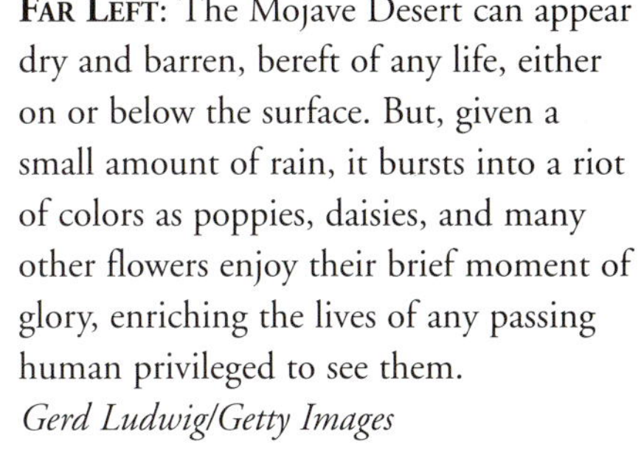

Far Left: The Mojave Desert can appear dry and barren, bereft of any life, either on or below the surface. But, given a small amount of rain, it bursts into a riot of colors as poppies, daisies, and many other flowers enjoy their brief moment of glory, enriching the lives of any passing human privileged to see them.
Gerd Ludwig/Getty Images

Left: Storm clouds gather over the Mojave Desert and two lonely beaked yuccas. This single-trunked arborsecent yucca reaches heights of up to fifteen feet and, as with the two seen here, develops a number of branches. The name "beaked" is derived from the shape of its fruit, which bears a supposed likeness to a bird's beak.
Gordon Wiltsie/Getty Images

Page 136: Two varieties of cactus, cholla (with purple flower) and saguaro (tall columnar plant) grow together in an Arizona desert. There are many species of cholla in the North and Central American deserts, but many are difficult to tell apart, even for experts, because they hybridize.
Annie Griffiths Belt/Getty Images

Page 137: Like many desert creatures, the Namaqua sand grouse has adapted itself to its harsh environment. The male bird has special breast feathers and simply by wading through a pool these absorb water; the bird then flies back to its nest, which can be up to fifty miles away, where the chicks drink the water from the feathers. This species has a unique, repetitive call, which can be transliterated as "kelkiewyn."
Peter Johnson/Corbis

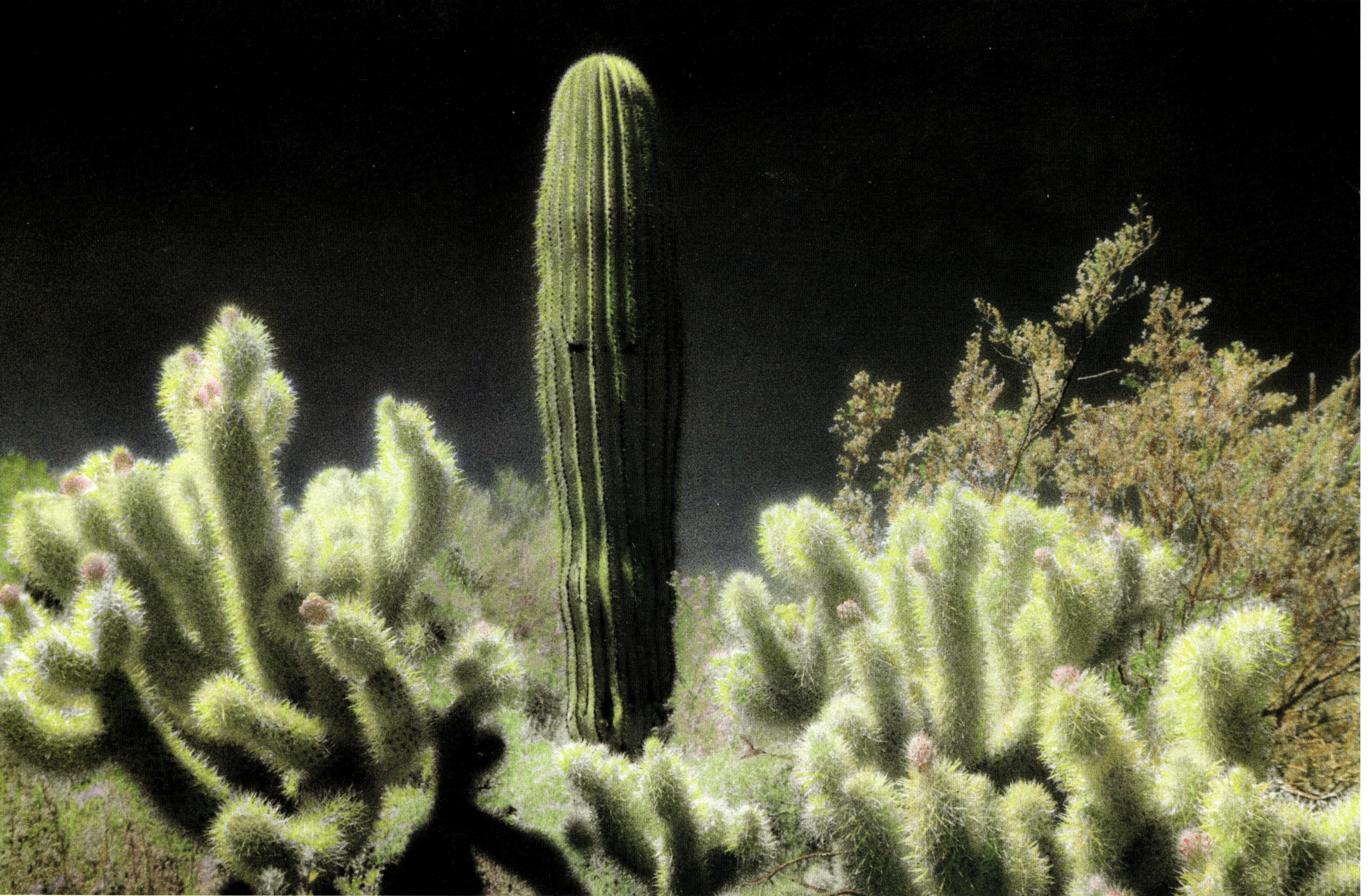

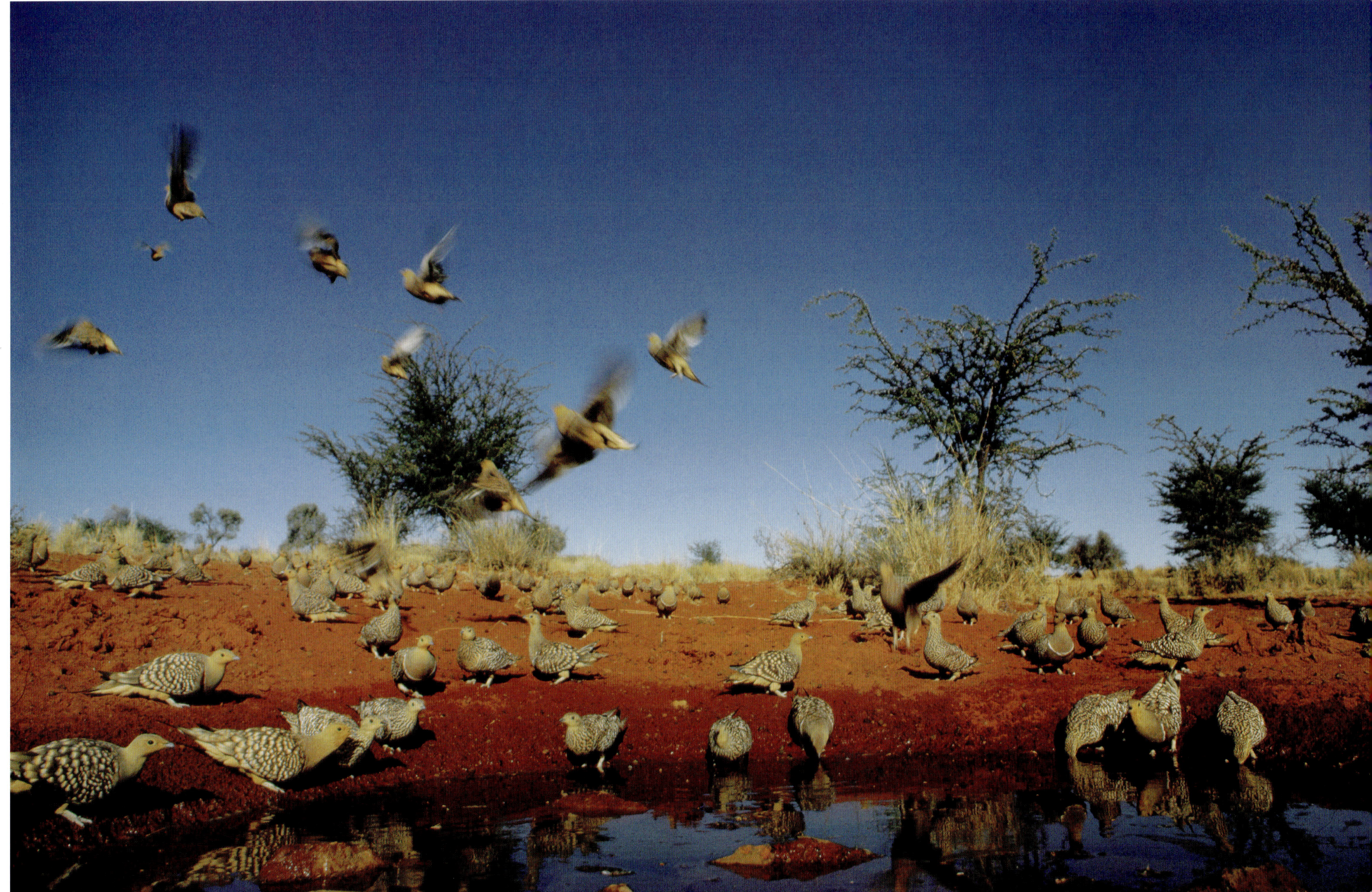

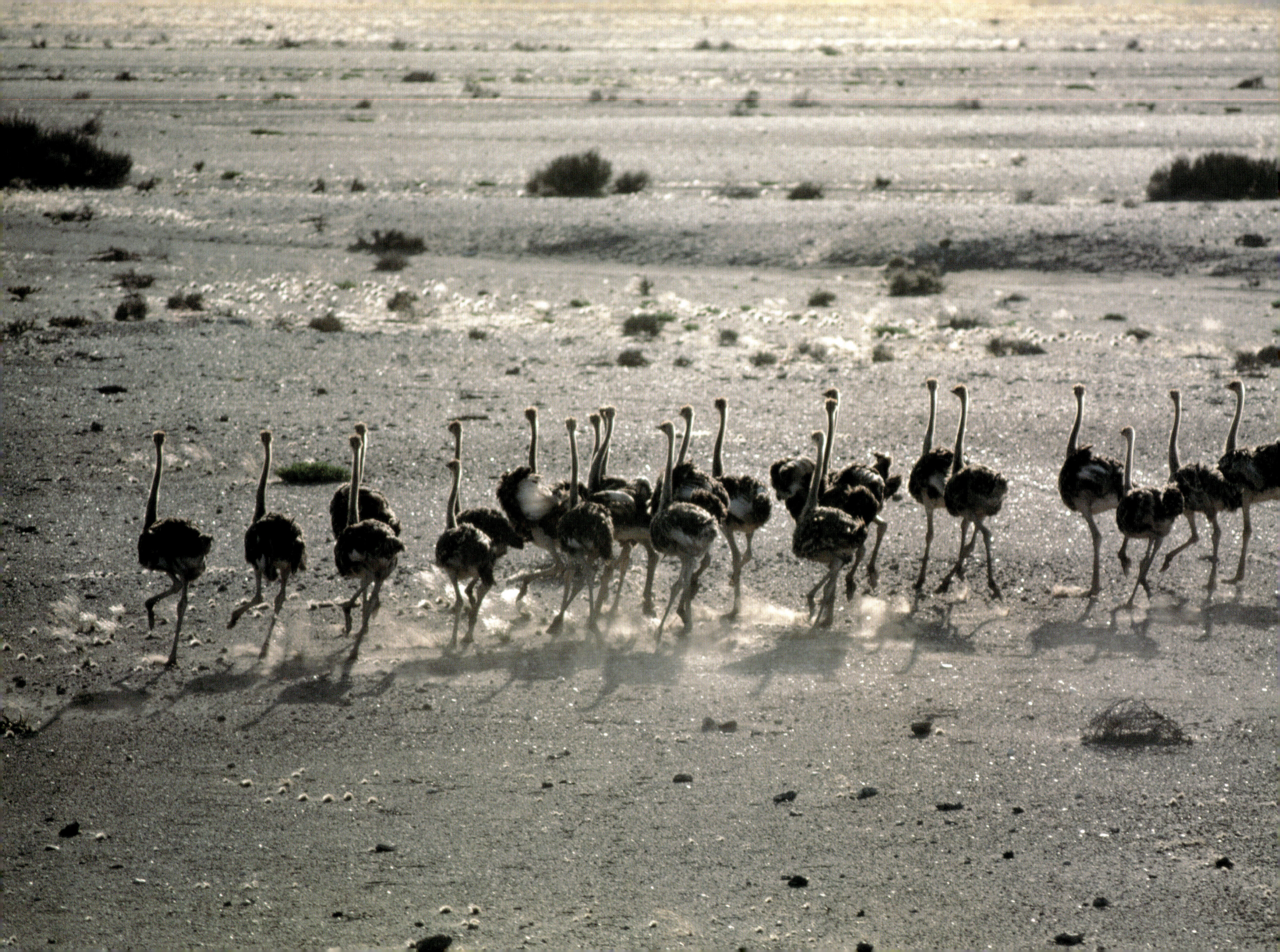

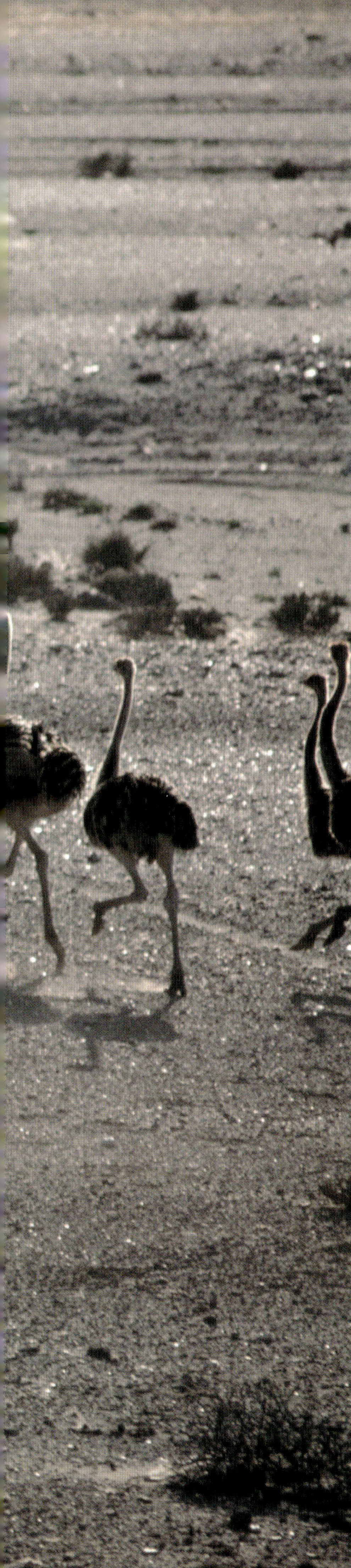

Left: Ostriches are the world's largest surviving bird species, and for most of the year they live in small, loose groups or even individually. During the five-month-long breeding season, however, they congregate into flocks of up to fifty, as with this group in the Kalahari Desert. Such a flock establishes a "territory" up to six square miles in extent. Ostrich eggs are greatly prized by the local Bushmen who use them as water containers, both to carry with them on hunting expeditions and also to form caches for use during the return journey.
Peter Johnson/Corbis

Right: The western capercaillie is by far the largest member of the grouse family, with the cock bird weighing some nine pounds, the hen approximately half that. The cock bird seen here in its native habitat in the Sonoran Desert is making its characteristic call, a mixture of "clicks" and "pops." The capercaillie feeds on berries, shoots, and stems.
Mattias Klum/Getty Images

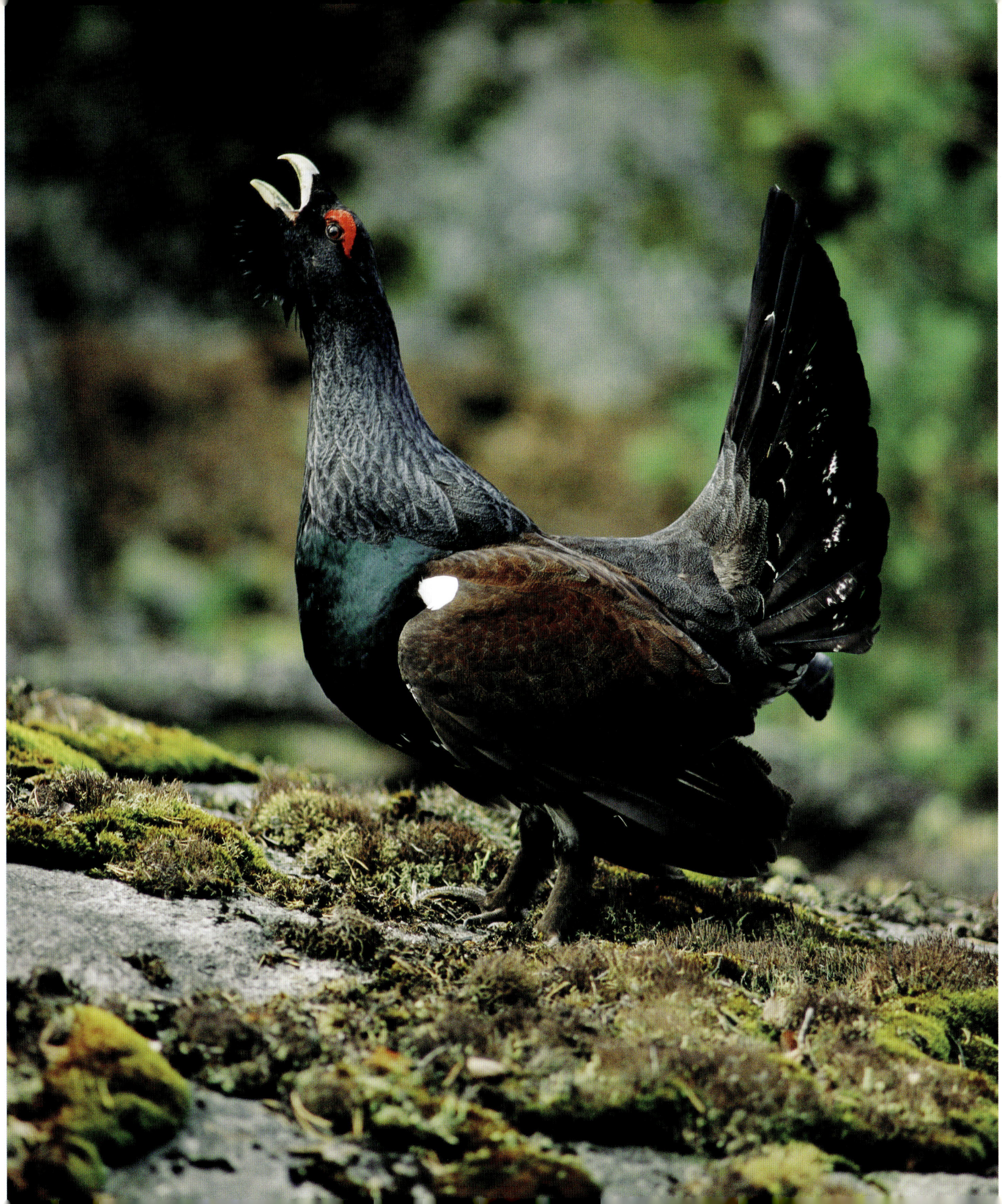

RIGHT: The diuca is a finch common throughout Chile. About seven inches long, it is normally to be found among shrubs in ravines and meadows, but it is equally at home among cacti in the Atacama Desert, as seen here. There are vast numbers and unlike many desert species it does not to appear to be in any danger of extinction.
Joel Sartore/Getty Images

FAR RIGHT: The Chilean flamingo is one of the most beautiful birds in the world. It is overall pale pink in color, while its wings are a darker shade of pink with some black mixed in, and its very long thin legs have dark pink bands and pink feet. The bill is bent in the middle, giving a rather imperious impression. The birds can be up to five feet tall and weight as much as sixteen pounds. They are found in many parts of southern South America and seem to have a particular liking for shallow salt lakes and marshes, as here in the Atacama.
Joel Sartore/Getty Images

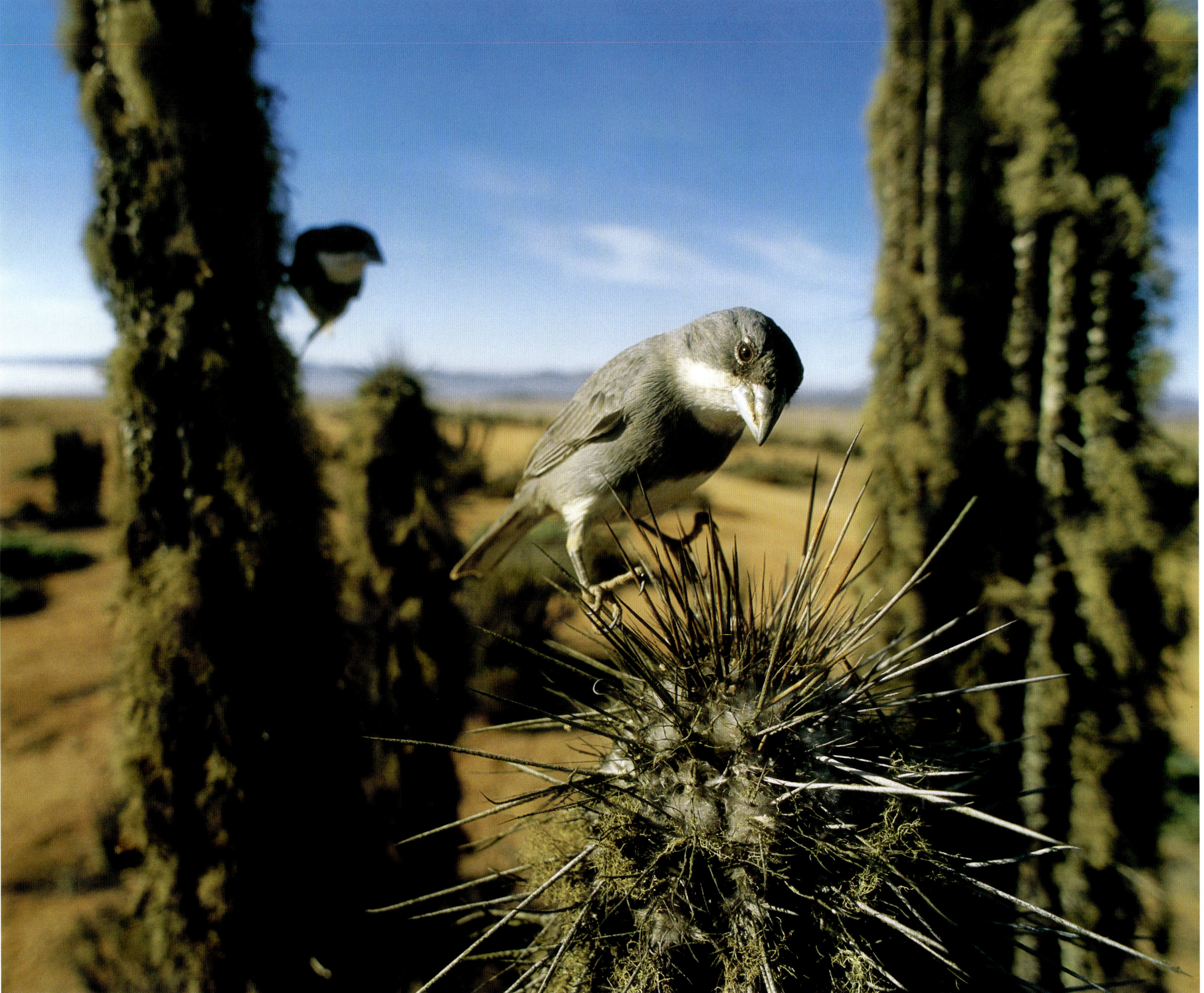

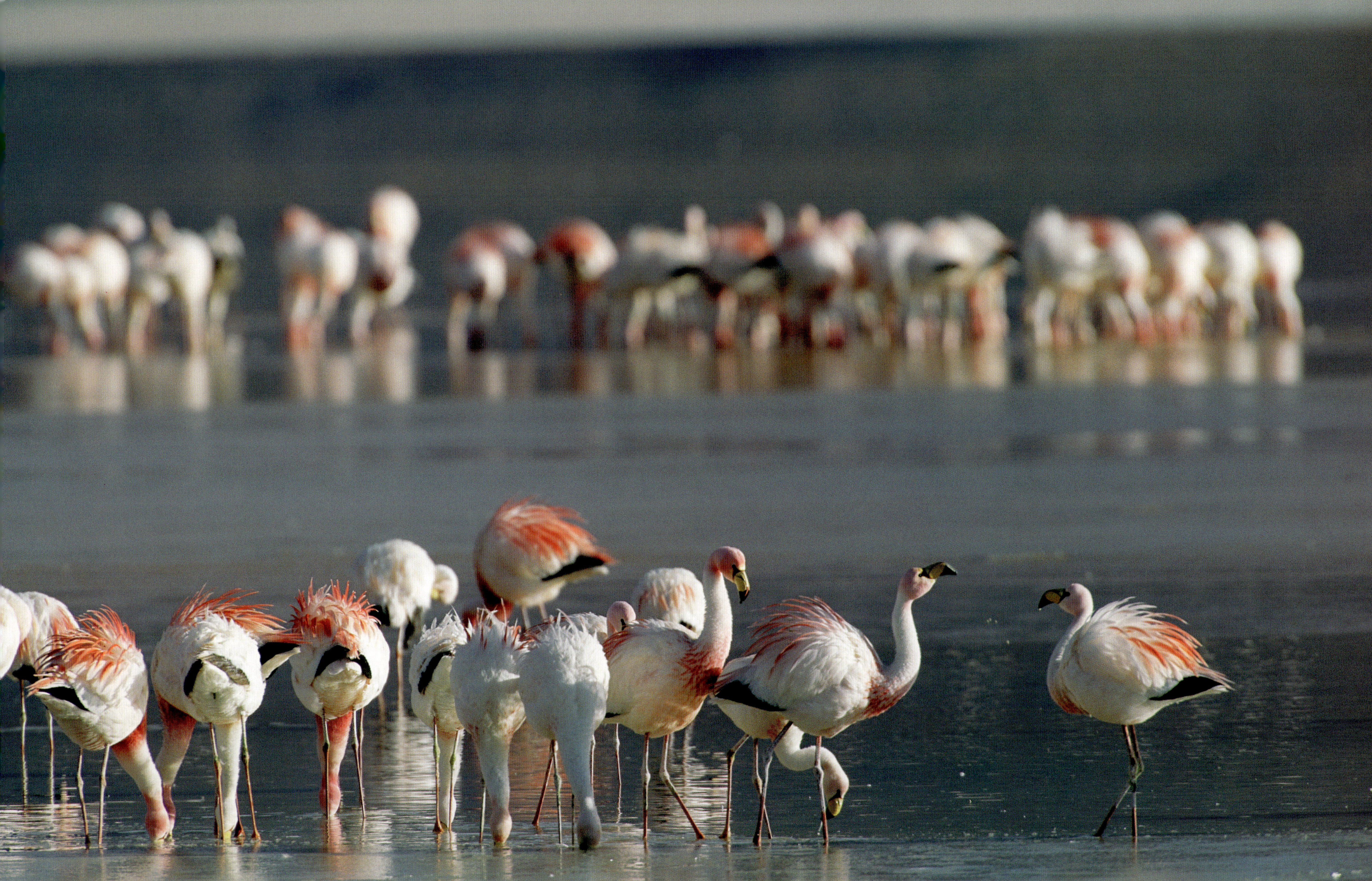

Right: Among the species to survive in the Australian Desert is the woma python (also known as the sand python), a normally nocturnal creature that digs temporary burrows in the sand to escape predators or extremes of temperature. It lives in semi-permanent burrows that it digs using its head as a shovel. It uses its very narrow tail as a lure to attract its prey, which includes reptiles, small mammals, and birds. Womas normally grow to about five feet in length, although specimens of up to nine feet have been found. In the background is Mount Uluru (also known as Ayer's Rock), a site of very special importance to Australia's Aboriginal people.
Michael & Patricia Fogden/Corbis

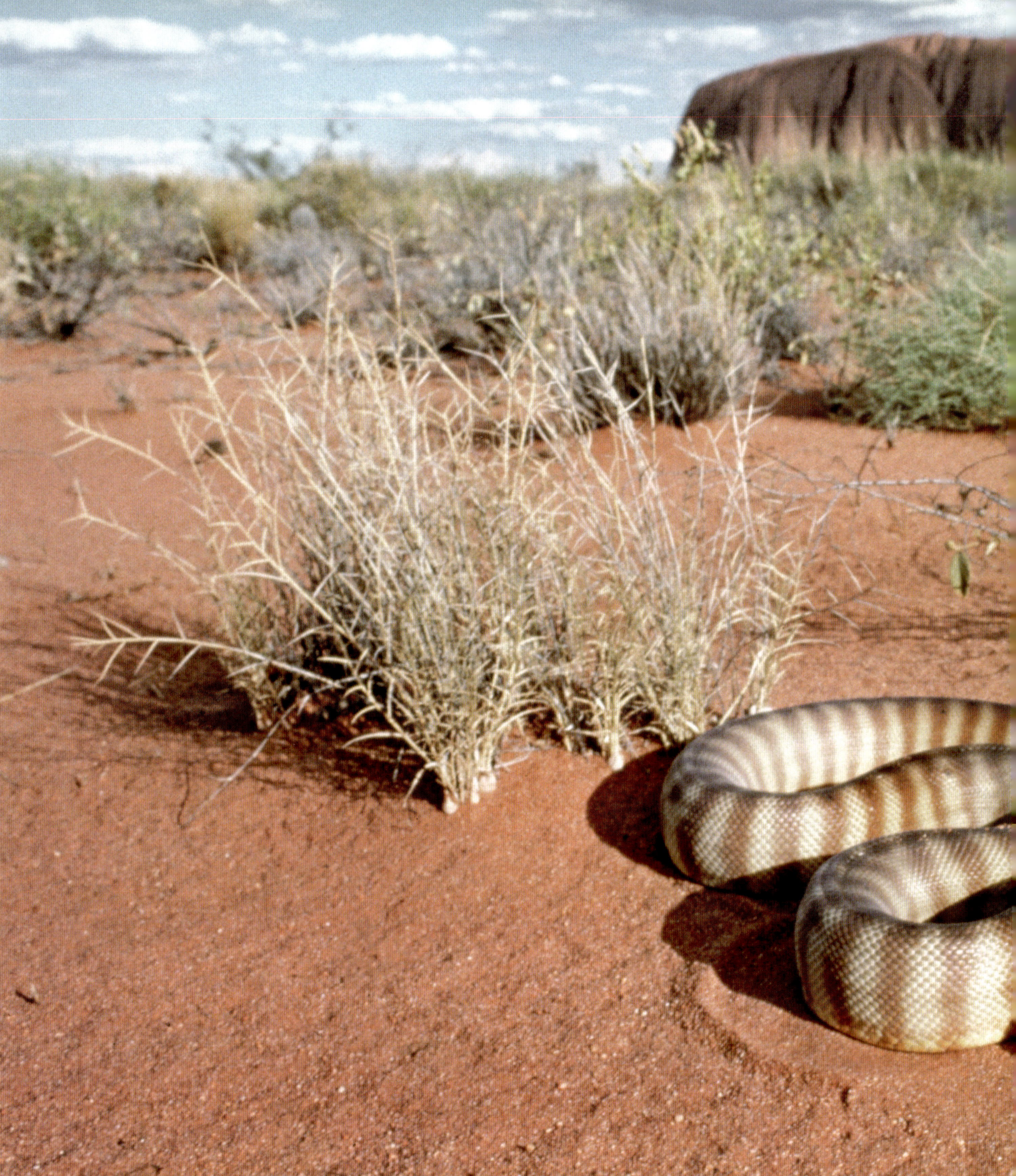

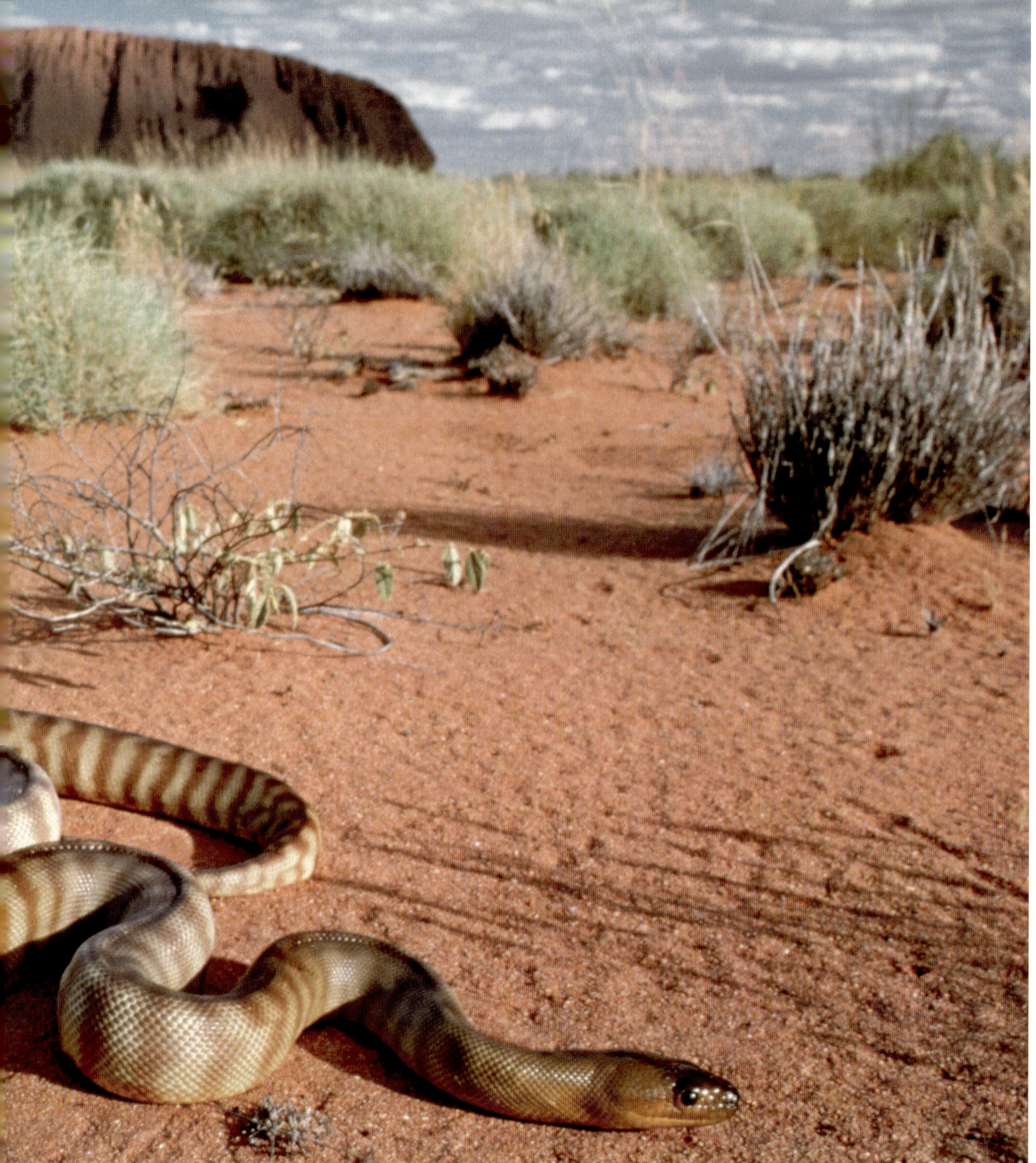

Page 144: This is quite definitely not the best angle from which to view a western diamondback rattlesnake, the most dangerous of the "rattlers" in the United States' southwestern deserts. The diamondback has an evil—and fully deserved—reputation and bites several hundred humans each year, although its normal prey are small mammals such as chipmunks, gophers, mice, rats, prairie dogs, and rabbits.
Joel Sartore/Getty Images

Page 145: An inhabitant of the Namib Desert's sand dunes is the Peringuey's adder (*Bitis peringueyi*), which moves with a sidewinding motion. During the heat of the day it normally lies embedded in the sand, with only its eyes showing, waiting for prey, usually lizards. It occasionally bites humans, its poison causing pain and discomfort but seldom being fatal.
Chris John/Getty Images

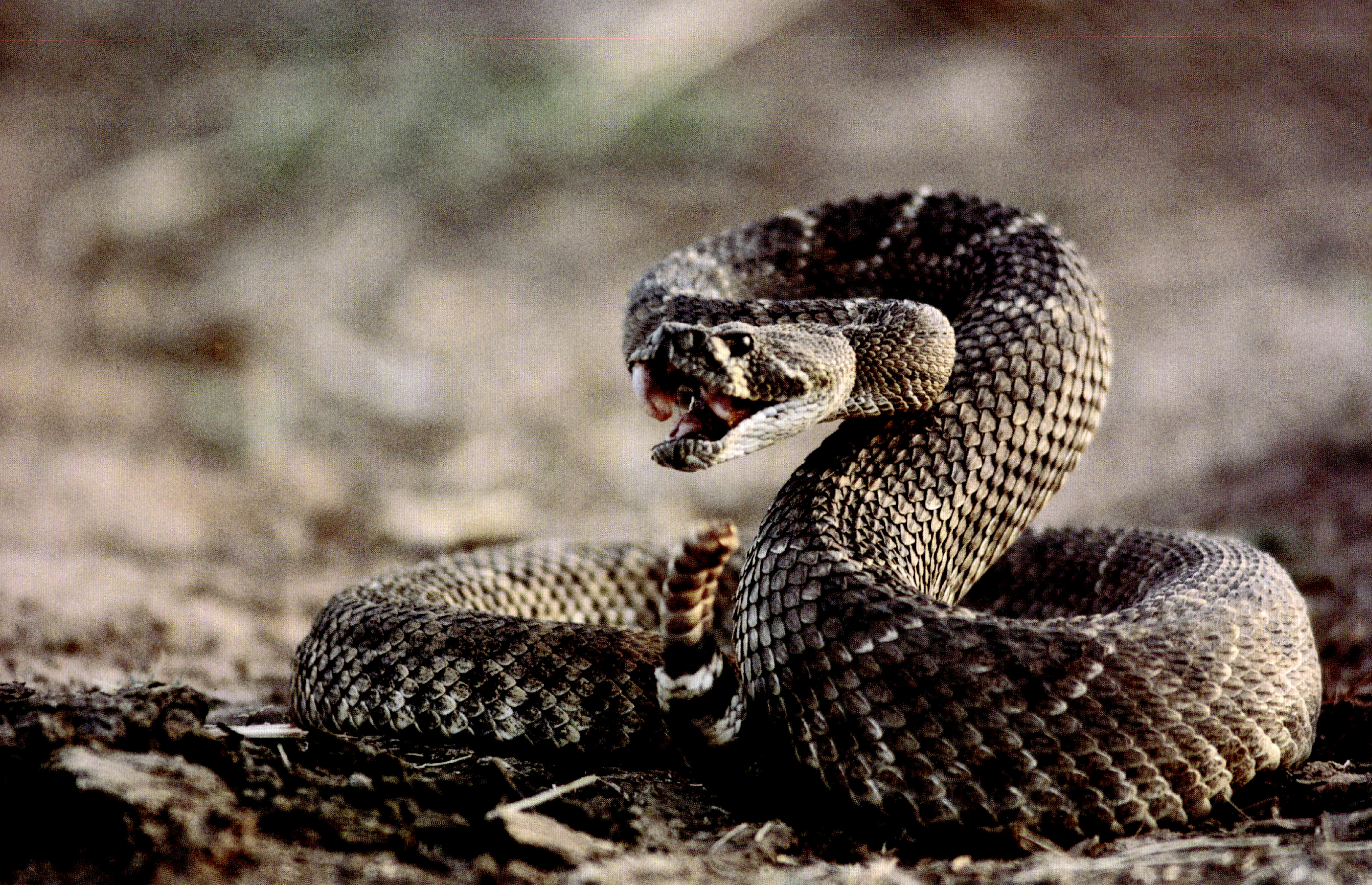

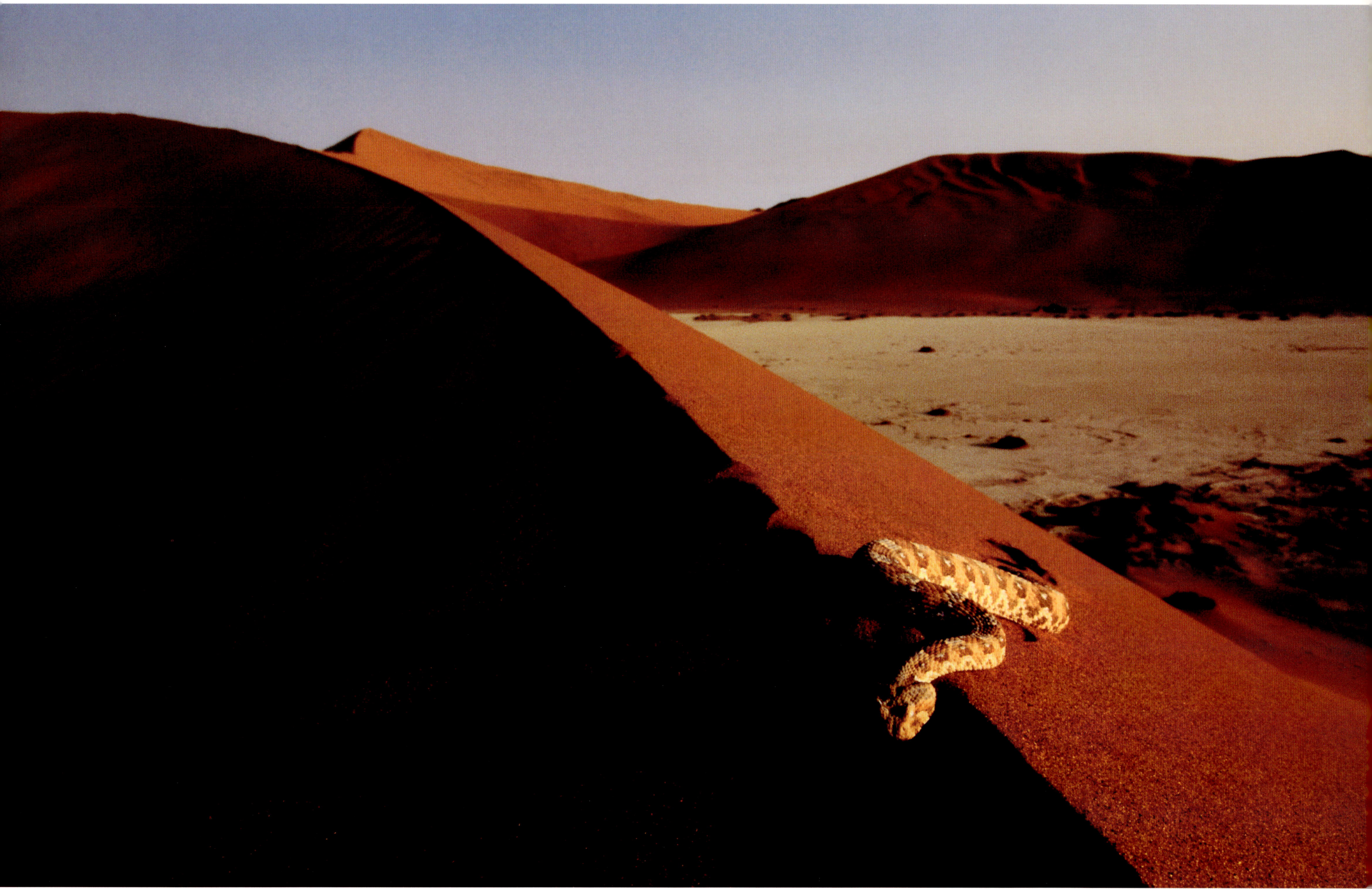

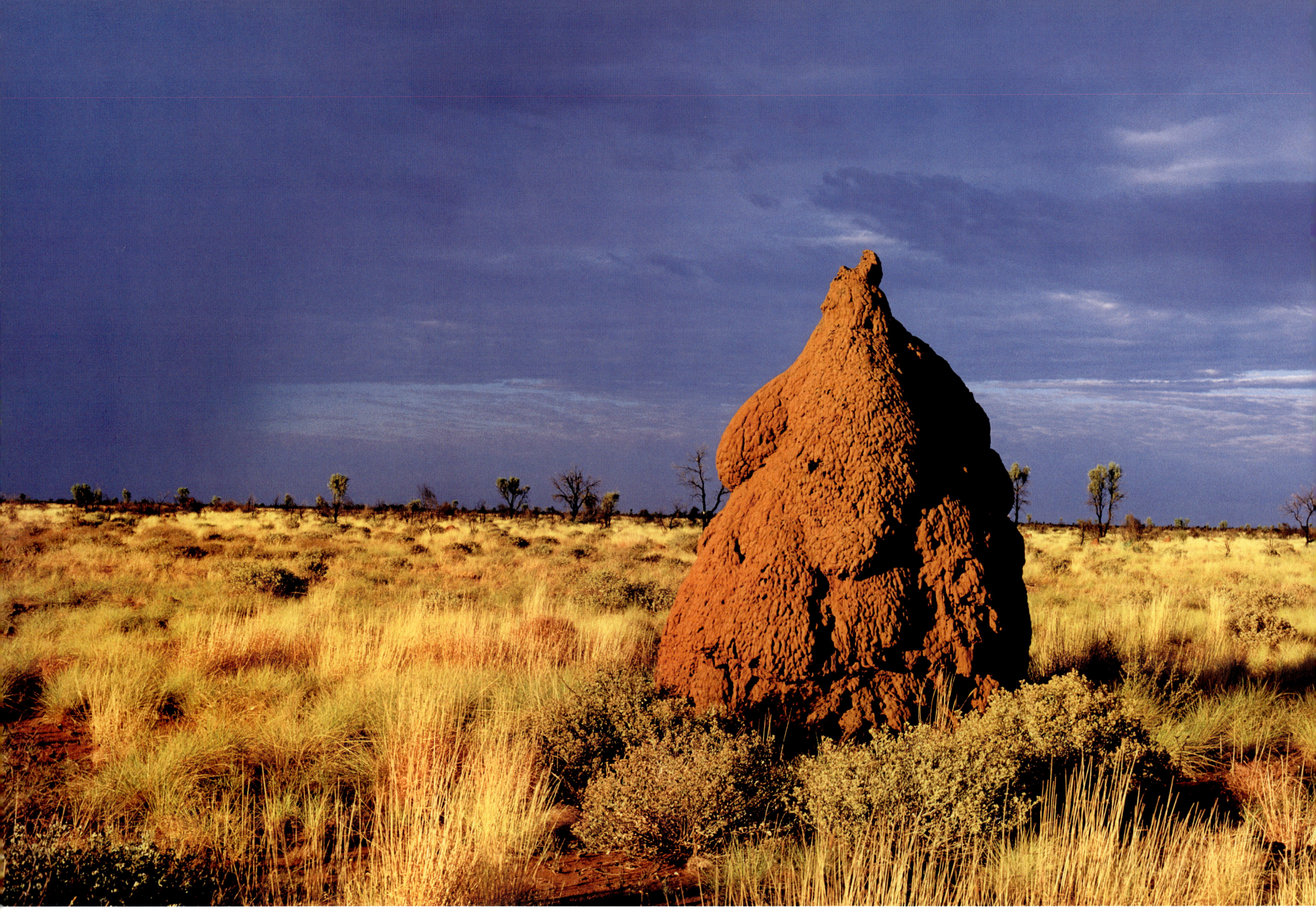

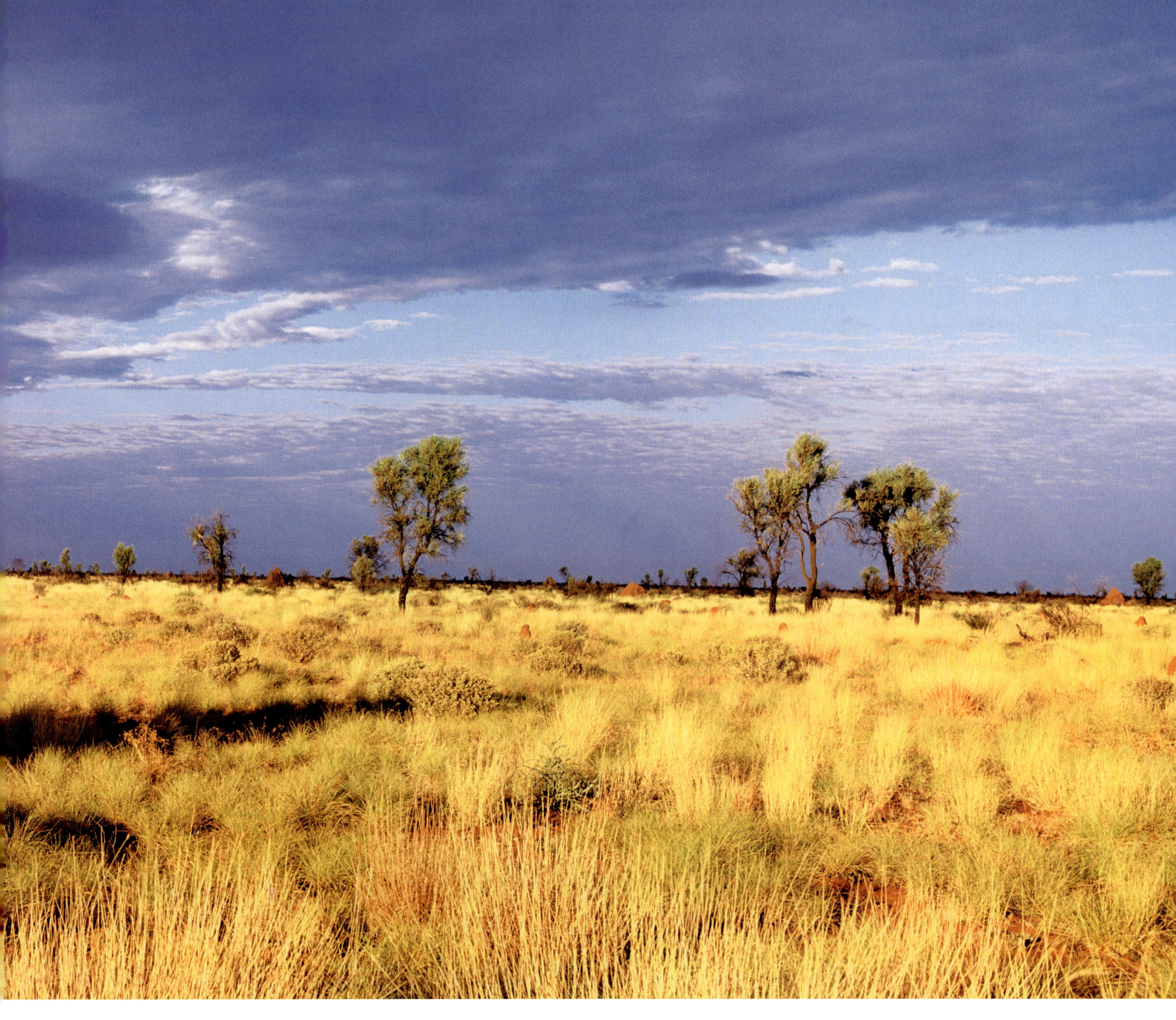

Left: A termite mound in the Tanami Desert in Northern Australia. One curious use of these structures is by kingfishers, which often nest in them. Their original penetration is made by flying flat out and head first into the side of the mound—a technique that is sometimes fatal. Once through the outer wall, the birds dig a tunnel some six inches long ending in a small chamber where the eggs are laid.
Theo Allofs/Corbis

Page 148: This scorpion, resting on a rock in Israel's Negev Desert, is one of a type of carnivorous eight-legged arachnid, consisting of some 1,500 species spread around the world and found in many environments and not just deserts. Its powerful poison is stored in the aculeus, or stinger, at the tip of its curved tail, seen here in the raised position.
Steve Kaufman/Corbis

Page 149: A spider at the entrance to its burrow on a sand dune in Australia's Simpson Desert. Under the ground the tunnel will extend for about three feet and is designed to give the pair of spiders a slightly humid atmosphere and relatively comfortable conditions in which to survive and breed their young.
John Edwards/Getty Images

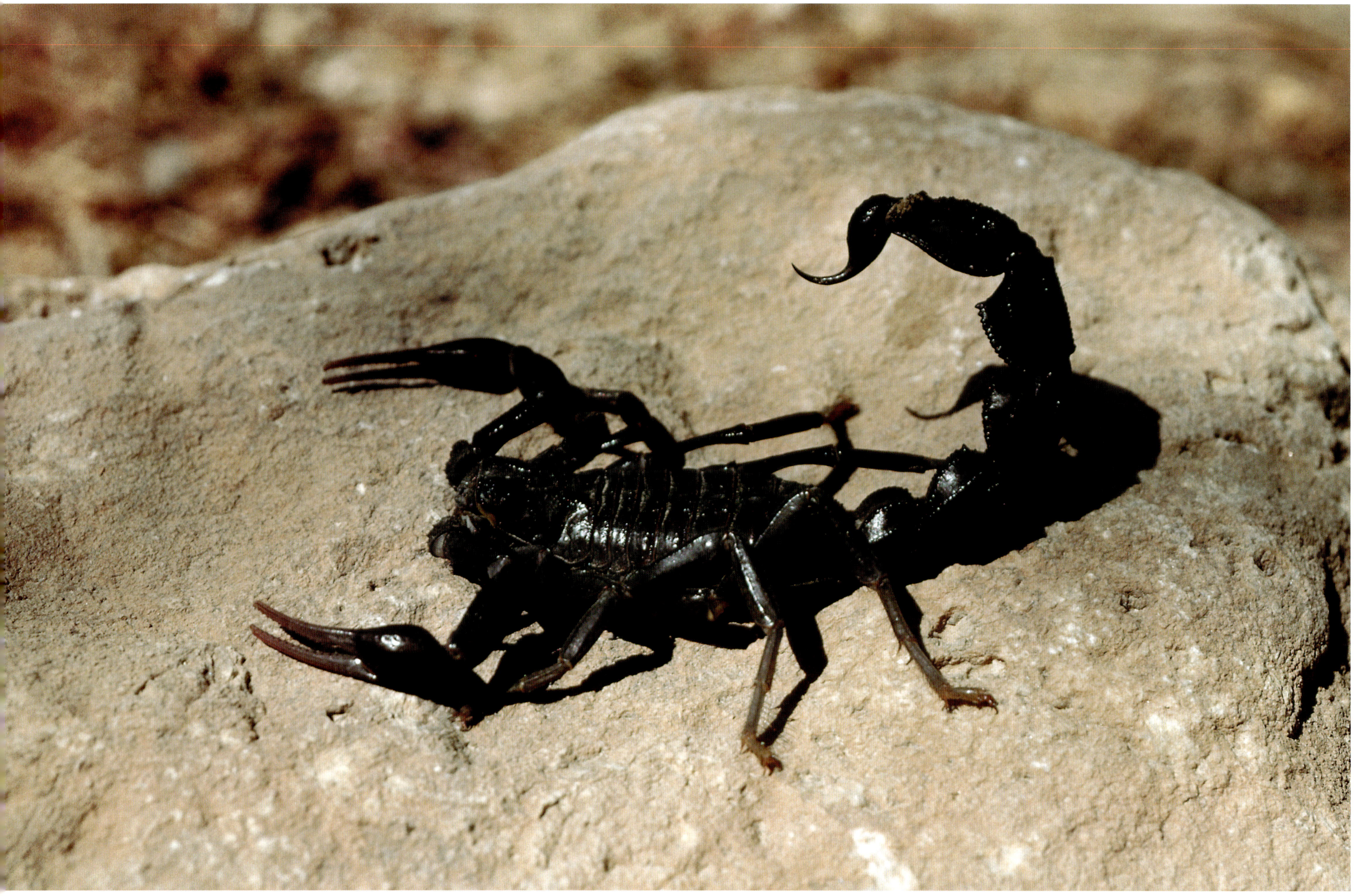

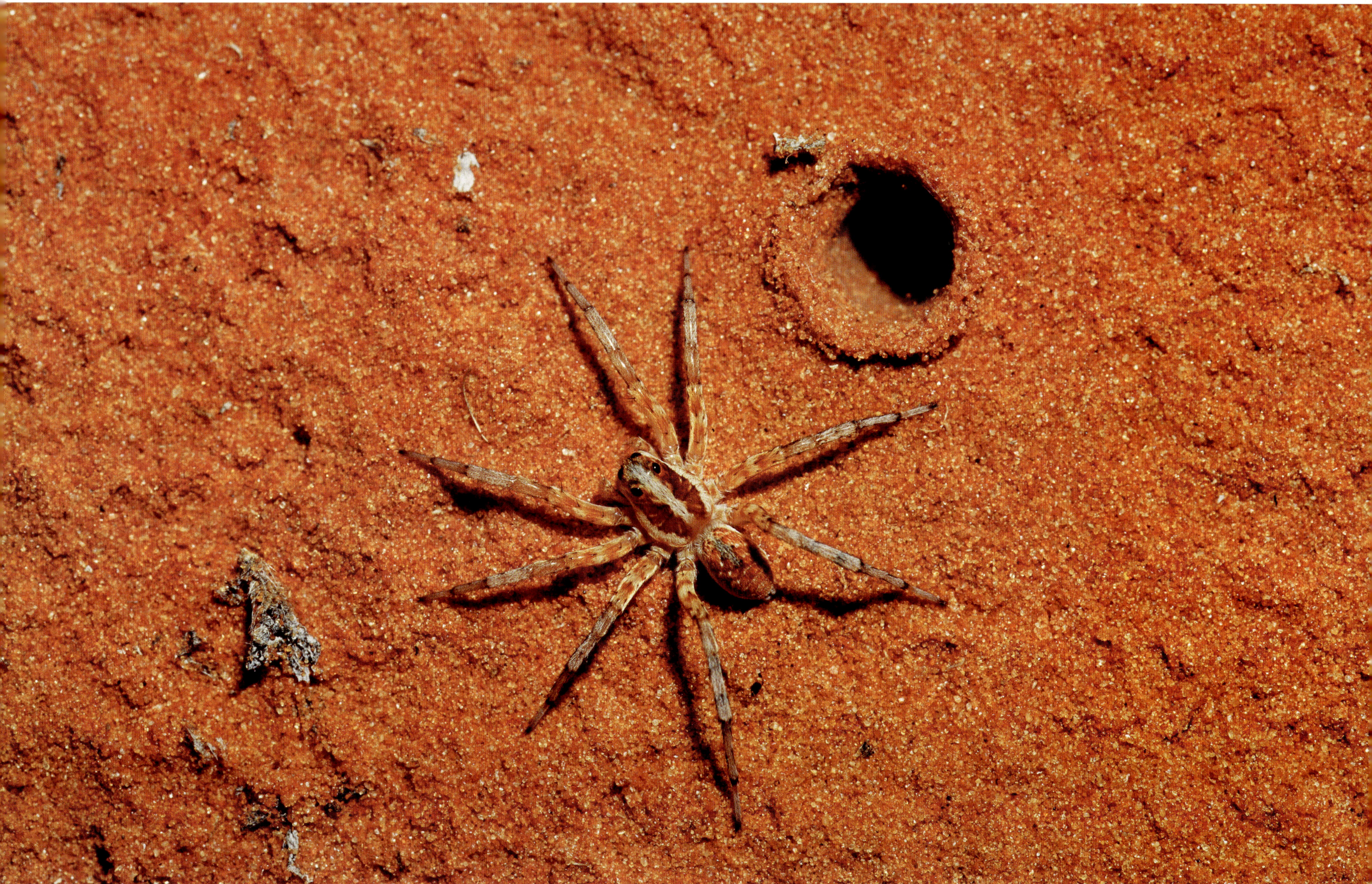

RIGHT: The scavenging circus beetle (*Eleodes hirtipennis*) is found in the sand dunes of Death Valley in California. It can be distinguished from others by the tiny hairs that cover its outer wings and by its ability to raise its rear abdomen and excrete a foul-smelling liquid if threatened. Note that despite its tiny size and very low weight it is leaving a very obvious track in the loose sand.
Paul Chesley/Getty Images

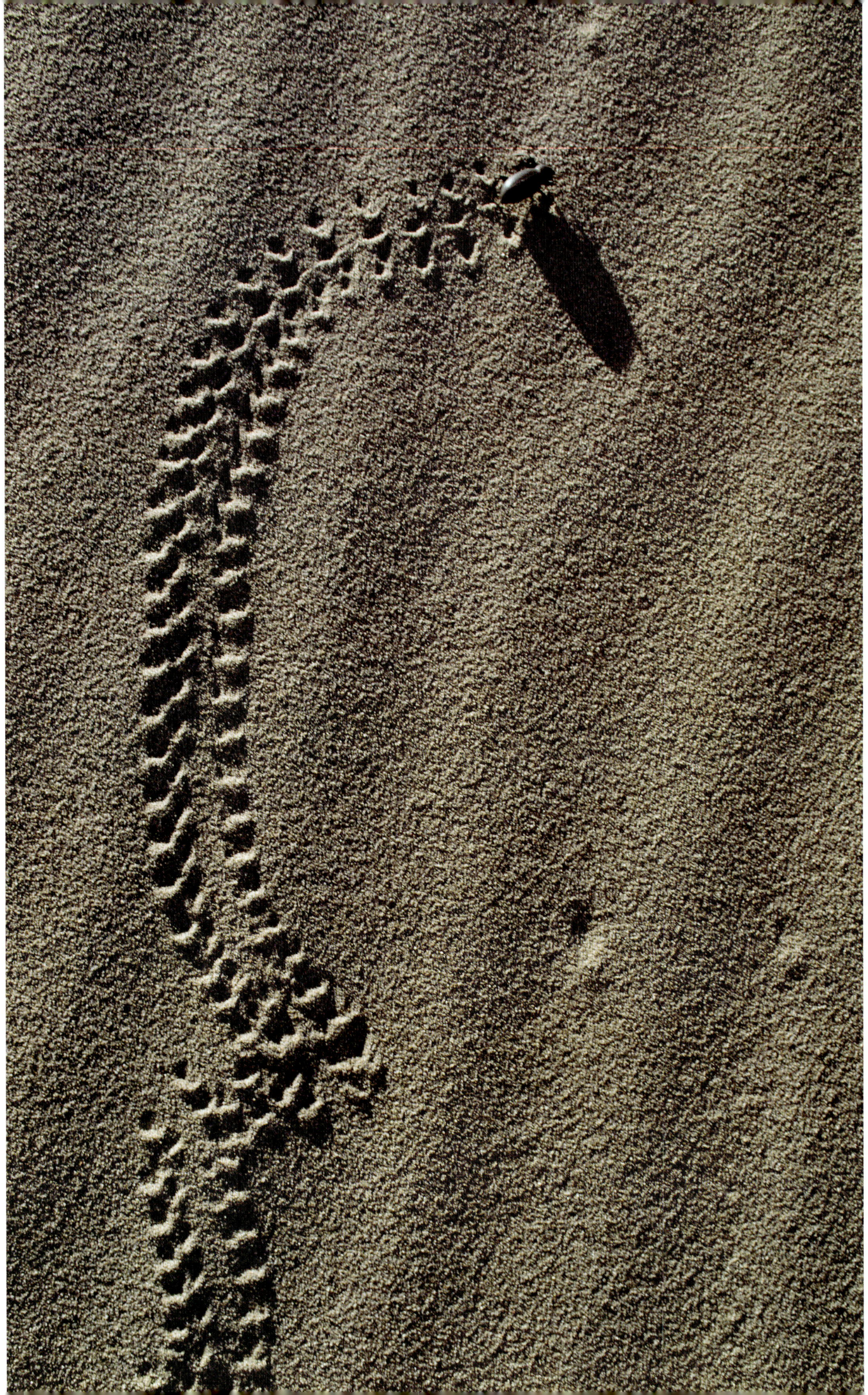

RIGHT: This splendid picture shows a mountain lion (also known as cougar, panther or puma) leaping from one rock to another in the Zion National Park in Utah, USA. An adult male can measure up to eight feet in length and weighs up to 150 pounds, while the female is somewhat smaller, being some seven feet long and weighing between 65 and 90 pounds.
George H. H. Huey/Corbis

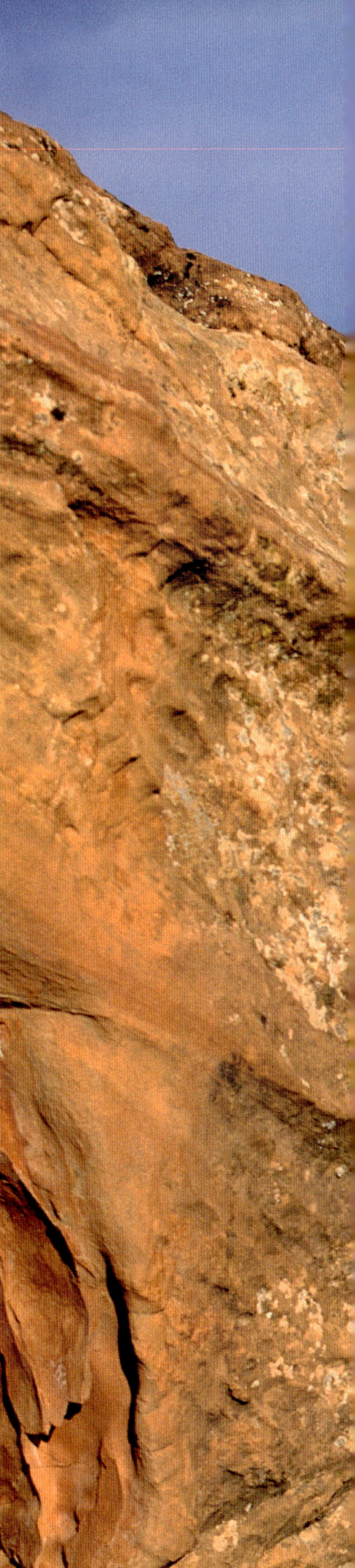

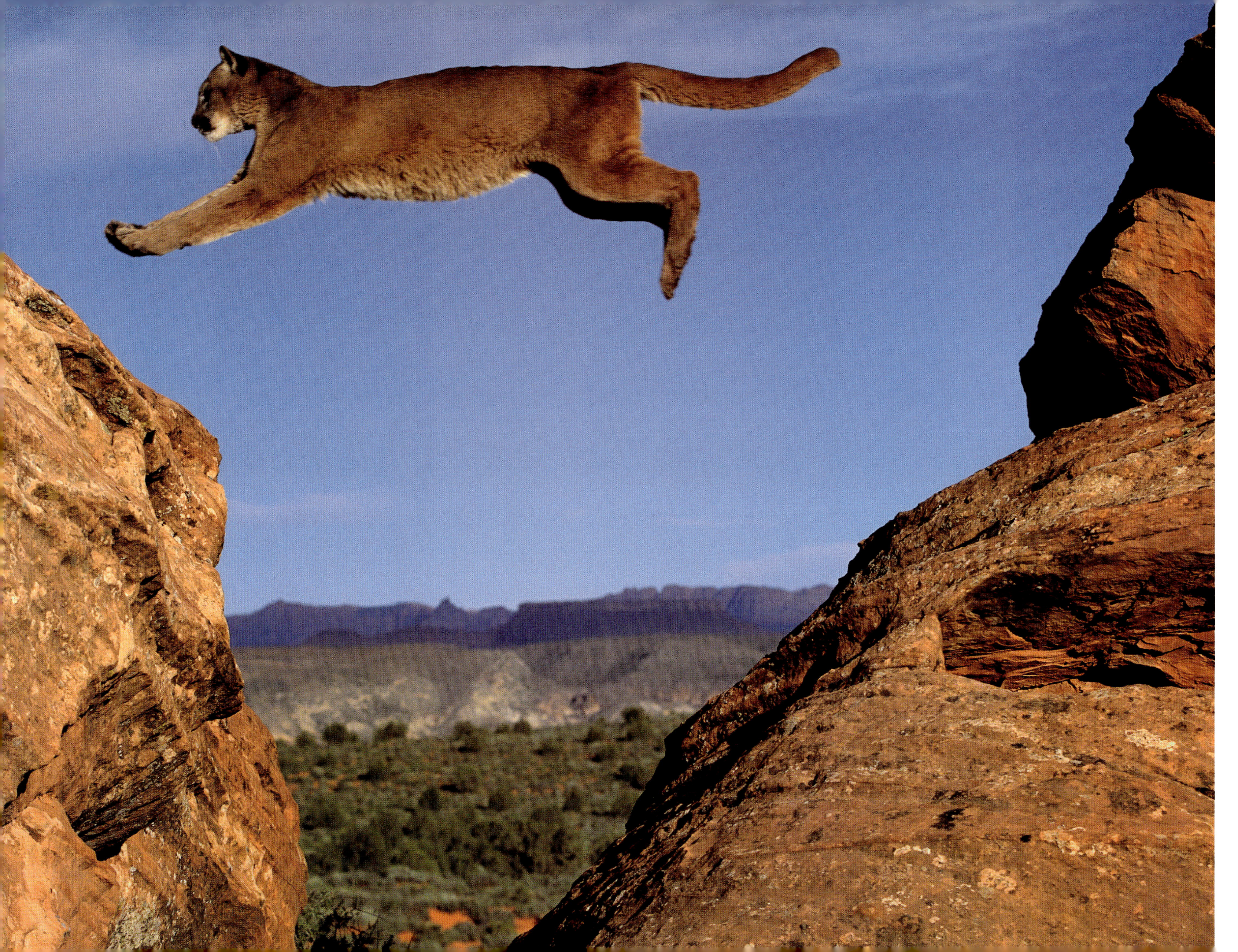

RIGHT: A pride of lions at dawn in the Kalahari Gemsbok National Park. This nature reserve covers an area of some 3,900 square miles of South African territory that abuts on Botswana's Gemsbok National Park, and since there is no barrier between the two, they combine to give animals such as these a territory of some 14,000 square miles in which to wander in reasonable safety.
Paul A. Souders/Corbis

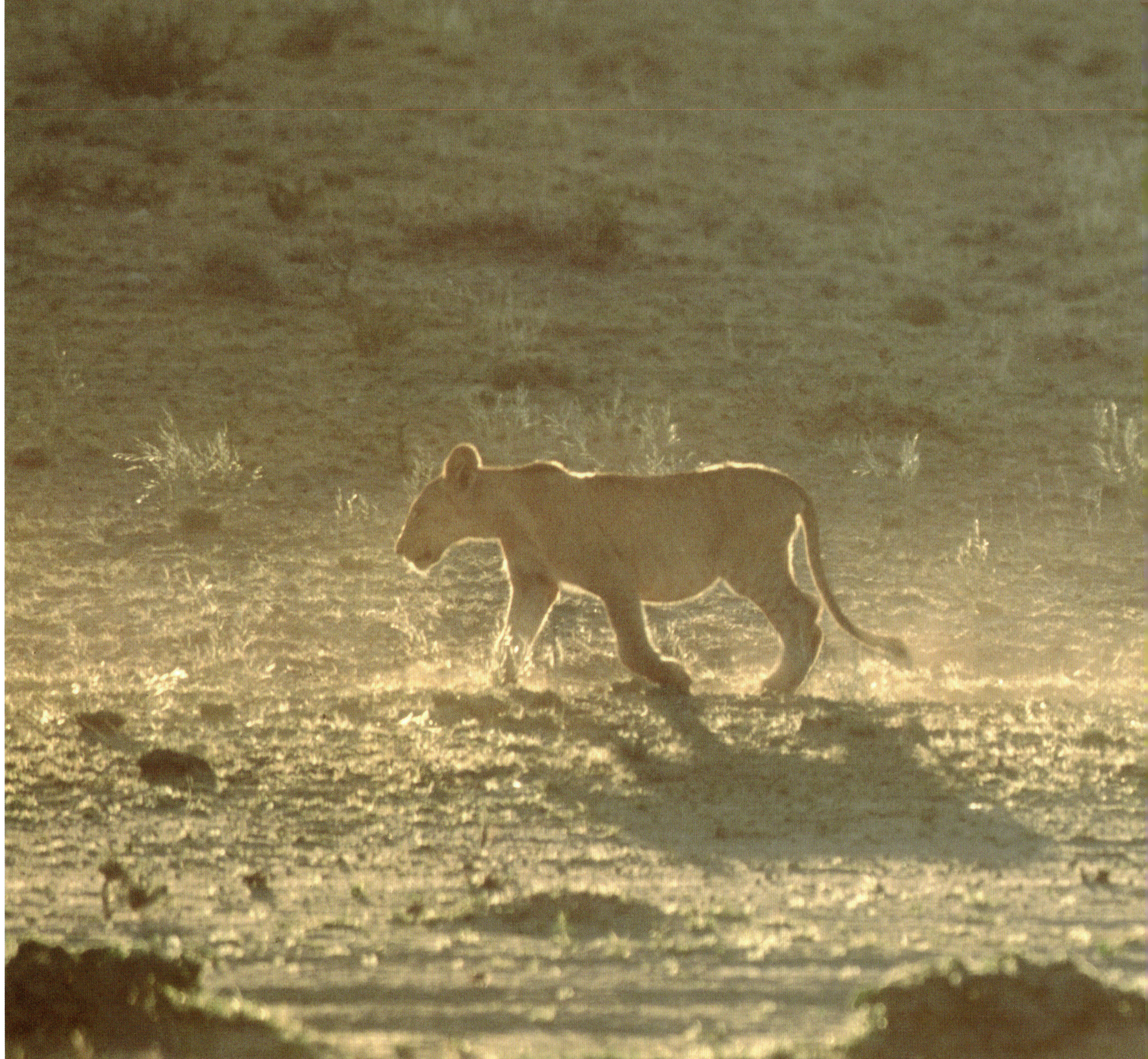

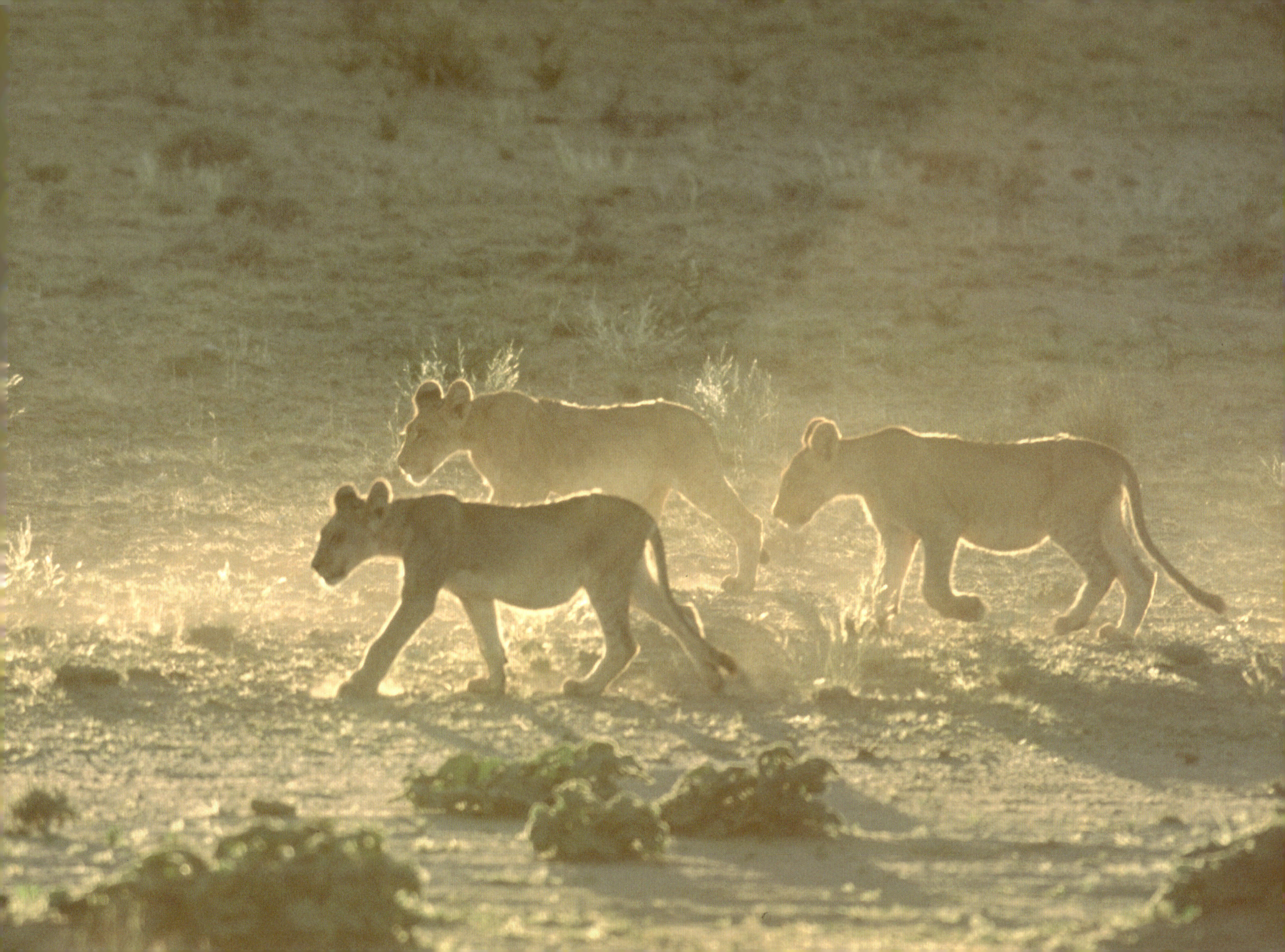

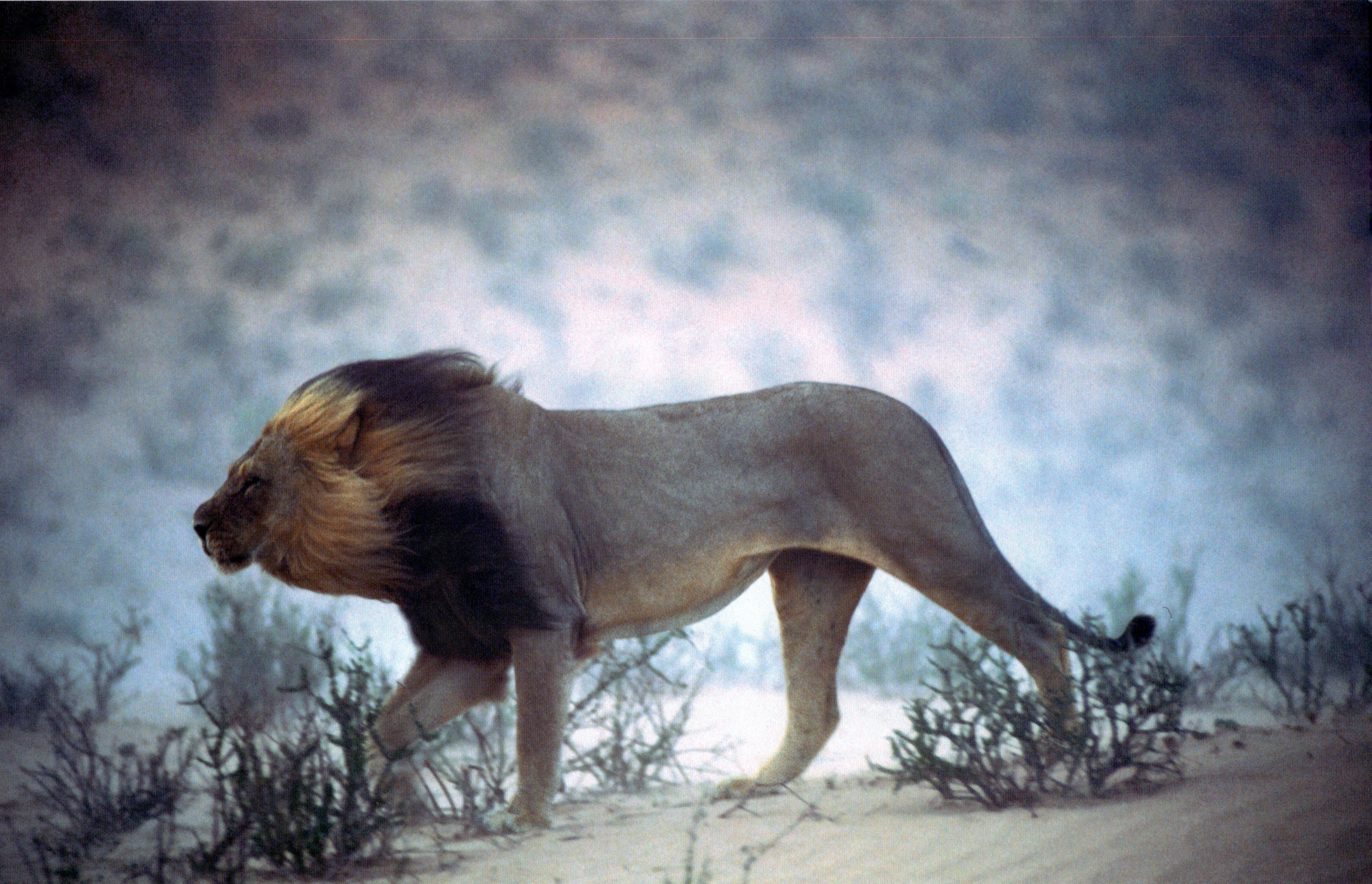

LEFT: Every inch the "king of beasts," this lion is hunting along the dried-out bed of the Nossob River in the Kgalagadi Transfrontier National Park. This is a joint venture between the Botswanan and South African governments. The Botswanan section, seen here, covers an area of some 11,000 square miles, in which these splendid animals are reasonably safe from the depredations of Man.
Chris Johns/Getty Images

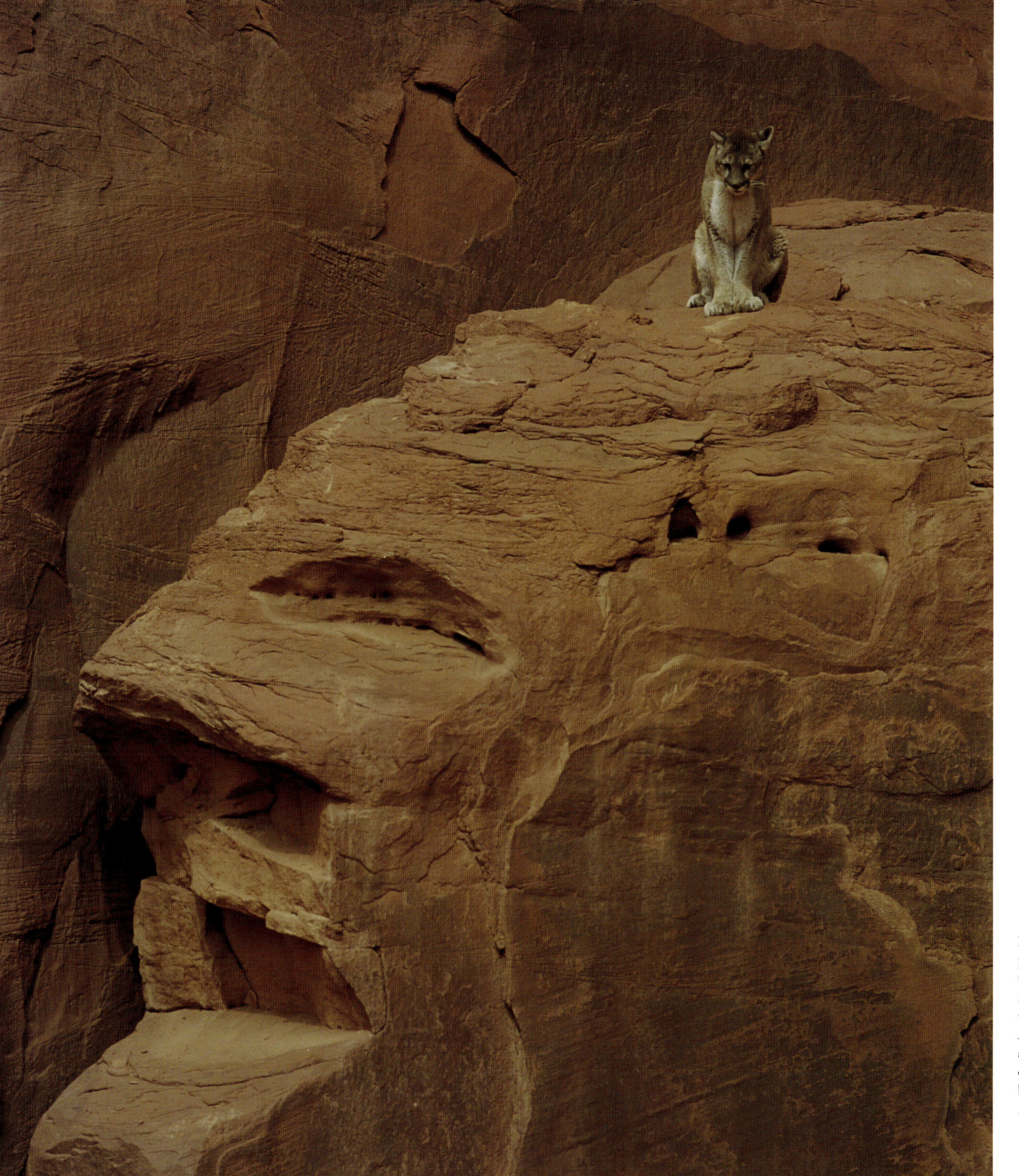

LEFT: Every now and then a viewer sees a photograph and cannot fail to ask how did the photographer manage that? This remarkable picture of a mountain lion in the Monument Valley Tribal Park. in Arizona must be included in that category, as the animal is clearly relaxed and at its ease, yet there is not a scrap of cover behind which the photographer could hide.
Norbert Rosing/Getty Images

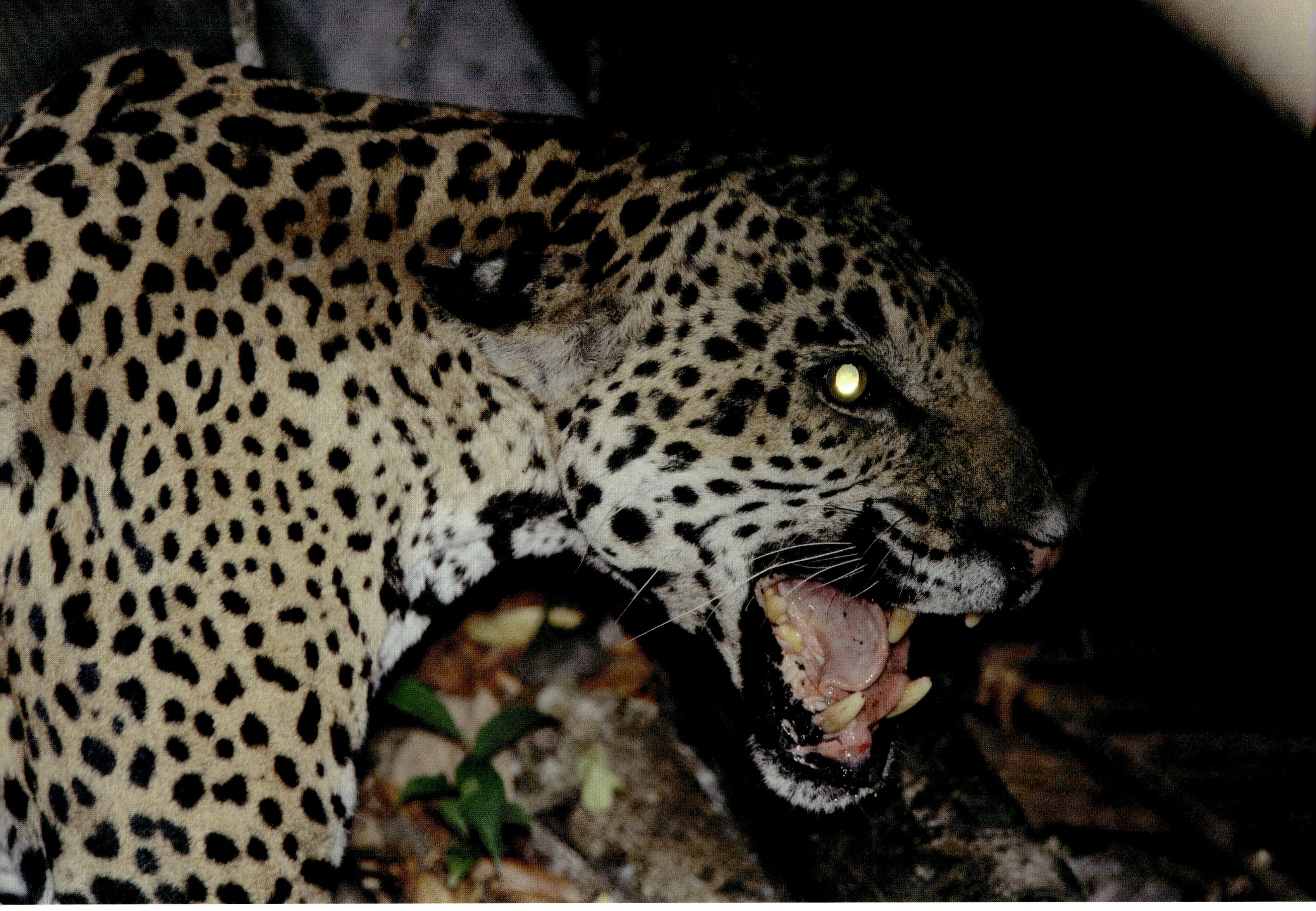

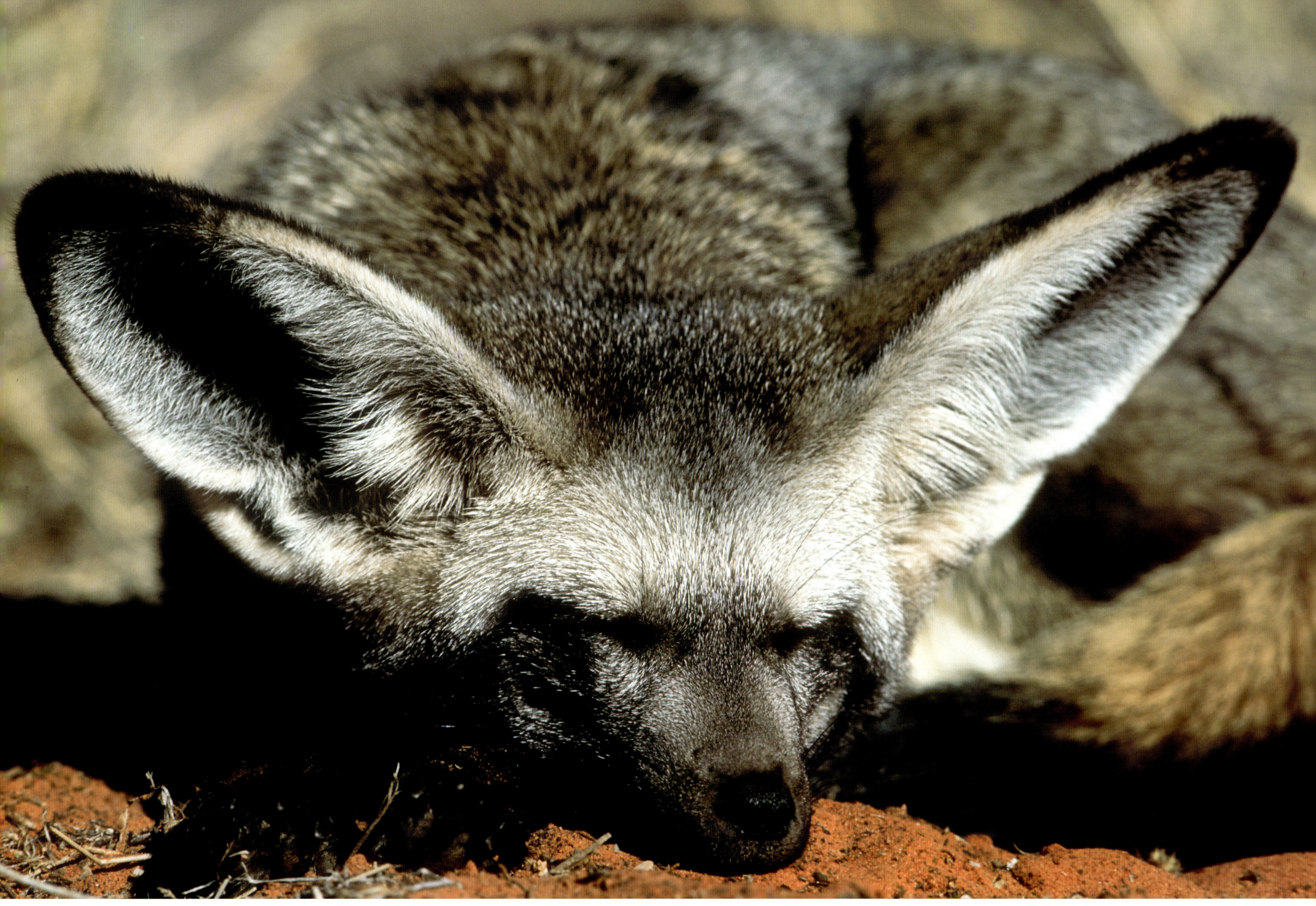

PAGE 156: The jaguar is the largest cat to be found in North America, although its numbers have decreased rapidly over the past few decades and only a few are believed to remain in Arizona. The jaguar is a formidable animal, reaching lengths of up to eight feet, weighing as much as 200 pounds, and capable of killing with a single bite, which can even pierce the armored shells of tortoises and river turtles.
Steve Winter/Getty Images

PAGE 157: Bat-eared foxes are found in eastern and southern Africa and their small heads and five-inch long ears make them unmistakable. They are the only members of the fox family to have virtually abandoned eating meat, their diet consisting mainly of fruit, scorpions, and insects such as dung beetles, although it is known that they occasionally eat birds or small mammals. This example is fast asleep in the heat of the midday sun in the Kalahari Desert.
Martin Harvey/Corbis

RIGHT: The bat-eared fox's disproportionately large ears are extremely sensitive, enabling it to find insects such as dung beetle larvae, even though they are underground. It initially makes an approximate location of the subterranean noise and then swivels its ears until it has pinpointed the source, whereupon it digs down at a frantic speed to catch the grub before it can move out of harm's way.
Mattia Klum/Getty Images

FAR RIGHT: The Andean fox occurs throughout the length of South America's west coast. This example is scavenging the carcass of a llama in Chile's Atacama Desert. They are very solitary creatures, with the males and females meeting only briefly in June to mate and then going their separate ways, leaving the mother to look after her litter of between two and six pups on her own.
Joel Sartore/Getty Images

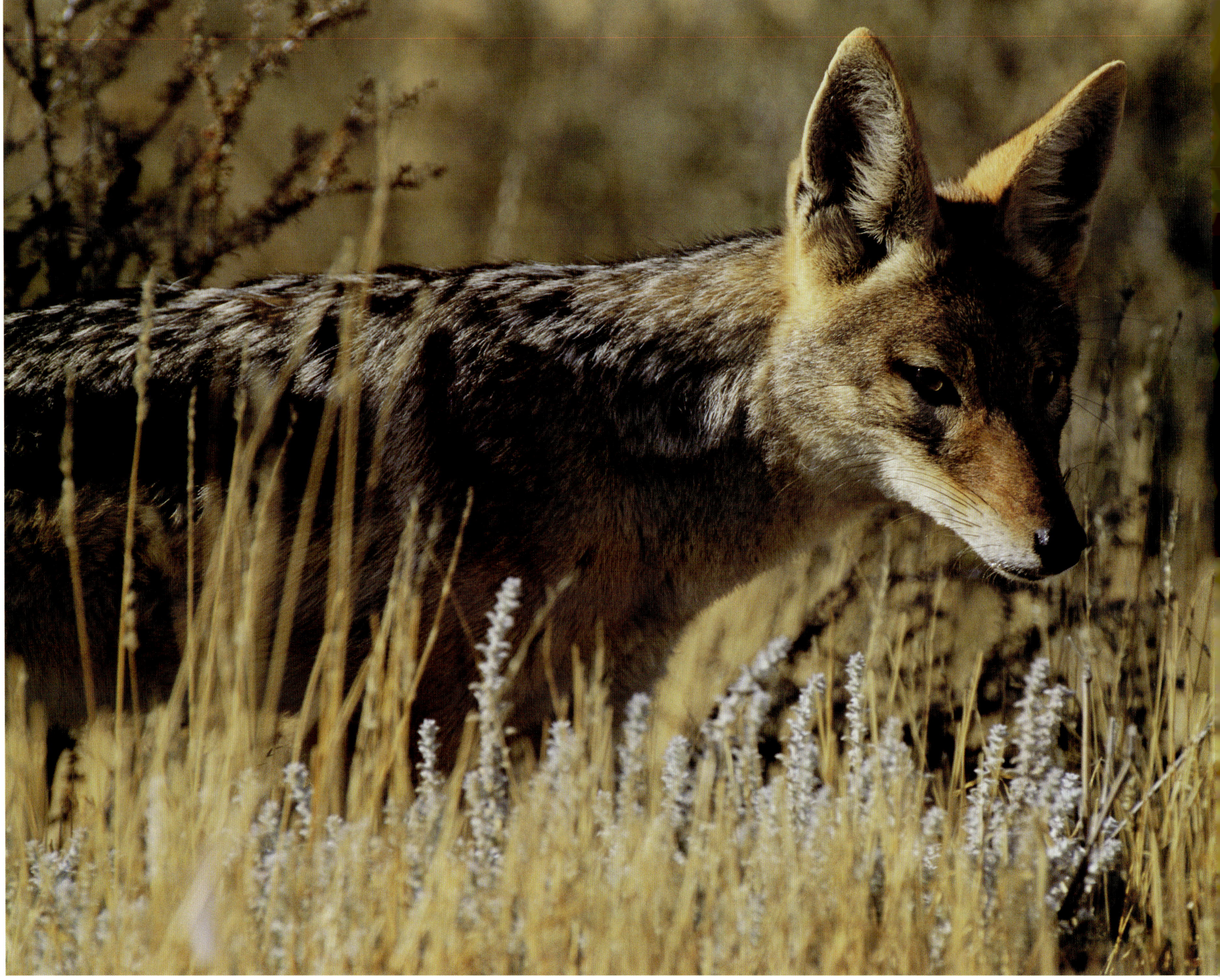

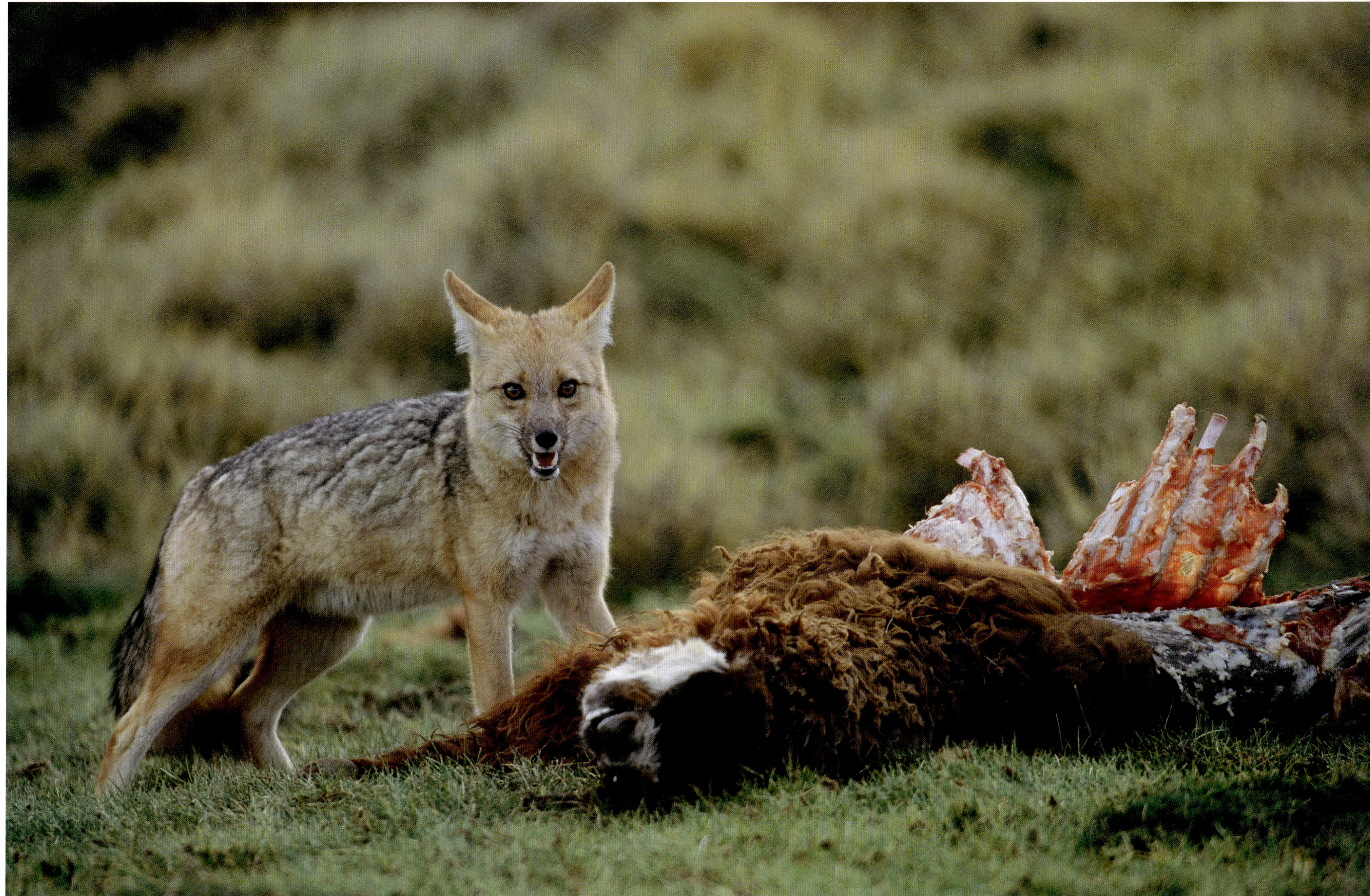

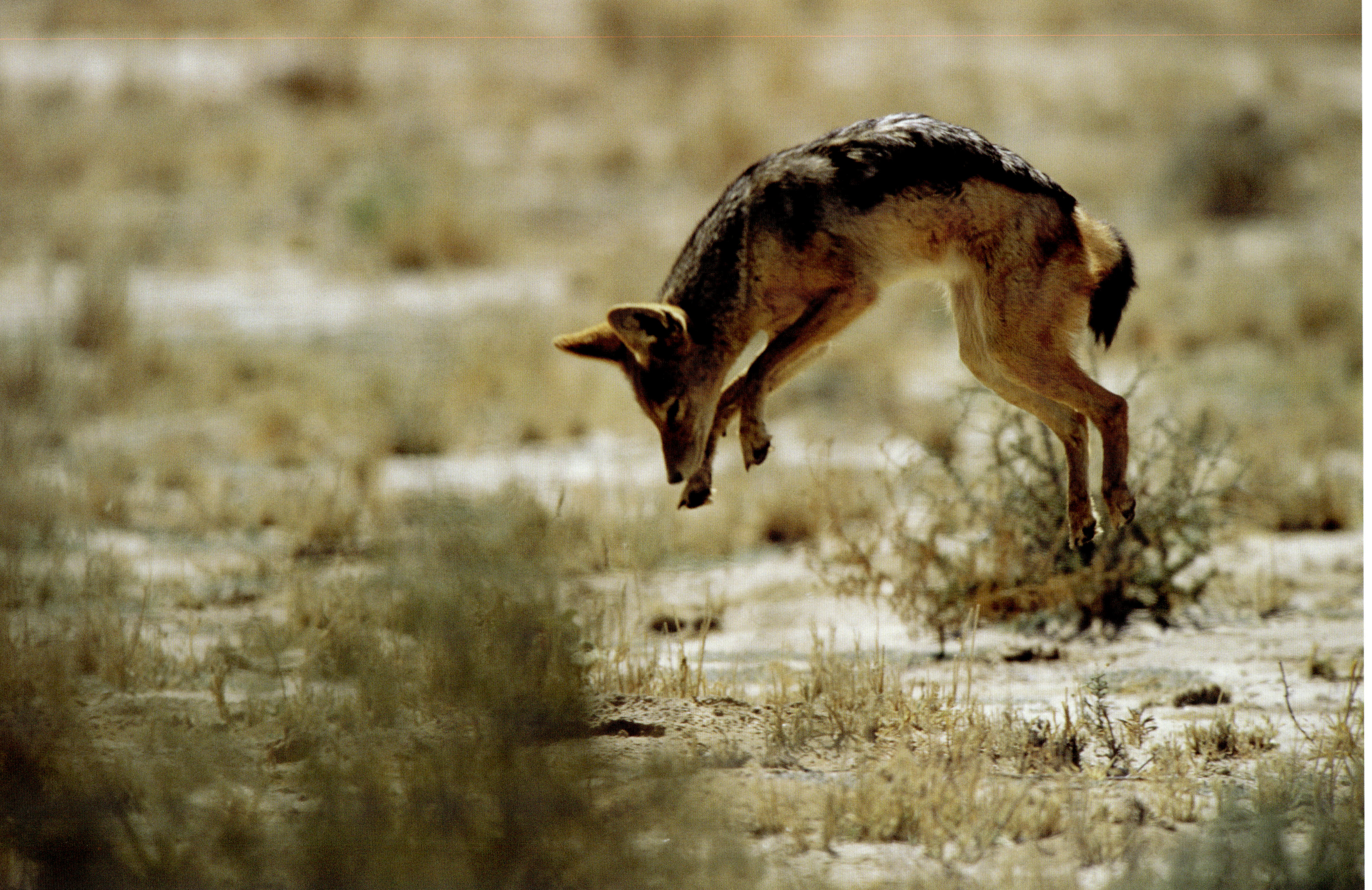

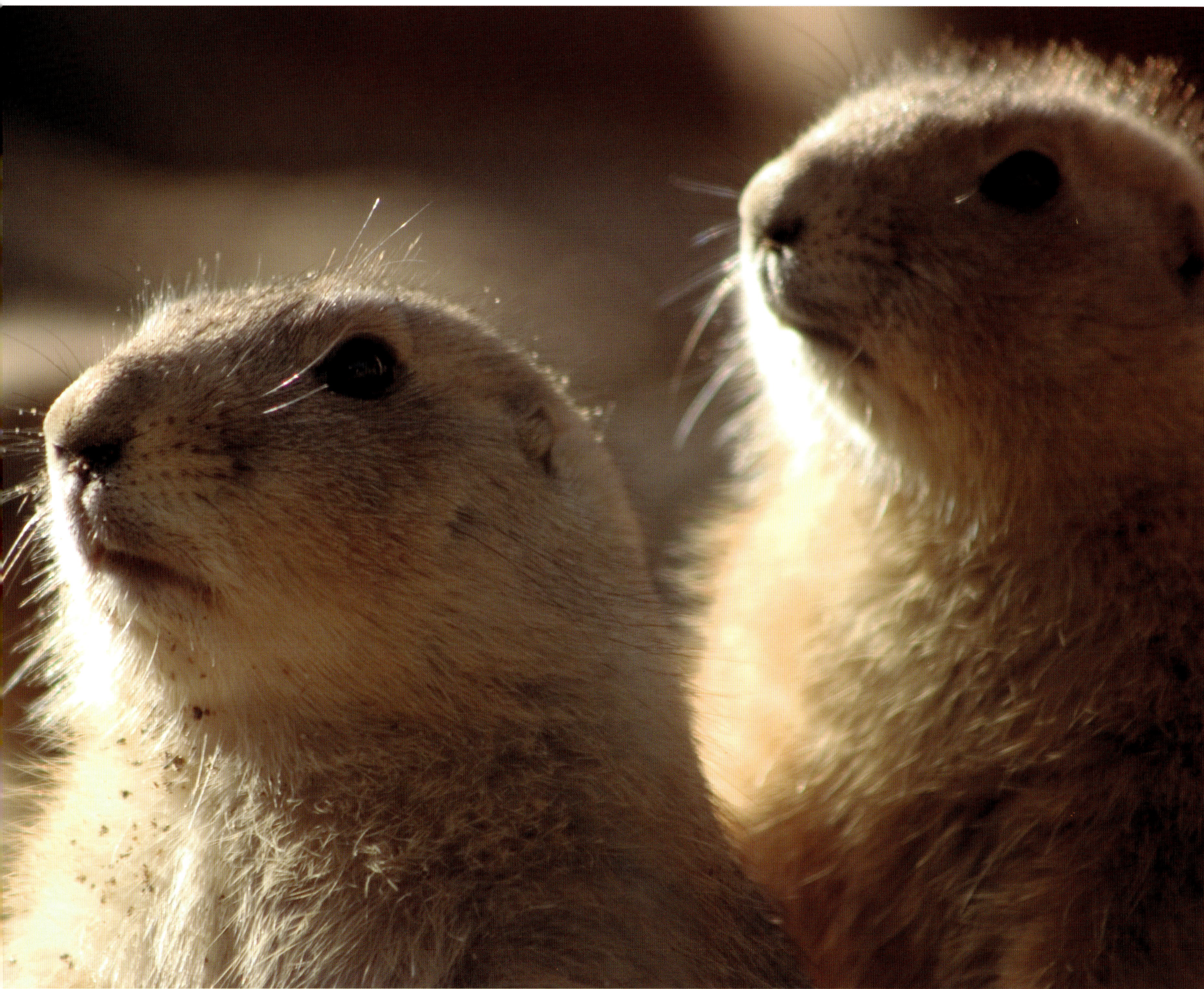

Far Left: The black-backed jackal is found in the desert regions of Southern and Eastern Africa. It is one of the smaller hyenas, the largest being about 40 inches in length, 20 inches tall, and weighing some 33 pounds. The jackal's diet consists of almost anything, ranging from small animals, such as meerkats, through carrion to fruit and berries. Jackals normally hunt by night but this specimen is attacking its prey during a daytime hunt in the Kalahari Desert.
Mattias Klun/Getty Images

Left: The North American prairie dog is actually a member of the squirrel family, but was given its name by the early settlers due to its danger signal, which is a barking sound, resembling that of dogs. Prairie dogs are ground-dwellers and dig burrows, which can be up to fifteen feet deep, with nesting rooms and a survival room for use in the event of flooding. They appear to drink little water directly, absorbing it instead from their diet of flowers, grasses, leaves, and roots.
Paul Chapman/fotoLibra

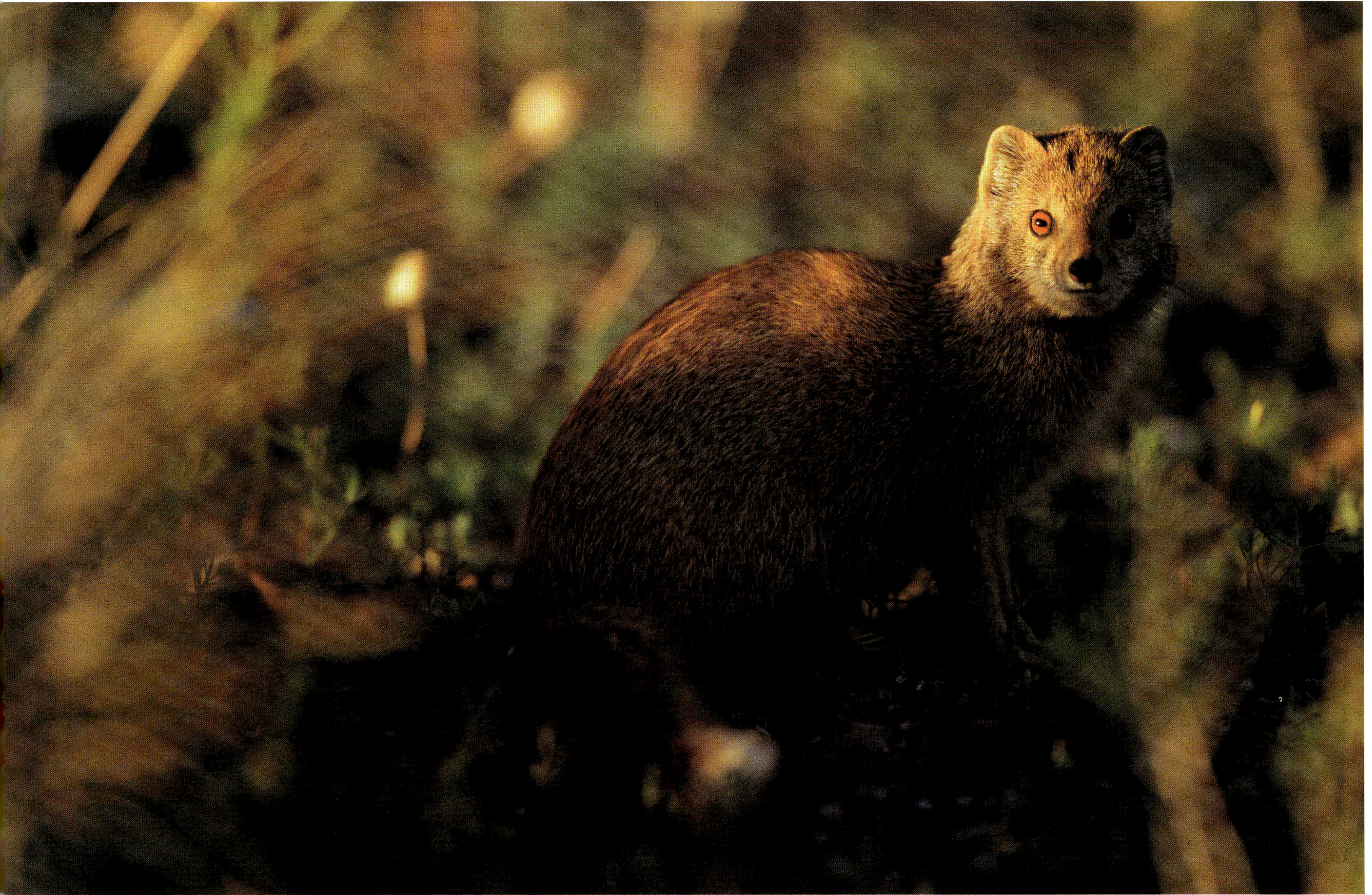

Left: Another denizen of the Kalahari Desert, the yellow mongoose is generally about twenty inches long. Mongooses are very sociable animals and live in large burrows, which they often share with meerkats. Their diet consists of mice, birds, eggs, and insects, while they, in their turn, are preyed upon by hawks, snakes, and jackals.
Mattias Klum/Getty Images

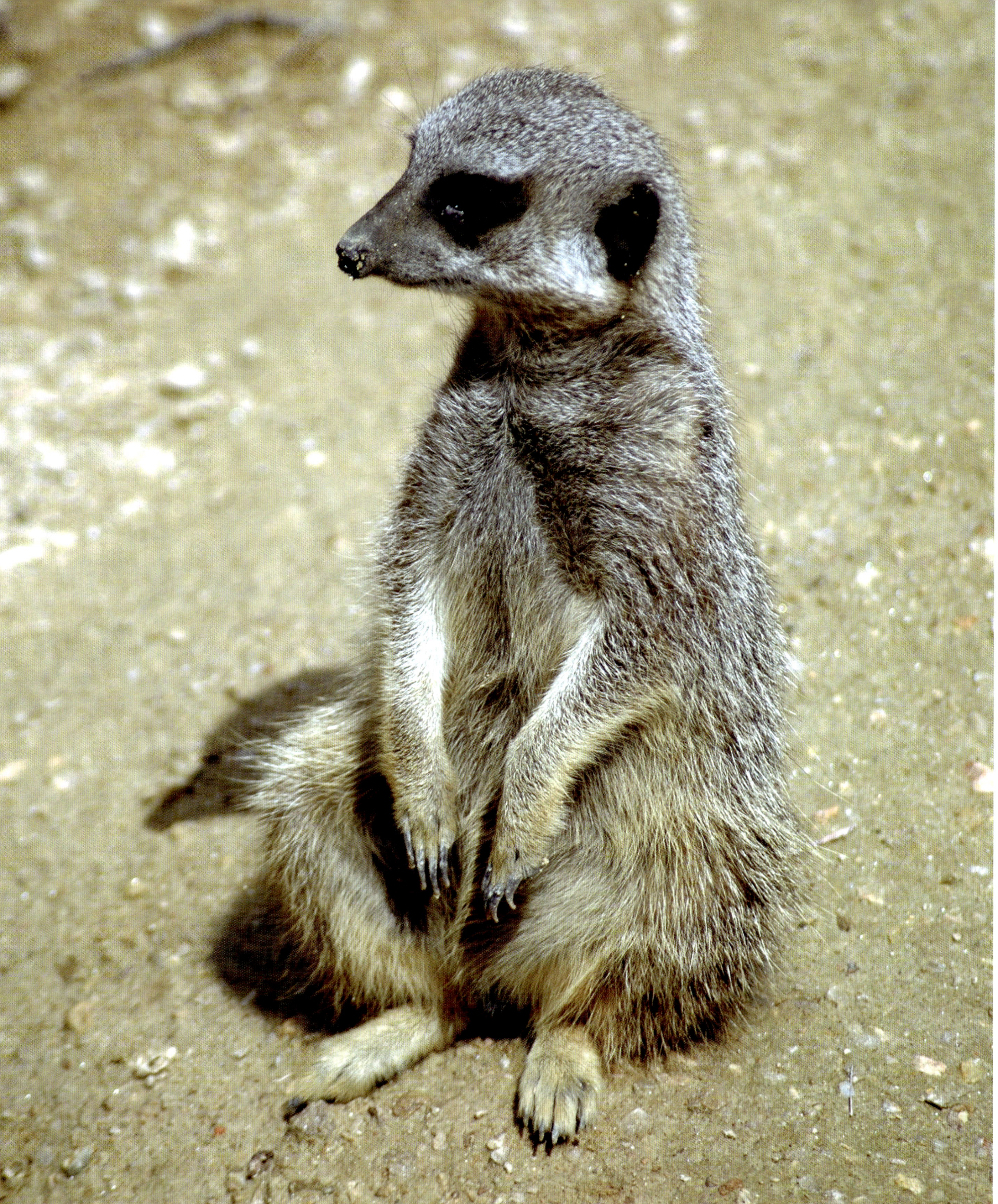

Left: Wildlife programs on TV have made the South African meerkat one of the most popular creatures on the planet, their natural upright pose and alert appearance, as in this picture, making them particularly appealing to humans. They belong to the mongoose family, but live in large colonies with a well-developed social structure. They feed mainly on insects, but also kill small snakes and scorpions, and are unusual in that they give absolutely no warning of an impending attack.
Magdalena Mayo/fotoLibra

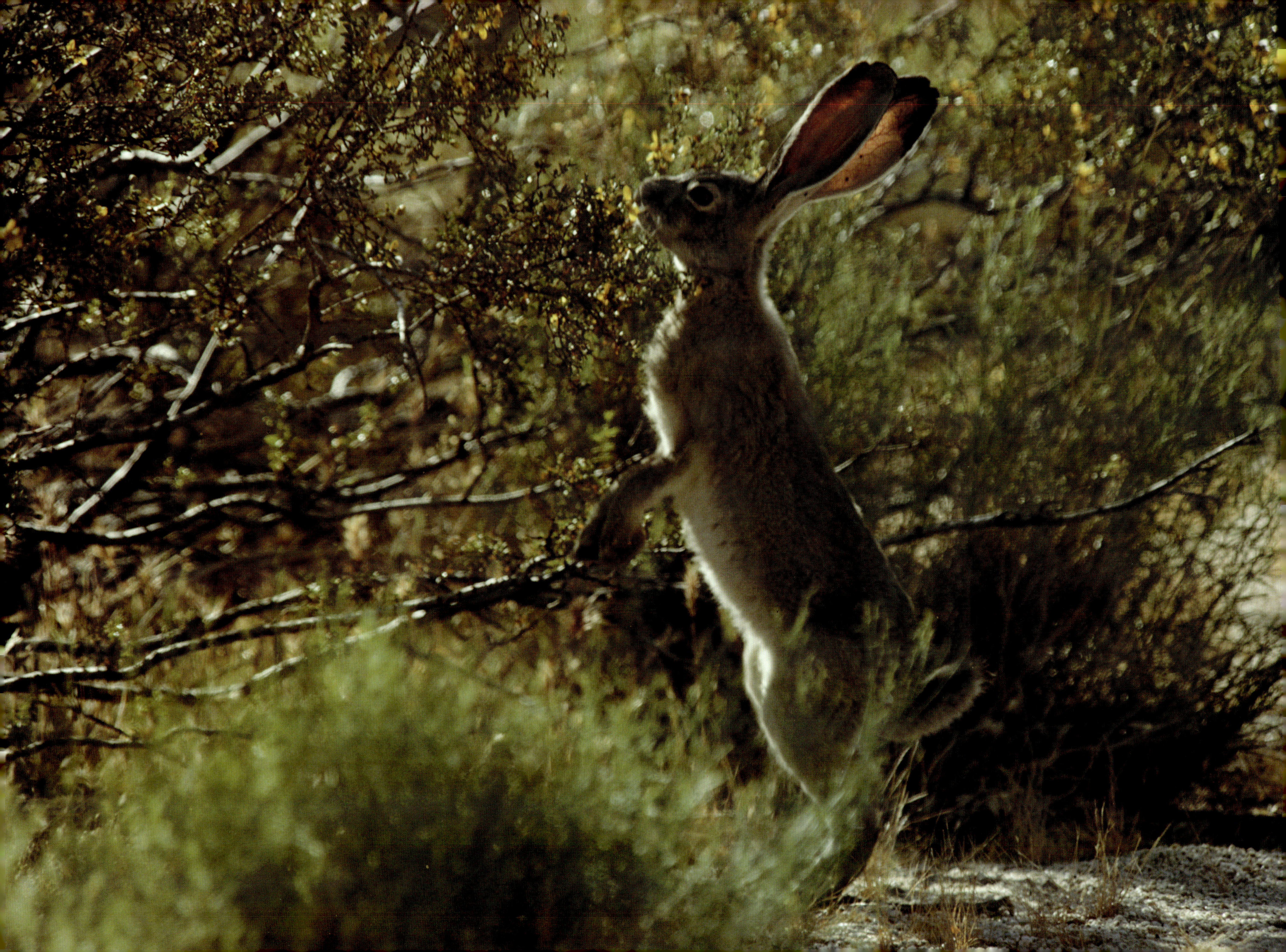

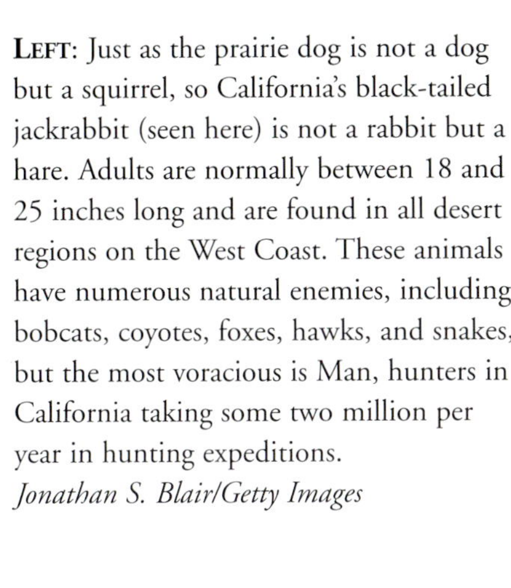

Left: Just as the prairie dog is not a dog but a squirrel, so California's black-tailed jackrabbit (seen here) is not a rabbit but a hare. Adults are normally between 18 and 25 inches long and are found in all desert regions on the West Coast. These animals have numerous natural enemies, including bobcats, coyotes, foxes, hawks, and snakes, but the most voracious is Man, hunters in California taking some two million per year in hunting expeditions.
Jonathan S. Blair/Getty Images

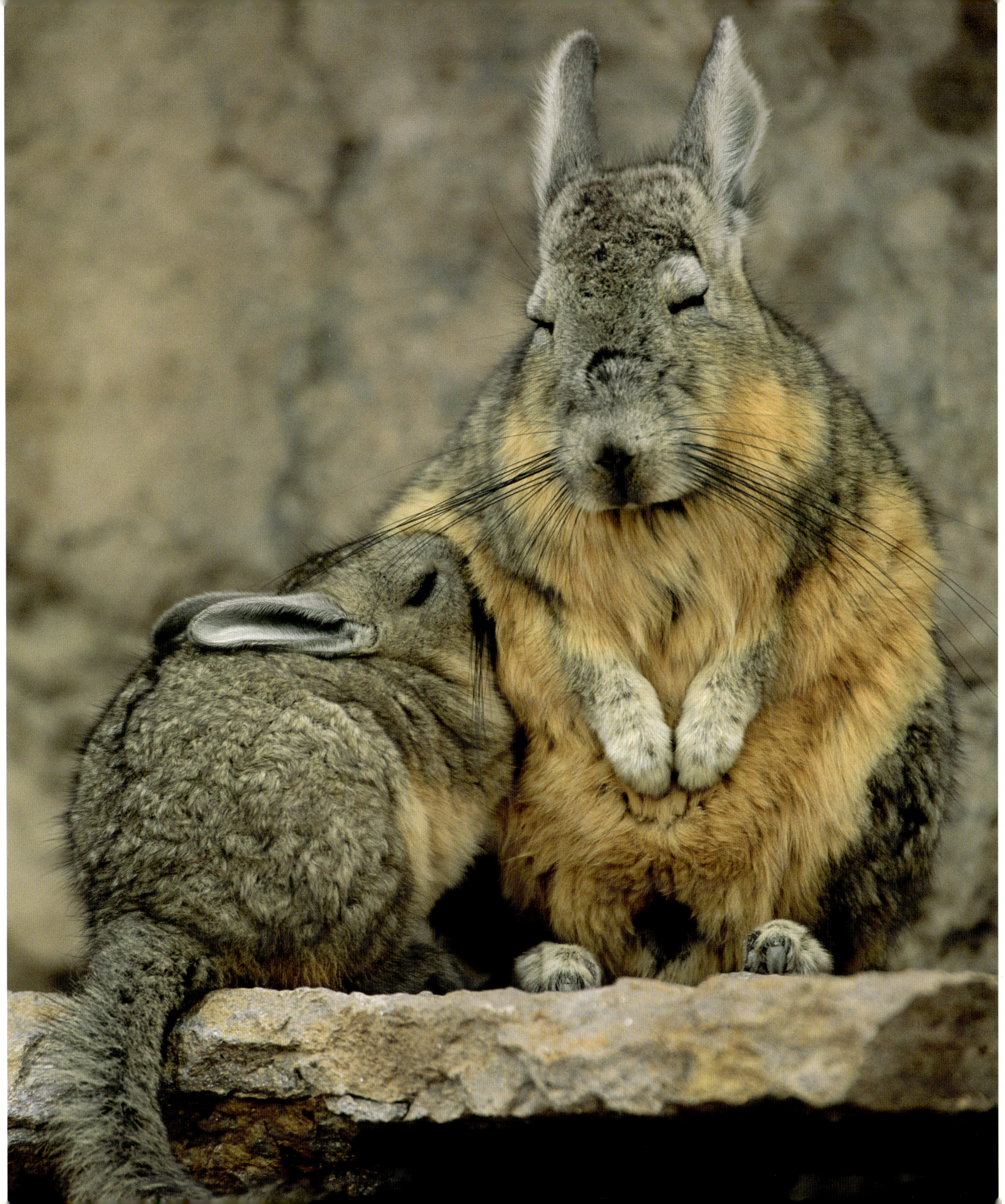

Left: A contented mother viscacha nursing her offspring in the Atacama Desert in Chile. This herbivorous rodent is related to the chinchilla and is found only in the southern parts of South America. Males weigh up to 17 pounds and can be 26 inches long with an 8-inch tail, the females being slightly smaller. The viscachas live in elaborate burrows, whose entrances are marked with dried bones and sticks. They are very fast movers and can change direction very rapidly.
Joel Sartore/Getty Images

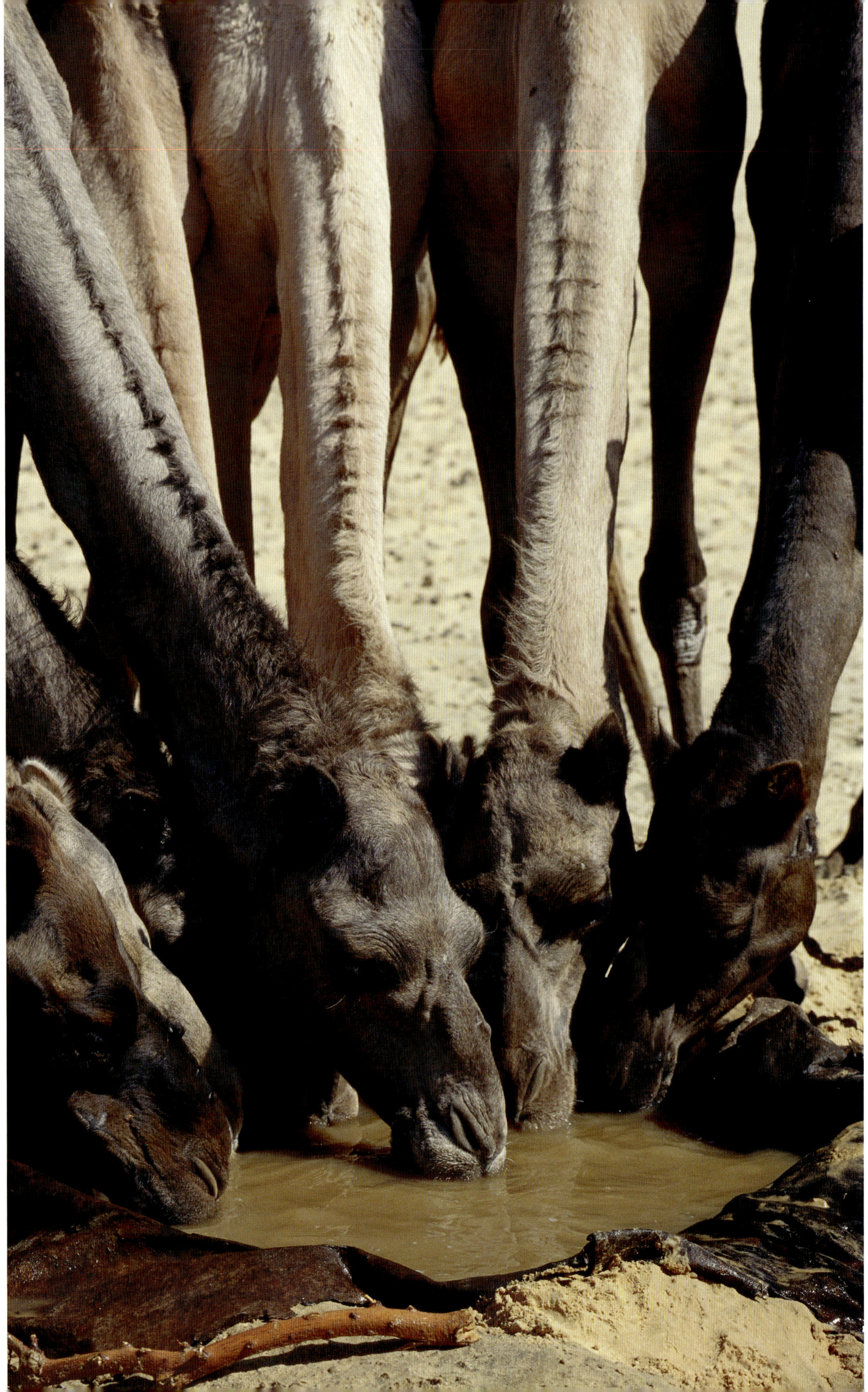

LEFT: All life on Earth revolves around water, a fact that those who have plenty of it tend to forget. In the desert, however, this need is only too apparent. Even animals that have adapted to such an environment, such as these camels, which can go without water for up to two weeks, must eventually replenish their stocks or die.
Michael S. Lewis/Getty Images

RIGHT: Llamas near the village of Caspana in the Atacama Desert, with ribbons in their ears to identify the owner. Llamas are camelids, belonging to the same family as the single-humped dromedary found in Arabia and the twin-humped Bactrian camel of the Gobi desert. Llamas are domesticated animals, used to carry loads, as a source of wool, and to supply both meat and dung for fuel.
Charles O'Rear/Corbis

PAGE 168: Mustangs run together in the Wyoming Desert. Most desert animals have spent many millennia adapting to their inhospitable environment, but some, such as these mustangs and the very similar wild horses in Namibia, have made the adjustment within a very short space of time.
Eastcott Momatiuk/Getty Images

PAGE 169: McCullough Peaks is an area of desert badlands, or high desert, lying south of Powell, Wyoming, and is home to a herd of wild horses, or mustangs, estimated to be some 130 strong. The herd has a very rigid social structure and the stallions seen here are fighting for the right to control the harem and establish breeding rights with the mares.
Steven G. Smith/Corbis

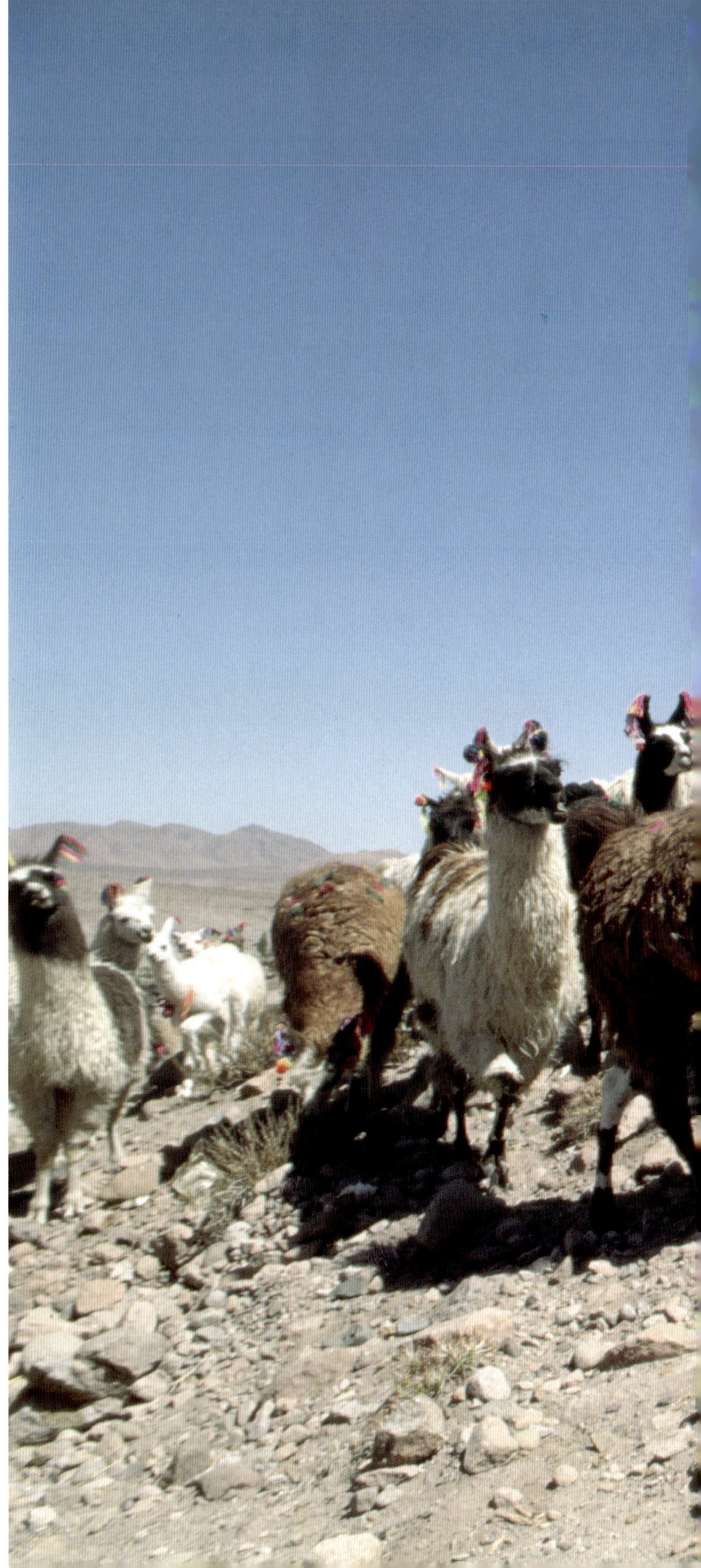

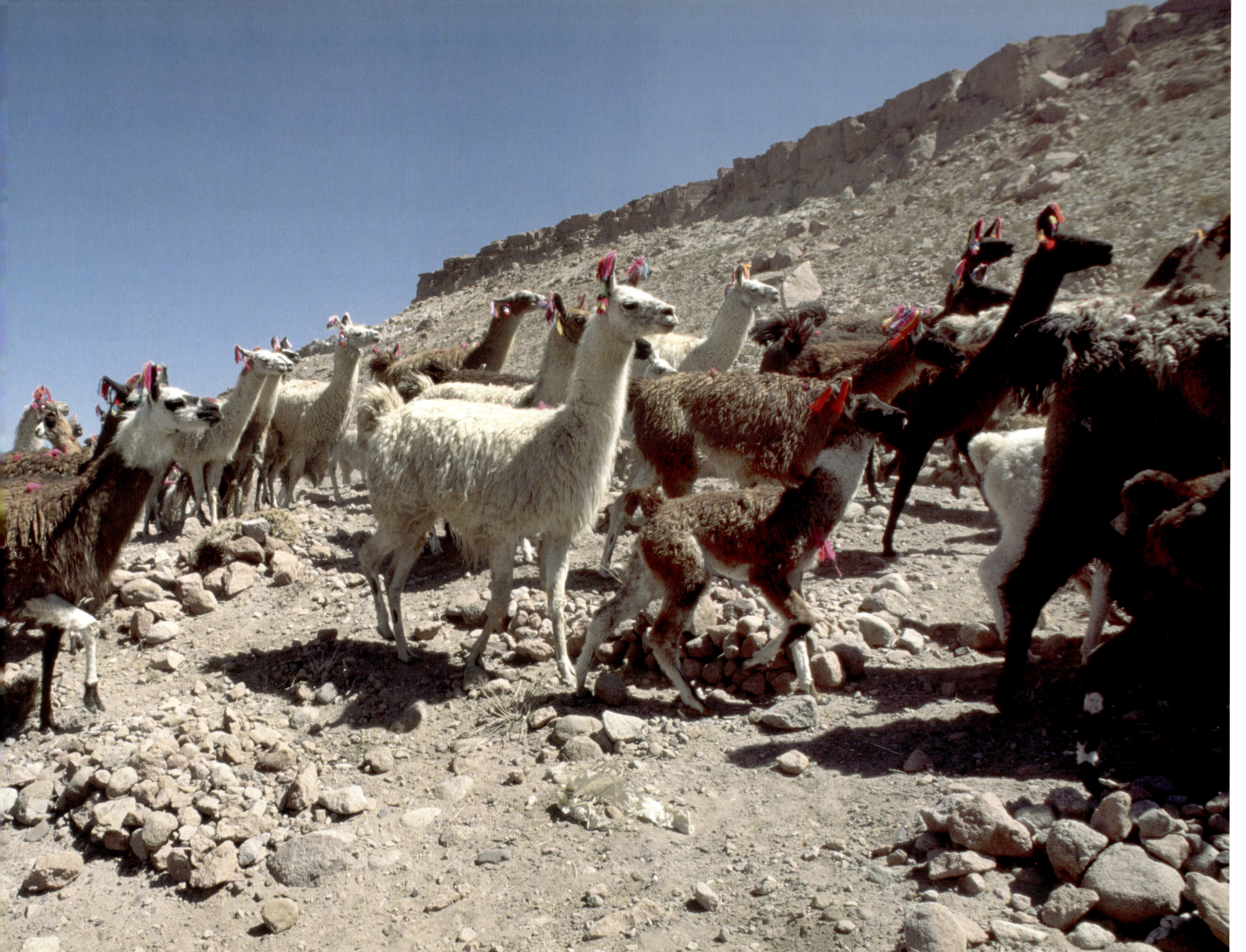

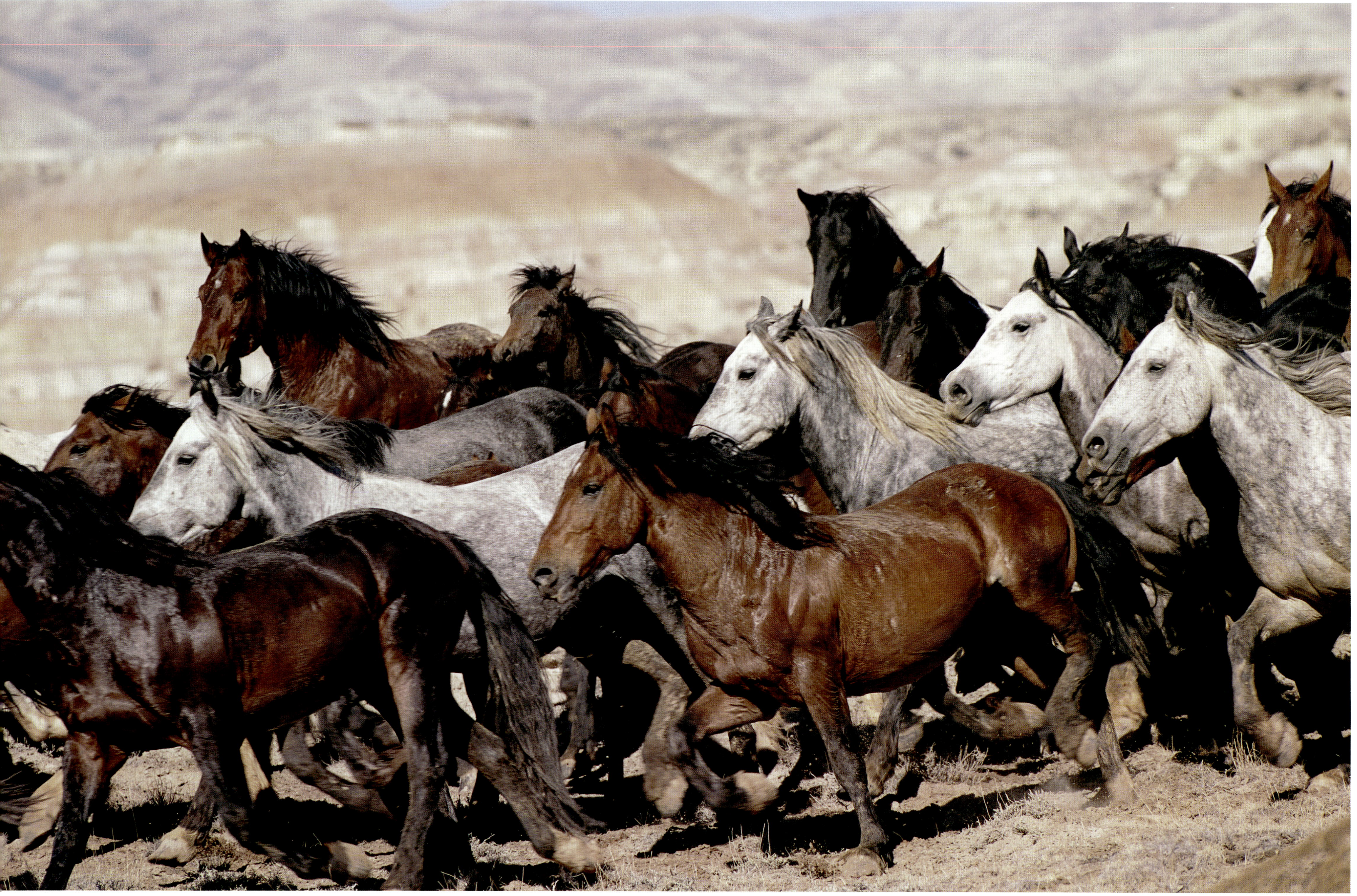

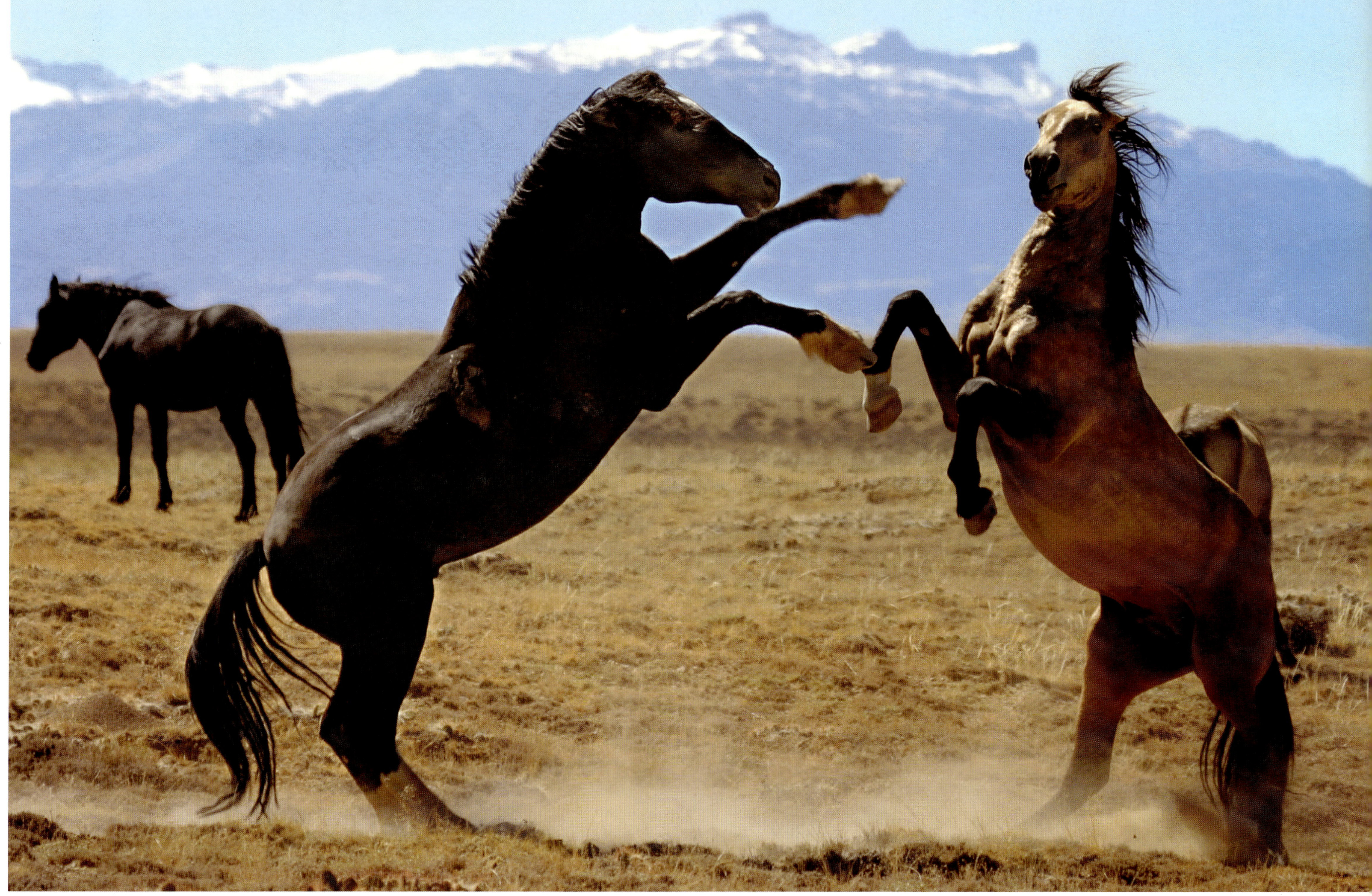

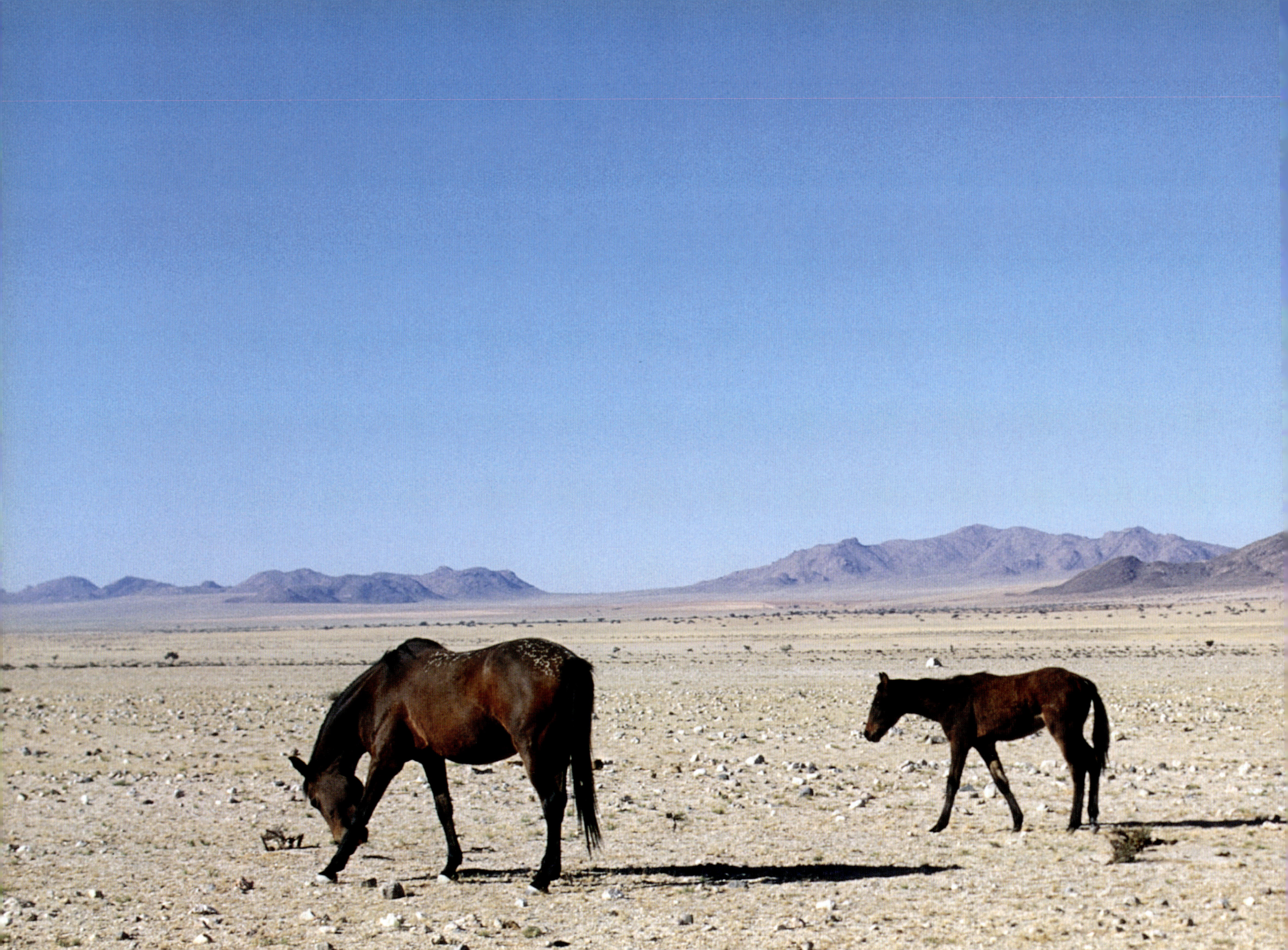

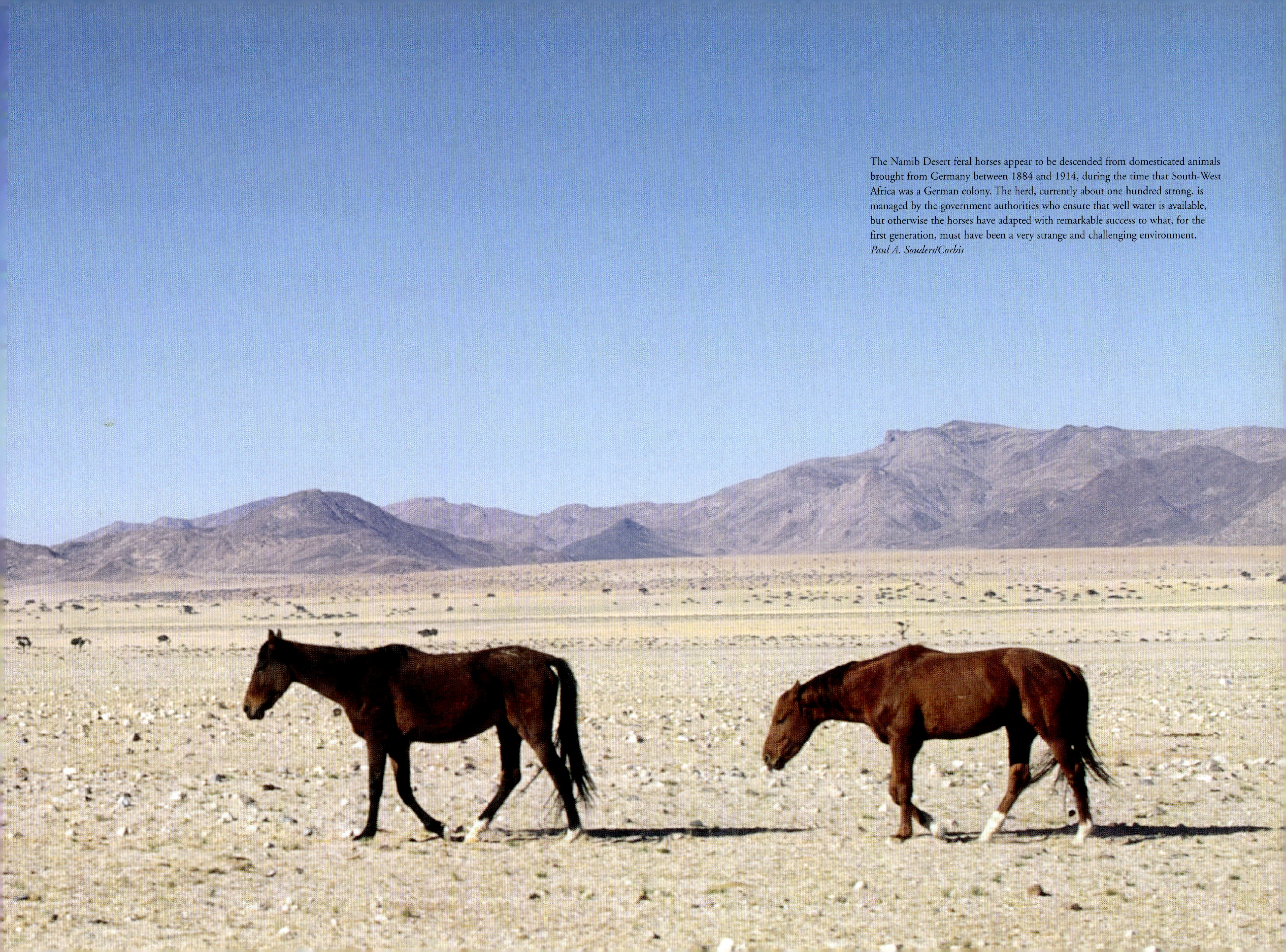

The Namib Desert feral horses appear to be descended from domesticated animals brought from Germany between 1884 and 1914, during the time that South-West Africa was a German colony. The herd, currently about one hundred strong, is managed by the government authorities who ensure that well water is available, but otherwise the horses have adapted with remarkable success to what, for the first generation, must have been a very strange and challenging environment.
Paul A. Souders/Corbis

RIGHT: The desert tortoise is found in southern California's Mojave and Sonoran Deserts, as well as in southern Nevada, Arizona, and Mexico. It spends some 95 percent of its life in a burrow and can survive even when the ambient temperature is as high as 145 degrees Fahrenheit. It is herbivorous and the outer shell (also known as the carapace) may be as long as fifteen inches. It is a protected species and it is illegal even to pick up a wild specimen.
Jonathan S. Blair/Getty Images

FAR RIGHT: The Thorny Devil lizard is found in many parts of Australia, this particular example being photographed near Alice Springs in the center of the country. It is quite unlike any other lizard, its 6-8 inch body being covered with conical spines. It has a variety of defense mechanisms including changing color, trying to look like a leaf, and rolling itself into a ball, but it has no known enemies apart from bustards and Man.
Theo Allofs/Corbis

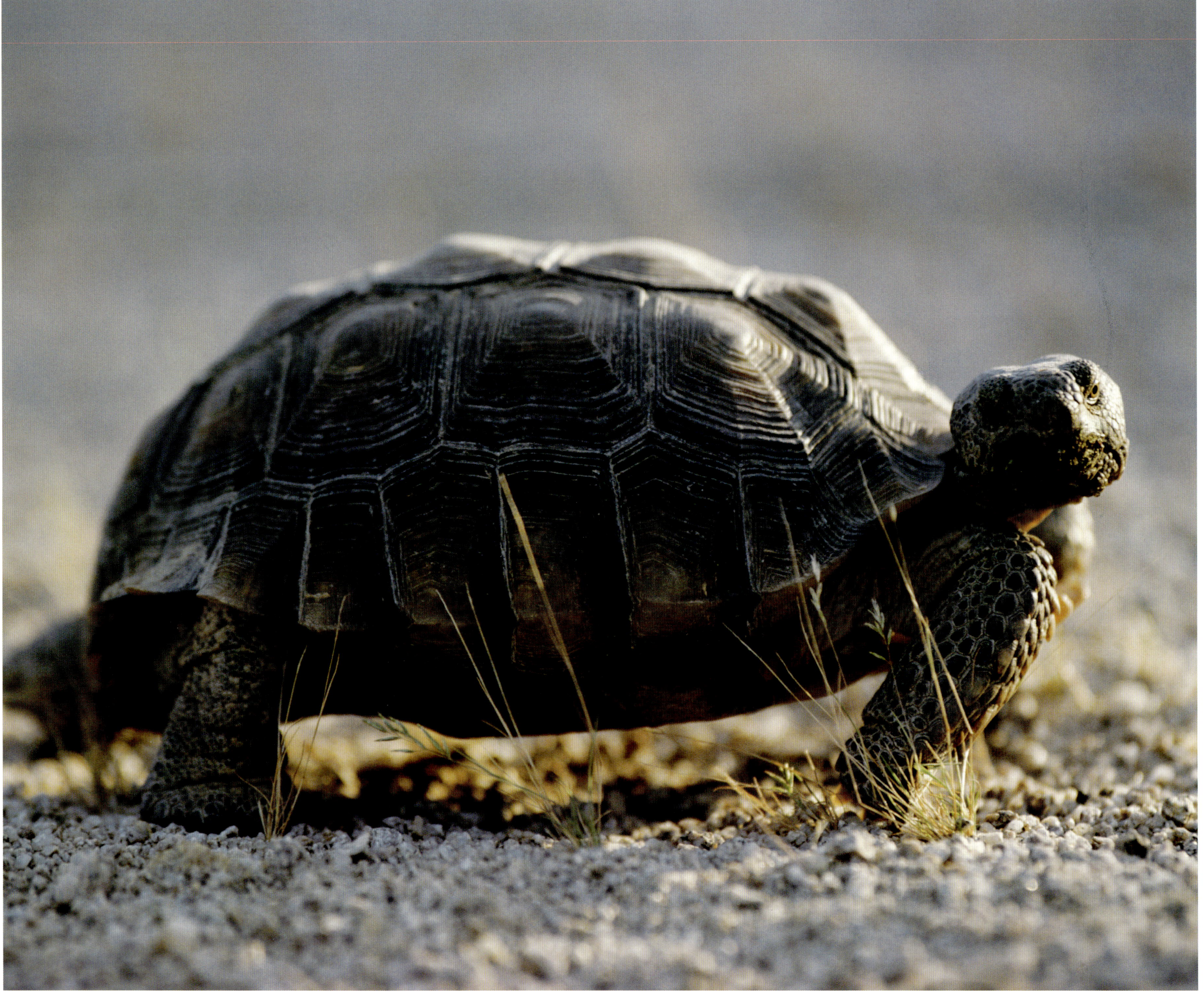

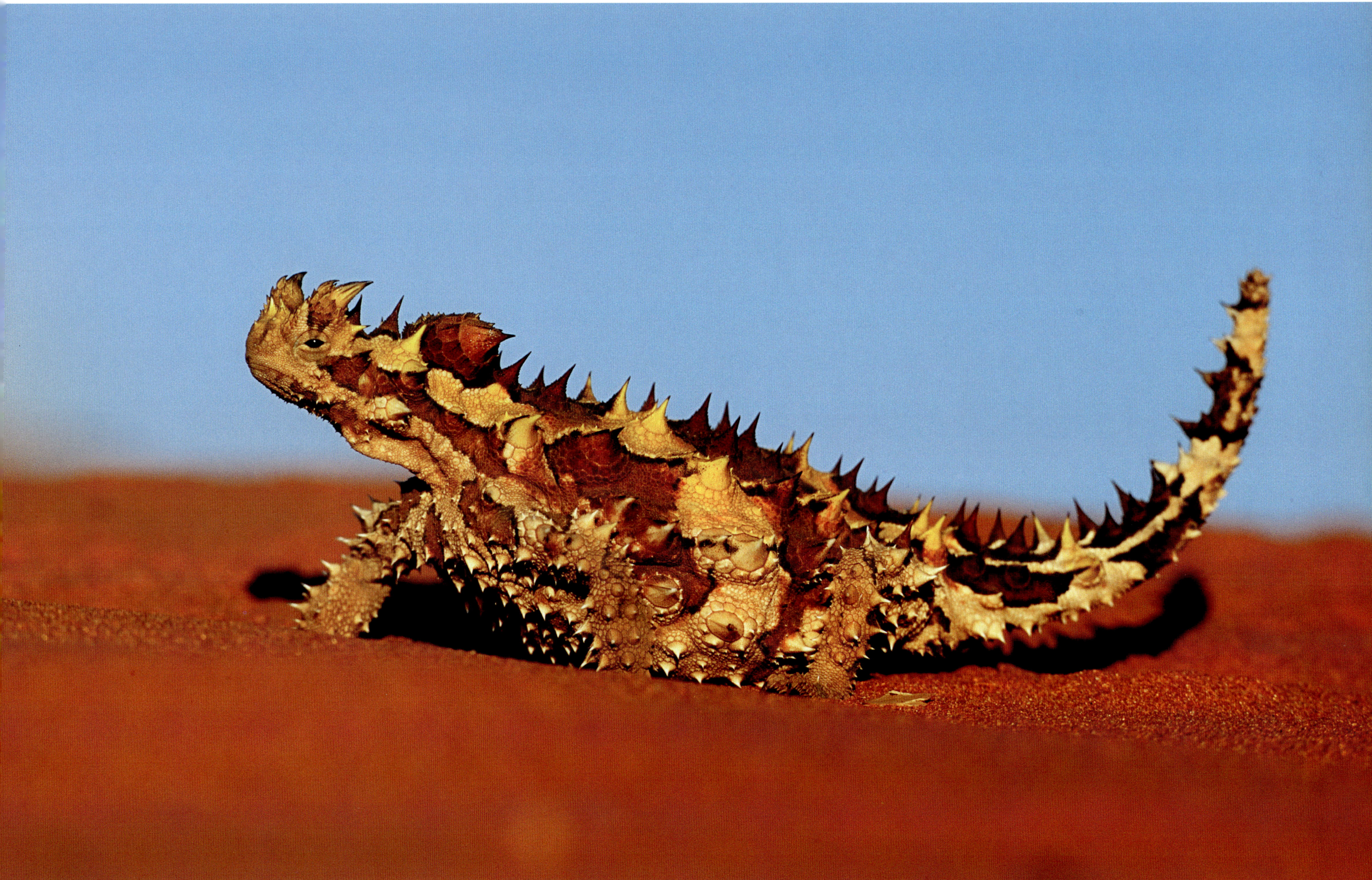

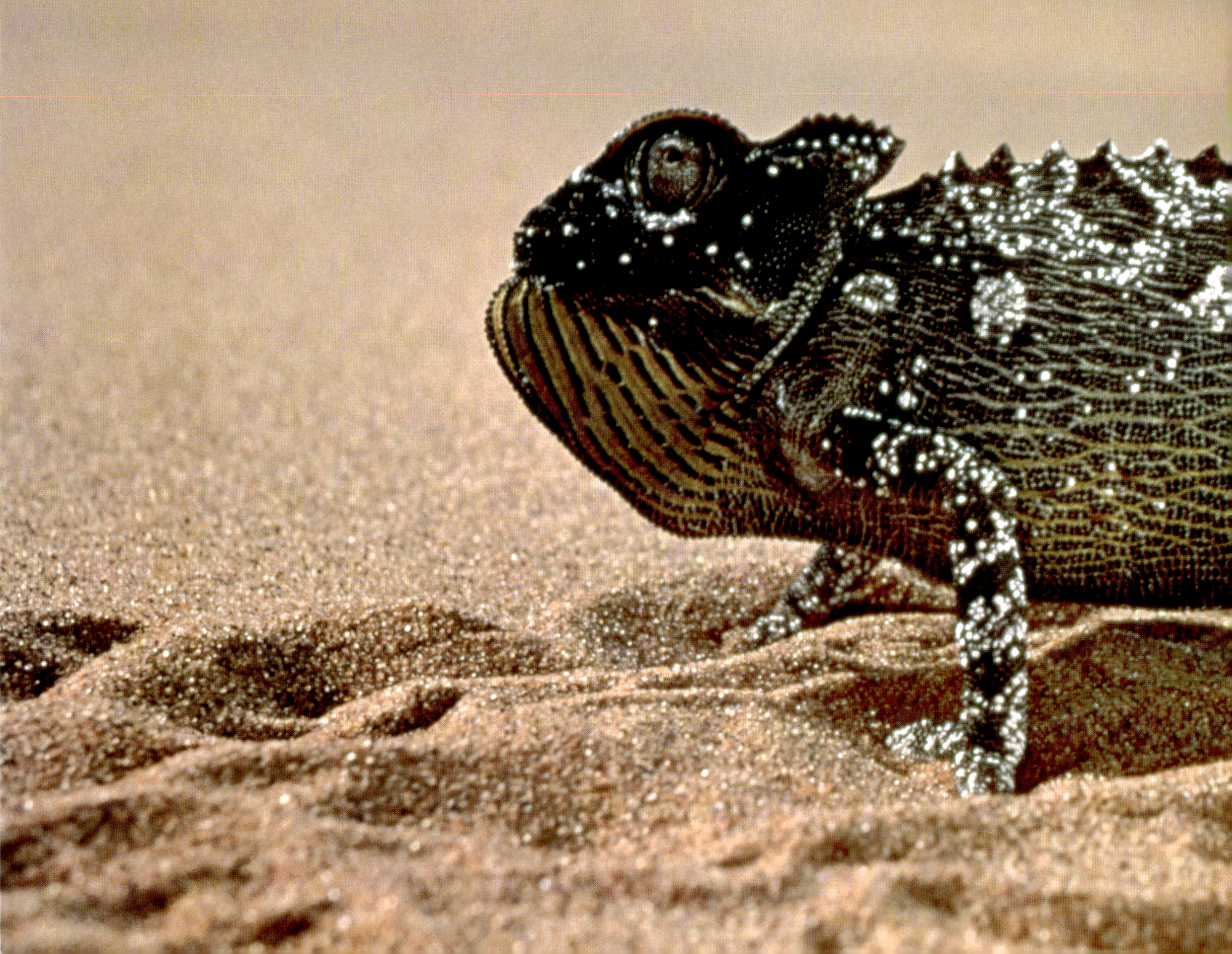

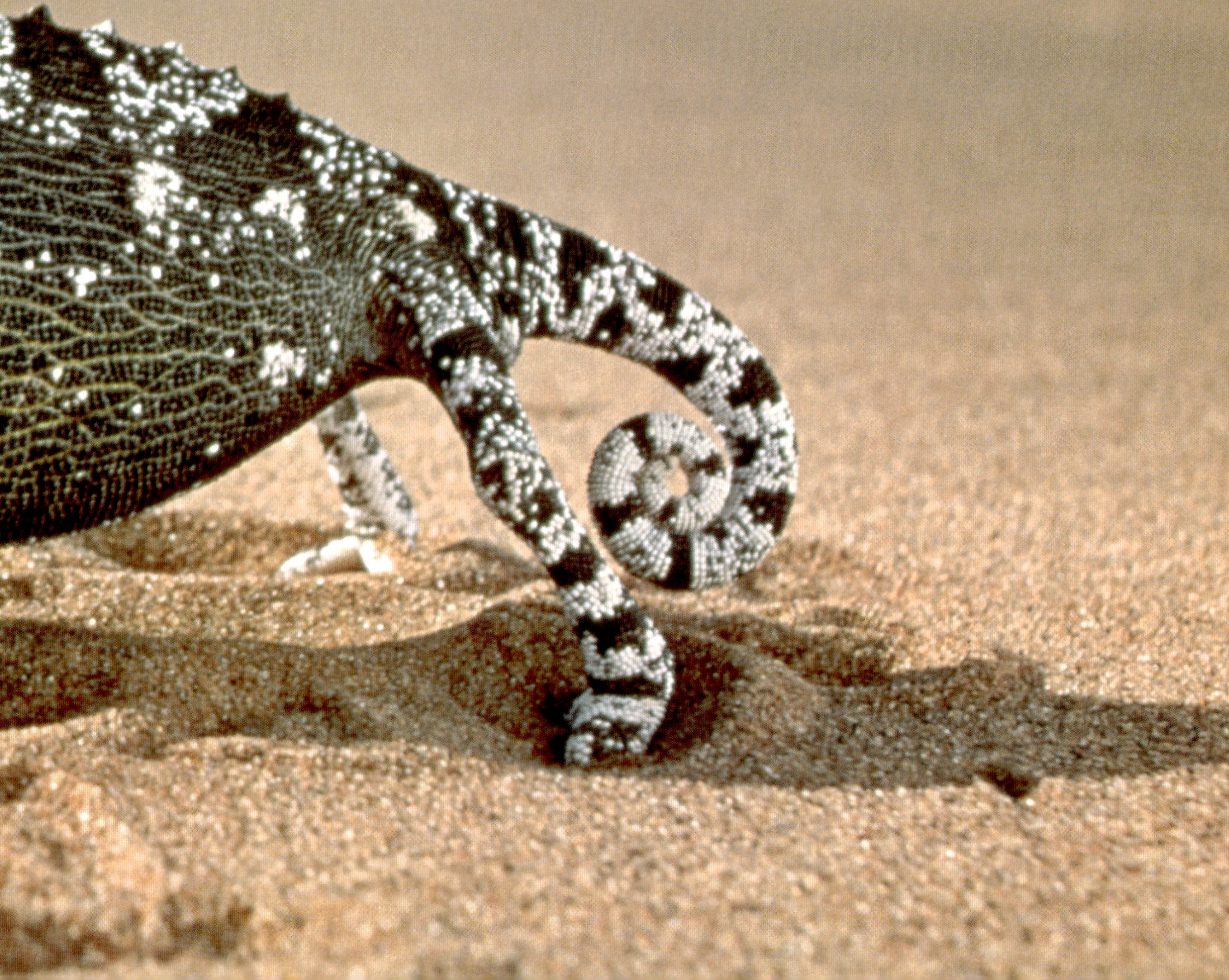

Left: The Namaqua chameleon is found only in southwest Africa, in Namaqualand and the Namib Desert. Belonging to the lizard family, the chameleon has a large head, very long tongue with a sticky tip, independently moving eyes and fused toes, but it is best known for its ability to change color. It has a curious gait, moving with diagonally opposed limbs, but is very fast, preying on beetles, crickets, locusts, scorpions, and small snakes.
Michael & Patricia Fogden/Corbis

Pages 176–177: The Australian blue-tongued skink is a desert-dwelling lizard, which eats both meat, such as insects, snails or worms, and plants, such as berries, flowers or fruit. The skink has a scaly body, very short legs, a short, thick tail (which can break off and be regrown), and the characteristic blue tongue. An adult measures some 24 inches in length and can live for up to 20 years. When threatened it sticks out its tongue and hisses, but is not dangerous.
Theo Allofs/Corbis

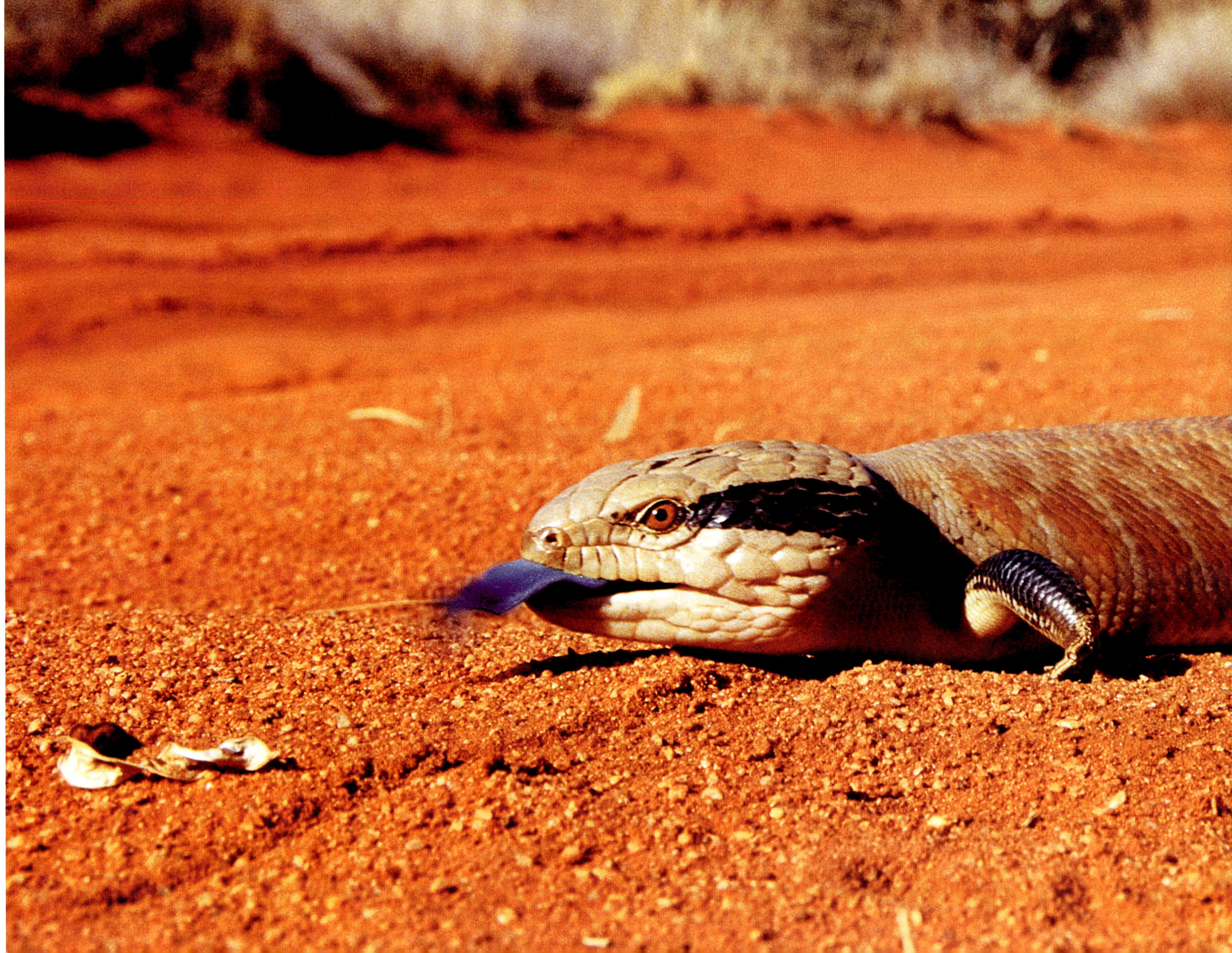

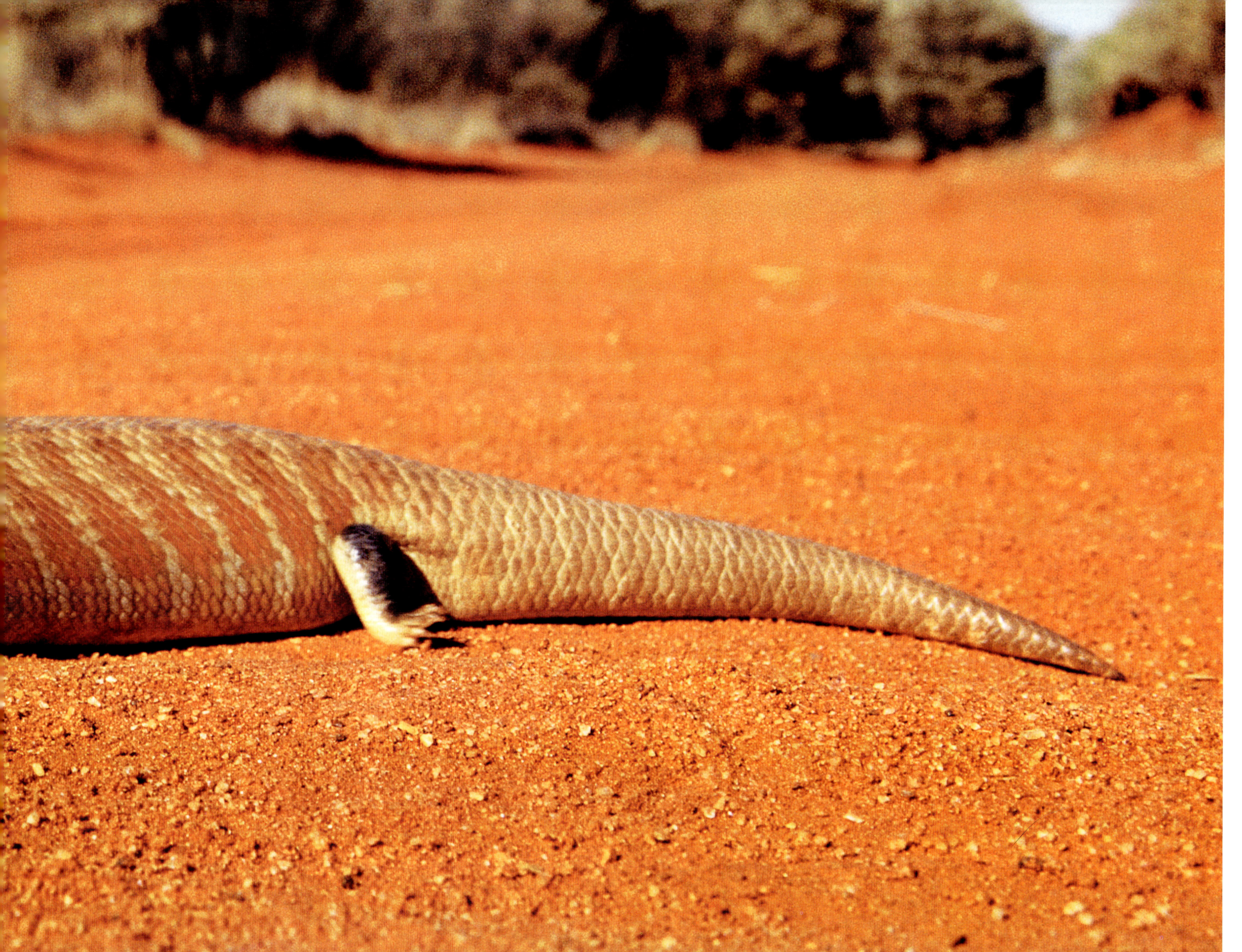

PEOPLE OF THE DESERTS

There are a very few deserts that do not have any inhabitants at all, while even in those that do, the population density is extremely low. Over many generations these people have adapted their behavior and survival techniques to their environment, learning to cope with the extreme conditions. Thus, people such as the Bedouin of the Sahara, the Touareg of the Arabian Desert, the Native Americans of the Great Basin Desert, and the Aboriginal People in Australia have survived, albeit in different ways. What they do have in common, however, is that their small numbers and unsophisticated way of life have not equipped them to resist the inexorable advance of the European settler or the urban dwellers.

Two developments set the past fifty years apart. The first is that in many cases there is an ever-increasing drift towards the towns or at least to static settlements on the fringes of the deserts, as people, particularly the younger generation, seek the benefits and greater comforts of urban life. Second, there is the increased use of deserts as tourist attractions and playgrounds for leisure activities such as cross-country driving with four-wheel-drive automobiles or motorcycles. There is, of course, a place for such enjoyment, but a balance must be struck to ensure that the weight of numbers or pollution caused by powered vehicles do not destroy Nature's delicate balance.

Right: The North African Tuareg are scattered across modern Algeria, Libya and other Saharan countries, the frontiers imposed by European imperialists in the late 19th century being essentially meaningless to such nomadic people. They used to indulge in raiding coastal settlements but this has now been virtually eliminated and the long-distance caravan trading, as seen here, is rapidly diminishing in the face of modern means of transportation, such as trucks.
Lynsey Addario/Corbis

Far Right: The very word "desert" conjures up pictures of great heat and this may be true (but not always) in the daytime, but nights are quite another matter and temperatures can approach freezing. Thus, there is a great need for fuel for heating, as well as, of course, for cooking. This Berber woman in the Grand Atlas Mountains of Morocco has collected a heavy load of firewood.
Robert van der Hilst/Corbis

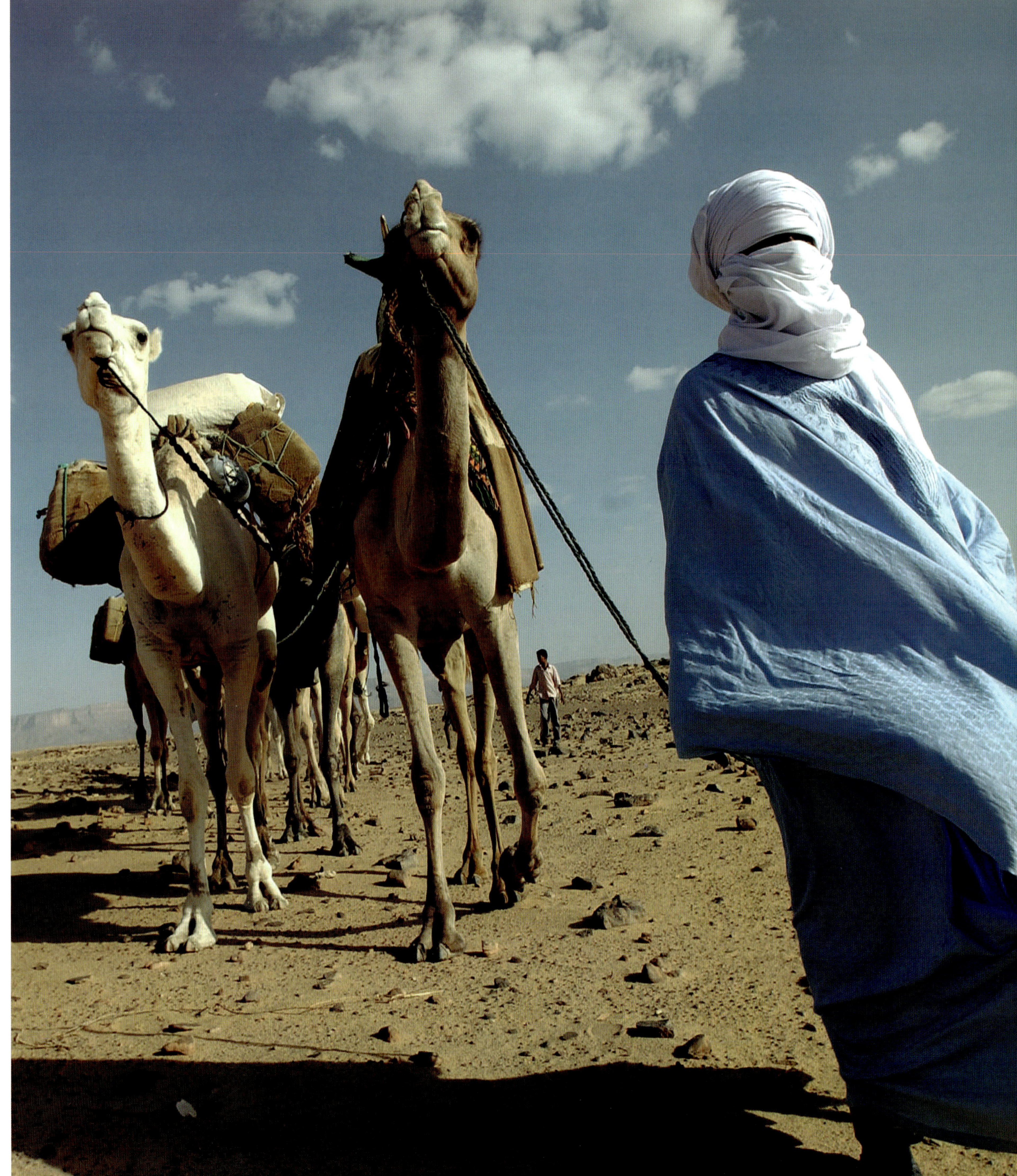

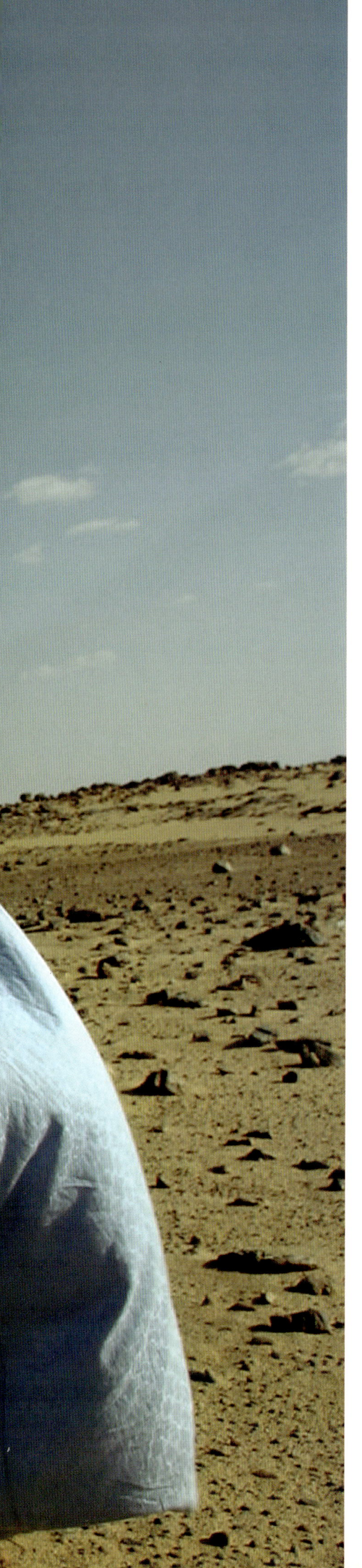

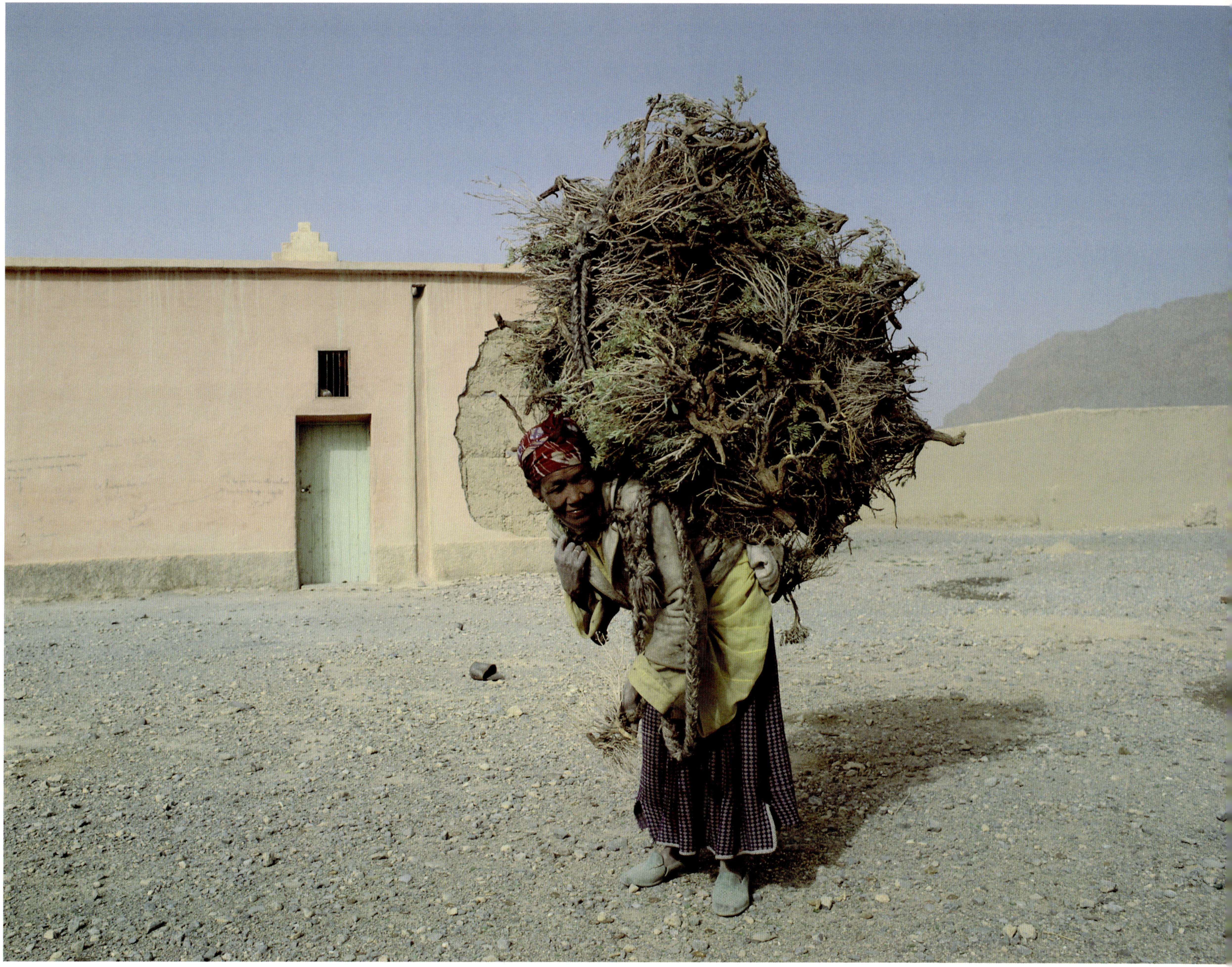

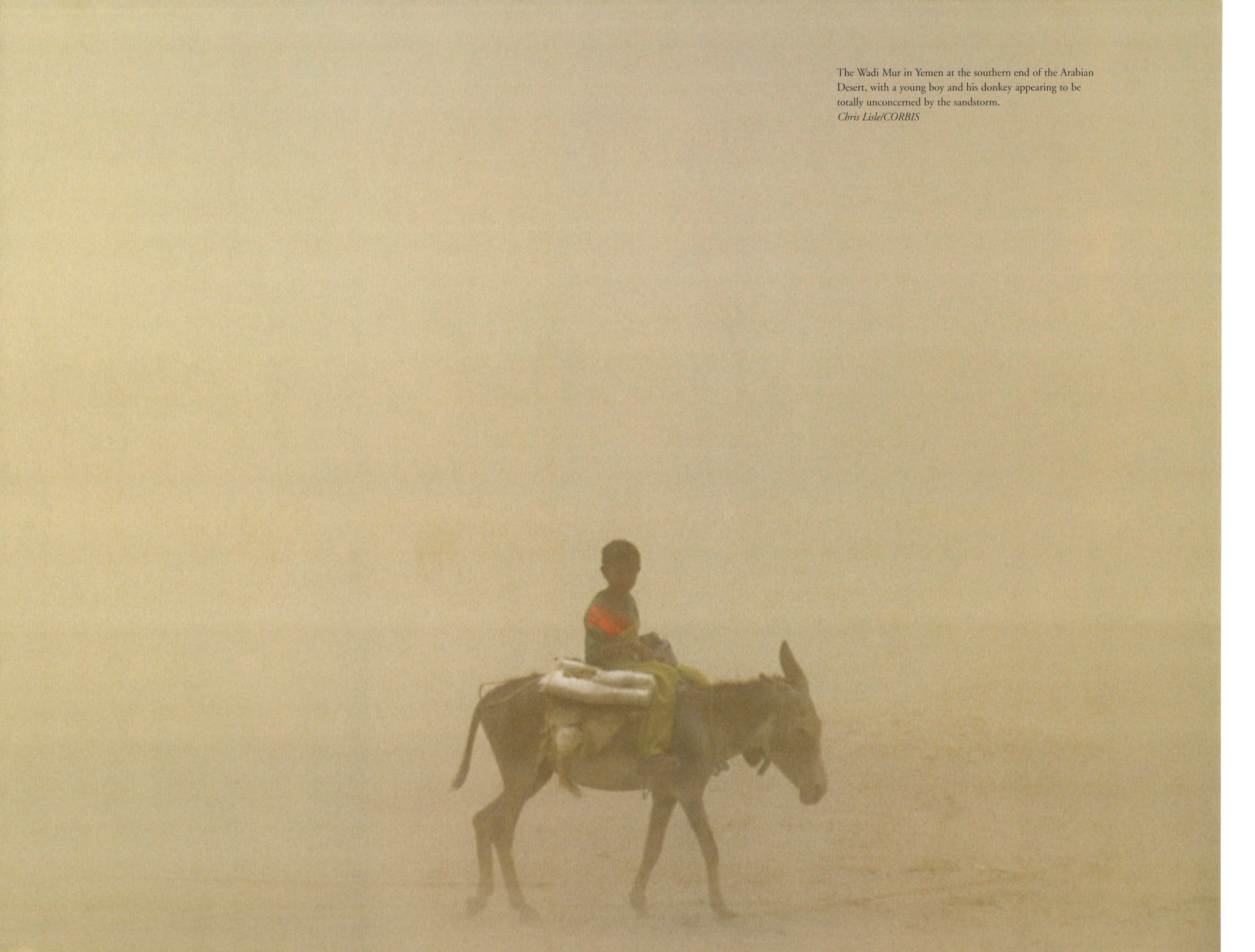

The Wadi Mur in Yemen at the southern end of the Arabian Desert, with a young boy and his donkey appearing to be totally unconcerned by the sandstorm.
Chris Lisle/CORBIS

RIGHT: A group of Bedouin women collect water from the well at a Saharan oasis between Zaafrane and Douz in southern Tunisia. People such as these are probably the last generation to experience such a traditional way of life; the creeping influences of tourism and modern comforts such as television, coolers, piped water, and automobiles will probably change things for ever.
Hans Georg Roth/Corbis

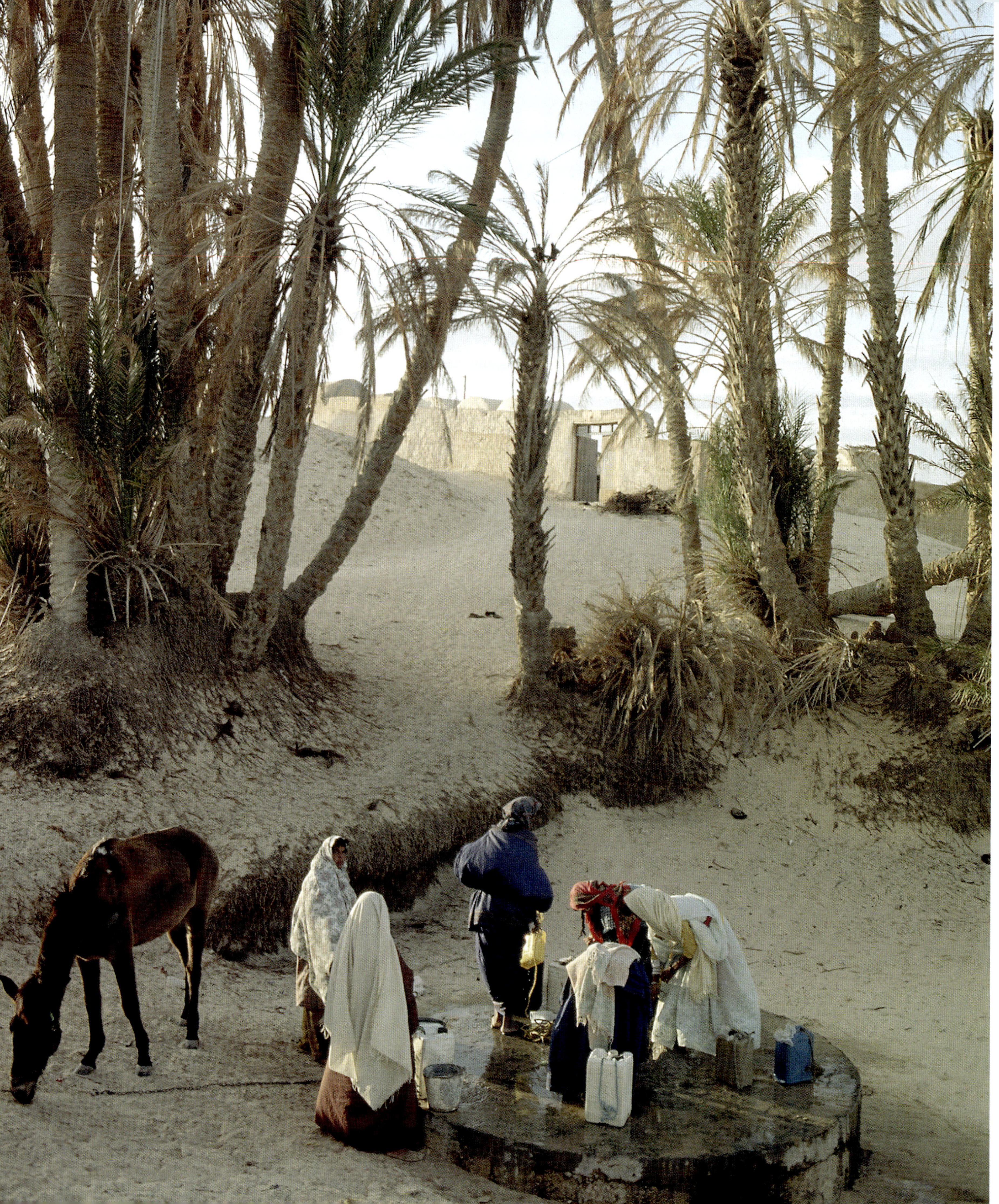

RIGHT: A Moroccan camel driver, wearing traditional dress, demonstrates his party trick by feeding his camel a baguette by mouth. For many centuries the camel has provided desert dwellers with a means of transportation, as well as milk and wool while it is alive, and meat and hide once it is dead. As such, its owners, like this one, treated it with respect and affection, but today its use as a beast of burden is decreasing rapidly and in many places it is now retained either for racing or as a symbol of bygone days.
Beth Wald/Getty Images

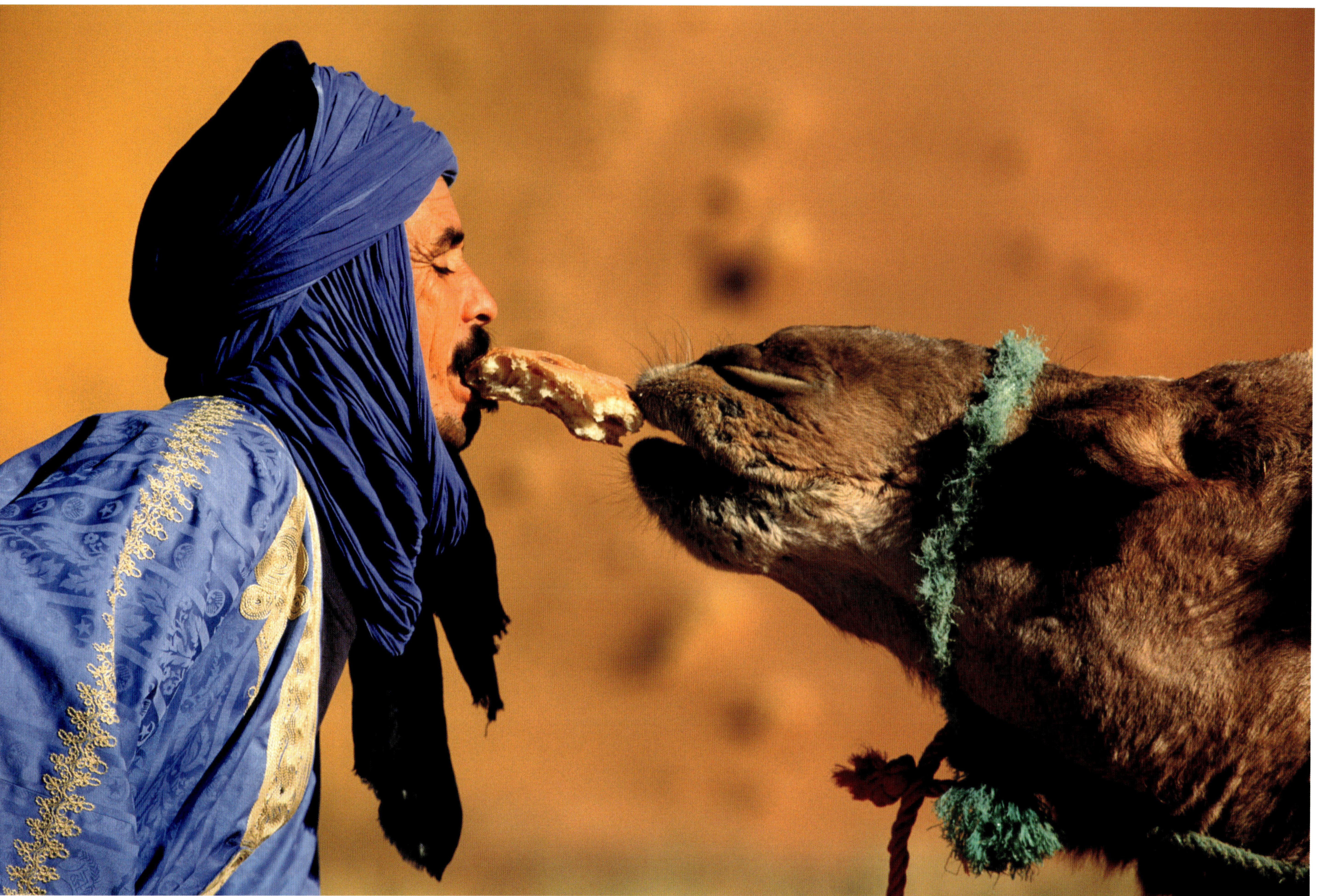

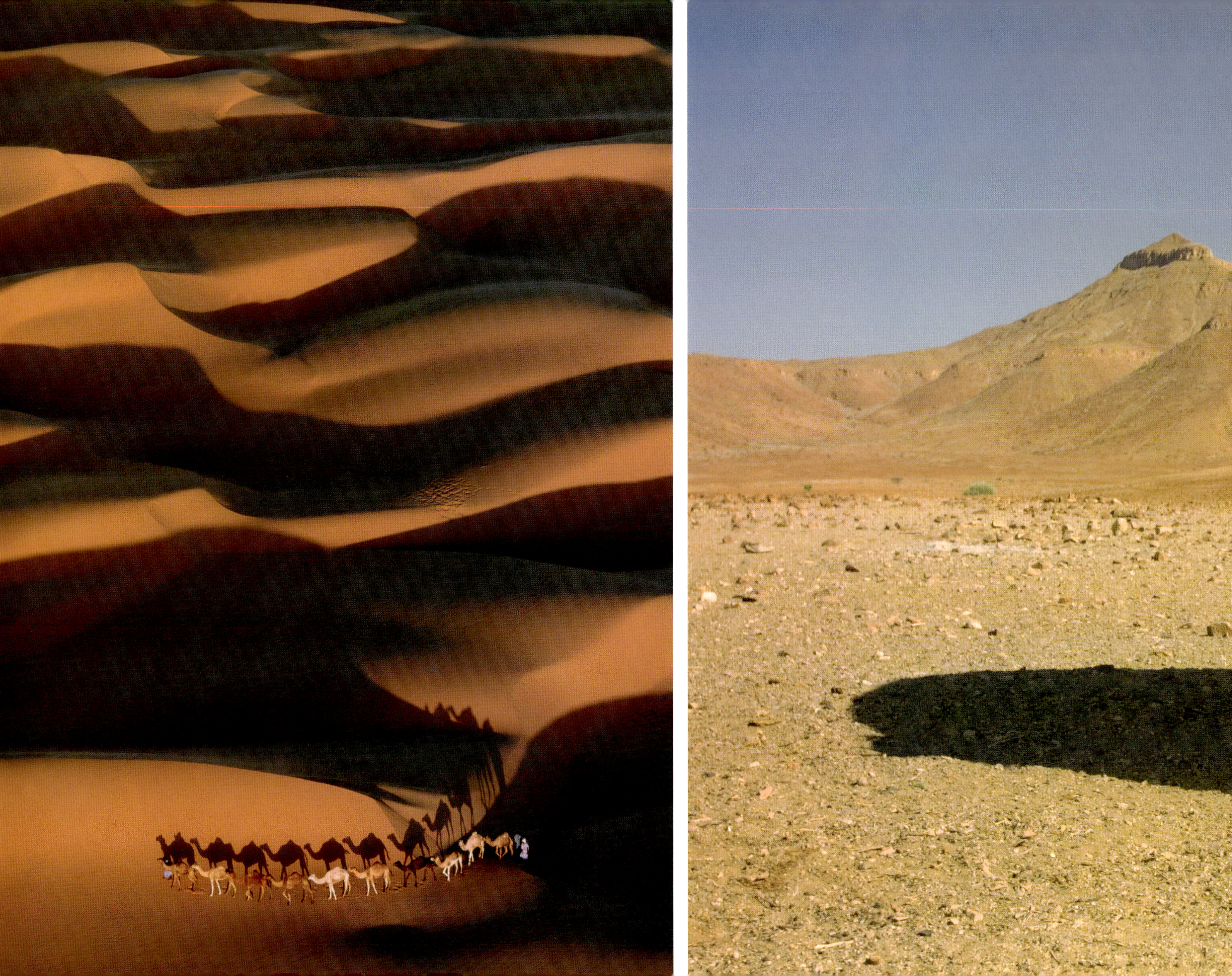

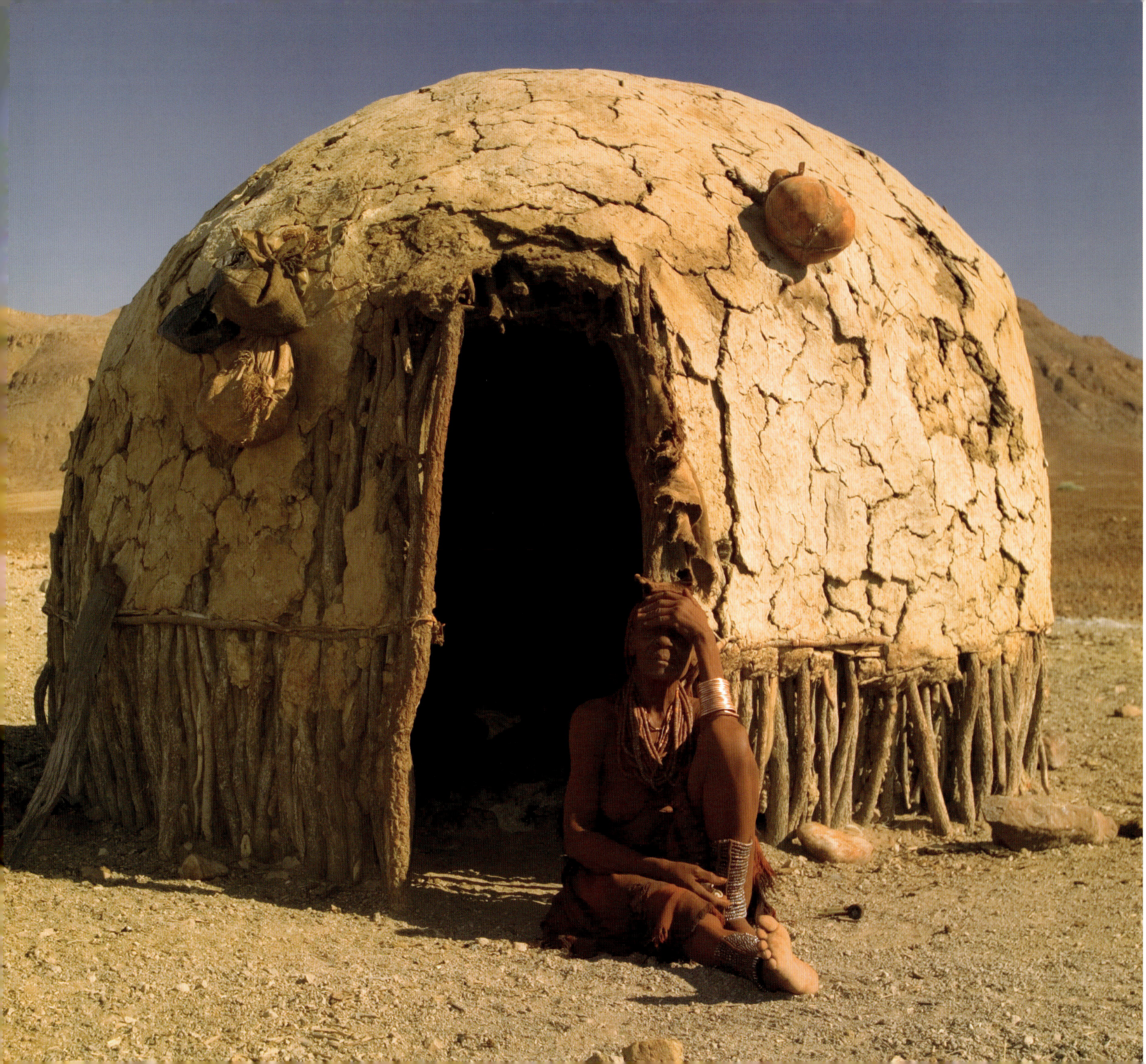

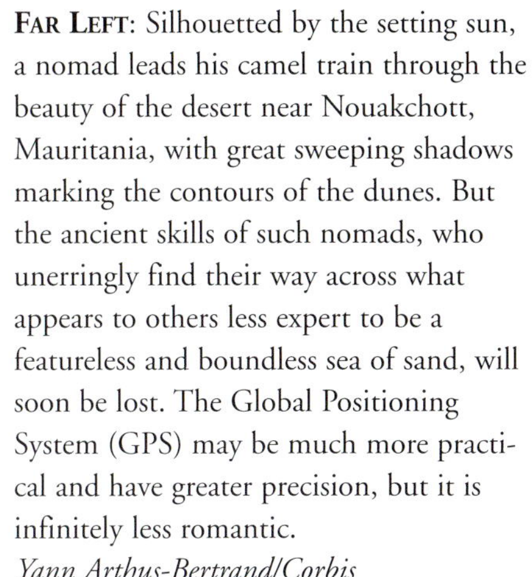

Far Left: Silhouetted by the setting sun, a nomad leads his camel train through the beauty of the desert near Nouakchott, Mauritania, with great sweeping shadows marking the contours of the dunes. But the ancient skills of such nomads, who unerringly find their way across what appears to others less expert to be a featureless and boundless sea of sand, will soon be lost. The Global Positioning System (GPS) may be much more practical and have greater precision, but it is infinitely less romantic.
Yann Arthus-Bertrand/Corbis

Left: This Himba hut on Namibia's Skeleton Coast makes an interesting comparison with the Mongolian ger; both have a circular plan with vertical walls and a conical roof. The Himbas use wooden poles and then cover the frame with palm leaves, which are sealed with mud and cattle dung. Unlike the Mongolians, the Himbas do not transport their huts, but leave one at each location and simply move back in when they return. It is, therefore, important for tourists to understand that an empty hut has not been abandoned—the owner is simply somewhere else.
Michele Westmorland/Corbis

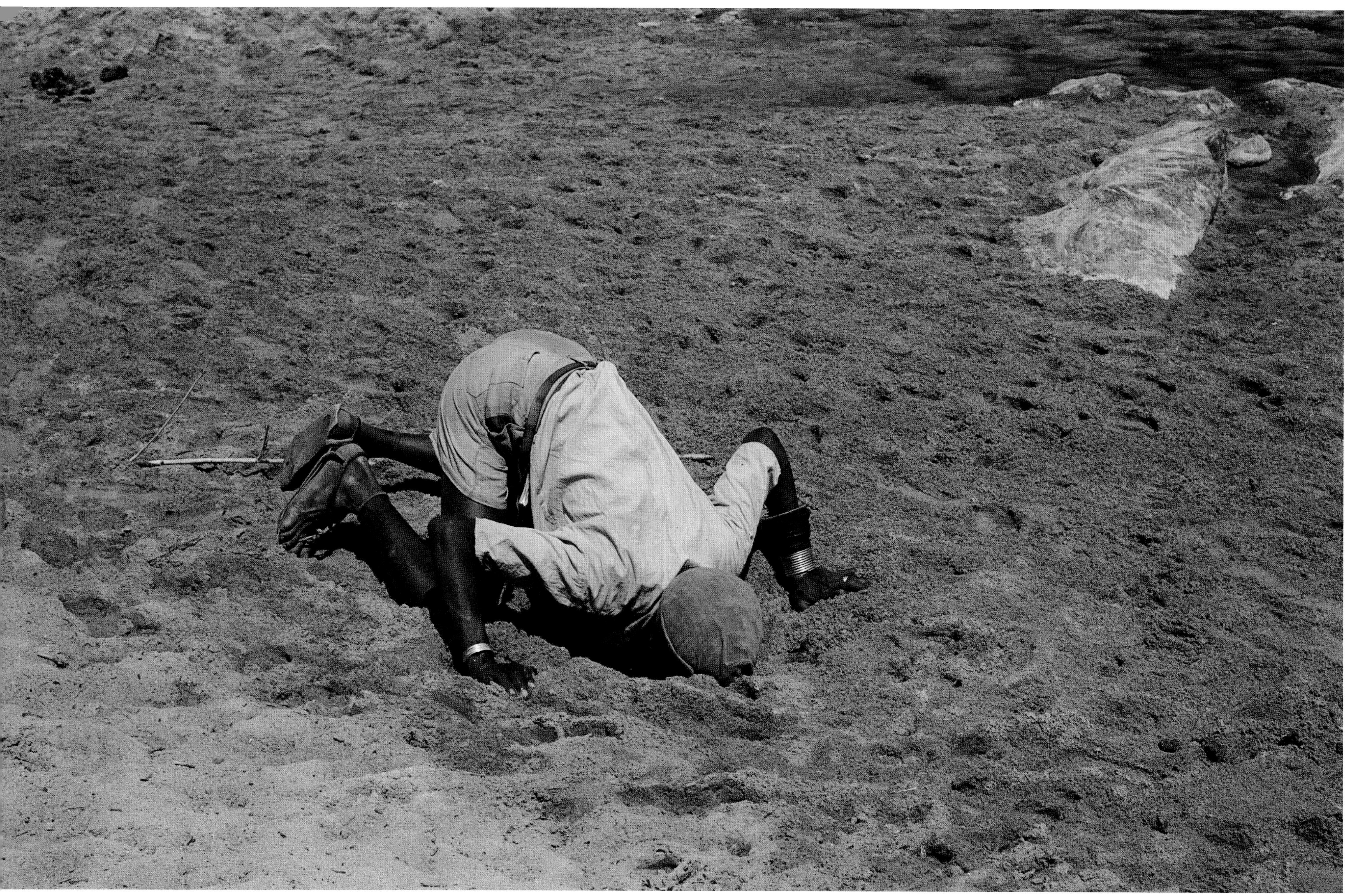

LEFT: This man in the African country of Angola has found water beneath the surface and is so desperate to drink that he cannot wait to scoop it up in a cup or even his hands. In the end, nothing is more important than water, and people will do almost anything to get it, particularly in a desert.
Volkmar K. Wentzel/Getty Images

RIGHT: In the country of Niger, the sun-bleached bones of an animal are gradually sinking below the sands of the Sahara, while some Bedouin, with their asses and a camel, pass, oblivious, in the distance. For all living creatures, every day is a struggle against the elements and above all the desert itself; as with this animal, the Bedouin know that the price of failure is death.
Steven L. Raymer/Getty Images

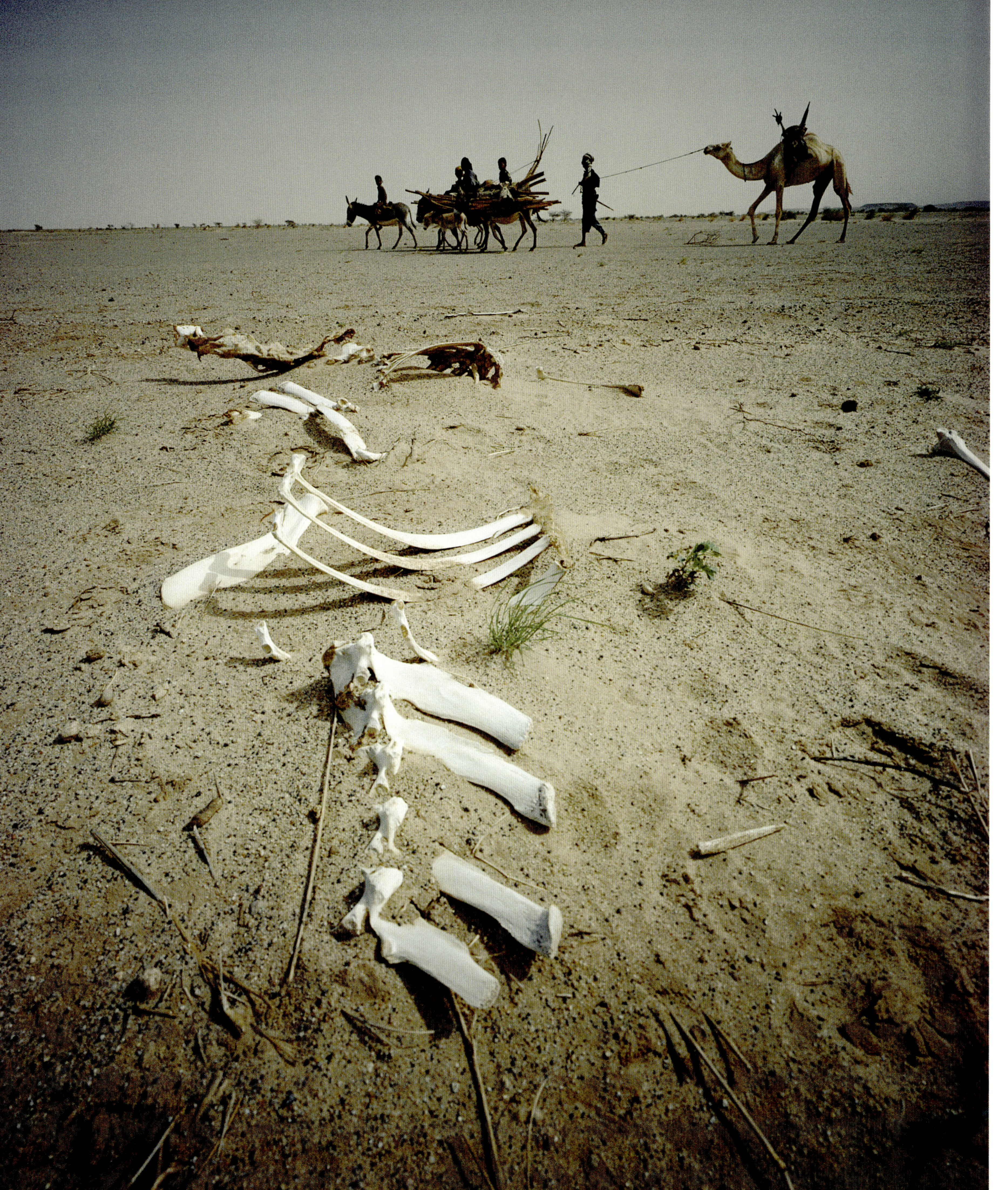

PAGE 188: San hunters (Bushmen) of the Kalahari Desert have traditionally used bows and arrows, but the arrows are so light that they will not, of themselves, bring down large animals. A poison is therefore applied to the arrowhead, derived from snakes, plants or certain types of beetle. Having been shot with such a poisoned arrow, few animals die quickly and the Bushmen must follow their quarry, which may cover some fifty miles or last up to four days before finally dropping dead.
Cyril Toker/Getty Images

PAGE 189: The Himba people of Africa's Namibia are nomads, herding and breeding cattle and goats. They travel with their herds from one watering place to another and have resisted change, preferring to stick to their traditions and way of life, although inevitable modern influences are beginning to be felt. Himba women, like the one shown here, are famous for their proud bearing, complicated hairstyles, and elaborate traditional jewelry; they wear very few clothes and coat themselves in red ochre to protect their bodies from the sun's rays.
Michele Westmorland/Corbis

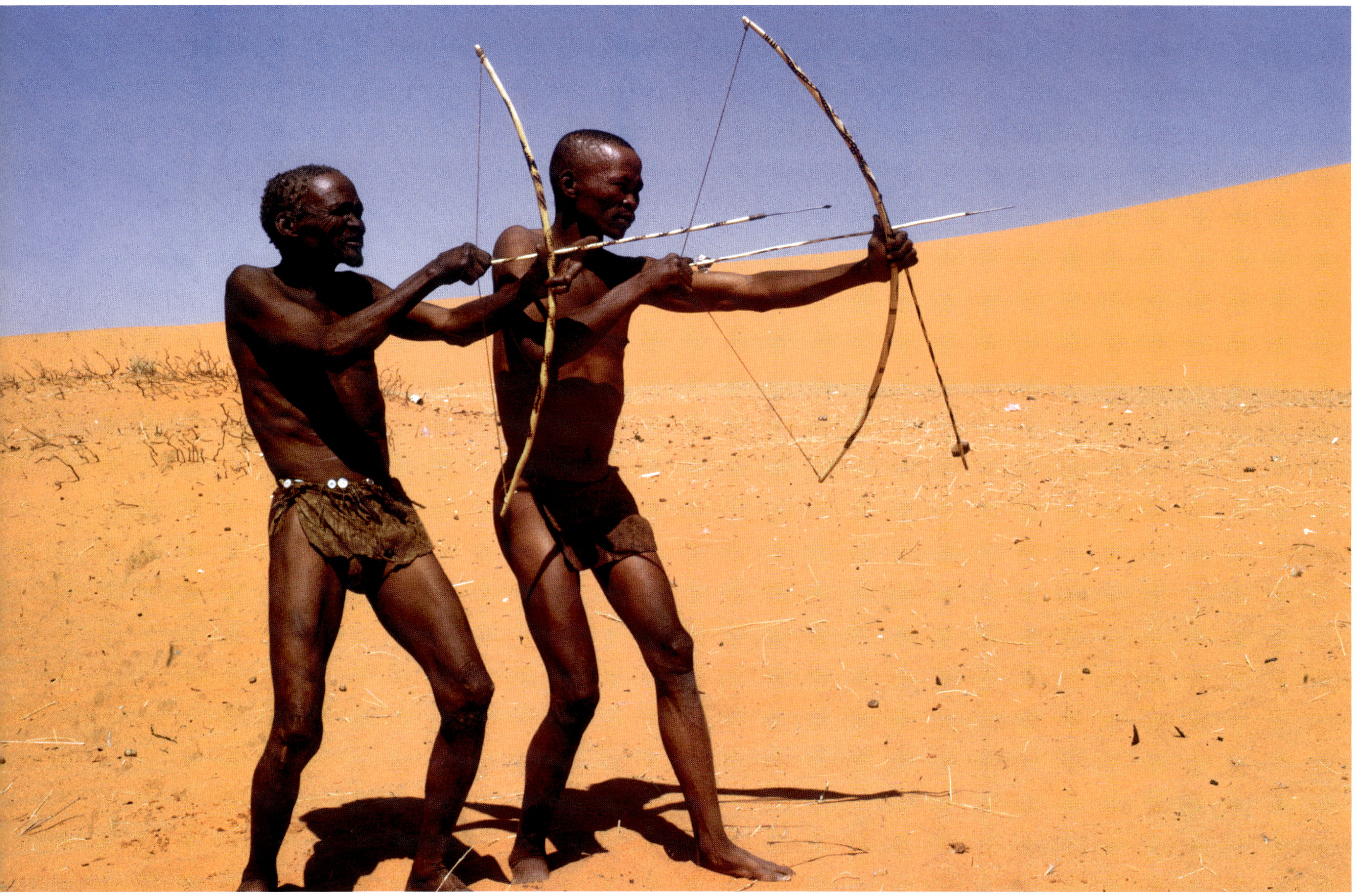

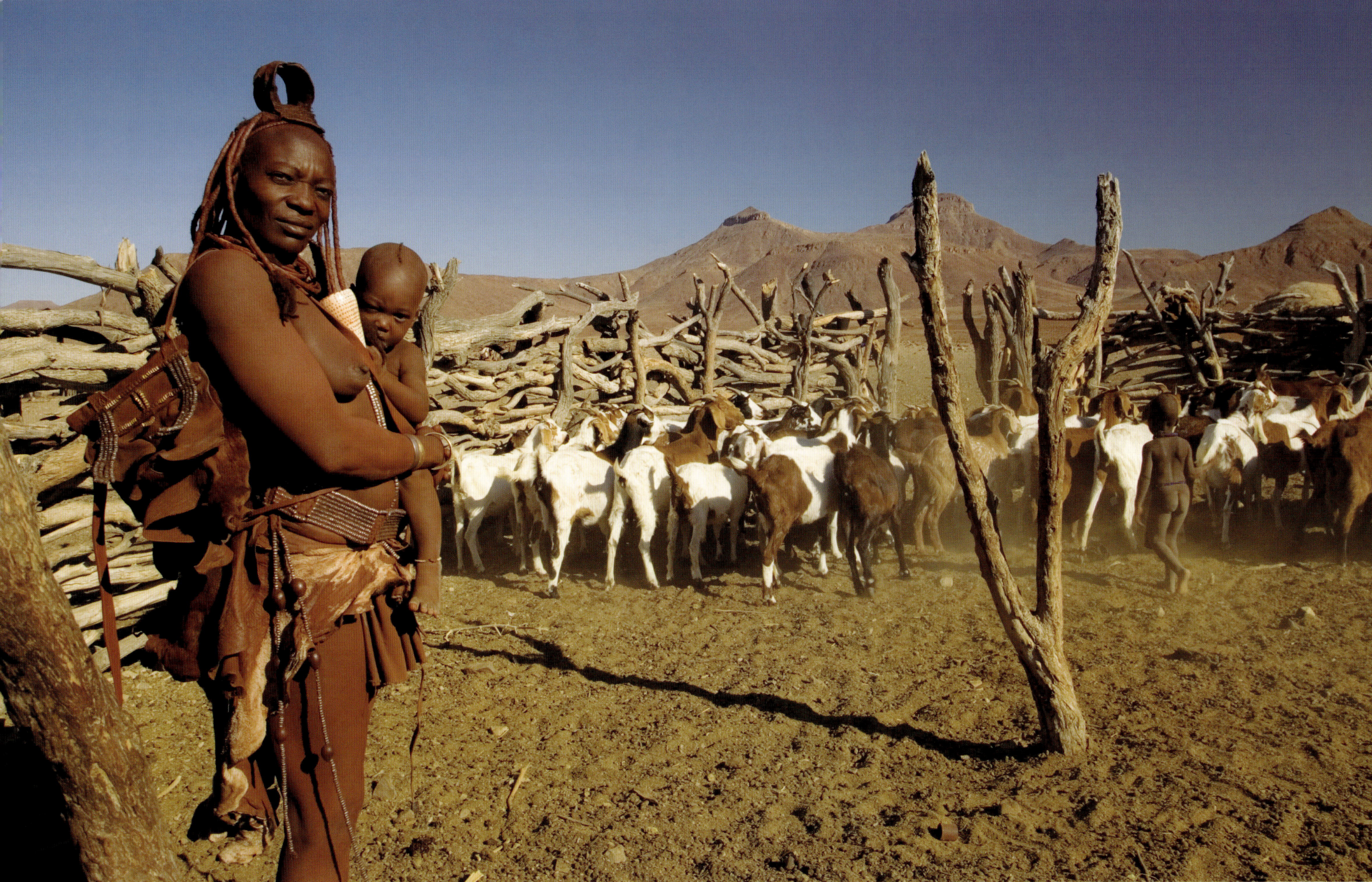

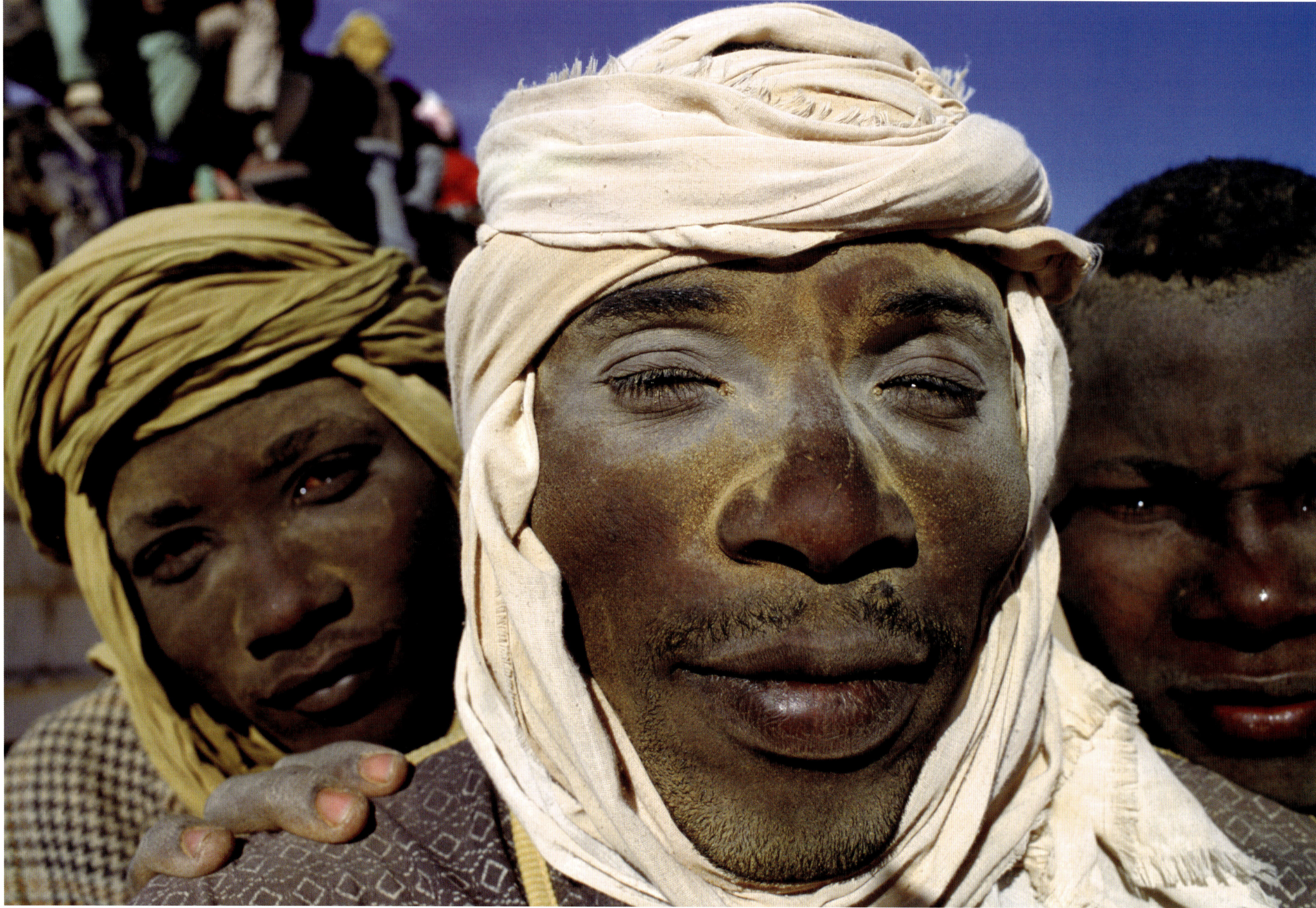

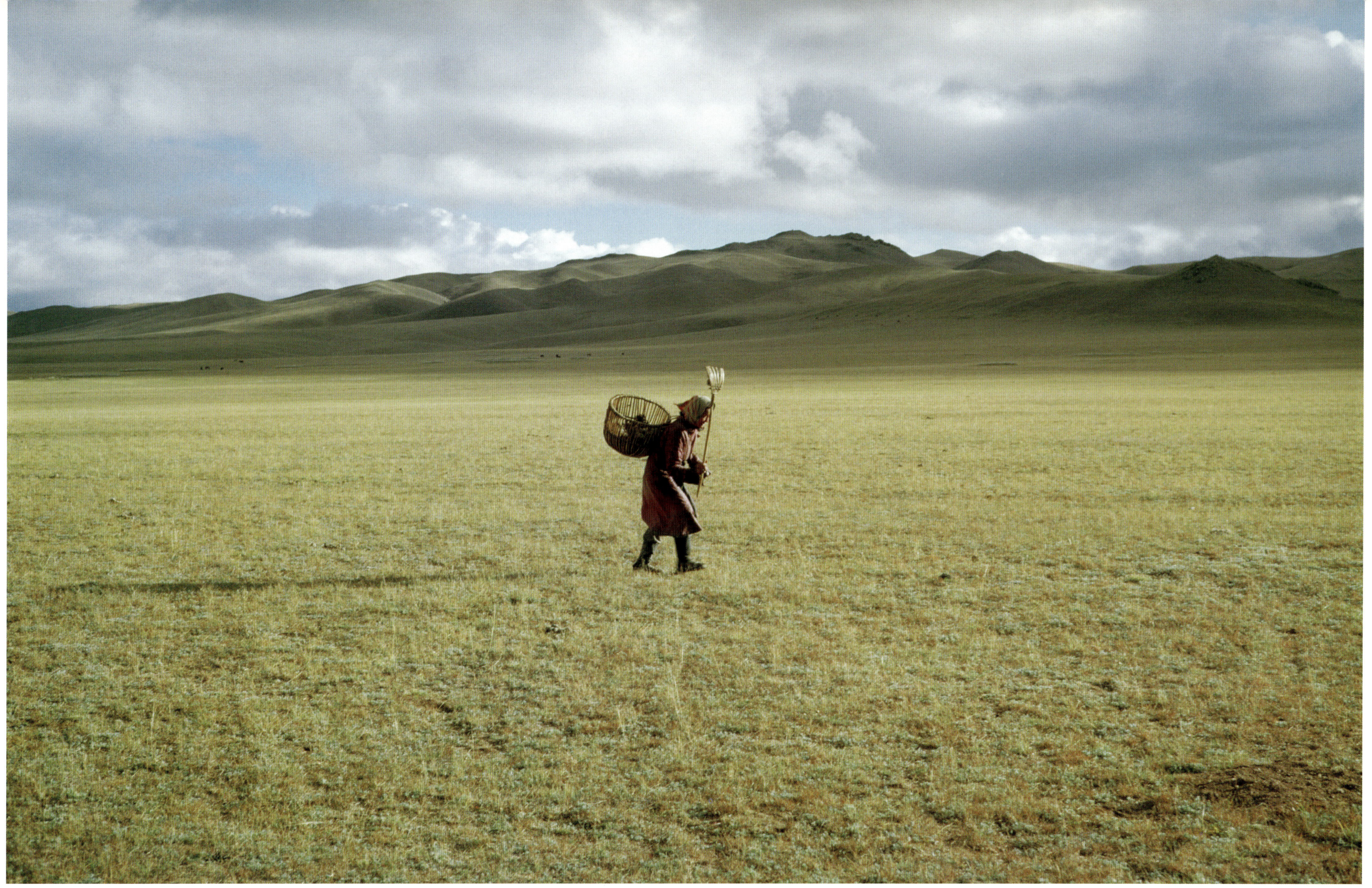

Left: Niger is a land-locked, former French territory that is today one of the poorest countries in the world, with little or no natural resources upon which to base national development. There is some mining, but the economy is largely based on agriculture, although this is often disrupted by extended droughts. As a result, many men must seek jobs abroad and these three are en route across the Sahara hoping to find work in Libya. *Chris Anderson/Getty Images*

Above: There are approximately 2.5 million people in Mongolia, with some 200,000 families still pursuing a nomadic way of life. As this picture illustrates, wood is scarce, sometimes non-existent, but animal dung is an efficient fuel, radiating a great deal of heat for both cooking and warming the tents. Dung is also plentiful since the national herd comprises some 28 million animals, including cattle, goats, horses, sheep, yaks, and, in the Gobi Desert, camels. Collecting this dung is a task for women and children, who use long-handled pitchforks or shovels to pick up the dung and place it in the baskets they carry on their backs. *Dean Conger/Corbis*

RIGHT: A village of Mongolian tents, known locally as gers, in the Gobi Desert (the name more usually used in the West is yurt, but this is a Russian word). The ger can be of any diameter, but usually between ten and forty feet, and consists of a dome-shaped wooden frame covered with felt and secured with ropes, which is easily transportable on animals; it can be erected by a small team in about thirty minutes and struck in less. At the center is a dung-burning iron stove with a chimney that projects through the roof.
Dean Conger/Corbis

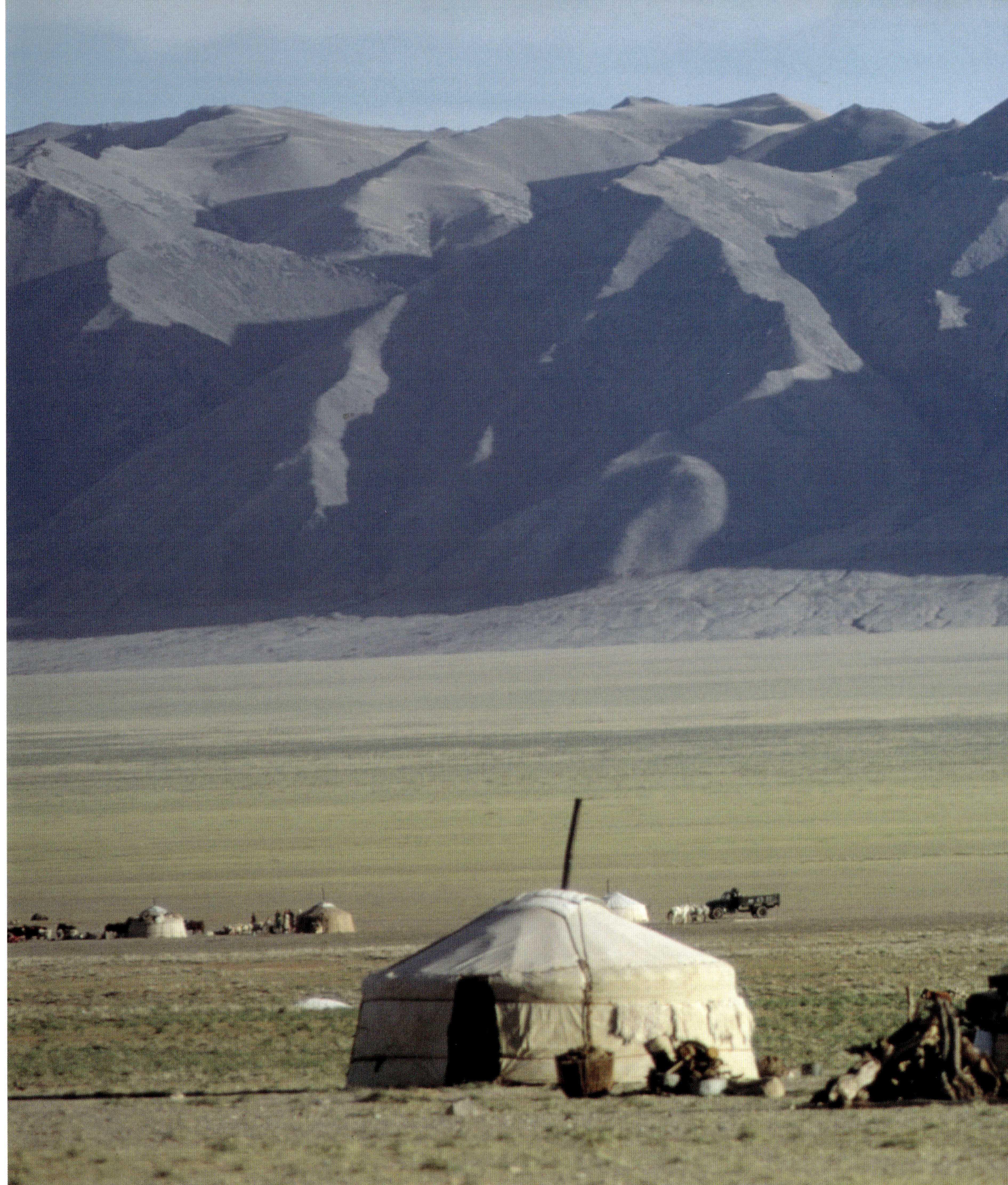

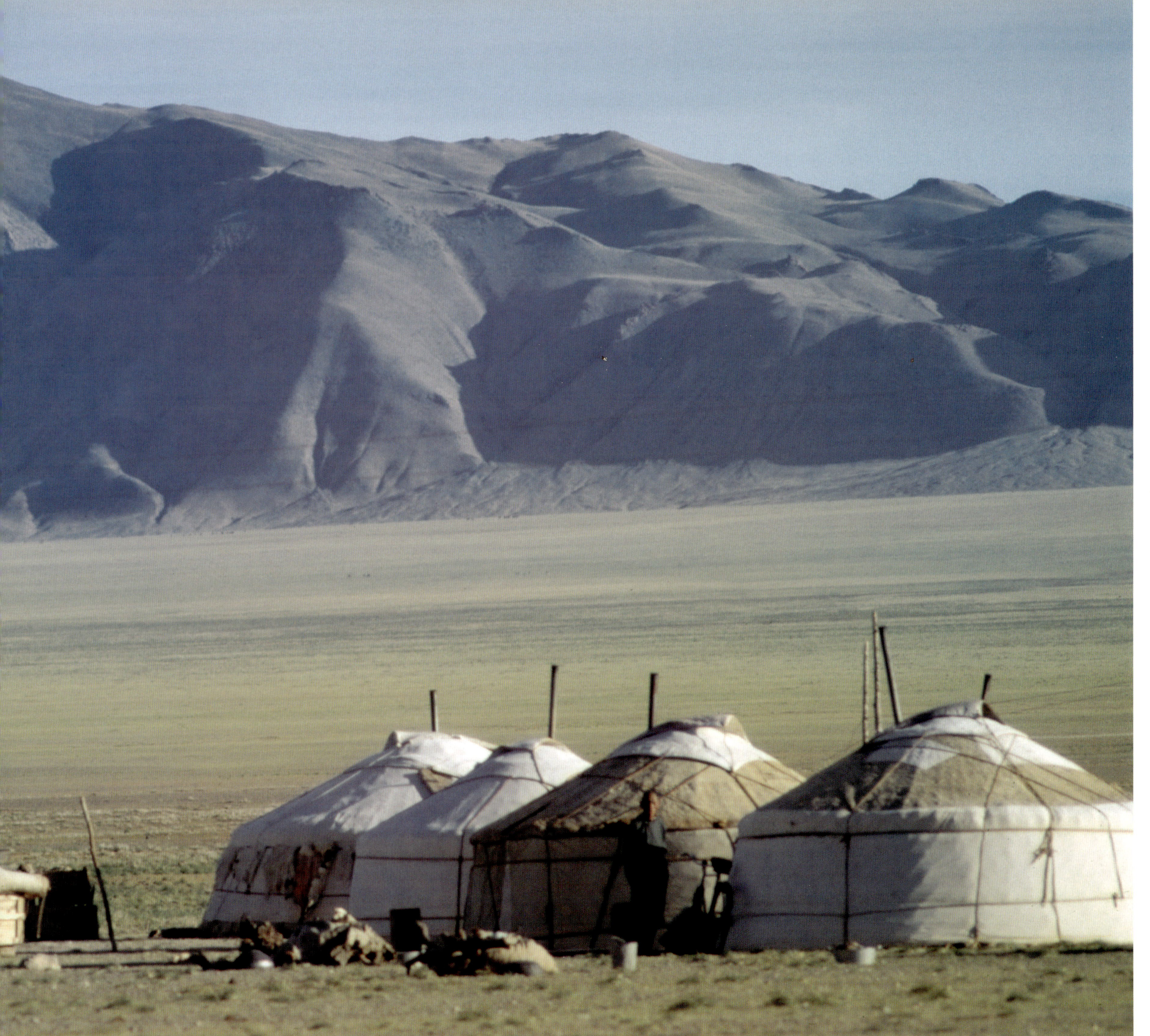

Pages 194–195 : The annual festival of Naadam (= game) is celebrated throughout Mongolia. The three-day festival starts with a parade that is followed by two days of sporting events, including horse racing. These races are designed to test the horses' capabilities, and the horses are split into six groups by age with the distance to be raced varying from ten miles for two-year olds, to seventeen miles for seven-year olds. The jockeys are young boys aged between five and thirteen and there is no preselected course—just a start and a finish. It is not surprising that Mongolian horsemen are so skilled. The third day of Naadam is reserved for eating and drinking, which are taken as seriously as the other sports.
SETBOUN/Corbis

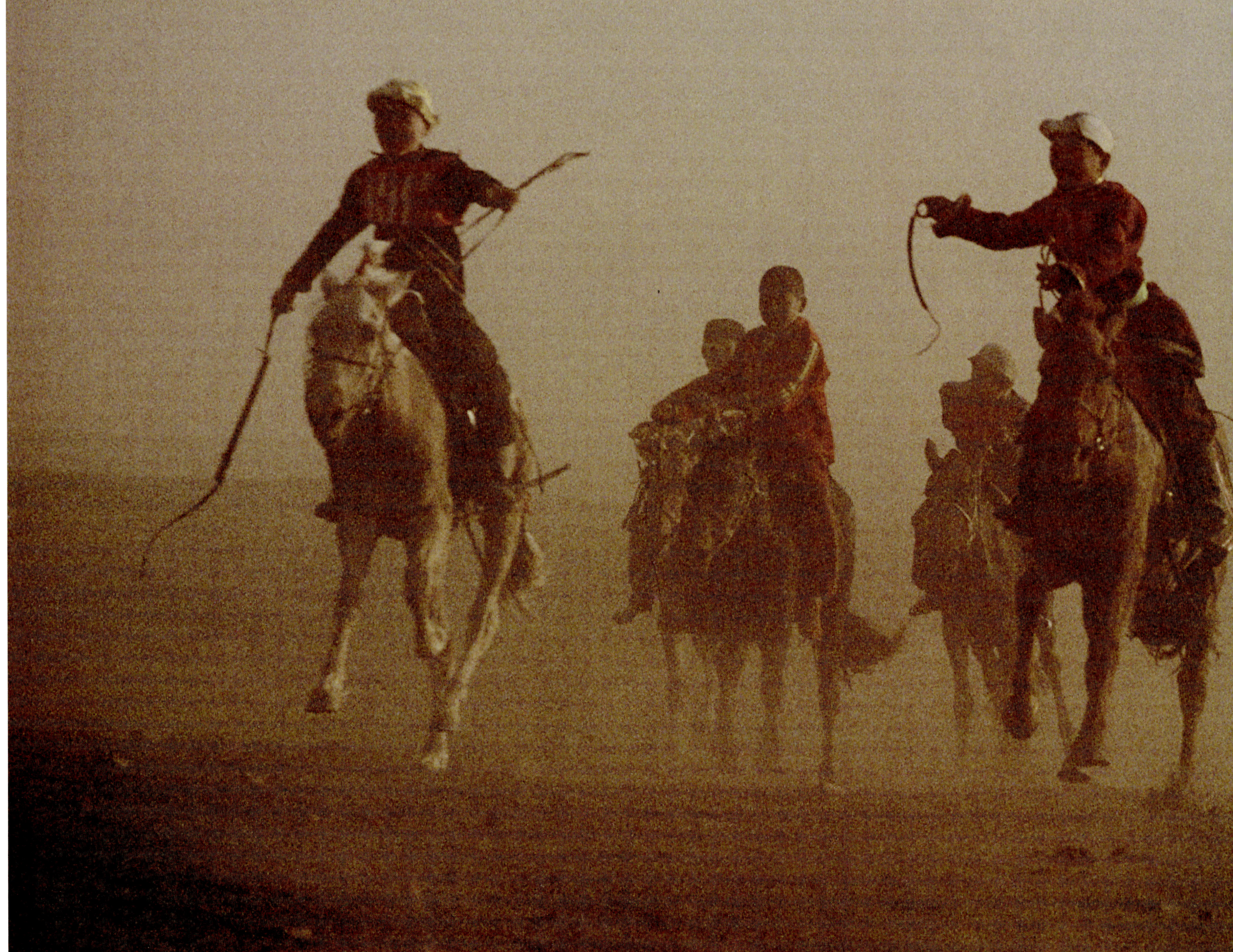

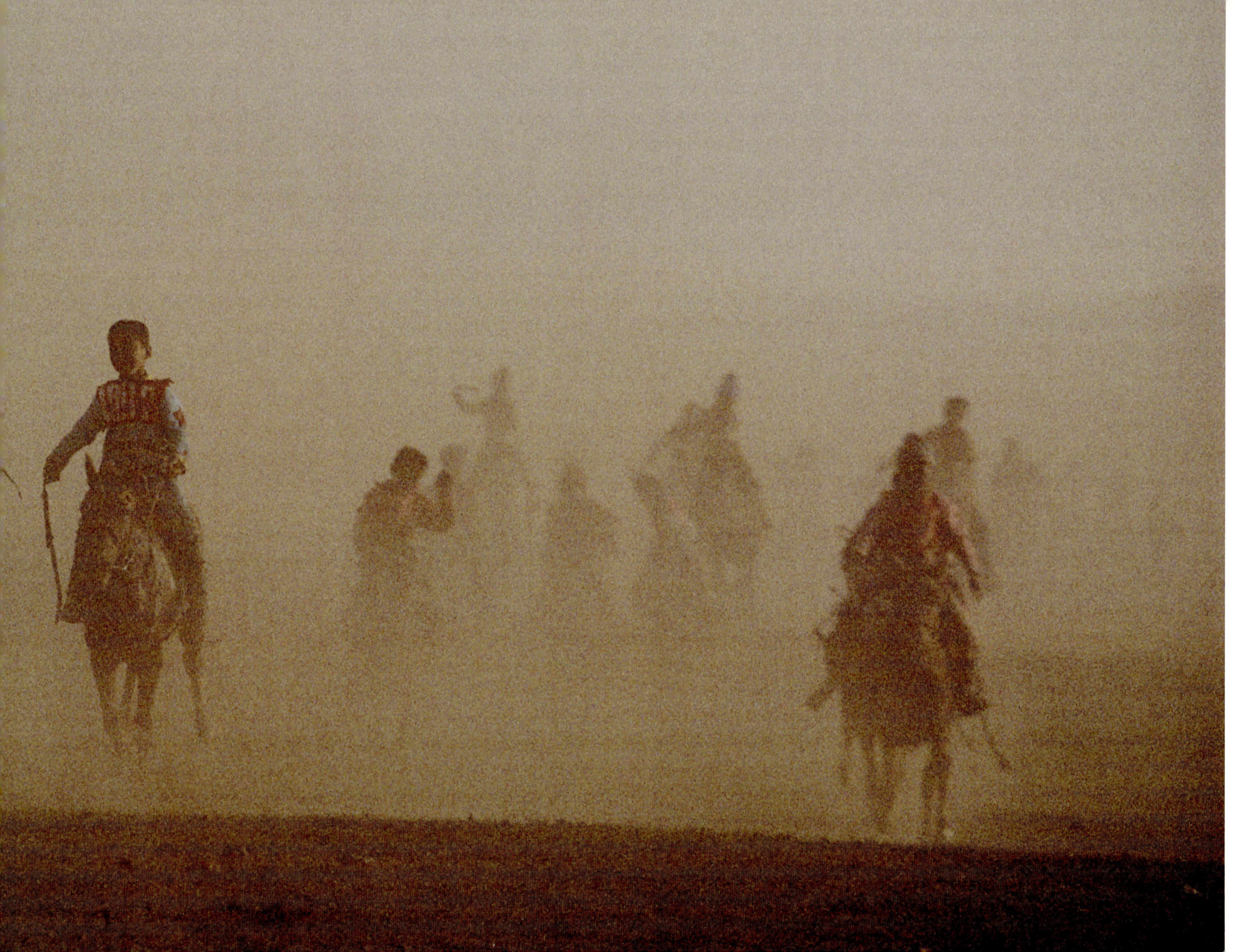

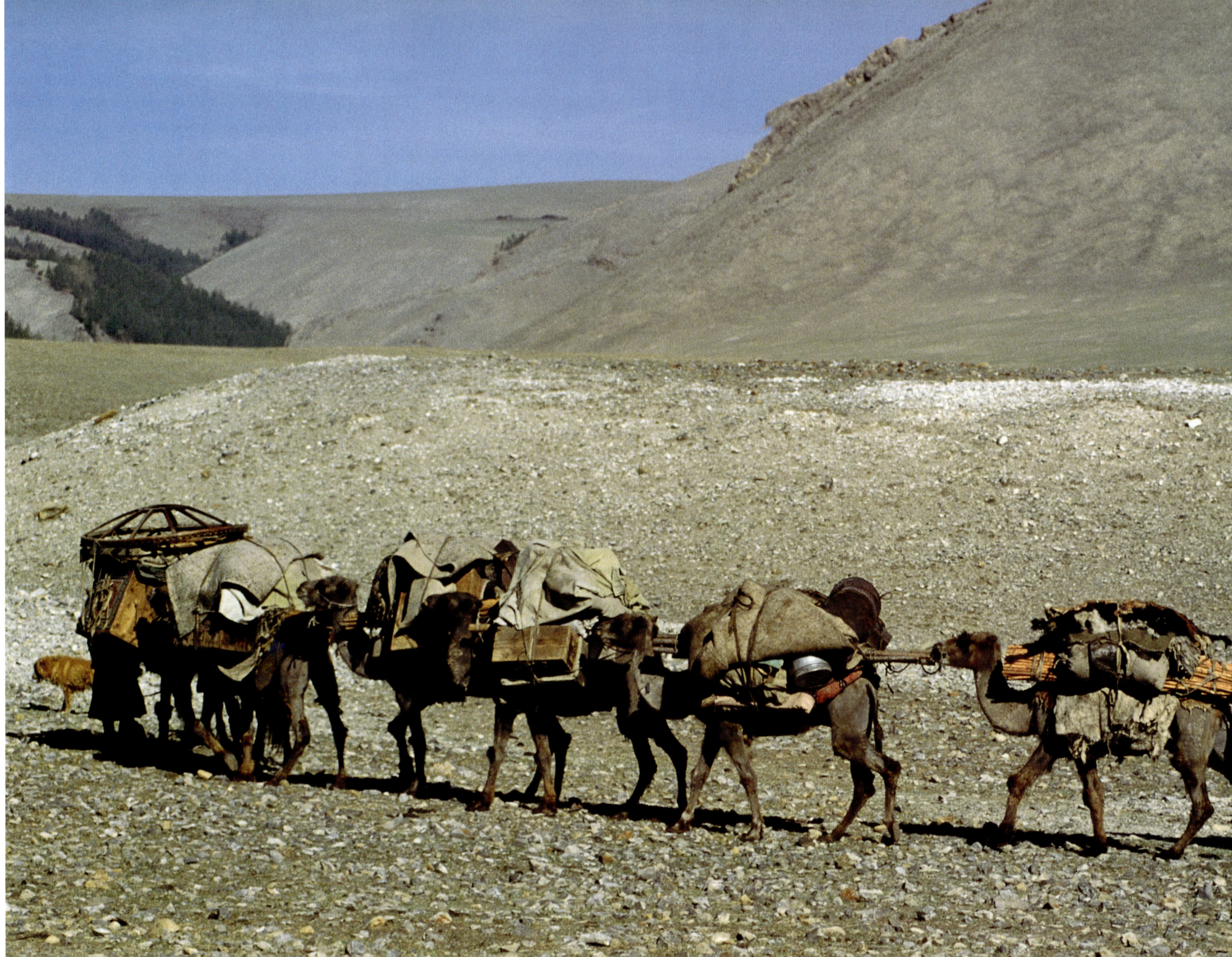

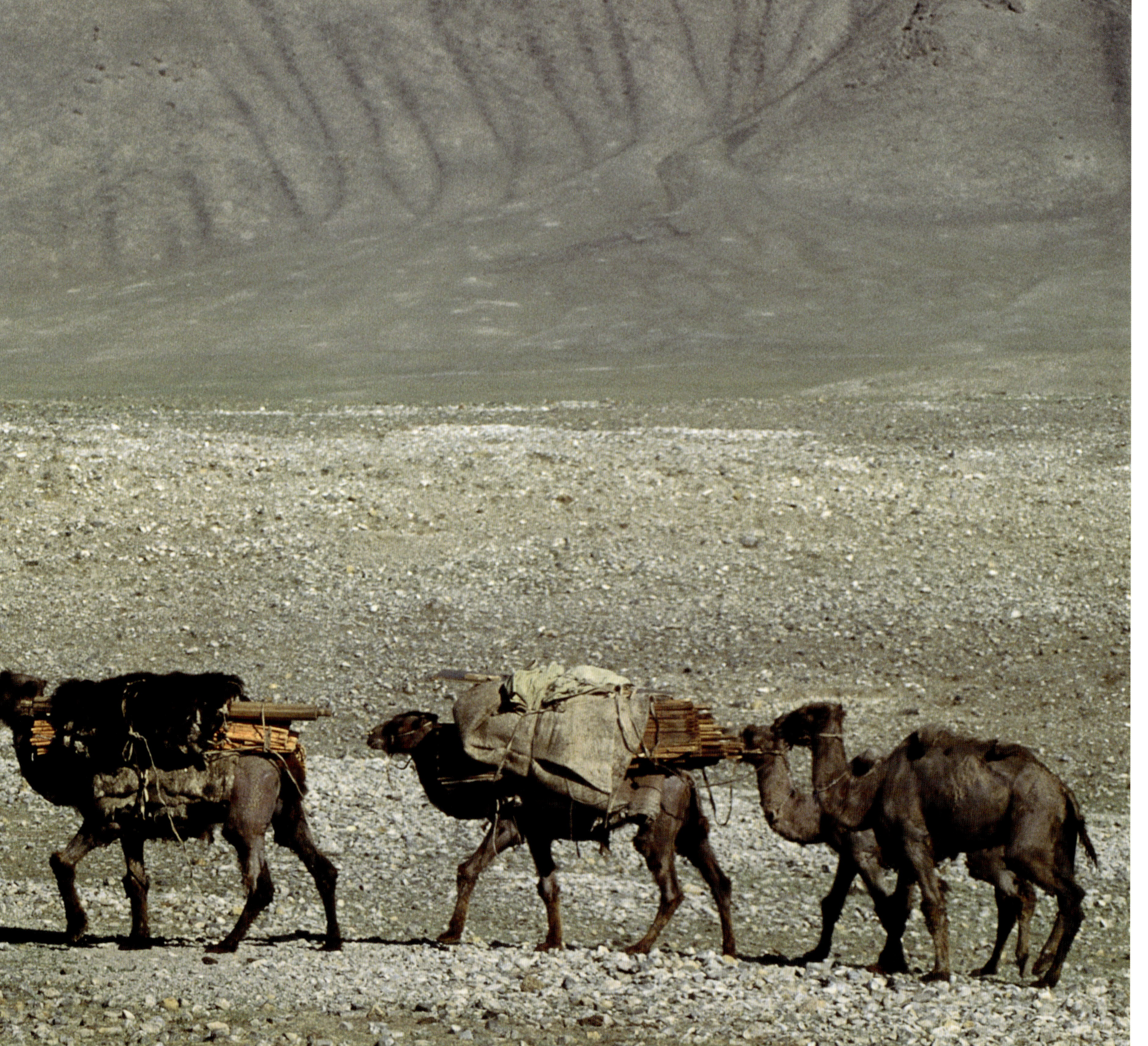

Left: The terrain and conditions are tough for both the Mongolian herdsmen and their camels. These twin-humped Bactrian camels are indigenous to the deserts of China and Mongolia. They have developed the ability to endure extremes of temperature, ranging from 40 degrees Fahrenheit below freezing in winter, to as much as 120 degrees in summer. As part of this process they grow a long, thick shaggy coat in winter, but shed it in summer. Bactrian camels can travel up to forty miles per day over rough terrain carrying loads of up to 600 pounds, such as these dismantled gers.
Adrian Arbib/Corbis

Page 198: Young Mongolian men herding goats in the Aymag (= region) of Omnogovi in Mongolia. This area, in the southern section of the Gobi Desert, is very sparsely populated and life is particularly hard. The goatherd on the left is astride a Bactrian camel, sitting between the two humps in a natural riding position. Goats have been herded in the Gobi for thousands of years and are not only hardy animals but are also an invaluable source of meat, milk, and hides, while their underdown is the basis of cashmere, which the Mongolians trade as one of the finest fibers in the world.
Jacques Langevin/Corbis SYGMA

Page 199: This Aymara woman in an Atacama Desert village is a member of an ethnic group, some two million strong, which has been spread for many centuries across the Andes in an area now encompassed by parts of what are now Argentina, Bolivia, Chile, and Peru. Once a rich and independent people, they were conquered by the Incas in the late 15th century and then by the Spanish, but they have retained their own language, also known as Aymara, with Spanish as a second tongue.
Joel Sartore/Getty Images

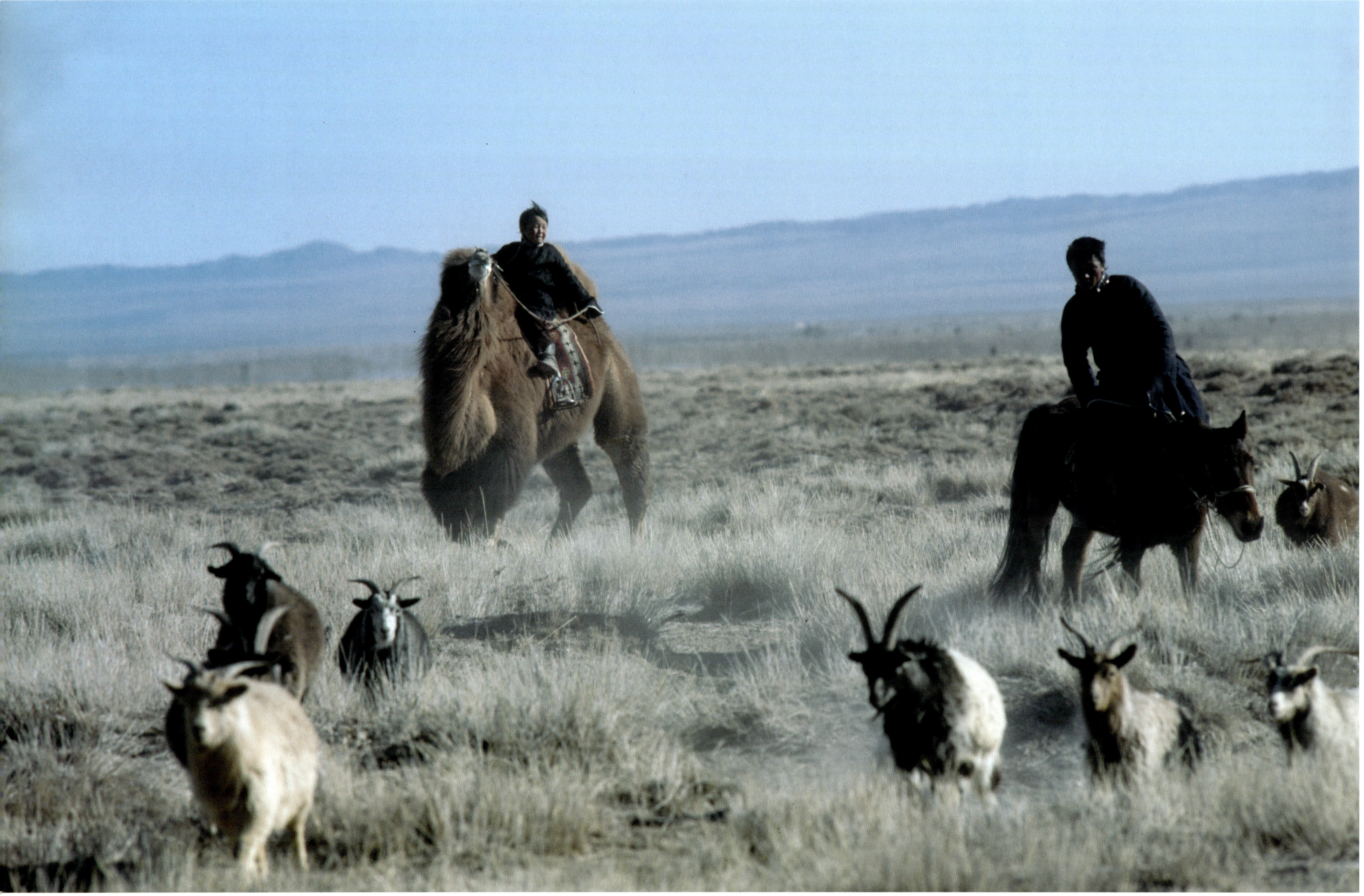

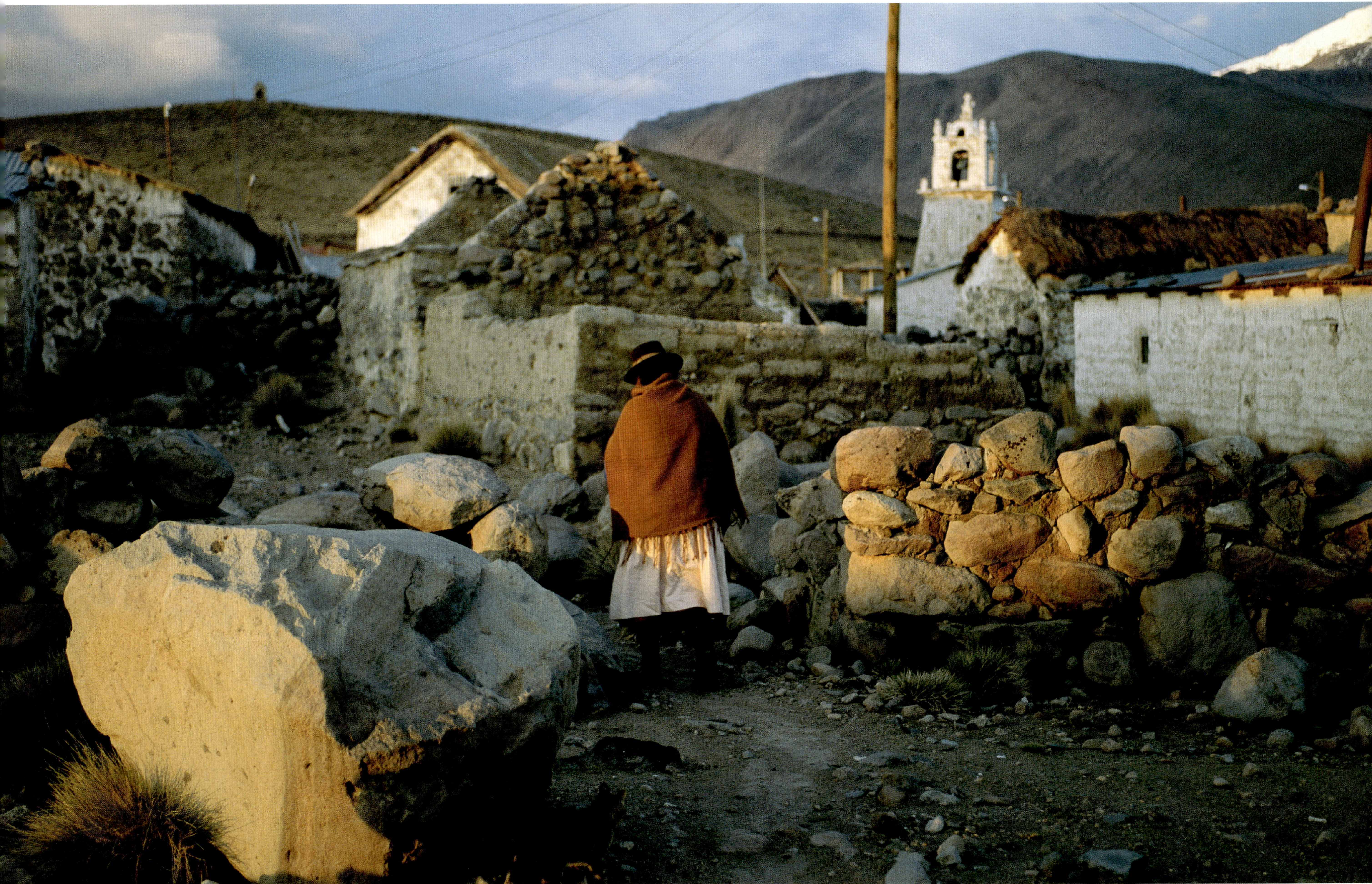

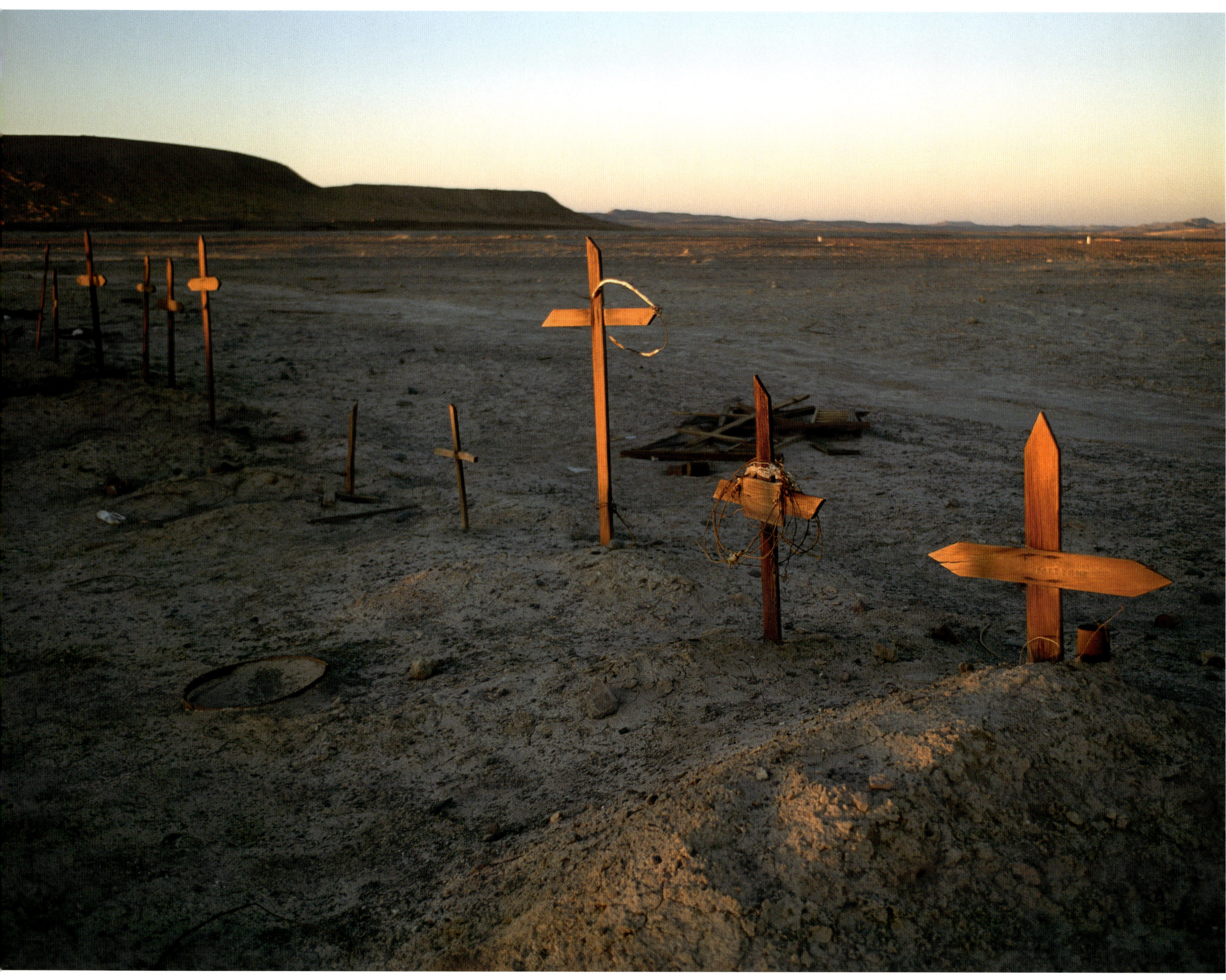

LEFT: Deserts are highly valued for the mineral wealth that lies beneath them, such as oil in the Middle East. Other deserts, such as the Atacama in Chile, are also rich and are being exploited as fast as commercial concerns can discover new deposits, whereupon local workers operate the mines and the transportation systems. The cost is high, as these weatherworn crosses in a miners' cemetery outside the town of Puelma in Chile's Atacama Desert testify.
Joel Sartore/Getty Images

RIGHT: Dusk and the end of the working day as buses take miners home from Chuquicamata Mine, the world's largest copper mine, in Chile's Atacama desert. The town of Calama, located in the middle of the Atacama, and some 125 miles inland from the port of Antofagasta, has a population of about 150,000 people, most of them either directly or indirectly involved in the copper mining industry.
Charles O'Rear/Corbis

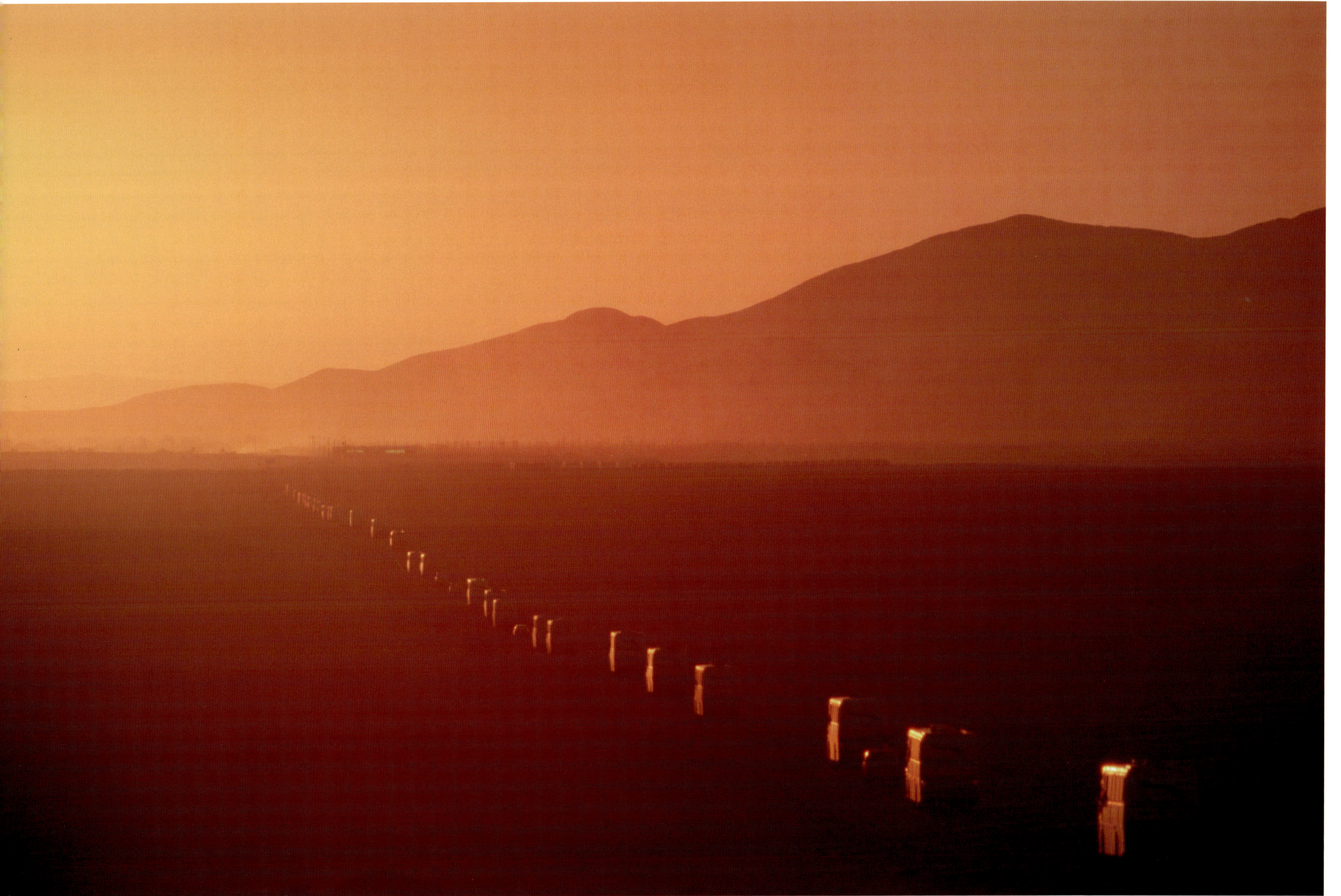

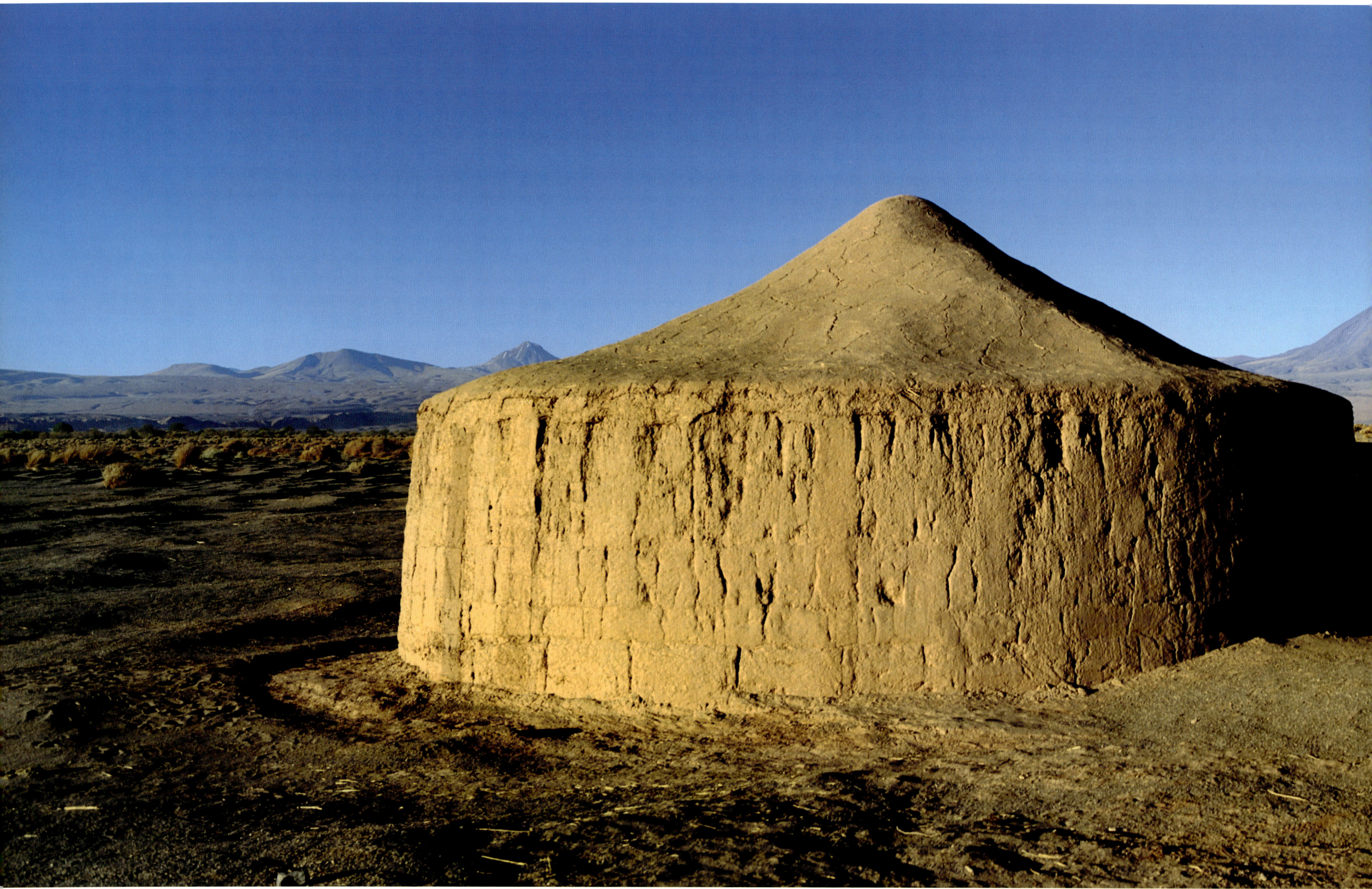

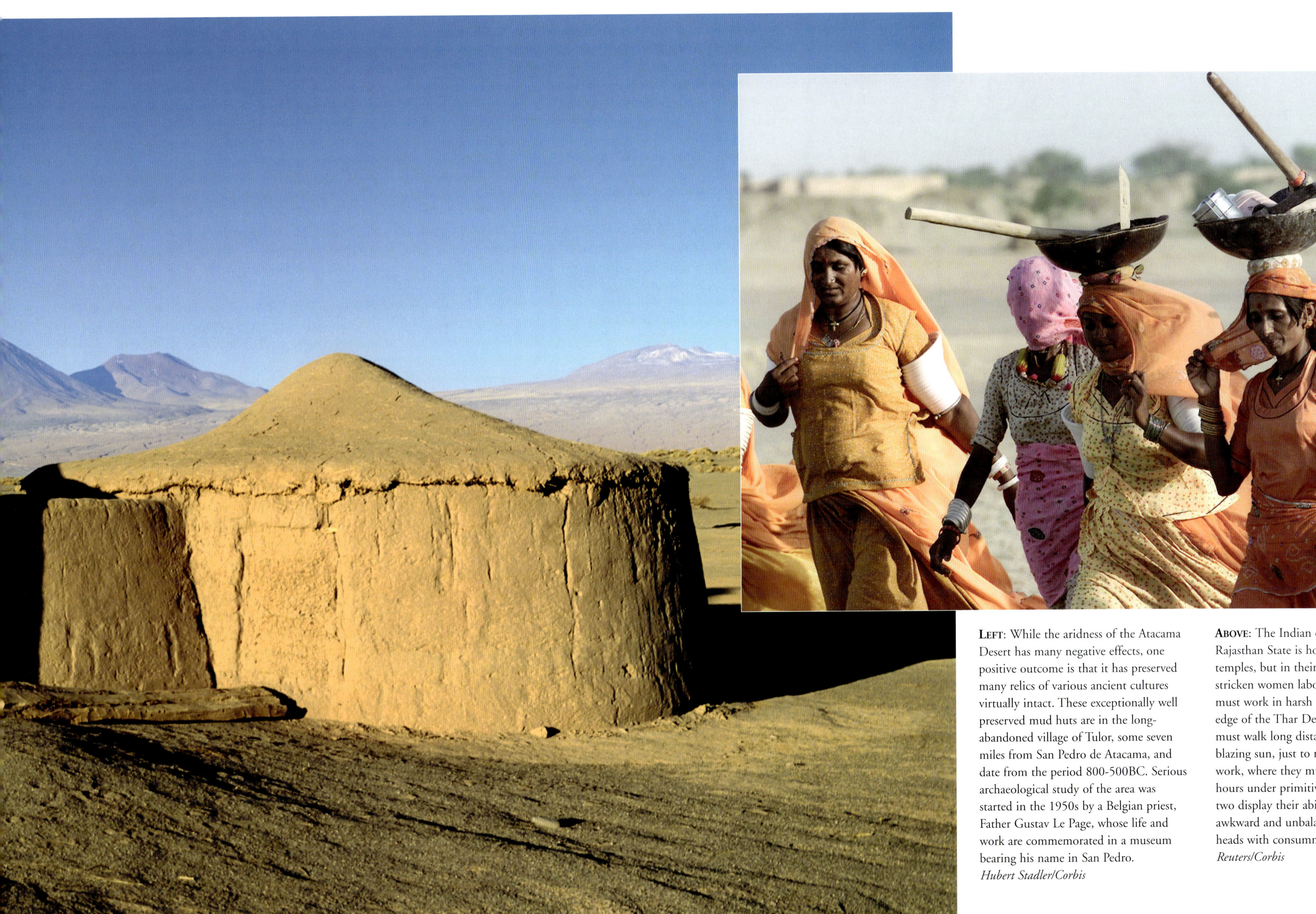

Left: While the aridness of the Atacama Desert has many negative effects, one positive outcome is that it has preserved many relics of various ancient cultures virtually intact. These exceptionally well preserved mud huts are in the long-abandoned village of Tulor, some seven miles from San Pedro de Atacama, and date from the period 800-500BC. Serious archaeological study of the area was started in the 1950s by a Belgian priest, Father Gustav Le Page, whose life and work are commemorated in a museum bearing his name in San Pedro.
Hubert Stadler/Corbis

Above: The Indian city of Jaisalmer in Rajasthan State is home to rich forts and temples, but in their shadow poverty-stricken women laborers such as these must work in harsh conditions on the edge of the Thar Desert. The women must walk long distances under the blazing sun, just to reach their place of work, where they must then work long hours under primitive conditions. Here two display their ability to carry seemingly awkward and unbalanced loads on their heads with consummate ease.
Reuters/Corbis

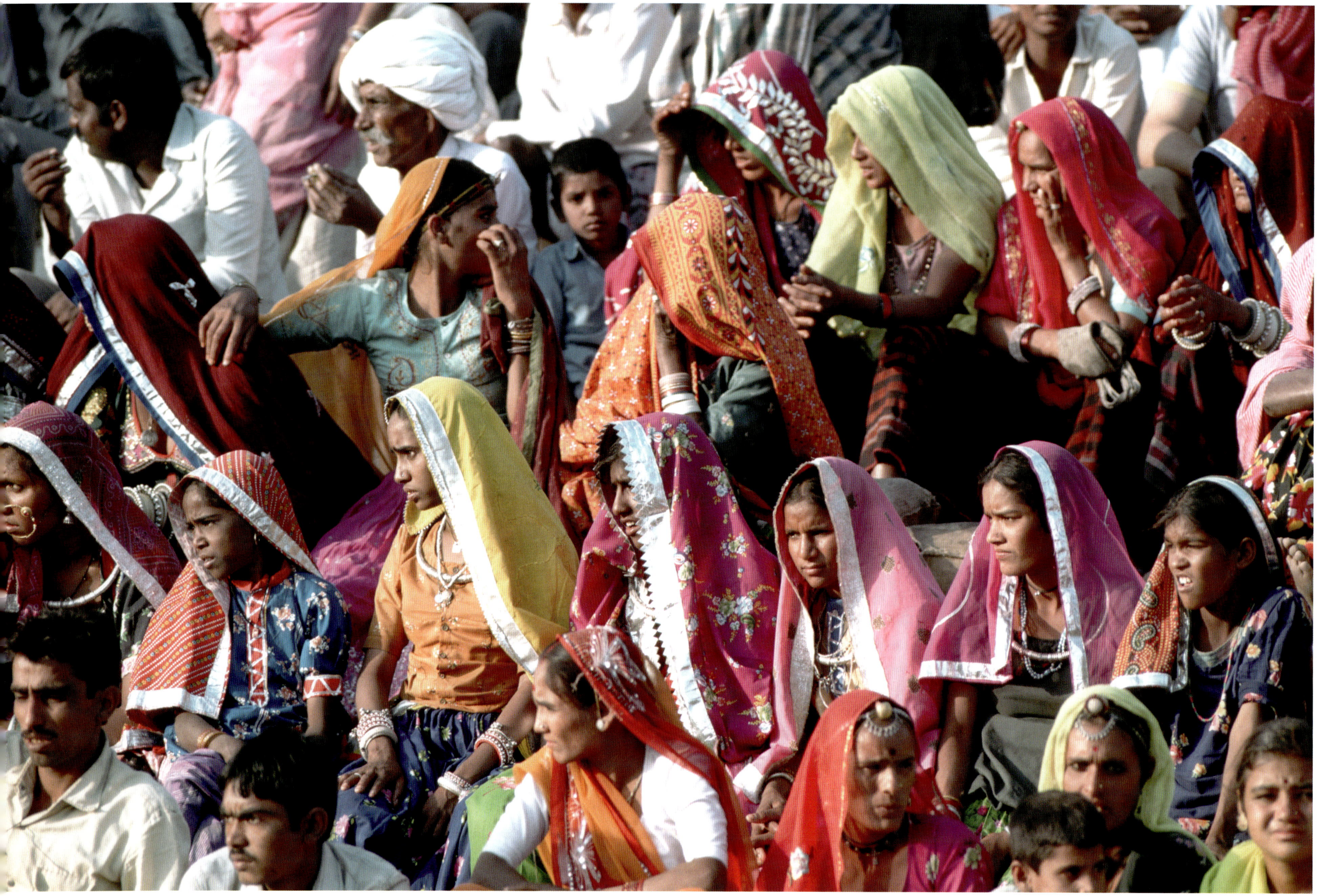

ABOVE: It is difficult to imagine a more colorful sight than these Rajput people watching the competitions at the Pushkar Mela, the annual Hindu religious festival and camel auction held in the Thar Desert in India. For such people the fair offers an annual celebration and a break from the poverty and struggle that characterize the rest of their year.
Brian A. Vikander/Corbis

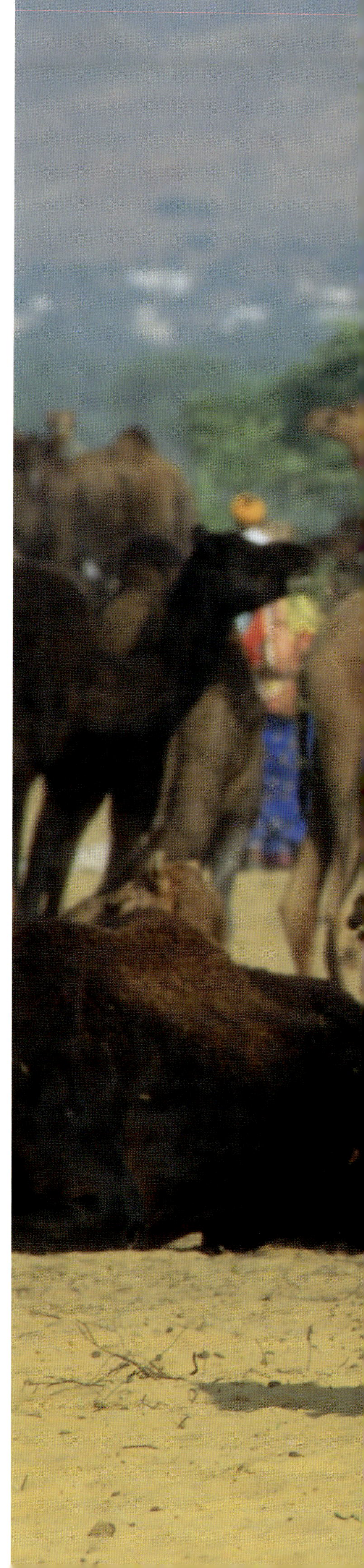

RIGHT: Selling and buying camel fodder are conducted by these women of Rajasthan, India, at the Pushkar Mela. Here the bargaining has been concluded and the money is handed over to seal the deal.
Brian A. Vikander/Corbis

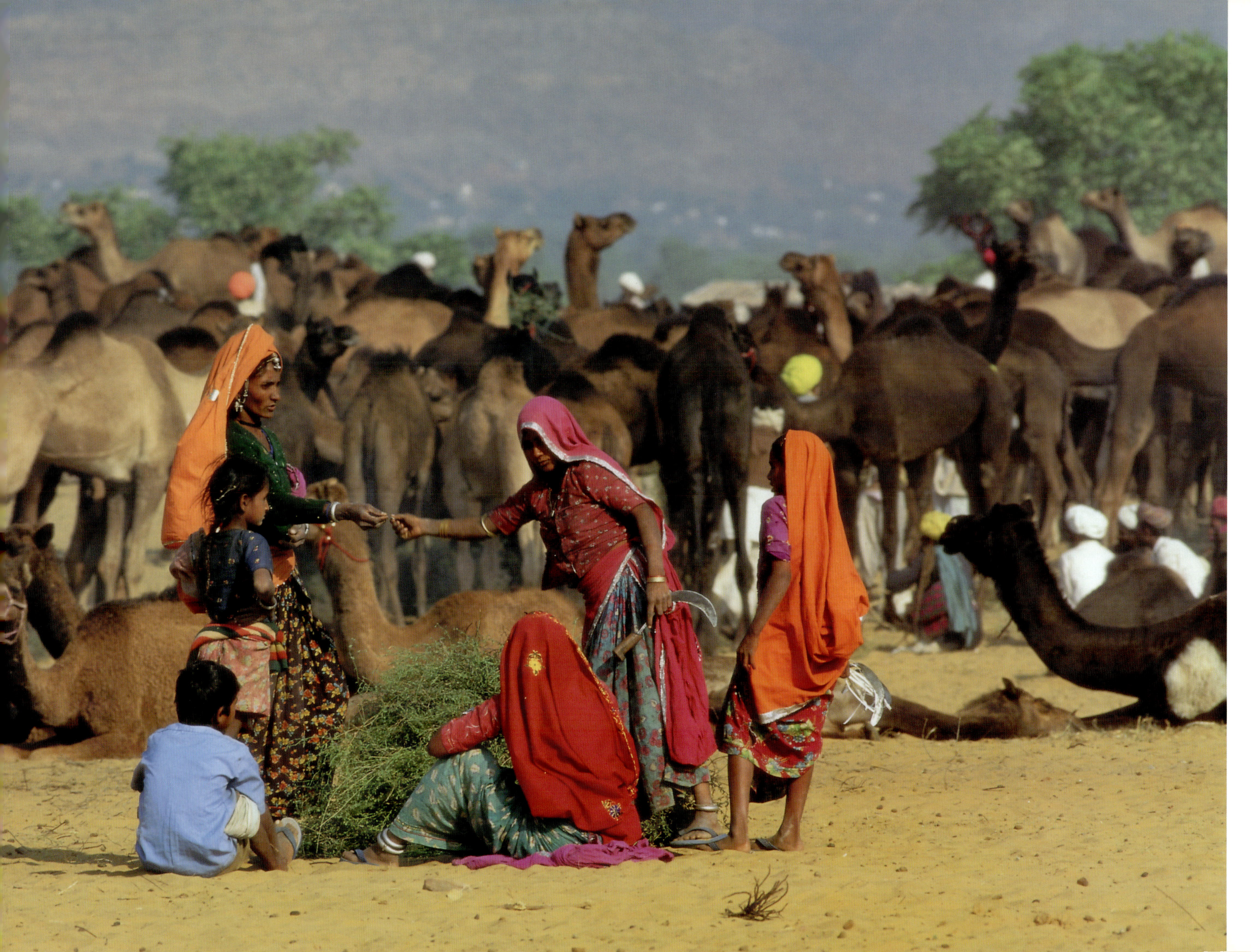

Right: A squad of border police on patrol in Turkmenistan's Kara Kum Desert. International borders are difficult—and sometimes impossible—to mark in a desert and constant electronic and aerial surveillance, backed up by guards such as these on the ground, is the only way to maintain even a modicum of security, as the United States knows only too well with its southern border with Mexico.
Robert Wallis/Corbis

Far Right: The 460-mile long Kara Kum Canal was built during the Soviet era to irrigate various areas in south Turkmenistan. The canal was completed in 1967, and was created by diverting some 40 percent of the waters of the Amu Dar'ya River, a major feat of engineering. The plan was carried out with the very best of intentions and undoubtedly brought great benefits to the people concerned, but about forty years later it has become apparent that the reduction in the flow of the Amu Dar'ya has been a major factor in the increasingly rapid disappearance of the Aral Sea.
Dean Conger/Corbis

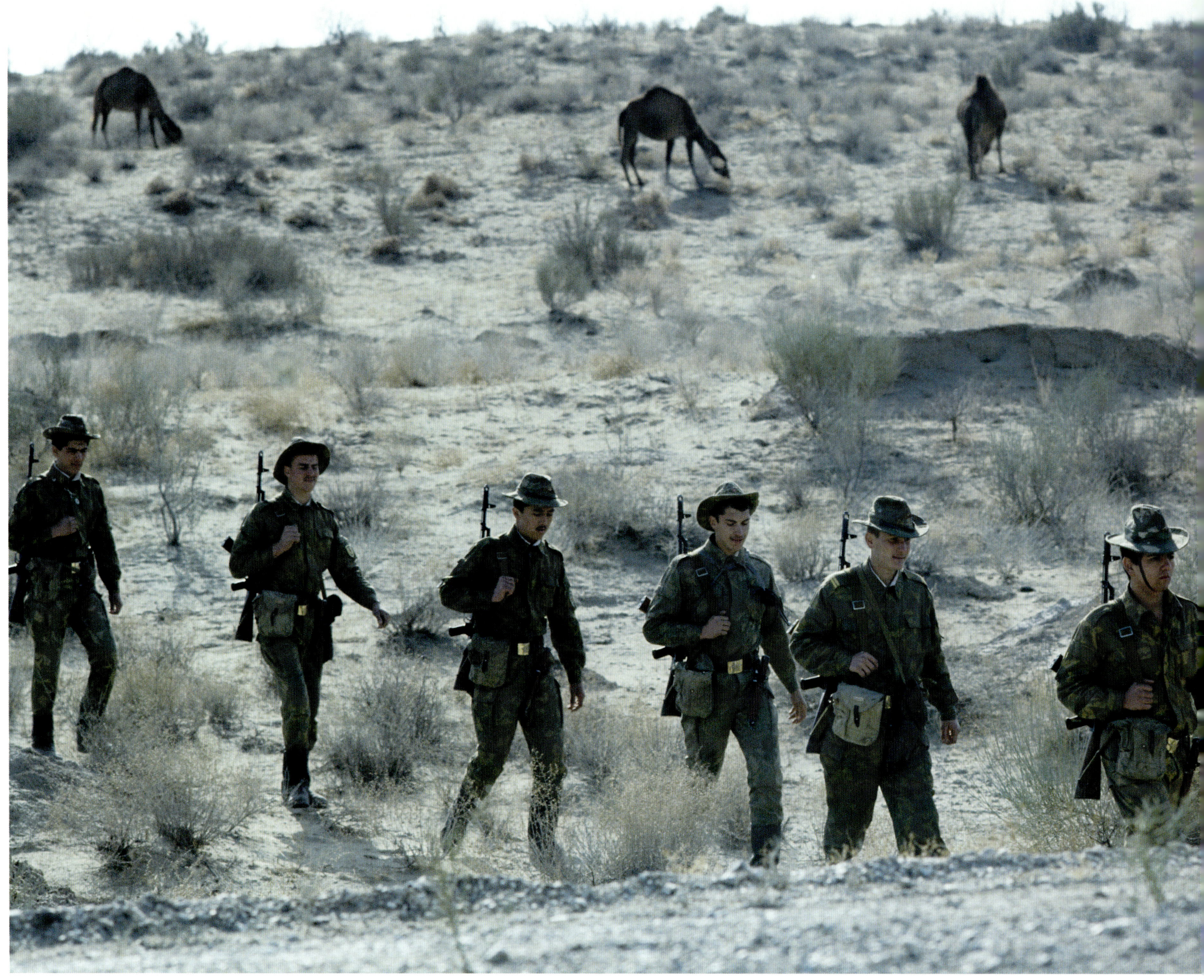

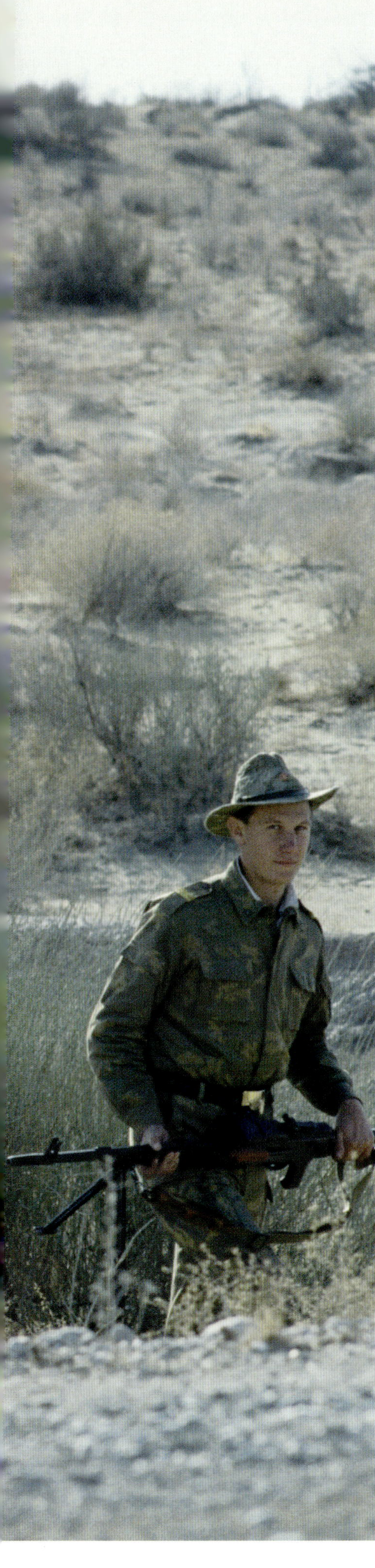

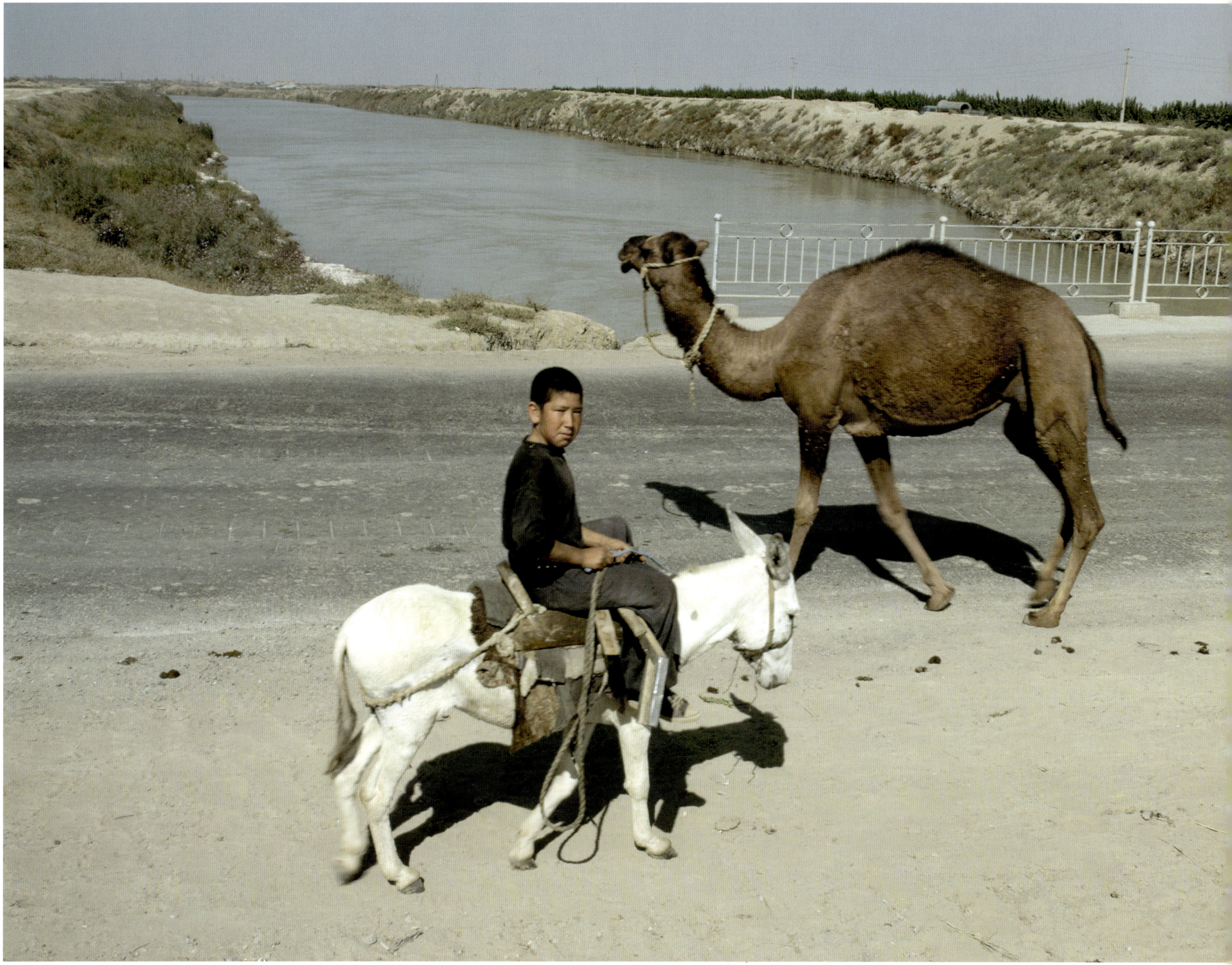

THE MARK OF MAN

Since time immemorial some people have made their homes in the deserts, coming to terms with the harsh living conditions, and, in particular, the great heat and the often desperate shortage of water. They have survived by hunting wild animals, herding domesticated animals, raising a few crops or trading, and they have made their marks, albeit mainly in a transitory way. Man has also made a few permanent marks, such as the mighty pyramids in Egypt, which will remain for ever as memorials not only to the kings and other nobles whose bodies occupy them but also to the skilled architects and industrious laborers who built them. Today, Man is still making his mark on the desert, but now it is by building cities such as Las Vegas, great wind farms and irrigation systems, wells to exploit the deserts' resources, and highways to facilitate transportation. Of deeper significance, there have also been men of many very different religions who have felt themselves to be closer to their gods in the vastness and tranquility of the desert, and who have built monasteries and shrines, many of which have become places of pilgrimage.

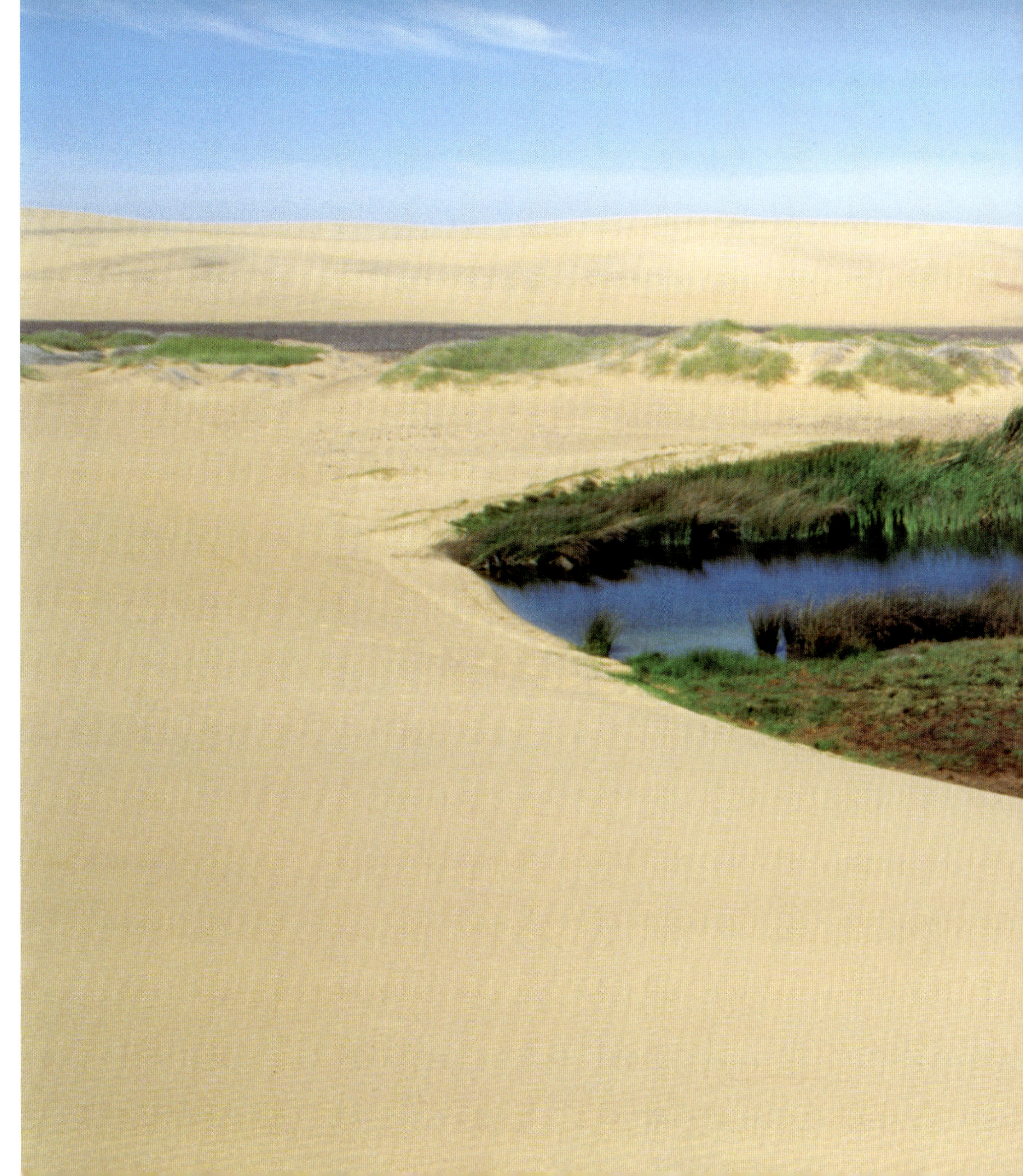

Right: This oasis in Namibia's Skeleton Coast National Park is centered around a natural spring. The limit of the fertile area influenced by the water is drawn with almost mathematical precision and shows how water can transform the apparently lifeless desert sand.
Sharna Balfour/Corbis

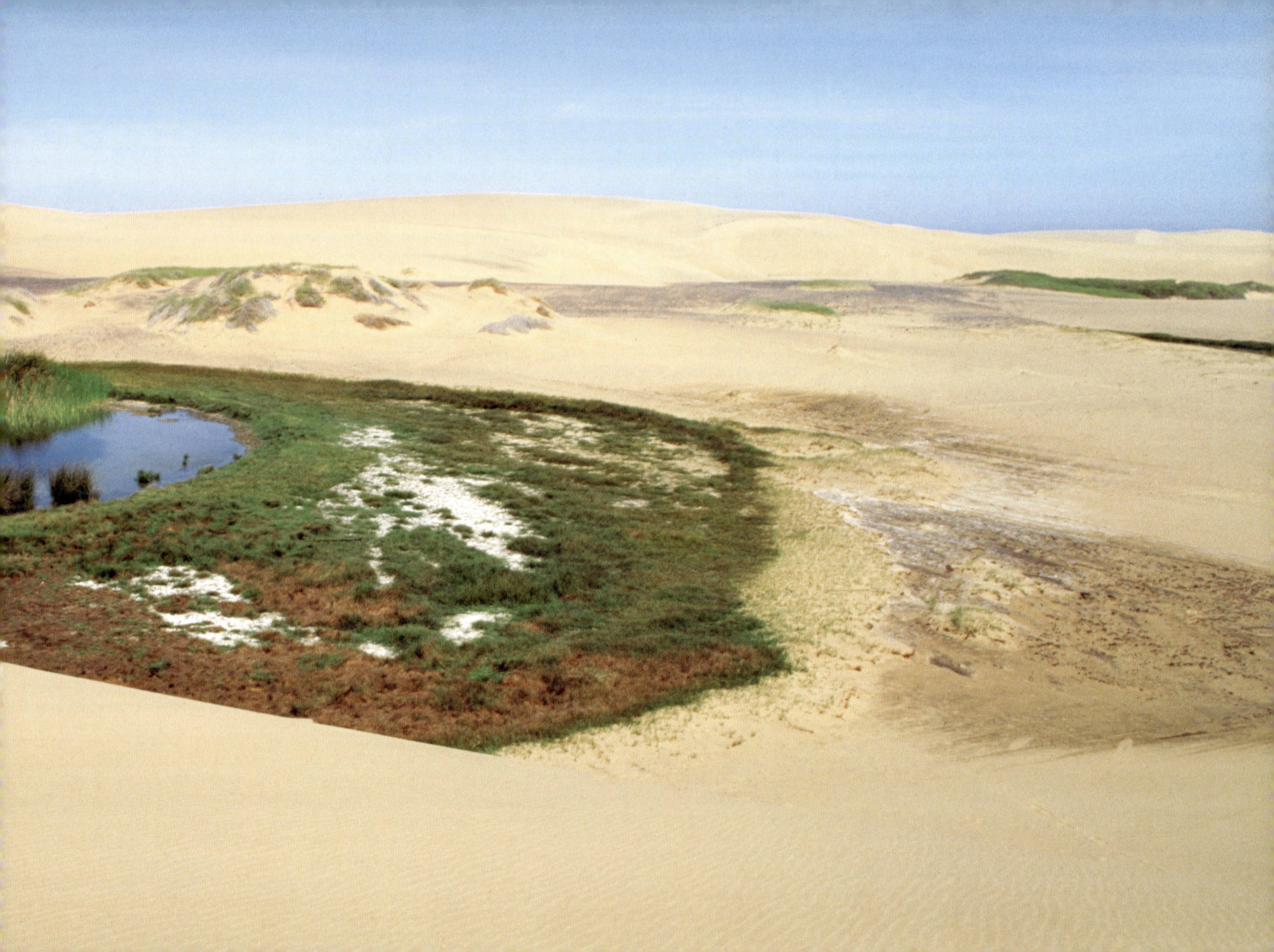

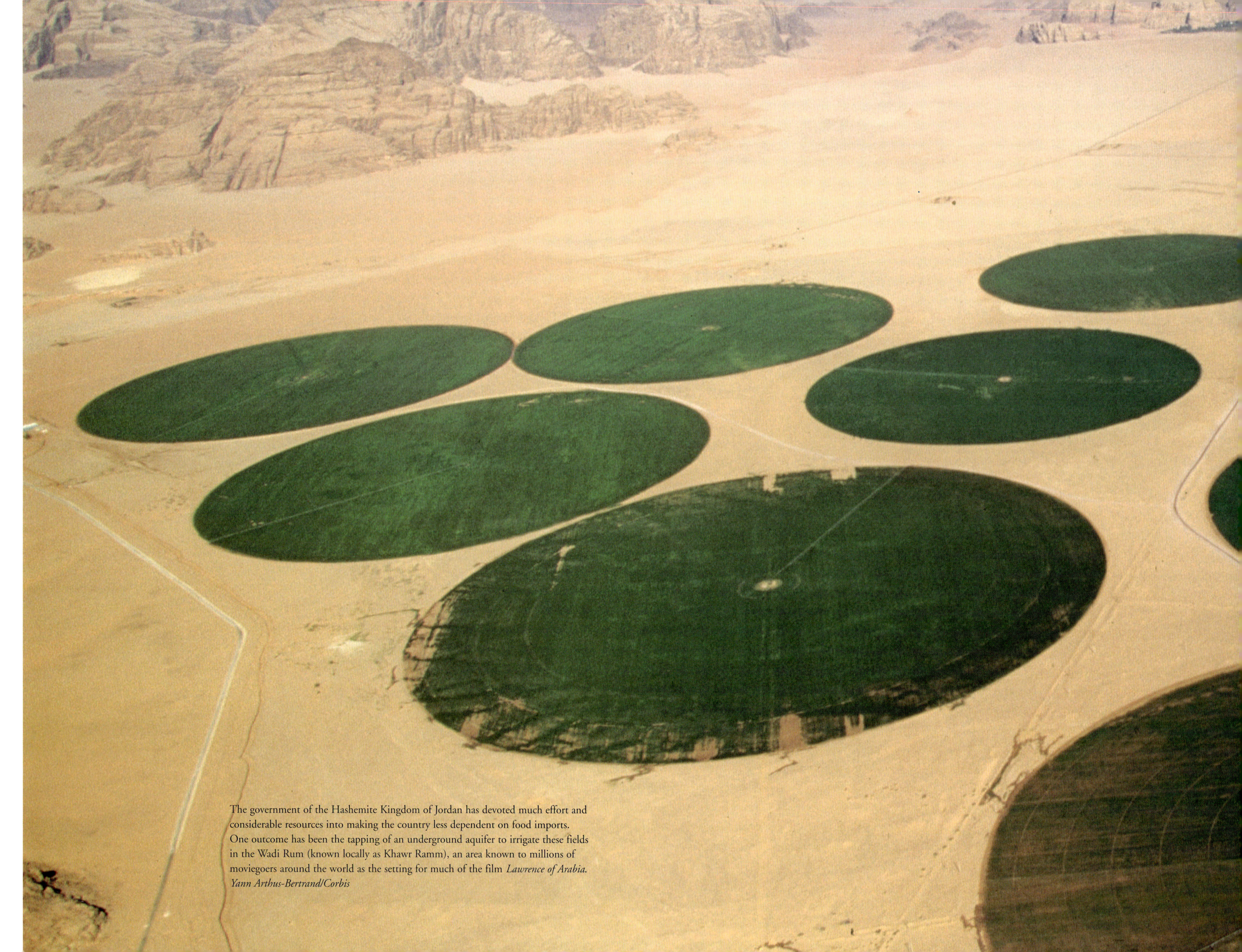

The government of the Hashemite Kingdom of Jordan has devoted much effort and considerable resources into making the country less dependent on food imports. One outcome has been the tapping of an underground aquifer to irrigate these fields in the Wadi Rum (known locally as Khawr Ramm), an area known to millions of moviegoers around the world as the setting for much of the film *Lawrence of Arabia.* *Yann Arthus-Bertrand/Corbis*

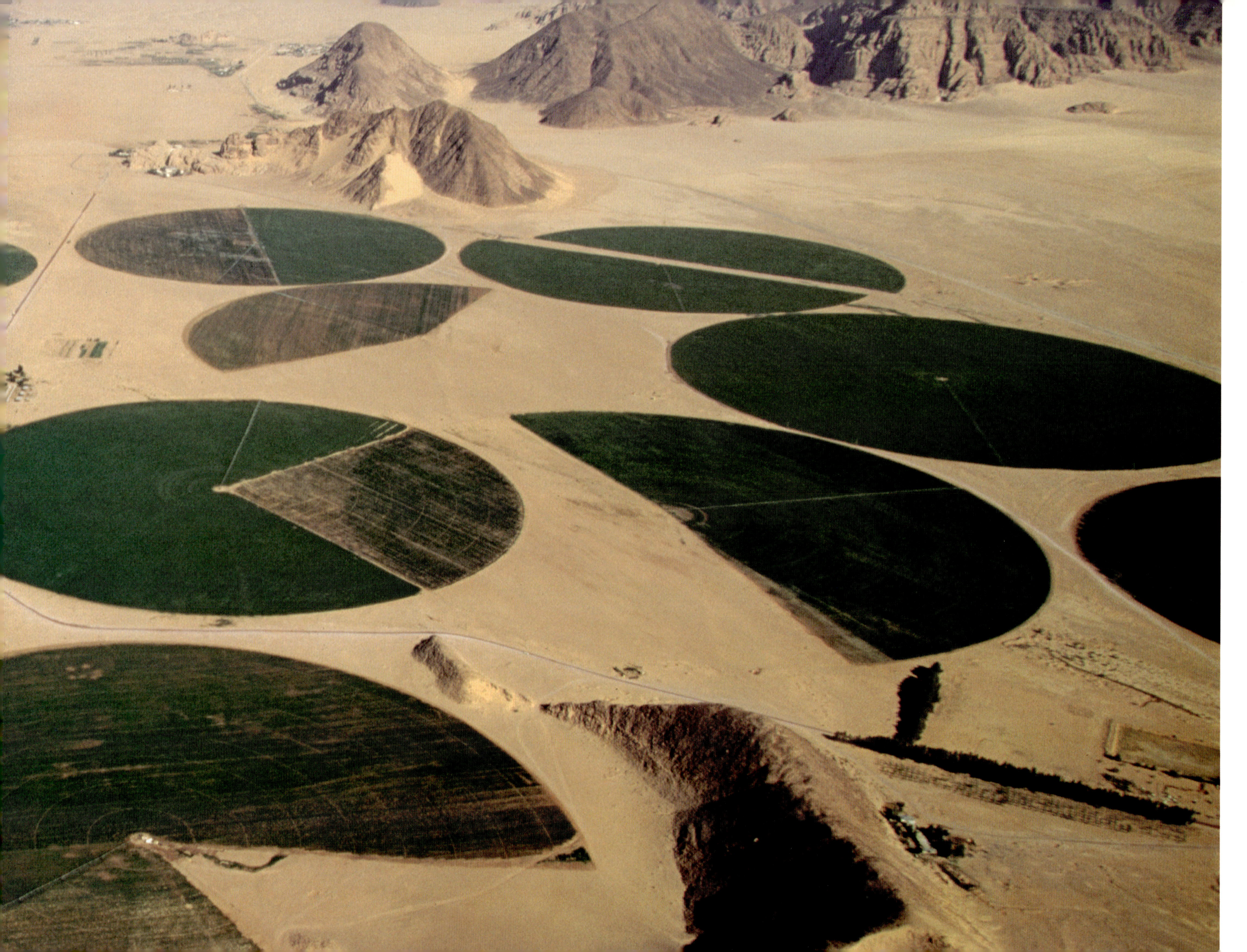

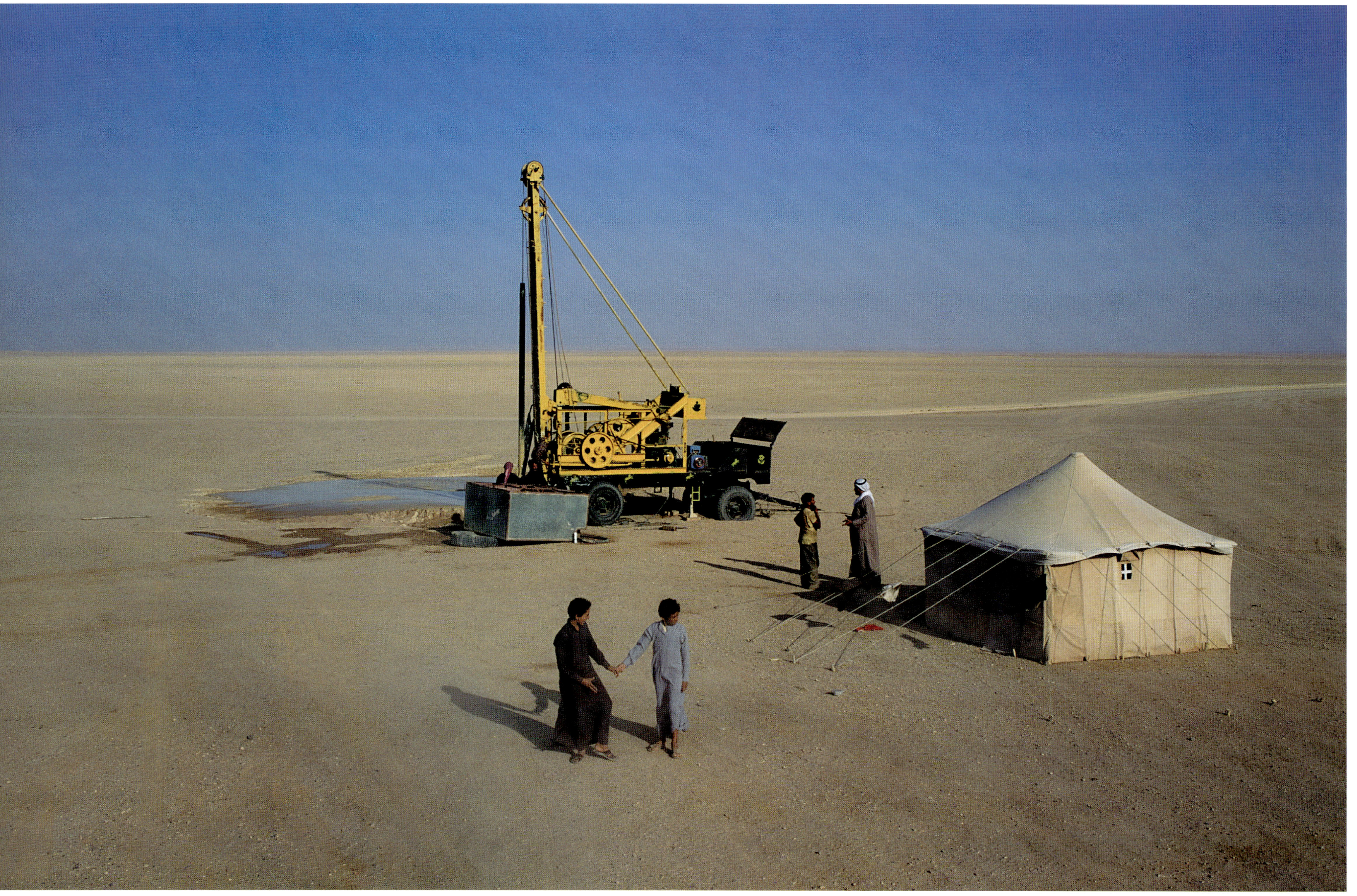

Left: The search for water is unceasing; these Bedouin workers are drilling for water in the Syrian Desert east of Damascus. They are searching for underground water reservoirs, rivers, or aquifers, which are porous layers of rock containing water. Until very recently these underground resources have been not only inaccessible but also unknown, although extreme care is necessary to ensure that they are not overused and run dry.
Ed Kashi/Corbis

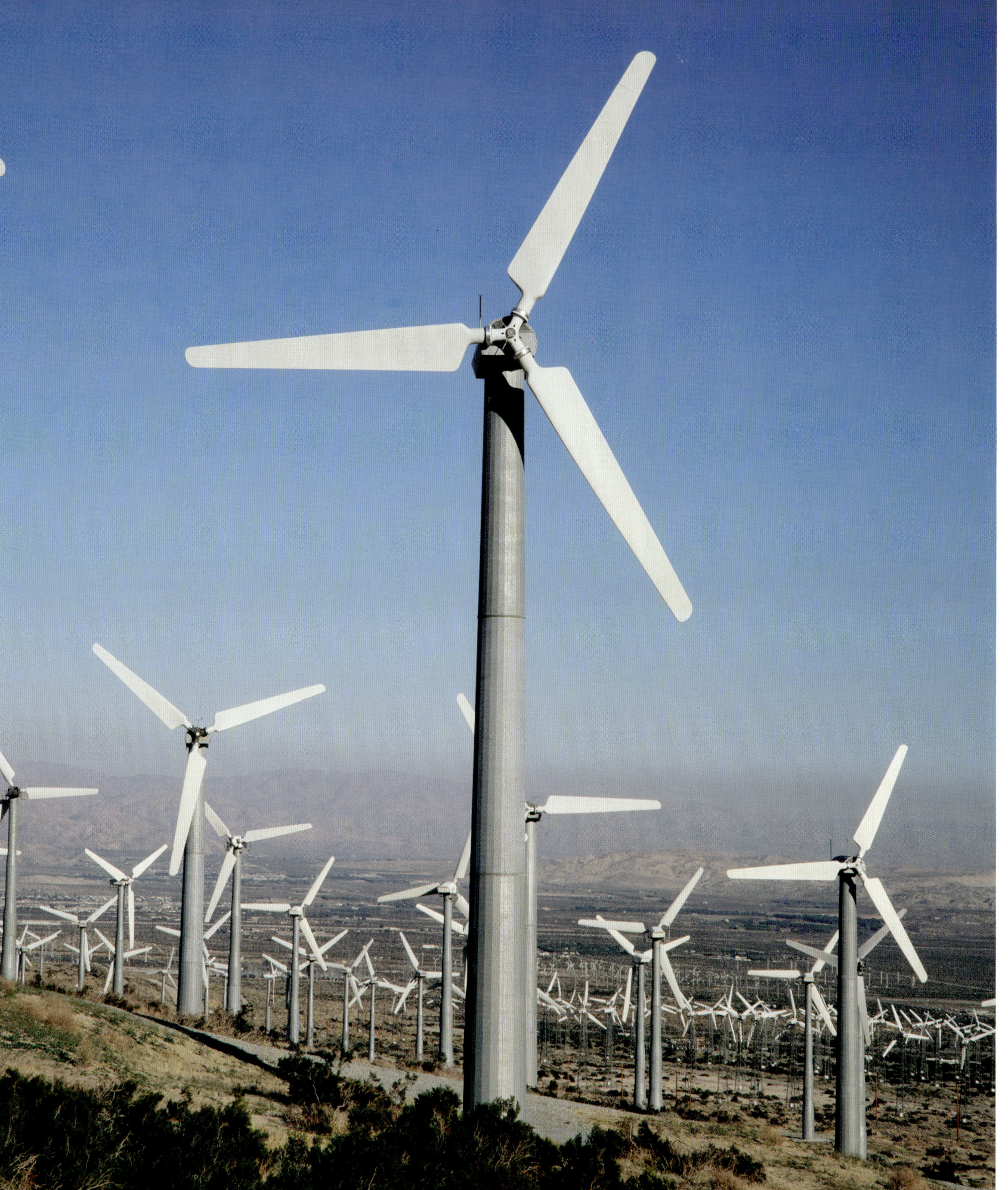

Left: One way of bringing power to the desert is using a wind farm, such as this one near Palm Springs in California, which contains some 4,000 individual windmills. The largest is 150 feet high and cost approximately US$300,000. Provided the average wind speed is greater than 13mph, it can generate some 300 kilowatts per hour.
Philip James Corwin/Corbis

Page 214: The town of Ourzazate in Morocco occupies a strategic position at the junction of various routes, which led to the French decision to build a fort and garrison town there in 1928, as part of their "pacification" program. In recent years major efforts have been made to irrigate the area, leading to these fertile fields.
Yann Arthus-Bertrand/Corbis

Page 215: A huge truck thunders along a highway through the Mojave Desert, near Las Vegas in the State of Nevada. The driver is cocooned in air-conditioned luxury, with radio communications for use in an emergency, but outside, and without his truck, he would find the conditions every bit as hostile as the intrepid frontiersmen and women of 150 years ago.
Walter Hodges/Corbis

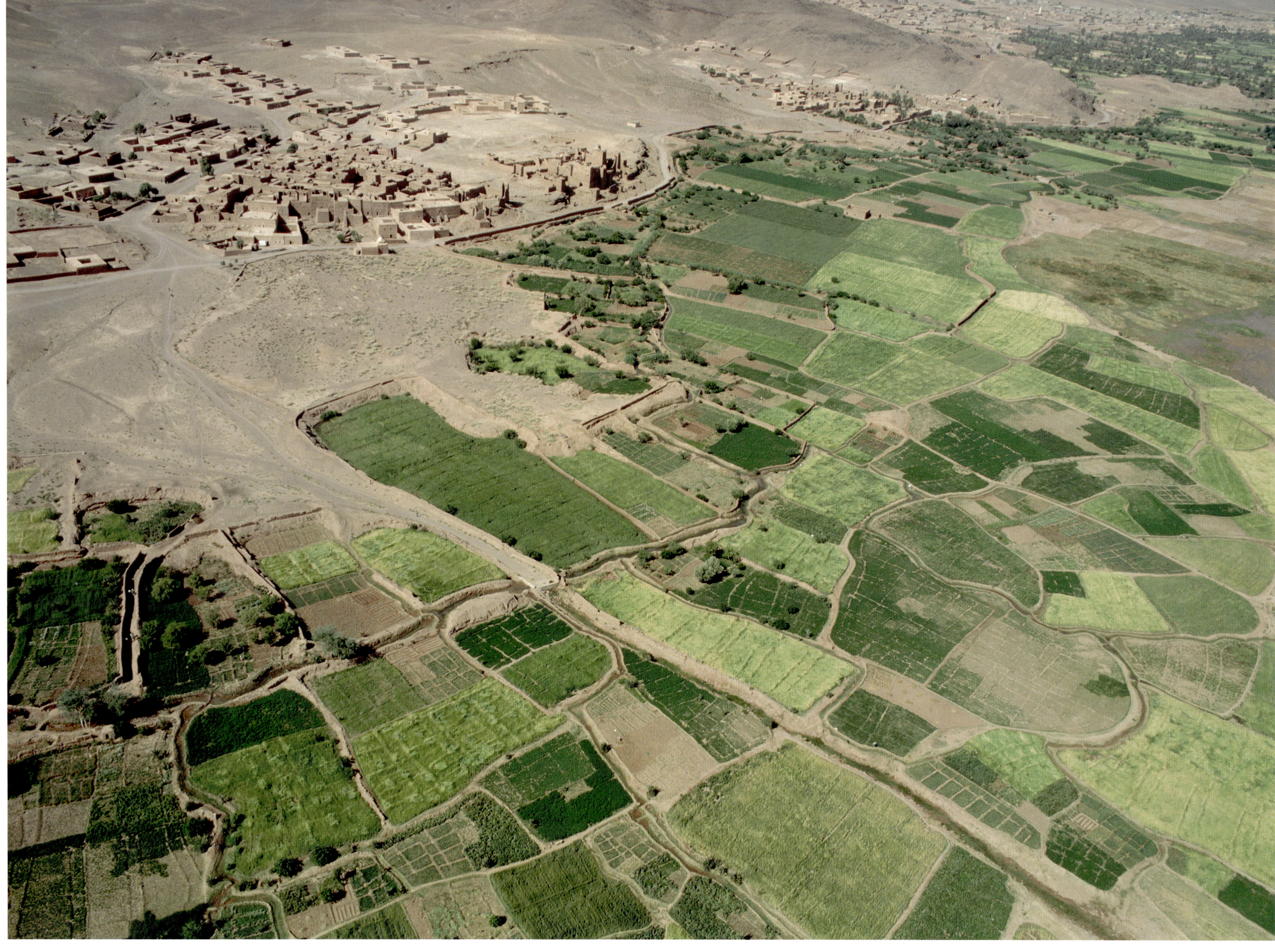

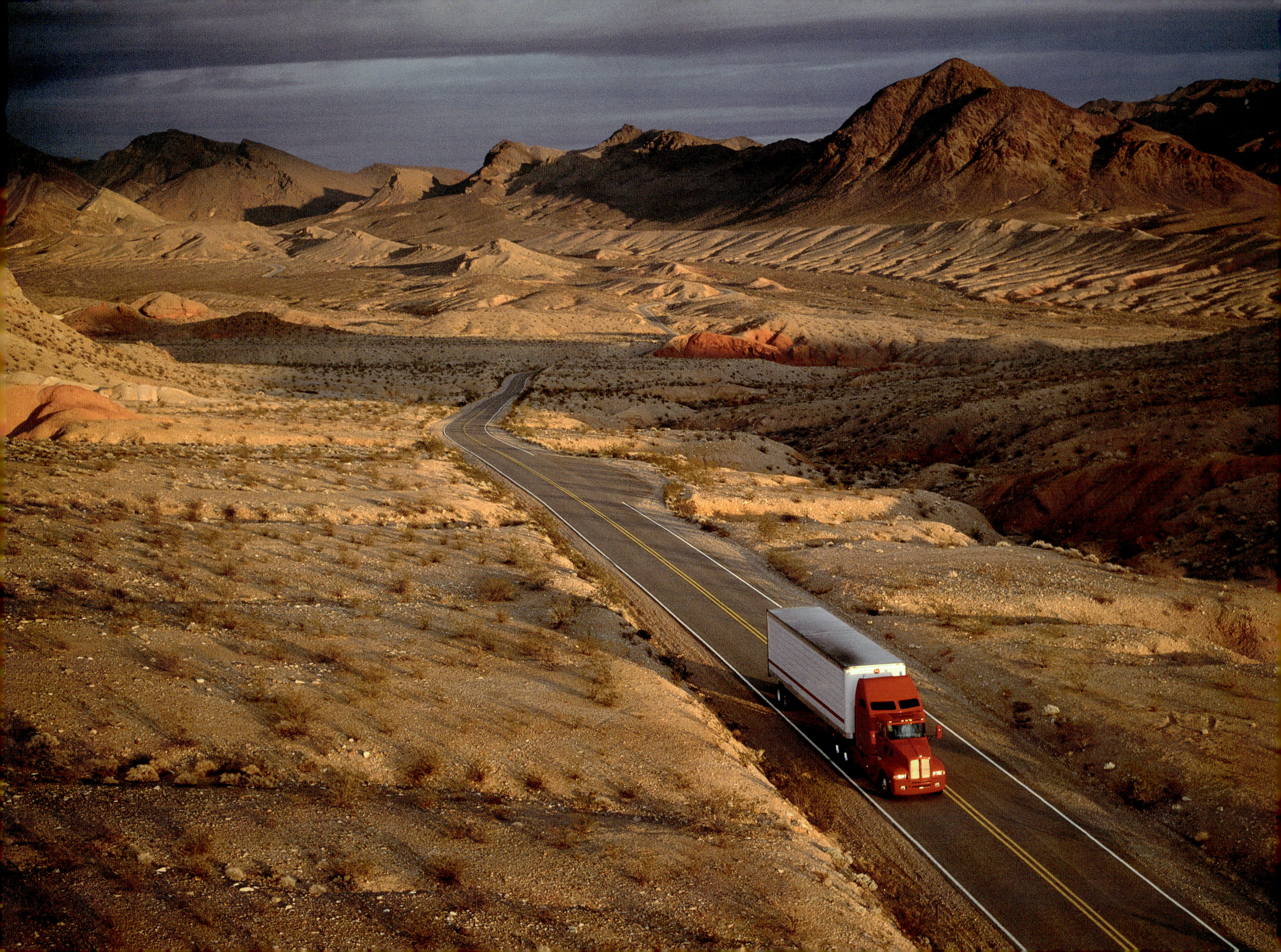

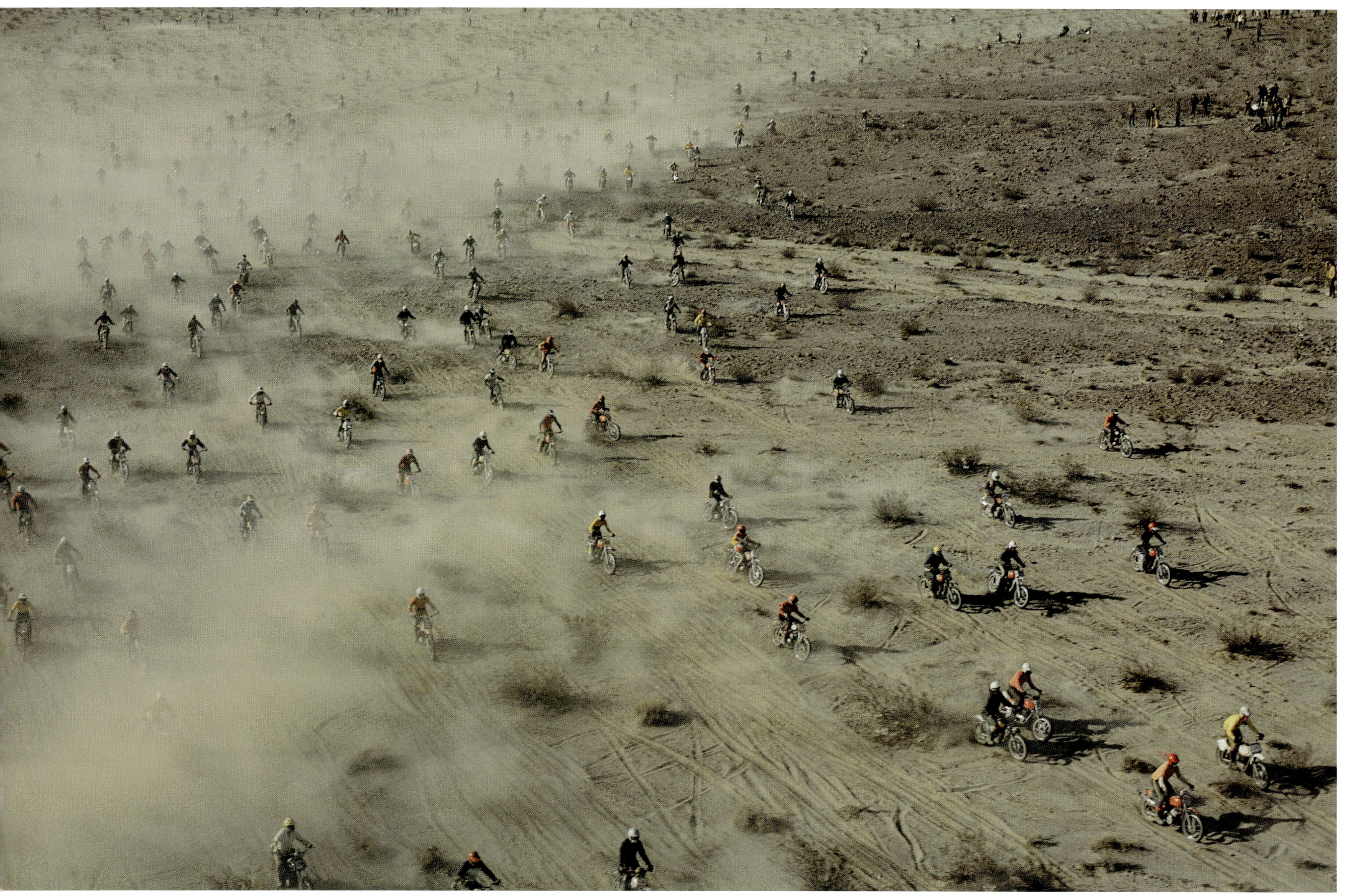

Left: Urban expansion from World War Two onwards has led to increasing use of desert areas for recreational purposes by city dwellers, who see the wide open spaces as offering opportunities for free-ranging activities such as this mass motorcycle race in the Mojave Desert near Los Angeles. At first uncontrolled, the rapid growth in the frequency of such events and the numbers taking part led to concern that the natural habitat was being destroyed, and conservation has become a hotly debated political issue.
Walter Meayers Edwards/Getty Images

Right: The El Mirage desert area in southern California is the scene of many leisure activities, including the use of motorcycles, all-terrain vehicles (ATVs), as well as less intrusive activities such as camping, hiking, and rock scrambling. El Mirage Dry Lake has a flat surface, which is used for Land Speed Racing (LSR), seen here, but also provides ad hoc landing grounds for ultra-light and small private aircraft. As a result, its use is now controlled by the Federal Bureau of Land Management, in cooperation with other Federal, State and County authorities, to coordinate these activities and to preserve the facilities.
Walter Meayers Edwards/Getty Images

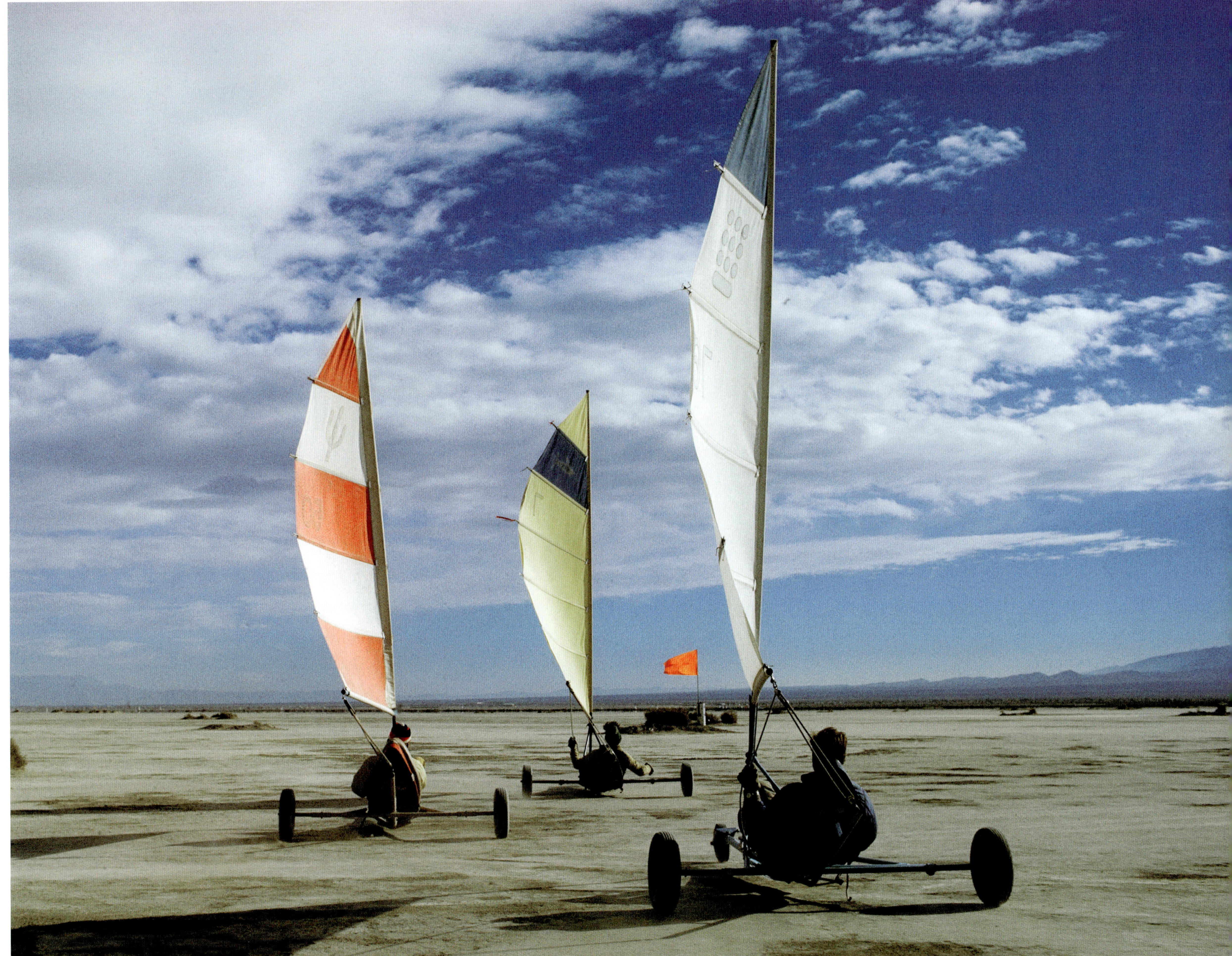

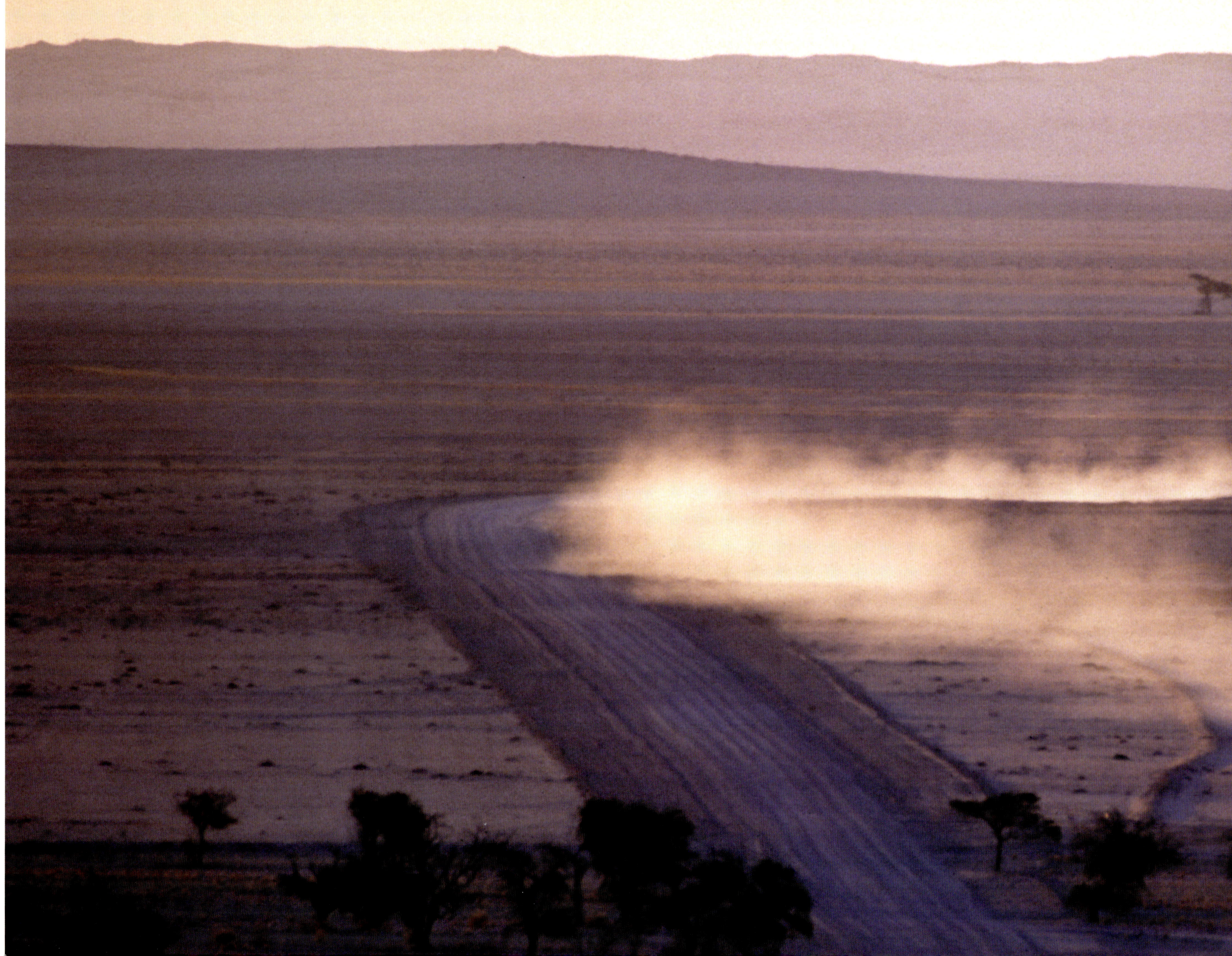

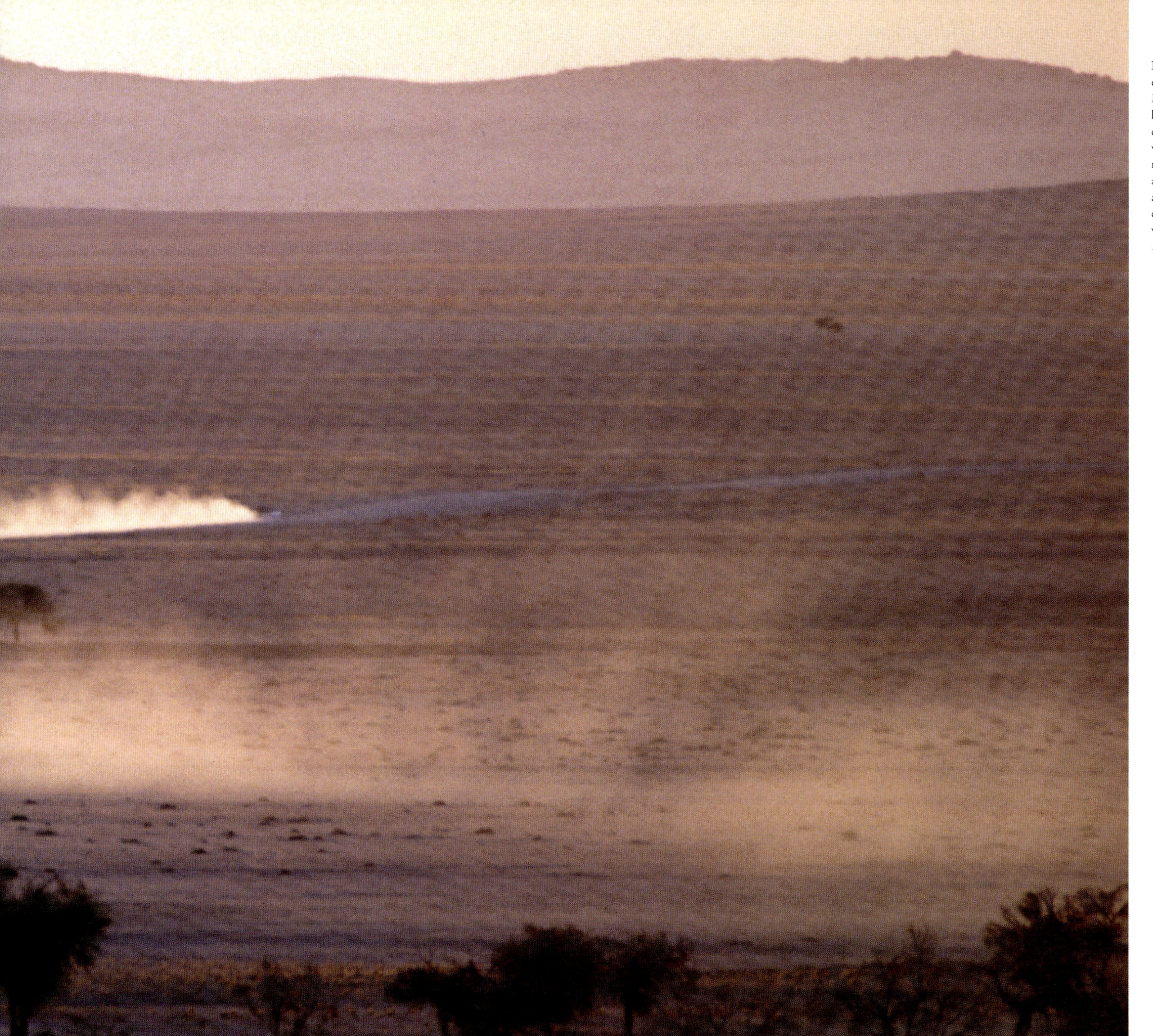

Left: In many parts of the world, Man is engaged in a constant fight with deserts. Many deserts are encroaching on settled land, turning it into a barren waste, while elsewhere men are trying to irrigate, cultivate and thus reclaim desert land, and make it fertile. In addition, many deserts are no longer physical barriers; roads, such as this one in the Namib Desert in southern Africa, enable people to cross them at will.
Lutz Wahlers/fotoLibra

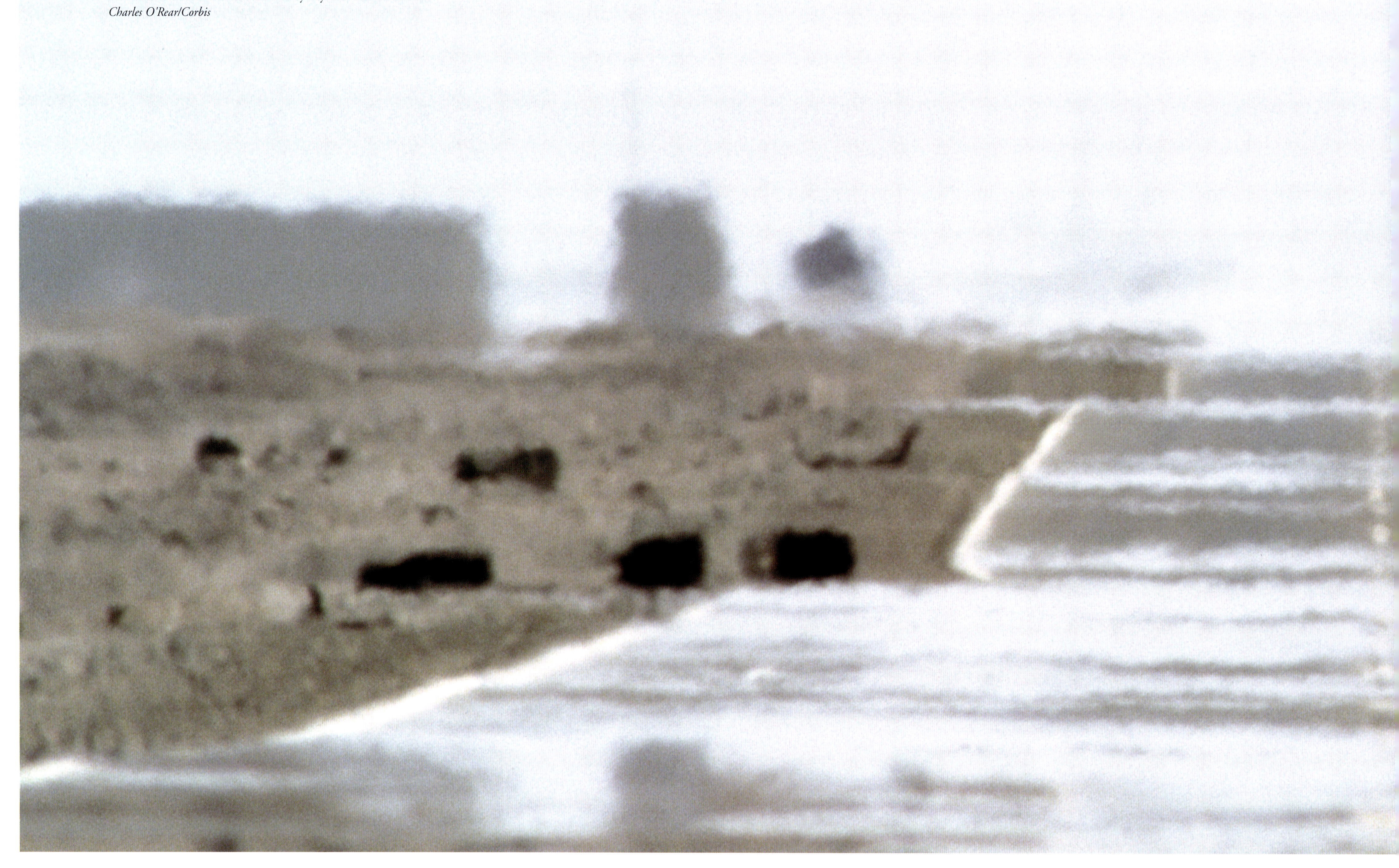

Where once men and animals would have died of thirst and exhaustion, the Atacama Desert is now crossed by Chile's Highway 25. Note the absence of drainage ditches alongside the highway, as these are completely unnecessary in an area where there has never been sufficient rainfall to be measured by any conventional means.
Charles O'Rear/Corbis

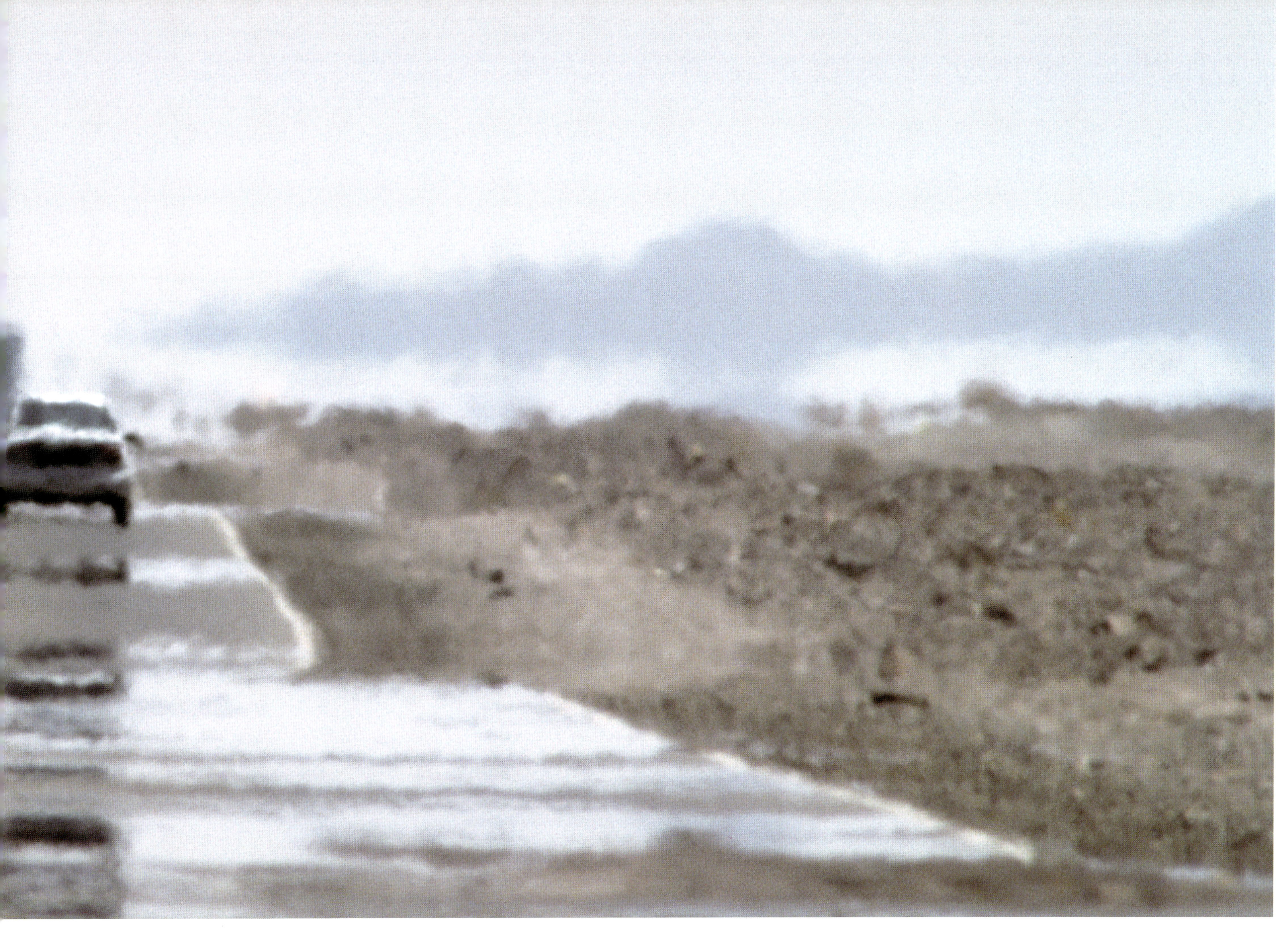

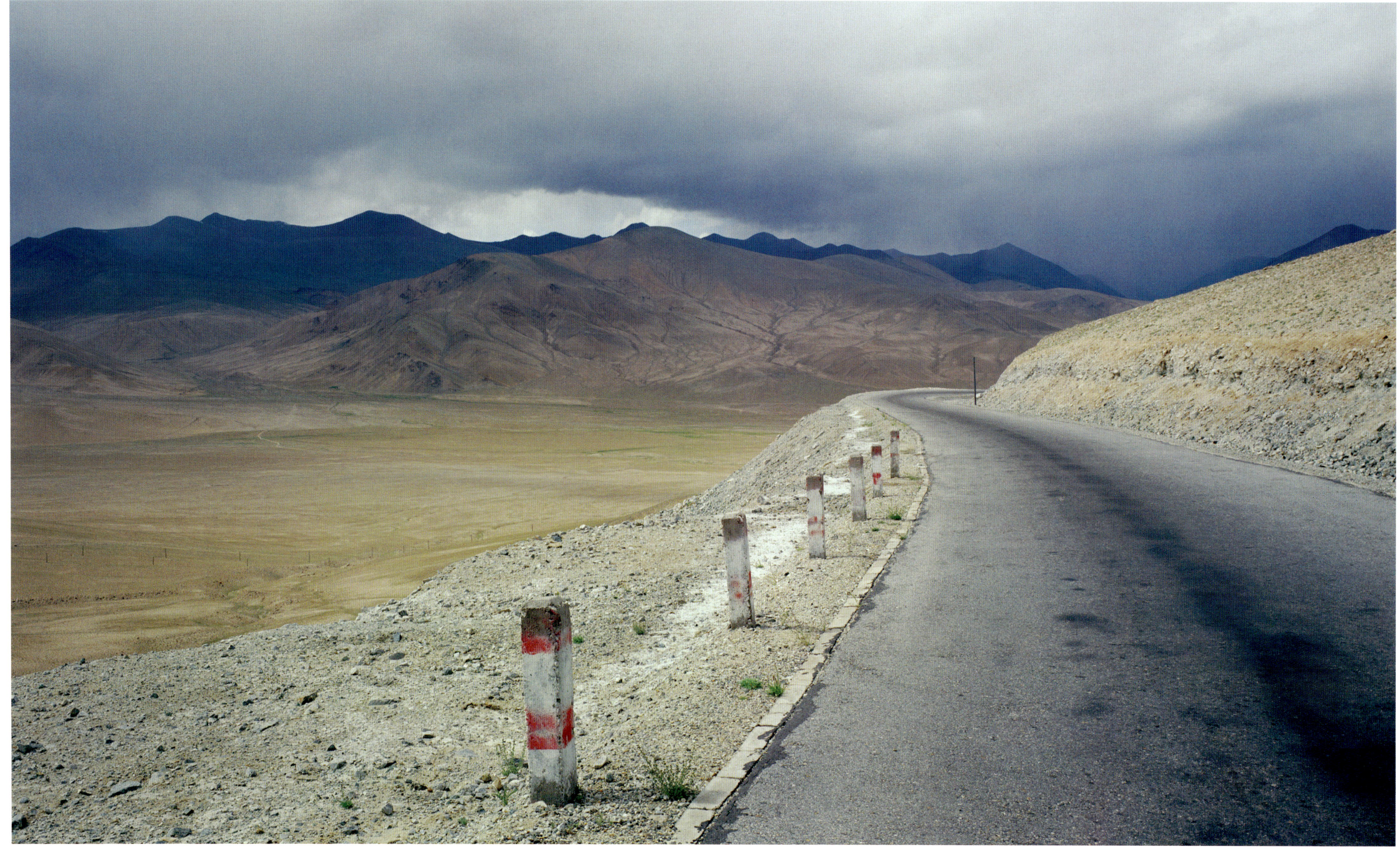

ABOVE: Almost everything about the Karakoram Highway makes sense; it greatly facilitates transportation between remote areas, and brings water, food, and relative prosperity to remote areas. But, on the other hand, it also brings atmospheric pollution from the exhausts of the trucks, and when trucks fail they are simply left there, causing other forms of pollution.
David Samuel Robbins/Corbis

RIGHT: An overturned cargo truck lies beside the Karakorum Highway in Chinese Turkistan. Obviously, if a truck breaks down in country such as this it will require a major effort to recover it to the nearest town and either repair it or scrap it. On the other hand, if it is abandoned, as here, the debris of civilization will gradually accumulate until it becomes a major visual and environmental problem.
David Samuel Robbins/Corbis

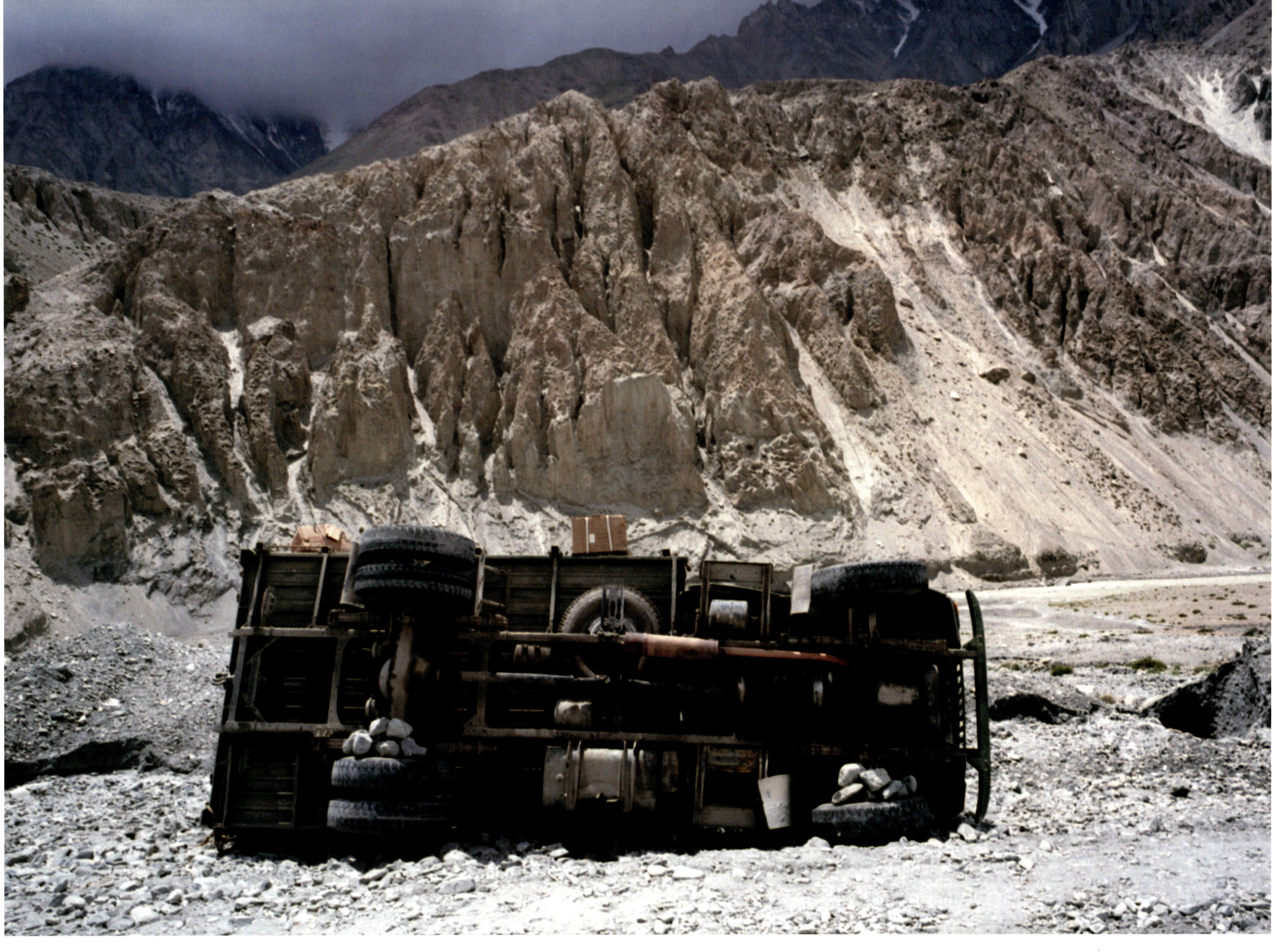

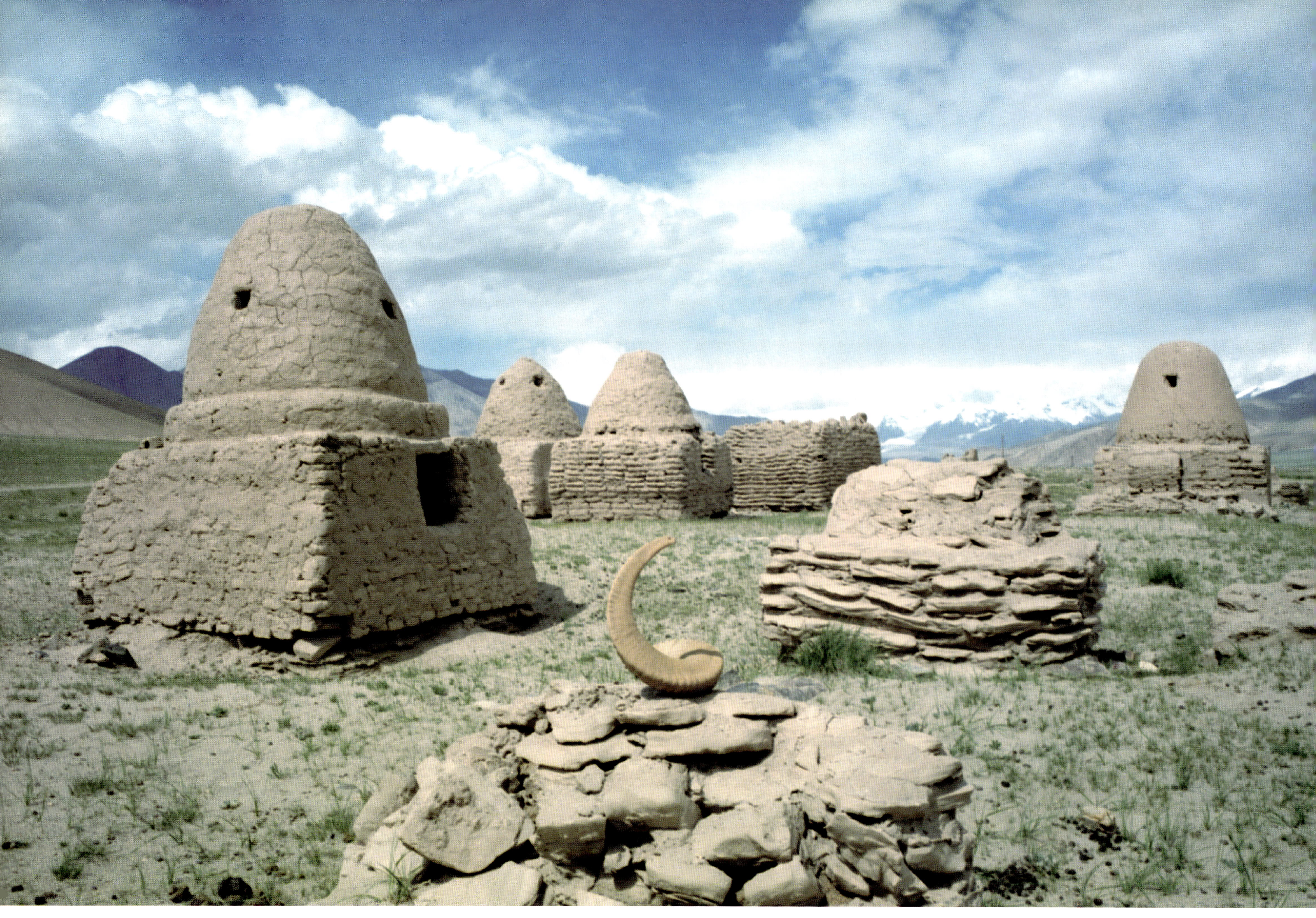

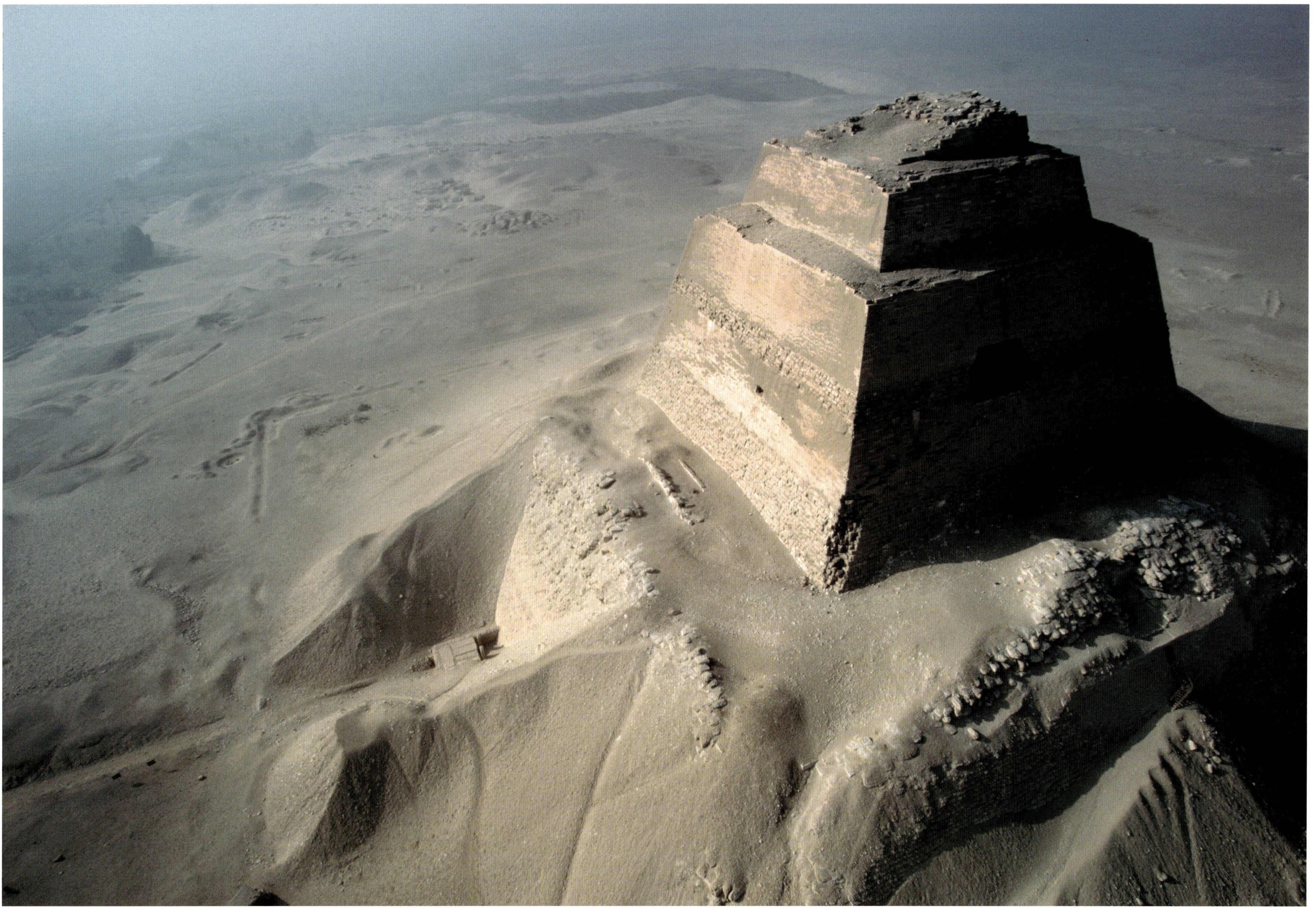

PAGE 224: Tombs made of dried earth and stones on the side of the Karakoram Highway. Many civilizations leave their mark on the environment, but most, such as these tombs, are dignified and blend into the landscape; roads and trucks do not.
David Samuel Robbins/Corbis

PAGE 225: By far the most famous buildings in any desert are the Egyptian pyramids, the earliest of which is this one at Maydum, near Memphis, on the west bank of the River Nile. The occupant was King Sneferu, the first ruler of the Fourth Dynasty. The pyramid was originally encased in an outer facing, but at some time, still unknown, this collapsed; this accounts for the debris around the inner core.
Yann Arthus-Bertrand/Corbis

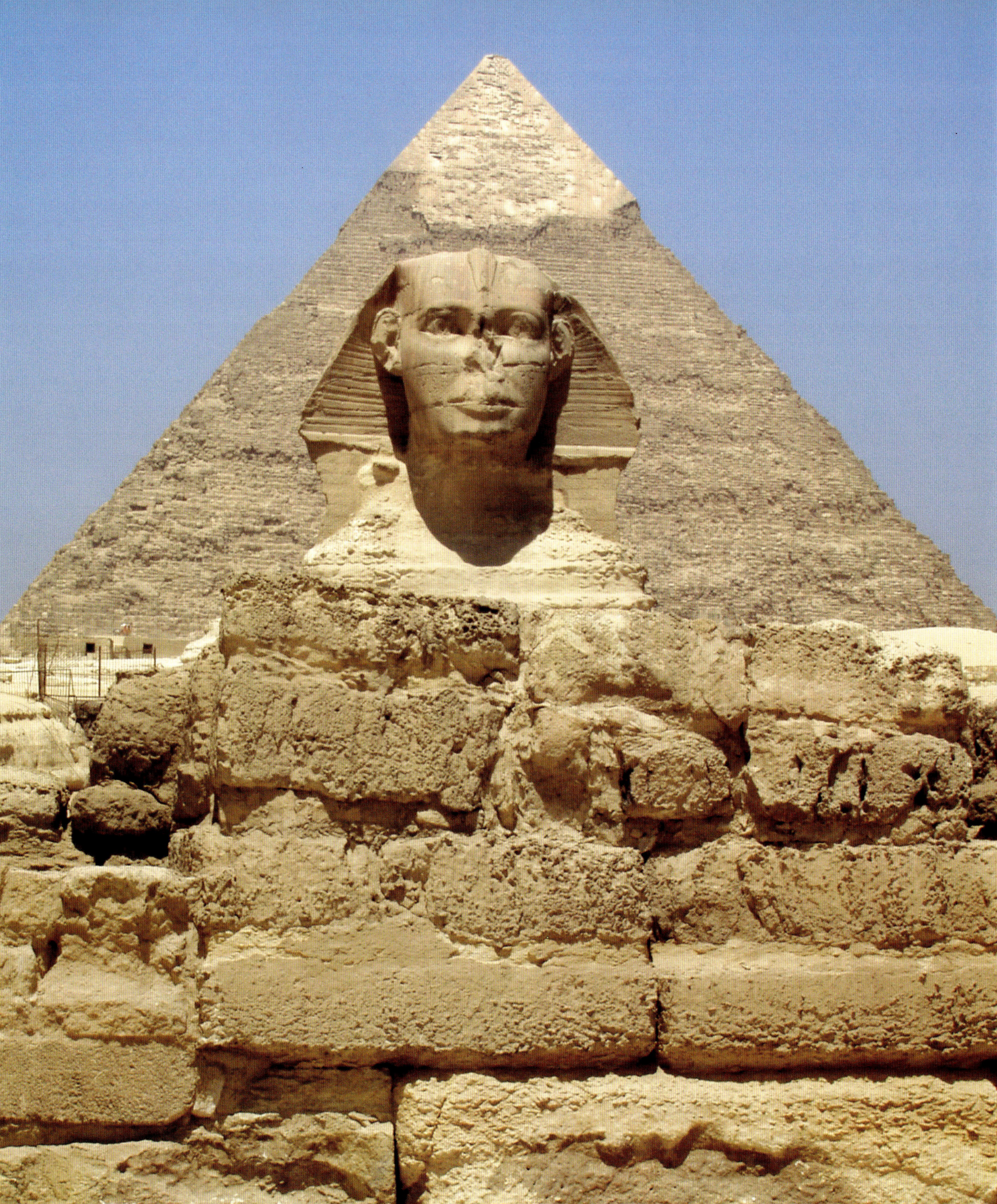

LEFT: The Great Sphinx of Giza has stared enigmatically across the Egyptian desert for several thousand years. It has the body of a lion with the head of a king or god, and, whatever the original intention, it has come to epitomize strength and wisdom. It is carved from the bedrock of the Giza Plateau and, because some of the layers of stone are softer than others, there has been an uneven rate of erosion. But, despite this and other slight damage, it remains magnificent and unique.
Brian Andrews/fotoLibra

RIGHT: Each side of the Red Pyramid at Dashur, Egypt, is 722 feet long and, with the sides angled at 42 degrees, it is 343 feet high, the two people in this picture setting the scale of this immense structure, which took some seventeen years of constant work to complete. The pyramids at Giza are better known and are so crowded with visitors that restrictions have been placed on numbers and access, while this pyramid is less well known and currently receives many fewer visitors. But, greater prosperity and cheaper travel are increasing the volume of visitors to all such sites, their sheer numbers helping to destroy what it is that they are going to see.
Stephen St. John/Getty Images

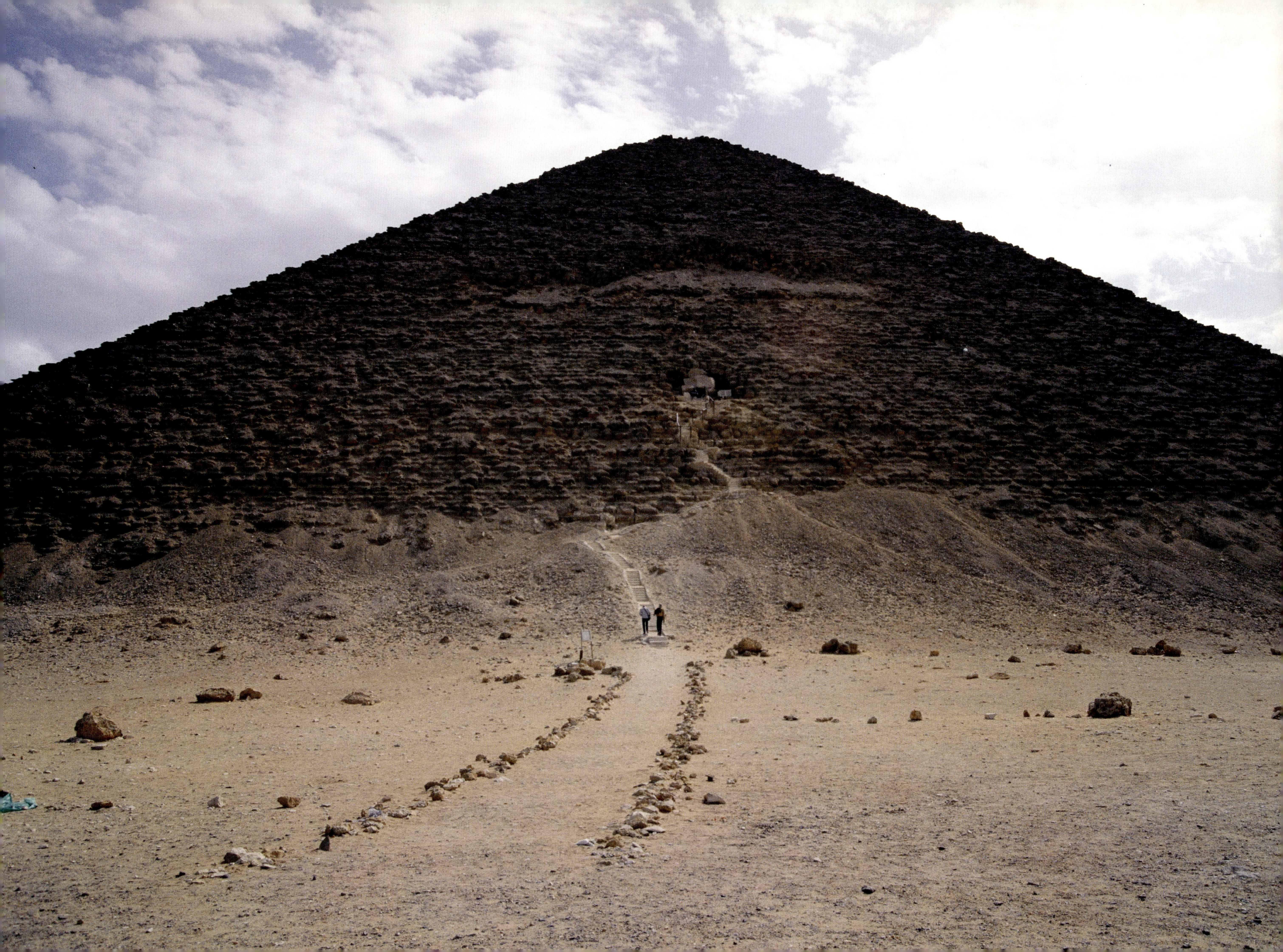

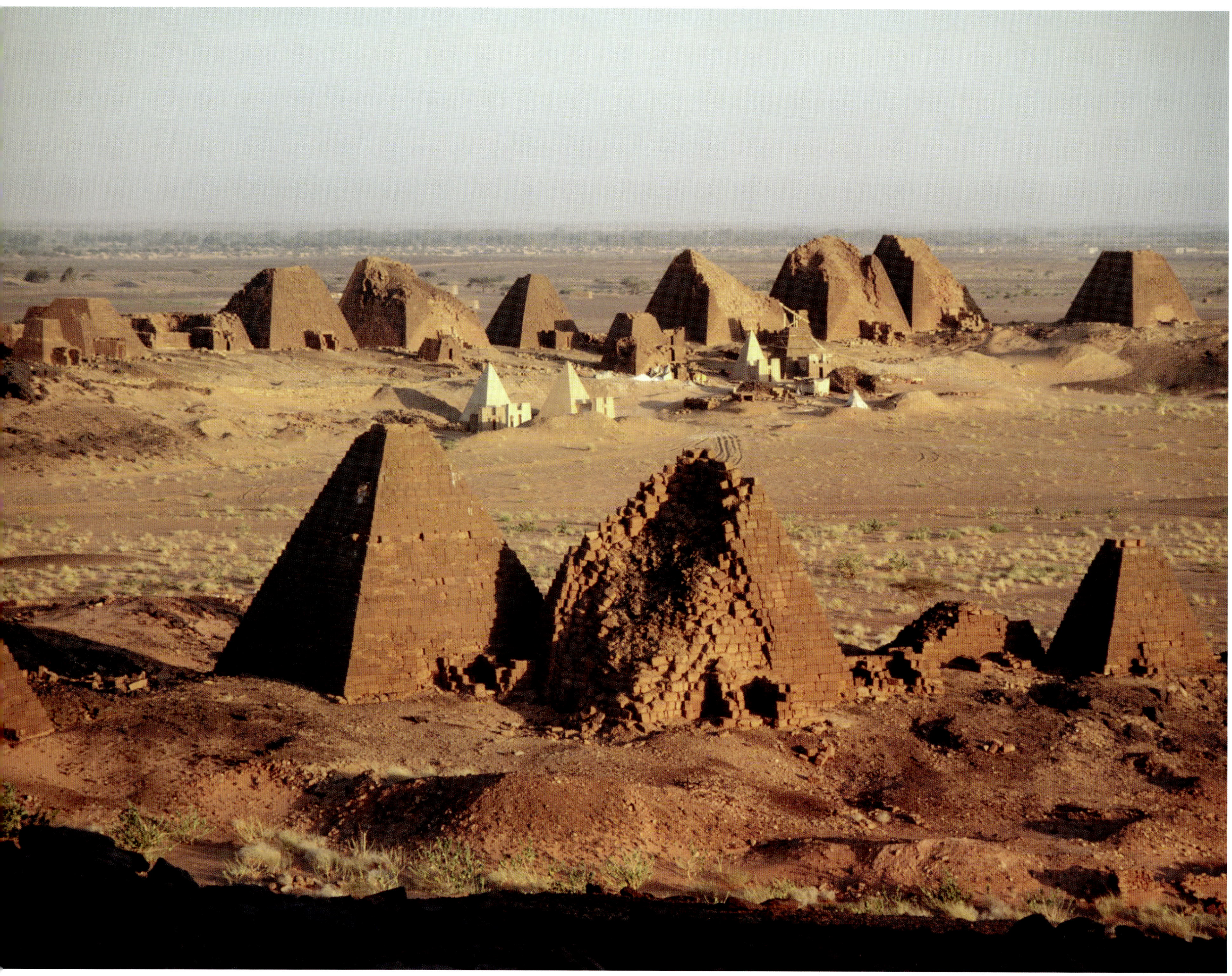

Left: Today's Sudan was known in Biblical times as Nubia, or the Kingdom of Kush, and the remains of this great and sophisticated civilization is marked by no fewer than 223 pyramids at Meroë in the Sudan. They were burial chambers for kings, queens and noblemen and, attracted by rumors of untold wealth, various adventurers have plundered all of them. The most notorious was an Italian named Ferlini who smashed the tops off forty of these invaluable historical relics—he found gold in just one in 1830, but this led to greater depredations by other fortune hunters.
Michael S. Yamashita/Corbis

Right: This man on his donkey riding past the Great Pyramids of Giza, in Egypt, represents a traditional way of life and a population pressure that were totally sustainable, although it would be wrong to deny that damage has not been done to such precious relics of the past by previous generations. But, it is the global population increase, the ever-growing urban sprawls, and the demands for leisure and tourist access that are combining to produce a major threat to the deserts of the world.
Kenneth Garrett/Getty Images

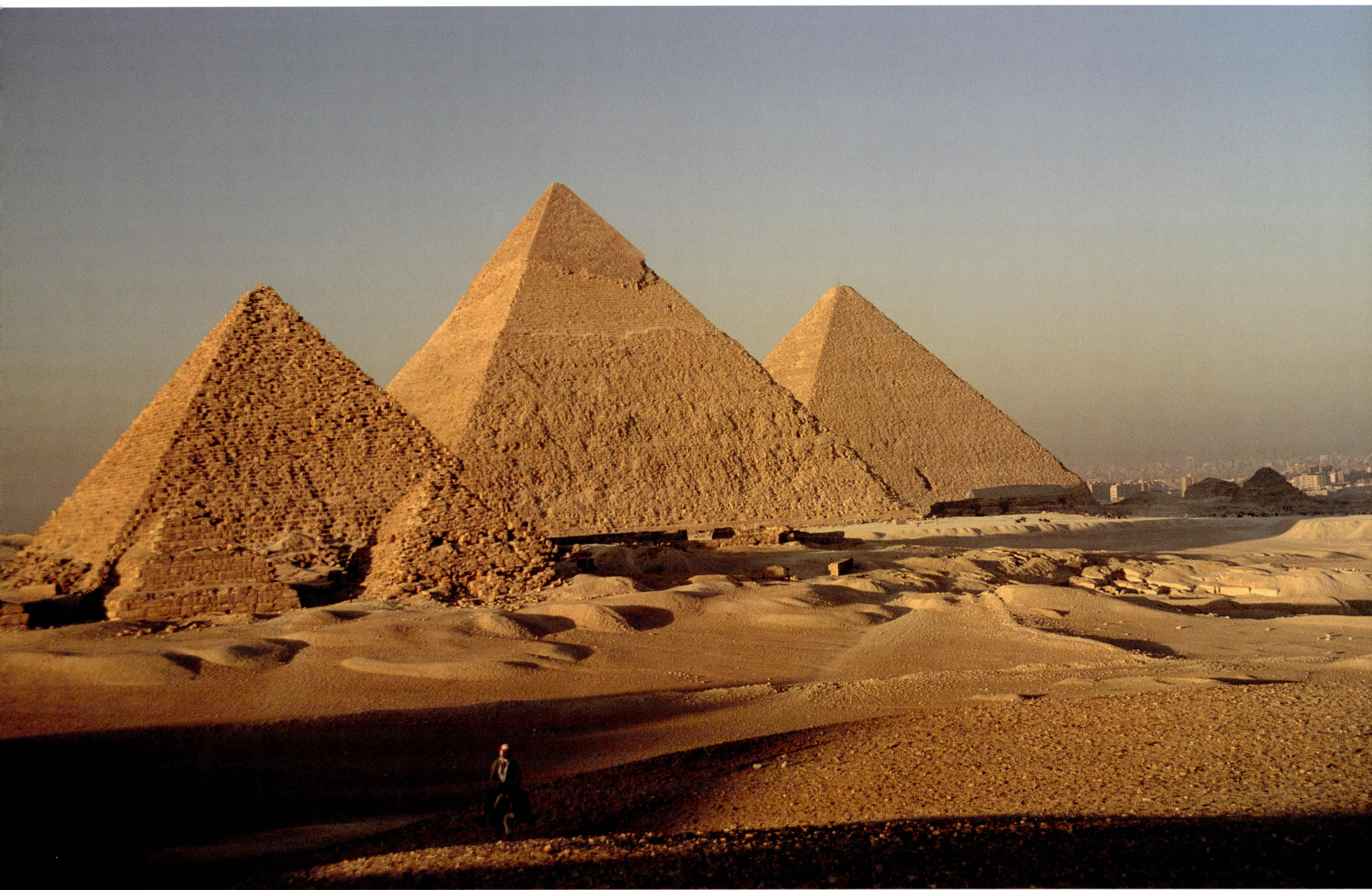

Right: The extraordinary city of Petra is almost entirely carved out of living rock. Located in the Great Rift Valley in Jordan, some fifty miles south of the southern end of the Dead Sea, it has had a checkered history, having been periodically forgotten and then rediscovered. It sank into obscurity from about 1000AD, but returned briefly during the 12th century under the Crusaders, only to be totally forgotten again until 1812 when it was visited by a Swiss explorer named Burckhardt. His reports sparked a succession of European and American visitors, but only in small numbers, until it featured in the movie *Indiana Jones and his Last Crusade*; now it has become a popular tourist attraction.
Terry Bugden/fotoLibra

Far Right: Palmyra in the Syrian Desert was originally a halting place for caravans and grew into a major city. It was taken over by the Romans, but treated well and flourished. It is remembered today as the capital of Queen Xenobia, a woman of exceptional talents, ability, and beauty. Unfortunately, she challenged Roman rule and in 268AD her armies overran most of Rome's eastern empire. Emperor Aurelian brought a vast army to retake the lost territories, capturing both Palmyra and Xenobia in 274AD. The queen took poison, but these ruins remain as mute testimony to a truly remarkable woman.
Richard T. Nowitz/Corbis

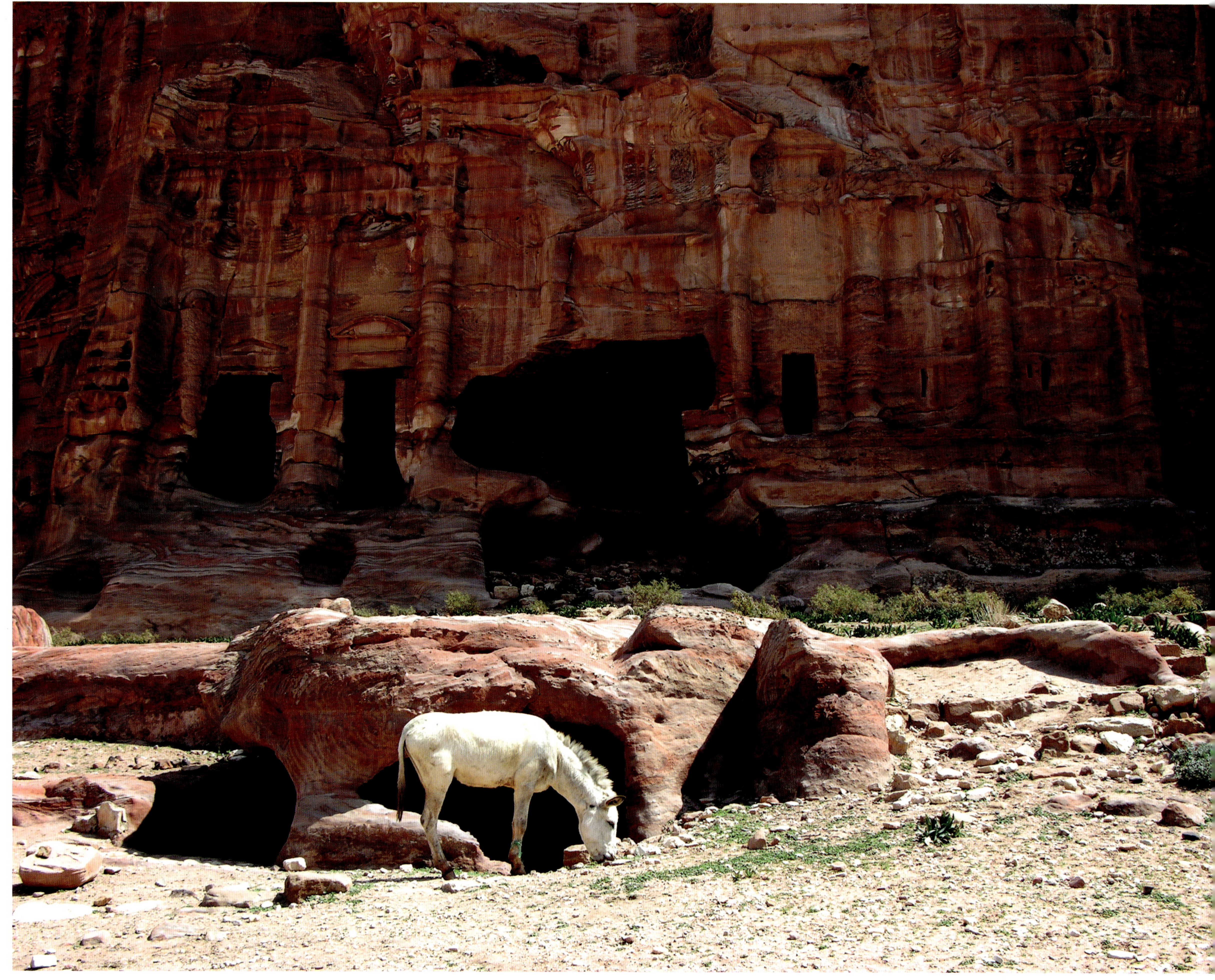

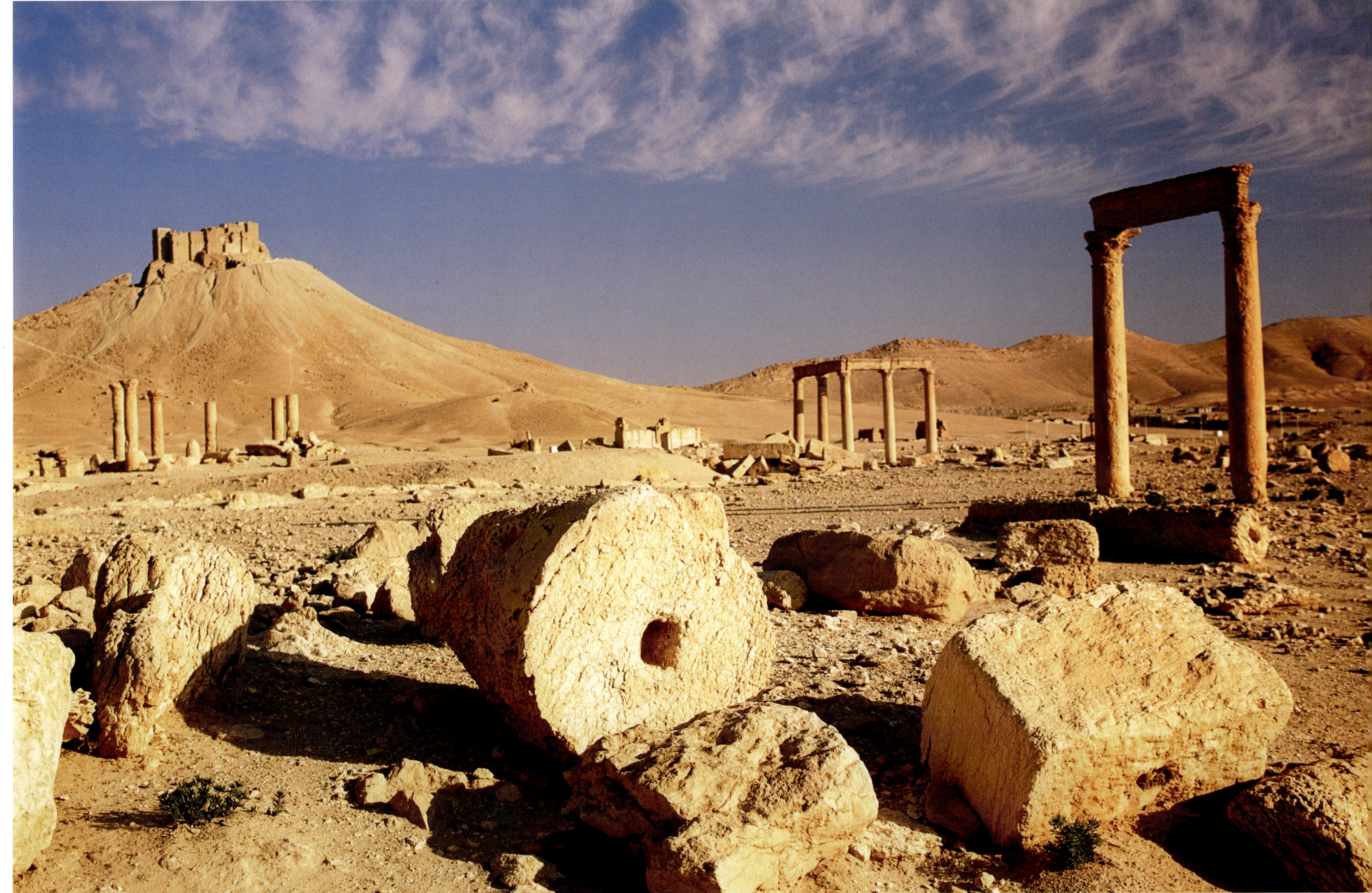

Right: This is one of a number of Coptic monasteries in the Wadi el Natrun in Egypt. The somewhat bleak exterior disguises the fact that the interior is very elaborate and, due to the design and the various air channels, very cool, despite the hot desert conditions outside.
Hans Georg Roth/Corbis

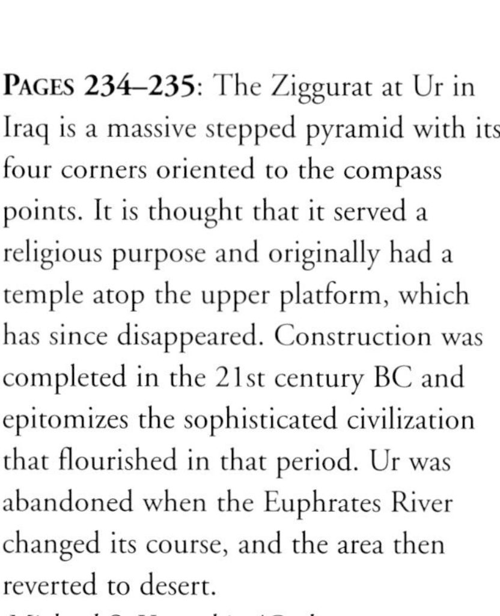

Pages 234–235: The Ziggurat at Ur in Iraq is a massive stepped pyramid with its four corners oriented to the compass points. It is thought that it served a religious purpose and originally had a temple atop the upper platform, which has since disappeared. Construction was completed in the 21st century BC and epitomizes the sophisticated civilization that flourished in that period. Ur was abandoned when the Euphrates River changed its course, and the area then reverted to desert.
Michael S. Yamashita/Corbis

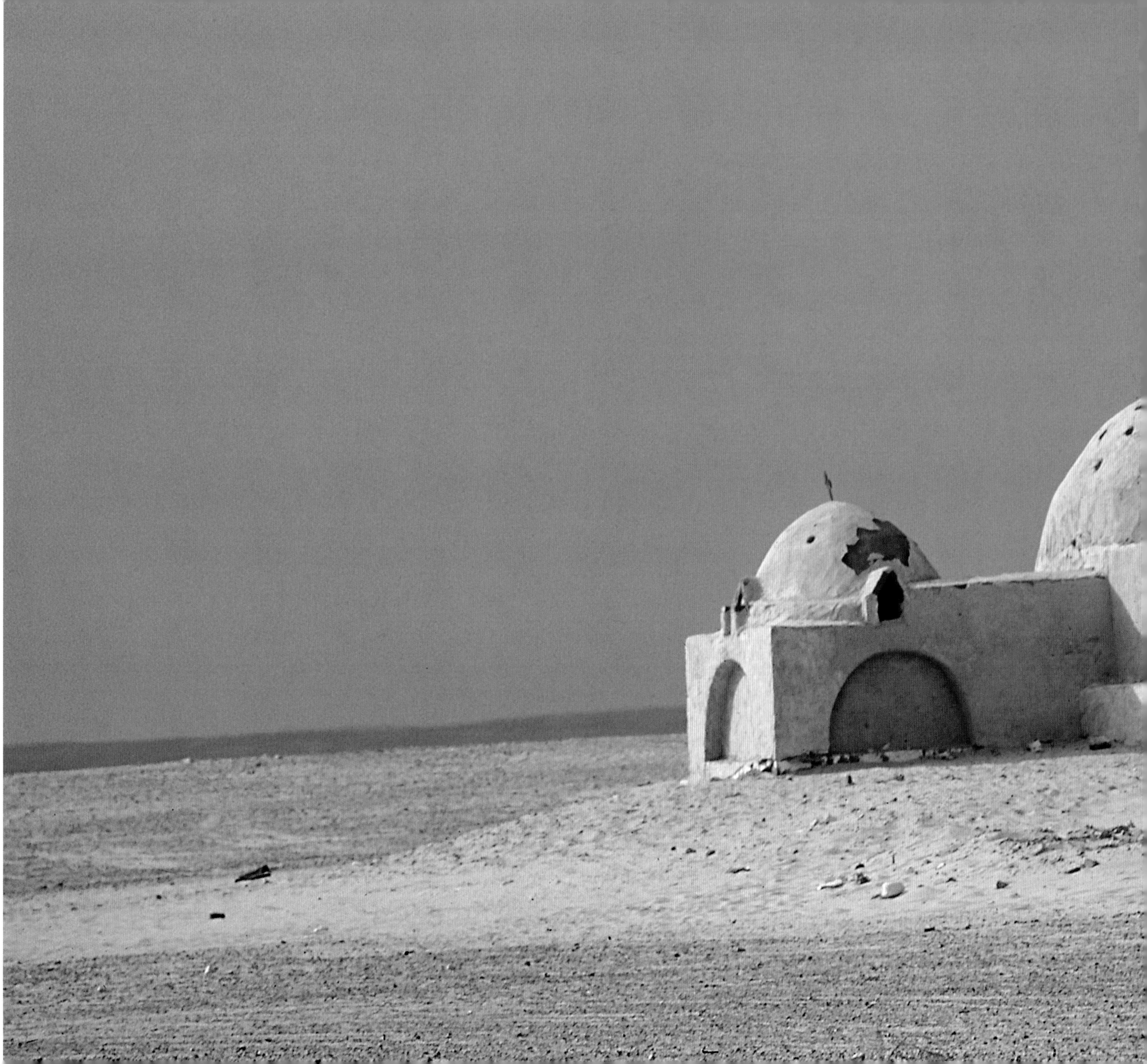

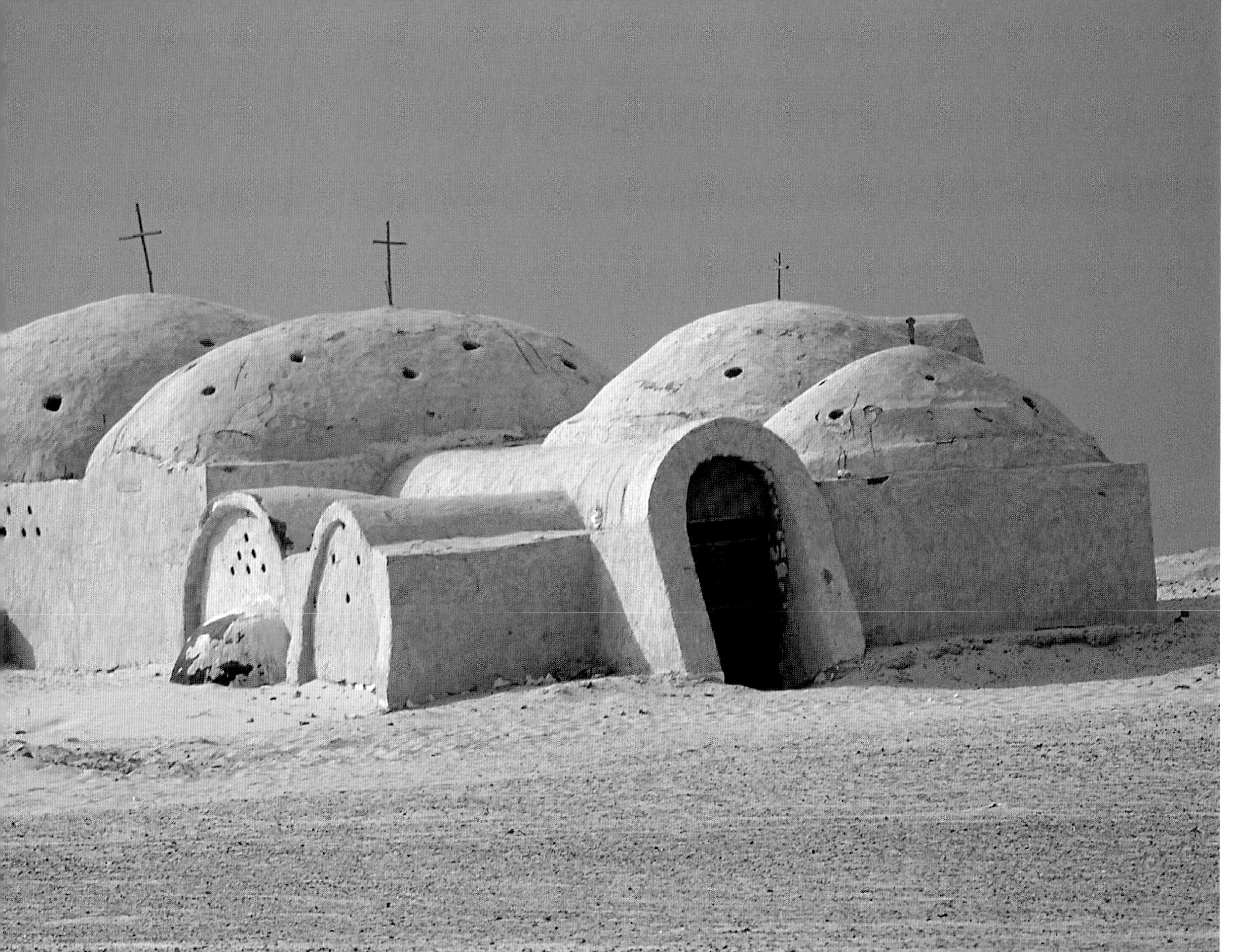

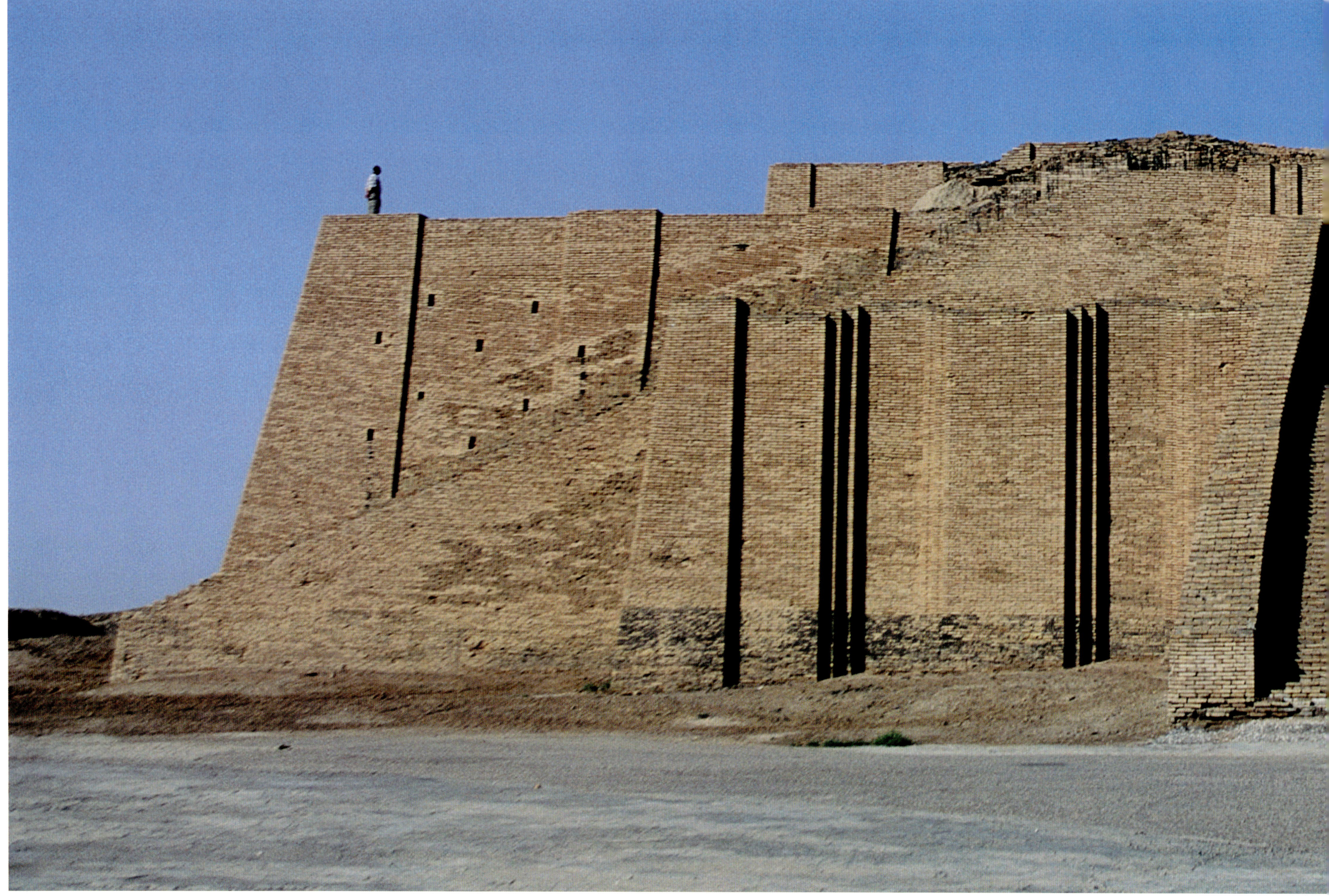

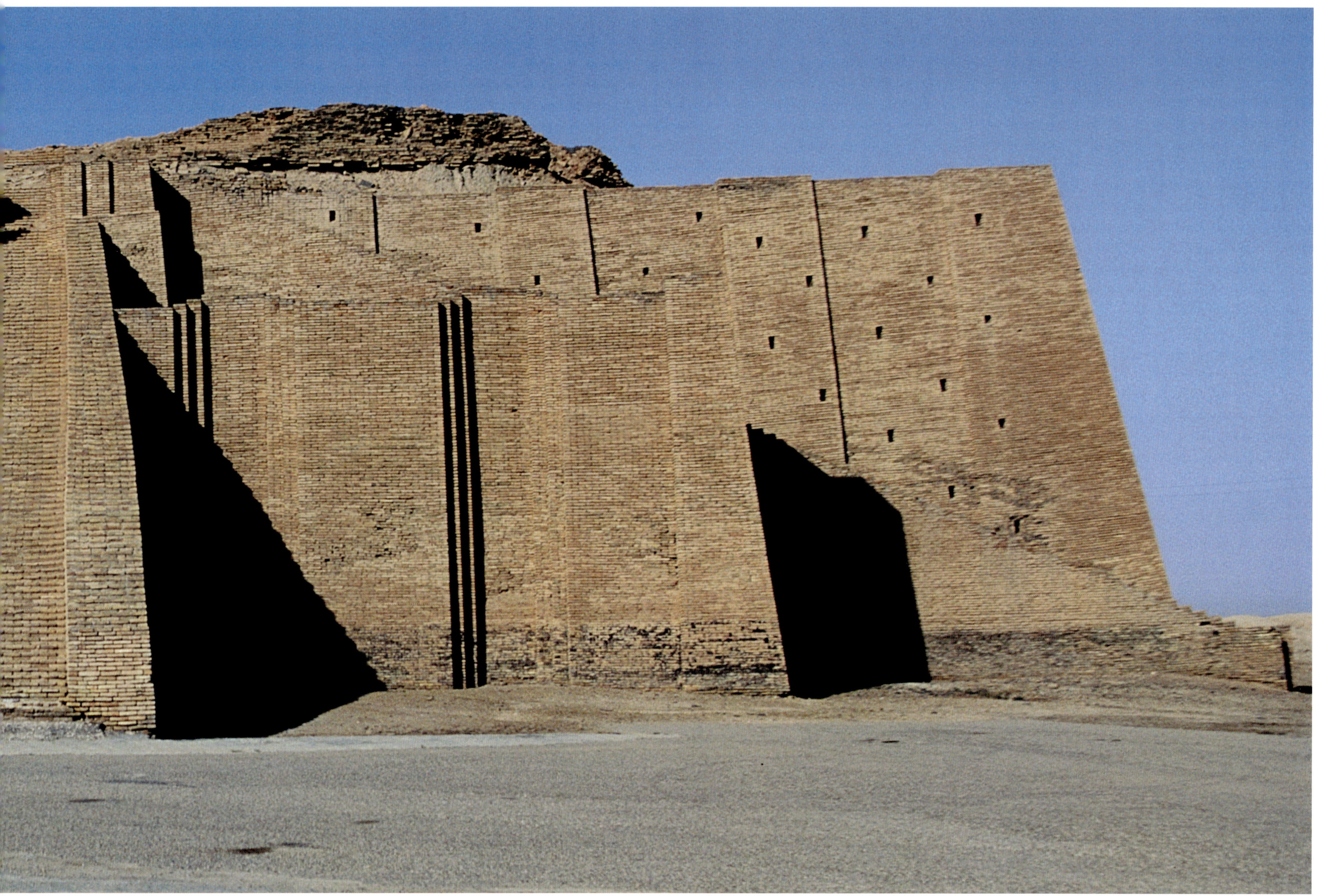

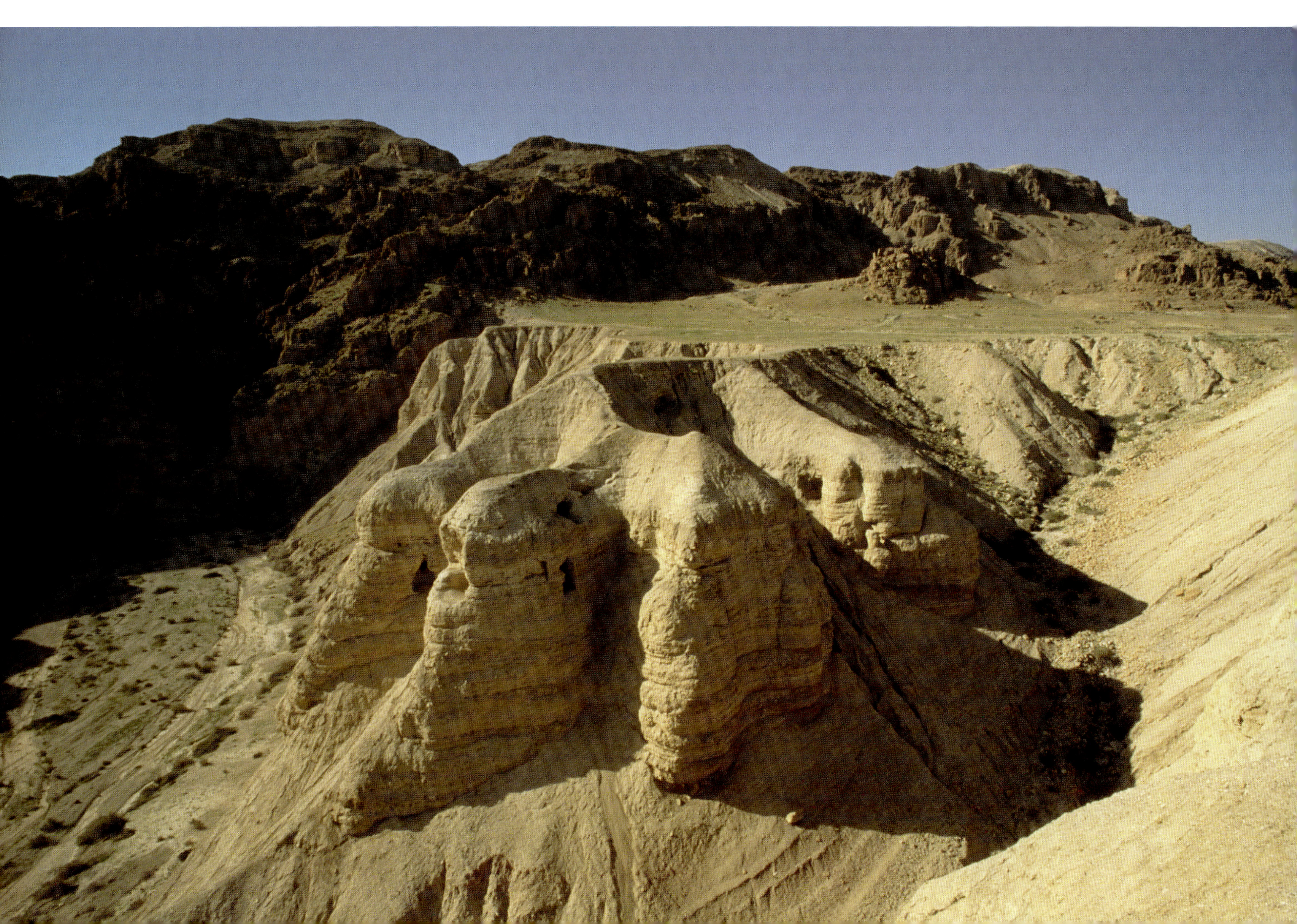

LEFT: These caves, situated above the ancient settlement of Qumran in Israel, are believed to have been occupied by the Essenes, a sect of Jewish scribes. These people are thought to have been responsible for the Dead Sea scrolls, which were discovered in the caves in the late 1940s. *Richard T. Nowitz/Corbis*

RIGHT: The two square towers at a site in Iran are known as badgirs in the local language, Farsi, and are designed to lower the temperature. The vents in the upper part of the tower are designed to catch the wind from whatever direction it comes, and cool it as it passes down the tower, thus making the rooms below more comfortable. If there is no wind, then the hot air from the rooms rises up the tower, drawing in cooler air from the courtyard. *Jose Fuste Raga/Corbis*

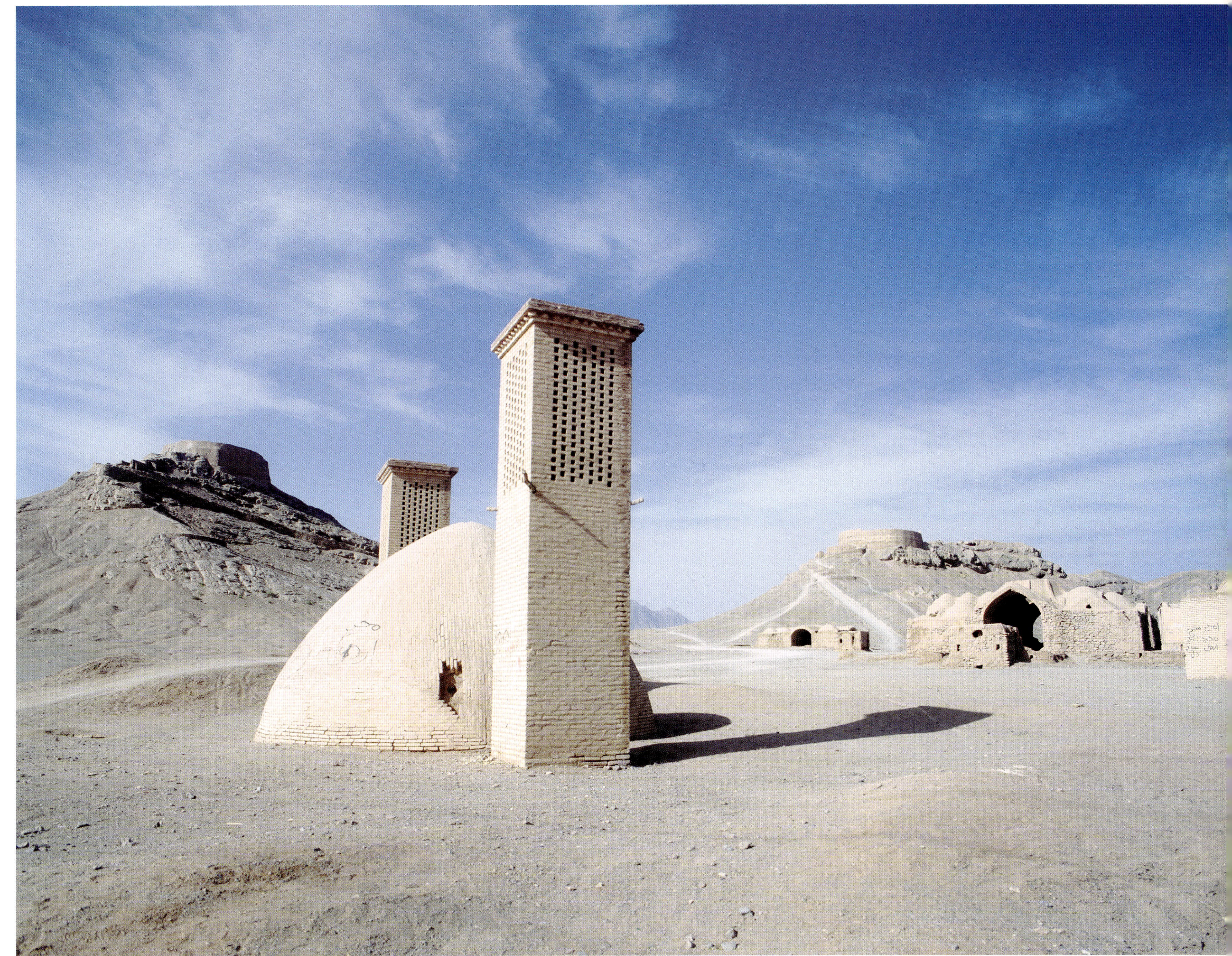

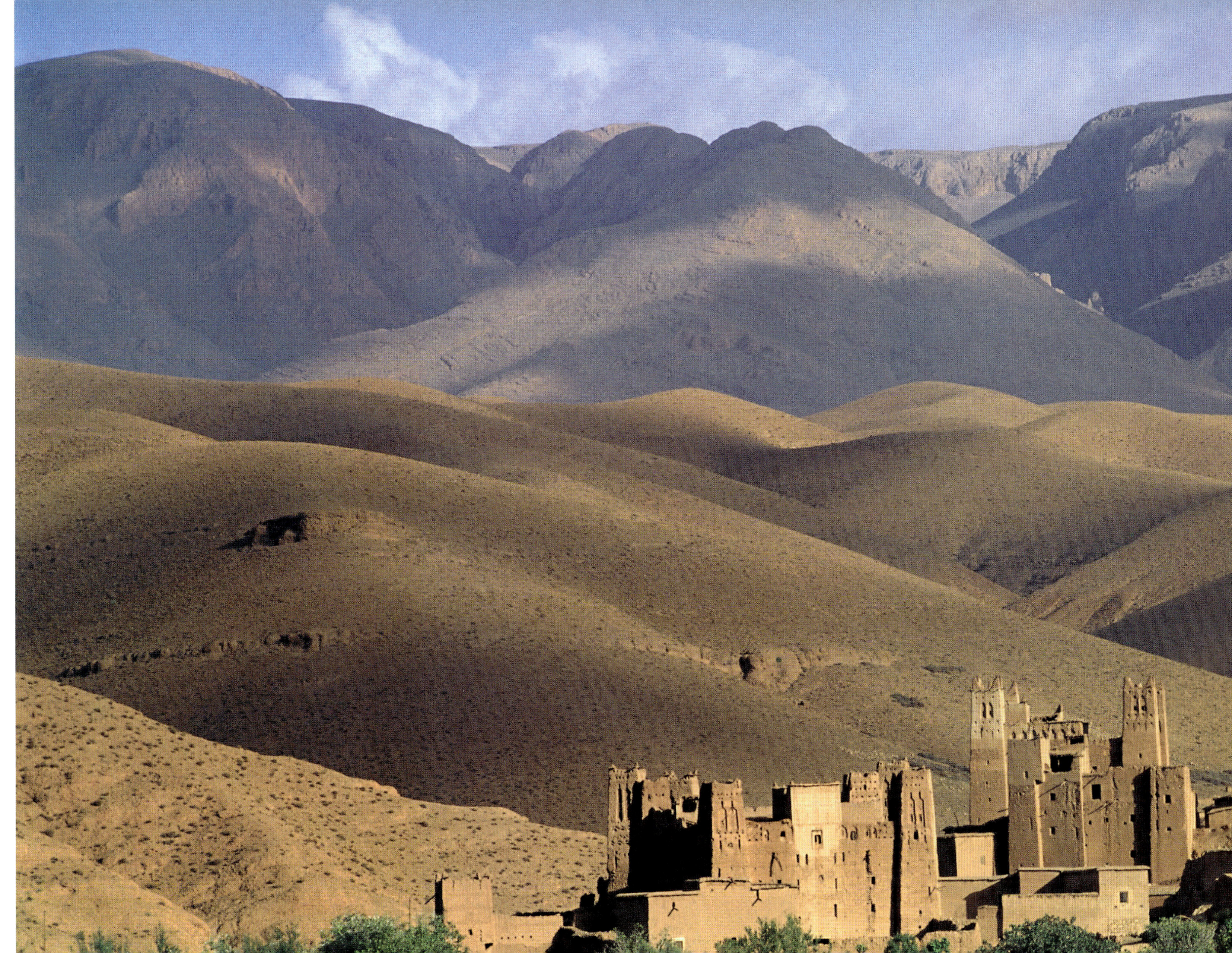

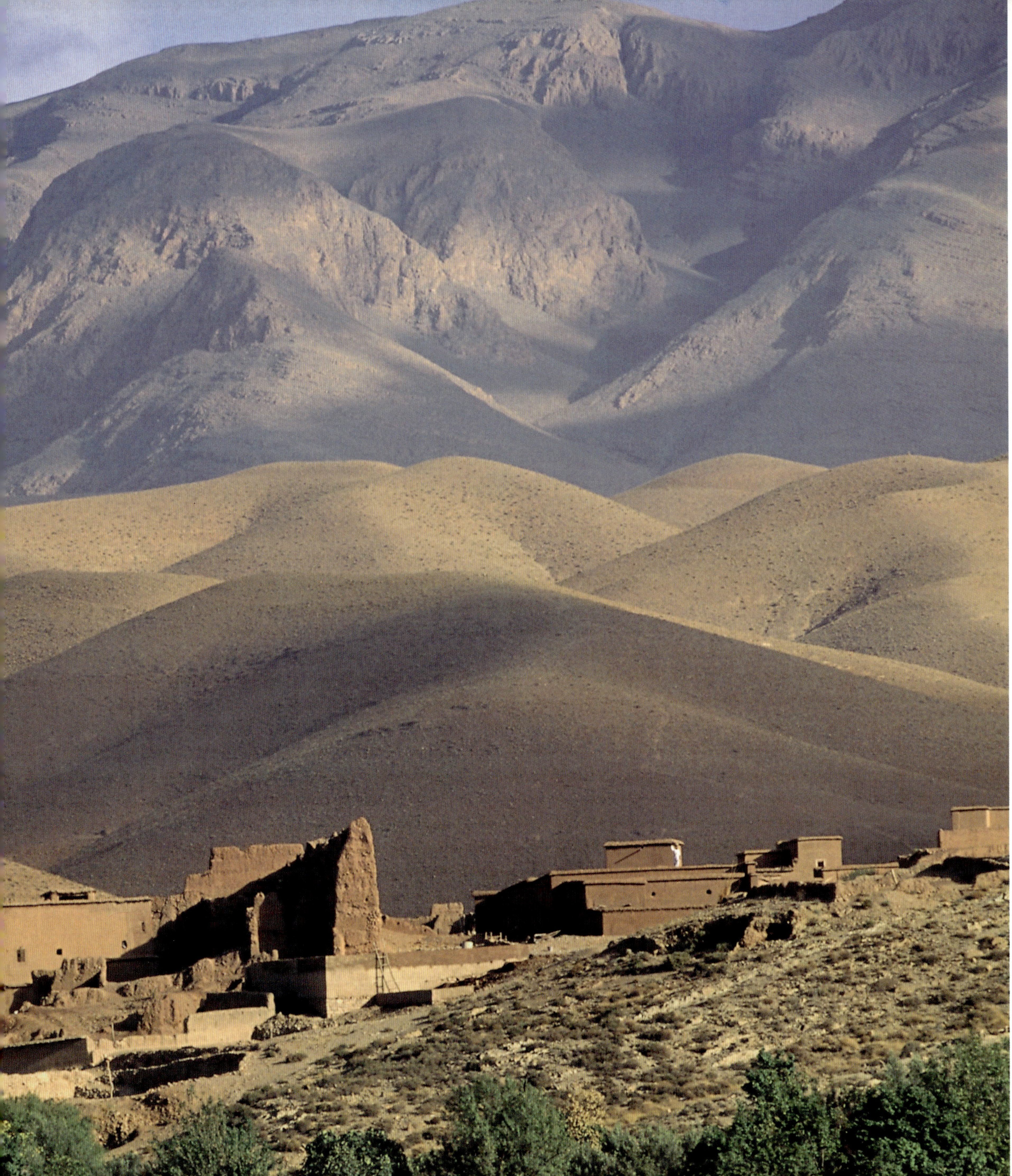

Left: Looking westwards towards Morocco's High Atlas Mountains, the deep V is the famous Dades Gorge, a feature of intense beauty, which, according to many travelers, exerts a magical effect on all those who pass through it. In the foreground is the rather more prosaic housing of the village of Ait Arbi on the western edge of the vast Sahara Desert.
Chris Lisle/Corbis

RIGHT: Lying in northern Saudi Arabia, Qasr Marid (qasr = castle) was built on top of a 2,000-foot hill overlooking the ancient city of Dumat-al-Jandal. The castle was built of stone and is reputed to be some 4 to 5,000 years old. Dumat-al-Jandal is famous for the Mosque of Omar, built in the 7th century and one of the oldest in the country, and also for the manufacture of swords, daggers, and carpets.
James Sparshatt/Corbis

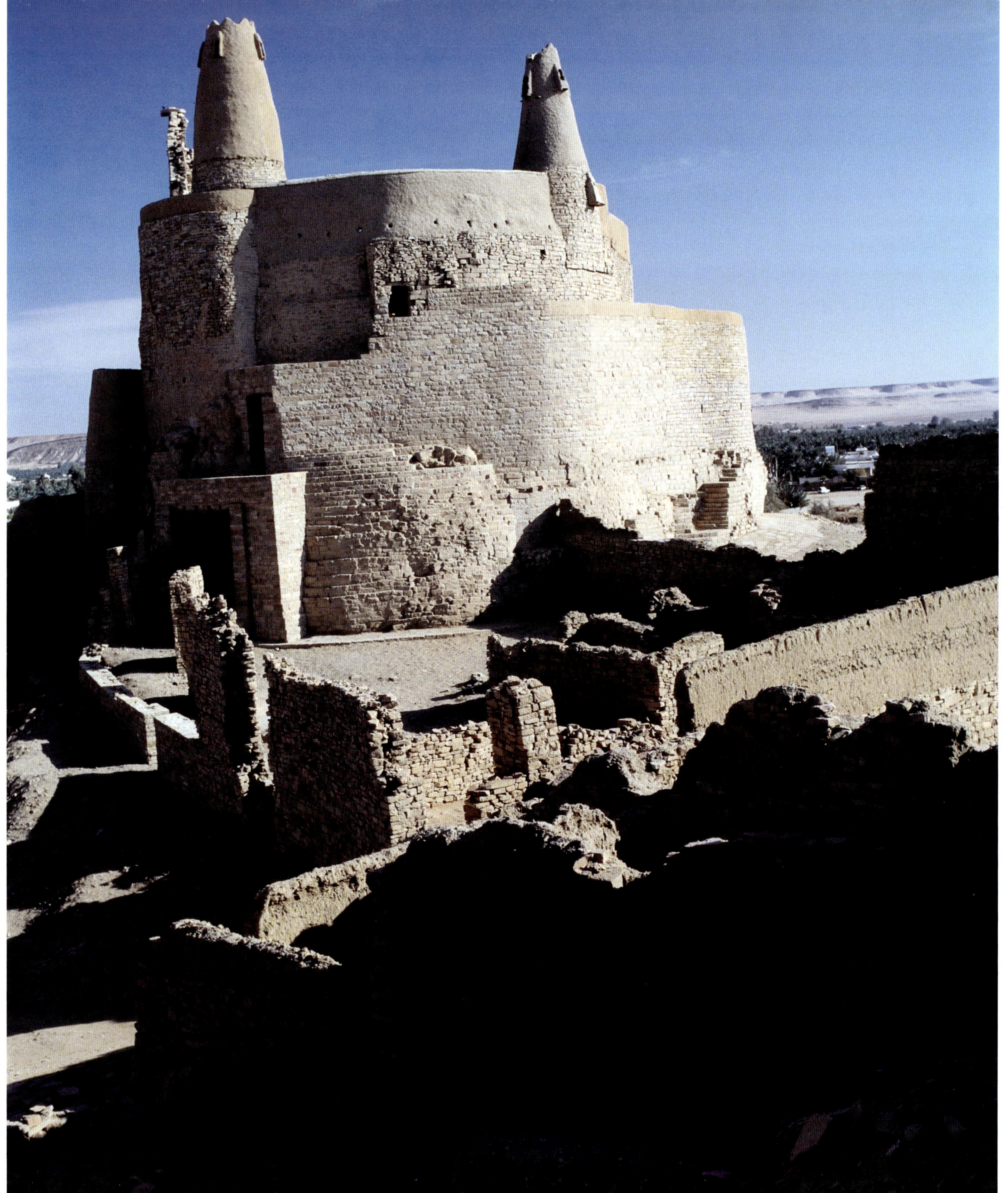

RIGHT: The Yeshi-O temple in Tholing, located in present-day Ngari Prefecture in Xizang Autonomous Region of the People's Republic of China. This area of western Tibet was once the Guge Kingdom, and this monastery was established in the early 10th century AD with the purpose of spreading Buddhism in Tibet. This area of high and cold desert is known as the Chang Tang, or "lonely place."
Craig Lovell/Corbis

PAGES 242–243: Chiu Monastery, seen here, is built on a hill overlooking the western shore of Lake Manasarover in Tibet, which is especially sacred to Buddhists. Guru Rinpoche, a famous teacher was brought to Tibet by the king to spread Buddhism in the country, remaining there from 822 to 876AD. During his journey home to India he stayed in a cave for a week, and the monastery is built around that cave. Indeed, the floor of the cave still has a footprint left by Guru Rinpoche and there is also a statue of the teacher, said to have been made by the Guru himself. The hard gravel below the monastery is typical of this desert region.
Craig Lovell/Corbis

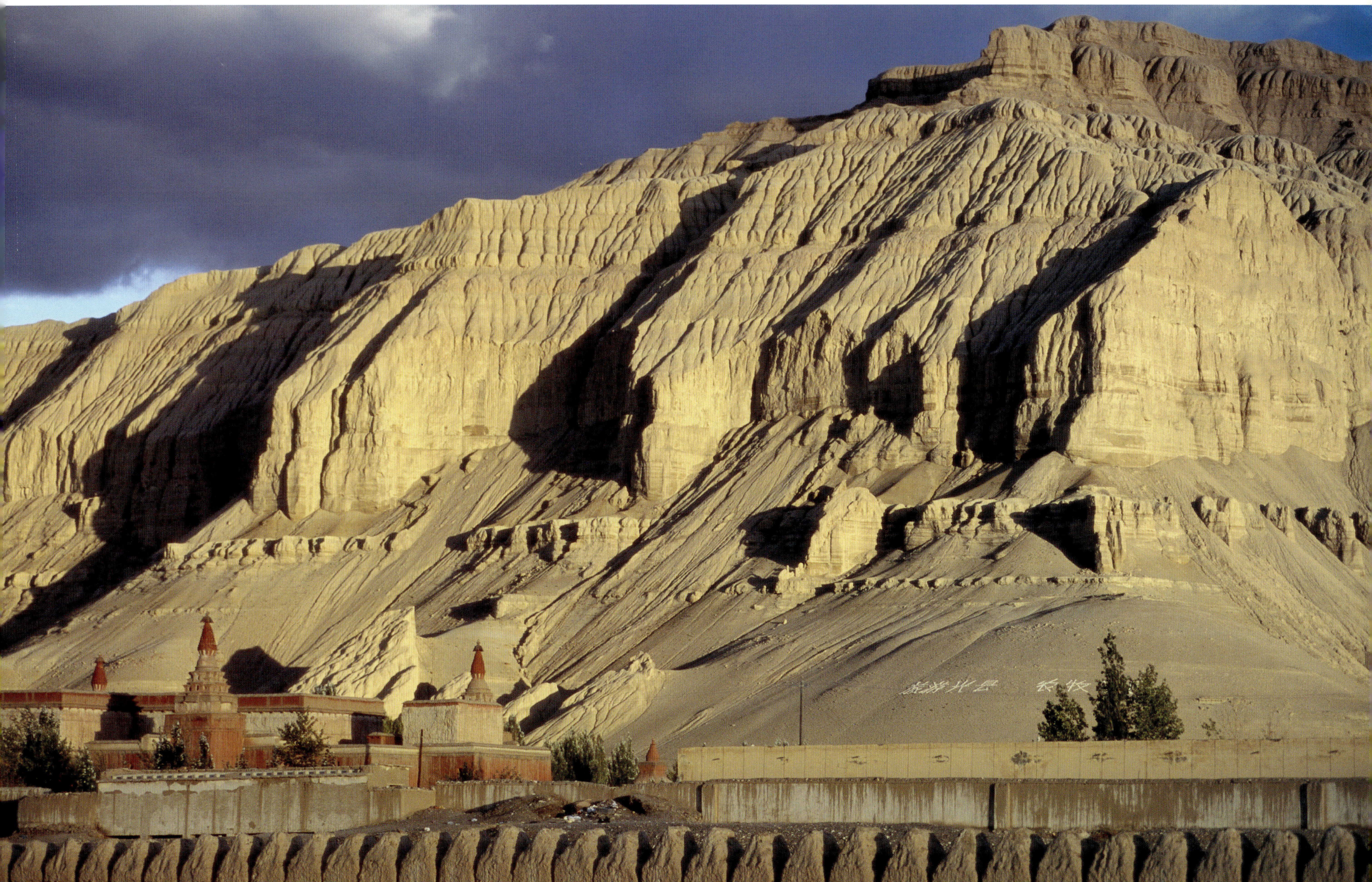

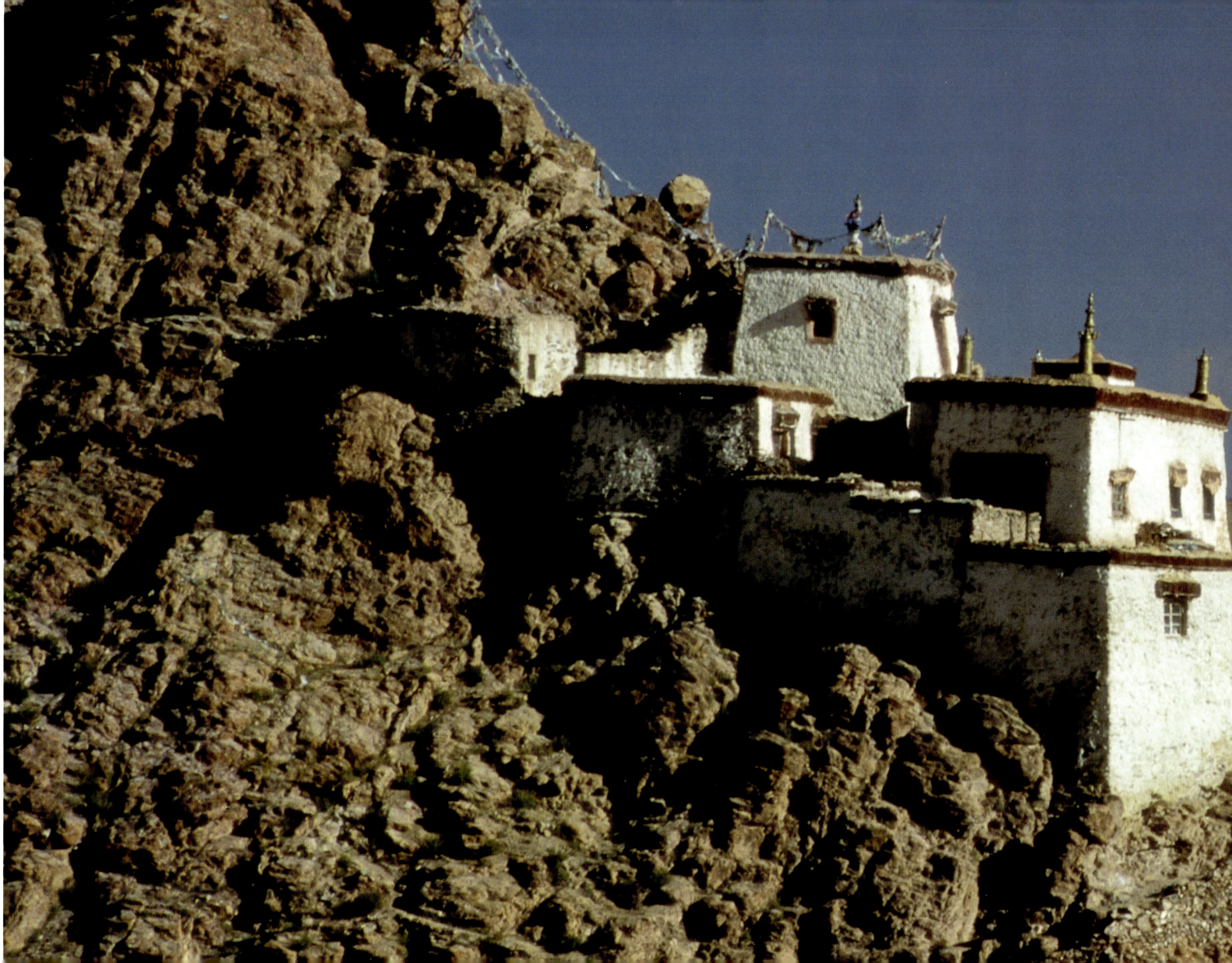

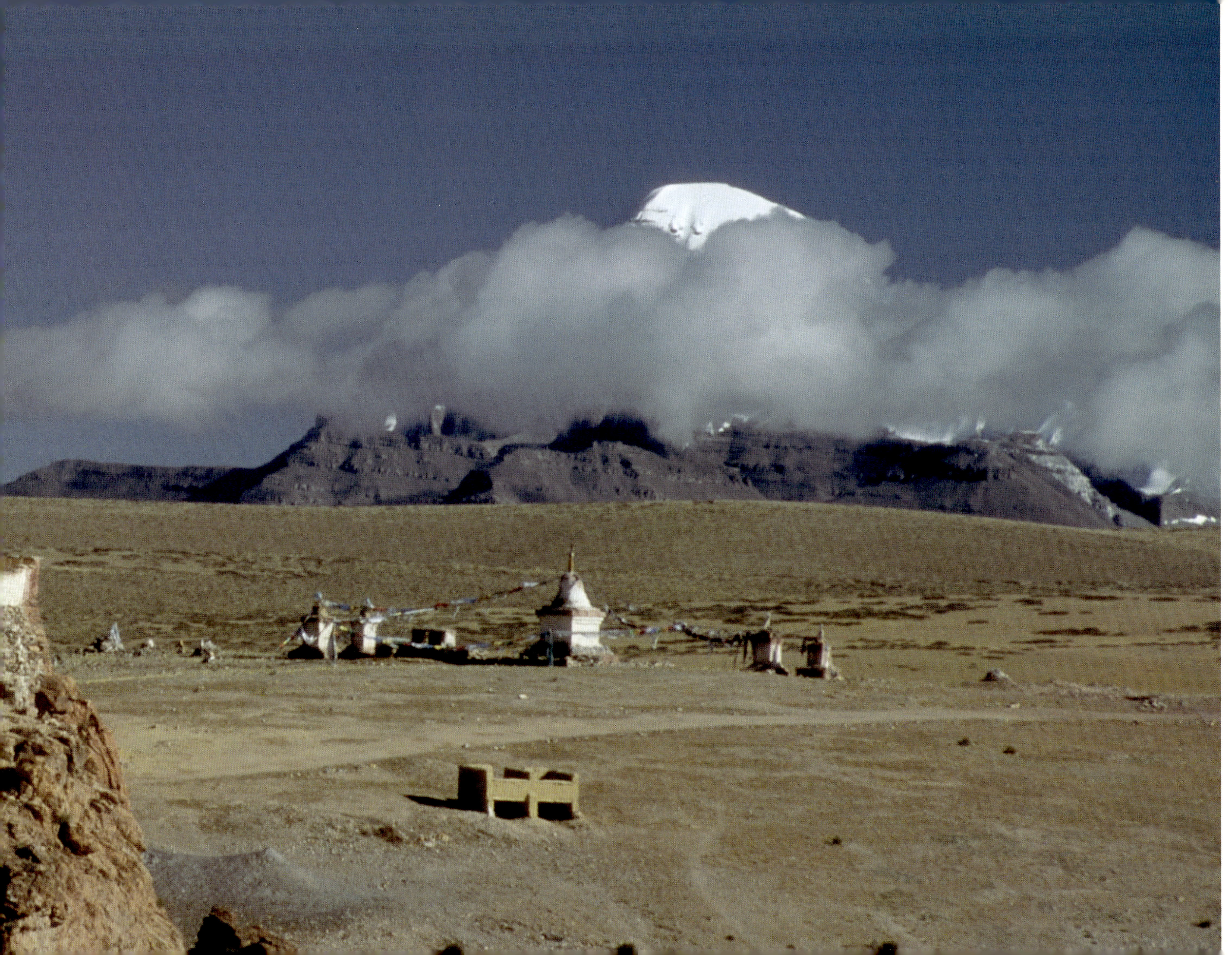

Right: The Desert View Watchtower gives every appearance of having been in position for two or more centuries, but was actually built as recently as the 1930s. Architect Mary Colter's brief was that the building must harmonize with its surroundings while acknowledging ancient Indian structures, and still give tourists an outstanding view of the Grand Canyon and surrounding desert. It is, by any standards, a triumph.
James Randklev/Corbis

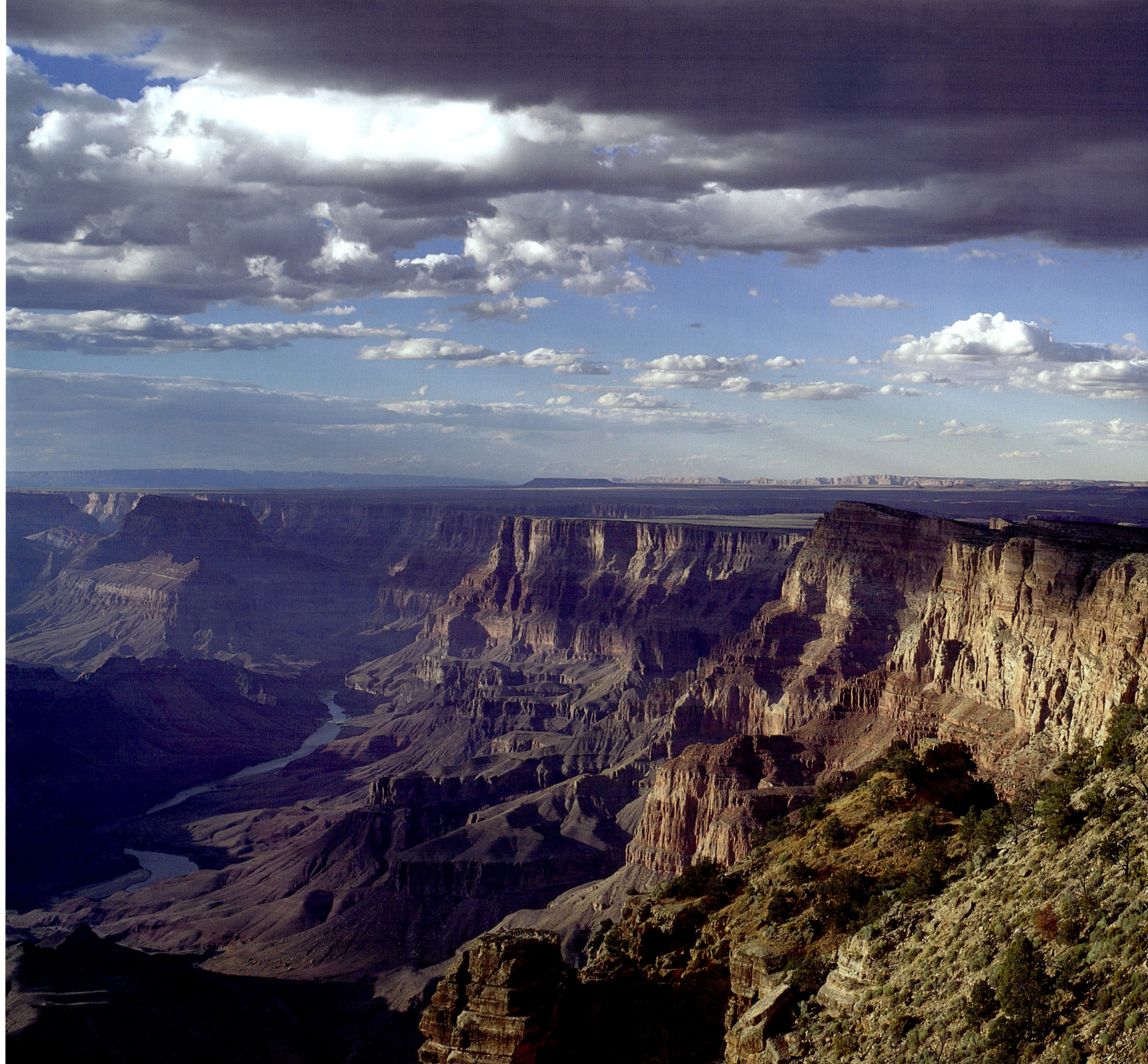

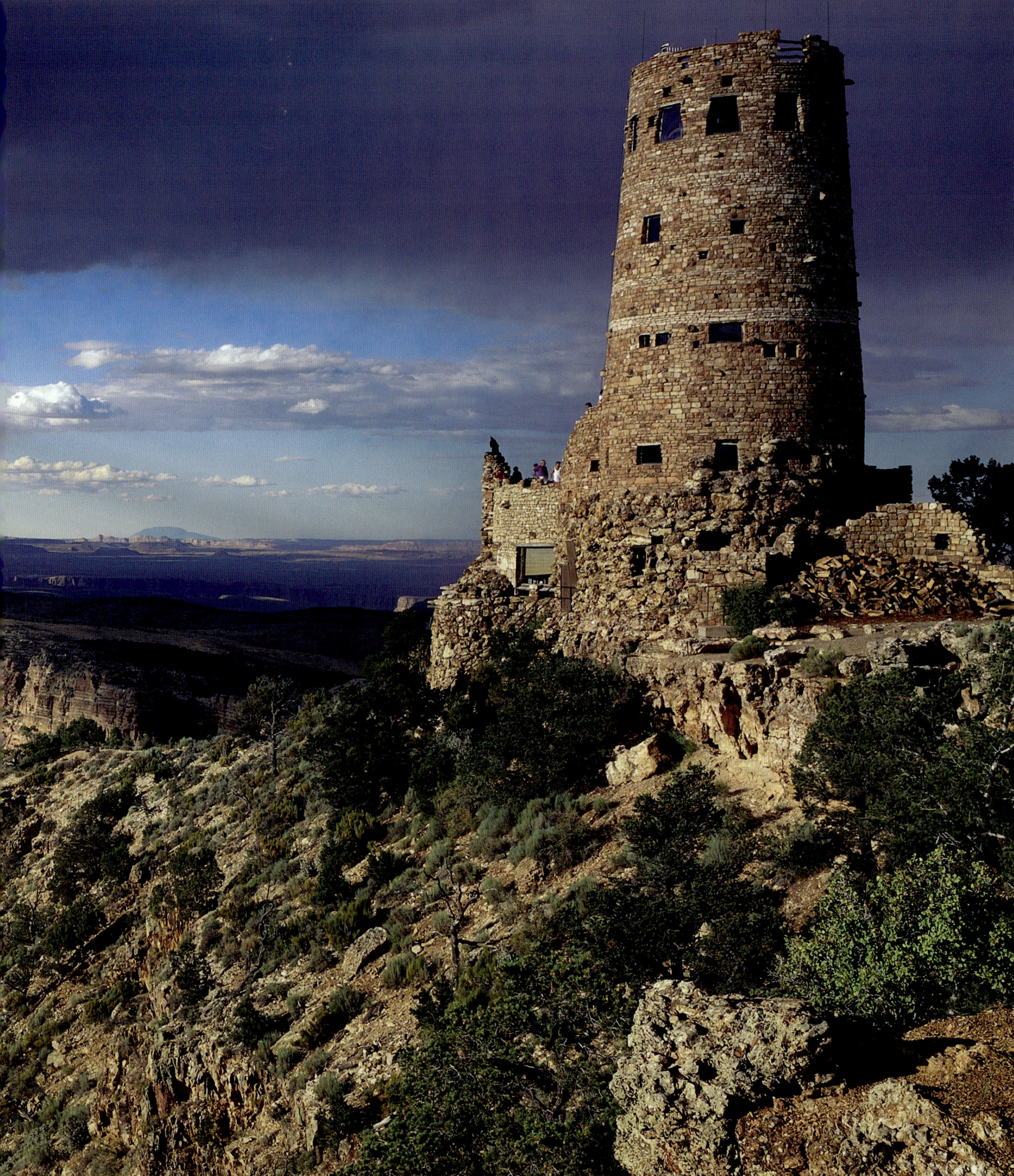

PAGE 246: This is the only road from the town of Calama to the village of San Pedro de Atacama in Chile through the Valle de la Luna (Valley of the Moon), so called because of its bleak landscape. The Atacama is the driest place on Earth but still Man manages to survive and even to prosper there, although Calama suffers from another type of modern malady as it has been the scene of numerous reports of UFO sightings over the past few years.
Joel Sartore/Getty Images

PAGE 247: Despite all modern scientific advances and the most painstaking historical and archaeological research, the world still contains some mysteries, among which are these geoglyphs at a hill named Cerro Unita in the Atacama Desert in Chile. As can be seen from the human figures in the foreground, these drawings are huge—and can, in fact, only be truly appreciated from the air. Some figures depict humans and animals, while others are geometric patterns, but nobody knows for certain who made them, why or when.
Joel Sartore/Getty Images

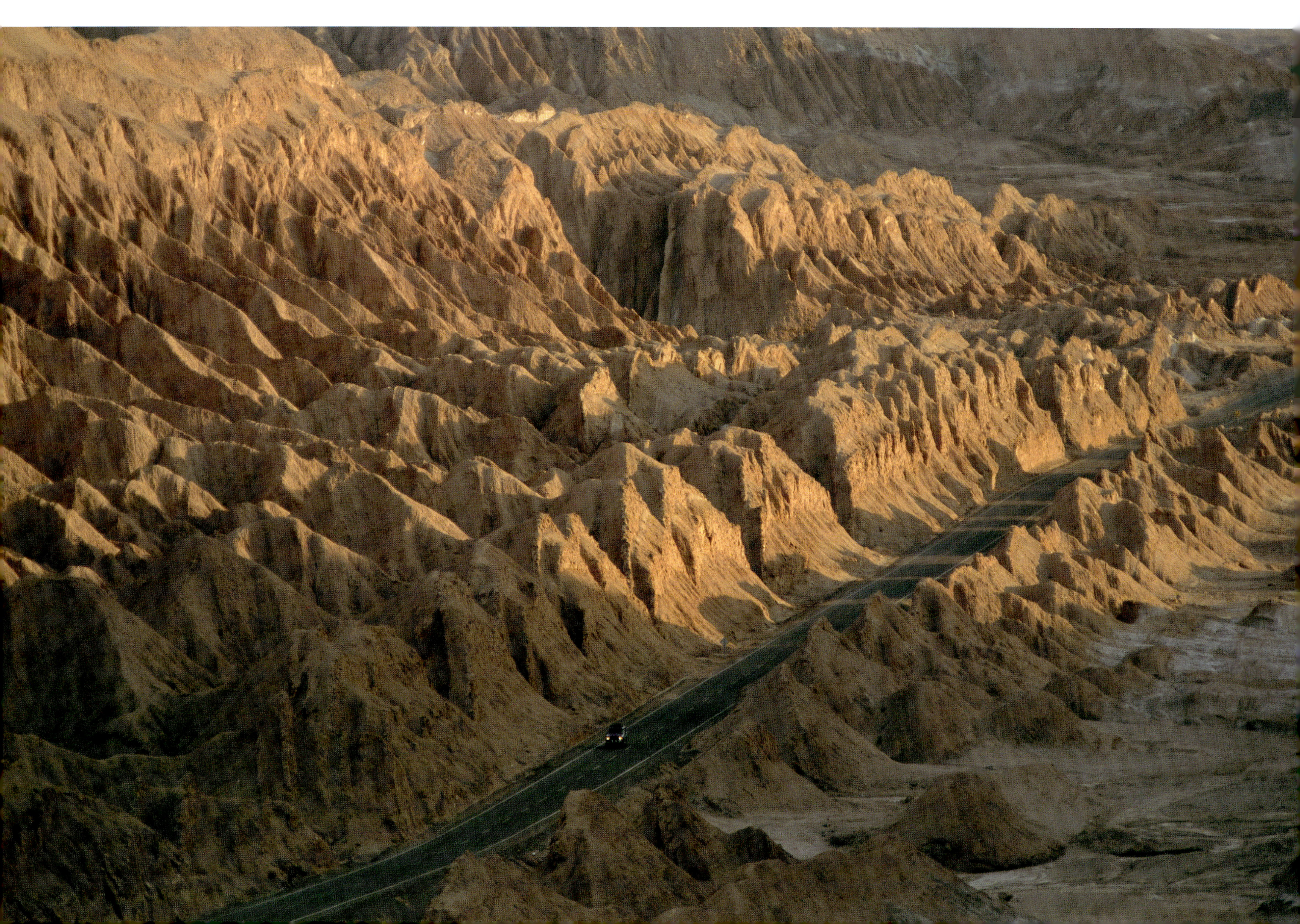

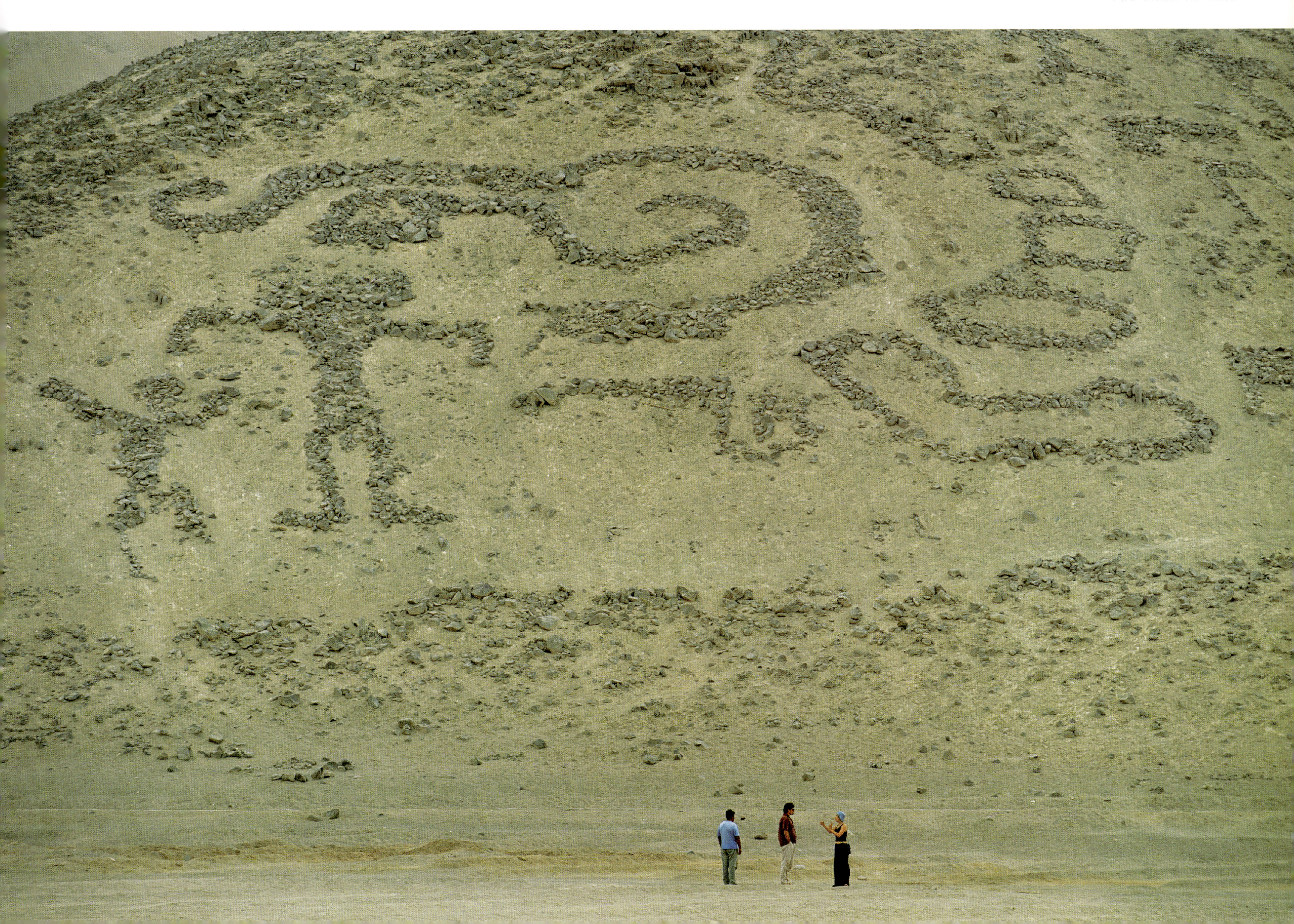

Right: Deserts provide such a harsh environment that it seems strange that people live there at all. For these villagers in the Thar Desert, in Rajasthan in northwest India, life is a constant struggle, with temperatures ranging from 122 degrees Fahrenheit in summer to below freezing in winter, and rainfall is but sixteen inches per year, at best. But, even though they sometimes have to trek great distances to find water or food, they almost always return to their hamlets as soon as it is possible to do so.
Brian A. Vikander/Corbis

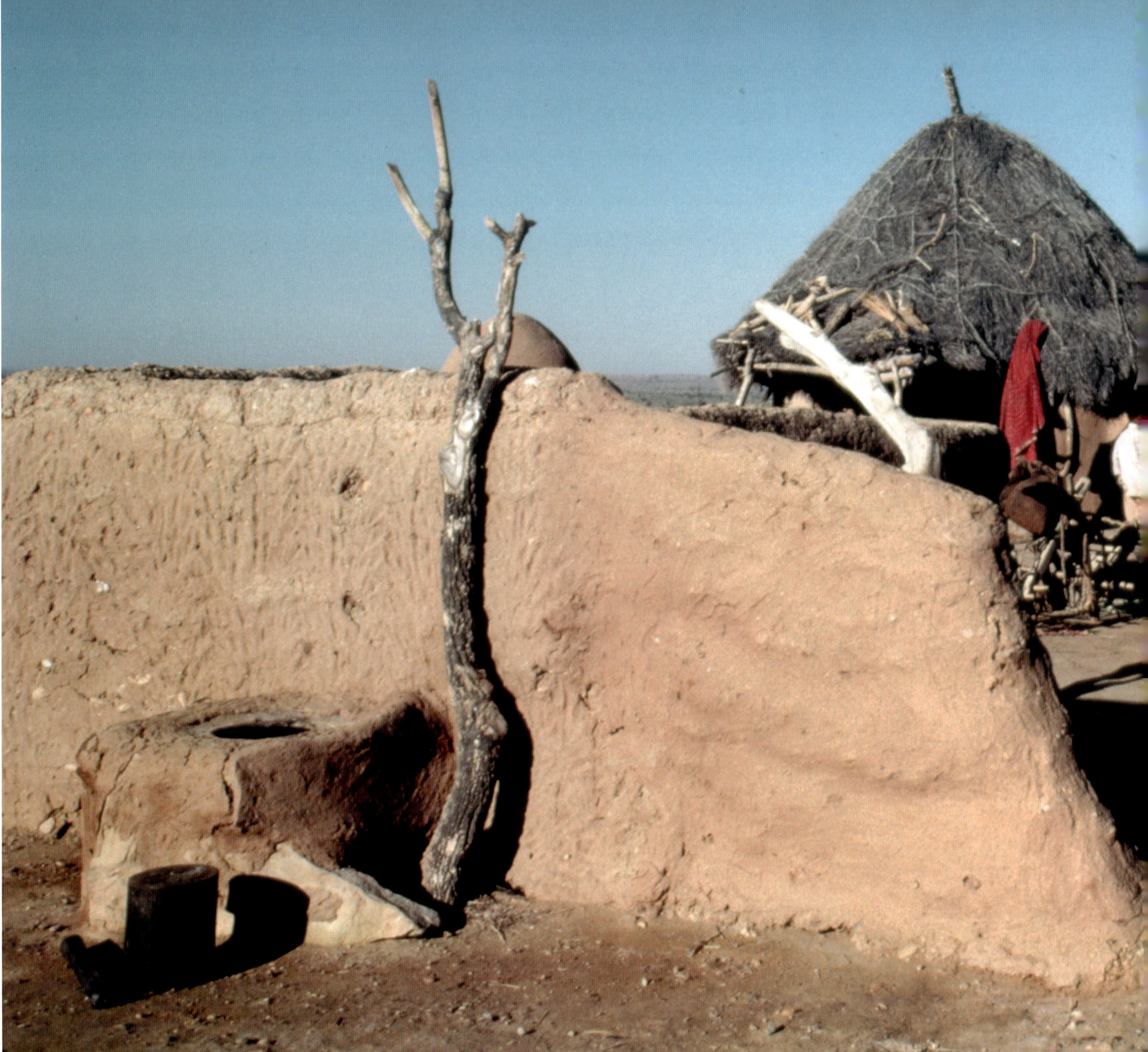

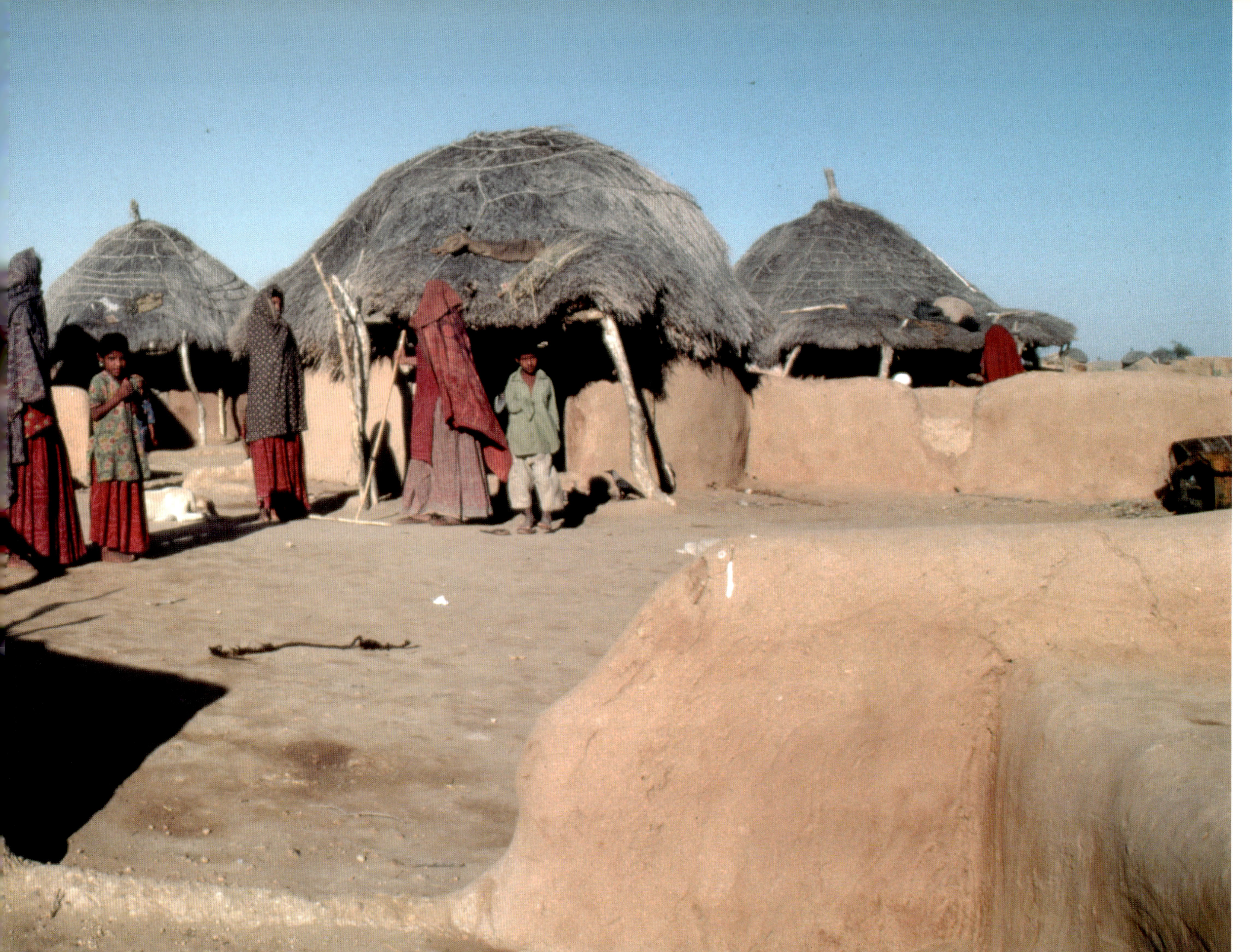

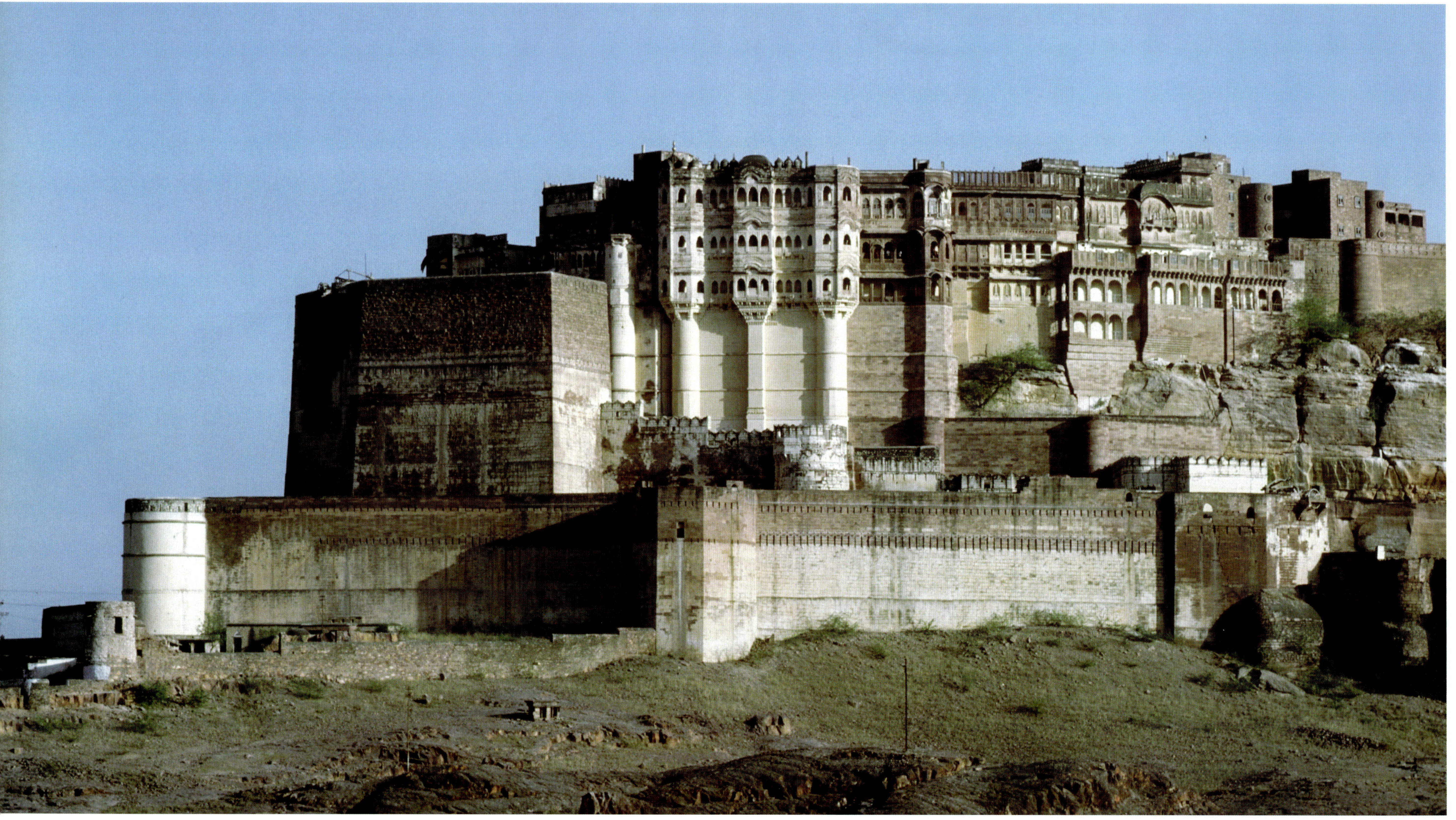

ABOVE: One of the most extraordinary buildings to emerge from any desert is the Meherengarh Fort, on a 400-foot hilltop above the city of Jodhpur in Rajasthan, India. The word meherengarh means "magnificent" and in this case is fully deserved. Building the fort started in 1459, but the greater part of what now stands was built in the 17th century during the reign of Maharajah Jaswant Singh (1638-78). There are seven concentric walls, with seven gates to be taken, and its design and construction make it one of the finest and most impregnable fortresses in the world.
Sheldan Collins/Corbis

RIGHT: The Kasbah of Ait Ben Haddou is one of the most famous kasbahs in the Atlas Region of southern Morocco. It has been used as a setting in a number of movies, including *Lawrence of Arabia* and *Gladiator*, and has recently been declared a UNESCO World Heritage Site.
Tim Graham/Getty Images

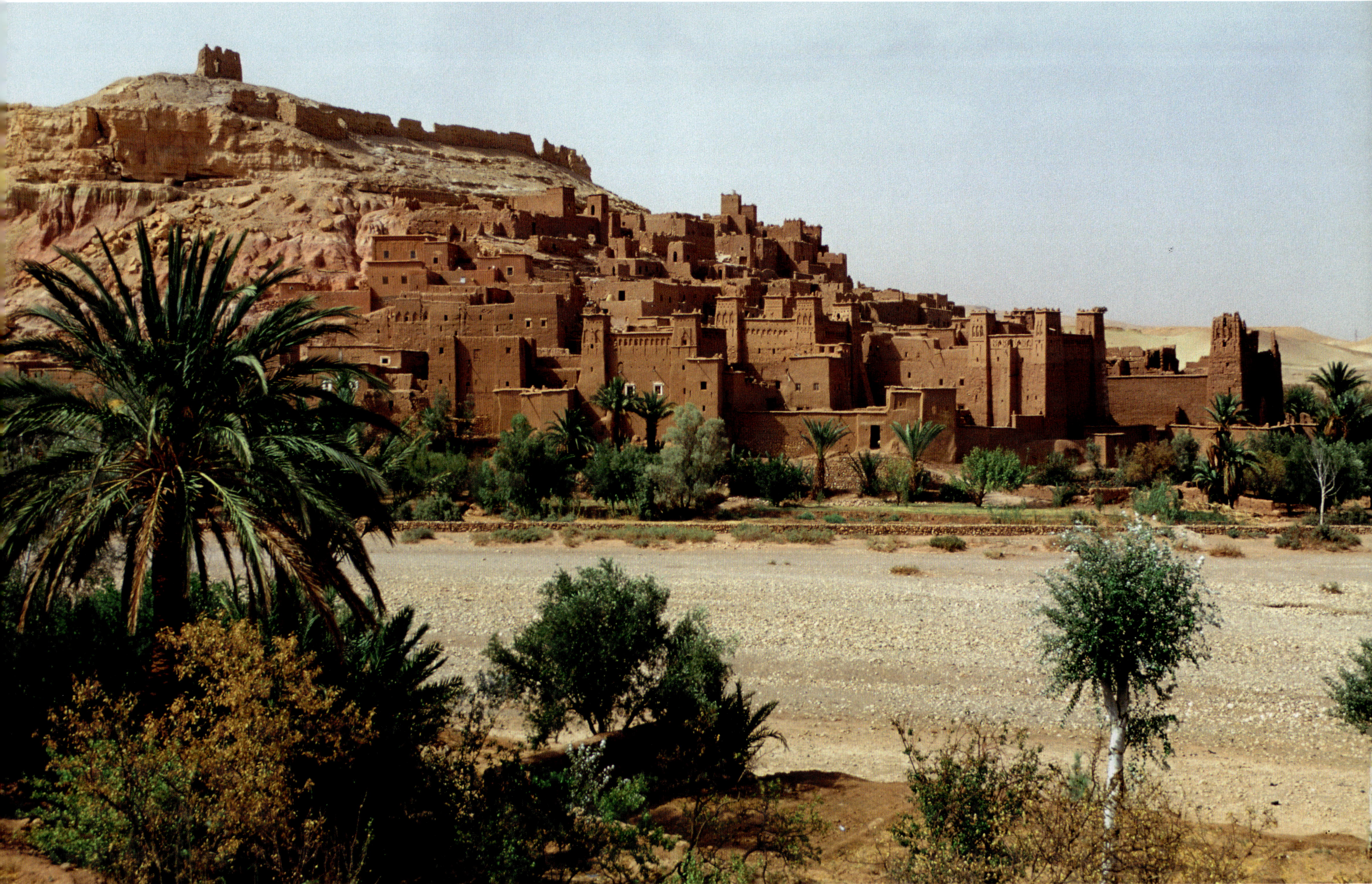

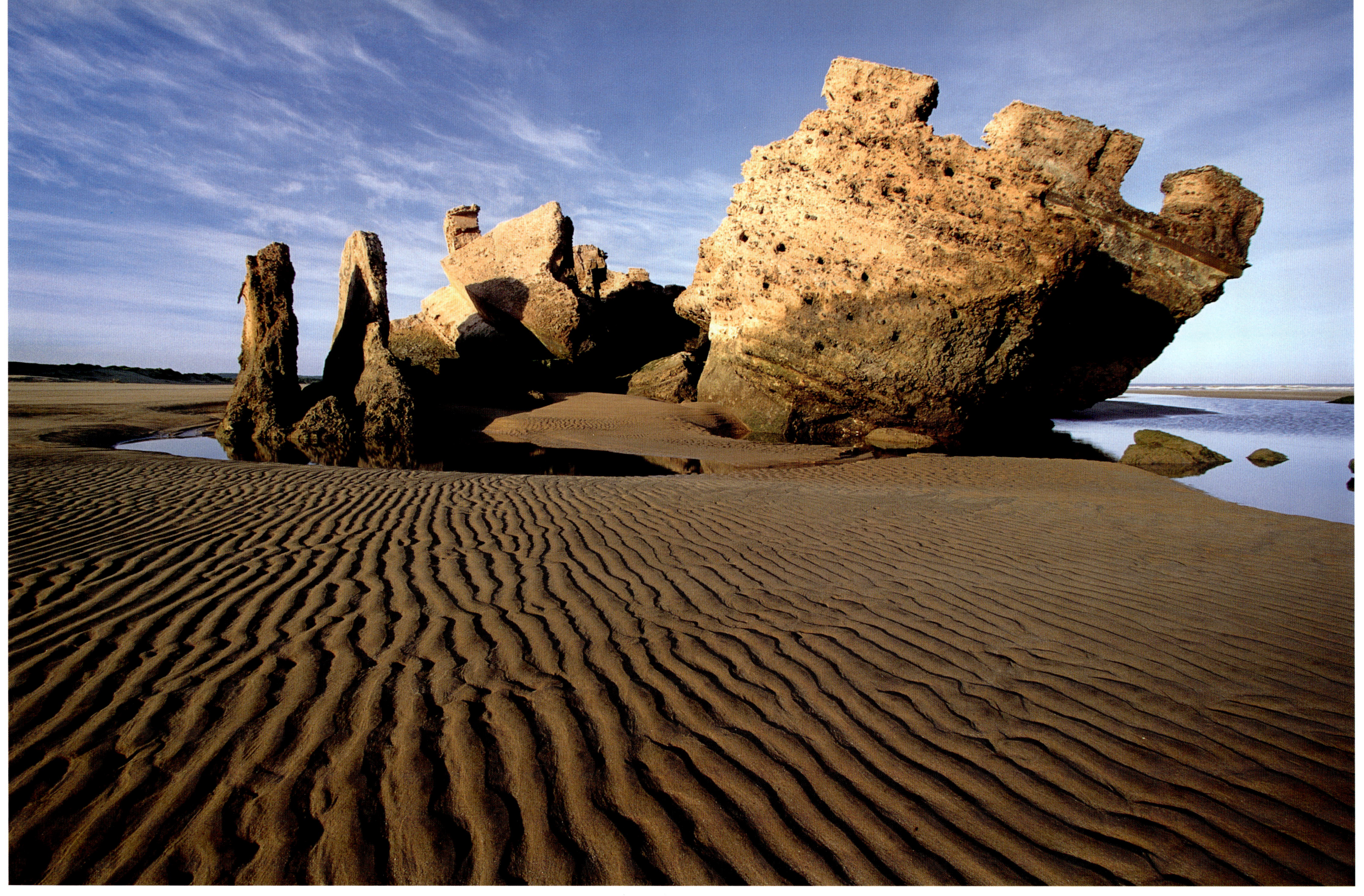

Above: Essaouira (formerly Mogador) on the Moroccan coast, some 125 miles due west of the capital, Marrakech, is a busy port. In the late 18th century it was totally fortified according to the latest European principles to protect it from the very active and fierce Barbary pirates. The walls around the town remain, but this outlying fort, known as Bord el Berod, has been abandoned and will soon disappear altogether, as the desert reclaims its own. It is reputed to have been the inspiration for Jimi Hendrix's song "Castles Made of Sand."
John and Lisa Merrill/Corbis

Right: The First Gulf War in 1991 ended with the Iraqi forces fleeing Kuwait in a desperate effort to get home, but vast numbers were caught on the "Highway of Death," where monumental tailbacks turned them into killing grounds for Coalition Air Forces. This is the scene after the routes had been cleared, the destroyed vehicles pushed to one side and bodies removed—it took years to sort it all out.
Peter Turnley/Corbis

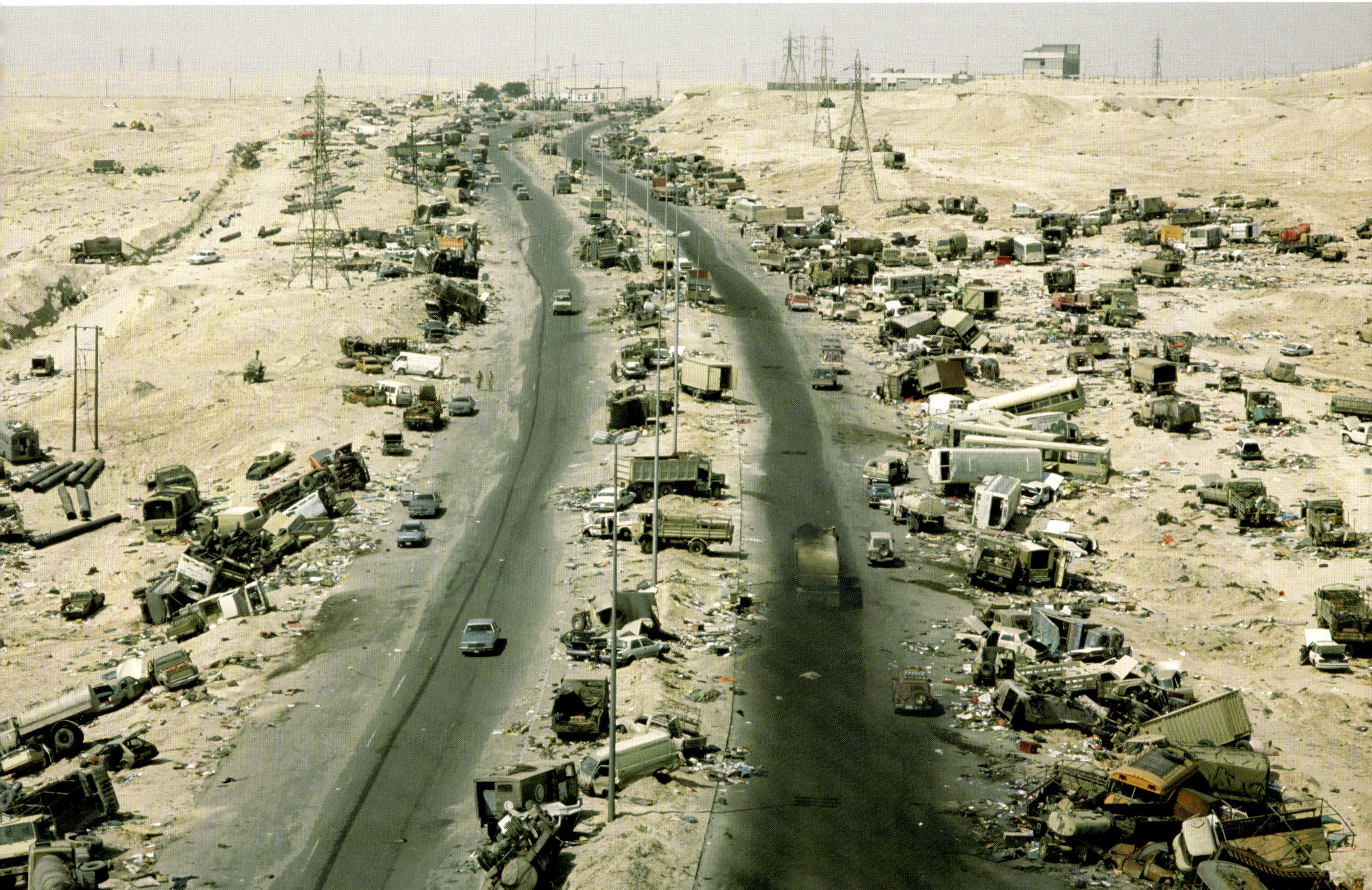

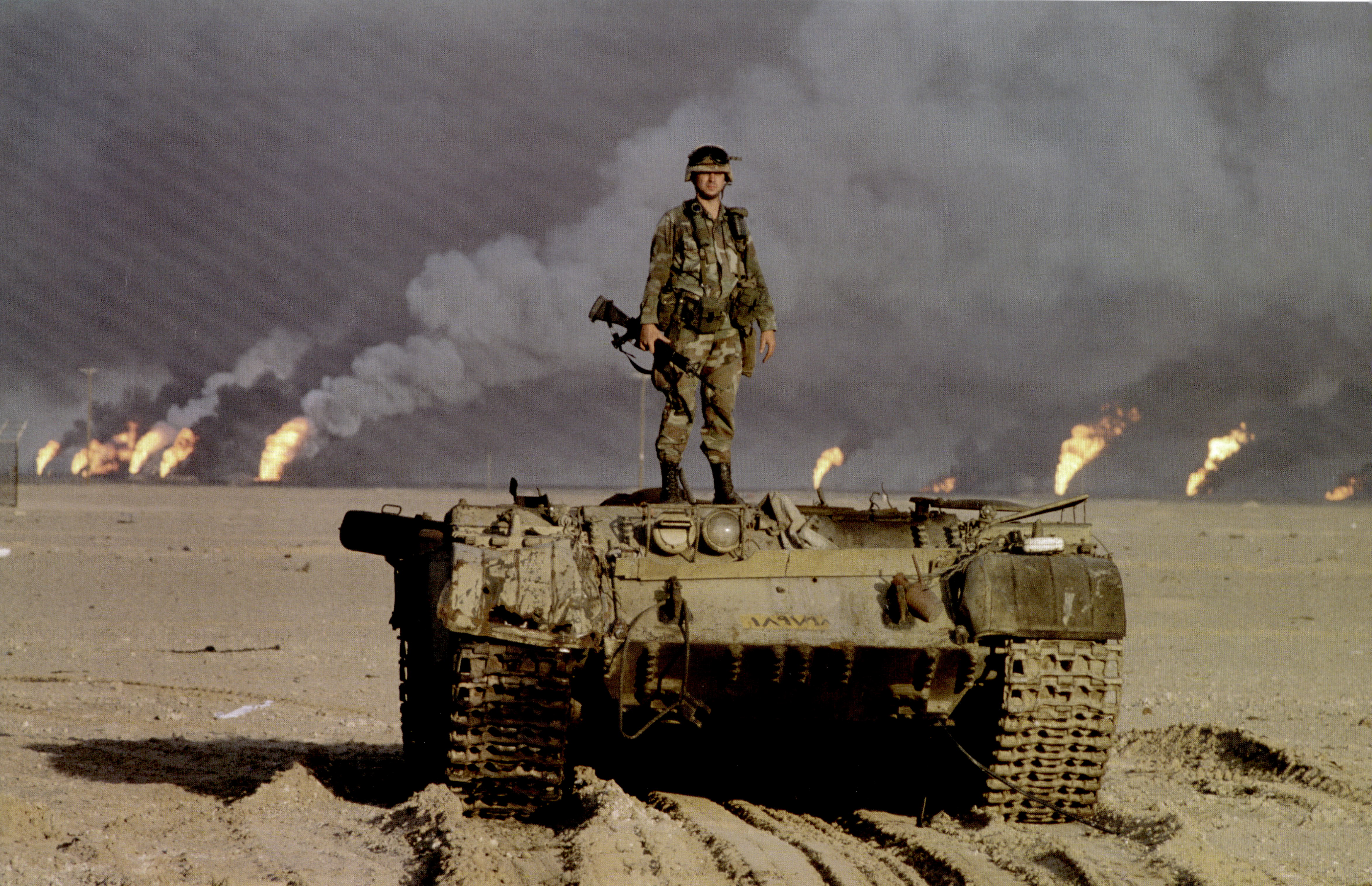

LEFT: A U.S. soldier stands atop a destroyed Iraqi tank, north of Kuwait, in March 1991. In the distance the oil wells burn, the "final hurrah" of Saddam's pathetic and totally defeated army as they fled homewards across the desert.
Peter Turnley/Corbis

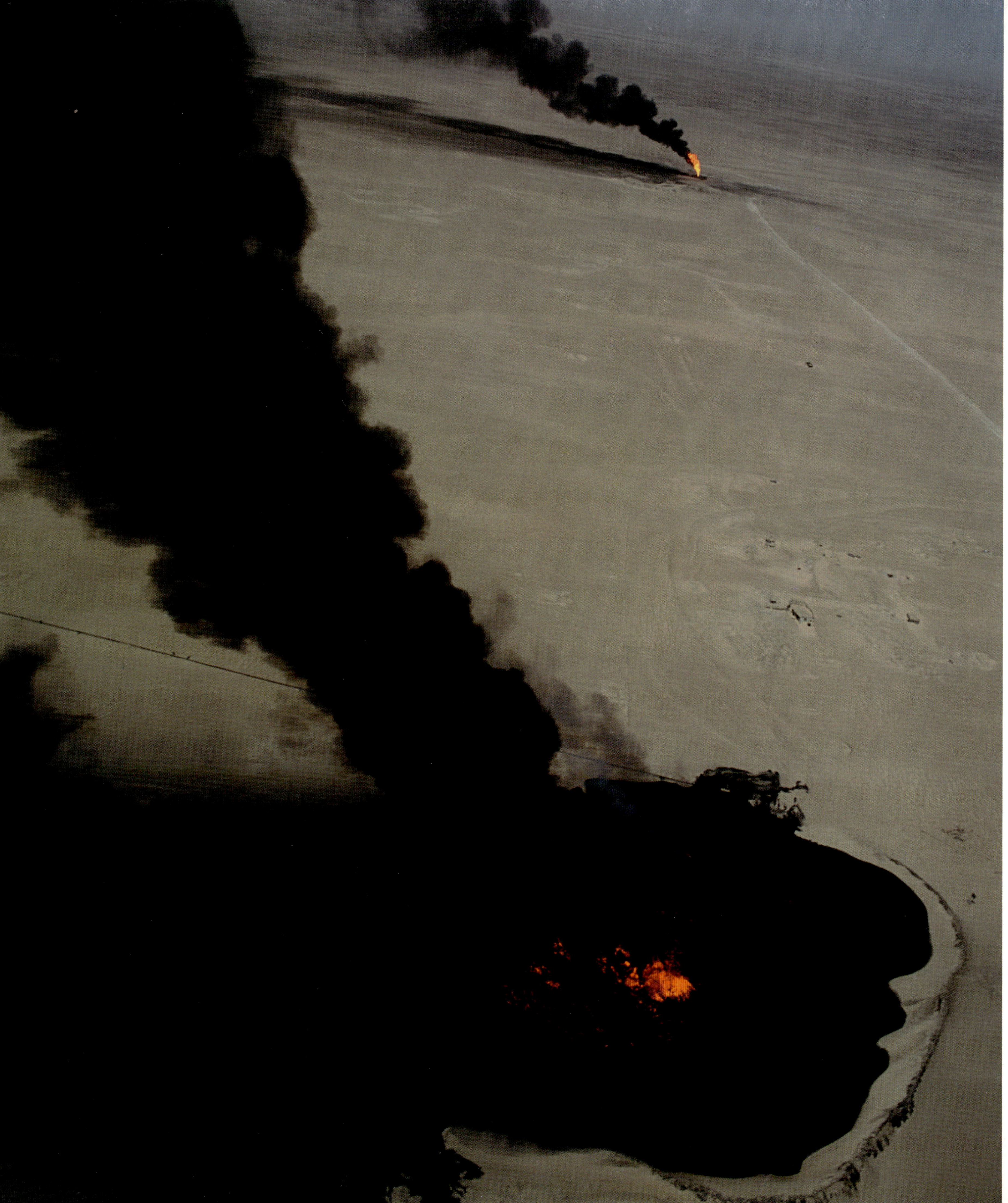

LEFT: Man has left his mark on the desert for many reasons; sometimes through carelessness or ignorance, and on other occasions in order to improve the lot of the people who live there. There has also been deliberate commercial exploitation, when making money has taken priority over care of the environment. Seldom, however, has there been such deliberate and calculated damage as when, at the end of the 1991 Gulf War, Iraqi dictator Saddam Hussein set fire to the oil wells in Kuwait, which, as seen here, burned for more than a year.
Sissie Brimberg/Getty Images

INDEX OF PLACES